MW01007824

THE BOOK OF CHANGES
AND THE UNCHANGING TRUTH

guide for finding the hexagrams

UPPER TRIGRAM / LOWER TRIGRAM	chyan ☰ heaven	chen ☳ thunder	K'an ☵ water	Ken ☶ mountain	K'un ☷ earth	sun ☴ wind	li ☲ fire	tui ☱ lake
chyan ☰ heaven	1	34	5	26	11	9	14	43
chen ☳ thunder	25	51	3	27	24	42	21	17
K'an ☵ water	6	40	29	4	7	59	64	47
Ken ☶ mountain	33	62	39	52	15	53	56	31
K'un ☷ earth	12	16	8	23	2	20	35	45
sun ☴ wind	44	32	48	18	46	57	50	28
li ☲ fire	13	55	63	22	36	37	30	49
tui ☱ lake	10	54	60	41	19	61	38	58

THE BOOK OF
CHANGES
AND THE
UNCHANGING
TRUTH

BY HUA-CHING NI
TEACHER OF AGELESS WISDOM

天地不易之經

倪化清著述

Shrine of the Eternal Breath of Tao
College of Tao
and Traditional Chinese Healing
SANTA MONICA

This book was accomplished with the assistance of the students who attended the classes.

We also wish to thank the Chinese National Museum for the use of the photograph on the cover.

Published by:
Shrine of the Eternal Breath of Tao
an imprint of Sevenstar Communications Group, Inc.
1314 Second Street #208
Santa Monica, CA 90401 USA

First Printing - August 1983
Second Printing - October 1989
Third Printing - October 1992

First Edition - Copyright 1983 by Ni, Hua-Ching.
Second Edition - Copyright 1990 by Ni, Hua-Ching.

Library of Congress Cataloging-in-Publication Data

Ni, Hua-Ching.
    The book of changes and the unchanging truth = [T ien ti pui chih ching] / by Ni, Hua Ching. -- 2nd ed.
       p. cm.
    ISBN 0-937064-29-7
    1. I ching.   2. T ien ti pui chih ching.
PL2464.Z7N5 1990   89-64438
299'.51282--dc20   CIP

This book is dedicated to
the Undivided Oneness of the Universe
and to those seekers of Truth
who choose to be like a mirror
reflecting its exquisite, immortal nature.

To female readers,

According to natural spiritual teaching, male and female are equally important in the natural sphere. This is seen in the diagram of Tai Chi. Thus, discrimination is not practiced in our tradition. All my work is dedicated to both genders of human people.

Wherever possible, constructions using masculine pronouns to represent both sexes are avoided; where they occur, we ask your tolerance and spiritual understanding. We hope that you will take the essence of my teaching and overlook the superficiality of language. Gender discrimination is inherent in English; ancient Chinese pronouns do not have differences of gender. I wish that all of you achieve above the level of language or gender.

Thank you, H. C. Ni

Warning - Disclaimer

This book presents information and techniques that have been in use throughout the orient for many years. These practices utilize a natural system within the body; however, there are no claims for effectiveness. The information offered is to the author's best knowledge and experience and is to be used by the reader(s) at their own discretion and liability. It can be beneficial or harmful depending upon one's stage of development.

Because of the sophisticated nature of the information contained within this book, it is recommended that the reader also study the author's other books for further understanding of a healthy lifestyle and energy-conducting exercises. You need to accept legal responsibility for doing a thing you do not thoroughly understand.

Because people's lives have different conditions and different stages of growth, no rigid or strict practice can be applied universally. Thus, it must be through the discernment of the reader that the practices are selected. The adoption and application of the material offered in this book is totally your own responsibility.

The author and publisher of this book are not responsible in any manner for any injury that may occur through following the instructions in this book.

CONTENTS

Part Four: Five Examples of Ancient I Ching Practitioners

Part Five: Epilogue 665

Prelude

The Subtle Essence conveyed by the teaching of the Integral Way is the deep truth of all religions, yet it leaves all religions behind to be the clothing of different seasons or worn in different places. The teaching of the Subtle Essence includes all things of religious importance, yet it is not on the same level as religion. It serves people's lives directly as all religions wish to do, but it surpasses the boundary of all religions and extracts the essence of all religions.

The Subtle Essence as conveyed by the teaching of the Integral Way is also the goal of all serious science, but it leaves all sciences behind as partial and temporal descriptions of this Integral Truth. Unlike any of the partial sciences, it goes beyond the level of any single scientific search.

The Subtle Essence is the master teaching. However, it does not rely on any authority. It is like a master key which can unlock all doors leading to the inner room of the ultimate truth directly. It is not frozen at the emotional surface of life and does not remain locked at the level of thought or belief with the struggling which extends to skepticism and endless searching.

The teaching of the Subtle Essence presents the core of the Integral Truth and helps you reach it yourself.

PREFACE

In this modern age, when mankind is so greatly benefiting from its technological advances, there is also the fearsome threat of its potential destruction. Nothing in human life remains untouched by man's scientific explorations. Nothing remains outside our challenging probes. Our zealousness and often impulsive endeavors have resulted in great confusion, both for society at large and for the individual, as ever new models of reality replace the old.

The human mind, master of all spheres of life, has become overwhelmed by its own creations. What is needed is a correct way of thinking which can guide all human activities to prosperity and safety - a way which will encourage the full development of individual life as well as the peaceful regulation of families and nations.

When individuals in a society fail to achieve high inner development, they can easily become the victims of opportunists who wish to seize the reins of social leadership. By stealing the will of the people through the insidious dissemination of false information and teachings in politics and religion, people of unbridled ambition become tyrannical leaders. Evidence of this process can be seen today in China and other parts of the world where people bear the burden of subjugation. The present hardships they endure are a direct result of a previous lack of inner growth over a long period of time. It would be a tragedy if people continued to make the same dreadful mistakes again and again.

It is an immutable fact that mind and spirit are the essence of an individual who is, in turn, the essence of society. In this modern age, we must seriously reflect on what is available that can nurture our minds and guide our spirits. We cannot rely on the general education that society offers to guide us in the correct way of living. Nor can we rely on the general religious education available. Based on inaccurate spiritual knowledge, it develops only prejudice and alienation among people.

What is needed now is the discovery of the inner light which enables human beings to see through the confusion of the mind and discover the subtle level wherein the truth of life resides.

In this overpopulated age, can people find a teacher or teaching that presents the correct guidelines for wholesome development? Is there any true authority that people can trust, totally and absolutely, for good advice in small matters and grand ones alike? Are there any good consultants who are ready and available to all people whenever needed? Though man now has the ability to develop highly useful machines, it is increasingly clear that he needs useful, appropriate and timely counsel to correctly direct his life's energies.

Awakened individuals should realize that common education is for common people and that special individuals need special education. Just as the fastest thoroughbreds need superior fodder, people who cultivate internal values need "superior fodder" for their growth, but where can modern man find this nourishment? In all his attempts to establish new ways of thinking and new modes of living, he has yet to arrive at insight sufficient to ensure a secure future for himself and his fellow man. We must turn, therefore, to ancient guidelines that were developed before human life became so complicated - not any primitive or simplistic methods, but true and appropriate solutions.

After reviewing the vast cultural and spiritual achievements of all times, the *Book of Changes* or *I Ching* comes forward. This ancient book holds the time-tested value of responding to the needs of mankind. The maturity of the pure minds of the ancients has the unique ability to provide the insight that is needed now. Those sincere individuals who examine, respect and make use of the *Book of Changes* today will discover that it serves as a good advisor and private teacher that can safely guide them through the trials of life.

Quite simply, rather than offering a dogma or doctrine, the *Book of Changes* teaches one to look for the most appropriate point in any particular behavior or event. This method is invaluable to an individual's self-discovery and self-alignment. The one who comes to understand this sense of appropriateness, incorporates it into his or her thought processes and adheres firmly to it as the highest "doctrine" of his or her own personal religion will benefit in all three spheres of life. Such a person will find clarity in the mental sphere, balance in daily life, and positive, steady spiritual growth.

I have therefore undertaken this translation and explanation for the modern mind. Examples and illustrations from the vantage point of my spiritual tradition are included to further clarify certain passages.

For interested readers, I offer the following historical background. Before written history, an ancient by the name of Fu Shi developed a "line system" to express the principle of appropriateness. It was not until about 1181 B.C., however, that the feudal lord, King Wen of the Shang Dynasty (1766-1121 B.C.) provided a written explanation of these lines and hexagrams. Much later, Confucius (551-479 B.C.) added his commentaries to the lines in his later years.

In my present translation, I have drawn from three ancient guides, who themselves are conduits of prehistoric wisdom: Lao Tzu (active around 571 B.C.), who continued the teaching of natural truth and the importance of sincerity in universal life; Confucius, who continued the ancient humanist teaching; and Mo Tzu (501-416 B.C.), who continued the teaching of a prehistoric religious faith in an indiscriminating, impartial Heaven. The commentaries of Confucius are absorbed in the explanation of each hexagram, while the new commentaries offered are from my spiritual training.

Without a doubt, the schools of Lao Tzu, Confucius and Mo Tzu were instrumental in preserving our ancient culture. If we use divisions of time to express the ancestry of these schools, Lao Tzu would represent the virtue of the Yellow Emperor (2698-2358 B.C.), Confucius the virtue of Emperors Niao (2357-2258 B.C.) and Shun (2257-2208 B.C.), and Mo Tzu the virtue of the Great Yu (2207 B.C.). After these three periods, beginning in the Sha Dynasty (2207-1767 B.C.), the corruption of human nature became increasingly serious. This debasement continued throughout the Shang Dynasty (1766-1121 B.C.) until finally, at the collapse of this dynasty, a tribal leader named King Wen responded to the situation.

King Wen deeply understood the influences that were corrupting people. Wishing to restore the ancient pure virtue, he dedicated himself to the reorganization and further explanation of the *Book of Changes* which contained ancient knowledge of human behavior. Promoting the *Book of Changes* as a system to guide the central government, heads of tribes and influential individuals, King Wen successful started a new epoch, the Chou Dynasty (1122-249 B.C.). Toward the end of the Chou Dynasty, however, the corruption of human nature again began to peak. At that time, many other sages came forth to respond to the situation and restore the pure virtue of life. Lao Tzu, Confucius and Mo Tzu were three of these. They each demonstrated the way of ancient unspoiled people in their own way: Lao Tzu through the love of nature and total integration with the pervading universal spirit; Confucius through the value of self-restraint in all human relationships; and Mo Tzu through selfless sincerity toward an indiscriminating Heaven. These three together represent the harmonious virtue of pure, original human nature and provide a healthy direction for society to follow. This is the essence of this book.

A bright new epoch starts with a correct philosophy, a philosophy which guides people to restore human nature to its original healthy condition and then encourages them to reach for further development.

People who know they are sick also know how they feel when they are well. Similarly, by observing the simple principles of behavior expressed by ancient, uncorrupted people, we can rediscover the value of naturalness and health. For this reason, I felt the time was right for this contemporary translation of the *Book of Changes*. It is aimed at reducing the dualistic thinking of "good fortune" or "misfortune" which pervades daily life. Instead, it leads one toward spiritual absoluteness and independence.

Sometimes my readers may be puzzled at the logic I present, namely that one plus one equals one plus one rather than the usual one plus one equals two. This is important spiritual logic, because things of nature exist simply by and for themselves. This logic is validated by natural existence and needs no recognition from the general mind. Conceptual existence is the playground of the mind and can be a far cry from the reality of natural existence. Because it cannot pierce its own shell, the common human mind cannot see the natural truth that surrounds it.

My purpose in making this present work available to my English-speaking friends is to share it with those who are sincerely interested in connecting with the earliest harvest of human cultural and spiritual achievement. You will find useful guidelines here for specific occasions, as well as a presentation of the fundamental path to take in daily life.

At this difficult time, when intense competition has led to bitter relationships with strife and contention among people, it is my wish to continue the work of all great-hearted sages. As the elucidator of an ancient pure culture and path of natural light, I join with those who would like to see all people find peace and brightness in their own minds and beings. Once people can see their fundamental mistake of separation, their pain and suffering can be eliminated.

It is my sincere desire that with this basic introduction to the *Book of Changes*, as in all the work I present, you may continue your work of self-education, self-discovery and self-fulfillment.

Ni, Hua Ching
March 21, 1983
Los Angeles, CA

Part One:
The Natural Truth Underlying
The Book of Changes and the Unchanging Truth

乾以易知，坤以簡能，易則易知，簡則易從。易知則有親，易從則有功。有親則可久，有功則可大。可久則賢人之德，可大則賢人之業，易簡則天下之理得矣。天下之理得，而成位乎其中矣。

化情書 癸亥吉日

Chapter 1

INTRODUCTION

The *Book of Changes*, also referred to as the *I Ching*, is an ancient work completed by the wise King Wen, a feudal lord, in the last generation of the Shang Dynasty (1766-1121 B.C.). People who recognize this as a remarkable work of profound wisdom which has been passed down from an ancient culture might also want to know how the ancient ones developed their integral vision of all aspects of life.

Long ago, before teachers of a cultural heritage existed, people relied on their own simple minds to develop a system of knowledge and solve the problems in their lives. Living close to nature provided them with their first teacher - great Nature herself. They learned that she provides for, supports and instructs all beings. After long periods of observation and life experience, the ancient ones not only gathered information about Nature, but they also discovered the laws behind its seeming diversity.

The system of hexagrams which we call the *Book of Changes* or *I Ching* was one of the first great successes in ancient man's attempts to find the laws which regulate all phenomena. Most significant was their discovery that the laws of great Nature are also the laws of humanity and that since Nature and humanity are one, harmony is the key to life. This conclusion was drawn after long internal and external searching which revealed the balanced way of life as the fundamental path.

This integral vision of the universe became the spiritual faith of ancient developed people. It was the broad and plain foundation for their discovery of spiritual truth and secret methods. Since life is the main theme of all useful knowledge, the *Book of Changes*, the *Tao Teh Ching*, acupuncture, internal medicine, and the internal work of spiritual cultivation all make living in harmony with nature their foundation.

In contrast, our overgrown human population, combined with modern city life, obscures the significance of nature in the lives of people today. Great Nature, however, always remains the true source of human life. To restore our understanding of this integral truth, we can use the line system of the *Book of Changes* to study the way in which people and events develop.

When we rediscover the usefulness of a natural life, we shall again learn to love great Nature. We will also learn that it is dangerous to violate our own nature, the subtle level of the natural order and the natural environment. We must learn to approach these ancient methods of integration with an appreciation for what they are: simple, non-coercive guidelines for harmonizing our deviated human nature with the unspoiled great Nature.

You will find these useful principles underlying all of the material that follows.

Chapter 2

THE NATURAL RHYTHM OF LIFE

The Rhythm of the Life Line

1. A perfectly straight line:

(FIGURE 1)

This line was drawn with the help of a ruler. It is perfectly straight, thus it is an artificial line.

2. A naturally straight line :

(FIGURE 2)

This line was drawn without the help of a ruler, thus it is a naturally straight line. A perfectly straight line is non-existent in nature, except in very short segments. In nature, all straight lines are slightly curved.

3. The development of human life, whether in an individual or society, is like a straight line with curves. It is a natural line. This is reality, but most people wish reality to be straight and smooth like a racing car on a cleared road. They cannot accept the fact that reality is not this way. They expect the environment to take responsibility for them, thus they naturally encounter pain.

4. A perfect circle:

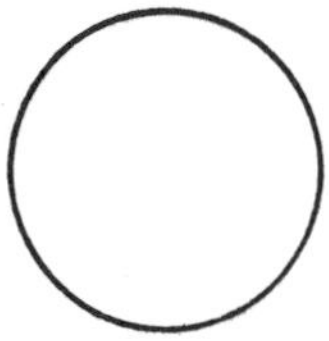

(FIGURE 3)

Likewise, an exact circle does not exist in nature.

5. A natural circle:

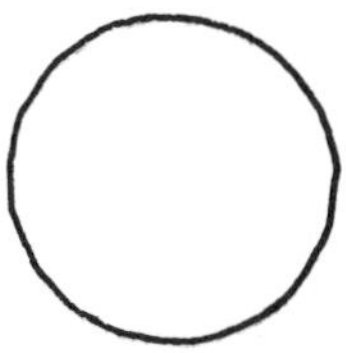

(FIGURE 4)

A real circle, or other round shapes in nature, would appear as a natural circle.

6. When a life is lived naturally, it looks like this:

(FIGURE 5)

7. Although a straight line with curves is natural, it is the responsibility of an individual not to augment the sharpness of the angles. When the human mind tries to impose the concept of imaginary perfection upon nature, the result is always unnatural. Destruction, disaster and agony are the inevitable result. Any stressful situation, either emotional or psychological, causes the curves of a straight line to become more angular:

(FIGURE 6)

When stress is expressed in a linear form, it looks like this:

(FIGURE 7)

In extreme cases, it looks like this:

(FIGURE 8)

Decreasing the Extremes

1. This is an idealistic baseline of a natural human life:

(FIGURE 9)

2. The baseline of a natural life has rhythmical curves:

(FIGURE 10)

This line shows that the peaks and valleys of a natural life are not too far from the baseline. The gently curved line is the real baseline. A precisely straight baseline does not exist in natural life.

3. When a line rises sharply, the following part naturally falls sharply:

(FIGURE 11)

4. Similarly, when a line sinks, the following part rises sharply:

(FIGURE 12)

5. Therefore, any extreme positive movement causes an extreme negative movement:

(FIGURE 13)

6. All extremes create other extremes. It can be said that when anything stands forth too positively, the benefits of being positive are transformed into negative results.

7. A balanced fundamental path is the baseline of a natural life.

8. Working to decrease the sharp angles of extremes wastes time. The best thing to do is not to create sharp corners in life by exaggerating emotional, psychological or conceptual attitudes.

9. Tensions and pressures may come from natural causes. However, the ancient integral ones observed that when nature creates trouble it can usually be escaped, but when people create their own trouble, it is fatal.

Lengthening or Shortening the Span of a Human Life

1. A natural, peaceful life can be expressed by a straight line with rhythms and easy curves:

(FIGURE 14)

2. A life under internal or external tension or pressure becomes denatured:

(FIGURE 15)

3. Generally, internal pressures are more serious than external ones. Internal pressure is expressed through impulsiveness, anxiety, anger, depression, tension, mistakes, etc.

4.   A natural life span is long, like this:

(FIGURE 16)

5.   If many curves are made on a straight line, it becomes shortened:

(FIGURE 17)

The length of this line is actually the same as the
one above in Figure 16.

6.   If the curves are sharpened, the length of the original straight line becomes even more greatly
shortened:

(FIGURE 18)

7.   To lessen the intensity of the curves actually
lengthens the span of the line. Below is a comparison
of a line with sharp curves and a line of the same
length with natural curves:

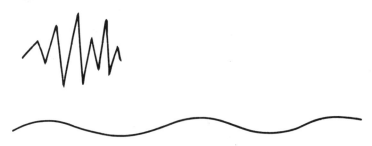

(FIGURE 19)

8.   As you can see, lessening extremes has the effect
of lengthening the life span. Which do you prefer?
In how many ways do you shorten your life span?
In what ways could you lengthen it?

9. Sharp curves deviate or stray from the baseline of a natural good life. They often represent crises in the development of an integral, normal life.

10. An individual should take responsibility for his or her own growth. Personal growth comes from incessant self-cultivation by which one can remove the emotional elements of love and hate, desire and impulse. It also leads one to know which external influences impede correct judgment and must be removed. Compromising adjustments to an unhealthy social or political system, the adoption of incorrect religious concepts or accepting modern, immature and fashionable education are some of the most important influences that can be removed. The overflow of such things often causes one to become unbalanced and extreme.

11. Internal and external pressures make a person deviate from the baseline of a natural good life. They indirectly form the curves of a person's life and constantly make these curves steeper. The unhealthy tendency of modern life is to denature the natural good life.

12. The teachings of Lao Tzu suggest that the Integral Way is to decrease extremes through personal cultivation.

13. The key guideline, which is often the teaching of the ancient developed ones, is to be natural. This means not artificially bringing a curve to its extreme by emotional or psychological exaggeration.

14. This also means that when curves are present, one should slow down, not speed up.

15. We should restrain our preference for any particular time or space and inwardly maintain naturalness so that we do not sharpen the curves of life.

16. As seen in the illustrations above, one should not trade a portion of one's life span for anything external.

Chapter 3

THE PRINCIPLE OF YIN AND YANG

A. The Two Forces

1. The two categories of yin and yang can be expressed as two different lines, one broken and one unbroken:

(FIGURE 20)

The unbroken line represents yang, the strong force. The broken or separated line represents yin, the weak force.

2. Yin and yang expressed by a slope:

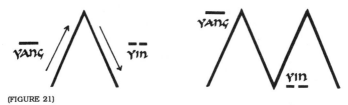

(FIGURE 21)

3. Yin and yang expressed by a circle:

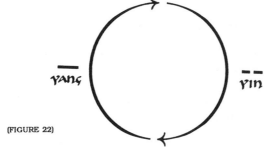

(FIGURE 22)

4. The interaction of yin and yang expressing the four phases of universal energy:

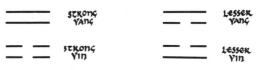

(FIGURE 23)

B. The Four Phases of Universal Energy

Expressed by a slope:

(FIGURE 24)

Expressed by a circle:

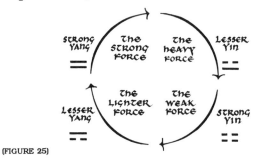

(FIGURE 25)

C. The Eight Phases of Universal Energy Expressed by the Trigrams in the Pre-Heaven Arrangement

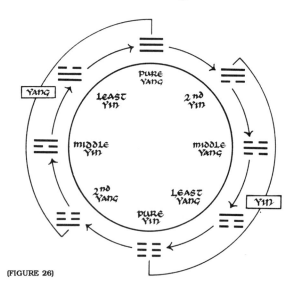

(FIGURE 26)

D. Finding the Balancing Force

1. Nothing exists in isolation. Even in the view of modern physics, everything is always interacting with everything else, and the most minute particle can be split again.

2. There is an organization within all things, regardless of how large or small they are.

3. In every organization, there are two groups or two important elements: yin and yang.

4. Within yin and yang there must be a balancing force.

5. In the case of pure yang and pure yin, the balancing force is expressed in the central line of the trigram. In general, this line signifies a leader, the force which holds the entire hexagram together or the most influential or decisive factor in the hexagram.

6. In most hexagrams, the ruling line is the fifth line:

(FIGURE 27)

7. In the combined energy formation of two different trigrams, however, any line can be the ruling line or center of the newly formed hexagram. For example:

    a.   In ☷, the center is the first line.

    b.   In ☰, the center is the second line.

    c.   In ☶, the center is the third line.

    d.   In ☳, the center is the fourth line.

e.   In ⚏ , the top yang line is the center, but it is not well centered. The hexagram itself is poorly formed, and the weak fifth line carries only the sense of leadership.

E. The Eight Natural Forces

The eight phases of universal energy are exemplified by the following images which connote the basic energy formations of nature and are named accordingly:

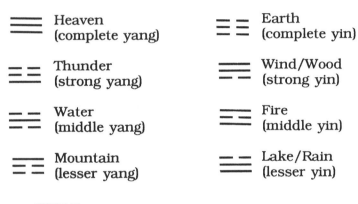

Heaven
(complete yang)

Earth
(complete yin)

Thunder
(strong yang)

Wind/Wood
(strong yin)

Water
(middle yang)

Fire
(middle yin)

Mountain
(lesser yang)

Lake/Rain
(lesser yin)

(FIGURE 28)

F. The Complete Cycle of the Eight Phases of Yin and Yang

The formation of a new kind of energy varies according to the composition of yin and yang. Not only is change affected by the quantity of yin and yang, but also by the position of the new forces that join to form the new energy phase.

In the following chart, all possible combinations of yin and yang, as expressed through the eight phases of universal energy, are represented. These combinations form the basic sixty-four hexagrams.

The Complete Cycle of the Eight Phases
of Yin and Yang

(FIGURE 29)

Chapter 4

THE FIVE ELEMENTARY PHASES OF CYCLIC MOVEMENT

A. The Five Phases of a Cycle

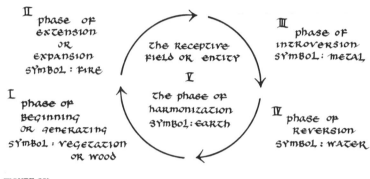

(FIGURE 30)

The four phases are expressed on a receptive field which is considered the fifth phase. The substance or entity of the receptive field activates the rotation of the four phases. This holding force, or harmonizing phase, is considered another basic phase, thus there are actually five phases of every cyclic movement.

(FIGURE 31)

In Figure 31 above, when one of the four phases dominates, the centering force yields, and when the dominating force weakens, it allows the central force to enter the transforming, transitional phase. The four phases of cyclic movement are what are most often noticed. The central force exists, but is unnoticed.

Characteristics of the Five Elementary Phases

"Wood"   symbolizes the beginning (sprouting or generating) phase as shown in I.

"Fire"   symbolizes the fully-grown or expanded phase as shown in II.

"Metal"   symbolizes the collecting or introverting phase as shown in III.

"Water"   symbolizes the reverting phase as shown in IV.

"Earth"   symbolizes the harmonizing phase as shown in V.

B. The Five Elementary Phases Expressed Through the Natural Energy Cycles

1. The Cycle of the Ten Heavenly Forces or "Stems"

甲 (Jia)   乙 (Yi)   Yang wood and yin wood as the generating phase or force of a cyclic movement.

丙 (Bien)   丁 (Ding)   Yang fire and yin fire as the expanding phase or force at the peak of the cycle.

戊 (Wuh)   己 (Ji)   Yang earth and yin earth as the allaying of the extremes of the other phases or forces: the harmonizing force.

庚 (Geng)   辛 (Hsin)   Yang metal and yin metal as the introverting phase or force.

壬 (Ren)   癸 (Quei)   Yang water and yin water as the reverting phase or force.

a) The Ten Heavenly "Stems" Represented in Linear Form

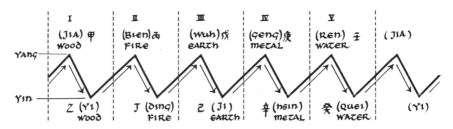

(FIGURE 32)

Note: The forces of natural cycle start with generation as Wood. This is also seen in the Post-Heaven arrangement of the eight natural forces (Figure 105b), which starts with Wood, moves upward to Fire, goes to the center as Earth, to the side as Metal and below as Water.

b) The Ten Heavenly "Stems" Shown in a Circular Manner

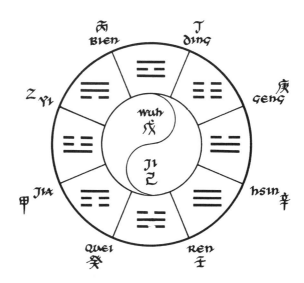

(FIGURE 33)

Note: "Earth" is the central element which holds the other forces together. It acts as a lubricant between the other conflicting forces and is thus a moderating force in the natural order.

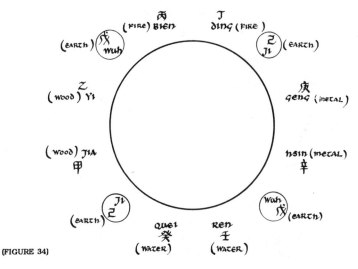

(FIGURE 34)

Note: Between each quarter of a cycle there is an "Earth" (circled above). In this figure, the Ten Heavenly or "Celestial" Stems are in the order utilized in the complete cycle of the sixty pairs of interacting energy phases which are discussed in Chapter Six.

2. The Cycle of the Twelve Earthly Forces or "Branches"

亥 (Hai)   子 (Tze)   Yin water and yang water of the force of earth.

寅 (Ein)   卯 (Mao)   Yang wood and yin wood of the force of earth.

巳 (Sze)   午 (Wu)   Yin fire and yang fire of the force of earth.

申 (Shen)   酉 (Yu)   Yang metal and yin metal of the force of earth.

辰 (Chen)   戌 (Shu)   Yang earth of the force of earth.

丑 (Chui)   未 (Wei)   Yin earth of the force of earth.

a) The Twelve Earthly Phases in Linear Form

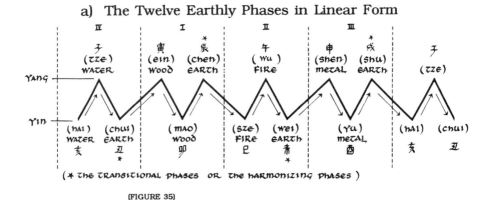

(FIGURE 35)

Note: The forces of Earth start with the returning force expressed by "Water." The natural order begins with "Tze" and reads thus:

子 丑 寅 卯 辰 巳 午 未 申 酉 戌 亥

b) The Twelve Earthly "Branches" Represented in a Circular Manner

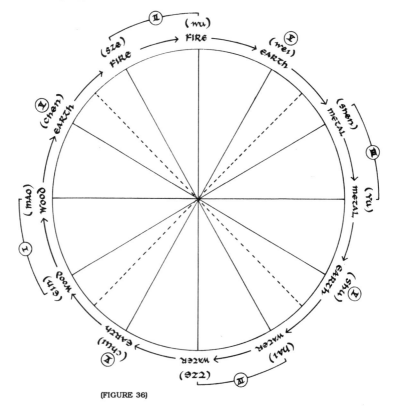

(FIGURE 36)

The dotted lines in both the linear and circular representations separate the four major phases. Notice that each phase shares the transitional phase ("Earth") represented by the Roman numeral V in Figure 36, and by the circled characters in the note to Figure 35. For instance, yin and yang water have a yin earth. Yin and yang wood have a yang earth, etc. The Roman numerals are in the order of the natural cycle that is expressed by the four seasons: Spring corresponding to Wood, Summer to Fire, Autumn to Metal, and Winter to Water. The cycle begins with IV, because the Winter Solstice is considered the beginning of a yearly cycle.

c) The Twelve Terrestrial Branches as They Apply to the Divisions of The Day, Month and Year

Application to the Daily Energy Cycle

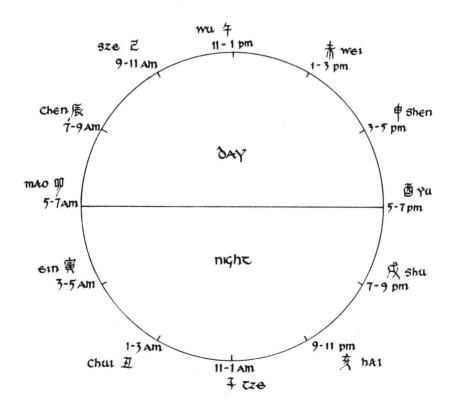

(FIGURE 37)

Application to the Months and Seasons

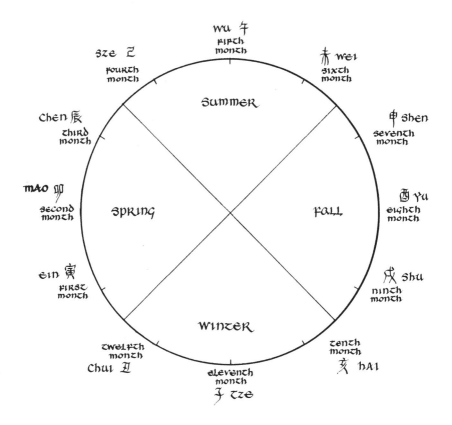

(FIGURE 38)

The various phases and cycles of vegetation can be described as follows:

Its growth is the phase of "Wood" or "Vegetation" and the season of Spring.

Its luxuriance is the phase of "Fire" and the season of Summer.

Its contraction is the phase of "Metal" and the season of Autumn.

The return of its vitality to its root is the phase of "Water" and the season of Winter.

The Ten Celestial Stems represent yang, the upper force which is the vitality of Heaven or the more subtle level of the universal life force.

The Twelve Terrestrial Branches represent yin, the lower force which is the vitality of Earth, the more gross, material level of the universal life force.

The universe comes into existence with the integration of both of these forces: "In the yang force there is yin, and in the yin force there is yang."

Tracing back to the basic source of the universe, neither matter nor the absolute subtle energy by themselves can be considered the foundation of the universe. Even in the most minute particle of the universe there is the integration of yin and yang. Using this key, the universe is clearly and objectively presented by the system of "Stems and Branches," at the root of which is the T'ai Chi symbol of integration.

C.   Dealing with Cycles, Phases and Forces

All movement, all change, is a pattern of the interaction of yin and yang. Each curve in the line of an individual life, or the life of the universe itself, is made up of three parts:

1) a generating phase
2) a phase of traveling far and reaching the summit
3) a decline and return to the origin

How we make use of and harmonize with these changes is a matter of importance in our lives. When we follow a gradual curve, we are not very conscious of change. When the curve is sharp or extreme, however, we are sure to meet difficulty. The appropriate psychological response to an extreme curve should be one of balance. Tension or severe emotions do not help anything. They are a way of denying that a curve or change exists.

When one faces a new situation, the mind is often on the past. This kind of thinking creates obstacles to an accurate, intuitive response which is more important than a conceptual understanding of the situation. General education helps people become well-versed in their thinking, but it destroys the correct use of intuition. As a result, tragedy can occur from an ordinary situation involving someone who is regarded as a good thinker.

Intellectuals and scholars may be very apt thinkers, but they often appear clumsy when direct instinctual or intuitive reactions are called for in daily life. They work hard at searching for an explanation or hidden meaning rather than having immediate contact with reality. The present, not the past, is the reality which should be faced, but most clever thinkers miss it. Thinking becomes an escape for intellectually developed people whose lives would be smoother if they worked harder at developing and using their intuition.

When a mind is detached from the past and also remains unattached to any details of the present, it can see the whole and thus find the way out of any situation. The minds of ancient sages may not have been any better than those of modern intellectuals, but they did not abuse or spoil their minds.

Everything is always, and without exception, in motion. Attachment to what one likes is a psychological defect and is unreal. In dealing with movement or change, the attitude which should be utilized is that of the phase of Earth. Its force connotes calmness, keeping to the root, perceptiveness, maintaining balance and not seeking extremes.

Cyclic movement is expressed in individual emotional life, psychological life, physical life, financial life, family life and social relationships as well as in historical development, the destiny of all mankind, the universe and all natural manifestations. You have only to open your eyes to see the bountiful evidence and examples of how to effectively deal with movement and change.

The Integral Way is a way of thoroughly understanding the universe. It is the best way of predicting human fortune; thus, our highly developed ancestors saved the Integral Way for all of us, their wise and fortunate descendants.

Chapter 5

AN ABSTRACT UNDERSTANDING OF HOW NATURE DEVELOPS ITSELF

The naturally developed mind in the very ancient time attempted to control the changes in its surroundings by adopting the abstract method:

The Early Stages of Natural Development

Stage I

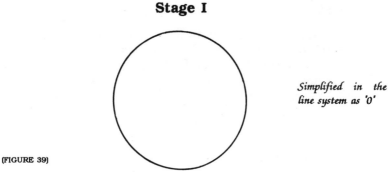

Simplified in the line system as '0'

(FIGURE 39)

Zero does not equal none. It symbolizes the fullness and the purity of nature as one life. It also can be illustrated as the origin of the universal impetus.

Thus, Nature starts from zero. Zero is the center of the universe. In the *Tao Teh Ching*, it is called "nothing" or the neutral.

Stage II

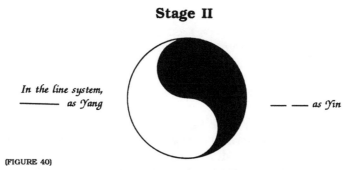

In the line system,
——— *as Yang*

— — *as Yin*

(FIGURE 40)

This figure demonstrates the division into two: yin and yang.

Stage III

In the line system,

≡≡
as Full Yang

═ ═
as Lesser Yang

═ ═
as Lesser Yin

═ ═
as Full Yin

(FIGURE 41)

Lesser yang (the small white circle) grows in the sphere of strong yin. This means the full yin sphere, once overextending itself, gives birth to lesser yang.

Lesser yin (the small black circle) grows in the sphere of strong yang. This means the full yang sphere, overextending itself, gives birth to lesser yin.

Nature Produces the Five Types of Energy

Nature itself is actually one energy. The different phases of this energy are expressed in the self-generating process of life.

Strong Yang or Pure Yang
This is the dominating yang force. It is the main energy of nature. It is constructive, creative, positive energy.

Young Yang or Lesser Yang
Before developing into strong yang, the energy that presses forward is expressed as "young" yang. This energy is conceptualized as "second strong" energy.

Strong Yin or Pure Yin
When strong yang energy over extends itself, it creates dominating yin energy. This occurs when yang energy seeks self-adjustment in response to opposition or resistance. It is a way of self-accomplishing.

Young Yin or Lesser Yin
This energy phase is the transition created by the movement of yang energy before it grows from weak to strong, less to full.

O This phase is the mild transitional force among the four apparent phases. Its function is to harmonize and hold the four phases together, thus enabling a cyclic function to be sustained.

The Adoption of the New Symbolic Meaning

Yin energy is produced by the movement of yang energy in an opposing and resisting manner in order to assist the effort of the yang. Thus it is the weak stage of yang energy which makes an alternating shift in order to continue generating itself.

The two line system of yang ———— and yin — — is inadequate to express this further discovered reality, thus the three line system was adopted and the five elementary phases were expressed with the following adaptations:

The Strong Force

Water, as the symbol of stretching and flowing, takes the emphasized double yang lines in the center of the new symbolic system.

The Weak Force

Fire, as the symbol of speeding, consuming and hollowing, takes the emphasized double yin lines as the center of the new symbolic system.

The Light Force

Wood or vegetation, as the symbol of growing, enlivening, rising and floating upwards, adds one yang line to the top in the new symbolic system.

☲ *The Heavy Force*

Metal, as the symbol of condensing and sinking, adds one yang line on the bottom in the new symbolic system.

O   *The Harmonizing Force*

Soil or earth, as the symbol of stabilizing, adds one yin line to the bottom of the weak force in the new symbolic system.

The Development of the Line System through Use:

The Four Energies Develop into the Eight Great Manifestations

By adding ▬▬ or ▬ ▬ to the four forces, the Eight Great Manifestations are developed:

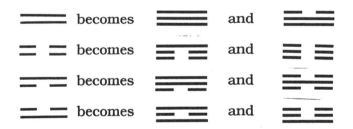

The tri-line system is completed by adding one yang or one yin line on the top of the already existing bottom lines of the two-line symbol to become the Eight Great Manifestations of Natural Energy.   Remember, the hexagram always expresses a development or order from the bottom up.

Afterwards, the hexagram or six line system was developed.   Doubling the trigrams with the same trigrams forms the eight symbols of the Ba Gua (octahedron). When the trigrams are paired with different trigrams, the 64 hexagrams of the I Ching are formed.

The Ba Gua Octahedron

(FIGURE 42)

The Division of Six Stages of Development

After the eight trigrams were developed from the four forces, they became a useful means of expression. Other than being used to symbolize the eight natural energies of ≡ sky, ≡≡ earth, ≡≡ wind, ≡≡ thunder, ≡≡ mountain, ≡≡ fire, ≡≡ water and ≡≡ rain, they are also used to express different stages of development of an event or situation. In natural developed medicine, for example, they are adopted to describe the depth of a physical disease; or they can describe the development of an event such as an historical period, a war or things of a small scale.

The six stages, symbolized by the six lines in a hexagram, reveal the two subdivisions or big stages in an event or situation: the yang or apparent stage and the yin or hidden stage. For example, an event can move from the stage of three yang: from ≡ full yang and ≡≡ strong yang to ≡≡ lesser yang. This progression means the matter is transforming from being superficial and becoming deeper. It also means the yang, positive energy, is gradually weakening. From this position of lesser yang, an event may transfer to the stage of three yin: ≡≡ lesser yin and ≡≡ strong yin into ≡≡ full yin. These trigrams express worsening development and the increase of a negative influence. This is called a proceeding regression.

In a situation of regression, we understand that there has been a change from apparent to hidden, from simple to complex and from easily managed to difficult. The reverse order, a proceeding progression, gives evidence of moving from deep trouble to a slight problem, etc. The recovery or progression follows the reverse process. However, here you notice among the eight trigrams that two of the eight trigrams, ☰ and ☷, have been dropped. They are not used as descriptive stages in such a situation because ☲ is used to govern ☰ to ☳ to ☶ which expresses fire, heating or expansive changes. This is the yang energy in a process of decreasing; it is moving towards becoming weaker and weaker. Similarly, ☵ is used to govern ☱, ☴ and ☷ which expresses the increasing of yin; this expresses watery, cold and deep changes. Regression and progression are illustrated in Figures 43 and 44. This six stage description is used in natural developed medicine to describe a physical situation.

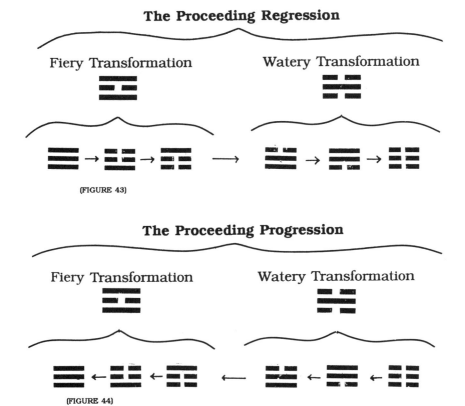

The Proceeding Regression

Fiery Transformation   Watery Transformation

(FIGURE 43)

The Proceeding Progression

Fiery Transformation   Watery Transformation

(FIGURE 44)

The Five Elements

After the line system was developed and used to express different natural energies and stages, it later came to be used in governing complicated phenomena such as physical or social situations. Following that, the concept of the five elementary relationships developed. The five elements are used to describe the harmonizing and conflicting relationships among the five constituents of a group relationship. These five elementary phases are widely used in governing complicated situations with simplicity. An illustration of the five phases can be seen in Figures 31 and 51, and in the charts in my book, *Tao, the Subtle Universal Law*. Studying such material can help train the mind; through the capability of arranging one's own understanding, one can understand a matter or situation. The Five Elements System is derived from the eight manifestations of natural energy, as described below.

The Meaning of the Eight Symbols by Trigrams

is full natural impetus. It is nature as an entirety.

is the full stagnancy of natural impetus. This is not movement or life. It is a foundation like the Earth.

is the natural impetus pushing upward. It is as the life of vegetation, Wood, Thunder or like life itself. It exactly expresses the great vitality of nature and the vital force in each individual life.

is the natural energy pushing forward like the flow of Water.

is the natural energy expressing in a hollow center, emptying a space. It is Fire.

is the natural energy covered by a slight obstruction. It is Lake or Rain.

is the natural impetus when it has moved too high. It is like a Mountain.

▬▬ is the natural impetus being active, and is above a
▬ ▬ solid base. It is like Wind.

Note: The words "Heaven," "Earth," "Mountain," etc.,
are verbal symbols used by the *I Ching* to describe a type
of energy. The items described are not literally what the *I
Ching* is referring to.   Such a misunderstanding would
damage one's understanding and study of the *I Ching*.

The Symbols of Five Elements

Thus the tri-line symbols of the five element energies
become:

▬ ▬
▬▬▬   as symbolic matter "Water"
▬ ▬

▬▬▬
▬ ▬   as symbolic matter "Fire"
▬▬▬

▬ ▬   as symbolic matter "Wood" which includes
▬▬▬   wind or airy energy.
       The ancient developed ones categorized
       Wind or airy energy in Wood, because no life
       grows without the need of wind or air. It is
       arranged in the diagram of the Ba Gua (Octa-
       hedron) between Wood and Fire, because it is
       used in the process of burning wood to be
       fire.   The necessary condition in creating a
       fire is the help of wind or air. Because Air is
       not concrete matter like the other symbolic
       four elements, the ancient developed ones let
       Wood govern the Wind.
       Wind is an energy in the phase between
       Wood and Fire. The transition from Wood to
       Fire creates the Wind type of airy movement,
       and from solid to empty as airy energy.

▬ ▬   as symbolic matter "Metal" which includes all
▬▬▬   heavenly bodies and the starry energy of the
       sky. The ancient developed ones consider all
       kinds of stars as the condensed natural ener-
       gy. Condensation is symbolized by using the
       image of Metal.

▬ ▬   as symbolic matter "Earth" which includes
▬ ▬   Mountain energy.

Note:
⚏ is not included in the five elements because it is Heaven. In nature, ▬ is impetus energy. ☰ means the full natural force of impetus. Thus, it represents all yang energy in one big category and cannot be further categorized to become one side of the Tai Chi diagram (which consists of two spheres, yang and yin).

The Meaning of the Five Elements

The trigrams represent more than what their names symbolize.

The energy represented by the name "Water" represents an energy which has the characteristics of fluidity, a liquid type of movement and a downward motion. It is cool and liquid. It is a gathering or dispersing type of movement. It can be gentle and slow but also may be quick. It is not abrupt or sudden. An example of this is the motion of rain water collecting in a beaver dam, which slowly trickles out through the stream. Another example is a crowd slowly filling a concert hall or football stadium, then slowly leaving after the concert or game is over. Another example is the breath of a calm person, slow and gradual.

The energy represented by the name "Fire" represents an energy of explosion and heat. It is a type of burning off; it speeds up the process of aging or being worn out. It consumes and destroys. It is beautifying. It is an airy type of reaction. An example of Fire energy, besides a bonfire, is a firecracker. Another example is the combustion inside an internal combustion engine. Another example of this is a person's untamed anger: quick, consuming and explosive.

The energy of "Wood" is an upward movement. It is expansive and creative. It consumes and creates something new. It is exemplified by small growing plants in the spring, which consume the seed, water and air to create a plant. It is like the root and sprout of a tree or any plant pushing up to break through the soil which covers it. Thus, it is also expressed by the movement of thunder breaking through the thick clouds. Another example is the expansive growth of a young, successful company. Another example is cooking, putting together the elements of a recipe or any creative action which combines different elements to form something new.

The energy described by the word "Metal" is contracting and heavy. Its motion is inward. It is cold. It is stagnant. An example of Metal energy is an overcast day in winter. Another example is the solidifying of water into ice. An example in the human realm is depression, which is imploding, stagnant energy.

The energy represented by the word "Earth" is stability. It is firm without being rigid. It is reliable and dependable. It is not movement, but it is not stagnancy: rather, it is a centered beingness. An example of earth energy could be the foundation of a house, which upholds and supports the structure of the building and provides a safe environment for life activities. Another example is the most responsible, stable person in a household. Another example is a person's physical body, which provides a base for one's thoughts, speech and actions in the world.

The above is a limited illustration with the purpose of giving a better understanding of the five elements system.

The Use of Numbers to Express the Law of Natural Development

One to five can be expressed as follows:

1 =   ━━━━   Strong (major or old) yang,
                the light force.

2 =   ━ ━   Strong (major or old) yin,
                the heavy force.

3 =   ━━━━   Lesser (minor or young) yang,
                the young light force, electromagnetism.

4 =   ━ ━   Lesser (minor or young) yin,
                the young heavy force, gravity.

5 =   O   The indiscriminable whole,
                the unifying force.

For further information regarding the line system, refer to Chapter 61 of the *Hua Hu Ching* in *The Complete Works of Lao Tzu* and *Tao, the Subtle Universal Law*.

The Traditional Lo Shih Diagram
as Pre-Heaven Order of Eight Manifestations

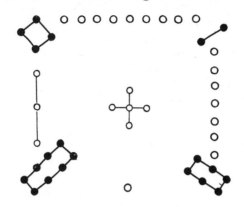

o = odd number   ● = even number

1 = Earth ▤ ▤   2 = Wind ☴

3 = Fire ☲   4 = Lake or Rain ☱

5 = 0   6 = Mountain ☶

7 = Water ☵   8 = Thunder ☳

9 = Heaven or Sky ☰

(FIGURE 45)

The Magic Square

4	9	2
3	5	7
8	1	6

(FIGURE 46)

The magic square is derived from Lo Shih. Any way the numbers are summed up, the total is fifteen. Now children use it as a game, but there is still profound natural meaning behind it. This nine house system has been developed for use in divination and spiritual practice.

The Eight Symbols Transfer to Five Elements

The Traditional Hu To Diagram

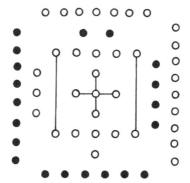

Number	Image	Symbol	Sense
5 = 6 - 1	Water	☰	light force
5 = 7 - 2	Fire	☲	heavy force
5 = 8 - 3	Wood	☳	strong force
5 = 9 - 4	Metal	☴	weak force
5 = 0	Earth	O	field of harmonization

(FIGURE 47)

The center of the above ancient mystical chart, Hu To, shows:

(FIGURE 48)

The middle "five" expresses the balancing force and is the unifying field, like the central element "Earth." The square expresses the universal basic energy as strong yang, strong yin, lesser yang and lesser yin.

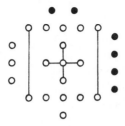

(FIGURE 49)

In this figure, the numbers one to four are expressed by the pyramid in Figure 50, as are the numbers six to nine as shown in Figure 45. The numerical combinations can also be expressed as shown in Figure 47.

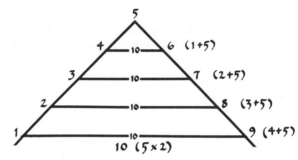

(FIGURE 50)

A. Five is a number whose function is to neutralize and unify. It is derived from 1 + 4 or 2 + 3 and is comprised of one odd yang number and one even yin number.

B. Five implies establishment.

C. The numbers six through nine are the repetition of the numbers one through five in a declining phase.

D. Ten is a number with the implication of stopping or decreasing the full growth of the yin and yang phases.

E. All numbers contain zero and one. The establishing factor is the number one, and that which is established is zero.

F. Thus the number five is an establishment which can be expressed by "zero" and contains the possibility of going further up or down.

G. One to five can be symbolized by the five natural phenomena:

1. Water
2. Fire
3. Wood
4. Metal
5. Earth

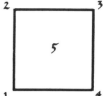

(FIGURE 51)

H. In the square in the above figure, the vertical lines express the rejection of each other.   The horizontal lines express the relation of generating.   Five is the neutralizing force which coheres the other Great Four, thus it is zero.

The Four Forces and Harmonization
Derived from the Combination of Lo Shih and Hu To

Hu To and Lo Shih are different systems of order. The number five emphasizes the expression of a new balancing point that should be found in each circumstance. The undisclosed spiritual practice is to realize this purpose spiritually, mentally and physically. This is the center of spiritual teaching, as in the *I Ching*, *Tao Teh Ching*, and other works.

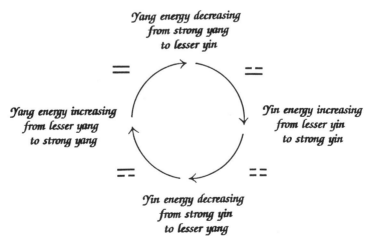

(FIGURE 52)

Left to right (clockwise) movement is the generating order. Right to left (counterclockwise) movement is the revolutionary order.

Chapter 6

THE VARIOUS ENERGY CYCLES
OF NATURE

I. Yin and Yang Expressed in the T'ai Chi Tu

A. The Tai Chi Symbol

(FIGURE 53)

Each T'ai Chi Tu has three aspects:

> yang (the white side)
> yin (the dark side)
> the circle representing their integration.

These two complementary spheres that exist together represent the relativity of all that exists, both in the physical and in the conceptual universe.

Located within each sphere is a small circle. The circle in yang is called "the yin in yang," and the circle in yin is called "the yang in yin." It is understood that further integration is brought forth in each sphere as the small circle increases into another T'ai Chi.

From the smallest element which composes the universe to the largest, the T'ai Chi Tu presents the integration of the universe in its totality.

Each T'ai Chi stands complete and independent while at the same time being one small part of the larger whole. This is illustrated in Figure 54 below. This precept can also be applied to the model of an individual human life. The universe itself is a unified existence like an individual human being, and an individual human life is a unified existence just like the universe.

Each T'ai Chi Stands Independent
as a Small Part of the Larger Whole

(FIGURE 54)

B. Four Ways to Present the T'ai Chi Tu

1.   This is the symbol that commonly represents the integration of yin and yang.   Yang is
generating, light energy, thus it rises to the higher
sphere.   Yin, its opposite, is receptive, heavy energy
and thus sinks to the lower sphere.   In general, yang
tends to rise, progress and increase, representing the
creative, active movement of nature.   Yin tends to
sink, reverse and decrease, representing the receptive
and less active movement of nature.   The principle of
equilibrium and balance is presented as the T'ai Chi
Tu, the interaction of the two different elements.

2.   This symbol expresses the energy state
of daily cycles, moon cycles, yearly cycles, and the cycles of an individual person's lifetime in general circumstances.   In a daily cycle, yang represents the
light of daytime and yin represents the darkness of
night.   If we bisect the T'ai Chi Tu with a horizontal
line, the lower half represents the period from midnight to noon.   The dark yin is exhausted and gives
way to the growing yang.   The upper half represents
the afternoon as yang energy decreases and gives way
to the growing yin toward midnight.

In presenting the moon cycle, the left (yang) side of the Tai Chi Tu expresses the moonlight increasing from the "new moon" upward. Around the fifteenth day of a Chinese calendar, the hypothetical vertical middle line is reached and the moon is at its fullest. Then the decreasing moonlight follows the next half of a moon cycle for around fifteen more days. The right side presents the darkness of the night.

In presenting the yearly solar cycle, the left (light) side represents the seasons of Spring and Summer and the right (dark) represents the seasons of Fall and Winter.

In presenting a person's general life cycle, the lower left expresses the first half while the upper left expresses the second half. The right side represents a person before birth and after death.

3. This orientation has the same meaning and purposes as the others, the only difference being to show the highest point of the cycle in the middle of the top curve. This is noon in a daily cycle, the full moon in a lunar cycle, the high point between Spring and Summer in a yearly cycle and middle age in a person's life.

4. This symbol more dramatically expresses the natural energy flow in its process of acceleration. The dimensions and states of the two opposite energy flows are clearly shown, as well as the important principle which says, "The faster the flow progresses, the more rapid its decrease." This principle can be understood in terms of natural phenomena, human physical force and historical events. The vivid movement, the active flow, and the principle that growth and decline are proportionally related are all pictured in this diagram.

There is another important principle expressed in the Tai Chi Tu which says: When yang reaches its fullest, yin grows, and when yin is at its fullest, yang starts on its way. All cycles follow this principle without exception.

There are still more principles and methods represented by the T'ai Chi Tu symbol which await one's further searching.

II. Use of Yin/Yang Cycles in Ordinary Human Life

A. Two Divisions

(FIGURE 55)

The yang (light) sphere represents life ——— .
The yin (dark) sphere represents uncertain death — — .

The basic structure of the universe, according to the Taoist view, consists of three spheres:

Heaven, or the spiritual realm, symbolized as ◯ .

Earth, or the material realm, symbolized as ● .

Mankind, containing all lives, symbolized as .

In the spiritual science of the natural spiritual path, represents a general human life before achievement. ◯ represents completed purification, total fulfillment, ascension or the pure yang body of an immortal one which is without any remaining yin. ● represents contamination, downwardness, ghosts, bondage and sorrow.

To be natural is to lengthen the yang or subtle cycle. To be supernatural is to eliminate the yin or gross sphere and become purely subtle.

In contrast, human life is usually spent chasing after death, and often the gross cycle takes charge of the entirety of one's life.

It is obvious that life belongs to yang and subtleness, while death belongs to yin and grossness. To understand this is to understand the foundation of spiritual truth, the great secret of which is immortal cultivation. One has access to the way of cultivation through all of my books.

B. Four Divisions

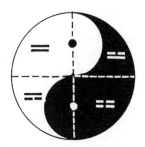

(FIGURE 56)

☰ represents the first quarter of life

☰ represents the second quarter of life

☰ represents the third quarter of life

☰ represents the fourth quarter of life

The length of each stage in an individual life is not determined by the length of time. Instead, the endurance of energy decides the length of time. Ordinary lives fill up a "frame" of time, such as how many years a person lives, but a "year" is only a mark of time. It does not actually represent the living situation of the person. When one's yang or subtle energy withers, life ceases. Therefore, in order to maintain life, subtle energy must be cultivated. There is no other way. This is the fundamental viewpoint of ancient naturally developed ones. Lengthening the yang curve of life's cycle is, in reality, lengthening life.

Ancient masters used metaphors to tell the truth which is lucidly expounded in my books, but it still requires daily self-cultivation to develop one's responsiveness and to experience the depth of the instruction. Total understanding and trust are required for development and achievement. Otherwise, my books would be no different from ordinary books.

From the understanding of the above, an individual should take responsibility for his life and apply the following virtuous practices:

self-adjustment   self-cultivation
self-communion   self-control
self-discipline   self-examination
self-government   self-improvement
self-knowledge   self-regulation
self-surrender   self-sustenance

As understood by the ancient spiritually developed ones, to consistently practice these virtuous qualities with sincerity is to grasp the meaning of the universe and of human life.

C. Yin and Yang in the Daily Cycle

Division of the Two Phases

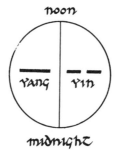

(FIGURE 57)

Note: In the natural spiritual way of cultivation, the hours between midnight and noon are composed of yang energy, while the hours between noon and midnight are composed of yin energy. Yang energy gives vitalizing support to human activity, while yin energy devitalizes activity. All important spiritual energy cultivation occurs during the yang part of the cycle.

Division of the Four Phases

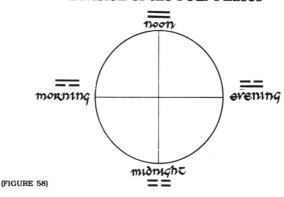

(FIGURE 58)

In this illustration of the four divisions of the daily solar cycle, the yang energy is shown rising through the morning hours and peaking at noon when the yin cycle begins. In the illustration below (Figure 59), maximum yang at noon is shown on the left.

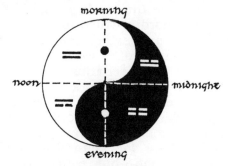

(FIGURE 59)

According to the energy differences, yang energy becomes too strong in the head area at the time close to noon. Although this is not a good time for cultivating, it is still okay for handling other daily affairs. The best time for self-cultivation is in the early morning when yang energy is not yet too strong.

In the first part of the yin sphere, the yin energy is still shallow and usable for some work. The latter part of the yin sphere, when the energy becomes deeper, is time for rest and not for engaging in work.

D. Yin and Yang in the Lunar Cycle

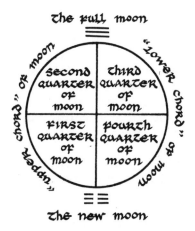

(FIGURE 60)

A "chord" is a straight line cut through a circle. Thus the Chinese call the half moon the "upper chord moon" when it is waxing in the left part of the sphere (Figure 60). They call it the "lower chord moon" when it wanes through the right half of the sphere. The new moon is called the "eyebrow moon."

The "upper chord," which develops from the new moon, is fresh, increasing, and reaches for the full moon. The "lower cord" is worn out and decreasing.

The tonifying and sedating effects of the moon's cycles extend to human emotional life. During the upper chord phases, one feels tonified, and during the lower chord sedated. One should regulate one's emotions in order to maintain balance during this cycle.

The correct time for self-cultivation is during all phases of the moon, but especially during the full lower chord moon. "No moon" is the end of the cycle when no light is visible from the moon. "New moon" is the very beginning of the new cycle, and is also called "eyebrow moon." New moon suggests new life or the beginning of a new cycle. It is beneficial to grow one's energy with the moon. For reasons of protecting the gentle energy sprout, emotional excitement and outbursts must be avoided during the new moon.

E. Further Applications of Figure 60

1.   On the day of the new moon one should fast or keep a clean, simple diet in order to benefit from the moon's refreshing energy.

2.   During the full moon (the fifteenth or sixteenth day of the lunar cycle) the tide rises. The liquid energy of the human body also rises at this time. During these days, one should avoid affairs which require a considerable amount of care, delicacy and gentleness. This is a good time for cultivating since it enables one to achieve clarity.

3.   During the closing days of the moon's cycle, before and at the time of no moon, the attracting or contracting force of the moon's energy is released. On the day when the energy is at its lowest, calmness should be maintained. One should avoid singing, crying or other emotional outbursts.

4. The phases of lunar energy influence the development of the brain of a newly conceived fetus. If conception occurs during a night with good moonlight, along with other normal conditions, the development of the brain of the future child will be benefited.

5. The moon influences the right hemisphere of the brain, whereas solar energy influences the left. The balance of the two hemispheres of the brain - the intuitive right side and the intellectual left side - is important for high development. The supporting, balancing energy from nature includes the Big Dipper, the first five planets, and the twenty-eight constellations, among others.

6. Parents do not give birth to the soul, they only provide the physical form. The great work of giving a body to a soul for mundane development is the primary work of the lunar and solar energy phases of the daily cycle. A good soul comes from the pure sphere of the universe for its voyage of continual evolution. When the parents have intercourse, an opportunity is created for the seed and egg to meet. Although pregnancy takes ten full moons to complete, the integration of a visiting soul comes to ride in this one particular moment of integration of paternal and maternal energies. The aura of the couple during intercourse is what attracts the soul, and a good soul will always make the correct choice without hesitation.

7. The variation among souls is enormous. Life's form is but a vessel; what is inside is most important. Parents only give life to form, they cannot give birth to a soul. Soul birth is the work of nature. All souls were once pure, but the contamination of worldly life has made them impure with "post-Heavenly" defects.

8. Lunar energy not only draws water from the ocean, but can also affect the ovulation and menstruation of a woman. The menstruation of ancient women always occurred during the full moon, thus the moon is the symbol of the female in spiritual symbology and the sun is the symbol of the male. This natural female cycle has become disordered, however, through social and intellectual activities which create internal disturbance and psychological problems.

Congestion in the uterus naturally increases from the time of the new moon until it is released during the full moon. Sometimes a woman's natural cycle does not correspond with the moon's cycle. Only when menstruation does not take place at all does one begin to see definite unnatural consequences.

F. Lunar and Solar Energies in a Yearly Cycle

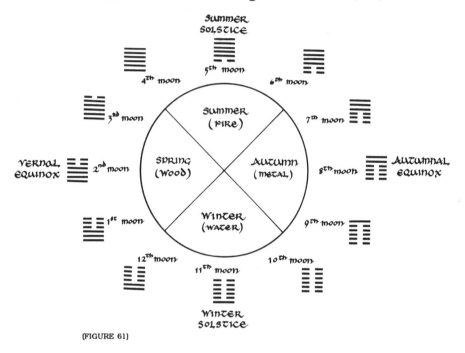

(FIGURE 61)

The cycles of the twelve hexagrams express the variations of solar energy at the beginning of each new moon. Notice that the Chinese New Year is characterized by the first moon in the early Spring. This roughly corresponds to February/March of the Western calendar.

III. A Deeper Observation of the Natural Energy Phases, Their Symbols and Meanings

A. Two Phases of Natural Energy

YANG   &   YIN

(FIGURE 62)

B. Four Phases of Natural Energy

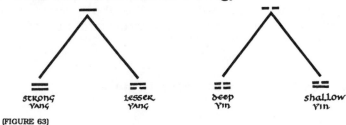

(FIGURE 63)

C. Six Phases of Natural Energy

The Yang Group

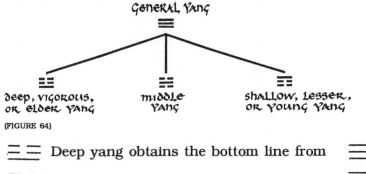

(FIGURE 64)

☷ Deep yang obtains the bottom line from ☰

☳ Middle yang obtains the middle line from ☰

☲ Shallow yang obtains the top line from ☰

The Yin Group

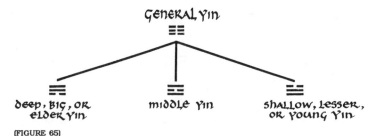

(FIGURE 65)

☴ Deep yin obtains the bottom line from ☷

☵ Middle yin obtains the middle line from ☷

☶ Shallow yin obtains the top line from ☷

According to a group of symptoms, any disease can be classified by the above six divisions of yin and yang, and the appropriate natural healing methods can be applied.

D. Eight Phases of Natural Energy

1. The Yang Group

☰ full or old yang   vigorous yang ⚎

☳ middle yang   shallow yang ⚌

2. The Yin Group

☷ full or old yin   deep yin   ☴

☲ middle yin   shallow yin   ☶

3. Diagram of proportionate expression

If we take the familiar circular expression of yin/yang proportionality from the T'ai Chi diagram ◐ and represent it on a linear place to illustrate the eight phases of the two great manifestations of one primal natural energy in gradation, we have:

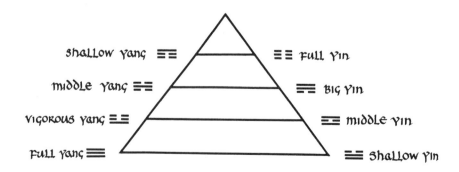

(FIGURE 66)

E. The Eight Phases and the Seasonal Changes

☰	☱	☲
Summer Begins	Summer Solstice	Autumn Begins
☳	eARth	☴
Vernal equinox	third moon of each season	Autumnal equinox
☵	☶	☷
Spring Begins	Winter Solstice	Winter Begins

(FIGURE 67)

IV. Universal Cycle Energy Phases

A. The Five Elementary Phases of Natural Energy

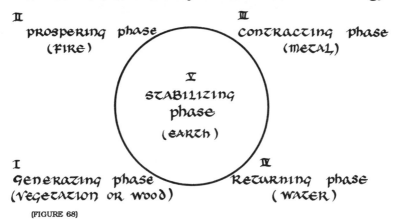

II
PROSPERING phase
(FIRE)

III
CONTRACTING phase
(METAL)

V
STABILIZING
phase
(EARTh)

I
Generating phase
(Vegetation or wood)

IV
Returning phase
(WATER)

(FIGURE 68)

The symbolic words Wood, Fire, Earth, Metal and Water are used in the Five Elementary Phases of Energy. They represent five classifications or phases of natural energy, but they cannot be rigidly interpreted. They represent the cyclic reality of natural energy and abstract the vast phenomena of nature into a series of interwoven relationships as expressed below:

1. Water gives life to Wood (vegetation).
2. Wood gives life to Fire.
3. Fire brings forth Earth (ash).
4. Earth creates Metal as the bone of Earth.
5. Metal can be transformed back into a liquid.

B. The Ten Celestial Phases

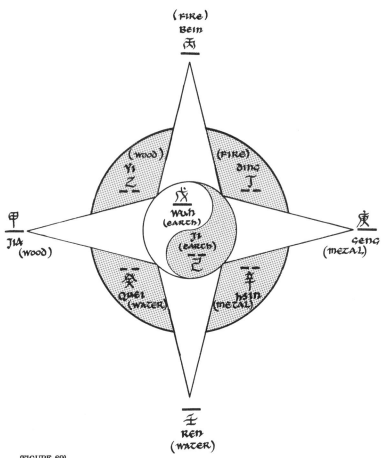

(FIGURE 69)

Jia	yang	Wood	strong generating force
Yi	yin	Wood	weak generating force
Bien	yang	Fire	strong developing force
Ding	yin	Fire	weak developing force
Wuh	yang	Earth	strong stabilizing force
Ji	yin	Earth	weak stabilizing force
Geng	yang	Metal	strong reforming force
Hsin	yin	Metal	weak reforming force
Ren	yang	Water	strong returning force
Quei	yin	Water	weak returning force

C. The Integration of the Five Phases With the Ten Celestial Stems

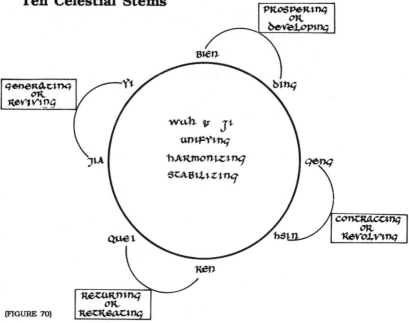

(FIGURE 70)

D. Understanding the Symbols of the Celestial Stems

甲 Jia (yang wood): the image of breaking through, like a sprout breaking through the earth.

乙 Yi (yin wood): the image of early growth with young, bending stems and branches.

丙 Bien (yang fire): the image of the life force expanding like a beautiful fire.

丁 Ding (yin fire): the image of a new life becoming fully grown.

戊 Wuh (yang earth): the image of luxuriant growth and prosperous development.

己 Ji (yin earth): the image of distinguishable features and attributes.

庚 Geng (yang metal): the image of the beginning of reversal, energy retreating until the next Spring.

辛 Hsin (yin metal): the image of withdrawing.

壬 Ren (yang water): the image of the life energy nurtured deeply within, like a pregnant mother nourishing the fetus.

癸 Quei (yin water): the image of regathering of a new life force. Underground and invisibly cultivated, it awaits a new breakthrough.

E. Relationships Found Within the Celestial Stems

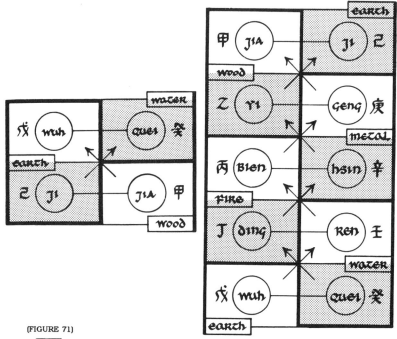

(FIGURE 71)

1. ⊟ indicates the same elemental phase (energy).

2. ○──◉ indicates an incorporated team.

3. ⤬ indicates fighting and conquering.

4. ▨▢ indicates yin and yang energy respectively.

5. The yin phase of any stem can conquer the same energy as the yang phase.

F. The Twelve Terrestrial Branches

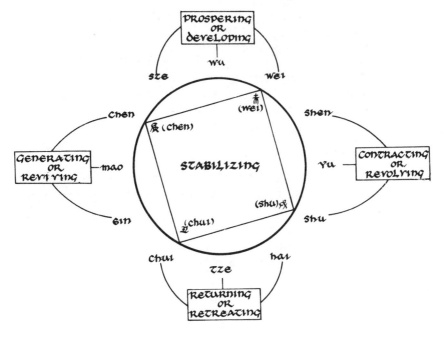

(FIGURE 72)

Hai	yin	Water	
Tze	yang	Water	Returning/Retreating
Chui	yin	Earth	Phase

Ein	yang	Wood	
Mao	yin	Wood	Generating/Reviving
Ch'en	yang	Earth	Phase

Sze	yin	Fire	
Wu	yang	Fire	Prospering/Developing
Wei	yin	Earth	Phase

Shen	yang	Metal	
Yu	yin	Metal	Contracting/Revolving
Shu	yang	Earth	Phase

G. Understanding the Symbols of the Twelve Earthly Branches

子 Tze (yang Water): the image of the reproductiveness of life, like a seed beneath the earth, absorbing moisture and nutrition for development.

丑 Chui (yin Earth): the image of a sprout before it reaches the surface. In other words, underground growth.

寅 Ein (yang Wood): the image of a crawling sprout as it meets the warmth of air, its final stretch out of the earth.

卯 Mao (yin Wood): the image of luxuriant vegetation dancing in the sunshine.

辰 Ch'en (yang Earth): the image of full awakening for the coming growth.

巳 Sze (yin Fire): the image of preparation for ripeness.

午 Wu (yang Fire): the image of growth as it reaches its peak.

未 Wei (yin Earth): the image of the sweet taste that expresses ripeness and mellowness.

申 Shen (yang Metal): the image of full ripeness and the time of harvest.

酉 Yu (yin Metal): the image of recollecting after a rich yield.

戌 Shu (yang Earth): the image of retreating from the visible excitement of life.

亥 Hai (yin Water): the image of the seed or core awaiting its next growth.

H. The Relationships Found Within the Twelve Branches

1) Harmonious Order

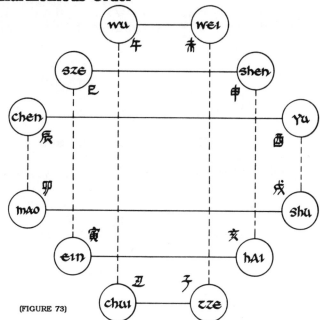

(FIGURE 73)

2) Enforcing Order

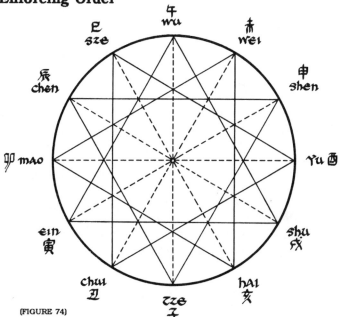

(FIGURE 74)

In Figure 73, horizontally paired phases inter-act harmoniously and vertically paired phases are antagonistic. Horizontal pairs combine to form one of the five phases. For example, Wu/Wei is Fire, Sze/Shen is Water, Chen/Yu is Metal, Mao/Shu is Fire, Ein/Hai is Wood, and Chui/Tze is Earth.

子 (Tze, Yang Water) and
丑 (Chui, Yin Earth)
come together to become "productive Earth."

寅 (Ein, Yang Wood) and
亥 (Hai, Yin Water)
come together to become "growing Vegetation."

卯 (Mao, Yin Wood) and
戌 (Shu, Yang Earth)
come together to be "useful Fire."

辰 (Chen, Yang Earth) and
酉 (Yu, Yin Metal)
come together to become "usable Metal."

巳 (Sze, Yin Fire) and
申 (Shen, Yang Metal)
come together to become "transforming Water."

午 (Wu, Yang Fire) and
未 (Wei, Yin Earth)
come together to become firey and light.

Each pair is in harmonious relationship and through mutual cooperation attains a new nature.

In Figure 74, the four triangles show phases that are mutually enforcing. The dotted lines show the phases that destroy each other. The triangles also form an element. Shen/Tze/Chen are Water, Hai/Mao/Wei are Wood, Ein/Wu/Shu are Fire, and Sze/Yu/Chui are Metal.

3) Persecuting Order

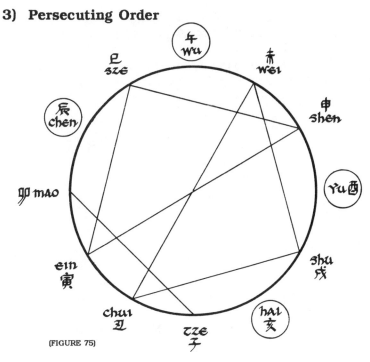

(FIGURE 75)

In Figure 75, the persecuting phases are shown in the following four categories:

Group persecuting:	Shen, Sze, Ein
Imbalanced triangle:	Chui, Wei, Shu
Mutually persecuting:	Tze, Mao
Self persecuting:	Chen, Wu, Yu, Hai

This situation is created by the different aspects of forming new relationships. Sze and Shen are friends in relationship, but Shen and Ein are in opposition. When the three come together, they form a new relationship as persecuting order.

Chui and Shu are in relationship, but Chui and Wei are in opposition. When the three come together, they form a new relationship as persecuting order.

When Tze and Mao come together, they form a persecuting relationship.

The above is created by the aspects as shown in Figure 75.

I. The Interrelation of the Ten Celestial Stems and the Twelve Terrestrial Branches

1) The Ten Stems With the Twelve Branches

JIA — EIN wood	JI. – CHUI – WEI earth
YI — MAO wood	GENG — SHEN metal
BIEN — WU fire	HSIN — YU metal
DING — SZE fire	REN — TZE water
WUH – CHEN – SHU earth	QUEI — HAI water

(FIGURE 76)

2) The Twelve Branches With the Ten Stems

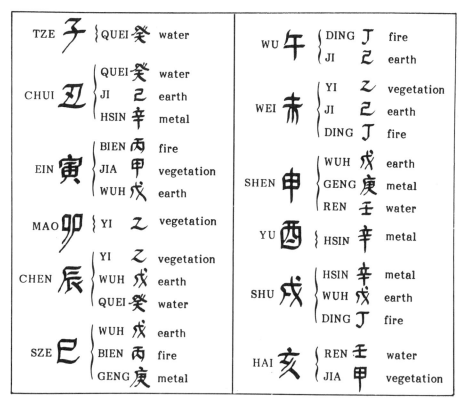

(FIGURE 77)

J. The Complete Sixty Cycle Energy Phases

1. Six Groups of Ten Cycles

A.

(1) 甲 (JIA) 子 (TZE) Yang wood / Yang water	(2) 乙 (YI) 丑 (CHUI) Yin wood / Yin earth	(3) 丙 (BIEN) 寅 (EIN) Yang fire / Yang wood	(4) 丁 (DING) 卯 (MAO) Yin fire / Yin wood
(5) 戊 (WUH) 辰 (CHEN) Yang earth / Yang earth	(6) 己 (JI) 巳 (SZE) Yin earth / Yin fire	(7) 庚 (GENG) 午 (WU) Yang metal / Yang fire	(8) 辛 (HSIN) 未 (WEI) Yin metal / Yin earth
(9) 壬 (REN) 申 (SHEN) Yang water / Yang metal	(10) 癸 (QUEI) 酉 (YU) Yin water / Yin metal		

B.

(1) 甲 (JIA) 戌 (SHU) Yang wood / Yang earth	(2) 乙 (YI) 亥 (HAI) Yin wood / Yin water	(3) 丙 (BIEN) 子 (TZE) Yang fire / Yang water	(4) 丁 (DING) 丑 (CHUI) Yin fire / Yin earth
(5) 戊 (WUH) 寅 (EIN) Yang earth / Yang wood	(6) 己 (JI) 卯 (MAO) Yin earth / Yin wood	(7) 庚 (GENG) 辰 (CHEN) Yang metal / Yang earth	(8) 辛 (HSIN) 巳 (SZE) Yin metal / Yin fire
(9) 壬 (REN) 午 (WU) Yang water / Yang fire	(10) 癸 (QUEI) 未 (WEI) Yin water / Yin earth		

C.

(1) 甲 (JIA) 申 (SHEN) Yang wood / Yang metal	(2) 乙 (YI) 酉 (YU) Yin wood / Yin metal	(3) 丙 (BIEN) 戌 (SHU) Yang fire / Yang earth	(4) 丁 (DING) 亥 (HAI) Yin fire / Yin water
(5) 戊 (WUH) 子 (TZE) Yang earth / Yang water	(6) 己 (JI) 丑 (CHUI) Yin earth / Yin earth	(7) 庚 (GENG) 寅 (EIN) Yang metal / Yang wood	(8) 辛 (HSIN) 卯 (MAO) Yin metal / Yin wood
(9) 壬 (REN) 辰 (CHEN) Yang water / Yang earth	(10) 癸 (QUEI) 巳 (SZE) Yin water / Yin fire		

D.

(1) 甲 (JIA) 午 (WU) Yang wood / Yang fire	(2) 乙 (YI) 未 (WEI) Yin wood / Yin earth	(3) 丙 (BIEN) 申 (SHEN) Yang fire / Yang metal	(4) 丁 (DING) 酉 (YU) Yin fire / Yin metal
(5) 戊 (WUH) 戌 (SHU) Yang earth / Yang earth	(6) 己 (JI) 亥 (HAI) Yin earth / Yin water	(7) 庚 (GENG) 子 (TZE) Yang metal / Yang water	(8) 辛 (HSIN) 丑 (CHUI) Yin metal / Yin earth
(9) 壬 (REN) 寅 (EIN) Yang water / Yang wood	(10) 癸 (QUEI) 卯 (MAO) Yin water / Yin wood		

甲 (1) 辰	乙 (2) 巳	丙 (3) 午	丁 (4) 未
(JIA) (chen)	(YI) (sze)	(BIEN) (wu)	(DING) (wei)
Yang Wood / Yang earth	Yin wood / Yin fire	Yang fire / Yang fire	Yin fire / Yin earth
戊 (5) 申	己 (6) 酉	庚 (7) 戌	辛 (8) 亥
(wuh) (shen)	(JI) (yu)	(Geng) (shu)	(hsin) (hai)
Yang earth / Yang metal	Yin earth / Yin metal	Yang metal / Yang earth	Yin metal / Yin water
壬 (9) 子	癸 (10) 丑		
(Ren) (tze)	(Quei) (chou)		
Yang water / Yang water	Yin water / Yin earth		

(E)

甲 (1) 寅	乙 (2) 卯	丙 (3) 辰	丁 (4) 巳
(JIA) (ein)	(YI) (mao)	BIEN (chen)	(DING) (sze)
Yang wood / Yang wood	Yin wood / Yin wood	Yang fire / Yang earth	Yin fire / Yin fire
戊 (5) 午	己 (6) 未	庚 (7) 申	辛 (8) 酉
(wuh) (wu)	(JI) (wei)	(Geng) (shen)	hsin (yu)
Yang earth / Yang fire	Yin earth / Yin earth	Yang metal / Yang metal	Yin metal / Yin metal
壬 (9) 戌	癸 (10) 亥		
(Ren) (shu)	(Quei) (hai)		
Yang water / Yang earth	Yin water / Yin water		

(F)

(FIGURE 78)

Charts A through F show the complete combination of the Ten Celestial Stems with the Twelve Terrestrial Branches in six groups of ten each, making up an entire cycle of sixty phases.

To figure out the energy of the year in which you were born, or any other year, work backwards or forwards from F-10 (Quei/Hai) which is 1983. 1973, for instance, would be E-10. 1963 would be D-10, and so forth. A quick way to calculate past or future years is to know that in the current cycle Quei/Hai is not only 1983, but also 1923, 1863 or 2043.

If you were to chart the sixty phases as a circle, each combined pair of phases would represent six degrees of the circle.

The upper or Celestial phases begin with the generating phase, Wood. The lower or Terrestrial phases begin with the returning phase, Water. Since the generating force comes from the vastness of the universe, the Earth responds with that which is substantial (water), the source of all earthly life.

2. Cross Reference Chart of Stems to Branches

CELESTIAL STEMS (Cycles)			TERRESTRIAL BRANCHES					
			CYCLE 1	CYCLE 2	CYCLE 3	CYCLE 4	CYCLE 5	CYCLE 6
1	Yang	(Breaking Through) 甲 (JIA) Wood	子 (TZE) Yang Water	戌 (Shu) Yang Earth	申 (Shen) Yang Metal	午 (Wu) Yang Fire	辰 (Chen) Yang Earth	寅 (Ein) Yang Wood
	Yin	(New Life) Growth 乙 (Yi) Wood	丑 (Chou) Yin Earth	亥 (Hai) Yin Water	酉 (Yu) Yin Metal	未 (Wei) Yin Earth	巳 (Sze) Yin Fire	卯 (Mao) Yin Wood
2	Yang	(Expansion) 丙 (Bien) Fire	寅 (Ein) Yang Wood	子 (Tze) Yang Water	戌 (Shu) Yang Earth	申 (Shen) Yang Metal	午 (Wu) Yang Fire	辰 (Chen) Yang Earth
	Yin	(Full Growth) 丁 (Ding) Fire	卯 (Mao) Yin Wood	丑 (Chou) Yin Earth	亥 (Hai) Yin Water	酉 (Yu) Yin Metal	未 (Wei) Yin Earth	巳 (Sze) Yin Fire
3	Yang	(Luxuriant Growth) 戊 (Wuh) Earth	辰 (Chen) Yang Earth	寅 (Ein) Yang Wood	子 (Tze) Yang Water	戌 (Shu) Yang Earth	申 (Shen) Yang Metal	午 (Wu) Yang Fire
	Yin	(Distinguish Attributes) 己 (Ji) Earth	巳 (Sze) Yin Fire	卯 (Mao) Yin Wood	丑 (Chou) Yin Earth	亥 (Hai) Yin Water	酉 (Yu) Yin Metal	未 (Wei) Yin Earth
4	Yang	(Begin Retreat) 庚 (Geng) Metal	午 (Wu) Yang Fire	辰 (Chen) Yang Earth	寅 (Ein) Yang Wood	子 (Tze) Yang Water	戌 (Shu) Yang Earth	申 (Shen) Yang Metal
	Yin	(Receding) 辛 (Hsin) Metal	未 (Wei) Yin Earth	巳 (Sze) Yin Fire	卯 (Mao) Yin Wood	丑 (Chou) Yin Earth	亥 (Hai) Yin Water	酉 (Yu) Yin Metal
5	Yang	(Return) 壬 (Ren) Water	申 (Shen) Yang Metal	午 (Wu) Yang Fire	辰 (Chen) Yang Earth	寅 (Ein) Yang Wood	子 (Tze) Yang Water	戌 (Shu) Yang Earth
	Yin	(Revitalize) 癸 (Quei) Water	酉 (Yu) Yin Metal	未 (Wei) Yin Earth	巳 (Sze) Yin Fire	卯 (Mao) Yin Wood	丑 (Chou) Yin Earth	亥 (Hai) Yin Water

(FIGURE 79)

To trace the cycle of sixty phases from beginning to end, read the Celestial Stems in the far left column, from top to bottom, and match them with the Terrestrial Branches of Cycle 1, from top to bottom. Then repeat the process, matching the Stems with Cycle 2, 3 and so forth.

3. Sixty-Cycle Interaction of the Five Elements

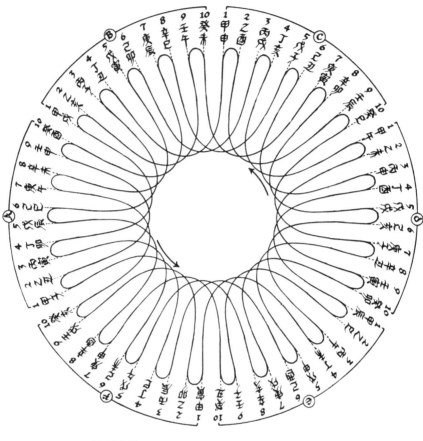

(FIGURE 80)

This chart illustrates the cyclic movement and interrelationships of the five phases of natural energy as outlined in Figure 70. Many important laws are expressed in this cycle. Moving counterclockwise, the law of generation - which is applied in the science of harmonics in music - occurs at every eight intervals among the Heavenly Stems. An incorporated team of two Stems occurs at every six intervals. The enforced trio of three Stems occurs at every four intervals.

Moving clockwise, an incorporated team of two Branches occurs each three intervals, and the destructive relationship of two Branches at every seven intervals.

When counting in either direction, take the first phase *after* the initial phase to which you are referring as #1.

4. Sixty Interacting Phases in Cyclic Rotation

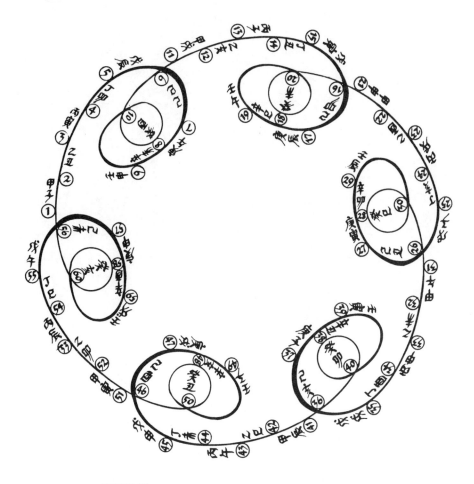

(FIGURE 81)

In the cycle of sixty, each individual unit of combined energy is a beginning, a transition and an end. It is complete unto itself. It is also a part of something else. The entire universe is comprised of such individual units of energy combinations in small circles of ten, as shown in the chart above.

These cycles of universal energy are far from being a matter of distant concern in our daily lives, but are actually the very context in which we live. This is the value of the knowledge passed down to us from the ancient developed ones.

5. The Spiral Unfolding of the Sixty Cycles

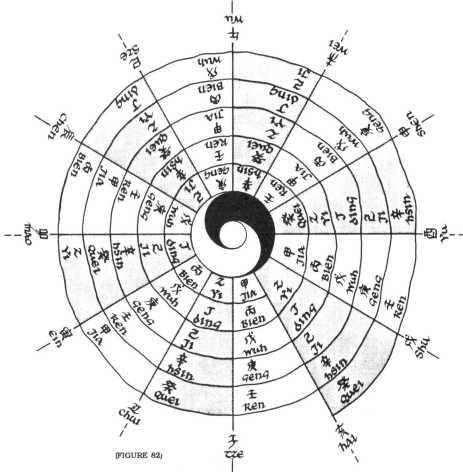

(FIGURE 82)

The T'ai Chi Tu at the center of this chart shows that as yang (the light half) expands, yin (the dark half) expands as well. In this illustration, the Twelve Terrestrial Branches are fixed, while the Ten Celestial Stems spirals outward in a clockwise direction, giving rise to the twelve major segments of yin and yang.

Once again, the Earthly Branches are coordinated with the Heavenly Stems in the following order: Jia/Tze, Yi/Chui, Bien/Ein, etc., continuously around the spiral.

Note that a yang stem is always paired with a yang branch. At no time does the yang of one category pair with the yin of the other category.

V. The Relation of the Sixty Cycles to the Natural Energy Calendar

A. Origin of the Calendar

The Natural Energy Calendar system began on the first day of the first year during the reign of the Yellow Emperor. The great astronomer of that time, Tai Chiu, a student of ancient astronomy, was assigned the task of formalizing an energy calendar from all the available sources. The Winter Solstice occurs during the eleventh moon of the year, and it is the time when yin energy ceases and yang energy begins. The eleventh moon was therefore chosen as the first moon of the first year of the Yellow Emperor's reign, in 2698 B.C., and this time of the year was recognized as the energy New Year.

Later, the Great Yu (2204-2197 B.C.), a great warrior of the pre-historic deluge, an outstanding astronomer and a man of spiritual development, established the third moon after the Winter Solstice (which is the first moon of Spring) as the first month of the year. This was done to coordinate human activities with seasonal variations.

Still later, during the Chou Dynasty, the eleventh moon (i.e., the full moon before the Winter Solstice) was again considered as the first moon. Subsequently, the third or "ein" moon which is now recognized as the seasonal New Year was considered as the first moon.

The following chart shows the ancient calendars of Tai Chiu and the Great Yu, as well as the corresponding cycle of Twelve Branches and their relation to the Western Calendar. At the top of the chart is the cycle order in energy language, with the birth of yang in the first month, increasing to its fullest expression in the sixth month, and followed by the birth of yin which grows to its full expression in the twelfth month.

NATURAL CYCLIC ENERGY ORDER	䷀	䷪	䷡	䷪	䷪	䷫	䷠	䷋	䷓	䷖	䷗	䷒
ORIGINAL ORDER ADOPTED BY THE YELLOW EMPEROR CORRESPONDING MONTH:	1	2	3	4	5	6	7	8	9	10	11	12
CURRENT CHINESE ORDER ADOPTED AFTER SHIA DYNASTY - 2207-1767 B.C. CORRESPONDING MONTH:	11	12	1	2	3	4	5	6	7	8	9	10
WESTERN ORDER BEGAN DURING REIGN OF JULIUS CAESAR. CORRESPONDING MONTH: THE MONTHS ARE ONLY APPROXIMATE	DEC-JAN	JAN-FEB	FEB-MAR	MAR-APR	APR-MAY	MAY-JUNE	JUNE-JULY	JULY-AUG	AUG-SEPT	SEPT-OCT	OCT-NOV	NOV-DEC
THE NATURAL CYCLE IN TERMS OF THE TERRESTRIAL BRANCHES	tze 子	chui 丑	ein 寅	mao 卯	chen 辰	sze 巳	wu 午	wei 未	shen 申	yu 酉	shu 戌	hai 亥

(FIGURE 83)

B. The Beginning of the Energy Calendar

The beginning of the generating phase of the upper universal energy system is 甲 Jia. The beginning of the phases of the lower universal energy system is 子 Tze. Therefore, the energy hour of 甲子 Jia/Tze, on the day of Jia/Tze, at the new moon of Jia/Tze 4681 years ago (in 2698 B.C.) marks the moment pf the first year of the Yellow Emperor's calendar. This system is the accumulation of many years of life experience from countless generations who followed the natural cycle. Thus came the instinctive, rhythmic response. By observing the twenty-four climatic periods of solar energy variation, the lives of Chinese people have been enriched, especially with regard to agriculture, spiritual activities, and nature in general. Along with Chinese integral medicine, this system is one of the remarkable achievements of the natural way of life. The names of these twenty-four periods and their relation to the Yellow Route (of the sun) and the Western Calendar are shown in the following chart (Figure 84).

	Seasonal Period	Yellow Route	Approximate Date
SPRING	●Spring begins	315°	Feb 4,5
	Rain water	330°	Feb 18,19
	Awake from hibernation	345°	March 5,6
	●Spring Equinox	0°	March 20,21
	Clear and Bright	15°	April 4,5
	Rain for grains	30°	April 20,21
SUMMER	●Summer begins	45°	May 5,6
	Grain buds	60°	May 21,22
	Bearded grain	75°	June 5,6
	●Summer Solstice	90°	June 21,22
	Slight Heat	105°	July 7,8
	Great heat	120°	July 22,23
AUTUMN	●Autumn begins	135°	August 7,8
	Limited heat	150°	August 23,24
	White dew	165°	Sept 7,8
	●Autumnal Equinox	180°	Sept 23,24
	Cold dew	195°	Oct 8,9
	Hoarfrost descends	210°	Oct 23,24
WINTER	●Winter begins	225°	Nov 7,8
	Little snow	240°	Nov 22,23
	Heavy snow	255°	Dec 7,8
	●Winter Solstice	270°	Dec 21,22
	Slight cold	285°	Jan 5,6
	Severe cold	300°	Jan 20,21

In the southern hemisphere, the seasons are opposite.

(FIGURE 84)

The Chinese system of solar energy variation defines the route which the sun travels (the Yellow Route) as beginning at the fixed point of zero degrees (the Spring Equinox) and moving eastward until it reaches 360 degrees. Each fifteen degree interval is a single seasonal period, thus establishing twenty-four equal periods. Each period has a special name which describes that climatic phase of the year. Twelve periods are seasonal changes, and twelve are dividing points called "Middle Chi."

C. Applications of the Seasonal Variations

The knowledge of climatic periods is very useful in agriculture, and colorful, meaningful festivals with all kinds of healthy activities at specific times of the year can help prevent emotional stagnation and refresh the spirit of life.

The eight dark circles in Figure 84 indicate the seasonal periods that are important for spiritual cultivation, inasmuch as they represent high energy days. At these times, highly evolved spirits are much more active, and these special days are very effective for such purifications as private confessions to the spiritual realm of nature, asking forgiveness for mistakes of which you are aware and unaware, prayers for good wishes and healthy spiritual fasting. During such a spiritual fast, one should abstain from tobacco, alcohol and sex, remain quiet and avoid meeting people or participating in needless activities. These fundamental procedures are necessary and should be practiced with sincerity, otherwise one's cultivation will have a negative result.

In the body there are twelve big ties which connect the soul to the body. This bondage is an obstacle for an uplifting soul, thus it is wise to utilize the power of forgiveness to dissolve these intricate ties. One can also take advantage of the eight main seasonal periods to dissolve these ties and reform one's personality.

There are many good spiritual practices which can be learned. The eight seasonal periods are very important for a person serious about cultivation. If you do a general spiritual practice, the seasonal periods can also help produce a good effect in dissolving the knots and ties. (For further information on this topic, please see Chapter 8.)

According to the phases of energy rotation, many people living in today's cities miss the "Springtime" of their day and struggle with the deep "Winter" of the night. They hibernate in the "Spring" or morning hours of the daily cycle and become active during the "Winter" or midnight hours. This is not in accord with nature.

The failures of many spiritual followers can be observed and used to benefit your cultivation. Their meditation is nothing more than brooding over their psychological problems. They may have noble intentions, but they stray too far from the course of nature and their own personal nature. Those who neglect the elements of nature and disregard the fundamental truths while searching for high spiritual achievement are blind. Wise people avoid this problem by being sufficiently and methodically equipped with the correct way.

By the careful study of the complete energy cycle, it can be determined which days are suitable or unsuitable for certain kinds of cultivation. Thus true and effective cultivation is intimately related to the rest of the universe. To know the energy cycles and live in harmony with them is very important to the one who wishes to make real spiritual progress.

So far we have seen the energy time system as it was originally adopted - the four phases of the bihourly cycle of a day, the daily cycle of the moon, the lunar cycle of the year and the yearly cycle of the sixty-year cycle. The unity of these individual cycles is sixty periods. The cycle of the current day and year can be determined by tracing back to the first year and first day of the cycle. The traditional Chinese calendar is a continuous record of these cycles and is available to everyone. To the person who learns to use it, this calendar can be of great benefit in utilizing cycles in the more important undertakings of general daily life circumstances as well as in one's personal cultivation.

D. Seasonal Variations with the Twelve Branches

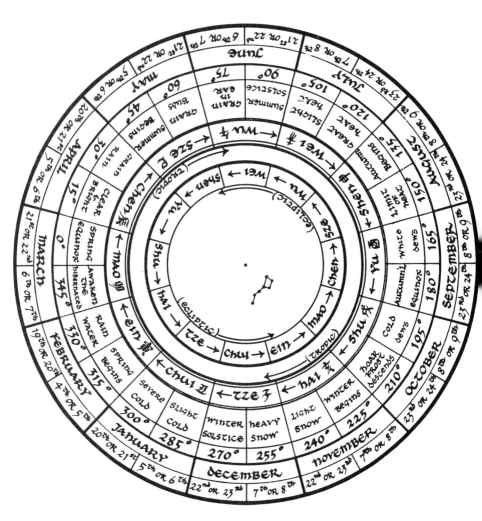

(FIGURE 85)

The inner ecliptic route and the outer tropic route of the Twelve Branches, as shown in Figure 85, illustrate the same harmonious relationships between phases that are shown in the horizontal pairs in Figure 73 and in the squares in Figure 95.

One can also note the correspondence of the Branches to the seasons of the year, as outlined in Figure 72, and also the complete cycle of twenty-four seasonal variations described in Figure 84.

E. Utilization of the Sixty Cyclic Universal Energy Phases

In ancient China, the sixty phases were used:

a. to mark the twelve bi-hourly division of energy in a day
b. to mark the days within different sixty-day cycles
c. to mark the twelve moons in a year
d. to mark years in different sixty-year cycles
e. to know the daily energy variations

The main reason for using the ancient energy-time system is to understand the nature of life. According to ancient spiritual understanding, time is neither the face of a plane nor a straight line. A unit of time is a phase of cyclic universal energy. It varies from the modern concept of time, which is represented by certain marks, measures or periods. Without different energy phases circulating, there is no sense of time or reality.

When the sixty-cycle system is applied to the hours of a day or to the phases of the moon, the lower Terrestrial cycle of energy phases is stationary. Its expression is always the same. The upper Celestial phases vary with the different hours or moons.

Understanding the daily energy variations is not only interesting but useful as well. Generally, cyclic energy has different influences on one's daily life. On Fire-energy days, for example, one's personal energy is primarily untamed. Important meetings should not be scheduled for these days, except for military purposes. Watery, cool food and slow, quiet music are better for Fire days.

For any changes which need to be made, metal days are best, especially a day in which the Celestial and Terrestrial phases are yang Metal. Interacting yang Metal energy indicates reformation or revolution. This is a good time for reforming bad habits and doing what is positive instead of destructive.

The three days of yang Wood/yang Water (Jia/Tze), yang Wood/yang Wood (Jia/Ein), and yang Metal/yang Metal (Geng/Shen) are all vigorous, energetic days that are very good for cultivating one's high, creative spiritual goals.

If one cultivates or wishes to obtain mystical power, the six yin Fire (Ding) days are especially suited for this purpose.

If one wishes to cultivate one's energy to become high spiritual energy, the six yang Wood (Jia) days can be used for this.

If one wishes to engage in sex for the purpose of enforcing vitality, the appropriate time is on yin Water (Quei) days when both individuals are more vigorous than usual.

When the energy cycles are applied to a year, the four major seasons are expressed as follows:

Winter (Water) is from　　亥 , Hai to 丑 , Chui

Spring (Wood) is from　　寅 , Ein to 辰 , Ch'en

Summer (Fire) is from　　巳 , Sze to 未 , Wei

Autumn (Metal) is from　　申 , Shen to 戌 , Shu

The Winter Solstice is a time when yin finally reaches the point of greatest regression and yang is generated. This is the beginning of yang energy and is an important time for people to nurture their vitality.

The Spring Equinox is when yin and yang are balanced and is the best time for people to harmonize their energy while undertaking creative activities.

The Summer Solstice is the time when yang has reached its peak and yin begins to grow. This is the best time for people to control their vitality and not over-extend themselves.

The Autumn Equinox is also a time of balance between yin and yang and is the best time for people to collect their vitality back to its center and strengthen their health for wintertime.

This is a general outline for spiritual seekers who wish to have some rudimentary knowledge. Knowing the effects of their personal cycle also provides people with a strong influence over general circumstances.

An entire day or year of meditating without knowing the supportive natural cycle is a form of self-indulgence. This type of meditation can be negative, sedative and devitalizing. Though it may sometimes help to calm the mind, it can be the cause of losing the correct way of spiritual life. This is not the way to prepare for "soul evolution." One may only ascend to the divine immortal realm by following the correct methods from a tradition of the natural truth. Meditation should never be used as an escape, an excuse or a pacifier. This would be self-deceptive. Cultivating a good life, in accord with the natural path, is the way to reach the supernatural. To be supernatural is to be in harmony with nature, to not act against either one's own nature or against universal nature.

Universal cyclic movement explains the influence of nature over human life and foretells no beginning or end to the universe. It is futile, therefore, to be anxious about a coming "doomsday." To know the cycles and adjust oneself accordingly ensures the fulfillment of one's life. Using this principle to organize and guide one's life will provide far greater benefit than blindly and irrationally following artificial doctrines.

F. How to Apply the Stems and Branches System to the Western Calendar

The Celestial Stems and Terrestrial Branches interacting on any day can be calculated by means of the following formula:

$$\frac{5(x-1) + (x-1)/4 + 15 + y}{60} = q$$

x = the last two digits of the year
y = the total number of days in the year, up to and including that date itself: be sure to check for Leap years when February has 29 days
q = the quotient
r = remainder, which is used to calculate the energy phases

In working this equation, drop all fractions. Do not round off to the highest number.

The number used to calculate the day is **not the quotient**, but the remainder left after the equation been worked. For example, if the numerator is 91, 91 divided by 60 equals 1 with a remainder of 31.

To determine the Celestial Stem for that day, divide the remainder by 10 and use the remainder again, not the quotient. For example, if you had a remainder of

31 from the original equation, then dividing 31 by 10 leaves a remainder of 1. Using Figure 86 below, 1 = Jia. If the remainder is 0, then it is considered a 10.

To determine the Terrestrial Branch for the day, divide the remainder by 12 and follow the same procedure outlined above. Again, if the remainder is 0, it is considered a 10. Using the same example of 31 as the original remainder, 31 divided by 12 leaves a remainder of 7. Using Figure 86 below, the Branch for the day is Wu.

If the remainder of the original equation happens to be less than 10 or 12, then it is considered the number for both the Stem and the Branch. An original remainder of 8, therefore, would be Hsin (Stem)/Wei (Branch).

If the date being calculated is in the twenty-first century, add 100 to the last two digits of the year. If the date is in the twenty-second century, add 200 and so forth.

Sample Calculations:

August 1, 1944

$x = 44$ $y = 214$ (31+29+31+30+31+30+31+1)

$$\frac{5(44-1) + (44-1)/4 + 15 + 214}{60}$$

$$\frac{215 + 10 + 15 + 214}{60}$$

$454/60 = 7$, with a remainder of 34

34 divided by 10 = 3, with a remainder of 4. The Stem is Ding (丁).

34 divided by 12 = 2, with a remainder of 10. The Branch is Yu (酉).

October 31, 1955

x = 55   y = 304
(31+28+31+30+31+30+31+31+30+31)

$$\frac{5(55\text{-}1) + (55\text{-}1)/4 + 15 + 304}{60}$$

$$\frac{270 + 13 + 15 + 304}{60}$$

602 divided by 60 = 10 with a remainder of 2
The Stem is Yi (乙) and the Branch is Chui (丑).

January 15, 2002

x = 102   y = 15

$$\frac{5(102\text{-}1) + (102\text{-}1)/4 + 15 + 15}{60}$$

$$\frac{505 + 25 + 15 + 15}{60}$$

560 divided by 60 = 9, with a remainder of 20

20 divided by 10 = 2, with a remainder of 0.   The Stem is Quei (癸).

20 divided by 12 = 1, with a remainder of 8.   The Branch is Wei (未).

Use this chart to translate the remainder into the corresponding Celestial Stem or Terrestrial Branch.

The Celestial Stems

JIA	Yi	Bien	Ding	Wuh
甲 = 1,	乙 = 2,	丙 = 3,	丁 = 4,	戊 = 5,

Ji	Geng	Hsin	Ren	Quei
己 = 6,	庚 = 7,	辛 = 8,	壬 = 9,	癸 = 10

The Terrestrial Branches

Tze	Chui	Ein	Mao	Chen	Sze
子 = 1,	丑 = 2,	寅 = 3,	卯 = 4,	辰 = 5,	巳 = 6,

Wu	Wei	Shen	Yu	Shu	Hai
午 = 7,	未 = 8,	申 = 9,	酉 = 10,	戌 = 11,	亥 = 12

(FIGURE 86)

This method of natural energy division was developed in ancient China to illustrate the various universal energy cycles. Since the original observations of these cyclic forces took place in China, the daily natural energy discernment was also determined there. Thus, it seems appropriate to use that geographical location as a standard for determining when these forces come into effect. If one agrees, then the Western Hemisphere is about one day late according to the corresponding Stems and Branches which occur on the same calendar day in both the Western Hemisphere and China. In other words, if it is November 28th in any given year in China, it will be November 27th in the Western Hemisphere. In real time, however, the natural energy cycle occurs on the same calendar day in both hemispheres.

For example, if a person in Los Angeles wished to observe a particular event noted on the Chinese calendar (such as Geng Shen day, when the natural energy renewal cycle beings), the correct day would appear to be a day late according to the Western calendar:

1983

Eastern Hemisphere (China)	Western Hemisphere (USA)
November 28 (Geng/Shen)	November 27
November 29	November 28 (Geng/Shen)

Confusion sometimes arises in the minds of modern students because of the several concurring cyclic systems. For example, one finds the yearly lunar cycle expressed in the twelve periods referred to as "months," 初 一 (1st), 初 二 (2nd), 初 三 (3rd), whereas the solar cycle is expressed by twenty-four seasonal periods, and the Stems and Branches are expressed in sixty increments.

It should be noted that the Stems and Branches can apply to seconds, minutes, hours, days, months (including the tropic and ecliptic cycles, with their respective twelve houses) and so on. The Stems and Branches system also expresses the five basic phases of natural energy rotation moving in different cyclic currents. It is a system which developed out of the integral vision of the ancient sages in an attempt to explain the multiple cycles of nature. One should be careful, however, to distinguish between the solar, the lunar and the Stems and Branches systems when making calculations. The Stems and Branches are a human metaphysical system and should be accepted as such.

Similarities of Yearly Cyclic Phases and Western Terms

子	(Tze)	Aquarius	午	(Wu)	Leo
丑	(Chui)	Capricorn	未	(Wei)	Cancer
寅	(Ein)	Sagittarius	申	(Shen)	Gemini
卯	(Mao)	Scorpio	酉	(Yu)	Taurus
辰	(Chen)	Libra	戌	(Shu)	Aries
巳	(Sze)	Virgo	亥	(Hai)	Pisces

(FIGURE 87)

See also related chart and information in *Internal Alchemy: The Natural Way to Immortality*, Eleventh Class.

VI. The Global and Universal View of the Four Directions

In the natural spiritual conception, directions indicate the variations in natural energy. The ancients believed that East and South, abundant in solar or yang energy, were generally more supportive of life. Thus South is the dominant direction on Chinese maps.

One may easily distinguish the vegetation of the eastern and southern sides of a hill as more luxuriant than that on the northern and western slopes. Even on the same tree one can notice that the sunny side bears more leaves, flowers and fruit.   In the ocean, fish will swim to the warmer, southerly currents before releasing their eggs. This phenomenon of energy quality is acknowledged in the *Tao Teh Ching*: "All lives embrace yang energy to sustain yin energy."

Two Views of the Four Directions

Another aspect of the "universal view" is that the generating energy of life emanates from the East and flows clockwise in a southerly, westerly and northerly cycle. South is positioned above, and the cycle begins in the East. North is below, and West is on the right. (See Figure 88 below.)

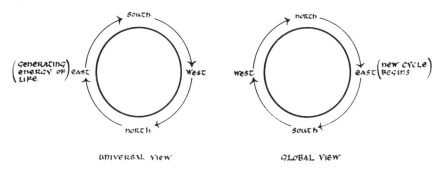

UNIVERSAL VIEW   GLOBAL VIEW

(FIGURE 88)

If you wish to acquaint yourself with the universal view, you must alter your conventional, habitual concepts in order to adapt to a new understanding. It would be a mistake to think that the universal view is simply the result of facing South. This metaphysical view is the product of ancient minds which took the vantage point of the North Star. When looking at the earth from that perspective, South is in front and North is behind.

The universal view is also a basic system to express the energy of a human body. South represents the head, or mind, and is at the top. East represents the liver and the nervous system, as the gathering and regulating source, and is seen on the left. West represents the lungs and skin, functioning as the respiratory and eliminatory systems, and is seen on the right. North represents the kidneys, bladder and reproductive systems and is at the bottom of the body. East corresponds to Spring, South to Summer, West to Autumn, and North to Winter.

The responsiveness between the brain and the rest of the body is the same as that of the spiritual realm to the earth. The correspondence and integration of the left and right sides of the brain to the left and right sides of the body is very similar to the correspondence between the higher realms and the human sphere.

The "post-Heaven" arrangement of the eight trigrams (see Figure 105b) and the twelve Earthly Branches system also utilize the universal directional system, which has the South at the top.

The ancient integral way is the way of self-discovery through natural energy centeredness. In the spiritual realm, however, there are no such distinctions as left and right, East and West. These serve only as a convenience for the discernment of the "post-Heaven" stage. Awareness and discernment of the variations of natural energy grows through cultivation. It was with such natural knowledge that the Yellow Emperor constructed the first compass and led his army out of a heavy fog to victory. In China, the compass has traditionally been called "the needle pointing southward."

For those who wish to refine their energy, it is important to clarify the order of natural energy. It is serious if one violates the natural order of energy in one's life and spiritual cultivation, especially after one has been awakened to the secrets of the universe.

Chapter 7

SPIRITUAL IMPLICATION OF THE SKY

I. Polaris

A. "The Emperor of the Stars"

Since the sun, moon and stars were so importantly related to their lives, the ancient inhabitants of Earth learned many things from the sky. They discovered that the most influential heavenly bodies besides the sun and moon were the Northern Stars. The stars comprising the Big Dipper and Polaris helped tell variations in the year and one's direction on land or sea.

The orderly universe inspired the innocent minds of the ancients, who organized society accordingly. They thought the North Star (Polaris) was the area from which Heavenly order began, so they accordingly named their emperor "Ti," which in Chinese means "divine center" or "divine one." They named the important ministers to correspond to the satellites of Polaris.

Human life, whether a society or an individual life, has to have its center. In vast nature, the ancient developed ones observed that Polaris always maintains its position in the sky as the other stars move around it. This is visible as the earth rotates. The ancient people respected the shimmering stars as their natural connection with heaven. They modeled their government and way of life after the stars with their peaceful order. With simplicity and sincerity the ancients lived their lives in peace. This type of natural life continued until some of their descendants did not understand the spiritual powers of simplicity, sincerity and living in harmony with the natural order of the universe. The descendants wanted to put themselves in the center rather than respecting nature as the center and adjusting themselves accordingly to the nature which was already there. Such ambition led them to corrupt the teachings of the old, traditional ways and destroy the naturally ordered society. So began the downfall of human nature. Human society began its own evolution, and changes in spiritual integrity are reflected by different eras of human society on earth. Typically, only when human beings become increasingly aware of dangerous conflicts do they reach new awakenings.

The North Star is the center of the star order from the human point of view of natural life on earth. The word "Ti," divine center or divine one, is derived from the meaning of the stem of a fruit. The North Star is recognized as the "Ti" or axis of the "vault of Heaven" and of the Earth as well. In English, its equivalent could be "God," but without the same connotations.

The spiritual potency of the Big Dipper will be explained later. One important point to know now is that the shape of the Big Dipper is not always the same. The position of the North Star alters about every twenty-five thousand years. Thus it is the natural truth that everything is an element of something else to which it is connected. Everything is in its own cyclic trail and is also a small part of a larger cycle. A larger cycle is one cycle of yet another larger cycle. In the end, all is changeable. Only the law that all is changeable remains changeless.

the GREAT Dipper over A span of 300,000 years

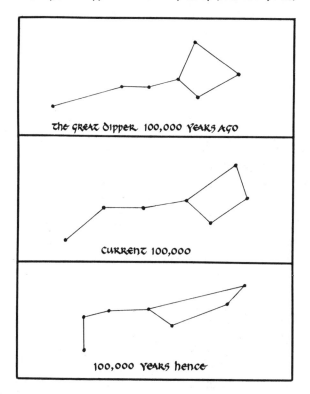

the GREAT Dipper 100,000 years Ago

CURRENT 100,000

100,000 years hence

(FIGURE 89)

B. The Polaris System

The Polaris system is traditionally comprised of Polaris (the North Star) and the Big Dipper.   The first star of the Big Dipper is called the "Pivot" of the sky 天樞. The second star is called the "Revolver" of the sky 天璇.   The third is called the "Rotator" of the sky 天機. The fourth, the "Leveler" of the sky 天權. The fifth, the "Balancer" of the sky 天衡.   The sixth, the "Generator" of the sky 開陽.   And the seventh is the "Harmonizing Light" of the sky 瑤光.

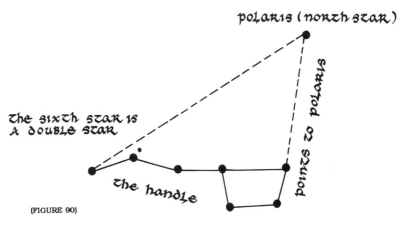

polaris (north star)

points to polaris

the sixth star is
a double star

the handle

(FIGURE 90)

The first four stars form the container of the "dipper," while the remaining three form the "handle."   A straight line extended through the first and second stars, which form the outer edge of the Big Dipper, always points to Polaris.   As the earth rotates on its journey around the sun and spins on its polar axis, the angle at which the Big Dipper is perceived changes on a daily, monthly and yearly basis.   The different directions in which it points, viewed from the earth, correspond to the different cycles of the moon as arranged in the circular order of the Terrestrial Branches.   After completing a 360 degree rotation, or twelve-moon cycle, they repeat themselves. (See Figures 83, 84 and 85.)

The Polaris system is somewhat like the hands of a clock, with the hands of the Big Dipper rotating counterclockwise, from North to East.   The ancient inhabitants of the "Middle Land" (China) noticed that the handle of the Big Dipper could be used to determine the season. In Winter the handle always points North, in Spring it points East, in Summer it points South, and in Fall it points West.

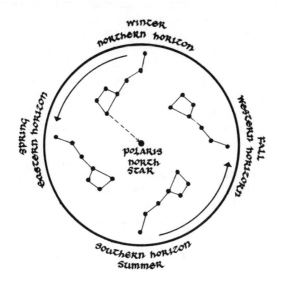

(FIGURE 91a)

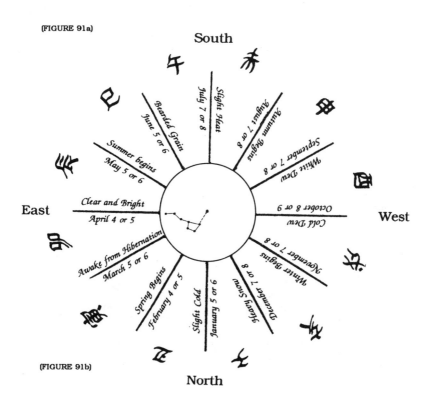

(FIGURE 91b)

If you hold Figure 91a directly overhead and face the North Star, with the northern horizon of the figure facing the realm northern horizon, you will see the stars and horizons exactly as they appear here during the corresponding season.

The common rotating star chart sold in most bookstores can help with the variation of seasons and hours. In Figure 91b, if you make due North the first degree of the circle, then every thirty degrees will mark the beginning of a new month, making twelve months in all. If you have enough training, your meditation can rotate to correspond with the direction of the Big Dipper whether you meditate in a room or in the wilderness.

Figure 92, below, shows the rotation of the Big Dipper in relation to the twelve phases of a yearly cycle. Notice that the Chinese New Year starts around February/March and that East is on the left. Many Westerners are confused when they read in ancient texts that the generating energy of the East comes from the "left." Because the sun moves in the southern quadrant, the ancient Chinese regarded South as being the most vitalizing direction and thus put South at the top. From this perspective, East will naturally be on the left.

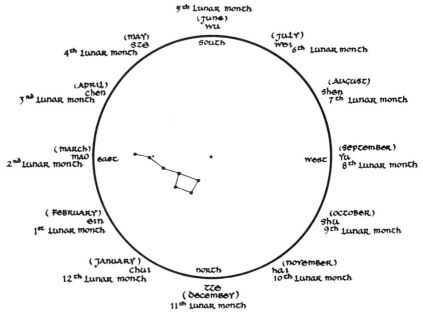

5ᵗʰ lunar month
(june)
wu

(may)
sze
4ᵗʰ lunar month

south

(july)
wei
6ᵗʰ lunar month

(april)
chen
3ʳᵈ lunar month

(August)
shen
7ᵗʰ lunar month

(march)
mao
2ⁿᵈ lunar month   east

west

(september)
yu
8ᵗʰ lunar month

(february)
sin
1ˢᵗ lunar month

(october)
shu
9ᵗʰ lunar month

(january)
chui
12ᵗʰ lunar month

north

(november)
hai
10ᵗʰ lunar month

tze
(december)
11ᵗʰ lunar month

(FIGURE 92)

When the Big Dipper points in the direction of the lunar month and one meditates facing this direction, one benefits from the invigorating energy. Meditation has many varieties and purpose. One who is well-developed makes self-cultivation his or her daily "energy meal."

Another way to explain this cycle is to divide the earth into 360 degrees, with the yearly cycle beginning at the Spring Equinox, which is 0 degrees in the East. Next comes the Summer Solstice at 90 degrees in the South, then the Autumn Equinox at 180 degrees in the West, and the Winter Solstice at 270 degrees in the North. As the cycle again moves to the Spring Equinox, a 360 degree revolution is completed and ready to begin again.

When the four 90 degree quadrants are divided into six equal parts, the twenty-four seasonal periods (Figure 84) are created. As the ancient book says, "Every five days is a small seasonal period. Every three small seasonal periods become one seasonal period. Thus there are twenty-four seasonal periods in a year, with two seasonal periods in every energy month."

C. The Earth's Rotation Clockwise Around the Sun; The Sun Moving on the Ecliptic, Counter-Clockwise

When the clockwise orbit of the earth is divided into twelve parts, Tze is put in the north to begin the cycle of seasonal periods. Each Terrestrial Branch represents a different energy phase. The sun's route is also divided into twelve equal divisions expressed by the same symbols but representing a different energy rotating in a counter-clockwise direction.

The Yellow Route is also known as the ecliptic. It is seen as the apparent annual path of the sun among the stars. The ecliptic is the plane of the earth's orbit around the sun, which is at an angle of 23 degrees 27 minutes from the earth's equator. The Red Route is the earth's equator and its plane in the sky which is also known as the celestial equator. In other words, it is the plane perpendicular to the axis of the earth's daily rotation.

The Sun's Path on the Ecliptic

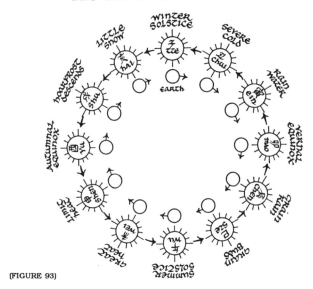

(FIGURE 93)

The four cardinal seasonal periods can also be explained as follows. After the Winter Solstice, around December 22nd, the sun moves on its ecliptic (the Yellow Route) from the South northward. Around March 21st, the sun crosses the equator (the Red Route); this time marks the period of the Vernal Equinox when the sun is directly over the Red Route and day and night are equal in both hemispheres. As the ancient book says, "Yin and yang appear and exit, moving upward and downward." When it comes to the "Equal Division of Spring," yang is directly in the East and yin is directly in the West. This is more commonly known as the Spring Equinox.

After the Spring Equinox, the sun moves northward until it reaches the Tropic of Cancer around June 21st. At 23 degrees 26 minutes and 59 seconds, the position of the sun is at the most northern point of the Yellow Route (ecliptic). This is called the Summer Solstice. In the Northern Hemisphere, this is the longest day and the shortest night of the year. In the Southern Hemisphere, the reverse is true.

After the Summer Solstice, the sun moves southward from the north. It crosses the Red Route again around September 23rd, which is the time of the Autumn Equinox. On this day the sun shines directly above the Red Route and the day and night in both hemispheres are equal again. The ancient book says, "Yin and yang appear and exit, moving upward and downward," until the "Equal Division of Autumn" when yang is directly in the West and yin is directly in the East. Because yin and yang are equally divided, the heat and cold of the year are evenly divided.

The Winter Solstice is at the southernmost point of the Yellow Route. When the sun reaches the southern latitude of 23 degrees, 26 minutes and 59 seconds at the Tropic of Capricorn, which is around December 22nd, it is the shortest day in the Northern hemisphere and the longest in the Southern hemisphere.

D. The Cyclic Relationship Among the Earth, Sun and the North Star in Seasonal Expressions

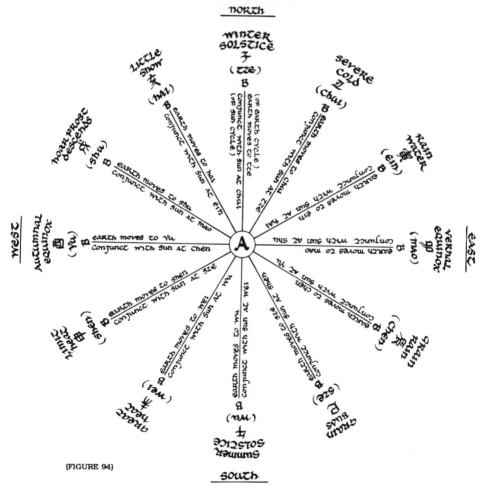

[FIGURE 94]

As the earth rotates around the sun, it goes through twelve seasonal changes which interact with the corresponding sun cycle. Each seasonal variation has two days ascribed to it (See Figure 84), because the beginning of each season varies according to whether it is a leap year or not. The twelve seasonal periods which appear at the first of each month mark the beginning of each energy month and are the seasonal periods of the earth. The other twelve, which appear in the latter part of each month, are the sun moving to its new position and creating a new harmonious relationship with the earth. (Notice that the energy month is not the same as the moon cycle.)

The Stems and Branches are hypothetical symbols whose subtle power and distinction come from the heavenly bodies and natural energy phases which they represent. These natural symbols have become active and effective characteristics in the natural and human multiple spheres.

Figure 94 above expresses the relationship between the different energies symbolized in the sun and earth cycles as follows. When the earth moves to Tze, the first spoke (A-B) from Polaris, it is conjunct with the sun. The seasonal period that is expressed is the Winter Solstice. In the earth's cycle the phase is Tze, while in the sun's cycle the phase is Chui.

When the earth moves to Chui, the second spoke of Polaris, it is conjunct with the sun, and the seasonal period expressed is Severe Cold. In the earth's cycle the phase is Chui, while in the sun's it is Tze.

When the earth moves to Ein, the third spoke of Polaris, it is conjunct with the sun, and the seasonal period expressed is Rain Water. In the earth's cycle the phase is Ein, while in the sun's it is Hai.

When the earth moves to Mao, the fourth spoke of Polaris, it is conjunct with the sun, and the seasonal period expressed is the Vernal Equinox. The earth's cycle is Mao, and the sun's is Shu.

When the earth moves to Chen, the fifth spoke of Polaris, it is conjunct with the sun, and the seasonal period expressed is Grain Rain. The earth cycle is Chen, and the sun cycle is Yu.

When the earth moves to Sze, the sixth spoke of Polaris, it is conjunct with the sun, and the seasonal period expressed is Grain Buds. The earth cycle is Sze, and the sun cycle is Shen.

This process continues until the earth makes a rotation through all twelve seasonal variations, thus completing one full year.

In Figure 95 below, one can see how the ancients made Polaris the center of the earth and sun cycles. Through the intermingling of these two great cycles, all seasonal changes occur. (The outer triangles read counter-clockwise, while the inner triangles read clockwise.) Although the North Star is considered the unchanging center amongst all this change, it must be remembered that even its position fluctuates.

The North Star will eventually be replaced by another star called the Wolf, which will usher in a new era. The true governing power of life, however, is the subtle law which balances all extremes.

The Earth Cycle and Sun Cycle in Relation to Polaris

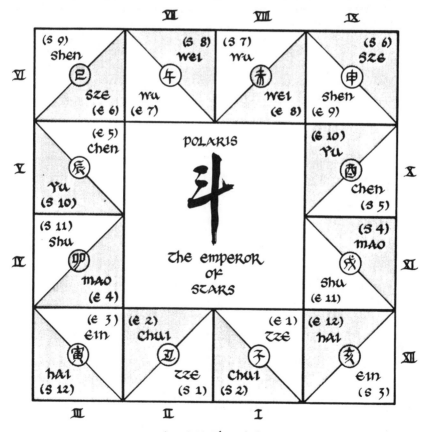

(FIGURE 95)

e: earth cycle
s: sun cycle

When the sun moves to the house of Tze I (S2) in the outer cycles, in a counter-clockwise direction, the earth moves to the house of Chui II (E2) in the inner cycle, in a clockwise direction. Tze, the sun "carriage," and Chui, the earth "carriage," meet each other harmoniously in House II of the twelve divisions of the Polaris-centered radii. This twelve-square method has many uses in Chinese astrology.

It is a precious thing if one can see both stars of the sixth star of the Big Dipper with the naked eye. It is believed that one who can see the "Star of Help," which is beside the "Generator" of the sky, will live a long and healthy life. Whether or not you can distinguish these stars, it is beneficial to learn how to observe the sky with bare eyes.

Anyone who would like to know the stars should first make himself familiar with the Big Dipper. As mentioned before, if you extend a line upward from the right side of the dipper, a little more than four times the length of the distance between the first star (Heavenly Pilot) and the second star (Heavenly Revolver), you will find the most noble North Star (Polaris) sitting at the end of the Little Dipper which is a star team of eight.

Another very important point of natural truth is that the natural order and its leading energy harmonizes without any deliberate competition. The order of the entire universe is supported by harmony. This is the unobstructed flow of the natural energy in its own channel. This is the great path of everything - this is Tao.

II. The Twenty-Eight Constellations

In the integral practice of individual spiritual cultivation, the Big Dipper, twenty-eight constellations, sun, moon and first five planets are highly valued and utilized because of their responsive natural energy and supernatural connection with life on earth. These heavenly bodies are actually the background for earthly energy. Each of them is in a different cyclic pattern, and they all have a direct and indirect influence on human life.

When the sun, moon and stars shine, their spiritual particles reach the earth. The overflow, insufficiency or balance of this energy shower influences a child's future life expression.   It forms a new energy picture; at birth, the new life receives its influence and becomes a symbol of the product of the natural energy at that time.   Conventional astrology interprets that fact in a way which may not be a perfect or complete expression of the energy affecting human people which makes them different from one another; however, one may like to use it as a good attempt at self-discovery.   More important and valuable is that the original spiritual understanding utilized the sky system as a symbol of individual spiritual formation.

The general area of the North Star is the center of the circle (See Figure 98), and it is from this center that the four directions are identified and located.   There are seven constellations in each direction, making a total of twenty-eight in all four directions combined.   The eastern seven are symbolized by a green dragon, the western seven by a white tiger, the southern seven by a red bird, and the northern seven by a black turtle.   The four colors distinguish the different subtle energy rays.

The number of stars in each constellation is not equal. For example, there are thirty-two stars in the eastern seven constellations, fifty-one in the western seven, sixty-four in the southern seven, and thirty-five in the northern seven.   All one hundred and eighty-two stars are set around the ecliptic of the sun.

Why did the ancient developed ones divide the fixed stars along the Yellow Route (the apparent annual path of the sun in the celestial sphere) into twenty-eight constellations?   There are two reasons.   First, the constellations are connected to the path of moon, which takes twenty-eight days to move from East to West among the fixed stars.   This is called a sidereal month.   The twenty-eight days are divided into twenty-eight regions which are courier stations or travelling houses for the moon.   Secondly, the ancient ones recognized that it takes twenty-eight years for Saturn to make a revolution around the sun. Just as the constellations are "on duty" for the earth, they are also "on duty" for Saturn.   The earth enters a new constellation every day, whereas Saturn enters another constellation each year.   This is called "holding authority over one constellation."

The shapes of the different constellations were originally drawn by using naked-eye observations, and a few constellations have changed since then.   The individual constellations are shown below in their original shapes.

The 28 Constellations

(FIGURE 96)

In the Eastern group are Chiao (the Horn), Kang (the Neck), Dii (the Bottom), Fang (the Room), Hsin (the Heart), Wei (the Tail), and Ji (the Basket).

In the Northern group are Dou (the Pipe), Niu (the Ox), Nu (the Damsel's Room), Zu (the Void), Wi (Danger), Shih (the House), and Bi (the Wall).

In the Western group are Kwei (the Champion), Lou (the Hump), Wei (the Stomach), Mao (the Rooster's Crown), Pi (the Fork), Tsu (the Beak), and Shen (the Interwoven).

In the Southern group are Jing (the Well), Kuei (the Ghost), Liu (the Weeping Willow), Hsing (the Star), Chang (the Drawn Bow), Yi (the Wing), and Chen (the Carriage).

95

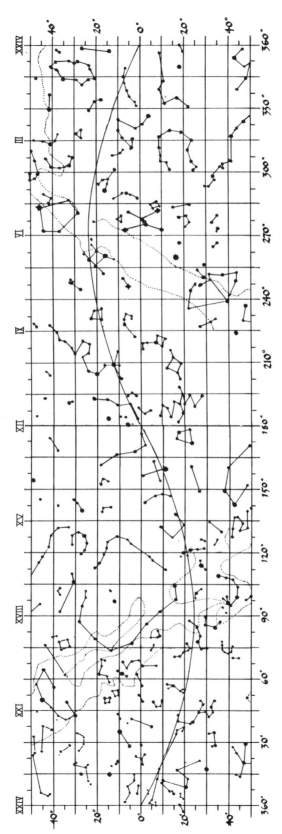

The 28 constellations

(FIGURE 97)

The Four Groups of 28 Constellations and Their Different Subtle Rays

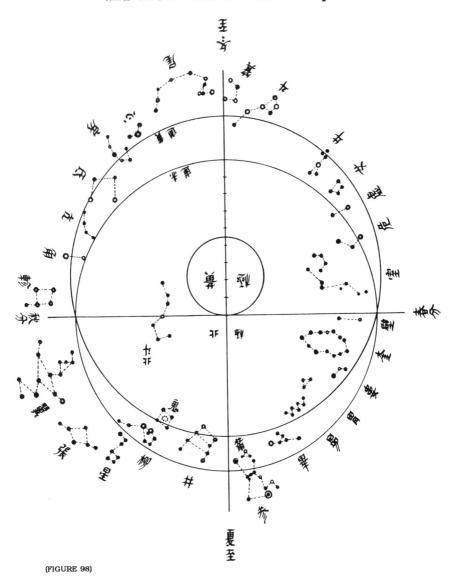

(FIGURE 98)

In the East, the seven constellations which form the shape of a dragon are:

角 ℮1, 亢 ℮2, 氐 ℮3, 房 ℮4, 心 ℮5, 尾 ℮6, 箕 ℮7,

Their energy is productive and their subtle rays are deep green.

In the North, the seven constellations which form the shape of a turtle are:

斗 n1 , 牛 n2 , 女 n3 , 虚 n4 , 危 n5 , 室 n6 , 壁 n7 ,

Their energy is destructive and their subtle rays are dark or black.

In the West, the seven constellations which form the shape of a tiger are:

奎 w1 , 婁 w2 , 胃 w3 , 昴 w4 , 畢 w5 , 觜 w6 , 參 w7 ,

Their energy is astringent and their subtle rays are white.

In the South, the seven constellations which form the shape of a bird are:

井 s1 , 鬼 s2 , 柳 s3 , 星 s4 , 張 s5 , 翼 s6 , 軫 s7 ,

Their energy is supportive and their subtle rays are red.

The ancient developed ones discovered that the main soul shapes itself in a flesh body with the endowment of natural energy. When a new life is born, a new company of the energy of nature is formed. The ancient astrologers thought that the sun, moon and the first five planets most influence a person's natural inclination and personality. However, far beyond the solar system, there are still the 28 constellations as four big energy formations on all sides which influence each life. In ancient times, the influence of society was much less and the influence of education was zero; thus the people were looking for explanations from nature. The people worked by themselves, governed themselves and developed themselves by special spiritual practices according to natural inspiration.

A. The Seven Day Cycle

1. The Correlation of Constellations To the Days of the Week

In the twenty-eight day constellation cycle, Sundays and weekdays have fixed dates. Their relationships to the constellations are as follows:

Correlations of Constellations to the Days of the Week

SEVEN DAY CYCLE	CORRESPONDING HEAVENLY BODIES	FIVE ELEMENTARY PHASES OF A DAY	EAST	NORTH	WEST	SOUTH
Thursday	Jupiter	Growing day of wood	角 E1	斗 N1	奎 W1	井 S1
Friday	Venus	Rigid day of metal	元 E2	牛 N2	婁 W2	鬼 S2
Saturday	Saturn	Reposeful day of earth (elementary)	氐 E3	女 N3	胃 W3	柳 S3
Sunday	Sun	Brilliant day of sun	房 E4	虚 N4	昴 W4	星 S4
Monday	Moon	Shimmering day of moon	心 E5	危 N5	畢 W5	張 S5
Tuesday	Mars	Consuming day of fire	尾 E6	室 N6	觜 W6	翼 S6
Wednesday	Mercury	Moving day of water	箕 E7	壁 N7	參 W7	軫 S7

note : the relationship of a week to the 28 constellations is from the moon's cyclic movement.

(FIGURE 99)

In the twenty-eight day cycle, Sunday must be the day of

房 E4 虚 N4 昴 W4 星 S4

Monday must be the day of

心 E5 危 N5 畢 W5 張 S5

Tuesday must be the day of

尾 E6 室 N6 觜 W6 翼 S6

Wednesday must be the day of

箕 E7 壁 N7 參 W7 軫 S7

Thursday must be the day of

角 E1 斗 N1 奎 W1 井 S1

Friday must be the day of

亢 E2   牛 N2   婁 W2   鬼 S2

Saturday must be the day of

氐 E3   女 N3   胃 W3   柳 S3

It is worth noting again that in the seven-day cycle, when the day rotates to 房 E4, 虛 N4, 昴 W4 or 星 S4, it will always be Sunday. The energy of Sunday is good for self-cultivation and spiritual development.

A week is only one quarter of a twenty-eight day constellation cycle. Sundays have the strongest regenerating energy in the four quarters because they are the middle day that points most directly to all four major directions. The kind of energy a Sunday provides is determined by the direction it is facing. The decision as to how to use different Sundays should actually depend on the energy of the particular constellation that is "on duty" for that day.

Not every Sunday is good for worship or cultivation. For example, an E4 Sunday is good for initiating things, while an N4 Sunday is not a good time to start anything new but rather a time to maintain the old, to worship and to cultivate. An N4 Sunday is also an appropriate time to participate in larger group activities. A W4 Sunday is a good day to remove obstacles and refresh oneself. A Sunday that is on S4 will be prosperous and good for celebrations and enjoyment. When Sundays are used for cultivating, the spiritual instructions will be different according to the energy.

2. The Daily Constellations

The fourth constellation of each quarter (which is always a Sunday) points directly to the due directions of East, South, West and North, as shown below.

Daily
Constellations

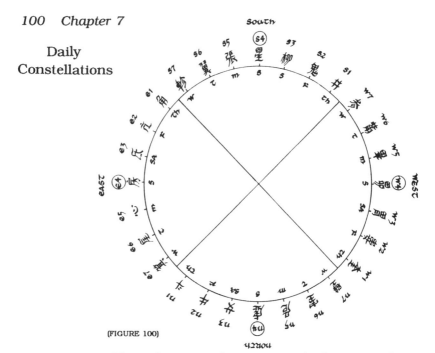

(FIGURE 100)

Note: This chart reads counter-clockwise and presents an idealistic arrangement of the constellations. Their locations are depicted only approximate to their true position.

3. The Days of the Week in Terms of Energy

The seven day cycle is one-fourth of a cycle of the twenty-eight constellations. It can be applied globally and is expressed in energy language as illustrated below.

(FIGURE 101)

In terms of energy, the days of the week occur in a decreasing phase. By Saturday the energy has become weak and ineffective and is expressed by ☶ . The recovery and revival of energy should be well-controlled at this time and one should not over-tax the body or mind. Sunday, or ☷ , should be a day for self-cultivation. In ancient Chinese it was called 來復日 or the "Day of Reviving," which begins with a yang line at the bottom. The seven-day cycle proceeds from Fu (Return), #24, to Po (Erosion), #23. One portion of yang energy must be retained in order to make the return cycle possible. The total exhaustion of ☷ , #2, should be avoided.

The energy language book that we call *The Book of Changes and the Unchanging Truth* corresponds with a seven-day cycle. There are sixty-four of these cycles, with each expressing a different pattern of natural energy movement.

For example, Hexagram #24, Revival (which also means return, review, regain, refresh, rediscover, etc.), is expressed in a seven-day period thus:

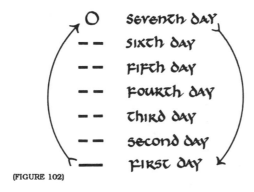

(FIGURE 102)

In this hexagram, the first line becomes the seventh after its movement through the six stages. Sunday can be considered as the last day of the week when used as a day of recovery and energy revival. It can also be considered as the first day of the new week. In a complete twenty-eight day cycle, Sundays are the middle days in each of the seven-day cycles; however, Sunday still remains the day to be used for the preparation of one's energy. Thus, Hexagram #24 illustrates one way to manage human work in terms of energy.

At this point it would be helpful to briefly review how the ancient sages discovered the natural
laws behind the complexity of all universal
phenomena. To govern the many events in their
lives, they organized a simple system based on the
knowledge they had acquired through observation
and insight over countless generations. Because
they had used the organs of the human body as instruments of observation, their vision was very
broad in scope. Especially important was their development of insight, which enabled them to reach
the true profundity of human life and the universe.
With regards to these important achievements, they
are still unsurpassed.

We have already mentioned the discovery of
the oneness of the universal, primal energy and the
two main expressions of this energy which are yin
and yang. From these two expressions come the development of the three spheres of yin, yang and
their integration, the four phases of full yang ⚏ ,
lesser yang ⚏, full yin ⚏ and lesser yin ⚏ , followed by the five basic phases of natural energy represented by Wood (generating energy), Fire (expansive energy), Metal (revolutionary energy), Water
(convergent energy) and Earth (harmonizing, unifying
energy).

Next we come to the sixty-four hexagrams,
each representing six stages of a particular energy
situation. These can be used to illustrate the concept of a seven phase cycle since each hexagram is
comprised of six individual lines which are an integral part of the larger continual cycle.

The six lines of a hexagram express a particular energy condition. Each line presents its own
situation and expresses a stage of development within the whole. A line can be strong or weak, its position correct, incorrect or confused, and its influence
on the whole hexagram can be either positive or
negative. It is preceded by a situation which
brought it about and will itself be followed by yet
another situation. For example, Hexagram #24
(Revival) follows the situation brought about in Hexagram #23 (Erosion). Although it usually remains
unexpressed, this transition from one hexagram to
another can be given the sign of zero. Thus we call

the cyclic formation of the hexagrams the "seven-phased" cycle.

In the seven day cycle, the natural energy of each day is different because the earth is under the influence of a particular constellation as well as the star "on duty" for that day. Since the earth is close to that star and that constellation, their energy is more accessible. Each day a different constellation becomes more responsive than the other constellations to life on earth.

The ancient Chinese paid much closer attention to the cycles of the moon and to the cycle of the twenty-four climatic periods of the year than to the seven day cycle. However, here the seven day cycle has been especially noted for its significance in self-cultivation since the spirit is the root of one's being, and the purpose of revival is to strengthen the root.

Although it has not been traced or recorded how or why those who lived outside of China adopted the seven day cycle (other than for religious purposes), it is interesting to note that Sundays occur on the same day everywhere.

B. The Relationship Between the Sixty Phase Cycle and the Twenty-Eight Constellations

There are twenty-eight constellations and sixty days in one energy cycle. It takes seven sixty-day cycles to make one complete rotation, thus it takes 420 days to accomplish one cycle of the constellations.

Each sixty day cycle has four constellations. The first, Jia/Tze 甲子 which is yang Wood/yang Water, starts from the eleventh constellation, 虚 N4 in due North. The second cycle starts from the fifteenth constellation, 奎 W1. The third cycle starts from the nineteenth constellation, 畢 W5. The fourth cycle starts from the twenty-third constellation, 鬼 S2. The fifth cycle starts from the twenty-seventh constellation, 翼 S6. The sixth cycle starts from the third constellation, 氐 E3. And the seventh cycle starts from the seventh constellation, 箕 E7. Then the new sixty day cycle begins again from the eleventh constellation. This describes the complete energy varying cycle.

C. Application of the Twenty-Eight Constellation Cycle

Constellations are the visible energy points of nature; similarly, there are many energy points in the human body. The twenty-eight constellation cycle can be arranged on the human body and used as the Celestial Stems and Terrestrial Branches. The main zone is the central line of the back and front of the body, which corresponds to the ecliptic path of the sun. There are many important energy points along one's "Yellow Route" which connect with spiritual health and development. If these points are successfully opened, a person's spiritual growth and capability will greatly increase.

Of the twenty-eight constellations, or spiritual energy points, only seven are familiar to some spiritual traditions where they are known as chakras. The opening of the entire ecliptic path is related to high spiritual growth, but this cannot be achieved by means of modern physical conditioning programs. T'ai Chi Chuan and Dao-In are ancient heritages which can aid in opening these points.

III. The Five Planets and Their Relation to the Natural Energy

Among the first five planets of the solar system, Saturn is considered the central force. Jupiter represents the East, Mercury the North, Venus the West, and Mars the South.

Applied to a human life as the assemblage of different natural energies, Jupiter is the liver, Mercury the kidneys, Venus the lungs, Mars the heart/mind, and Saturn the stomach.

In relationship to the five phases of cyclic movement, Jupiter is the planet of Wood, Mercury the planet of Water, Venus the planet of Metal, Mars the planet of Fire and Saturn the planet of Earth.

Qualities and Forces of the First Five Planets

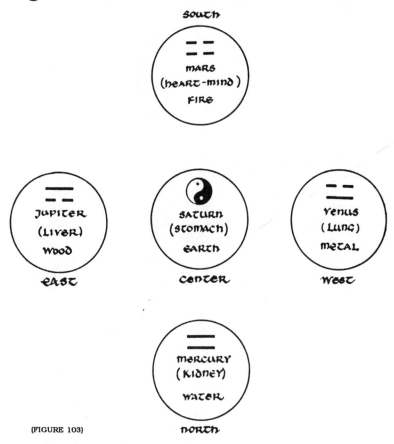

(FIGURE 103)

The natural energy of all the stars were distinguished and classified by the ancient developed ones and put into the system of the Five Elementary Phases, as were the planets. It would be incorrect to make these five planets the only source of the five different energy forces which influence the earth. The earth is the combination of all universal forces.

IV. The Unmanifest and Manifest Spheres

Above the manifest sphere is the unmanifest, the ultimate sphere of the interaction of yin and yang. This ultimate is called Wu-Chi, the unlimitedness which can also be expressed by the T'ai Chi symbol. It is more commonly expressed, however, by zero or by the neutral sign of Wu-Chi Tu.

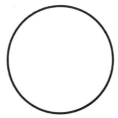

(FIGURE 104)

In the ancient tradition of cultivation, the "unlimitedness" is called Wu-Wei. A fundamental practice in meditation and in daily life, Wu-Wei expresses a state of purity, centeredness and neutrality from which all creative action comes forth. When one maintains this state of mind, one can develop the flexibility which leads to spiritual freedom.

In the T'ai Chi symbol, yin and yang are expressed as paired energies that assist each other. In each system there is an ongoing interaction of yin and yang. In the total sphere, the upper or Celestial cycle phases are expressions of universal yang energy, while the lower or Terrestrial cyclic phases are expressions of earthly yin energy. Their interaction is an internal movement in the manifest sphere.

With the integration of yin and yang comes power, a power which, when wisely applied, can ensure one's spiritual life. Utilizing this principle harmonizes the relationships between any parts of the whole, either in a male/female relationship or among all the elements of an individual body/mind/spirit. In all, this simple philosophical expression, the bountiful harvest of mature human insight, contains the secret guidance for single and dual cultivation which allows one to achieve the energy harmony and refinement that can lead to divine immortality.

Pre-Heaven and Post-Heaven

The universe is the first expression of primal chi. Because the movement of primal chi has phases, we have differently expressed phenomena. When we talk about primal chi as the unmanifest sphere, there is no way to express it. When we reach the manifest sphere, the following expressions can be used:

- the complimentary elements of yin and yang
- the four stages of yin and yang
- the five elementary phases
- the eight trigrams
- the ten Celestial Stems
- the twelve Terrestrial Branches
- the twenty-eight constellations
- the sixty cycles
- the sixty-four hexagrams

All of these energy phases apply to the manifest realm.

In the entire universe, according to the understanding of the ancient developed ones, the phenomenon of "flesh" life can be explained as the interaction of two basic energy elements which are the energy phases of Fire and Water. Fire energy is less controllable, while flowing Water energy is more stable.

In the earth's development, the beginning phase was Fire. After some time, the Fire cooled and the energy condensed into a shell, thus forming Earth. At that stage, an atmosphere formed and much Water was created.

The existence of life on earth can be explained in the same way. The sun represents Fire, and Water represents the only possibility for life as we know it. With the intercourse or interaction of these two kinds of energy, a new life develops. Since different natural environments received sunshine under varying conditions, the life phenomena that was created differed accordingly.

Pre-Heaven Order   **Post-Heaven Order**

(FIGURE 105a)

(FIGURE 105b)

In discussing the eight trigrams, we note that there are two different orders for their arrangement. One is the pre-Heaven order, and the other is the post-Heaven order. Pre-Heaven order is expressed by the eight trigrams stably positioned in a cyclic order (Figure 105a). The way to distinguish pre-Heaven order is by the top and central trigram, which is Heaven or light energy. Opposite Heaven in the pre-Heaven order is Earth or heavy energy. In the post-Heaven stage (Figure 105b), the top and central trigram is Fire, and the lower central trigram is Water.

While these four energies can be used to identify the different arrangements, the two orders are viewed differently according to the interaction of the energies. Pre-Heaven (Figure 105a), when viewed as evolving clockwise, shows the rise and decline of yin and yang. The top trigram ☰, shows yang at its fullest, which gives way to ☴, showing yin entering from the bottom. In the image of Water, ☵, yin surrounds the yang, and in ☶ it pushes the yang out at the top, leaving only pure yin ☷ at the base. The cycle continues as yang enters at the base and surrounds and pushes out the yin until there is only pure yang once again.

Post-Heaven order (Figure 105b), however, is viewed by looking at the oppositely paired images. For instance, Fire ☲ and Water ☵ , Wood (Thunder) ☳ and Metal (Lake) ☱ , Wood (Wind) ☴ and Metal (Heaven) ☰ . Through their interaction and integration these opposing forces create all phenomena. Only the images of Earth (Mountain) ☶ and Earth (Earth) ☷ harmonize, thereby stabilizing all opposing forces.

The pre-Heaven arrangement shows the self-generating cyclic movement of the different energy phases whereas the post-Heaven arrangement shows the interaction of opposing energies that actually brings about creation.

By looking deeply, we can discover that energy has phases and that after the integration of these different phases, a new life begins. All life and all existence is the multiple transformation of primary chi. On a superficial level, one can gather discriminating information and see differences, but at the very core of energy there are no differences. This leads to the spiritual level. However, a person needs to deal with the superficial level in order to understand the traceable natural phenomena that can help one control one's self-cultivation.

Chapter 8

NATURAL ENERGY IN HUMAN LIFE

I. The Nature of the Universe and the Human Body

The energy language system which expresses all natural phenomena completely can also be applied to the human body. Human life is nature's offspring, not a human production, and the phenomena of living beings cannot be separated from nature. It follows that the ancient energy language, therefore, will express phases and situations of human energy.

Most of us are familiar with the statement that the human body is a microcosm of the universe and that the universe is but a macro-human body. Now let us analyze how the ancient sages used this system in two different areas.

A. The Meridian Systems

First, the microcosmic orbit (the main energy channel of the human body) is located on the central line along the front and back of the body. Thus, the two lines form a complete circle around one's body. The front central meridian is often called the "Stewardess" (任 脈) and it is the general yin meridian. Its energy symbol is ☰☰ The back central meridian is often called the "Governor" (督 脈) and it is the general yang meridian. Its energy symbol is ☰ .

In the upper and lower parts of the body there are twelve different meridians or energy channels. Starting from the hands, there are three yang meridians and three yin. There are also three yang meridians and three yin starting from the feet. The yang meridians of the hands and the feet are symbolized by ☰☰, ☱☱ and ☲☲ . The yin meridians of the hands and the feet are symbolized by ☷☷ , ☶☶ and ☴☴ .

When the "Stewardess" and the "Governor" are combined with the twelve meridians, there are fourteen energy channels in all.

B. Energy Channels of the Human Body According to Natural Energy Language

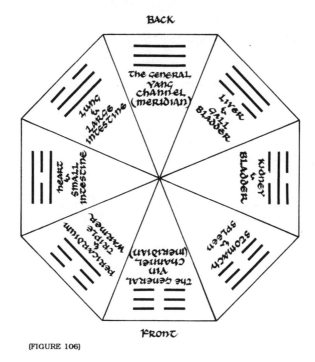

(FIGURE 106)

C. Correspondence of the Ten Celestial Stems With the Ten Organs of the Human Body

甲	gallbladder	己	spleen
乙	liver	庚	large intestines
丙	small intestines	辛	lungs
丁	heart	壬	bladder
戊	stomach	癸	kidneys

(FIGURE 107)

The ten Celestial Stems are symbols of the distinctly different energy phases and forces of the universe, thus these organs in the human body express the different energies and their functions, and they communicate with nature in the same channels as shown above.

The natural daily energy circulation in the human body is shown in the following diagram (Figure 108). By studying this diagram one can see that the natural energy connection begins with the lungs, circulates throughout all the different organs, and ends with the liver.   Each breath or absorption of natural energy makes a complete circulation of these energy channels to sustain a normal life.   If a meridian is damaged, either by internal or external causes or by the artificial disturbance of surgery, the natural energy circulation will be incomplete.   Even in such cases, however, with the cultivation of a good mind spiritual energy circulation will not be incomplete.

D.   Physical Energy Flowing in the Human Body According to the Twelve Earthly Branches

The General Spheres of Chi Circulation

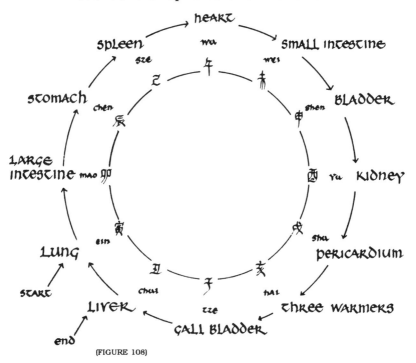

(FIGURE 108)

Natural energy not only connects with the skin, lungs and other organs of the body, we are totally enveloped in it like fish in water.   Fish, however, are not aware of this energy; however, we have the chance to realize it.

A natural environment is of first importance to a natural life. For example, an avocado tree can be made sterile by neighboring plants. There are many different trees which can cause an avocado tree to be "white-washed," and more than a thousand different trees which can make the tree fruitless.

Specific natural environments can also cause people to develop differently. People from New York are different than those from Texas, although such differences are minor and of no great importance. Problems only arise when there is a great energy dissonance between people.

Some specific natural and social environments such as a family, an office or a society can hinder the normal development of a person. This is like the damage done to an avocado tree by other trees. Human beings should take responsibility for the pollution of their natural and personal environments. A free society is surely a better environment for positive individual and personal development. The order of the Five Elementary Phases of Energy clearly expresses this fact.

The cycles of natural daily energy circulation explain the strong flow of energy which occurs in a certain hour within a certain organ. This helps with diagnosis and treatment in the traditional Chinese integral healing practices and is especially useful in acupuncture treatment. These cycles also help those of self-cultivation to do internal harmonizing work in different sessions of daily meditation. Kung Fu experts utilize these cycles in self-defense for overcoming an aggressive enemy at the appropriate moment.

One way of using the energy system in Chinese medicine is to divide the symptoms into yin and yang categories. Yang indicates that the trouble is easily diagnosed and shallow. Yin means the opposite. Though yang diseases are easily cured, they can turn into deep yin diseases if improperly treated. The first division of a disease is into categories of yin or yang. Within each category there are subdivisions according to the width and depth of yin or yang. Thus three yang and three yin categories have developed with the following symbols:

yang+	yin-
yang++	yin--
yang+++	yin---

In Chinese medical terminology:

yang+	represents young yang
yang++	represents middle yang
yang+++	represents old yang
yin-	represents young yin
yin--	represents middle yin
yin---	represents old yin

If one has a cold with a slight headache, a stiff neck and some chill, the disease is at the stage of yang+. If the symptoms are not cured or naturally healed and the patient begins to cough, has side pain and pale eyes, the disease is in the second stage of yang++. If stomach pain and high fever occur and are not controlled, then mental symptoms appear and the patient becomes delirious. This condition may be encephalitis. The disease is at the stage of yang+++. This is the top phase of the yang category of a cold and was caused by the same virus. The depth, location, symptoms and severity of the cold, however, are all different. If the high fever is not handled properly and medicine is used merely to suppress to fever, it turns from a shallow problem into the consuming yin category. The patient may develop an exhaustive low fever, perhaps with dysentery, thus becoming a case of yin-. If the patient becomes very drowsy or restless and sleepless and the heart muscle holds heat, the disease has become a case of yin--. If the disease is not cured at this stage, a nervous disorder develops and confused symptoms appear, alternating with different types of fever. Because of ineffective control at the beginning of the phase, serious organ disorders now arise. A common cold or flu can develop into many serious diseases.

This is one example of using energy language to describe physical problems. Human physiology is connected with the principles of yin and yang and the Five Elementary Phases of cyclic energy phenomena. Accurately applied in the practice of Chinese herbal medicine, these principles can be used to conquer or generate a response. This is only a slight introduction to a vast field.

II. Practical Matters

A. Birth

When a new life is born, it is important how and where it is born. For example, a baby is naturally born on a particular day at a certain hour. If a drug or pituitary extract is taken by the expectant mother, however, the new life energy is violated.

There are many cases of interference with the natural right of birth. For example, on the human head there are many points which are connected with the development of the mind. If forceps are misused on a baby's tender head, damage is certainly caused, not only physically but spiritually as well.

It is a beautiful and auspicious beginning if a child is born during the full moon, on a fine day, in normal weather. The place where the new life is welcomed should be a natural setting with the ceiling not too far from the sky, the floor not too far from the earth, and the space throughout filled with fresh air.

A child is fortunate to be born close to a peaceful natural environment such as a mountain or a lake. The baby will be calm and earnest if it is conceived and born on a mountainside. If it is born by a lake, it will be more intelligent.

B. Death

We have a friend whose grandfather is dying in a hospital. The doctors are trying to keep him, a deteriorating old man, alive. My friend, however, does not agree with the doctors' treatment of the old man's symptoms. She feels that medicine is no good for those who are dying of natural causes.

I can understand the vision of this girl. It is like a ripe apple on a tree - it should naturally fall to the ground, but someone develops and uses powerful techniques to keep it on the tree longer.

In modern medicine, death is determined when the heart no longer beats. Real death, however, does not occur until seven days after the heart has stopped beating. During that time, the deep consciousness is still alive. The invisible "umbilical cord" between the soul and the body has not yet been severed. For the duration of those seven days, if the corpse is put in a refrigerator, it experiences the cold. If it is burned to ashes, it experiences pain from the heat. Apparently, many people's loved and respected ones are persecuted by their closest relatives.

Appropriate action should be taken only after seven days and not before. Moreover, when a person is passing away there should be no interference or disturbance. Such disturbances prevent a natural death and thereby damage the formation of the soul. Generally, seven days are needed for the soul to grow and leave the body and thus appear as a new ghost.

C. Natural Medicine

In human life there are two basic classifications of people: "heavy" and "light." Herbal medicine, acupuncture and other healing arts of the same family are for "light" people who are sensitive enough to react to "light" medicine. "Heavy" medicine, which has developed along the same level as modern industrial technology, serves "heavy" people. Such plumbing techniques that require complicated operations and strong medicines are very popular in treating many human medical symptoms.

This principle applies not only to medicine but also to the spheres of religion and politics. "Heavy" religions and political systems suit the needs of "heavy" people. Light wine is not for vodka drinkers. No one can promise that "light" measures will solve all human problems, however - especially when the tendency of humanity is to become "heavier."

Because of the evolutionary and devolutionary phases of individuals, it is not easy to distinguish who belongs in which category. A person may defer from one thing to another or revert to yesterday's habitual behavior. The mass production of today's educational system tends to build "heavy" students who are restricted in their own development. Although some people escape being molded in such a way, many become poor victims.

D. Mental Illness

People who have mental or spiritual illness often strive for spiritual achievement, but such a search is unrealistic. Spiritual achievement depends on sanity, on having a sound mind in a sound body. Also, spiritual growth does not occur suddenly. If one is unaware of one's own problems yet tries to follow a religious ritual, one is only looking for something to cover up those problems. The harder one works, the less will be the results. In a case such as this, great nature is a good cure.

If one wishes to improve one's mind by self-reflection and introspection in order to reorganize his life, I recommend the *Tao Teh Ching* which guides one to return to one's own nature and thus to the nature of the universe.

Drugs and electrotherapy many have an effect on evil spirits which menace and attach themselves to the patient, but they also hurt the patient's energy. This kind of treatment is like using chemical insecticides to protect vegetables: the vegetables can also become poisonous.

E. Confusion for Spiritual Students

Spiritual cultivation is not equivalent to participation in groups. Such practices are only on a social level. Real spiritual cultivation means looking for inner balance, spiritual independence and self-mastery. As described in the *Tao Teh Ching*, people of real spiritual independence and self-mastery do not seek attention; thus they do not show off or chase after fame, position or worldly luxuries. Nor do they ever reveal the profound nature of their spiritual authority or power to others. Even though a spiritually achieved person may never reach spiritual authority, he must nevertheless always follow the fundamental spiritual path without compromise.

F. The Elixir

The "divine golden medicine" is the most important metaphor for the process of spiritual cultivation in the ancient tradition of integral spiritual development. Are you aware of how much gold can be gathered from tons of sand? In an ordinary life being there may also be "gold" - the essence of life. Through the process of spiritual cultivation, one refines oneself, disposing of the "sand" and retaining the "gold." Having obtained the "gold," one then has the necessary material for refining the "divine immortal medicine."

Spiritual cultivation involves removing the coarse and keeping what is truly precious. This process involves a great deal of work. Many teachings emphasize throwing away what is coarse, but too often they throw away the essence at the same time. Some teachings even use that essence in exchange for what is false. These kinds of teachings are very popular in today's world. True cultivation requires much time and daily practice, whereas conceptual achievement can be immediate.

G. Application of the Twenty-Eight Constellation Cycle

Constellations are the visible energy points of nature; similarly, there are many energy points in the human body. The twenty-eight constellation cycle can be arranged on the human body and used as the Celestial Stems and Terrestrial Branches. The main zone is the central line of the back and front of the body, which corresponds to the ecliptic path of the sun. There are many important energy points along one's "Yellow Route" which connect with spiritual health and development. If these points are successfully opened, a person's spiritual growth and capability will greatly increase.

Of the twenty-eight constellations, or spiritual energy points, only seven are familiar to some spiritual traditions where they are known as chakras. The opening of the entire ecliptic path is related to high spiritual growth, but this cannot be achieved by means of modern physical conditioning programs. Tai Chi Chuan,

Chi Gong and Dou-In are ancient heritages which can aid in opening these points.

H. The Return of Energy and Cultivation

From the twelve phases illustrated in energy language below, one can clearly see the increasing process of yang energy.

Once yang reaches its fullness, it begins to decrease. The following illustration can help you visualize the decrease of yang energy in a steady, gradual process.

From the illustrated energy language above, one should be able to recognize which of the hexagrams expresses the return of energy or beginning of a new cycle: it is , Revival.

In a daily cycle, the time of return or revival is just after midnight. In a yearly cycle, it is just after the Winter Solstice when the shortest day in the Northern Hemisphere has ended and the days begin to lengthen. The opposite applies in the Southern Hemisphere.

Thus, there are two time periods which are essential for energy cultivation and during which the energy should not be violated. One is midnight in the daily cycle, and the other is during the Winter of the yearly cycle. If damage is done to a seed when it is just sprouting, it will affect the entire life of the plant. One the other hand, this early stage is a good time to nurture the seed. Cultivation just after midnight, and indoor cultivation beginning at the Winter Solstice, reap the benefit of the time when yang energy is increasing. When this twelve-phase cycle of energy language is applied to cultivating the human body, the energy is used to open the corresponding energy channels illustrated below.

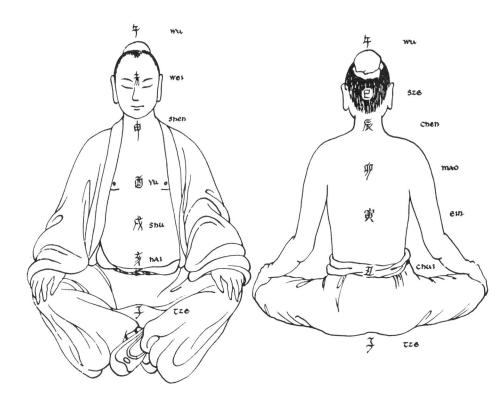

(FIGURE 109)

The natural time of revival for the human body is just after midnight. At this time the sexual member stirs naturally, without stimulation or temptation. It is the appropriate time to cultivate chi rather than using hormones or other artificial methods of rejuvenation. After the bitter coldness of deep Winter and before the Spring Equinox comes, a subtle warm current starts at your feet and gradually ascends. This is the return of yang energy and is the time to cultivate this energy and make it grow.

Although the seasons are opposite in the Southern Hemisphere, this principle is global. It can be applied anywhere and is especially beneficial to people of self-cultivation. A developed being knows well that yang energy always maintains and supports life on earth.

Cultivation that is based on the returning nature of energy will not mislead you, unless you do not know how to utilize it. It is a pity to turn away from what really supports our life inwardly by searching for fragmented help from the outside, superficial world. No discovery is greater than the discovery of that which supports all life.

In the body there are twelve big ties which connect the soul to the body. This bondage is an obstacle for an uplifting soul, thus it is wise to utilize the power of forgiveness to dissolve these intricate ties. One can also take advantage of the eight main seasonal periods to dissolve these ties and reform one's personality.

In response to questions from the readers of the first edition of this book, there is a particular spiritual practice that dissolves those blockages. This practice is contained in Volume 1043 of the Taoist Canon which was edited during the Ming Dynasty, at the time of Chen Tun.

You might like me to simplify that practice for you. Each person is an individual child of nature, and the spiritual system in each individual is naturally built-in. Each person has his or her own level of spirituality or spiritual potential. The spiritual levels are conventionally divided into three: Heaven, Earth and the Underworld. There are heavenly people, earthly people and people whose minds reflect the underworld and whom we will call "hellish" people.

The truth of an "underworld" does not necessarily reflect the conventional conception of a place where one is punished after death. Punishment is decided and meted out while you are still alive. Generally speaking, this can be more easily understood by talking about those twelve ties or blockages.

People have illnesses because their bodies are blocked in one place or another. Once there is blockage, sickness will be expressed. Spiritual blockage, however, is usually not as easily understood as physical blockages. Take the example of a husband and wife who have differing attitudes toward a matter of conflict with somebody. Let us say that one would like to take a very extreme approach while the other would like to take a more humanistic way to solve the problem. The difference in attitude, idea or approach is due to two different levels of spiritual living. The person with more spiritual blockage inside will understand a matter very differently than the person whose spiritual energy flows more fluently within the body. This is one way to explain this.

Another way of explaining spiritual blockage is at the level of the semi-spiritual, semi-physical. For example, sometimes when you have bad dreams the reason could be physical. Laying in a position that blocks the circulation of internal energy will make it difficult to wake up. When the waking spirit struggles inside to move from the lower body to the head, that struggling will express itself as a bad experience in a dream. In this case, practically speaking, the bad dream is a physical blockage. If one is not sick, such dreams could be caused by other simple things like being overly tired, sleeping under a blanket that is too heavy, bad air or an odor in the room.

Once we experience worldly life, we have desire and wish to satisfy it. If you act on that desire and you have a blockage, one portion of your energy becomes over extended and weakens another part. Then the blockage becomes stronger because the weakened energy does not support a balanced life being. In our spiritual practice, we do meditation, Tai Chi, Dou-In (Do-In) and Chi Gong to improve the energy flow inside the body. When that internal flow is very good, then you are not troubled physically.

Spiritual cultivation follows the same process, but it is harder to understand. The practices I mentioned above are not like athletic exercises which are totally physical; they are semi-physical and semi-spiritual. A person can still develop or withdraw further to concentrate totally on the spiritual level to make the energy flow.

When a person who is not spiritually achieved has sexual desire, the sexual energy in the abdomen is so strong that the person cannot manage it except by doing something to oneself or to a partner, or by going out to do something improper just to satisfy that momentary need. People with spiritual blockages live at this level, which could be said to be a hellish way of life.

Another example of spiritual blockage is when a person needs money, but does not have any good way to obtain it. Such a person will start to scheme or cheat, play tricks on people, become mischievous or even become violent or brutal. Why are they so strongly affected by their desires or ambitions and cannot see that there is another way to achieve them that is much more healthy and acceptable? It is because they are spiritually blocked, the upper part and the lower part of their being cannot communicate. Therefore, they will do whatever they like rather than follow a better way.

Another illustration might help make this more understandable: a twenty-four rung step ladder can be likened to the human spinal column. A healthy person's vertebrae are well joined, but without cultivation, the spiritual energy cannot go through any section of the bones because each step is blocked. As the energy rises up the spinal column from the bottom, there is a block in each vertebrae that needs to be opened, one at a time. Some people never can open all the blocks, so desire, interest and personal outreach all originate from the internal organs of the life being. The energy of a spiritually achieved person moves easily through each section, so he or she naturally looks for a balanced, good approach for their life energy. A person whose spiritual energy is blocked, on the other hand, will take an approach or make demands that are based on a partial vision. He or she cannot see the benefits and disadvantages of things, whether a situation or action is proper or not, or whether what is done is accomplished by good means or bad means.

Dark energy in a person's aura can be caused by two conditions. One is that the person is physically blocked, is sick, and is going to die. The other condition is that the person is mean and has done many bad things. We would not necessarily call the person "bad," but the person's spiritual energy is definitely blocked and cannot be seen, it cannot shine. When it is blocked completely, a dark aura appears and you know that person is extremely negative in nature.

This is why we need to dissolve those ties, those internal blockages. Physically or spiritually, a person always needs, subtly and slowly, to reform and connect the energy flow between each one of the chakras or each one of the blockages. Chakra is the word used in yoga. Each chakra is very powerful. If energy goes through each chakra, it is excellent and a person can achieve something. If energy does not go through, if it is blocked, then there will be some kind of trouble. In our system we call the chakras checkpoints. There are many,

many checkpoints inside of us. On the physical level, more than a thousand acupuncture points have been discovered which can also be related to human physical problems. In our system there are eight extra meridians applied in spiritual cultivation. In each meridian of these extra energy channels - channel is a better word than meridian - there are special points needful for your spiritual opening. Why do you need to achieve this? It is needed because a blockage prevents spiritual achievement. Once these blockages are removed, the energy can go anywhere. You can manage it just like an urban transportation system, smoothly flowing everywhere with no traffic jams.

The physical sphere can help you to understand the personal spiritual sphere so that you can achieve yourself. In this world, in this lifetime, a person can be a heavenly being, an earthly being or a hellish being. Generally speaking, everyone is born as an earthly being. This is fundamental. Even if you are a heavenly being, you sometimes need to take an earthly approach to matters. Otherwise, you can only live in the air. If you can achieve that high level, it is beautiful, but never extend yourself to the lower realm to become an infernal being of the underworld. Always reach higher. Once you have become a hellish being, it is very hard to save yourself and your soul.

About the matter of saving the soul, we like to have freedom in the world. Let me ask you: do you have freedom within yourself and in your own soul? Many people do not have freedom even in their own body. The soul is a tiny but essential portion of physical life; it is no larger than the tip of a hair. When it descends to the lower region of your body while you sleep, there may be some places it cannot pass through. If it is shut up in darkness and is looking for help, it becomes panicked until you wake up and it enters the head again. It is important to wake up.

Now about that special practice I was talking about that dissolves the blockages; as long as you do the main practices I have recommended, the specific ones like that do not matter. I have witnessed many highly spiritually achieved teachers who do not pay attention to the minor practices, and they only do the main things to achieve themselves. But those practices do exist, for security.

Some people are very happy when they take advantage of somebody else. They do not know that their own bad acts increase the thickness and strength of the blockage. For this reason, it is important not to take advantage of any other people. Also, do not be negative or narrow minded. Those things would only cause your own spiritual downfall.

So you see, people do not have to fall into pandemonium after death. Lifetimes of accumulated evil doing, or even bad acts after entering the world in this life, build the blockages that create hell. When your eyes are spiritually opened by your own achievement, you can see that there are so many people who are hell-beings. This is why the ancient sages preferred to stay away from the majority of people.

I am glad that in an open society like America, most people are only naive. If they make a mistake, it is because they do not know. When people in India or China do a bad thing, they know what they are doing. They have the knowledge, but they doubt that knowledge because they are blocked. Those people who vaguely know suffer much worse than the people who do not already know better. So I am happy to be working in such an open society like the United States and other areas. The young people I see may be scattered or negative and have no purpose to their lives, but they are not demonic or hellish people. They only need to be spiritually awakened; then there will be hope in their lives.

When a society declines, it is because a majority of bad souls reincarnate or re-enter life in that society. Likewise, when a society is in a high, good cycle, it is because so many good souls have re-entered or reincarnated as its citizens. The society that suffers more is the one that has a spiritual background. It has half or incomplete knowledge, but still does worse things than what its ancestors taught it. These people are really unhelpful unless they find light and change themselves, because spiritual things change much faster than anything else. If a person finds the right teacher and the right moment, however, then salvation is there for that person.

The important correction needed by worldly religions is the transformation from external religious teaching to truthful internal spiritual reality. The so-called Heaven is the spiritual sphere of each individual life.

The so-called man is the mind which we have all educated to serve our worldly life. Earth means our physical foundation of bodily life. Hell is associated with earth, so it is also called the earthly hells. The mind of people, correctly functioning, is a medium which can reach the spiritual sphere of each individual's life being and can also communicate to the physical sphere of each individual life being. The learning of most people, however, has been limited by their life experience, thus creating a strong blockage which keeps them from communicating with their own spiritual sphere. The result is a truly hellish experience and reality.

In early times many religious leaders externalized this fact and presented it to people who were at the stage of a mixed life and whose minds were of the underworld; thus, religions were created. People's intellectual development today is adequate to comprehend the truth of the three levels of life energy which are contained in each individual life. They should be self-responsible for their spiritual growth.

A healthy life being should attain the development of all three spheres. Otherwise, the individual life is incomplete. It is dangerous for world leaders in all fields, because many of them only have two spheres: the mind and the body, or the man and the earth. Without the spiritual connection, these leaders inflict their own confusion, disorder, turmoil and shortsighted leadership on the world, bringing downfall to all.

In ancient times spiritual teachers used the word "karma" to describe such an accumulation of bad behavior and habits. Parents should not only accumulate wealth to give their children. It is much safer to accumulate good deeds in a lifetime. Your children may not be able to enjoy your wealth and money. Many youngsters cannot manage their lives because they cannot manage the spiritual condition of their life being. Lots of demons live in the youngsters bodies because of the parents' bad karma. There is nothing wrong with karma, but the conventional explanation of it may mislead some people, because it gives the impression of an external authority that punishes people. They do not realize that the spiritual system is a built-in system inside the body of each individual. Many things you do are against the spiritual system or God inside of you, so when God leaves you in hell, it is the result of your own actions.

There are many good spiritual practices which can be learned, and the eight seasonal periods are very important.   If you do a general spiritual practice, the seasonal periods can help produce a good effect in dissolving knots and ties.

III.   General Energy Arrangements for Self-Cultivation

The integrity of the cosmos in the pre-Heaven stage is inexpressible.   When it reaches the expressible level of the post-Heaven stage, polarity and duality become its main characteristic.   Yang (——) and yin (– –) become the two great spheres.   The continuous multiple development of the universe is the perpetual variation of those two great forces.

Wherever there is a phenomenon of yang, there must be one of yin and vice versa.   An expression of yang actually contains yin, and yin contains yang.   On a deep level yin and yang are indivisible.   This sphere of indivisibility reaches to the core of the cosmos.

Life is the offspring of the indivisible cosmic nature.   It is like the blossoms on a tree; they come and go, but the tree always remains.   The way to restore oneness with the cosmos is to dissolve duality and eliminate or integrate polarity, not only on a conceptual level but also in the real cultivation of inner eternal life.

Practically speaking, we cultivate ourselves on the basis of yin and yang.   In expressing the continuous restructuring of yin and yang in human life, there is nothing better than using energy language as a guide.   On the subtle level of the pre-Heaven stage ☰ and ☷ are the two great complementary forces.   On the practical level of the post-Heaven stage ☵ and ☲ express the interaction and interdependence of Water and Fire as the two complementary forces that accomplish each other in the process of creation.   Male and female energy need each other in order to achieve independence.   After the middle line of each trigram in ☲ is exchanged with the middle line of the trigrams in ☵ , then ☲ becomes ☰ and ☵ becomes ☷ .   Thus, the purity or integrity of each is achieved.

The entirety of the universe is but energy arrangement or energy formation.   Practicing self-cultivation without the

fundamental knowledge of energy rearrangement causes
negative results.   To help give a basic understanding of
this truth some examples are given below.

A. Examples of Poor Energy Arrangements in Sitting Cultivation

When in a state of calmness, a person can be divided into six energy regions from top to bottom.   Following are several ways you can violate or help your
energy in those regions.

☰ This arrangement exemplifies unnecessary and
irrelevant thinking in one's sitting cultivation, causing
the energy to rush into the head.   This imbalance can
become serious and dangerous.   If a person is ill, only
a small amount of yang energy (liveliness) is left, and
death is not far away.

☷ This arrangement exemplifies an abundance of
energy in the middle area and resembles a building
with strong beams but weak pillars.   In human terms,
it implies a stomach too full of food.   This imbalance
can be particularly dangerous in sitting cultivation.   If
a person is sick, stuffiness or suffocation can occur in
the middle area and cause death.

☷ This arrangement exemplifies Fire beneath the
Earth and implies that one's sexual impulses are too
strong.

☲ In this arrangement Fire is above and Water is
below.   Since they are not interacting in one's sitting
cultivation, nothing constructive occurs.

☰ In this arrangement the scatteredness of the
Wind below causes the yang energy to disperse.

☵ This arrangement represents dual cultivation in which there is no communication between the upper and lower partners.   In self-cultivation this indicates no communication between the upper and lower parts of the body.

B. Examples of Appropriate Energy Arrangements in Sitting Cultivation

☶ In this arrangement the yin energy descends from above and the yang energy rises from below, thus the integration of the two energies transpires.   In dual cultivation the partners meet and male and female energy are subtly integrated.

☶ In this arrangement there is an interaction between the Water above and the Fire below, thus the sitting cultivation can be successful.

☵ This arrangement exemplifies a correct gathering of energy in the middle region.

☳ This arrangement shows that clarity of mind is attained, as indicated by the fifth line which symbolizes an unpreoccupied and flexible mind.

☵ This is a comfortable arrangement in sitting cultivation.   The energy is kept deeply within.

☳ This arrangement represents the calm image of water in a well.   The water is a lively fountain but not a surging tide.

IV. Appropriate Matches of Natural Energy

Seeking a match as general male and female.

1. Full yang looking for a match. ☰

    a. ☰ meeting ☷

        If ☷ is in the superior position, this means great peace.

        If ☰ is in the superior position, this means divorce.

    b. ☰ meeting ☳

        He loves her only. It is a difficult match.

        She also loves him. It is a good match.

    c. ☰ meeting ☳

        A great love.

        A great match.

    d. ☰ meeting ☱

        Careful conduct brings a happy relationship.

        Gentleness brings total trust.

2. Vigorous yang looking for a match. ☳

    a. ☳ meeting ☷

        A comfortable match.

        A progressing match.

    b. ☳ meeting ☳

        If the male has loved with constancy, then it is a good match. If he has often changed his interest, then the female needs great tolerance to maintain a good relationship.

        A beneficial relationship. The male has the total support of the female.

c. ☳ meeting ☳

☲ A burning love affair. It cannot last long.

☳ A quarrelsome relationship that matures both individuals.

d. ☳ meeting ☷

☲ A good marriage.

☳ A good fellowship.

3. Middle yang looking for a match. ☵

   a. ☵ meeting ☷

☲ Companionship for a specifically good reason.

☵ Teaming up for an externally positive purpose.

   b. ☵ meeting ☴

☲ A quietly supportive relationship.

☴ A good relationship will depend on removing emotional obstacles or on personal improvement.

   c. ☵ meeting ☱

☲ A loving relationship.

☱ A difficult relationship.

   d. ☵ meeting ☶

☷ A good relationship involving self-restraint on both parts.

☶ A good relationship that encounters difficulty from its surroundings.

4. Young or shallow yang looking for a match. ☱

a. ☰ ☷ meeting ☷

☳ The yang energy will be damaged.

☶ Rich, motherly love.

b. ☰ ☷ meeting ☳

☵ A corrupt match.

☴ A gradually built friendship.

c. ☰ ☷ meeting ☶

☲ A lodge on the journey of life.

☵ Traveling mates.

d. ☰ ☷ meeting ☴

☳ The male side is more supportive.

☴ A mental correspondence.

The above situations also apply to a female seeking male energy.

V. Good Partnerships in Terms of Natural Energy

A partnership in business is not the same as a relationship between male and female. People of different sexes may become partners in business, but business relationships can generally be expressed as yang with yang or yin with yin.

Yang Partnerships

1.　　This represents an incidental partnership. The outcome will be a surprising result in either a positive or negative direction.

This represents a strong team, if it is without internal difficulty.

2.   ☰   This represents an argumentative partnership. Both sides need more relational strength.

          ☰   This represents a passive partnership. Helpfulness comes after the dispersion of doubt.

3.   ☰   This represents a retreating situation. Since the opposite partner or external situation is not yet reliable, one should take care of oneself.

          ☰   The strength of one's partner is needed. It can be obtained with tolerance and calmness.

Yin Partnerships

1.   ☷   Promoting opportunity comes with this partnership.

          ☷   Helpful partnership by watching the high model. Reaching out in the right direction brings a broad perspective and personal growth.

2.   ☷   The partnership will shift from the bright to the dark.

          ☷   A progressive partnership.

3.   ☷   A beautiful partnership that cannot last very long.

          ☷   A partnership is gathered, however, it needs the correct direction.

In observing the different kinds of relationships in either category (matches or partnerships), the basic symbols presented above should be flexibly applied and interpreted in order to discover the significant information for the next positive use.

Chapter 9

THE NATURAL TRUTH
OF THE SPIRITUAL REALM

The Spiritual Realm

The truth of spirit is very different from ordinary descriptions in literature and religion or the general imagination of people. The existence of spirits is a fact of nature. They do not belong to the imaginary realm at all.

The difference between spirits and ghosts is an important one. The two great spheres in the subtle realm are the divisions of yin and yang. Spirits belong to the yang category. They are natural beings who are invisible, inaudible and intangible to ordinary people. To a spiritually developed human being, however, spirits are visible, audible and touchable, and in some way are just another kind of living entity.

Spirits are the essential beings of the universe before they take form. Ghosts, on the other hand, belong to the yin category of the subtle realm and are of a much heavier energy that comes from the recent life experience which they have just left.

People like to imagine spirits as being like themselves, but in some respects this is very inaccurate. For example, spirits, especially high spirits, can transform themselves into any size. During the day, and in crowded places, spirits can display a much larger size.

Since they depend on the absorption of natural energy, they are very much affected by the energy cycle. Generally, spirits are active at the hour right after midnight (Tze 子) when they are invigorated by the returning life energy. They disappear at 3:00 a.m. (Ein 寅) or at 5:00 a.m. (Mao 卯) or whenever they have invigorated themselves with the dawn energy.

The capability of spirits to transform themselves is incredible. To adapt to the human environment, they may transform into flies, mosquitoes, bugs or ants. When a spirit is in a star, he is so enormous that he can "break your gall" and terrify you tremendously.

Spirits may simply appear in one's inner room, at one's desk, or anywhere one imagines oneself free from intruders. As human beings we think very much of the sacred privilege of privacy. To spiritual beings, however, this notion is a great human hallucination. Wherever one is, there are spirits. An ancient Chinese proverb says: "You think your mind is as quiet and deep as a bottomless abyss, but your thoughts are as loud as thunder." Nothing can be hidden from spirits.

One may wonder why their transformation is not into more attractive shapes, such as beautiful girls or handsome boys. Good spirits do not want to confuse you. They know the appropriate occasion and form in which to appear. Most people would not be annoyed by spirits that transform as sweet hummingbirds. An important truth of the spiritual world is that spirits like to ride on birds. However, spiritual birds, like spiritual people, are not easily distinguished by undeveloped eyes.

If they wish, spirits will let you touch them. Their bodies are as ethereal as a piece of untouched silk or the web of a spider in a bamboo grove on an autumn morning. They are soft but not fragile. One may actually feel the spirit's touch on one's skin. On some occasions high spirits come to humans like wispy strands of clouds. A spirit's appearance may be white or dark, and it may fly gently in front of people who are of high spiritual development. All of these forms serve as a way of communication. The human concept of form, however, is invalid in the spiritual realm.

With distinct communication, one can verify that such an occurrence is not a hallucination. If to see means to know the truth, then this approach may excite spiritual students to attain these opportunities.

Spirits can also make sounds by borrowing something material. Sometimes these sounds resemble noises that human beings make, like walking on a floor, for example. Spirits can also make noises in the air by themselves. Some of these noises are signals or warnings and others are quite pleasant, but most have a specific meaning or message.

The speech of spirits is at too high a frequency for the human ear to distinguish. They have a complete language, like human language, but it is spoken on the level of subtle energy waves, which a well-developed receiver may be able to understand after some training.

Since spirit language is a touch of energy waves, any place on the human body can be a receiving station. Normally, high spirits communicate with one's head, middle level spirits with one's trunk, and general spirits with one's feet. Spirits can communicate any time of day or night. For example, if a writer makes a mistake while working in his office, a spirit who is in another room can make a noise to let the writer know of his error. The function is limited by the writer's ability to catch the mistake in what he worked on. In reality, spirits can know people's thoughts at astronomical distances.

Spirits offer their services by staying with their spiritually developed human friends. They can also disclose the personality of a new acquaintance and warn habitually kind and tolerant people of impending danger. Spirits can also read documents in any language and tell if signing such a document is safe. They can foresee visitors and telephone calls, and they can foretell mental, physical and financial problems that people will have. Spirits can locate physical problems, diagnose illnesses and prescribe herbal medicine as well as a trained doctor. They also know whether food is edible or not. Actually, spirits respond quickly to any new situation and can thus easily find solutions.

What a very sagacious person can do, spirits can also do. They do not, however, have the physical strength to do hard work, and they also lack the psychological persistence to endure certain trivial tasks. A gathering of numerous spirits, though, can accomplish what human beings never could. They can stop an electric current for as long as they wish, be mischievous with a mechanical system, or control certain points of the human nervous system and cause paralysis for protective reasons or other intentions.

Generally, spirits are very, very small. They can enter your body as easily as you would enter a house without walls. One might assume that since a spirit is so small it can easily be controlled, but this is not completely true. A spirit is such because it is the essence of a being. It does not have eyes, ears, nostrils, entrails, hands, feet or wings, yet its functions are complete. Spirits may do as they wish.

One may ask if there is a "police force" among spirits, and the answer is yes, but spirits are numerous and unaccountable and cannot be completely controlled. Good spirits stay with good people and bad spirits are the tenants of bad people. Since they know what is fatal to the human body, they can easily make people ill. Cancer and other incurable diseases can be actions of revenge from spirits.

The significant difference between spirits and ghosts is that spirits are essential, light and pure whereas ghosts are the opposite. Spirits come from the formation of nature; they are pure and mild. Ghosts are souls that have recently departed from human life and are still contaminated with their life experience. A spirit is much lighter than a ghost. Ghosts usually sink into the ground.

It generally takes a new ghost seven days to completely withdraw its energy from its deceased body. The situation is different, however, in the case of accident or war. When a trauma is too sudden for a ghost to withdraw its complete soul energy, various parts of the ghost's ethereal body may be lacking in energy. Since these people did not fulfill their allotted natural years, they may come back to the human world sooner than others, often with parts of their new shape weakened, depending on the trauma they suffered. Since ghosts have "heavy" energy, they sometimes appear in human form at night and attack people. Actually, this seldom happens.

The sudden interference of an evil-intentioned ghost can cause vehicles or machines to completely stop and thus create land or air accidents. Such a ghost can also attack women and impregnate them with a "ghostly" embryo or disease of the womb. Many diseases, both in men and women, are caused by ghosts, with or without reason. Many of the troubles of the human world also exist with or without true reason and are the work of "satan." This is real whether or not it is in accord with your knowledge. The ghosts in an inferior negative sphere are more apparent and can easily reach a person's level of emotion, such as fear, or of feeling, such as chilly. It is difficult to be immune from the influence or encroachment of the spiritual world on all levels.

When one person persecutes another, he or she can seldom escape the revenge of a future ghost, but should fear of such revenge prevent one from disciplining people? No. Righteousness is protection for one's soul. When truly evil people are restrained or punished, they cannot take revenge against you in the spiritual realm. Your own good spiritual elements are your positive, protective power. Good spirits connect with Heaven, and with Heaven behind you, why should you fear Hell?

If a human being follows the right path and maintains the right process of purification, he can return to be a spirit. The highest level of ghosts can also cultivate themselves. With concentration they can shrink to the size of a gentle peck of a mystical bird and communicate with their spiritual friends on the soles of their feet. They are smart and can express their opinions very well. Such ghosts are highly developed intellectuals with good moral standards. They are called "Kwei-Shien" which means spiritualized ghost. This is close to what human beings can achieve when they are pure yang energy. Other levels of ghosts are far behind them in spiritual rank.

A pure spirit is a natural spirit and is thus related to natural truth. It has no connection with vulgar religions which associate the spiritual world with death. This is a serious mistake. Spirits are part of nature even though they do not have physical bodies like human beings.

Around the Big Dipper are two subtle spots which accompany the seven stars of the Dipper itself. This is where the highest natural deities reside. Next to these are the natural deities around the twenty-eight constellations. Correct prayers can evoke their response. These prayers, however, are only revealed to those with a wise and blessed nature, for nothing from the treasures of nature can be taught to a shallow, worldly mind.

There are nine levels in the high spirit's domain of Tai Ching (太清), the Realm of Great Purity and the first of the three high pure realms.

1.	*Supreme Divine Immortals*	上仙	*The Top Shien*
2.	*High Divine Immortals*	高仙	*The High Shien*
3.	*Great Divine Immortals*	大仙	*The Great Shien*
4.	*Virtuous Divine Immortals*	玄仙	*The Virtuous Shien*
5.	*Heavenly Divine Immortals*	天仙	*The Heavenly Shien*
6.	*Natural Divine Immortals*	真仙	*The Truthful Shien*
7.	*Spiritual Divine Immortals*	神仙	*The Spiritual Shien*
8.	*Responsive Divine Beings*	靈仙	*The Responsive Shien*
9.	*Reachable Divine Beings*	至仙	*The Reachable Shien*

Above this realm are two higher divine realms, Shan Ching (上清) and Yu Ching (玉清).

Because spirits have no form, one's mind can imagine whatever form it feels for them. The forms of spirits depend on what they wish to communicate to a person and also on one's own subjective emotional reaction. A person with a beautiful heart always meets beautiful spiritual beings. Someone who is fearful always sees terrifying ghosts, monsters, goblins and demons. Actually, the image is created by one's own feelings. This is similar to the spoken language of a spirit in that it is real, but the way it is received and interpreted depends on the degree of clarity or unclarity of the person.

Do spirits actually have a form of their own? Yes. They are subtle beings with flexible forms of subtle energy.

It is really marvelous that spirits and ghosts are not substance, yet their capabilities are so human-like. This is why spiritually developed people cannot help but accept them as important living entities.

You may be interested to know what spirits generally like, dislike and fear, even though they do not have sensory organs. They respect high deities and high spirits. At some levels they dislike strong sunshine. They fear thunder, although in some cases they create thunder. They dislike airplanes and jets. They dislike bad odors. They like the beauty and sweet fragrance of flowers. They appreciate beauty, truthfulness and goodness of any kind. They like music played with natural instruments. They like opera and other delicate, graceful music, especially dramatized historical tales of ancient people and the exaltation of virtue in the true human way. One kind of refined Chinese opera called Kun Chui (昆曲) is hard to understand, even by highly educated people, but high spirits understand and enjoy these operas greatly. All high spirits love the pure, ancient cultures. This is something which I can verify.

Music is heavenly language. Some of the most elegant human minds have been truly inspired by heavenly beings to create beautiful music. The highest level of music is that of nature, such a breeze whistling through the bamboo, or a murmuring stream, or birds chirping in a weeping willow. All spirits enjoy the beauty of such subtlety. Higher even than this, however, is the voiceless, wordless and soundless heavenly melody that is enjoyed by spirits and by highly developed spiritual human beings as well.

Spirits do not like to touch blood or anything that is decayed. They like things that are alive and natural such as a piece of stone. Generally, spirits are not afraid of fire or water or poison or anything else, but they are subject to higher spirits.

Do spirits eat food? Yes. High spirits who have achieved independence do not need ordinary food, but sometimes they may ride on their human friends and go to restaurants just for fun. General spirits obtain food energy through a human body. One may wonder if this is safe. In the right situation it is, because human beings often waste their energy anyway. Bodily energy offerings can be a practice of real piety and faithfulness to the spirits. On the other hand, young men and women who sleep in the nude often create opportunities for ghosts to attack them. Many nightmares are actually ghosts pressing the body and sucking energy.

"Demon" is a human name given to evil spirits. If the spirit is really evil, then it deserves this name, but in many cases the so-called demon is just a natural spirit without any experience of human life. Such a spirit is "wild" until it becomes familiar with the human mind. Then it is no longer a "demon."

Generally, all natural spirits are pure spirits, but when they are encountered at the human level, conceptual discriminations of good or bad develop. Through thousands of years of artificial cultural and religious life, human beings have put more and more conditions on life. Although life was once a matter of natural harmony, there is now much discrimination between what is "good" or "bad," based on new habits and modes of acceptance.

In the same way that human knowledge of the natural spiritual world is not fully developed, "wild" spirits' knowledge of the human world is not fully developed either. What ordinary people perceive as good or bad may not necessarily be the way the natural spirits perceive it. Because these spirits are still "wild" and "uncivilized" before they have contact with the human realm, they sometimes create havoc for human beings.

In the ancient tradition, the most valuable and useful guidance for subduing such spirits was virtue. Stable, virtuous behavior and good naturedness can earn the friendship of the spiritual world. Exorcism only does a small job. If the exorcist is not highly disciplined and virtuous, the revenge from the "demons" he exorcises can be dangerous. Some religious leaders of past epochs were victims of this when they displayed hostility toward "wild" spirits by treating them as "demons."

Even though the preceding information is correct, one need not wonder whether truly evil spirits exist. Evil spirits and ghosts actually do exit and many people suffer harm, illness and disharmony because of them. When people deviate from their natural way of honesty, opportunities develop for demons to come to live with them and generate negativity.

Spirits and ghosts, especially real demons, can incite riots through morally undeveloped people who come together as a mob and who are often used without even knowing it. These people carry out the evil wishes of such spirits in order to persecute one who is righteous and has fulfilled his moral duty and actually protected people from the harm of these demons and evil spirits. In most cases, demons and evil spirits cannot carry out these actions themselves. They must be enacted through morally undeveloped people whose inner darkness is reflected in their ignorance and vicious behavior.

The practice of virtue protects one from this level of evil spiritual influence or interference. One should neither please nor offend evil spirits. According to the teaching of Lao Tzu, "When one follows the way of natural morality, all gods and spirits follow the same natural way and become powerless to harm people. Thus one integrates the potency of all beings in a great harmony, in absolute oneness." Another effective exorcism for evil consists of prayers to powerful, natural deities.

Four possible reasons why general spiritual problems happen to people involved with real spirits are:

- Troublesome spirits haunt troublesome people. The kind of energy a person has will attract a spirit of like energy. Thorough spiritual purification can have a good effect on these problems.
- If a real spiritual problem occurs, improper handling of the problem will make it worse. This is due to a lack of spiritual experience and/or correct spiritual education.
- Spiritual naivete and curiosity can invite spiritual problems. One may open the prohibited "magic box" prematurely. This is like mistakenly touching electricity.
- Sometimes people who wish to strengthen their spiritual power and augment their spiritual protection

find an incorrect spiritual path and make a bad connection with an improper spiritual source. These people bring trouble on themselves through their own ambition.

Although problems occasionally occur, spirits are part of the natural world and interacting with them is no different from dealing with other beings in the physical realm. Just as reincarnation follows the law of familiarity, people with a certain kind of energy attract spirits of a similar energy. A virtuous and kind individual should not have any trouble with spirits.

If you wish to attract a high spirit as your own beloved one, then you must purify and cultivate yourself. Such preparation takes generations to accomplish. A virtuous family conceives good seeds. On the other hand, a baby might be payment for a debt from a previous life, but this is seldom known until one breathes his last breath. A newly pregnant mother's dreams can tell her what kind of spirit she has attracted. These dreams are messages from her own energy and are the bodily language of her inner communications.

Do not mistreat your father or mother when you are a child or forget to discipline your own children when you are a parent. If one is undutiful, one's debts will not end. If you wish to achieve yourself spiritually, fundamental obligations such as these need to be fulfilled first. Social and family systems have varied greatly since ancient times, but the fundamental patterns of human life have not changed, unless one is conceived in a test tube! Such a person is then the sole being of their test-tube lineage.

Modern day man may be proud of his industrial and technological achievements such as taking a once-large object and making it compact, like cameras, tape recorders, computers and so forth. Such machines have highly complex functions for their small size, but compared to a spirit human advancements like these mean nothing! There will never be a machine that can take the place of a spirit.

The Natural Truth of Spirit

What appears in this section of the book is only a fragment of the whole picture. Actually, the entirety of the spiritual world is as vast as the universe. Though there are many kinds of life, human beings are the most rare and precious species on earth. Earth is also a rare and precious place within the vast range of the entire universe.

Mankind has been to the moon and may land on other planets in the future, but they have been and will continue to be disappointed in not finding living entities like themselves there. This should never be a disappointment, however. There are spiritual entities on all the planets, moons and stars in the universe. These living beings are the direct sons and daughters of natural energy, not flesh and blood like the human species, which is unique in that it encompasses both the material and spiritual spheres.

The first natural spirits took life forms as part of the materializing process of evolution. All lives are actually spirits in different forms. Spiritual energy has many different levels. The shape of a human being is an expression of inner adjustment and is the result of self-cultivation through many lifetimes. In certain ancient books there are illustrations of our ancestors. The first beings had nine heads on a snake-like body. Possibly each head did one job at a time, like the intellectual mind does now. The beautiful simplification of the human form and mind evolved through millions of years to have many functions, with one head and two hands and feet instead of many invisible feet beneath the belly. This is like using many different kinds of knives, forks and spoons to eat a meal which can just as easily be eaten with a pair of chopsticks or a spoon.

The human form is an artistic work of spirit. If the spirit is correct, it will sooner or later take the right shape. This is similar to a great artist who spends years mastering the skills of his art, yet the value lies in what is actually produced with the skills that were cultivated. Skill is not a totally external development. Inside a great master is the spirit which was there from infancy, waiting to be correctly shaped.

This is how we attained the human form we have today. Correct spiritual energy is the seed of the shape of human beings. It is very important to have a good seed. The next step is cultivation in order to develop the seed. This cultivation, or development of virtue, is a fundamental part of life involving service, internal improvement and continuous evolution.

Have you ever heard of a person with ten souls? You might think such a person should be in a "nut house," but this is not so. This person is you. Ordinary spiritual education teaches "one person/one soul," but this is a fantasy. Have you ever heard of a person who was a jack of all trades or who was highly achieved in several areas? Have you ever dreamt of being a totally different person? Why are you never alone in your dreams yet you remain isolated from the others in your dream? Have you ever surprised yourself when you were alone by speaking out loud on a subject you were not thinking about? The human mind has the power of reason, from which different theories originate, but the following answers come from natural spirituality, not from the mind.

A highly achieved person, someone of great versatility, has a well organized government of unified souls. A person whose mind is "spoiled" has, in reality, disharmony among his ten souls. The different people in your dreams are active souls taking the form of people you have met, imagined or fear. They communicate their feelings about your internal and external environment in story form, and they may exert pressure to notify you that they have been mistreated by your "solo" desires or decisions. A good government does not initiates action but responds correctly and appropriately to its "people."

Sometimes one becomes excited by mundane matters and the sophisticated mind tries to maturely express the matter. Your souls, however, are as naive and wild as children and they like to express themselves as well, so they do it privately when tensions are few. Thinking is our personal internal discussion before this energy reaches the tongue and is expressed by the voice. When a second thought denies the first, the two ideas come from different sources. It is one soul protesting the nonsense of another. When you act against your general personality, whether in reality or in your dreams, the action has come from a different source than the one you customarily act from.

Of the ten souls of an ordinary person, three are of the high sphere of personal spirit and are deeply related to spiritual life. These are called "Hun." Seven are of the low sphere of spirit and are strongly related to physical life. These are called "Po." The Hun belong to the yang category and the Po to the yin. With the integration of Hun and Po, one receives life. If one is born with an incomplete number of Hun, he is an idiot. If he is born with an incomplete number of Po, he will never completely develop physically and there is no medicine that can ever help with the growth. One can be born with the correct number of Hun and Po but lose some of them in life's journey. An ordinary person may, through many years of work on enhancing his Hun and Po, highly develop his inner and outer being.

In my book, *The Heavenly Way*, one can find ninety-four examples of what can cause people to lose their souls. This material is the standard elucidation of Chapter 71 of the *Tao Teh Ching*. Other examples of what can cause the rapid loss of spiritual potency and how to remedy this can also be found in *The Heavenly Way* in a treatise called "Tai Shan Kan Yin Pien" (Straighten Your Way). Instruction for saving a lost soul can be found in the same book in the chapter called "The Silent Way of Blessing," which is the elucidation of Chapter 54 of the *Tao Teh Ching*. The real and precious guidance that enables one to integrate Hun and Po (the two spheres of the entirety of the universe) is found throughout the *Tao Teh Ching*. People need to integrate their inner being of Hun and Po with the outer world of duality.

From this illustration, one can better understand the first line of Chapter Ten of the *Tao Teh Ching* which says, "Embrace your Hun and Po to be one without divergence." (Although I have translated this line differently to avoid confusing my readers, the exact meaning is given above.) This explains how one's soul energy may be lost because of one's way of life and other psychological reasons. One's soul energy can be enriched by leading a proper life and correctly cultivating one's essence.

Why does a human being have three Hun and seven Po? Because human lives are the children of nature. Thus, they are installed internally with yin and yang energy as their mother in such a proportional difference because they carry more physical influences. We know from the natural truth that there are ten main energy beams which are the celestial energy of the upper sphere of the universe and twelve main energy rays which are the terrestrial energy of the lower sphere. The upper and lower energies are constantly interacting in a rotation which brings forth all phases of universal life, thus the universe is an everlasting deep energy. A human being is the offspring of the interacting paternal energy of the upper sphere and the maternal energy of the lower sphere; thus, one is a small model of the universe itself. One's life is composed of three souls from the ten celestial energies and seven souls from the twelve terrestrial energies. That is, what one receives for life is three out of ten from the upper sphere of universal energy and seven out of twelve from the lower sphere. Thus a human being can be an independent, high-level being among all offspring of the universe. However, one's cyclic phases are not complete and thus not as everlasting as one's life source, the universe. On the human level, one may be complete, but the human level itself is incomplete. The possibility of divine immortal life comes with the completion of all celestial and terrestrial energy spheres. It is impossible to achieve this by endeavors that reach only the superficial phases. Behind all phases is the unmanifested root, the primal chi.

On one hand, spiritual cultivation is self-integration. On the other, it is universal integration. On one level it is the process of self-transcendence. On another, it is the process of transcending the entire universe, not only in the manifest sphere but in the unmanifest as well. Spiritual achievement is meant to be a complete life and to develop the flesh; a small universe of self-completion. A true way was discovered for achieving this goal and it has become the central practice of the Integral Way.

When I was a student of Tao (I am still a student of the Divine Immortal Way), I wondered which among the ten souls was me. Which soul would achieve divine immortality and which souls would be expelled? This was a problem of self-integration. The souls of the lower sphere (the animal souls) can become traitors to one's self-cultivation, especially in the process of purification and self-sublimation. This thought was troubling to my fast mind. Real achievement, however, only comes with beautiful, harmonious cooperation within one's entire being. This comes without even mentioning the expression of total harmonization of the internal and external as a T'ai Chi. The universe is a big T'ai Chi of the integration of yin and yang. A human being is a small T'ai Chi, complete and integrated on another level.

Answers to Basic Questions in This Chapter

Q: *If a sneeze can be caused either by a strong smell or by a spirit that wants to enter a person's body, how can one tell which is the real cause of the sneeze?*

Master Ni: This is an elementary spiritual capability or awareness which is achieved as the result of a personal breakthrough. A breakthrough occurs only when one finally gives up or breaks through an obstacle which has been hindering one's forward movement. Serious students of the Integral Way cultivate themselves so that they can achieve these breakthroughs.

There are six different major spiritual breakthroughs:

1) Generally, people do not understand or know their fortune or destiny, nor do they know the meaning of life or why they have taken the form of human life. Once students achieve the first breakthrough, they know their future and the mandate of their life. This developed mental capability is called "Personal Destiny Breakthrough."

2) Normally, people cannot see very far, not to mention seeing a thousand miles away. Nor can they see what is happening inside a room when they are not in it. With the second breakthrough comes the capability to see thousands of miles away, even on the stars or anywhere else in the universe, like the developed ones of the past whose knowledge was based on their cultivated transpiercing vision. These ancient masters could see things that were far away and they gathered accurate knowledge without the use of equipment. This is called the "Breakthrough of the Heavenly Eye."

3) You cannot hear what people say at a distance, whether it is only a block away or a thousand miles. It is not important what people say behind your back; however, it is a known achievement on the spiritual level that one can hear things from thousands of miles away. This is called the "Heavenly Ear Breakthrough."

4) It is not too difficult to find one who is capable of reading others' minds. If such a capability is obtained through self-cultivation, it is called the "Breakthrough of the Mind." One can know what another holds in his mind. Even though the contents may not be known, the intentions can be known. When one has achieved this capability, one will also know what is in his own mind. With a reflecting mind one can easily read the minds of others, whether they are present or not.

5) The spiritual world has many levels, just like the material sphere with which most people are familiar. The only difference is that the spiritual world is behind an in-

visible, inaudible and intangible divider. When observing the development of spiritual students, the different levels of the spiritual world present themselves accordingly. An incomplete spiritual vision can be obtained by a person with some cultivation, but it can also leave him confused. While obtaining complete vision is rare, even partial vision can help one achieve a correct understanding of and definite connection with the spiritual world. Unfortunately, revealing it is usually forbidden. This capability is called the "Breakthrough of the Spiritual Realms."

6) In the sixth kind of breakthrough, one may experience whatever one wishes. Suppose someone wishes to be wealthy or in an important position or to have an unusual experience. Just by extending one's mind there can be an immediate experience. One does not really need to be the other person in order to have their experience.

West Lake of Hanchow in the province of Che Chiang of Mainland China is extraordinarily beautiful. The light of the water is enchanting. After achievement, if one wishes one can see or hear the water and be there immediately without any separation whatever.

Another example is knowing something you have never learned before, perhaps how to play a musical instrument or the contents of a book. Once it is touched, one will immediately know it and do it well. It is one's spiritual development which enables this kind of breakthrough known as the "Breakthrough of Transferable Capability."

These breakthroughs are famous in spiritual cultivation. Not everyone has these capabilities, yet to some it is a natural gift. They usually occur as side effects to spiritual development, even though they can be cultivated for their own sake through methodical and systematic cultivation.

Q: You mentioned that spirits sometimes cause people trouble with or without reason. Does that mean that both good and bad spirits come to stay with the same person?

Master Ni: Yes. Most people are a combination of good and bad, depending on the level of purification they have achieved. According to the law of spiritual correspondence, which is that any energy will attract another energy of the same frequency or vibration, the high, pure spirits come to be with someone whose energy is high, and lower spirits come to be with someone whose energy is not as pure. As a general rule, however, it is not appropriate to discriminate between good spirits and bad. A particular spirit may help you develop in a good way on one level and encourage the development of negativity on another. It is more a matter of one's own level of development.

Q: Do you mean that a person invites a negative spirit by his own negativity?

Master Ni: Yes. This is certainly so.

Q: If a person fears a disease, will he invite a spirit of this illness?

Master Ni: This is a different matter. A distinction must be made regarding what belongs on the psychological level.

There is a story about a man who believed that in middle age he would have cancer of the back and die as a result of the disease. When he was still young and strong he began telling this story to all his relatives and friends. It was clear to him that this would occur, but those around him all denied it. The disease did occur, however.

There are two explanations. One is that the man's psychological beliefs were so strong he caused it to happen. The other is that his intuition or precognition was correct. Both are possible.

People like Joseph Stalin and Mao Tse Tung, when they were alive, would tell themselves many times, "I don't care what happens after my death." What was going to happen, however, was worse than they could ever imagine.

Maintaining good psychological health is necessary to leading a balanced, harmonious life that supports one's spiritual development. For example, one should try to eliminate fears or the strong need for security. It is best to work on developing your intuition so that you will naturally connect with the many good things in life. If you dwell only on mental or emotional fears, you will connect with the negative aspects of life. This leads to incomplete development. One should, therefore, develop the positive, virtuous aspects of the mind rather than the negative. If negativity is allowed to develop, then one actually undermines oneself at every moment.

Q: Do different spirits associate with the different souls of a person?

Master Ni: There are generally two levels of soul energy in a human being: three of the ten portions belong to Heaven and seven of the ten belong to Earth.   Heavenly energy is spiritual and lighter than Earthly energy which is heavier and closer to the physical sphere.   If one does not practice self-cultivation and become well integrated, then at night when the central nervous system is relaxed, one's souls become individually active and may invite other soul friends to play in one's being.   This causes strong result in dreams.

Cultivation is necessary to keep one's soul energy properly channeled.   If the soul energy is not regulated, then regardless of whether one is an emperor or a beggar, his souls will start to scatter and he is no longer himself when he closes his eyes.

When human beings are born, the fetus is connected to the mother by the umbilical cord.   The souls in people's bodies also have an invisible umbilical cord connected to physical life.   When one is asleep, the souls become active.   Since they are confined by the umbilical cord, the souls usually just wander within the body.

The relationship between one's life and one's souls is similar to the relationship between a mother and a fetus.   In a negative sense, the invisible umbilical cords become the bondage of a free soul, and "untying" these knots through one's cultivation is an important step in achieving spiritual freedom.   Spiritual freedom depends on integrating one's soul successfully and cutting their "umbilical cords" to the physical body.   Without this, one sinks to the ground with the corpse.   This is usually more of a problem for people whose physical strength is excessive.   On the other hand, children and those who are weak may easily lose their souls because of the fragile connection between the souls and the body.   Good balance, therefore, is as necessary as spiritual freedom.

Q: Can a disease be retribution from a past life, even though the person has been very kind in this lifetime?

Master Ni: Yes.   It can also be retribution for the deeds of one's parents or ancestors within a seven generation span.   Often it is from a past life or lives in which the person himself did not take responsibility for his own life.

Individualism is very popular in the modern world, but the natural truth cannot be altered. A new generation is the continuation of the old generation, externally as well as internally. In most cases, the souls of the ancestors come to live in the next generation. This is called the soul's connection and continuation. If one does evil, then not only is one responsible oneself, but one's ancestors and even future generations suffer for the wrongdoing.

Many people seek riches so that their second or third generation can enjoy it, but they never realize that the accumulation of subtle virtuous merit is a more important protection and blessing for future generations. When wealth alone is passed on, it usually becomes a poison.

The spiritual development of a human being is a good influence for all of one's connections. Virtuous inheritance is much more important than material inheritance. When a father or mother gives a child money or invests in a trust for their children or grandchildren, such actions often result in the future generation's psychological misery or disability.

Q: Is it possible for the spirit of a parent in a previous generation to come back several generations later as a child in the same family lineage?

Master Ni: Earlier I introduced the natural fact of incarnation and the principle of family priority. A grandfather, for example, may come back into the same family to collect what was owed him or to repay a debt. (Such debts are usually on the emotional rather than the material level.) Thus, cultivating one's virtue among family members is more important than giving gifts. One who is wise does not look for material wealth. Virtuous realization cannot be consumed, but it can bless future generations.

Q: Does the cultivation one does during one's lifetime also affect one's ancestors?

Master Ni: Yes, it does. If a person achieves divine immortality, seven generations of his ancestors will also be benefited, although the benefit they receive will depend on how highly achieved they are themselves. Likewise, if one does evil, seven generations of ancestors and the seven future generations will all suffer one's misdeeds. The only remedy for this is purification to cleanse the contamination of the bad influence.

Q: *When one has a difficulty or illness to overcome, is it always a case of spiritual retribution or could it also be subtle guidance?*

Master Ni: When one has trouble or trials, one needs to either overcome them or let nature take its course. Generally, all highly achieved spiritual people have many obstacles during their lifetime. If a disease cannot be easily overcome, it means that the root of the disease is deeply embedded, perhaps seven generations back.

In this world there is no one who is without trouble. Whether one is a winner or a loser all depends on one's personal sincerity and virtue in solving the problem.

Q: *Is it possible for a human being to increase the three Hun souls to ten and the seven Po souls to twelve so that the Heavenly and Earthly cyclic phases are complete?*

Master Ni: There is no way to fill the gaps in one's spiritual development except through cultivation, and one can only use virtue to remedy inadequacy. Soul energy can be richly enhanced by accepting pain, taking trouble honestly, being dutiful, and always taking the unfavored part with ease and without complaint.

Another way to enrich your soul energy is to cultivate the Integral Way. When one becomes spiritually developed, the harmonious extension of one's spiritual being can doubtlessly help also. Trouble shall then be effortlessly dissolved.

Without the benefit of cultivation and virtue, some soul energy is bound to be lost or buried deeper in the physical sphere just through the process of life or through doing evil.

Q: *Is there a difference between the revenge of a spirit and the revenge of a ghost?*

Master Ni: Suppose you are an evil person, and have killed someone who becomes a ghost. In the spiritual world, revenge has validity and the ghost is allowed to take revenge. There is no escape, and the debt will be fulfilled whenever one's personal high energy cycle is over. If a person is in a low energy cycle, any ghost at all can bully him - even a dog can bite him.

A spirit on a high level has the freedom and the authority to punish evil people or evil ghosts, but this is not considered revenge.

A more fundamental way to influence all lives is by the retribution of the subtle energy of the universe. It is the real unruling ruler of all. High beings and spirits know that subtle energy and subtle law are one. It is what all spiritually developed beings respect and hold in great awe. They follow its way without deviation and avoid any emphasis on individual spiritual authority.

Q: How can we tell the difference between the actual spiritual level of life and our own idealism or imagination?

Master Ni: The mind is a kind of energy with good capabilities, but most people attach importance only to its conceptual aspect. This conceptual level is the level of idealism, and the significance that people generally give to conceptual or idealistic mental activity greatly limits the mind's other natural capabilities. Ordinary thinkers and intellectuals stay on this mental level.

The spiritual level is not the idealistic level. If one's mind is purified and sublimated, it can function as a vehicle to carry one to the deep sphere of the spiritual realm.

Q: Would you say more about "family priority?"

Master Ni: This is discussed in detail in my book, *The Taoist Inner View of the Universe and the Immortal Realm.* It is the result of an emotional or affectional connection. In their lifetime, ordinary people do not extend their affection (or their hatred) beyond a small circle of family and friends. This deep emotional involvement is what makes "family priority" so solid. Family members reincarnate into the same family over and over.

This natural phenomenon can only be corrected when people are alive. That is when they have the opportunity to dissolve all bad connections and reach high achievement on the spiritual level.

The blood connection also makes one return to the same family, but a high spirit does not follow the natural law of the lower sphere. This is a reality of achievement and is actually supernatural.

Q: *You mentioned that a spirit can tell a human friend about the personality of a new acquaintance, but don't human beings have that capability themselves?*

Master Ni: Sometimes this capability is equal in a human being and a spirit, but the spirit is often much faster at discerning the true character of a new person.

Q: *Can you say more about how spirits can control an important energy point in the human system and paralyze people for long or short periods of time?*

Master Ni: This is new information to Westerners, but it is ancient knowledge to the Chinese. Some Kung Fu and Chi Kung practitioners who are highly achieved do not need to defend themselves by force. They just touch certain points of the body and one is paralyzed. In the nervous system of the human body there are weaknesses. Ordinary people protect themselves with muscles, but a good Kung Fu practitioner whose energy is developed can easily locate the points of weakness. By lightly touching these points, he can make his enemy suffer. This can easily be illustrated through acupuncture; however, acupuncture is only used as a healing art.

Q: *Does one receive the communication of spirits through intuition?*

Master Ni: Intuition is the direct utilization of spiritual energy. Spirits communicate on a general rather than intuitive level. You actually feel an itch or heat or cold or pain, it is not an intuition. This feeling is very accurate. Sometimes it is like a light touch or kiss from another person. Other times it may be like an acupuncture needle or a bee sting or mosquito bite. "Wild" spirits may be a little rough in their communications because they are unfamiliar with the human social code of behavior.

Q: *Can a lower spirit transcend? How do spirits develop?*

Master Ni: Low spirits have usually lost their flexibility. A human being usually has more potential than the lower level of ghosts. Sometimes we say that there is no separation in the entire universe, but a separation can be made. For example, the distinction between spirits is strong, and a long process of evolution is necessary in order to go from a low spirit to a high spirit. Positively speaking, all beings move upward and forward, thus one cannot say that low spirits have completely lost their chance. You could say, however, that they have not yet found their way. A human spirit is also in the process of evolving from a lower to a higher level.

Q: *Does a high spirit ever descend to become a human being?*

Master Ni: Among all beings, higher and lower, a human being is an inter-medium or transportation point. A high spirit who takes human form probably has either a mission or a single wish.

When a low spirit takes human form, it has the great opportunity to continue its soul evolution. Evolving to this level of profundity would take many lifetimes, each becoming more essential by condensing one's spiritual being.

A human being who has self-awareness has no time to lose in negative things. One should work diligently on one's own cultivation. I keep this door widely open to the beautiful individuals of the Western world who have high aspirations and virtue and who wish to continue achieving themselves. This is how I follow the example of the ancient ascended masters who left the door open for future comers.

Q: *Does a spirit remain with someone throughout many lives?*

Master Ni: Yes, it could for some special reason. Generally it does not "remain," but rather returns when the being takes a new life in order to help awaken the old soul.

On an energy level, people change every day. This law also applies to the spiritual world. Every minute of every day there is a new organization of human physical life, and one always has the chance to either stagnate or become revitalized. Thus one always needs to be well prepared.

One's good energy naturally invites high spirits, but when one is bad these spirits surely leave. Daily cultivation is important, therefore, not in the general religious sense of pleasing an external god, but in order to keep oneself high.

Q: *Does a person carry around the ghosts of their past lives?*

Master Ni: Yes. All people carry their old ghosts around, and some people never give them up. They will hold onto them from their childhood until old age. People who do this can never refresh their spirit.

Q: *Does a person ascend to become a spirit or descend to become a ghost according to how he has lived his life?*

Master Ni: Unless a person practices natural, genuine cultivation, he usually becomes a ghost. Good religions, at best, are for people who are trying to control themselves. Ordinary religions, however, hinder undeveloped humanity. Faith in an imaginary god touches the blind spot of people's minds. There is no salvation in their self-deception. Real salvation can only be accomplished by oneself. No one can do it for you. There is no mass production in the real spiritual world. Spiritual development is not an industrial process.

Q: *What is the difference between deities and spirits?*

Master Ni: Spirits are extensions of positive universal nature who can transform into positive beings. Without their presence human beings would not be safe from invisible enemies for a single second. Although the spiritual development of spirits is never less than that of humans, it may vary on different levels.

In some ways, gods and deities are high and remote. Natural, pure spirits are the medium between high divine spirits and human beings. They serve as messengers and guardians on most occasions. Since these spirits are the followers of high divinities, they are the helpers of spiritually developed human beings.

In describing a good friendship, one thinks of such words as friendly, kind, intimate, close, faithful, affectionate, nice, sweet, etc., but the real meaning of such words can only be known by experiencing friendship with spirits. They are fatherly, motherly, sisterly, brotherly, husbandly, wifely, like a good teacher, a kind nurse, or a dutiful son or daughter. Moreover, they are considerate, understanding, tolerant, helpful and virtuous. No other words can accurately describe the spiritual relationship between the spirits and humans. If a distinction were to be made, one might say they are the kindest, sweetest and most faithful of friends. They may need a little training and discipline from their spiritually developed human friend, however.

The significant aspect of spirits is that without their assistance as spiritual guardians and "pilots," no one on the spiritual path could achieve anything real. It is an honorable and precious occasion to have these guardians and pilots whom the high god sends. The sweetness of spiritual achievement is lost to those who lack a true spiritual connection; empty imagination and sour philosophies are their only results.

The Yellow Emperor, in his struggles with the vicious Che-Huy, received the help of spirits in obtaining the righteous power of the universe. With the instruction of these spirits, the compass was invented and victory was assured.

Long after the Yellow Emperor, the Great Yu overcame the deluge, and this too was because of the subtle merit of natural spirits.

Both of these ancient sages thereafter put their energy into spiritual methods and further connecting with the spiritual world. All secret spiritual practices were handed down at that time. The great accumulation of spiritual treasures from the ancient divine hermits was made by devout emperors such as these. This is the real strength of the natural spiritual tradition.

Some methods can only be passed to a qualified student, which may occur only once in a thousand years. Other methods can be passed down to only three people in seven hundred years. Such high spiritual treasures are not well known. As for self-cultivation, these methods are also reserved for the appropriate person.

It is a serious matter when the corruption of human nature becomes deeper and deeper. Most people cannot be trusted with these invaluable secrets, nor do they have the capability to give orders to helping spirits.

Q: *Would you explain your statement that "real spirits do not want to confuse you, but animal spirits may do so?"*

Master Ni: One cannot expect a high spirit to come if one is mentally or emotionally confused or if one has a confused way of life. In this case one can only attract impure ghosts and animal spirits. If one does not summon such confused ghosts, then one's growth is directed in a more pure way.

It is not that the animal spirits like to confuse a person. It is his own life and vibration that attracts this lack of well-organized spiritual self-government and practice. The animal spirits can also join the person and become a part of the spiritual organism of life. The entirety of the individual needs high spiritual guidance to conduct his life.

Q: *How did the ancient sages know so much about the universe? Does their knowledge meet scientific requirements, and is their way congruent with the scientific way?*

Master Ni: As I understand it, the development of the mind has two main directions which exemplify yin and yang. There is the analytical, generalizing mind on which modern science is based, and there is the high intuitive, or integral, mind which enables the truth to be presented in the right way. The integral mind, which differs from the modern intellectual mind, is the basis for the knowledge of the ancient sages. It sees the whole picture at a deep level, thus the discovery of the entire truth of the universe was possible.

It undeniably took capable minds to connect with this good source of knowledge. From the six breakthroughs mentioned earlier, one can understand that an ordinary mind can be cultivated and developed to a level that can respond to the subtle truth of the universe. This ancient capability which can abstract a very complicated, detailed phenomenon and use a single word or picture or diagram to express it is not usually available to the ordinary human mind of today and is thus not easily understood, but we must recognize that the human mind is capable of such a high achievement.

Many words and books are needed to explain the natural sciences of the modern world, and only after specializing can one understand even part of the truth. Through the Integral Way, one needs only to look at one simple picture to achieve real learning. From this illustration one can understand that the function of these mental capabilities are different.

I am not saying that one way of knowledge is greater than the other, but I do think that each has different functions and that the values of each should be equally recognized. Intellectual knowledge can, of course, help explain integral knowledge of the natural truth.   Words, language and descriptive methods can all serve and carry the message of truth; however, they are not the truth itself.   The integral mind participates directly with the truth; the intellect is only its messenger.   Only one who knows the truth can accurately explain it.   Such knowledge comes from the inside out, as opposed to intellectual knowledge which comes from the outside in.

This is the divergence between ancient and modern knowledge.   If you agree that knowledge is the harvest and mind is the tool, then you must also agree that the harvest is limited by its tools.   Without the guidance of the integral mind, how can one fuse all other known elements of the mind?

Q: *Can Western students who follow the Integral Way achieve themselves as highly as Chinese students?*

Master Ni: The six breakthroughs are personal developments that are achieved through self cultivation.   The technological way of the West encourages people to become externally oriented and spiritually lazy.   Personal development has lost its spiritual priority and people have been taught to develop and become dependent on machines and technology.   Even the new techniques in acupuncture use machines.   Originally, an ancient healer had to develop his own sensitivity and natural energy in order to know the energy points and meridians.   Now that machines have been designed to locate these points and administer the treatment, many acupuncturists no longer need to use their intuition.   The result is that they have lost an opportunity for their own inner development.   This may be acceptable at some level, but on the fundamental level much damage will result.

Machines are helpful at a practical level.   For instance, with their help we have more time for personal cultivation.   Modern people have the intelligence to develop many useful things.   This does not mean, however, that we should take more time for play or decay.   By taking pride in one's new inventions, one loses the chance for personal development.

Many people in the East are too introverted, while those of the West tend to be too extroverted and superficial.   In the West, things may be better organized externally, but in the East, for instance, one can determine the blood pressure by feeling the pulse and looking at the color of the tongue or the ears.   Yet this cannot be expressed numerically without a machine.

It is not unusual for a patient to be examined by modern trained doctors and also visit a traditionally trained Chinese healer for the integral way of healing.   This may be a good cooperative approach and a good prospect for future medical practices.   One way is more academic and the other is more practical.   The same approach applies to the integration of Eastern and Western culture and to the balance of personalities.

In spiritual development, the same method of external organization can be applied.   People in the West can organize very strong and wealthy churches, but searching for the truth in their teachings is like having a big pot of boiling soup, only to discover that inside is a skeleton with no meat.

The shortcoming of most Western students is that they touch only what is superficial without reaching for the deep truth.   If they wish to achieve any breakthrough they must first stop trying to invent or use machines instead of doing things for themselves.   Otherwise they will need machines to do their self-cultivating!

Q: *What is the significance of dreaming about someone being pregnant, other than a pregnant mother?*

Master Ni: If a boyfriend or husband dreams of his wife or girlfriend being pregnant with a big belly, it means that she is hiding something inside herself, perhaps a secret plot.

Q: *Would you tell us more about the spiritual world?*

Master Ni: We have discussed the general pure spirit, but we have not connected it to human religious conceptions which proclaim that spirit is "holy" and human is "dirty." The human being and the spiritual being can connect on the level of purity.   The spirit is pure and divine, with no evil.   If a human being is pure, he is a spirit.

What I describe in my work are primarily the divine spiritual beings, not the ordinary ones.   Impure or undeveloped spirits have the will to develop themselves once they are enlightened.   Human beings, however, know what is evil and impure and still do such things for material gain and profit, failing to consider the final result.   This is like taking a little poison at a time.   One finally poisons

oneself. It is a pity that people who look only for excitement and temporary solutions to their problems are not
more aware of this.

In ancient China, the word heaven had two different
meanings, one of which was the complete and integral
universe. Although people did not make Heaven the final
judge, they did believe the laws of Heaven to be universally just. Heaven is the fatherly energy, the source and
authority of life. Methodical spiritual cultivators often refer to
the thirty-six heavens. In this realm, there are many subtle
spots where heavenly beings live. These are the subtle
energy islands where spiritual beings live. This is not a
matter of religious faith, but the fruitful result of the exploration and cultivation of many generations of true spiritual scientists and pioneers. The possibility for personal
spiritual cultivation and achievement is not lost to the
modern student. The method and the way are still here.

It is difficult to describe the subtle energy spots of
heaven, but one can look at each star, each planet and
each constellation as a special energy island. Among
these are the earth, the sun and the moon. Since energy
forms differently on each star, the beings of each star are
also different. Ordinary human beings like to use themselves as the standard for all beings. If they do not find a
flesh and blood being on a star, they deny the existence of
any being there. This attitude yields inaccurate information which can have a negative influence on the growth of
future beings.

Stars are the source of all living creatures, and every
star has starry beings. Practically speaking, heavens are
places to go and tour. There are thirty-six special communicating places, and besides the close connection of the
first five planets in the solar system, sun and moon, there
are still other reachable spiritual places such as the twenty-eight constellations or the Big Dipper. The Pung Lai immortal isles are a spiritual place on the Heavenly River
(the Milky Way) where those who have achieved the refinement of the internal immortal medicine especially like to
visit.

All heavenly energy spots are reachable by developed
souls. The fundamental principle of achievement is the
integration of Hun and Po into a complete and transformable spiritual being. Although such a being does not depend on the nostrils to receive oxygen, he may still depend on something more subtle. With their indescribable
forms, spirits can tour all the stars of the heavens.

The well-known Three Realms of Purity may be above all thirty-six heavens. They can also happen anywhere as one's personal spiritual achievement. By consistently cultivating oneself spiritually, one can become developed and have the capability to be on any of the energy islands, whether visible or invisible. An achieved one can even have a star resort for one's own cultivation.

A universal being can go anywhere in the starry heaven. Someone may say, "I can move to England if I don't like being here," and if he does not like England he can move to France, and if he does not like France he can move to Spain. He may be a global being, but he is not yet a universal being. One can be a universal being by eliminating conceptual discriminations, but this is only on the mental level. The truth is that one can be anywhere, not in the flesh but with the light energy one accumulates from the world. This light energy is part of spiritual methodology, the real science of spiritual cultivation which is not the same thing as religion. Ordinary people psychologically need religion to maintain social morality. The true expression of morality, however, comes from natural law. If one wishes to be supernatural, one must first eliminate what is not natural. To illustrate this, an important example is the question how far is it from earth to one of the divine stars such as one of those in the Big Dipper? Surely it is many light years away. With developed spiritual energy, however, one can cause a response as quickly as the snap of a finger and the starry being will stand right in front of you, exactly as summoned. We cannot expect such high divine ways to be taught or demonstrated to the majority of people. They are truly holy.

The way of life that can lead one back to Mother Nature and reach for being supernatural has already been clearly outlined in the *Tao Teh Ching*. There is no better way to restore purity and relations with all natural beings.

Earth is a toyroom for starry heavenly beings who watch human struggles in the same way that a child plays with toy soldiers that fight and destroy each other. The shallowness and ignorance of undeveloped human beings create trouble for people who wish to use Earth as a place for self-cultivation and continual development.

Are the beings of other planets as ignorant as human beings? No, starry beings do not have the heavy, inconvenient flesh body of human beings. They have a subtle form and a higher capability. They are not separated from the primal energy. They do not cultivate, they are natural and are very developed. That is why the ancient sages call them heavenly beings. Their level is far higher than that of human beings.

One may wonder if there are any evil beings in the universe. This has been discussed earlier. They are not evil, they are rough. Natural beings are never the same as human beings who are tricky, greedy and rough. Pain, agony, excitement and frustration happen only on Earth.

Ascension to heaven does not seem very important to modern people who are under the pressures and tensions of practical life, who demand immediate, visible pleasures, and who do not consider their spiritual future but merely indulge in the material life. When they become ghosts, they suddenly become aware of the importance of ascending to heaven with the freedom of a universal being, but by this time their potential to become light has been lost and they can only sink deeply into the ground with a heavy separation from all living entities. One's heaviness becomes his limitation and confinement, and in this sense one builds one's own hell. So here I remind you, my good reader, that it is important, if you still value your precious soul, to live not only for the short period of your human life, but to live long and free with all those important stars and with the whole nature of the universe.

I do not wish to see this toyroom of the high beings destroyed before some good humans have the opportunity to achieve and transform themselves.

Natural Cultivation and the Taoist Canon

Throughout millions of years, human beings developed from the constant cycle of nature. By observing the hibernating insects and animals around them and the yearly cycles of vegetation, they responded naturally to all the seasons. In Spring they were lively, in Summer vivacious, in Autumn they gathered themselves, and in Winter they prepared for return. Thus mankind achieved an existence here on earth that was in harmony with the divine order of the universe.

Before the stage of separation between Heaven and Earth, the natural and supernatural were one. After life in a form became distinct from spirit, the supernatural quality of natural life started to diminish. In spiritual cultivation, it is understood that the highest achievement of a human life is to restore what is most natural in order to reach the possibility of the supernatural. Thus the regimen of self-cultivation and all methods of spiritual development are practiced according to the natural cycle of the season.   Seasonal periods mark significant times which are beneficial for undertaking special cultivation for specific purposes.

For those who have the high understanding and the will to achieve themselves spiritually, to unite themselves in their own short lifespan with the deathless spiritual realm, the precious methods of the ancient achieved ones are left in various sacred and secret books, some of which are preserved in different *Taoist Canons.*   Their great value and worth are only for the true aspirant who, by devoting his entire life to learning one or two of these methods, can remake himself or herself.

The largest *Taoist Canon* of 1,487 books was compiled during the Ming Dynasty (1368-1643 A.D.) and completed during the reign of Chen Tun (1436-1505 A.D.).   It is known as the *Chen Tun Canon.*   The main part of this work is the remainder of collections made in the Tang Dynasty (618-906 A.D.) which were unfortunately damaged and widely scattered in the political rebellion of Hwang Tzau (880 A.D.).   After this, different collections were made, but many of them were lost and disordered.   Although the natural spiritual heritage is enormous, the easiest and most widely understandable natural background is presented by this book, the *Taoist Canon* which was re-collected and re-compiled at the time of Chen Tun.   I sincerely hope that someday the translation of these incomparable treasures of human development can be made available and respected in the modern world.

The content of the *Chen Tun Canon* falls into several different categories, including the philosophical works of Lao Tzu, Chuang Tzu and many others.   It also includes natural religious rituals, ceremonies and practices which were developed and which in the course of time incorporated the customs of rural Chinese villages.   It also became intermingled with Hindu and Buddhist scriptures prior to Chinese Buddhism as it was formalized after the Tang Dynasty. New and different translations were made by Indian monks, who were versed in the teachings of Lao Tzu and Chuang Tzu, for the express purpose of integrating the two teachings of Taoism and Buddhism.   This made the translations easily accepted by the Chinese people, because at an ideological level they superficially carried the same basic understanding of life.

Other parts of the *Canon* include traditional Chinese medical texts and internal alchemy, which takes up a good part of the *Canon* and is written in esoteric, hidden language. The names of metals and stones are used as metaphors to describe the way to achieve spiritual immortality. The key to understanding these writings was passed down orally from a truly achieved one to his students. I still believe that it would be improper to fully reveal those methods to people who do not value their life and even to those who do value their life but are unvirtuous.

The last part of the *Canon* contains the essence of spiritual truth and methods. It is only one part of the whole, but I truly and deeply respect those invaluable materials. Only a very few people can utilize this information. It can be of use only to the one who has surpassed his own intellectual strength after achieving the utmost level of intelligence.

As descendants of the integral truth of life, we owe a debt to past emperors who used their political power to seize and collect those sacred and secret books for their personal royal libraries. However, neither political power nor financial power nor intelligence nor wit can break those ancient riddles and make use of them. Their truth can be discovered only by the one whose personal evolution reaches a point of spiritual attainment.

This most valuable spiritual treasure of mankind, which cannot be obtained anywhere else is available only as a small part of the *Taoist Canon*. It can easily escape the eyes of prominent Chinese scholars and smart students whose intellectual pride and confused worldly knowledge hide the truth from them. To those of spiritual aspiration it is not just a problem of a language barrier (either the Chinese language in which it is written or the esoteric language of the text), but rather the twistedly educated mind which now and then becomes the obstacle to entering the profound spiritual ocean.

I encourage those who sincerely aspire to spiritual achievement to learn the Chinese language for the purpose studying spiritual classics or Chinese medicine. You may wish to learn Chinese for other purposes, but it never seems to have any special value other than its own intrinsic characteristics. Language, however, is a communication tool, and it seems that the picturesqueness of Chinese characters serves better in learning integral spiritual development than other languages do. Thus I limitedly recommend it to those seekers who have reached this level.

Photo Credit: Marvin Smallheizer, T'ai Chi Magazine

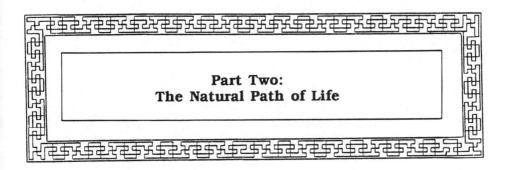

Part Two:
The Natural Path of Life

一陰一陽之謂道，健之者善也，

成之者性也。仁者見之謂之仁，

知者見之謂之知，百姓日用而

不知，故君子之道鮮矣。顯諸

仁，藏諸用，鼓萬物而不與聖

人同憂，盛德大業至矣哉。

富有之謂大業，

日新之謂盛德。

Chapter 10

BASIC GUIDELINES
FOR DAILY LIVING IN ACCORDANCE
WITH THE NATURAL TRUTH

The sixty-four hexagrams of the *I Ching* give guidance for specific circumstances. The two classics, "The Great Learning for Everyone" and "The Fundamental Path of a Plain Good Life," which follow, offer more general guidance. Both works were written by Confucius during his old age, after his audience with Lao Tzu.

"The Great Learning," believed to have been put in writing by Cheng Tzu who was an eminent student of Confucius, has provided many generations with a basis for building the foundation of a balanced personality. This work also provides the proper foundation for the further study of Tao, the path of integration, and for cultivating oneself to become an Integral Being. Since pure spiritual cultivation is useful at all times during one's life, it is wise to start when one is young. I myself was trained in this way.

"The Great Learning" can also be used to illustrate the fundamental steps for self-cultivation as outlined in Chapter 54 of the *Tao Teh Ching*:

"Virtue will be genuine
when one cultivates oneself.
Virtue will be sufficient
when one cultivates oneself with his family.
Virtue will grow rich
when one cultivates oneself with those of his village.
Virtue will abound
when one cultivates oneself with those of his nation.
Virtue will flourish universally
when one cultivates oneself with all people under
Heaven."

The Great Learning for Everyone

1

The great way of learning and developing one's personality is this: to understand that one's virtue comes from nature, to renew one's virtuous being from time to time, and to settle one's mind on the perfectly attainable virtue.

Knowing where and how to settle the mind,
*   one will be calm.*
Having attained calmness,
*   one will be undisturbed.*
Having attained an undisturbed mind,
*   one will have peace.*
Having attained peace,
*   one's mind will respond correctly*
*   to all situations.*
One who responds correctly to all situations
*   will find the way.*

Everything has roots as its main part and branches as its secondary parts. All matters have a beginning and an end. One who knows what is fundamental will not stray far from the way.

From ancient times to the present,
*   one who wishes to extend virtue*
*   to all people under Heaven*
*   should first have a well-governed nation.*
One who wishes to have a well-governed nation,
*   should first have a well-organized family.*
One who wishes to have a well-organized family
*   should first cultivate his personality.*
One who wishes to cultivate his personality
*   should first regulate his mind.*
One who wishes to regulate his mind
*   should first be honest with his consciousness.*
One who wishes to be honest with his consciousness
*   should first attain true knowledge.*

To attain true knowledge, one should look deeply into all matters. Thus, the essence and balance of life will be reached.

2

The ancient sage teaches: "Reveal your original, pure and virtuous nature."

The ancient book teaches: "Purify the pristine, virtuous nature which Heaven has bestowed."

The ancient classic teaches: "Clearly perceive the great, virtuous nature of your life."

All the above sayings teach people to truly know and recover their original, untainted, virtuous nature. But this nature is covered by many layers of contamination which are accumulated from many lifetimes of experiences. Thus, the clarity of one's nature becomes lost. In the beginning, there was no separation between individual and universal nature. Once this separation occurred, people began to experience the thousands of pains which result from being attached to the problems of life and death.

3

The motto engraved on an ancient fountains reads: "If today we wash ourselves and clean the filth from our bodies, then we should continue to wash the filth away daily. We should constantly refresh our bodies and our minds. Our life should always be kept refreshed."

The ancient sage teaches: "Be new people."

The ancient ballad says: "Although the state of Chou is old, it accepts the Heavenly will. By always renewing itself, it is always new."

People of self-cultivation continually renew themselves. Thus, they help themselves and others.

4

The ancient ballad says: "Though the central territory of Shian has only a thousand miles, it is a good place for people to gather and live. The little yellow birds sing tender songs as they perch on the luxuriant bushes of a small, warm hillside."

The ancient sage says: "The little yellow birds know where they should perch. Are human beings less wise than the little birds?"

The ancient ballad says: "The king wishes to extend his virtue and continue his work justly and openly. With equanimity he holds to the grand task."

Thus, to be king, one should be kind. To be a minister, one should work dutifully. To be a son or daughter, one should be faithful to his or her filial duty. To be a parent, one should love his or her children. To be a friend, one should be truthful.

Another ballad says: "Look at the other shore of the River Chi. The green bamboo flourishes where the virtuous King Wei lives. He is as deliberate in his studies as if he were cutting and polishing a piece of jade. He is careful and accurate in his actions and firm in principle. He is a person of self-cultivation and a truly unforgettable model."

Another ancient ballad says: "Alas, the virtuous models of past kings are unforgettable!"

From such examples, one of self-cultivation recognizes the virtuous and wise and respects them. One who cultivates himself knows who to be near. He is content with what is simple and useful in life. Even after the virtuous pass away, their merit continues to flourish.

5

To know what is fundamental is to possess the greatest knowledge.

To work with what is fundamental is to be one of self-cultivation.

6

The ancient sage says: "When I listen to people's arguments I have consideration for both sides. If they look deeply within their hearts, they forget the straight and the twisted, and the argument can be naturally resolved."

One who is not fundamentally truthful does not listen to his heart but rushes into arguments. Surely, the argument could be settled through clarity of mind, yet one is usually afraid to acknowledge and recognize this clarity. Nevertheless, the answers lie within.

To learn to follow the fundamental truth is to have the key for settling all problems.

7

To be honest with one's deep consciousness means not to cheat oneself. Be truthful to feelings of disgust at decaying odors or pleasure in beautiful colors. Keep away from things of decay. Be attracted to things of beauty. Thus will true happiness be found. One cannot cheat one's own feelings. Bad odors and sweet smells are real. One must keep away from the things which are corrupting and accept what is beneficial.

One of self-cultivation is aware of himself when alone. Those who are shallow indulge in all kinds of corruption when alone. When they face a virtuous one, they try to cover their lack of virtue, but the lack of virtue cannot be hidden from those who are truly virtuous. One who cultivates truthfulness inside naturally expresses it outside.

Do not be indulgent when you are alone. The ancient sage said: "Even when you are alone, act as though ten people were watching you and pointing their fingers at you. How significant it is to be sincere!"

Riches beautify one's house. Virtue enriches one's life. When the mind is at peace, the body is at rest. Therefore, the most fundamental thing in life for one of self-cultivation is to be honest with his deep consciousness.

8

To cultivate virtue means to regulate the mind. When one is angry, in conflict or worried, the mind loses its original balance. When one's mind is distracted, things are watched but not seen, listened to but not heard, eaten but not tasted. Therefore, regulating the mind is the basis for self-cultivation.

9

Why does harmonizing one's family depend on self-cultivation? Because one would be deferential to those one loves and feels close to, yet discriminate against those one dislikes and looks down on. One would also be deferential to those he respects, fears, pities or admires.

Usually, when one loves another, flaws are overlooked. When one dislikes another, seldom can the goodness be seen.

The ancient proverb says: "People seldom perceive the evil of their attachment to a favorite possession. Nor from envy do they know how well their own crops grow as compared to their neighbor's."

This is why cultivating a centered, balanced mind is the strong foundation of an orderly family.

10

Why is a well-governed nation based on the orderliness of well-ordered families? One who has a disorganized family cannot really help his nation. Thus, one who cultivates can help his nation without leaving home.

He treats his parents faithfully, and with this same virtue, serves his nation.

He treats his elders with respect by listening to their experiences, and with this same virtue he also treats his superiors with respect.

He treats those who are close with kindness, and with this same virtue commands the majority of the people.

The ancient teaching says: "Embracing a nation is like caring for a new-born baby. Experience is not necessary in order for a caring mother to protect her baby."

Thus, serving one's nation with an honest mind is not a difficult task.

If the family practices impartial love and is non-combative, the whole nation will be benefited. If one person is selfish and cruel, the whole nation will be in turmoil. The real key to an orderly society is this simple.

One wrong word can destroy a good relationship; however, one good person can lay down a good foundation for the safety and order of a society.

11

Why does the foundation of a harmonious world depend on the orderliness of nations?

If the leaders of a country respect the old, then the people will do the same.

If the leaders of a country pity the lonely and helpless, then the people will do the same.

Therefore, one of self-cultivation follows this principle of conduct:

> "What you do not like from the one above you,
>   do not do to the one below you.
> What you do not like from the one below you,
>   do not do to the one above you.
> What you do not like from the one in front,
>   do not do to the one behind.
> What you do not like from the one behind,
>   do not do to the one in front.
> What you do not like from the one on your left,
>   do not do to the one on your right.
> What you do not like from the one on your right,
>   do not do to the one on your left."

This is the fundamental principle of conduct.

The ancient ballad says: "Happy is the virtuous one. He becomes the parent of all people."

He likes what all pure people like and rejects what they dislike. This is called being the parent of all people.

Another ancient ballad says: "Look to the South Mountain. Its rocks are tall and well-founded. It resembles the great minister of a nation. All people look up to it."

A leader has to be careful and upright. If one is prejudiced, the world will be damaged.

The ancient ballad says: "The beginning rulers of Er had virtue which matched that of Heaven, but their descendants lost their virtue and thus they lost their people. This example can be used as a reminder to maintain constant virtue."

The way which allows one to gather people also enables one to lead a nation.

The way which does not enable one to hold people also causes one to lose a nation.

Therefore, one of cultivation must first be careful and nurture his virtue.

With virtue, people will follow.
With help, one can have land.
With territory, one can have wealth.
With wealth, one can provide things that have use.

Virtue is fundamental; wealth is last in importance.

One who considers wealth the most important of all things and virtue the least important, robs others of their wealth.

When wealth is hoarded, people scatter. When wealth is distributed, people come together and grow.

The ancient virtuous kings applied kindness in leading their nations, and people followed them willingly. The ancient tyrants applied force in leading their nations, and people also followed them, but when leaders command others in ways that go against their own nature, people should not follow them.

Virtuous beings cultivate virtue before asking others to follow. If one does something which is not harmonious within, then he should not ask others to agree and follow.

One never gains respect and understanding from others by being unjust and unkind. In order to govern a nation one should first put one's family in order.

The ancient ballad says: "The beautiful peach tree is growing. Its leaves and branches are thriving. A very beautiful girl will marry the right man. A good family has begun."

The faithful love of young people is also a good thing for an entire society.

Another ballad says: "One's example is flawless. With this example, the neighbors are influenced."

That which can be applied between fathers and sons, and among brothers and sisters, can be useful guidance for all people. With these examples, bringing order to the nation by first bringing order to one's family is illustrated.

Similarly, when absurd words are spoken, the response is absurd as well. Goods and wealth obtained in an absurd way will depart in the same way.

The ancient teaching says: "Blessings do not belong to everyone." Only the virtuous one receives them; the unvirtuous one loses them.

The book of Chu says: "In exile, we have nothing to treasure but kindness."

The vow of the country of Chien reads: "If we have only one minister for our nation, and if that person has many talents but is lacking virtue, then he is not dependable. One's heart must be grand and one's receptivity ever open. If the people have talents, then a minister of virtue would treasure their talents as if they were his own. If the people have wisdom, a minister of virtue would treasure it as if he possessed it himself. His great tolerance can protect the people and their descendants. If he embraces the nation, then the nation is benefited. A minister of the opposite persuasion will be jealous of people's talents, create hindrances for people of wisdom, and be intolerant. Such a minister will not want others to succeed. He will not be able to protect the people or their descendants. Such a person is indeed a danger!"

Only one with impartial love can drive the wicked into the wilderness and not allow evil to remain in the midst of society.

Only one who is impartial knows how to be kind to people and at the same time firm.

If a leader holds to what is harmful instead of what is virtuous and wise, he is acting counter to human nature, and destruction occurs. The true Way of a good leader is this: virtue allows one to gain; pride causes one to lose.

The way of material prosperity is this: production should be more, consumption should be less; production should be fast, consumption slow. This is like a person who makes more than he spends.   Thus, wealth will always be sufficient.

A virtuous being extends virtue with wealth.   The unvirtuous sacrifices virtue for wealth.

It never happens that if a leader practices impartial love toward people, the people will in turn practice unrighteousness toward him.   Nor if a leader practices helpfulness toward the people will the people leave him stranded.   The wealth of a nation is building each individual to be the asset of the nation; then the nation is truly powerful.   Thus, the wealth of the country should be in the homes of all people.   It is not the government that should control all the wealth; thus, the national wealth can never be stolen.

A leader's profit should not be personal or material; instead, it should be that of support.   Virtue is the real profit of the leader; material profits are not needed.

The Fundamental Path of a Plain Good Life

In ancient China, at the end of the Chou Dynasty (1122-256 B.C.), came an era of confusion, competition and wars which marked the decline of the spiritual origins and naturalness of human nature.   All seemed to be lost, but fortunately a great student named Kon Tzu (Confucius, 551-479 B.C.) responded to the momentous task of preserving the essence of the ancient teachings.   He exerted great effort in collecting and compiling manuscripts and writings of the ancient developed human beings whose natural minds were unspoiled.   This work was the essence of his old age, and it was written after he had interviewed Lao Tzu and had studied the *I Ching* so diligently that the three leather straps which bound the book wore out from use.

The important conclusion of his many years spent cultivating the ancient treasures was "The Fundamental Path of Life."   Living a plain life is the most fundamental spiritual cultivation a person can do before achieving oneself, and has been exemplified in the lives of many developed ones in Chinese history.

Lao Tzu, the great elucidator of the Simple Natural Path, has become widely admired by our contemporary spiritual world.   Unfortunately, his simple message has been misunderstood by many new spiritual students.   For this reason, the work which follows is important in assisting those who follow the Way to cultivate a better understanding of human relationship. its primary importance lies in the fact that the fundamental path of a plain, good life endures for all times and for all of humanity.

1

What is innate within the universe and human life is nature. To follow nature, or to cultivate and regulate oneself, is the fundamental path of life.

One of self-cultivation must be attentive to what cannot be seen with outer eyes and humble toward that which cannot be heard with outer ears.

There is nothing clearer than to know things which, to the mass mind, are hidden. There is nothing more explosive than to be shown things which, to the ordinary mind, are too small to be seen. Therefore, one of cultivation must be very cautious with what he cannot see or hear, what appears to be hidden, or what seems to be too small and superficial. All these things are knowable and can be known by one with high awareness.

When joy, anger, sorrow and pleasure are not exaggerated, this is called harmony or being centered. When they are expressed in an appropriate manner, this is called balance.

2

Centeredness in the unmanifest sphere is like a seed before it develops - it is the greatest source of the universe. Balance is the underlying principle of all things. Therefore, the attainment of inner centeredness and balance reflects the orderliness of the universe and the abundance of all that lives.

The Balanced One says: "One who cultivates himself lives by the principle of centeredness and balance. One of inferior virtue goes against this principle. One of self-cultivation also lives by the principle of regulation. One of inferior virtue goes against this principle by indulging."

3

The Balanced One says: "The highest virtue is to be inwardly centered and balanced. However, people are seldom able to maintain it."

4

Why is the fundamental path of life not widely practiced or widely understood? The wise miss it by being superior; the unwise miss it by not being high enough to reach it. Everyone eats and drinks, but there are only a few who know the real taste.

5

The Balanced One says: "Shun was a great wise man. He was not assertive, but he was inquisitive. He always paid close attention to the discourse, letting go of what was not useful and absorbing what was. He avoided extremes and applied the balanced way to people. For this, he was a great wise man!"

Note: Shun, a former Emperor of China, began his 48-year reign in the year 2257 B.C.

6

The Balanced One says: "All people say, 'I know,' when they are caught in nets, traps and pitfalls, but not one of them knows enough to stay away.

"All people say, 'I know,' when the fundamental path of life is shown to them, but not one of them can keep to it for as long as a month."

7

The Balanced One says: "Wei was a good human being and followed the fundamental path. When he attained a new virtue, he thoroughly obeyed it and never lost it."

Note: Wei is the abbreviation for Yeng Wei who was the favorite student of Confucius. Confucius adored him because he was a truly spiritual person who firmly adhered to the way of the plain life. Once Confucius said, "Many people would worry about living in a narrow house with only a gourd ladle of water and a bamboo basket of food, yet Wei never lost the happiness he attained by living in such a simple way." (Yeng Wei was used as an example of meditative practice in the book written by Chuang Tzu, an influential spiritual book.)

Wei was also noted for never having transferred his anger to a third party and for never repeating the same mistake twice. He was happy with a very simple way of life and did not deviate from the way in order to improve himself materially. Nor did he trade his truthful being for glamour or undeserved glory. To him, being truthful was much more valuable than pursuing wealth or fame.

8

The Balanced One says: "The world may be made peaceful, a noble position may be given up, a sharp knife may be trod on, but the fundamental path is not easy to follow consistently without deviating. This is why we place daily honest virtues above momentary miraculous performances."

9

Tze Low asked which people are stronger, and the Balanced One replied: "What strength do you wish to achieve? The strength of the South or the strength of the North?"

To guide people with gentleness and tolerance and not repay evil with evil is the strength of the South. This is where people of self-cultivation live.

To sleep on a hard bed, wear metal armor and have no fear of death is the strength of the North. This is where ordinary people live.

Although one of self-cultivation is a lover of peace, yet his principles still remain firm. Such a person is strong, independent and does not take sides in conflicts. When a nation is in order, one of self-cultivation does not need to bend in the face of difficulties. When a nation is in disorder, his virtue remains constant, even under threat of death. Therefore, he is the strongest of the strong.

10

The Balanced One says: "Looking for things that are obscure and behaving eccentrically may draw the attention of others and be remembered for generations to come, yet such ways are not for me. Although many people follow the fundamental path, they may give up halfway. Neither is this way for me."

One who cultivates, follows the fundamental path of plain living, avoids social honors and gives up his name does not regret being and remaining unknown. This is the way of the highly virtuous.

11

The path of self-cultivation is broad yet subtle. It can even be put into use in the simple life of a husband and wife. Yet, at its most profound, it cannot be comprehended by the intellectual mind, even of a wise person.

In the vastness of the universe much is unknowable to the human mind. The greatest of things on the path cannot be found in the manifest sphere; the smallest of things on the path are too small to be split by anything in the manifest realm. Between the manifest and unmanifest spheres of the universe, there are numerous levels of beings and things. The path is applicable to all levels.

An ancient ballad says: "Birds fly high in the sky, fish jump in the water. All stay in accordance with the Way and thus express the Way in their every movement."

The path of self-cultivation starts with the "ordinariness" of human life. Its extensiveness is revealed through everything in the universe.

12

The Balanced One says: "Although the path of all fulfillment is not far from people, they believe it is so. Thus, they make the path inaccessible to themselves."

As an ancient ballad says: "When using an ax to cut a new handle, the model is at one's hand, but by looking at it this way and that, it can never appear the same." One is unaware of his own change.

One of self-cultivation extends his awareness to know people and correct himself. Being honest with oneself and considerate of others, the fundamental path is fulfilled.

As the ancient teaching says: "What is not acceptable to me, I will not do to others."

This suggests a fundamental discipline for all people.

Note: This is not the same as interfering in the lives of others by "doing unto others as you would have them do unto you." This can actually bring a negative result.

Here are four general guidelines for following the path of self-cultivation. Most people have difficulty achieving even one of them:

1) One should not expect from his sons what he cannot do for his parents.
2) One should not expect from his subordinate what he cannot do for his superior or leader.
3) One should not demand from his younger brother or sister what he cannot do for his older brother or sister.
4) One should not ask from his friends what he cannot do for them first.

Thus, one of self-cultivation honestly watches one's own speech and behavior. If inadequacies are discovered in meeting the fundamental path, self-discipline is applied. The behavior of the cultivated one matches his speech, and speech matches behavior, but this person is not proud of being virtuous. Virtue is just how a person of self-cultivation fulfills life.

13

One of self-cultivation is content with himself and does not look beyond his own position or capabilities.

When one is rich, one adapts to wealth. When one is poor, one adapts to poverty. When one is in a foreign country, one adapts to foreign ways. When one is in trouble, one adapts to difficulty. One is not ashamed of or troubled by what one is naturally. One does not pretend to be what one is not; instead, one stays on the fundamental path of life.

When one is in a high position, one does not suppress subordinates; when in a low position, one does not become attached to those in power as a means of securing unjustified promotions or unearned benefits. One corrects oneself without complaining or making any demands on others. One does not blame others for not being supportive, nor accuse Heaven of not providing help. One of self-cultivation keeps to what is, and is thus at ease all the time. He knows the appropriate time for change. He is not like those of inferior virtue who like to take chances.

The Balanced One says: "The way of self-cultivation is like the art of shooting: if the target is missed, first check to see what is wrong with yourself."

14

Self-cultivation resembles beginning a long journey or climbing a mountain. In either case, the trip begins from the home or from the base of the mountain.

The ancient ballad says: "In the harmonious life of a family, all members are gathered. This is like the harmony of musical instruments. They get along together well and create a happy union."

The Balanced One says: "The parents of this family must indeed feel content!"

15

The Balanced One says: "How great is the power and virtue of divine beings? One looks but cannot see them. One listens but cannot hear them. They are everywhere - above you and at your left and right. Nothing is excluded from them. They are the true source and reservoir of all that lives. In a subtle way, they make sensitive people recognize them. People may acknowledge this relationship by making offerings."

The ancient ballad says: "The coming of spirits is unpredictable."

One must be careful when performing ceremonies that lead to reconnecting with spirits. How powerful is the sincerity of the human mind which causes the subtle realm to communicate with the manifest!

Note: In the ancient Chinese text, the terms "qui" and "shen" were used. The literal translation of these two characters when used together means "ghost" and "spirit." "Spirit" indicates the subtle essence of all things which live on after their earthly existence. Everything has its own spirit. Even a seed, before it develops into its appropriate form and distinguishable shape, has spirit. Nothing is without this subtle essence. It is the first stage of all beings, the real source and reservoir of all lives. Since there is no real death, all life naturally returns to it.

Cheng Tzu, an eminent scholar of the Sung Dynasty (960-1279 A.D.) says: "Spirits are the potency of the universe, a trace of the process of creation and transformation."

Chang Tzu, another eminent scholar of the Sung Dynasty, says: "Idealistically speaking, if we put the primal chi into two divisions, spirit and ghost, spirits are the positive potency of yang and ghosts are the inertial potency of yin. Actually, in the preliminary unmanifest sphere, they are one chi. Their virtue expresses their function and nature. They are formless and silent. They are the beginning and end of all matter and all lives. The emergence of matter and life is the convergence and dispersion of chi as either yang or yin. Yang and yin manifest as the subtle essence of matter and life. Nothing in nature can be without them."

The Developed One says: "When chi generates upward, it becomes Heaven. From this, all things derive their life. All life is evidence of spirits; no life can exist without them."

The world is a place where souls have come for the process of purification and refinement.

16
Sincerity or genuineness is the way of Heaven. To be sincere or genuine is also the way of humanity.

With sincerity, one can find the way.

17
To be centered on the Way without struggle is to be highly achieved, virtuous and wise.

To be sincere means to choose the right way and stay with it persistently. When one is sincere, one's mind is clear. When one's mind is clear, one is naturally sincere.

18
Only the most sincere person under Heaven is aware of his innate nature. His being is harmonized with his innate nature. He can know the nature of all people; thus, he can be harmonious with the nature of all people. Knowing the nature of all things, one can help their growth by living selflessly. Thus, a sincere person is one with Heaven and Earth. There is no separation between his nature and that of the universe.

19
A person who has difficulty in spiritually breaking through the separation between his own nature and that of the universe should begin by working on particular things. Any simple motive, plan or idea can be pursued if done with sincerity. Once formalized, it can blossom and become bright with growth. This brightness and growth generate movement and are very useful.

Only one who is sincere can effect change, internally or externally, in the material or social world.

20
Ultimate sincerity can give foreknowledge of future events. Auspicious signs can foretell even the future of the nation. When a nation is to become extinct, there will be ominous signs. These signs can be observed by using the *I Ching*, and also by one's own intuitive responses.

The coming of both fortune and misfortune can be foreseen. When a person reaches ultimate sincerity, he is equal to a divine being.

21
To be sincere is to be self-realizing and self-accomplishing. The fundamental path is the path for the growth of all things. With sincerity, things are started and accomplished. Nothing can be done without it.

Therefore, it is important and valuable for one of self-cultivation to be sincere. To be sincere not only completes oneself, but also completes others. To complete oneself is to be wise. To complete others is to be kind. Being kind and wise is the virtue of our nature.

This is the way to unite the internal and external aspects of our being. Kindness and wisdom are applied to every moment and every circumstance by one of self-cultivation.

22
Those who are sincere never cease; thus, they are long-enduring. Being long-enduring, one's virtue can be expressed. To be self-expressing is to become far-reaching. Being far-reaching, one becomes broad and deep. Being broad and deep, one becomes high and brilliant.

With broadness and depth, one can carry others.
With highness and brilliance, one can guide others.
With endurance, one can fulfill oneself and others.
With broadness and depth, one can match Earth.
With highness and brilliance, one can match Heaven.
With endurance, one can be limitless.

If one can accomplish this, one becomes worthy without being known. Without actually moving, one may effect change by being in accord with the movement of nature. Thus, one's work is accomplished without strain.

23

The Balanced One says: "Shun was a person with a sense of great duty. He made Heaven and Earth his parents. His virtue made him sacred. He became the Heavenly son who had sovereignty over human beings. He considered all the wealth held within all the seas as his own and equally cared for it all. His spirit is worshipped with a majestic temple and is protected by all his descendants. Therefore, any such great and virtuous being must enjoy high position and rewards, a good name, and longevity. All lives and all things of heavenly birth must develop accordingly. The one who cultivates will be reinforced. The unvirtuous will be destroyed."

The ancient ballad says: "One of self-cultivation is upright and happy. His virtue is brilliant. People make him their leader. Heaven sends rewards to the one of self-cultivation and he is protected by the Heavenly Emperor. Therefore, the great and virtuous one will be blessed."

24

The carefree one was King Wen! He had the support of his virtue even during times of great adversity. His grandfather and father established their nation not with aggression but by being kind and yielding.

After returning from captivity of the tyrant Jou, King Wen became yet even more prosperous. Two-thirds of the enormous empire gave him their support. King Wen's son took action against the tyrant and succeeded immediately. The son was then enthroned and became responsible for one large, unified nation.

Thus, a new, virtuous and long-lived era, the Chou Dynasty, was begun.

25

The King of Lu asked the Balanced One: "How does one properly manage public affairs?"

The Balanced One replied: "Taking good care of public affairs depends on the proper person. Such a person must cultivate the fundamental path. Impartial love is the most important virtue in handling public affairs. This virtue is developed from two important bases: first, one should take care of his parents and extend this same kind of service to all people. Second, one should respect the virtuous and wise, for they are indeed the nation's true leaders and the only ones who actually know the Heavenly Way."

There are five essential forms of human relations:

1) the relationship of leader and follower
2) the relationship of parents and children
3) the relationship of husband and wife
4) the relationship of siblings
5) the relationship of friends

There are three virtues to cultivate in order to fulfill these five relationships. They are: understanding, love and the courage to recognize one's inadequacies.

These three virtues can be simplified into one word: sincerity. With it, all relationships can be fulfilled and maintained.

It furthers one to learn through experience and reflection. But if there is sincerity, it enables one to have the highest understanding that the way of Heaven and Man is one.

One who studies diligently will have a deeper understanding. One who practices diligently will have more kindness. One who knows the inadequacy of his being will develop more courage. Having these three is the basis of self-cultivation.

When one knows how to cultivate oneself, one will then know how to direct others. When one can direct others, one will be able to direct the nations of the world.

26

A goal can be reached with proper preparation. Without this, no goal is attainable.

A speech studied beforehand has no flaws.

A job planned beforehand has no obstacles.

Behavior considered beforehand will give no cause for remorse.

A way of life determined beforehand will not be misled.

27

A good plan for learning has five steps:

1) Learn broadly.
2) Examine completely.
3) Ponder carefully.
4) Discern clearly.
5) Practice exactly.

If one has not learned anything, it does not matter, but once one begins to learn something, he should be thorough in his studies.

If one has not seen anything, it does not matter, but once one looks at something, he should not stop before knowing it completely.

If one has not thought about anything, it does not matter, but once something is pondered, one should not stop before understanding it.

If one has not recognized anything, it does not matter, but once something is distinguished, one should be clear in his discernment.

If one has not developed a skill, it does not matter, but once something is practiced, one should be exact.

If there is something which can be done by someone "smart" with one portion of his strength, then let me, an honest person, achieve it with tenfold of my strength if I am less than he.

If there is something which can be done by someone with ten portions of his strength, let me achieve it with a hundredfold of my strength if I am less than he.

The foolish who follow this earnest principle can be enlightened and the weak can become strengthened.

28

The Way of the universe can be summarized in a word: oneness. It is oneness, or sincerity, with oneself. Or, it is oneness or sincerity with both Heaven and nature.

Look at the universe. Although it straightforwardly gives birth to all lives, its creativity is unfathomable. From its development, broadness, profundity, highness, brightness, expansiveness and endurance, it gives birth to time and space. Time and space are indivisible as reality in the development of the universe.

The sky can be small,
    but its development is infinite.
The earth can be small,

but its development is incalculable.
The mountain can be small,
    but its storage is immeasurable.
The water can be small,
    but its use is unlimited.

The ancient ballad says: "Heaven is called Heaven because incessant sincerity, or oneness, makes it so."

29

Great is the way of the virtuous and wise! The Great Ones limitlessly continue the development of the universe. Their height can reach Heaven. They are broad enough to receive all people and things.   There are thousands of good things that await the coming of the virtuous and wise.   It is said, "If there exists no high virtuous being, the highest goodness cannot be manifested in the human realm."

Therefore, one of self-cultivation respects his innate virtue and develops it through continuous learning and cultivation.   Such a being achieves the greatest, the subtlest, the highest and the most brilliant state, yet stays on the fundamental path. He reviews the past and thus knows what is to be. Although he is very deep in nature, he is also willing to adapt to current social manners. Therefore, when one is in a high position, he is not proud. When one is in a low position, he is not rebellious.   When the nation is in good order, he helps it prosper. When the nation is in disorder, his silence and tolerance preserve him.

The ancient ballad says: "With crystal clarity and wisdom, one's life is protected."

30

The Balanced One says: "If a person is foolish and self-assertive, inferior and stubborn, he goes against the fundamental path which has been followed by all generations on the road of history. Calamity must surely befall such a person."

Only one of true sincerity is wise enough to have the insight to know the right way from the wrong and to understand the implications of such discernment.   Such mental and spiritual capabilities are sufficient to be open to everything and everybody and to provide help.   One's gentleness and softness express tolerance.   One is firm and dauntless in maintaining one's principles.   One is solemn, balanced and worthy of respect.   One is deliberate and accurate in judgment.   With these virtues, one is like an unfathomable fountain which unceasingly gives of itself in order to support all life.

32

Only the most sincere can organize a good constitution and the foundations for harmonious cooperation in order to cope with the natural development of the universe.   One relies on nothing but sincerity.   One's kindness is pure, profundity infinite, and greatness connected with Heaven.   One develops the insight to see that Heaven's nature is one's own nature.   Therefore, the cultivated one is able to give to all things and all beings.

33

The ancient ballad says: "Let shining silk and satin be the undergarments and plain cotton be the outside clothes."   Being conspicuous and shining is not in accordance with nature.   Therefore, the way of one who cultivates himself is not to be outwardly showy, but to work inwardly.   True brilliance comes from sincere and long cultivation.

The way of the inferior person is to be outwardly beautiful, but without any real value inside.   Make-up that is used each day loses its effect.

Although one of self-cultivation appears plain, he is never ignorant.   His character is simple and gentle, with natural depth and the fullness of truth.   One of self-cultivation knows great expansiveness from within and how the apparent develops from the subtle.   Following the way, one enters the unfailing realm of virtue.

Chapter 11

INTRODUCTION TO THE GUIDANCE OF THE SIXTY-FOUR HEXAGRAMS

The Value of Using the Sixty-Four Hexagrams

The *I Ching* is an ancient book that teaches about the changes and the unchanging truth of nature, human society and individual life. It was initiated by the quest of mind which wanted to find the rules in life of how to behave and respond to life situations in order to bring about good results.

In many situations in today's life, we do not know in advance what is right and what is wrong, or which movements will lead us to good fortune or which ones bring misfortune. Sometimes we cause trouble by making a wrong move. Sometimes when we do not move, instead responding passively to a situation, we also cause trouble. Thus, we need to know when it is right to do something and when not to act. To help guide people in such circumstances, all kinds of divination were developed, such as spirit channeling, oracle searching and magic writing. However, these things do not usually help one obtain an objective vision of a matter. They do not produce a real or good solution because they can be inaccurate depending on the person giving the channeling or interpretation. Spirit channeling and oracle giving resulted in the development of religions, spiritual misunderstanding and illusion of the human mind.

For a long stage of history, the ancient spiritually developed ones used the *I Ching* as the spiritual consultant for their lives. From doing so, they slowly produced the general guidelines which are useful and effective in all general circumstances. The production of the *I Ching* system was based on the principle of the responsiveness of spiritual nature, both within and without.

Thus, the *I Ching* does not give you subjective answers to your questions. Nor does it make decisions for you. Rather, the use of the *I Ching* is to give you inspiration for making your own decisions. It inspires you to view a matter differently. What it does is assist your development. It is not like religion, which puts a cart in front of the horse; instead, it shows you how well you can drive.

Although we cannot consult with the *I Ching* about each movement in life's activities, the *I Ching* binds with each moment of our life. After people used the *I Ching* for divination purposes for many years, they learned the general guidance of the book which they could then follow from remembering the reading. Thus they knew the guidance without having to throw the coins or use the seeds. An illustration that can help us understand how this works is that a well experienced driver, or the user of a machine, has no need to refer to an instruction booklet to operate or repair his machine. He already knows how to keep it operating smoothly from his experience. This comes from his familiarity with it. Perfection in skill comes from practice and more practice.

The *I Ching* is too big a book to carry around and use each time we need to make a change or respond to change, make a move or decide not to move. Even a very meticulous fortune telling system cannot help a person make a good and correct response in each decision of his life. Thus, one's ability to respond to situations becomes a matter of personal growth. The use and study of the *I Ching*, assists that growth.

The subtle spiritual levels of the *I Ching* are almost endless. This is why the study of the *I Ching* presents such a great challenge. Though the words are not difficult to understand, that which lies between them is another matter. When one really understands how to use the *I Ching*, the nature of personal problems and the entirety of the universe can be perceived.

The *Book of Changes* is a compact vision of universal reality and can simultaneously be seen as an enlarged vision of human life. Its scope is so vast and encompassing that it can be used for the very small or the very large, depending on the breadth of one's life and mind.

By continuously studying the *I Ching*, many levels of truth gradually unfold. Why is this so? The *I Ching* serves as a key to unlock the inner rooms of one's psyche, which are in turn connected to all the inner rooms of the universe. The truth buried in one's consciousness at a particular stage of development is not always easy to perceive. However, the *I Ching* can reveal all of this and more. Nothing can be hidden from its subtle and penetrating insight.

The human mind, by its very nature, has the potential to know future events. Although this ability can be developed, most people do not know how. Studying the *I Ching* not only enables one to develop this ability, but also counsels one on how to respond to or change future events. If a problem is not sensed and positively corrected before it occurs, then that event, in effect, is predestined and one must suffer unnecessarily.

The value of foreknowledge alone has very little significance. A true prophet not only sees that which will happen, but also has the wisdom and ability to respond appropriately to the situation. Therefore, the *I Ching* really deals with two different aspects: the development of foreknowledge, and the capacity to use this foreknowledge correctly.

Unfortunately, the spiritual capabilities of most people are not sufficiently developed to take advantage of the *I Ching*'s wise counsel, nor do they realize how much their attitudes determine the outcome of their lives. Lacking this awareness, they are not receptive to the teachings of the *I Ching* and never progress to the subtle levels it makes accessible. A true *I Ching* practitioner, on the other hand, develops high spiritual capabilities such as seeing subtle beings and even the ability to live among them. Ordinary people also have visions, but they are frequently the result of psychological disturbances and have no real value.

A true *I Ching* practitioner must live a spiritual life if he hopes to use the *I Ching* for personal and spiritual development. The subtle rays of the universe only respond to an achieved being. Such a being is aware that as the mind vibrates, so does the subtle ray, thus producing a response from the *I Ching*. Unfortunately, most modern people have such an over-developed intellectual function that it is difficult for them to get a clear and accurate response. Since the intellect is only part of the overall mind, a condition of imbalance, or a "twisted mind" as it was called by the ancient sages, arises.

An unbalanced mind is not "straight" enough to allow the overall picture to be accurately reflected or perceived. The intellect first goes through its externally programmed thought patterns before it responds to a situation, thus it can never truly reflect what it is presently experiencing, but can only reflect that which has already been programmed. As the ancients said, "One who sees things in a twisted way lives a twisted way."

When the mind is no longer complete and natural, questions and solutions also become unnatural. Even if one stumbles on a natural solution, in this state of mind he will still doubt it and insist on going ahead with the programmed response. Emptiness, isolation and confusion are the results of responding only to what was previously learned.

A true mind will respond to truth and an unnatural mind will respond to what is unnatural. Modern people are more willing to understand and control the future by means of a hard-earned and expensive education than by trusting a simple, whole mind. If people would concentrate deeply and allow time for their minds to quiet down, the function of their essential mind would appear naturally, but modern people always need to have things explained. To over-explain everything solidifies the mind, and a rigid intellectual mind degrades and enslaves itself.

Reading many artificial, authoritative books has also created great conflict in people's lives. Most educators only know how to fill their students with more useless information. They do not realize that true education is the cultivation of a flexible and responsive mind. Learning is not just a matter of accumulating information. Gathering more and more information only leads to an unquenchable thirst for more information.

When this attitude is applied to spiritual cultivation, it actually prevents high achievement. The intellectual mind denies or ignores direct experience and intuitive knowledge of the inexplicable and thus develops a "twisted" kind of thinking or prejudice which values only that which can be analyzed under a microscope. This tendency prevents most modern thinkers from appreciating the spiritual achievements of their forefathers.

Even today, when things such as T'ai Chi Ch'uan, acupuncture, and the practice of Chi Kung have been proven to be of definite value, that which is visible and shallow receives recognition while the deeper, unseen level of human endeavor, the integration of Heavenly and Earthly energies, remains unnoticed. Modern people are almost totally ignorant of the real significance of these energies in their lives and thus do not realize the need to improve lives spiritually as well as materially. The result is that the world appears to be rapidly changing for the worse.

Through the practice of the *I Ching*, a person can see that over-intellectualization has violated the order of the natural, wholesome mind. By following its guidance, people of truth will no longer be limited to superficially looking at life.

The *I Ching* is actually a tool to prove the truth of life. At the moment a true, natural mind reaches as far as it can, things are seen from within and reflect what comes from without. This is not the ego, but the response of the whole mind as it connects with the vibrations of the totality of the internal and external universe.

Continued *I Ching* practice can also allow one to know oneself. However, "self" cannot exist without something that is "not-self." "Self" signifies the mind when it is motivated and reacts. "Self" disappears when the mind is at peace. Only at the moment of opposition does the "self" emerge as a function of the mind.

The inner part of one's being and the so-called outer world actually go hand-in-hand and cannot exist independently of one another. Likewise, the intuitive, integral, responsive mind and the intellectual mind are interdependent aspects of one whole mind, like two wings that harmoniously work together to carry a bird higher and higher.

Actually, good fortune and misfortune are only vibrations to which the mind responds. A whole, natural mind always responds appropriately to external stimuli and is thus in control of its reaction. The simplest way to receive a whole mind is to work with the *I Ching*. Through it, one sees the reflection of one's mind as a whole and one soon learns that what is regarded as good or ill fortune depends completely on how a situation is approached and what actions are taken to deal with it.

Is sitting around worrying about what will happen beneficial? The *I Ching* can help one see beyond an emotional level to a deeper reality as it presents itself in any moment. Life is not determined by the future, it is determined by this very moment. Although past actions still affect a person, it is the present moment which is decisive.

Is it possible to control one's fortune and destiny? One can learn by studying the *I Ching* that fortune depends entirely upon how changes are approached and dealt with. People usually want their lives to get better and hope that all will happen just as they wish. However, if they did not insist on things always happening as they wish, then good things would naturally occur. The *I Ching* is not intended to make one a fortune teller, but it can help restore the wholesomeness of one's mind, which will allow better control of one's life.

Many people think their minds are clear, but their actions indicate otherwise. There should be no divergence between what people know and what they do. People of awareness understand that intellectual development is only partial and that cultivating or restoring an integral mind takes years. To develop foreknowledge is one thing; applying that knowledge skillfully is another matter. Both can be developed by studying the *I Ching*. Indeed, this is its true value.

Fundamental Benefits of Using the 64 Hexagrams

Although the *I Ching* was formulated almost 6,000 years ago, few scholars have actually understood its true depth. People generally misuse the *I Ching* by categorizing its response in terms of good or bad fortune and consulting it to reinforce their own narrow viewpoints instead of recognizing its broader applications. If one wishes to become an illusionist, a poet or a novelist, the *I Ching* is a poor teacher, allowing little room for imagination. The *I Ching* tells the truth through the medium of a very special and accurate language. If one is receptive to its advice, one will be able to respond to a situation which may occur in a few days, a few months, or even generations to come.

Each line of the *I Ching* is based on a fundamental principle of natural law. Therefore, each sign contains the entire truth of the universe. Behind its entire system of 384 lines, there is only one truth. *I Ching* training can show people what will happen in the future and what the truth was in the past.

Many examples exist which prove that people born thousands of years ago achieved themselves by following the guidance of the *I Ching*. There are records of ancient *I Ching* practitioners who made predictions several thousand years into the future by engraving their predictions on stone tablets and burying them in special places. When they were discovered, these tablets accurately described events which had been prophesied and which had taken place within that span of time.

In practicing the *I Ching*, a beginner should look very closely at the interpretation of the hexagram and be aware that, even with the interpretation, wrong judgments can still be made. Sometimes one does not easily accept the fact that its guidance responds to one's true needs;

instead, one interprets the hexagrams as a response to one's desires. The *I Ching* never tries to please. The vibration of the mind, along with the situation in question, always come together and are represented unerringly by the appropriate hexagram. Indeed, what we are given is the truth.

In the early stages of working with the *I Ching*, do not become discouraged by unfavorable signs. One will do well to find the guidance which is ultimately beneficial. Even if a clear interpretation cannot be made, the *I Ching* still gives valuable guidance by preventing one from rushing thoughtlessly into the situation being considered. If this can be recognized and appreciated, then true progress has been made.

Taking time to use the *I Ching* indicates that one's attitude is cautious and objective. It also allows one to recognize which elements of the situation are favorable. Another benefit that one can receive from studying the principles of the *I Ching* is that of self-education.

I Ching study is still the best method of education. Many of life's situations are difficult to understand. However, by practicing the *I Ching*, one will be able to abandon narrowness and adopt correct attitudes as one develops spiritually. It will also help control impulsiveness, cultivate wisdom and broaden one's point of view. The day will eventually come when no artificial means of foreknowledge will be necessary. One will reach a level where the truth of life is clearly revealed, just as it was to the enlightened sages of antiquity.

When one becomes spiritually developed, it is no longer necessary to stuff the mind with information. At such time, neither religious nor political propaganda will be confusing to a person who is one with the truth. All questions will have been answered and, with this new knowledge, one will be able to determine the best way to live. Thus, the *I Ching* can not only be one's best friend, but one's most reliable consultant.

The following five guidelines are important for the correct application of the principles of the *I Ching*. Always adhere to them carefully.

1. As a way of life, always follow the fundamental principles and guidance in the *I Ching*. For specific problems you should refer to the hexagrams and lines.

2. In the beginning, use the predictive system only for practical, down-to-earth matters.   Do not ask questions about spiritual achievement, virtuous aspirations or artistic accomplishments.   Responses to such questions may actually weaken one's good motives by fostering self-doubt.

3. Do not use the *I Ching* to support your own self-righteousness.   Using the *I Ching* correctly can promote growth, but using it incorrectly will create great obstacles.

4. Do not use the predictive system after something has already been undertaken to find out if it was correct.   The system should be used before an event rather than after it.   This guideline applies to all relationships and practical matters.

5. Always remember that good fortune is not contained within the seeds, coins, sticks or any other instrument.   It is contained within one's own refined essence.

The Underlying Principles of the Sixty-Four Hexagrams

The *I Ching* is composed of sixty-four images called hexagrams, which represent different stages of transformation or change.   Everything in the universe goes through these changing states.

Within each hexagram, a situation unfolds into six different stages, each represented by one of these six lines, thus there are 64 x 6 or 384 different states of transformation, each having a particular significance.   There are also further multiple transformations which continue unceasingly and follow many different cyclic patterns.   However, for all practical purposes, these 384 situations are sufficient to work with.

According to legend, the six-line symbols of the *I Ching* were created by Fu Shi in early times.   The third or fourth edition of the *I Ching* was compiled around 1143 B.C. by King Wen, who systematically organized the sixty-four hexagrams as we know them today.   Extensive commentaries were added to the basic text over the next 1,500 years, the most important of these being the "Ten Wings" ascribed to Confucius (551-479 B.C.).   My commentaries at the end of each hexagram incorporate the essence of the "Ten Wings."

The *I Ching* system as a whole originated from careful observations of natural universal development which begins with yin — — and yang ———. These polarized energies contain and complement each other. As they begin to multiply and interact, however, four basic manifestations result: full yang ═══, lesser yang ═══, full yin ═ ═ and lesser yin ═══. By further interaction and multiplication, the fundamental eight trigrams develop. These symbols can express all events in the universe in a simple and concise manner.

☰ Complete yang	☷ Complete yin
☳ Strong or deep yang	☴ Strong or deep yin
Middle yang	Middle yin
Shallow yang	Shallow yin

The eight trigrams represent the eight stages of universal energy whose interactions produce a given situation. Each is distinct from the others, depending on its composition of yin and yang, and their interaction yields sixty-four permutations of energy.

Each trigram has many distinct attributes and also represents a particular member of a family, as shown below:

Complete yang	☰	Chyan, Heaven, father
Complete yin	☷	K'un, Earth, mother
Strong yang		Chen, Thunder, eldest son
Strong yin		Soen, Wind, eldest daughter
Middle yang		K'an, Water, middle son
Middle yin		Li, Fire, middle daughter

Lesser yang   ☶   Ken, Mountain, youngest son

Lesser yin   ☱   Tui, Lake, youngest daughter

Each hexagram and every line is an image that represents and reveals a different aspect of the universe. Although absolute truth cannot be expressed through words, it can become visible through the symbolic language of the *I Ching*. One must be careful, however, not to become attached to the literal translation of the symbols, for example Lake or Thunder, otherwise the true meaning will be missed.

By studying the *I Ching* one can see that there is a sense of time and space which is produced by movement. As the stages of movement are divided into sections, sequences of space and time appear. However, in the reality of the universe, there is no definite way of dividing space or time. In other words, the division of time and space is not absolute, but relative. One can learn by studying the *I Ching* that our perception of space and time is, in fact, merely a product of movement.

Systems of time and divisions of space are only tools of measurement to describe the relative sphere. Insisting on any relative standard such as physical measurement damages our capacity for flexible spiritual discernment. The dominant, mechanistic view of nature in early modern times created the same kind of darkness as that caused by social or religious dogma. The basis of all modern knowledge systems is limited to the relative sphere. In order not to become entrapped by this superficial dimensionalism, the *I Ching* uses a series of signs and numbers, such as one, two, four, eight, sixty-four, etc., to express the flux of natural phenomena.

There are two principal configurations of the eight trigrams, commonly referred to as the "pre-Heaven" and "post-Heaven" realms expressing the integrated nature of the universe. Pre-Heaven (Heavenly) refers to the unmanifest realm, and post-Heaven (Earthly) refers to the manifest realm (see Figures 105a and 105b).

All manifestations of nature occur in the post-Heaven realm. In this realm the forces of yin and yang come into play. In the interaction of yin and yang, concepts, thoughts and the order of the physical world manifest as patterns of relative development.

Deep within the core of one's spirit, in the reality of the universe, is the primordial integrity of "pre-Heaven" and "pre-Earth" energy which is beyond all time. The pre-Heaven realm is invariable, but in the post-Heaven stage everything changes.

Universal Being, or Tao, contains both the variable and invariable. In order for one to be able to make a clear distinction between the two, one must maintain a balanced life. This is why balance is the key to all spiritual cultivation.

The unmanifest, natural subtle law of the universe becomes manifest through its operation in the world. With the help of the *I Ching*, the unmanifest becomes known. By following the *I Ching*'s guidance, one can reunite one's life with the natural potency of this unmanifest subtle origin. Though the physical being of a developed one is in the post-Heavenly or manifest realm, his spirit can extend to the pre-Heaven realm.

Studying the *I Ching* enables one to restore the natural wholeness of one's mind. This whole mind serves as an intermediary between the spiritual and physical realms, and by continuously studying and applying the principles of the *I Ching* to one's life, one will be able to harmonize outer universal natural reality with one's true being.

The purpose of studying the *I Ching* is not to exercise the intellect, but to help one understand wholeness on a much deeper level than would ordinarily be possible. By studying the *I Ching*, the function of intuition, or what is called "straight awareness," can be developed. This is the direct perception of reality without thought or judgment.

How to Evaluate and Interpret a Hexagram

How can the *I Ching* be used as a predictive tool with which to enhance one's life? To begin with, the *I Ching* synthesizes all possibilities of human life into sixty-four essential patterns. Within these broad categories, more subtly defined specific stages are represented by the lines, which illustrate varying degrees of evolution and response to the whole situation.

To establish a basis for evaluating specific situations, eight words are frequently used. Four are blessings, or positive developments:

Yuan   元   Natural and original; no deviation

Hung	亨	Smooth and enjoyable; full growth.
Li	利	Profitable and promising; benefit.
Tsing	貞	Upright and firm; perseverance.

The four words expressing the consequences of deviating from the right path are:

Shung	凶	Danger
Jye	咎	Fault or Blame
Hwei	悔	Remorse
Ling	吝	Humiliation

There are also two more words which support these eight words as they apply to various situations:

Wang Ji	往吉	Proper
Wang Ling	往吝	Improper

How accurate is a response from the *I Ching*? I would say one hundred percent. How great is the possibility of misinterpretation? Again, one may also say one hundred percent. Misjudging or misinterpreting the *I Ching* is always a possibility for novices; often they do not really understand its guidance, but simply create interpretations to satisfy their superficial desires.

How can the *I Ching* be used with one hundred percent effectiveness? With familiarity, it cultivates the mind, fostering development and achievement.

A hexagram is composed of two trigrams which, in turn, contain two inner trigrams. The two inner trigrams then integrate to form the inner hexagram.

(FIGURE 110)

The individual lines express different levels of development within a given situation. Just as infancy, childhood, adolescence and adulthood are stages of human growth, the six lines are different expressions or levels of a particular situation. They show the transformation of a situation as it moves upward through the hexagram. The first or bottom line expresses the beginning stage, and the top line expresses the stage of completion or excess. Each line also has a specific energy and a correct position. Reading from the bottom up, the positions 1, 3 and 5 are odd-numbered and should be yang——. Lines 2, 4 and 6 are even-numbered and should be yin — — . In other words, yang lines are normally odd-numbered and yin lines are normally even-numbered.

Furthermore, each line of the lower trigram has a special relationship with a line in the upper trigram. For example, line 1 corresponds with line 4, line 2 corresponds with line 5, and line 3 corresponds with line 6. These relationships are essential in determining the harmony and appropriateness of the individual lines.

Another important relationship among lines is between neighboring lines: 1 and 2, 3 and 4, and 5 and 6. To be correctly related, a yin line should always be paired with a yang, either as its direct neighbor or through its correspondence with another line. For example, when a yang line in the first position matches a yin line in the fourth, mutual support and correct conduct is usually indicated. When this is reversed, that is, if the first line is yin and the fourth line is yang, there may still be something of a correspondence between the two. However, this reversal of inappropriate position may be the cause of the existing problem. This also applies to the correspondence between the second and fifth lines and the third and sixth lines. If this principle of yin paired with yang does not apply to these lines (1 and 4, 2 and 5, 3 and 6) then one looks at the relationship between lines 1 and 2, 3 and 4, and 5 and 6 in order to decide the appropriateness and harmony of the situation.

Since the hexagrams are composed of two trigrams, the upper one and the lower one, similarities exist between the positions of the three lines of each trigram. For example, the first and fourth lines are often cautioned against premature action. The second and fifth are the leaders of their respective trigrams, the fifth line usually being the leader of the entire hexagram. The third and sixth lines, at the top of each trigram, usually express excessiveness. It is important to remember, however, that these characterizations are only tendencies of a particular position rather than absolute characteristics.

Each hexagram expresses a unique interaction between two trigrams, which together symbolize two of the eight basic natural energies: Heaven ☰ , Earth ☷ , Fire ☲ , Water ☵ , Thunder ☳ , Wind ☴ , Mountain ☶ , and Lake ☱ . Each of the eight basic energies has many different attributes. With an understanding of these energies and how they interact with other energies, one may know the truth of any situation and the proper action to take.

In the *I Ching* there is no moral distinction between "right" and "wrong," only between that which is appropriate or inappropriate. Nothing is rejected. Instead, one is shown how any situation can be transformed into an appropriate one. There is no such thing as an unchanging situation. Circumstances exist as one shapes them, and they are continually subject to change.

Most problems are created by going against one's true nature or that of the circumstance. By following the natural course of nature, there is a continuous movement towards harmony with the Way. For example, the nature of water is to flow. If there is an obstruction and water still continues to flow, it will become dammed up, creating an unnatural accumulation which may result in flooding. However, if the water finds an alternate route and moderates its flow, the obstruction ceases to be a hindrance. Actually, an obstruction can be used as a catalyst for change and provides an opportunity for overcoming an obstacle.

When one consults the *I Ching*, the particular hexagram gives the general background of the situation, while the lines give the specific circumstance and the correct way in which to handle the matter. A good decision can only be made after careful analysis of both the hexagram and the lines.

One's main focus should be on the guidance presented in quotes at the beginning of the hexagram, and secondarily on the guidance at the beginning of each line. The guidance of each line is further explained and expanded upon below each topical quote. Ultimately, the ability to correctly interpret the guidance of the original text depends on one's personal cultivation and life experiences.

When interpreting the guidance, examine the elements of the hexagram and the relationship of the lines to one another. You will find the instruction needed comes from the principles expressed by the arrangement of the lines. Furthermore, this is good training for developing intuition. The subtle, natural laws expressed through the oracle can truly show the situation objectively and indicate what action is appropriate to it. If one has resistance or becomes frustrated by the response, this indicates that there is some barrier which must be broken through. Therefore, one should contemplate not only the answer obtained from the *I Ching*, but one's reaction to it. This method is very useful in developing both personal insight and the ability to solve problems.

The movement toward balance is a fundamental principle of the *I Ching*. This fact is of utmost importance when interpreting the hexagrams. When one is impeded by obstacles or adversity, the *I Ching* always offers hope and a reminder that the condition will surely change. During times when movement is difficult, one should gather energy and prepare for change. On the other hand, there are times when "crossing the great water," or partaking in a new venture, is necessary; to be still would cause one to lose the opportunity. There are other times when everything progresses smoothly. In these circumstances, the *I Ching* cautions not to become smug but to remain calm and centered.

There is always a hint of warning in prosperous times, for they too will inevitably change. When something reaches fullness, decline will surely follow. The basic premise of all guidance is to maintain the "middle way" and thereby avoid all extremes and excesses.

Each sign of natural energy exemplifies a virtue. Accordingly, one will be advised to remain adaptable and flow like water, or to keep still like a Mountain, to be receptive like the Earth, to be creative and forward like Heaven, to be innocently joyful like a Lake, to have the clarity and brightness of Fire, to be gently influencing like the Wind, or to be awakened by the call of Thunder to break through obstruction. A hexagram can also symbolize a virtue to be emulated, such as Ching 井 (the Well), or Ting 鼎 (the Cauldron).

When trying to understand a situation, look at the relationship between the upper and lower trigrams to see whether they conflict or harmoniously integrate with one another. This relationship depends upon several things. The degree and position of yin and yang energy determine how the energies will interact. For instance, in T'ai 泰

(Harmony/ Prosperity), the yang energy below ascends and the yin above descends, thus coming together peacefully and harmoniously. Conversely, in Pi 否 (Misfortune/Disharmony), the yang energy above continues to ascend while the yin energy below continues its downward movement. They can have no communication because they are moving apart.

Another consideration is how the nature of the tri- grams interact in the natural world. For example, Water and Fire can be either destructive or creative in their relationship. The creation of all life is the result of the harmonious integration of Water and Fire; yet, if there is not a proper balance, Fire will be extinguished or the Water will evaporate.

If a hexagram is comprised of five yang lines and one yin line, one should then look to the yin line for the significance of the hexagram. Likewise, if all of the lines are yin except for one yang, then look to the yang as being of particular significance. If these energies are equally proportioned, the judgment will depend on their arrangement. If you practice the *I Ching* with a method other than seeds, it is possible that all will be moving lines but one. If there is one single still line, or if only one line moves, look at that line. Look at the entire process in order to know the full meaning. Another important influence in the hexagram is the inner trigrams which are formed by lines 2-3-4 and 3-4-5. These show the inner influence of the hexagram and lend different meaning to the lines.

Generally, in a relationship with another person or material thing, the lower or interior trigram represents you and the upper or exterior trigram represents the other. However, this changes according to your respective roles. For instance, if you are the buyer of something, then you assume the exterior (i.e., outsider) or upper trigram position, you being the one to enter the situation, while the seller is in the lower, or interior trigram position.

Additionally, there is often a suggestion of time in the guidance. For instance, if a question is formulated around the period of a year, then each line represents two months; if a week, then each line represents a day (see Figure 102); if a day, then each line represents four hours. In other cases, time may be more vaguely expressed, such as when the guidance speaks of "three days." In reality, this may mean three months or three years, or it may simply mean a long time. Often a hexagram represents a time period preceding or following an undertaking or event. None of the times mentioned can be rigidly held to because of the many facets of each hexagram.

From studying the *I Ching* one will come to learn that everything is relative and that nothing with form is static. One can also learn not to be overly rigid or assertive. *I Ching* practice enables one to discern good fortune from bad fortune in any situation and to respond appropriately with a good positive attitude. You, yourself, become the main factor for changing your fortune and destiny.

Guidance for Consulting the Sixty-Four Hexagrams

For maximum effectiveness in consulting the *I Ching*, the following steps should be followed:

1) Find a quiet place for making the divination. It should be clean, with no bad odors or sweet smelling incense. Be mindful to cleanse your body as well.

2) Do not consult the *I Ching* when you are in a hurry or just after a meal when your energy is congested in your stomach. Early morning is also not a good time, because you may not be sufficiently attuned yet to what the day has to offer. The *I Ching* responds to the primary image in your mind, so if your mind is still asleep or if you have particular expectations, the response will not necessarily reflect what is actually important for that day. If the primary image in your mind is unknown to your consciousness, you will get a response that does not seem to relate to your question. It is therefore best to wait until you become more sensitive to the energies of the day and to your own consciousness. The best time to ask a question is between meals or late at night when the activity of the day has subsided and you are alone without distractions.

3) Keep a special notebook for recording your questions. Each time you make a divination, write down the date and the question. Make your question as simple and direct as you can. If it is not clear there can be no correct response. Since your objective mind is the medium to which the *I Ching* responds, how you form your question is very important. If you ask in a

positive way, your positive energy will be reflected in
the answer. Similarly, your doubt or confusion will also influence the response. So, before you make a divination, be sure to calm yourself. Your breathing and
energy must be even and quiet. If your mind is scattered or full of thoughts, or if you have just completed
physical activities, you will not receive an accurate response. Your mind is like a pond of water; when the
water is quiet, the image is clearly reflected. If you
throw a stone into the pond, the reflection becomes
distorted. The *I Ching* is a mirror of your mind, thus
it is of great importance that it be still and lucid.
Then, as you consult the *I Ching*, the right image will
appear because your outer and inner energies will be
in accord.

When formulating a question, it is wise to consider
your approach. The function of the *I Ching* is to guide
us in harmonizing our dualistic nature.   Therefore,
questions which require a yes or no answer are not
appropriate.   To ask the consequence of an action or
undertaking under consideration, or the appropriate
conduct within a particular situation, are examples of
the correct way to approach the *I Ching*.

4) When you are ready to ask your question you can
focus on your lower mind and your upper mind, and
enhance your concentration by using one of the following prayers:

    I. Invariable, kind virtue of the universe,
        please respond to the variable question of my
        human life.
        Show me the consequence of:

        _____.

        Tell me through the hexagram (and line)
        what my sincere mind seeks.

    II. Heaven and Earth,
        Divine Spirits and Ancient Masters,
        Your son (daughter) has a question:

        _____.

        Please respond to me
        through the system of the *I Ching*.
        I will accept this response,
        whether it shows me good fortune or
        misfortune.

5) Initially, I do not recommend using sticks for making divinations since their use is more complicated, takes more time and requires prolonged concentration. In the beginning, any method which is simple and fast is preferred. I recommend using seeds. One good type are the seeds of cassia tora which have a beneficial effect on vision and are thus called "wise decision" seeds in Chinese medicine. However, any type of small seed or short grain rice will do. I generally do not recommend using coins, because they roll about and make noise which may disturb one's tranquility during divination. But, if you do not feel troubled with coins or sticks (or any other method), then feel free to use them.

How to Use the Seeds

Pick up a few seeds between your middle finger and thumb. Carefully and respectfully place them on a sheet of clean paper. This is done six time in succession. Each small cluster of seeds is placed so as to form a line starting from the bottom of the sheet working upward. Each cluster represents one line of the hexagram.

Next, translate the six clusters into the language of yin and yang in order to find the hexagram. This is done by counting the seeds in each group. If there is an even number of seeds, this will be translated as a yin line, (· ; or − −. An odd number will be a yang line, (·) or ——.

Following is an illustration of this process. Remember that the order is always from the bottom upward.

If the sixth (top)	group has 8 seeds:	Yin	— —
If the fifth	group has 7 seeds:	Yang	——
If the fourth	group has 6 seeds:	Yin	— —
If the third	group has 5 seeds:	Yang	——
If the second	group has 4 seeds:	Yin	— —
If the first (bottom)	group has 3 seeds:	Yang	——

Now, to determine the hexagram you have received, you can consult the chart listed on page 213. Since the hexagram is read from the bottom up, the lower three lines in the example given above compose the lower trigram or ☲ , Fire; and the top three lines compose the upper trigram or ☵ , Water. By looking down the left column and locating the lower trigram Li, Fire, and then moving across until you are below K'an, Water, you will find number 63, the hexagram Chi Chi, "After Crossing the Water."

You now have an overall response to your question. In order to know where your specific circumstance lies within that overall view, you must find the line which most specifically reflects your situation. To do this, you ask your question again and pick up one more cluster of seeds. If you have six or less, then whatever you have - 6,5,4, etc. - is the number of your line. If you have more than six, then subtract six from the total number, and the remainder indicates the number of your line. For example, if you have nine seeds, three is your line; if you have six or twelve seeds, the top line is your line; if you have eleven seeds, five is your line, and so forth.

This line is not the same as the changing line which might be obtained if you used the coin or stick method of divination. When using the seed method, only one hexagram and one line are obtained, providing the general background and specific guidance for your question. A more complicated system is not necessarily more effective. One can become confused by too many changing lines. With too much information, it is difficult to make a good interpretation; thus one loses the benefit of using the *I Ching*. Therefore, the simpler method of using seeds is recommended to insure greater accuracy.

If you approach the *I Ching* with composure and centeredness, you will receive a clear answer. In general, it is appropriate to ask a question only once. When one is anxious about some matter and receives a hexagram or line which does not affirm one's wish, the tendency is to ask again. To ask the same question a second or third time will not necessarily bring a proper response; even worse, you may even get a "scolding" from the *I Ching* for lack of faith or disrespect. However, if you really do not understand the response at all, it is allowed to rephrase the question and ask again, but never ask a third time.

It should be pointed out that occasionally, when you ask a particular question, the *I Ching* will respond with an answer that refers to something other than what you asked. This indicates a response to your deepest and most urgent problem rather than to your more superficial question. Do not be so rigidly focused on your question that you fail to recognize a warning concerning a much more serious circumstance that surrounds you. The *I*

Ching responds to your total being, but unfortunately most people are not consciously aware of all that goes on in their lives. Always remain open to the possibility of a response to something deep within your being. The practice of *I Ching* is not involved with your conscious mind alone. Correctly speaking, the practice of divination is involved with the depth of your spiritual cultivation and the response of the Divine Realm to it. Often people do not know what is going to happen, but the *I Ching* knows.

You may hesitate to consult the *I Ching* because you are afraid it will discourage you from acting upon your wishes. This is unfortunate, because even if the guidance is contrary to your desires, it will always give you constructive advice. There is no reason to distrust or fear the *I Ching*. It is always a faithful, trustworthy friend. It understands us with a depth that greatly exceeds our own limited vision, and it always speaks the truth. The problem is that we sometimes fear the truth, but in the *I Ching* truth and safety are twins.

It is often very difficult to accept information about something which is troubling you. If you ask for advice or guidance, you must always be willing to hear the response. Be honest with yourself and try to recognize your own level. Do not fool yourself by asking a question when you are already attached to the anticipated answer. To hold fast to one way of thinking will only keep your mind narrow and your life devoid of greater possibilities.

There are often times when a situation is too overwhelming for one's mind to remain detached and objective. If you are confronting such an emotional matter, sometimes the very process of making a divination has a centering effect that can calm your impulsiveness. If not, it is wise to seek the help of a professional *I Ching* consultant or an adept practitioner. This is how the *I Ching* has been used in China by professional people and the general public.

The methods and information contained in this book are the most fundamental. There are more complex and specific uses of the *I Ching*, but they should be learned only after you have a firm grasp of the basics.

Photo Credit: *Marvin Smallheizer, T'ai Chi Magazine*

guide for finding the hexagrams

UPPER TRIGRAM / LOWER TRIGRAM	chyah ☰ heaven	chen ☳ thunder	K'an ☵ water	Ken ☶ mountain	K'un ☷ earth	sun ☴ wind	Li ☲ fire	tui ☱ lake
chyah ☰ heaven	1	34	5	26	11	9	14	43
chen ☳ thunder	25	51	3	27	24	42	21	17
K'an ☵ water	6	40	29	4	7	59	64	47
Ken ☶ mountain	33	62	39	52	15	53	56	31
K'un ☷ earth	12	16	8	23	2	20	35	45
sun ☴ wind	44	32	48	18	46	57	50	28
Li ☲ fire	13	55	63	22	36	37	30	49
tui ☱ lake	10	54	60	41	19	61	38	58

(Figure 111)

易與天地準，故能彌綸天地之道。仰以
觀于天文，俯以察于地理，是故知幽明
之故。原始反終，故知死生之說。精氣為物，
游魂為變，是故知鬼神之情況，與天地相
似，故不違；知周乎萬物，而道濟天下，故
不過，旁行而不流。樂天知命故不憂，安
土敦乎仁，故能愛。範圍天地之化而不過，
曲成萬物而不遺，通乎晝夜之道而知。故
神无方而易无體。

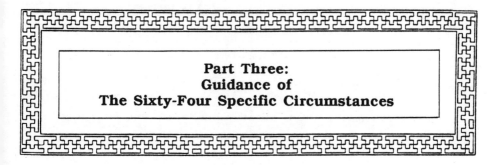

Part Three:
Guidance of
The Sixty-Four Specific Circumstances

The SIXTY-FOUR HEXAGRAMS

no.	Chinese	Close English Meaning	Familiar Spelling	Pinyin Roumaji	no.	Chinese	Close English Meaning	Familiar Spelling	Pinyin Roumaji
1	乾	positiveness the creative	ch'ian	qian	33	遯	retreat	tun	dun
2	坤	receptiveness	k'un	kun	34	大壯	great strength	ta chuang	da zhuang
3	屯	to be stationed to assemble	chun	zhun	35	晉	progress	jihn	jin
4	蒙	the undeveloped one	meng	meng	36	明夷	the time of darkness	min yin	ming yi
5	需	waiting stagnation hesitation	shiu	xu	37	家人	family	chia jen	jia ren
6	訟	dispute (litigation)	sung	song	38	睽	opposition disharmony	kwei	kui
7	師	military leadership	shih	shi	39	蹇	obstruction	jien	jian
8	比	fellowship	beh	bi	40	解	dissolution of the problem	hsieh	xie
9	小畜	small accumulation	shau chu	xiao chu	41	損	sacrifice decrease	suen	sun
10	履	conduct	lu	lü	42	益	benefit, increase	yi	yi
11	泰	peace harmony good opportunity	tai	tai	43	夬	resolution	kui	guai
12	否	misfortune	pi	pi	44	姤	encounter meeting together	kou	gou
13	同人	uniting with people	tung ren	tong ren	45	萃	congregation gathering the essence	tsui	cui
14	大有	great provider great harvest	ta yuo	da you	46	升	rising	sheng	sheng
15	謙	modesty, egolessness	chien	qian	47	困	besieged entrapped exhausted	kun	kun
16	豫	comfort	yu	yu	48	井	well	jing	jing
17	隨	compliance following	sui	sui	49	革	revolution reformation	gir	ge
18	蠱	correcting the corruption	ku	gu	50	鼎	caldron harmonization & stability	ting	ding
19	臨	advancing	lin	lin	51	震	the arousing force of thunder	chen	zhen
20	觀	contemplation point of view	kuan	gaan	52	艮	keeping still impediment	ken	gen
21	噬嗑	biting through hardship	shih ho	shi he	53	漸	gradualness	jen	jian
22	賁	adornment, beautification	be	bi	54	歸妹	marriage	kuei mei	gui mei
23	剝	erosion, decline	po	bo	55	豐	over, capacity	fong	feng
24	復	revival, renewal	fu	fu	56	旅	traveling	lu	lu
25	无妄	innocence unexpected happening	wu wan	wu wang	57	巽	gentle wind submissiveness	soen	sun
26	大畜	great amassment	ta ch'u	da chu	58	兌	joyousness	tui	dui
27	頤	providing nourishment	i	yi	59	渙	dispersion	huan	huan
28	大過	great excess	ta kuo	da guo	60	節	self-restraint	chieh	jie
29	坎	the abyss	k'an	kan	61	中孚	faithfulness	chung fu	zhong fu
30	離	radiance	li	li	62	小過	minor excess	shiao kuo	xiao guo
31	咸	mutual attraction	hsien	xian	63	既濟	after crossing the water	chi chi	ji ji
32	恆	constancy	heng	heng	64	未濟	before crossing the water	wei chi	wei chi

(Figure 112)

1 乾 chyan ䷀

positiveness · the creative

GUIDANCE: *"Be creative with these basic yang virtues: initiative, progressiveness, supportiveness and persistence."*

The great Oneness expresses itself through the perpetually interacting and integrating energies of yin and yang. Of the two, yang is the primary mover and initiator. When it moves, it creates time and space and transforms all things in the manifest universe while, at the same time, remains beyond time and space. Being self-generating and self-motivating, it has no creator and is therefore sometimes confused with a personalized concept of God. Universal yang energy is the true creator, positive performer and endless generator of all that exists. It is beyond conceptualization.

When yang moves, yin becomes apparent. Like an object and its shadow, these two energies cannot exist separately. Although yang is the initiator, it is not correct to think that it precedes yin, for at their deepest levels the creative and receptive beget one another, the dynamic and responsive sustain one another, the progressive and recessive exist in one another. Whereas yang is expansive, stimulating and transforming, yin completes, structures and accomplishes what has been initiated by yang. Yin perfectly complements yang by being responsive, consolidating, sustaining and conserving.

It must also be remembered that there is always yin within yang and yang within yin. Their relationship is best symbolized by the T'ai Chi symbol ☯ , which represents both their duality and unity. When these two energies interact, all things manifest and evolve. However, the ultimate truth is that they have never separated, and dualities of every kind are only the result of a fragmentary and incomplete view of the great Oneness.

The hexagram Chyan ䷀ is comprised of all yang lines. Yang energy is symbolized by the image of a dragon which usually represents any powerful natural force. A swift, violent electrical storm, a raging fire or a powerful wind all represent "dragon" energy. These natural forces were understood and utilized by ancient achieved ones whose minds, spirits, lives and beings never separated natural and supernatural influences.

For a human to express "dragon" energy, he must have all four yang virtues. Once this is accomplished, one's life is natural and normal, blessed with plainness, smoothness and joyfulness. Thus, this hexagram teaches the virtues of being positive, creative, progressive and persevering, all of which build a strong foundation for a universal life.

Our spiritual value is not dependent on pleasing some conceptual God. It is the result of the way we harmonize our yin and yang energies. The truth is that human nature already is Heavenly nature, and Heavenly nature is human nature. There is no other nature. Even our lowest impulses are part of this nature. We do not create them, nor is anyone else responsible for them. What is important is how we integrate our energies and how we express our nature. We have the choice to indulge our impulses or to spend our time cultivating inner and outer harmony.

Because it is the nature of the human mind to see things single-mindedly, people generally recognize only one side of an issue and tend to emphasize that side over another. They are either blindly religious or blindly materialistic. They tend to over-react or under-react to different situations in their lives. This hexagram and the entire text of the *I Ching* helps us learn how to respond appropriately in different circumstances, as well as when and when not to extend our 'dragon' energy. Only then will we fulfill our natural virtue.

Most people neglect the fact that all things have both a yin and a yang aspect and that true progress is made only when they are in harmony. Yin and yang are like two wings that, through their own natural movement, can help us rise above our worldly problems. Because our artificial cultures encourage us to seek fulfillment outside ourselves, most people never take the time to look within and harmonize their yang and yin aspects. They never learn that their simple, natural being is already whole, and if they would only maintain their own naturalness and normalcy there would be no need to do anything else to make them great or holy.

In ancient times, sages did not need external devices to help them. They were guided by their own integral natures. Through sincerity and purity, the door of universal natural truth was opened to them. By following the examples of nature, they fulfilled their lives and provided us with pure examples of how to live in accord with the universal integral path.

True sincerity is the integration of our being and is the highest power and virtue that one can have. With sincerity, one becomes pure and egoless. Thus, one can reach the Heavenly Realm and alter destinies of individuals, families or even entire nations. One's sincere mind is as powerful as a "dragon." It is the highest universal energy and can even make things manifest and become substantial. What once was subtle and hidden becomes visible and powerful.

LINE 1: *"When the potency of a dragon has not yet emerged, it is not time to try to use it."*

In the first stage, one's positive, or yang energy, is still hidden. The I Ching advises self-cultivation because it is not yet time to take action.

LINE 2: *"The powerful dragon appears on a vast field. It is time to meet the Great One."*

This line responds to the fifth line. One needs to set one's sights on a great and just goal and offer one's energy to a great leader.

LINE 3: *"The dragon is cautious and uses its power wisely. One of self-awareness cultivates in the daytime and is alert at night. This is difficult but correct."*

The positive energy of the lower trigram now develops and pushes upward to the higher spheres. This is a precarious situation and one must be very cautious; the result could go either way.

This line is an especially important one for the individual who practices self-cultivation. It advises one to beware of temptation and be cautious throughout the entire day. One should also avoid anything that causes deviation from the path.

LINE 4: *"The dragon jumps into the water and disappears. No fault."*

In this line, the dragon has matured and is strong enough to do as he wishes. However, he is wise enough to know that he cannot compete with the strength of the leader in the fifth place. Thus, he remains in a helper's position. In order not to cause disorder and confusion for himself and others, he does not push forcefully ahead.

The fourth line shows the importance of harmoniously adapting to whatever situation one might be in.

LINE 5: *"The dragon flies in the sky. It is the right time for the Great One to make full use of his energy and presence."*

Anything can be accomplished at this time because one is at the height of one's energy. Do not miss this golden opportunity to extend your energy and make full use of your cultivation. Understanding this, the wise one does not hesitate to take action, yet knows when to stop. Power can endure only when one uses it correctly.

LINE 6: *"The dragon extends too far. Extremes bring remorse."*

During these times, one should be aware of the natural law that when anything reaches its fullest it must decline. Here the dragon's power has begun to weaken, for it has been pushed to its extreme. Any extreme action should be avoided.

SPECIFIC GUIDANCE

PERSONAL FORTUNE: You should be diligent and cultivate virtue.

MARRIAGE: It will be a good marriage. The woman is beautiful and upright. However, beware of a troublesome "matchmaker" or someone else who might cause some miscommunication.

HOUSING/FAMILY: It is not peaceful, but do not move to another country.

TRADE/BUSINESS: It is profitable to buy goods.

SEARCHING FOR SOMEONE: They will come late, maybe after ten days.

LOOKING FOR SOMETHING LOST: It can be found. Go to the Southwest or someplace where there are trees and stones. Look among them, it is there.

HUNTING FOR THIEVES: They are difficult to find. They are hiding in the woods or mountains.

LAWSUIT: Peace can be made.

CLIMATE: There will be a great drought until autumn when there will be rain. With this sign, there is also the possibility that the weather during the day will be fine, but it will rain at night.

TRAVEL: Not good to travel alone, it will be a happy occasion if you travel with company. (The reason is that, in this hexagram, six yang energies are connected together as a team.)

DISEASE: The malady is exhaustion or edema. The energy is not flowing in the proper channels; there is disorder. The energy flowing upward creates discomfort. It may be a very serious disease. If you are asking about a serious disease, this sign could indicate death.

PERSONAL WISH: Nothing can be achieved in a hurry. Movement brings remorse. To retreat brings no trouble. Untimely action loses the opportunity. If a woman gets this hexagram, it means she may be too strong, and she should be careful of that.

COMMENTARY
The Primal Chi

How can the universe be alive? Because it is the continual transformation of primal chi, the pivotal energy and living soul of the universe. Primal chi functions as the subtle connection of the universe in the same way that the nervous system functions in the human body. It extends itself primordially as the self-nature of the universe. It then extends itself further as the main spheres of reality, the manifest and the unmanifest.

In the unmanifest sphere, called pre-Heaven, there is nothing describable nor discernible; there is only absolute, undivided oneness. In the manifest sphere of post-Heaven three-dimensional developments are revealed as spirit, matter and life. The diversification of primal chi becomes the multiplicity of individual things and beings.

Although the manifestations of primal chi are many, the reality is one. Expressing the oneness of the universe, it is given the name "Tao." Expressing flexible and transformable reality, it is given the name "chi."

When primal chi is unexpressed and untransformed, it is the essence of the universe with inexhaustible potency. When it is expressed, it takes the form of the mother giving birth to her child.

By understanding that all things in the universe are just different expressions of chi, one can see why the sages have always said, "All things are one, and the one is all things." Without the outreach and withdrawal, the giving and returning of chi, the transformation of all things would be impossible.

According to spiritual thought, Heaven is not separate from the material sphere as it is in most Western religions. The natural heaven has many energy levels that include all spheres of manifestation. In other words, everything in the universe is a manifestation of Heaven, and everyone is potentially a heavenly being.

The four great realms of heaven include: chi as the first, spirit as the second, matter as the third and life as the fourth. The pure and light chi develops into spirits. The impure and heavy chi develops into matter. From the integration of both comes life, thus chi is spirit, chi is matter, and chi is life. Chi is the basic essence of the universe. Nothing that exists can be without it, though it is not everything itself. When regarded as the invisible, untouchable, inaudible, insubstantial substance of the universe, the primal chi is Tao, the path itself. All things manifest or develop from it. In this same way, chi as life can also be differentiated.

A well-trained Kung Fu expert can break stones with his hands as easily as one can cut through a watermelon, and in numerous other ways he can demonstrate his truly unusual powers. It is the chi he has gathered and cultivated which enables him to do these things.

Look at the person who can walk on glowing coals. It is chi which enables him to do so. Look at a psychic who moves a chair from one side of a room to the other by either gazing at it or thinking of it.   It is chi which makes this possible.   Or the woman who gives birth to a dozen children and still looks young and healthy.   Again, it is chi which makes this possible.   And look at the exceptionally long life of a developed one who lives in the mountains.   It is chi which makes this possible.

In an integral or holistic life, the word "chi" has many usages.   There is chi in spiritual cultivation, chi in integral, natural medicine, chi in philosophical discussions and chi in everyday use, as in the atmosphere and one's general condition.   The usage of the word corresponds to its particular application.   Similarly, the discovery and understanding of chi corresponds to the level of one's personal development.

Spiritual cultivation is totally involved with the knowledge and technique of nurturing and managing chi.   After thoroughly understanding chi, one's perception of universal reality becomes deepened, and with it comes the possibility of high spiritual achievement.   The summoning of a spirit becomes as sure and trustworthy as extending an invitation to a good friend.

Ordinary religions believe that God can do things that are impossible for human beings to accomplish.   This is not completely accurate, unless one thoroughly understands that God is chi and, at the same time, spirit.   By understanding chi it becomes clear in one's mind that all things are possible by managing chi.   What you beseech God to do for you does indeed happen.   But what actually makes it happen?   It is chi.   How does chi make it happen?   Since one's personal cultivation corresponds to the chi, it responds.   This activity goes on, not only on the spiritual level, but on the everyday level of life.

To become "pure chi" is the goal of this immortal tradition.   When one's chi becomes purified, one's spirit becomes complete.   Then a new immortal is born in the Immortal Realm.   Is this not an important and serious matter for everyone?[1]

---

[1](See the author's work *Tao, the Subtle Universal Law*, for more illustrations of chi.)

2 坤 K'un

⚏⚏

Receptiveness

GUIDANCE: *"Receptiveness, like a mare following its mate, brings good results. It is beneficial for one of righteousness to pursue his goal. There may be confusion in the beginning, but one eventually finds the right way. Due to the energy correspondence, one finds support in the southwest and unfriendliness in the northeast. Being peaceful will enhance your receptivity and will bring good fortune."*

K'un represents the virtues of Earth. Chyan represents the virtues of Heaven. Heavenly or yang energy is the active, initiating force of the universe and is creative, productive and progressive. Earthly or yin energy allows all things to become manifest and is cooperative, obedient, submissive and receptive. It is symbolized by a mare or a cow, while Chyan is symbolized by a stallion or a dragon. The cow and ox, animals renowned for their submissiveness, supply the patient labor that has powered agriculture and life for generations. Therefore, Chyan and K'un, stallion and mare, are naturally paired.

K'un needs the creative Chyan to be its leader. Each line of this hexagram encourages one to follow a great person, a great goal or a great principle. This hexagram also expresses the essential process of self-development. Becoming a good follower requires practicing the highest virtues of K'un, as expressed in the teaching of the *Tao Teh Ching* where the great sage Lao Tzu emphasizes being soft, gentle, compliant and humble. These virtues are the essence of K'un and also of the Earth. Too many people struggle to be above, and this has led to all the disturbances and wars in the world. People never realize that their true significance and worth reside in the very being of their individual lives, and that mother Earth and the entire universe embrace all beings equally. Is there any true advantage in being "above" someone else? If people stopped this useless vanity, there would be no more contention in the world.

Every truthful individual life is like the Earth, low and receptive, motherly and gentle, giving support to everyone and everything selflessly without discrimination. To be like the Earth is to be like Heaven.

K'un and Chyan exemplify yin and yang in that they complement each other. Developed beings know that yin and yang are expressions of oneness; only the one whose view is partial thinks their energies are in conflict. In the image of T'ai Chi, ☯ , however, one can clearly see their harmonious relationship.

Through the interaction of yin and yang, wholeness is expressed and all life is produced and nourished. All movement and matter in the universe is an expression of yin and yang. Male and female, inhalation and exhalation, sound and silence, subject and object: nothing exists that is not an integration of these energies. In spiritual cultivation, every person can experience yin and yang energy within himself. Since a person is a microcosm of the universe, by balancing these natural energies, one will be able to realize a complete "universe" within oneself.

The movement of natural energy is constant, cyclic and takes place on many different levels at the same time. Some cycles are easy to recognize on this planet, such as the change of seasons. The earth spinning on its axis and traveling around the sun helps illustrate the variations of earthly cycles, which in turn are influenced by all the heavenly cycles. In keeping with the spirit of K'un, the abundance of Earth is derived from its receptiveness to all beneficial Heavenly influences.

The guidance suggests that one is able to find friends in the southwest but not in the northeast. This refers to the location where King Wen's virtuous leadership resided and offers the clue to follow the virtuous and wise one.

In the search for truth, people often lose themselves in the beginning because they do not know exactly what truth is. Though initially there may be some difficulty and misfortune, clarity gradually develops with experience. One may discover that it is the quest for truth that provides the real security and unfailing guidepost in one's life. The result of this search is a continuous expansion of inner vision. This is the only correct understanding to have until you discover that the direction of your life is the integrity of life itself.

One should also be cautious on the pathway because it is easy to become lost when one insists that the point that has been reached is a final or complete truth. If one's mind is active and attached to things on a general, discernible level, the truth can never be reached. In the beginning, it is important to proceed with caution. As the journey is accomplished, that which was not formalized or stabilized in early life will become solid and correctly supported. Thus, good fortune will result. When the right inner and outer goals have been found, one must continue to work on them until they merge into one. The result is true integration of one's being.

LINE 1:   *"When walking on frost, be careful; ice is surely ahead. One should be circumspect in beginning."*

In Chyan, the first line represents an unexpressed potential. Here, the first line remains gentle and cautious in order to not create difficulties when beginning new tasks. In Autumn, dew turns into frost and water into ice. A harmless-looking frost may have ice under it, thus danger may be just underfoot.

The early stages of an undertaking always require tact and caution. Just as one should walk carefully on ice, one should proceed cautiously in beginning the journey toward one's goal in life. Initially one frequently experiences confusion as to the best approach to take. Lacking clarity, one may meet with unnecessary danger.

One who pretends to have complete knowledge for the sake of saving face becomes trapped by foolish pride. There should be no shame connected with being careful in the beginning.

LINE 2:   *"By being upright and natural, things naturally go well."*

In both Chyan and Kun, the virtue of the second line is to earnestly seek guidance from a great advisor or teacher. This line simply suggests: "Be honest like the Earth." There is nothing more honest than the Earth. Just be as plain and honest as you are by nature. Surely this is a blessing! With Lao Tzu's deep vision of nature, his primary guidance for practical life is to be honest like the Earth.

This line is guided by the balanced light of the fifth line. Because this is a valuable guide, the second line obeys it with total compliance. Therefore, a great harvest is reaped from what has been planted.

LINE 3:   *"Being humble is beneficiaL   Work for the public good.   Proceed with care."*

In Chyan, good fortune is brought about through unconcern for external things and through practicing self-cultivation.   In this hexagram, the third line is benefited by being unconcerned with personal matters and by being devoted to the work of the Great One.   Thus one's achievement assists the leader's accomplishment.   This line selflessly contributes energy in order for things to develop beautifully and does not seek credit for its good work.   Its offering is without vanity or attachment.   There is great good fortune for this kind of follower.   As the *Tao Teh Ching* teaches: "When a great task is accomplished, leave the honor behind and go forward."   The third line encourages one to follow this guidance in order to complete his true being.

LINE 4: *"Be self-contained.   No fame, no fault."*

In both Chyan and K'un the fourth lines stay safe by remaining self-contained.   This is a position of strength in both hexagrams, but here humility is recommended in order not to encourage one's enemies.   This wise and brave follower carries out his responsibilities and, at the same time, is like a closed sack; nobody knows what is inside. At this time, one's eagerness to express oneself should be restrained in order to avoid unnecessary disturbance.

Generally, a follower or student should be receptive to advice and put it into the closed "sack" of one's mind without passing it on to others.   It should become part of one's being before it is given to someone else.

LINE 5:   *"Great good fortune will be brought forth by being correctly centered, like yellow light among all the colors of the spectrum."*

In Chyan the fifth line represents great power.   In K'un this line represents the great light.   The greatness of each is perfectly complemented by the other.

According to ancient knowledge of the colors of all heavenly bodies, yellow is the light of the earth.   It is a rich, conspicuous color, signifying broadness and kindness.   This leader has a subtle, tactful and natural approach.   It is compelling without controlling; yielding, yet surrendering nothing.   It is beautiful, natural and selflessly virtuous. If world leaders were willing to follow this natural earthly virtue, there would be nothing wrong in the world.

LINE 6: *"Dragons fight in the wilderness. Their blood blends together."*

In the top positions of Chyan and Kun there is remorse for being excessive. Here the yin principle reaches its ultimate, but instead of integrating with its yang complement, tension arises. By being overly strong, yin competes with yang, which eventually leads to destruction.

Competitive energies bring destruction. Cooperative energies bring harmony, thus integration results when two harmonizing energies meet.

SPECIFIC GUIDANCE

PERSONAL FORTUNE: Gradually things become smooth. If you work for someone, there may be some hard work.

MARRIAGE: The marriage will be good, but things should not be hurried.

HOUSING/FAMILY: The location is a good one. Good fortune.

CHILDBIRTH: The delivery will be a safe one; the baby will be a boy. A changing first line indicates danger for the mother.

LOOKING FOR WORK: Do not hurry or you will lose some money.

SOCIAL/GOVERNMENTAL POSITION: It is possible to earn a good position and become famous.

TRADE/BUSINESS: Good.

WAITING FOR SOMEONE: Although they will not come, they will leave a message.

LOOKING FOR SOMETHING LOST: It is difficult to find, but may be found in the Northwest.

HUNTING FOR THIEVES: They have run to the Northwest and can be caught.

LAWSUIT: There is conflict over rent. One should attempt to make peace; otherwise, the suit may be lost.

CLIMATE: It will rain. However, within a twelve-day cycle, the fifth and sixth days will be fine.

TRAVEL: Westward travel is good. It is not good to go North or East.

DISEASE: Serious.

PERSONAL WISH: It can be achieved, but there are obstacles. Therefore achievement will be late.

COMMENTARY
The Balance of Life: Integrating the T'ai Chi

In the previous hexagram, Chyan ☰ , the universal first nature is discussed. The recognizable trace of the universal nature can be sensed as the qualities of initiative, persistence, forwardness, creativeness, productiveness and positivity. It symbolizes masculinity and fatherhood.

The hexagram K'un ☷ means to accomplish, continue, receive, follow, realize, formalize, shape and stabilize. It symbolizes femininity and motherhood, and expresses the self-balancing nature of the universe. Self-balancing means harmonizing with all beings and things that are brought forth.

Hands are a good example of how Chyan and K'un express themselves in the human body. Gentleness is expressed by the soft left hand, while strength is expressed by the strong right hand. Developed people value the left hand; undeveloped people value the right hand. Actually, both hands assist each other in the practical sphere of daily life.

This example also relates to the yin/yang principle and the Taoist physiology of the left and right sides of the brain and their different functions. Generally, the left side of the brain controls the sequential processes of logic, analysis, rational and scientific behavior, the right side of the body and the special processes of intuition, creativity and dreaming. A dominance in either side of the brain is apparent by observing the behavior and actions of an individual or nation. "Military aggression" can be associated with an overly dominant left side of the brain and "the strong right." Since consideration and sensitivity are associated with the right side of the brain, it is easy to see how "gentle people value the soft left hand." The Integral Way is the balance and cooperation of both hemispheres of the brain: "Use upright measures to govern the country, use a surprising approach to win the battle and to lead the world, do not apply interference or disturbance."

These ancient discoveries have been accurately utilized in natural diagnosis and acupuncture practice since the Stone Age. Right and left side brain controls are of utmost importance in acupuncture treatment. For example, in the case of someone who has become paralyzed or twisted, acupuncture needles would be applied to the side opposite that of the paralyzed side.

Pulse diagnosis in natural healing uses the different functions of the left/right sides of the brain which influence pulsation, thereby yielding the secrets of the body. The most accurate time for reading the pulse is early morning, before any mental or physical activity has had a chance to disturb or change the pulse rate.

In ancient times, some developed ones also used pulse reading as the basis for telling a person's fortune and predicting what would happen in the near or distant future. They knew that the development of both sides of a person's brain divulged the secrets and decisive factors of one's life. This same principle is also applied in palm reading, where the lines of the palm tell the secrets of the brain and thus the influence the lines have over one's whole life. When one's customary patterns of life change, the lines of one's palm correspondingly change.

Ancient integral cultural development was based on the natural reality of balance between the right and left sides of the human brain. Today that balance has obviously been lost. The modern "right-hand" culture of logic is accepted, while the ancient "left-hand" intuitive cultural achievement is mistakenly rejected.

On a more mystical level, the natural evolution of the human race in both the eastern and western hemispheres can be observed. Their tendencies and habits are interestingly contrasted with each other. Since Earth is shaped like the brain, the different developments of the east and west sides of the globe should also serve each other in beneficial ways. However, it appears that the left side of the brain is overused in today's society. The T'ai Chi symbol ☯ expresses complete balance of both sides. It resembles the brain, with even right and left halves, and the globe of the earth, with balanced east and west hemispheres. This symbol of balance, development and integration can be applied to all things and all events.

In spiritual guidance for human life, the left hand expresses harmony in the world as well as in human cultures. Earth is not only a mixture of soil, rocks and minerals, but is also a vast living organism. It is a life.

When people abuse the Earth, this behavior becomes suicidal for the entire human race.

Damage to one's integrity may also be caused by specialization. A well-trained athlete takes a long time to excel at his or her special event. One may be good at javelin throwing, hammer throwing, discus throwing, and so forth; however, the result of this type of special training generally makes the arm and leg of one side thicker than the arm and leg on the other side. In some situations, the same imbalance can seriously influence one's brain, organs, personality and total health. People who train with iron-made devices and use machines for building their muscles will probably experience a mechanical reaction in their personalities, due to the lack of natural-ness and flexibility of their bodies and minds.

Not only do physical training and sports produce unnatural results, but much learning, specific training and some professions also produce adverse effects. These effects often limit one's capabilities and interactions with others. Specialists often see only the trees without seeing the forest.

In order to achieve harmony, it is necessary to balance and integrate yin and yang as one unit. This balance is the subtle yet sustaining power of the universe. Every positive manifestation in the universe comes forth as the result of the creative, harmonious union of yin and yang energies, and each manifestation has its own unique ener-gy arrangement and pattern of movement.

Following the inherent order of the universe results in harmony and balance. Opposing this principle of natural order causes destruction. Anything that is one-sided is incomplete.

Balance can also be illustrated by the operation of the T'ai Chi principle. T'ai Chi is universal movement, a con-tinual sequence of yin and yang movements. That is how T'ai Chi Chuan originated as a form of integral cultivation. Thus, all movement, as an expression of yin and yang, should be balanced. Nothing should be excessive. If there is upward movement, there must be downward movement. If there is movement to the right, there must also be movement to the left. Inhalation and exhalation should also be coordinated to maintain balance. One should integrate the principles of T'ai Chi into one's own life. By understanding all movement, one will be able to lead a balanced, integrated life.

3 chun ䷂

to be stationed · to assemble

GUIDANCE: *"Be stationary and firm; do not move. It is helpful to establish leadership in a new community."*

In this hexagram, Water is above Thunder. Thunder indicates strong yang energy that pushes forward and is capable of breaking through obstructions. The upper trigram K'an, Water, symbolizes an abyss. Any premature movement by the yang energy is blocked, and the image of a stockpiling of energy or an assemblage of people is created. This is like water in a dam that is unable to move and therefore accumulates. Since movement in this situation will bring trouble, one can benefit by remaining stationary, gathering energy and waiting for the situation to change. Thus, there will be no negative response.

This hexagram is similar to K'an, ䷜ (#29, the Abyss), in which the trigram Water is doubled. The obstruction in K'an is more serious, however, since it is already present and will not go away. In Chun, the blockage is ahead. It is a temporary situation and will change by itself. The only problem could come from an untimely move brought about by impatience. For this reason, the hexagram advises one to be still while gathering energy and friends for a later move. When danger is present one should maintain balance and adhere to correct principles.

LINE 1: *"He lingers for a while. It is suitable to stay and settle down."*

The first line is the key line and illustrates the situation of the entire hexagram. "He" is the strong thunder. During a time of hindrance and impediment, he finds himself unable to move, thus he stays to unite others in a similar situation.

LINE 2: *"Difficulty in proceeding, like riding a horse and moving unsteadily on the way. The man is not accepted and is thought to be an invader. After many years have passed, an understanding is reached and the virtuous woman accepts his advances."*

The second line is like a weak person who is riding a strong horse (the first yang line) and is having difficulty controlling it. The fifth yang line is the correct match for the second, but because of obstructions (represented by the third and fourth yin lines), their marriage is prevented. However, their union will eventually be achieved.

The difficulty can also be illustrated by the yang line in the first position. He is very close to this line and wishes to marry her; however, he is not right for her. If she hastens to marry the first line, remorse will follow. Because she is so close to the first line, the fifth line seems like an intruder. As she has not yet understood that he is her real mate, it will take ten years for her to accept him.

LINE 3: *"Hunting without a guide, one is certain to be lost in the forest. One of balanced virtue would give up rather than follow his desire for adventure."*

The third line faces the abyss, which is represented by the upper trigram, Water. It has no correspondence with the second and fourth lines, because they too are yin energy. Thus, it is isolated and in a dangerous position.

Although the goal of this line is to reach the fifth line, a dangerous abyss lies ahead. This is like going into a dark forest to look for a deer. The goal cannot be successfully achieved and will end in trouble. Do not be tempted or stirred by illusions of possible victory.

LINE 4: *"One rides a horse hesitantly on the way to propose marriage. Go ahead; nothing will go against you. Good fortune is awaiting."*

The first line is the correct match for the fourth, and a good partnership is possible. The first line is yang, whose energy naturally ascends; the fourth line is yin, whose energy naturally descends. The opportunity for union and harmony exists, but these two lines are separated by two yin lines, which are two women who come between them and make their union a bit unsteady.

From another perspective, the fourth line represents a minister to the fifth. The relationship between the fourth and first lines is one of a good minister soliciting a trusted aide to help the leader in the fifth line.

LINE 5: *"Energy is impeded.   One cannot achieve great things, only small things."*

The fifth yang line has creative energy, is in the position of leadership and wishes to help those below him. However, his energy is blocked by the yin energy of the fourth and sixth lines.

In this position, misfortune can be changed into good fortune by cultivating and improving oneself. By improving oneself, the situation will also improve. Instead of having the qualities of the water of the abyss, one can become substantial like the earth.

LINE 6: *"Riding on a stumbling horse, blood and tears flow. This cannot continue."*

The top line does not respond to the third line and is isolated. The fifth line is limited and cannot be of any help. The difficulty seems insurmountable, thus continuing only leads to misfortune. The one way to survive this bad time is by cautiously and prudently changing oneself. Change does not come by sitting around crying.

SPECIFIC GUIDANCE

PERSONAL FORTUNE: This is a good time for personal enjoyment.

MARRIAGE: This is not a good match; hurrying makes it difficult to achieve.

HOUSING/FAMILY: Repair is needed in the northern or eastern part of the house.

CHILDBIRTH: There is difficulty. The child will be a boy.

LOOKING FOR HELP: Only with repeated begging can help be received.

SOCIAL/GOVERNMENTAL POSITION: Difficult to achieve.

TRADE/BUSINESS: Difficult to achieve.

SEARCHING FOR SOMEONE: Hurry. Even if you cannot meet them, you can still find where they live.

WAITING FOR SOMEONE: They will come.

LOOKING FOR SOMETHING LOST: It can be found where trees and grass grow luxuriantly. However, after three days, it cannot be found.

HUNTING FOR THIEVES: Search for them in the North or the West.

LAWSUIT: Be careful of trouble from a woman. By being patient and taking your time, peace can result.

CLIMATE: It will be cloudy, and it appears as if a storm is approaching.

TRAVEL: It is best to travel North and West.

DISEASE: The disease is serious and due to something stagnating inside, such as an obstacle in the chest. If the third line is received, extreme danger is indicated.

PERSONAL WISH: Difficult to achieve in a short time. It is best to remain calm.

COMMENTARY
Self-Cultivation - The Golden Key

The hexagram Chun ☷☳ means to assemble, station, or stockpile. The yang energy is blocked in both the upper and lower trigrams. In the lower trigram, ☳, the first yang line is stopped by the two yin lines. In the upper trigram, ☵, the yang line is limited by the yin lines on both sides of it. In this situation, the growth of yang energy is needed more than immediate movement. Therefore, cultivation should be applied in order to accumulate the yang, original energy.

It can be said that cultivating chi, practicing subtle virtue and attaining enlightenment are one and the same. When we do things, we also learn them. When we practice things, we also nurture ourselves. The process is almost indivisible. However, it is necessary to keep a balance among the three. On the one hand, we should always be diligent about the cultivation of bodily fitness, healthy attitudes and the correct practice of virtue and capability in our work. At the same time, we should put our cultivation to good use. Both sides of one's outlook and nature need to be balanced; this is the principle of cultivating oneself or training spiritual students in the Way.

The development of our capability, integrity, uprightness and efficiency comes from the constant work of cultivation. Without cultivation, one never has the chance to reflect on what one's life has been.

The effect of your self-cultivation shows who you really are. If you do not take the chance to correct or improve yourself, you will stay at the same undeveloped level. For example, in the practice of T'ai Chi Chuan, you can learn the complete form in three to four months. But over many years, and with daily practice, you learn the details, the breathing and the corresponding internal energy movements. Many people spend a lifetime practicing, but it never benefits them. What matters most is the internal work. T'ai Chi is not limited to superficial movement.

Self-cultivation is also one way to deepen your capacity for appreciation. The highest appreciation is the appreciation of nature's simplicity and plainness. If you have not developed the capability of deep appreciation, then your life runs down wrong alleys, and everything loses its real meaning, including your personal life. To lose the meaning of your personal life is very dangerous. It can cause great self-indulgence or even death.

In the Integral Way of life, work is very important. Before you reach enlightenment, you should use all your energy to break through the darkness. This is the pursuit of enlightenment. Because you are not enlightened, you live in darkness. Beginners often think they are enlightened, but the teachings of all great masters and spiritual books are usually completely beyond the ones who claim to understand them. This is like taking the tusks of an ancient elephant, so rare, valuable and beautiful, and putting them on a dog's mouth. The dog is still a dog. You can put the tusks of an elephant on your own mouth or you can read all the great works of the ancient masters, but without enlightenment you are still exactly the same.

People sometimes think that by staying in their present positions, without self-improvement, they can become immortal. What kind of immortal do you wish to become? Perhaps you can become an immortal bug! Improve yourself first. Some of the things you are taught with a positive purpose can motivate you to change yourself.

What is enlightenment? What is truth? What makes it so interesting? In the latter part of his life Confucius said, "If in the morning I know the truth, I am enlightened. Then, if that very evening I am dying, I am satisfied." Are you satisfied?

Equal to the importance of enlightenment in spiritual cultivation is the gaining of chi. You may think you already have chi. Surely you do. Don't you think that poison oak has chi also? All life has chi, but different people accumulate different kinds of chi in their lives. What is really valuable is to accumulate and refine your personal energy to gain divine immortal chi, which is the most refined, supreme chi of all. If you had only a little of that chi, your whole personality would be different. Having divine chi is like being a person who has a piece of jade in his bosom yet wears coarse clothing.

What kind of chi do you have? Through enlightenment, through the practice of virtue and through practical and technical cultivation, you can gain the highest chi. Without this, you are like a donkey who bears a golden saddle. You may think you are enlightened, but you are still a donkey. A spiritually achieved person is a flying horse; nobody can even catch sight of his shadow.

Practically speaking, supreme chi can be gained through correct cultivation and the consistent practice of virtue; these surely change one's being. As one's sensitivity to the natural flow of life increases, one's personal thought patterns and inner awareness begins to harmonize with truth, and enlightenment naturally follows. Through the practice of virtue and correct cultivation, one can gain the supreme chi.

The way is so simple. Work on your enlightenment in order to change your darkness. This does not mean that enlightenment itself has such a high value; the value is taking away your darkness.

How do you take away darkness formed by many lifetimes so that you finally become enlightened? By working hard to become spiritual? Unfortunately, for many, this is like putting the cart before the horse and can even increase the darkness. Rather, look toward the purification, refinement and cultivation of your being to bring forth your awakening. As you work to eliminate your darkness, your spiritual eyes will naturally open.

Equally important is the consistent practice of virtue and development of personal conduct in accord with what is positive and good, vital and enlivening. Your virtue is the energy and fragrance of your life and your golden key to crystal clear vision. If your personality has become contaminated, work on cleansing it. Be assured that when you change yourself inside, it is naturally expressed outside. There is no need to buy and wear a golden saddle - just become a special donkey.

The core of the Integral Way is not a matter of faith. Religious faith is connected with what and how you believe. Faith works by belief. It is like being taught that fire is cold. If you believe that fire is cold, even when burned by it, if you have survived, you will still think it is cold. The Way does not promote rigid, blind faith which can induce psychological or hypnotic effects that are fragile in truth and lacking in durability. The Integral Way is a matter of understanding and doing. The Integral Way inspires, enlightens and opens you up for higher integration. With this training, you might become an authority over mundane and eternal life. The Integral Way teaches openness; through openness you reach the essence in order to develop your being. It is the path of open-ended growth. The secret of eternal life is beyond conceptual exploration. It is the highest scientific secret, expressed in riddles, puzzles and metaphors. No wise person can decode them or fit the pieces of understanding together into the whole picture unless he is a real student, guided by divine immortal selection. At this level, it is not only extremely difficult for a pupil to find a teacher, it is also difficult for an achieved one to find the right person to whom he can pass the knowledge of divine immortality. It is not a matter of closeness, as the relationship of father and son. It is a matter of being the "right one."

The *Tao Teh Ching* says that Tao is invisible, inaudible and untouchable. This description is appropriate for the spiritually undeveloped, but to those who are spiritually developed the truth is visible, audible and touchable. It always exists. However, as all forms are the form of Tao, no particular form can be insisted on as being Tao.

4 meng

zhe undeveloped one

GUIDANCE: *"Go ahead to enlighten undeveloped ones, but it should be the undeveloped one who makes the request, not the teacher. He should approach with sincerity."*

This is also the way to consult the I Ching. The correctness of the answer received depends upon the sincerity of the request. If the same question is asked many times, the mind will become scattered and the energy violated. Thus, a correct response cannot be reached.

In this hexagram, Water is at the foot of the Mountain, creating the image of fog covering a mountain range. Such a condition represents one who lacks clarity. At the base of the mountain there are many small streams that flow in various directions. This represents a condition of bewilderment and confusion because of too much divergence. On a human level it symbolizes a person who is undeveloped, unguided or uncivilized.

Mountain, $\equiv\!\equiv$, represents an uneducated youth. Water, $\equiv\!\equiv$, represents an experienced, middle-aged man. The young man has presumed and put himself above the developed one instead of following him. Such actions mean that one follows impulse instead of wisdom. When the Chinese word "meng" is used as a verb, it means to cover in darkness.

Scattered energy and people with no direction are basically useless. In order to be fully used, one's energy must be properly channeled or stored. This is the meaning of cultivating oneself and refining one's character.

Both this hexagram and the previous one, Chun, represent the beginning of the process of development. This is the time of a new beginning for an uncivilized society and is like the early stage of a seed, newly sprouted and still covered with earth.

The yin lines of this hexagram represent the student, and the yang lines represent the teacher. Their interaction on various levels is expressed by the explanation of each line. The first line represents the undeveloped, unenlightened one who has many difficulties due to ignorance. Everyone has gone through this stage. Regardless of how old one is or how much one already knows, there always remains much to be learned. The second line is responsible for enlightening and educating others. He is a teacher, not a ruler, so he must have patience and be tolerant of the uneducated when instructing them. The third line represents one who is ambitious, ignorant and unreceptive to proper guidance. The fourth line exhibits another type of foolishness - pride. Since he does not listen to the teacher, he becomes trapped in difficulty and bitterness. The fifth line represents the wise one who constantly seeks self-correction and self-cultivation. He is pure, receptive and willing to take the good advice of others. Certainly one so wise will be blessed with good fortune. The top line is beyond help. At this point, education alone will not suffice; discipline is also needed as a protection and a correction.

LINE 1: *"When enlightening the undeveloped, restraint and discipline should be applied. If the undeveloped ones are left unregulated, there will be trouble later on."*

Punishment and regulation should be established and imposed in order to restrain one's wildness. This kind of restraint serves as a channel to regulate one's energy so that one may become useful. This line symbolizes the early stages when one needs strict guidelines as the framework within which to develop.

LINE 2: *"Having tolerance toward the undeveloped brings good fortune. This simple virtue also applies to family life. If one's child knows this, he will become a responsible person."*

The second yang line, the only teacher in the hexagram, is surrounded by four yin lines which represent the uneducated. He must have the tolerance necessary to educate them according to their individual levels and needs. Thus, good fortune results for all.

This line can also apply to marriage. Because it has the proper correspondence with the yin line in the fifth position, a harmonious marriage may be achieved.

The second line is responsible for giving the hexagram a positive overall perspective. Within the context of a family, it represents a mature, responsible son who has a good relationship with everyone. In fulfilling duties and responsibilities to the family, one's energy is positively channeled.

LINE 3: *"Do not marry a woman who only seeks a wealthy man. There is no benefit in this marriage."*

The third line represents an ambitious woman (a yin line in a yang position) who is seeking marriage to someone in a high position. The top line, a yang line in a yin position, is also in an incorrect position. He has wealth, but no virtue. Because they do not come together out of true love, the marriage is of no benefit.

One may wonder why the relationship between the second and fifth lines, so similar to that of the third and sixth lines, can have such different consequences. Though they are complementary, none of the lines are in their correct positions. The second and the fifth lines, however, are centered in their own trigrams and are responsible for what they do.

Each hexagram has a certain balance, and within that structure, the second and fifth positions are usually the lines responsible for harmonizing the other positions. Although their energies are inverted in this hexagram, they fulfill their duty with the highest virtue. On the other hand, the third and sixth lines also have a yin/yang correspondence and have the same inverted relationship. In their positions of excessiveness, however, it is difficult for them to achieve true harmony.

LINE 4: *"Stubborn and ignorant, one is helpless."*

By holding onto an unreceptive, stubborn attitude toward the wise, or being unwilling to seek the advice of a teacher, one brings about misfortune and humiliation. One who is ignorant must be willing to learn and accept correction. If one is satisfied with being ignorant, then one is a helpless fool! Isolation and ignorance will become a trap, and one will be unable to find one's way back.

LINE 5: *"Enlightening the undeveloped and innocent. Good fortune."*

The child is willing to receive an education. (He can follow the second line as a teacher or the top line as an advisor.) Good fortune comes naturally by being receptive and flexible. Accepting teachings and advice with an empty and humble mind, one is assured of positive growth and high achievement.

LINE 6: *"Punishing the undeveloped is a good, protective measure. Thus, the pupil will not be tempted to repeat the same mistakes."*

The third line is the "pupil" of the top line. The pupil is incorrect in behavior, the teacher is justifiably stern and punishment is applied. Thus, correction produces cooperation.

Also symbolized is the correct attitude when defending oneself. One should rightfully defend oneself, but not attack others. One should not use the ways of robbers to deal with robbers. A true peace lover does not use war to stop war.

SPECIFIC GUIDANCE

PERSONAL FORTUNE: One will have lots of hard work.

MARRIAGE: Difficult to achieve.

HOUSING/FAMILY: Housing will be good if located close to a mountain with water.

CHILDBIRTH: It will be safe.

LOOKING FOR HELP: In the beginning, there is no cooperation. Later on, with the help of a negotiator, the goal can be achieved.

SOCIAL/GOVERNMENTAL POSITION: If it is a promotion, good fortune will follow.

TRADE/BUSINESS: It will be achieved later.

SEARCHING FOR SOMEONE: They are difficult to find because they do not have a stable place to live.

WAITING FOR SOMEONE: They will come late because something has happened on the way.

LOOKING FOR SOMETHING LOST: It is in a house, grave or garden.

HUNTING FOR THIEVES: They are difficult to find.

LAWSUIT: The trouble may have been started by other people, but it can be settled as you wish.

CLIMATE: It will rain.

TRAVEL: Dangerous. You will lose money, or it will be a terribly expensive trip.

DISEASE: There is an internal spasm or difficulty, perhaps with diarrhea. It will be difficult to cure in a short time.

PERSONAL WISH: In the beginning, there is difficulty, but later it can be achieved.

COMMENTARY
The Light in One's Personality

Following what is right
is like a stream flowing toward the ocean.

Keeping one's innate virtue
  is the true foundation of happiness.
Through practicing great virtue,
  one can change one's personality
  and alter one's life.
One's life will then be peaceful and long.
Persevere in doing things
  only of a giving and constructive nature,
  and your heart will become pure and free of
  negativity.

Extend the care you cultivate in your own family
  to all things and creatures surrounding your house,
  such as the plants and the animals.
When you make an error, correct it as best you can,
  and do not harbor guilt within.
Be earnest in all you do.
Soften your disposition,
  and be thorough in your good conduct.
Do not do anything that cannot be exposed to
  daylight;
  it will be seen in the subtle realm of Heaven
  as a flash of lightning.
See virtue as your main goal in life,
  and enjoy helping others.
Never let an opportunity to help pass.
To be honest, faithful, trustworthy and sincere
  is to be carefree.
If your virtue and your talents are equally good,
  you are a superior person.
If you want your good deeds to be seen by others,
  the good is lost.
Do good for the sake of doing good,
  and do not expect anything in return.
Take care of little things;
  be diligent in caring for life.
Educate others by setting the right example,
  not by preaching.
Do not promise lightly;
  and when you promise, keep it.
Never tire of the pursuit
  of the actualization of your inherent virtue.
Turn your mind to what is deep,
  abandon the shallow.
Develop a strong heart with the virtues of
  benevolence, humanitarianism, justice and kindness.

Care for all without partiality;
  be sincere and guileless.
Maintain right conduct, control passion.
As one's virtues increase daily, so will one's health.
Do not express any negative energy
  in thought, word or action.
Humility is the root of virtue,
  but being overly humble is artful and false.
Exercising excessive pride causes decrease,
  exercising humility causes increase.
It is better to acknowledge your faults
  than to tell a lie.
Righteousness in thought, word and action
  is how the upright person preserves his integrity.
Of all vices, lewdness is the worst offender.
Do not deceive others in word, action or thought;
  know that the subtle energy responds accordingly.
Remember the law of attraction;
  what you are, think and express,
  attracts corresponding energy.
Without fail, you will meet the results
  of your positive or negative thoughts and actions.
Do not separate spiritual practices
  from your conduct in daily life;
  they should move on one channel
  and be tuned into each other.
Burning incense, sitting in meditation,
  and not correcting your behavior
  is perilous and leads nowhere.
Always remember that your true nature is virtuous,
  and by practicing diligently the virtues of life,
  you will reach purity and clarity of being.

5   霈   shiu   ☰☵

waiting · stagnation · hesitation

GUIDANCE: *"Stagnation. To overcome it, one needs faith, patience, and sincerity. Proceed with hope as if embarking on a new adventure."*

In this hexagram, Water is above Heaven, suggesting the image of clouds in the sky. Although rain is expected, it has not yet come, and anticipation is created by the delay.

Heaven expresses the energy of initiative, creativity and strength. Water symbolizes an obstruction to this heavenly energy and indicates that danger lies ahead. Though one wishes to fulfill one's needs, nothing should be done in a hurry. There is difficulty in moving forward at this time. If one advances recklessly, one will plunge directly into the "abyss." However, by gradually moving forward, the goal can be achieved.

Crossing dangerous waters is not an easy task. Therefore, one should prepare for the undertaking as one waits for the water to calm down or recede.

The possibility of achieving the goal is hinted at by the inner trigrams, Li ☲ and Tui ☱ , which symbolize warmth and excitement or enjoyment. A feast or celebration is implied due to overcoming the obstacles. In the meantime, one should focus clearly on the direction that has been set and maintain a strong conviction of success. One can easily become entrapped by Kan ☵ , the top trigram, which is ahead. Therefore, it is important to remain well balanced and maintain control. Do not give in to impulses that can lead to radical behavior.

Anxiety, expectation, need or desire can cause people to act recklessly. This is a time when either virtue or self-destruction may be achieved. The *I Ching* does not disparage the present difficulty, but emphasizes that one should do and accomplish what is needed. All things of great value are difficult to attain; nothing truly worthwhile can be attained without difficulty. The most valuable achievements and the highest goals are fraught with difficulties. The process of overcoming these obstacles is what enables one to develop inner strength. After the difficulty is overcome, one can enjoy oneself and begin to prepare for the next challenge.

The image of "Shiu" shows clouds in the sky, but only when yin and yang harmonize can the rains come. To rush around worrying or complaining will not make the rains come any sooner. The virtue of sincerity is the only power that can cause a response from nature or heaven and make all difficulties disappear. This is the most meaningful thing to be learned in life.

Each line indicates time or distance from the danger. The danger draws progressively nearer as one moves forward on the way.

LINE 1: *"Waiting in the countryside. If one is patient, there is no problem."*

The situation is not yet dangerous. The abyss, or danger, is still far away. The allusion to a rural place far from the city means that one should keep a calm and peaceful attitude. Although one feels anxious or needy, one should not rush into anything that might create disturbance.

LINE 2: *"Hesitating in the sand. A little difficulty, but the final outcome is hopeful."*

The distance from the danger or abyss has lessened and can be compared to the sand at the edge of the water. Though one may be implicated in scandalous gossip or a disagreement, it is not a serious matter. The idea of scandal comes from Tui, the inner trigram. It is associated with the mouth and represents one who speaks insultingly of another. It may also mean that one creates tension for oneself with careless gossip.

If one has patience and self-control in this situation, no real problem will manifest, and good fortune will eventually result. Maintaining calm in the midst of rumors, insults, agitation and gossip is always the best policy. Do not be discouraged or distracted by such worldly actions. By focusing on one's own goal, the disturbance will pass.

LINE 3: *"Hesitating in the swamp creates an opportunity for robbers to attack. Be cautious."*

The third line is very near the danger. It is also the middle line of the inner trigram, Tui ☱ , which represents a lake or swamp where movement is difficult. Since one is in so vulnerable a position, it is not a good place to stay. One got into this position by recklessly moving forward. However, by being extremely careful, this self-created trouble may not cause much difficulty. On the other hand, further recklessness will cause one to sink even deeper into the mud.

LINE 4: *"Hesitating in blood. Follow the strong one out of the danger."*

The fourth line of the hexagram is the first line of the upper trigram, K'an or danger. Because of the anxiety and anticipation caused by the danger, there is the tendency to run into trouble.

Because the fourth and fifth lines are in their natural order, with a yin line in the fourth position and a yang line in the fifth, a good possibility exists for cooperation between them. If the fourth line takes advantage of this opportunity and agrees to obey and cooperate with the fifth line, it will receive the support needed to get out of danger.

LINE 5: *"Waiting with wine and food, stay centered. Good fortune."*

During this time of waiting, make yourself comfortable by enjoying food and drink. Since this line is a strong yang line which is in the correct position and has the power to overcome any existing trouble, there is no reason not to enjoy oneself. However, one should remain centered and not be restless or over-indulge. Otherwise, one may invite danger.

LINE 6: *"Finally, one enters the abyss. Three unexpected guests arrive. Be nice to them because they bring good fortune."*

The top line completes the cycle of danger. There is no more need for hesitation. Three unexpected guests, who are all strong yang lines (as represented by the first, second and third lines) come to help. It is the third yang line that corresponds to this line, who brings the others. The top line responds with gentleness and caution, which can change the situation to one of peace.

SPECIFIC GUIDANCE

PERSONAL FORTUNE: Good fortune and good times have not yet come. If you push ahead, there will be trouble.

MARRIAGE: Difficult to achieve. However, if the first or fourth lines change, it can be achieved.

HOUSING/FAMILY: Now is a difficult time to be peacefully settled.

CHILDBIRTH: The baby will be a girl. There will be no problem in delivery.

LOOKING FOR HELP: It can be profitable.

SOCIAL/GOVERNMENTAL POSITION: You spend a lot of money but do not achieve any position.

TRADE/BUSINESS: Quarrels will hinder achievement.

SEARCHING FOR SOMEONE: They are now staying somewhere near you. You will meet them soon.

WAITING FOR SOMEONE: They will either be late or not come at all.

HUNTING FOR THIEVES: They are hiding with acquaintances in the North and can be caught.

CLIMATE: There will be rain for a long time (5-7 days) without stopping, then good weather will come.

TRAVEL: Good fortune. You will meet helpers and experience some happy times.

DISEASE: Headache, vomiting or alcohol poisoning.

PERSONAL WISH: Difficult to achieve in a short period of time.

COMMENTARY

As you walk ever more firmly on the path of Tao,
*   you will leave impurity and lust behind.*
Needs that once were, are simply no longer.
If at first the six sense organs
*   become enemies and obstructions,*
*   in time they will prove the wealth*
*   of your cultivation.*
Be sincere in the Tao,
*   and there will be a change in your body and heart.*

Observe these six dangers closely:

*   One: Do not confuse what is*
*   with what you want it to be.*
*   Your will cannot preside.*
*   (Besides, it is not yours).*
*   You cannot change the direction of things.*
*   To try is to intrude.*

Two: Release all concepts
that come into your mind.
Do not cling to any of them.

Three: There is nothing that is necessary. Nothing.

Four: The sovereignty of Nature is just that.
Do not impose on it nor act in place of its authority.

Five: Do not rebel and challenge the law of Nature.
This is foolish and destructive.

Six: Remember, your mind is not your own.
It is a gift of life from Nature.
It is imperative to use it positively, constructively.
To do otherwise, to use it for worry, anger
or negativity, is to abuse the mighty gift.

A mind united with Tao
  is devoid of thoughts that are a constant ramble,
  even thoughts pondering utmost wonders
  and mysteries.
A sincere cultivation is done naturally, easily,
  in the here and now.
Only in calmness can one see infinity.
So, if you are a beginner,
  close your eyes and search inside your soul,
  head and body upright, keeping the heart at peace,
  the mind calm.
Discontinue showing a false front
  to others and to yourself,
  whether in your way of living or thinking.
It is not you and thus is dishonest
  to your true nature.
Keep your integrity,
  no need to search the outside world for your soul.
Again and again you will see,
  it is with the pure mind only
  that you can become one with Tao.
It is with the pure mind only
  that you can bask in the radiance
  of the true spiritual sun.
In this way, you will be allowed
  to be the seed of a whole being.

6 SUNG 訟

DISPUTE (LITIGATION)

GUIDANCE: *"Keep to the facts. One should restrain emotion and not over-react to the situation in order not to aggravate the trouble. Endless dispute is harmful. It is beneficial to meet with the Wise One for advice in settling the dispute. It is not beneficial to go ahead adventurously."*

In this hexagram, Heaven is above Water. Because heavenly energy naturally ascends and water naturally descends, this hexagram is an expression of diverging energies. Furthermore, there is conflict in the relationship between the unyielding strength of Chyan, ☰, and the strong energy of K'an, ☵. Since there is no beneficial communication between the upper and lower trigrams, disharmony and dispute are indicated. On a personal level, this situation implies an uneasiness between body and mind. Among people, conflict is indicated.

Sung describes a situation in which each side has great difficulty earning the trust of the other, even though both might be sincere and righteous. One should, therefore, be especially truthful in such circumstances. If one can uphold this virtue, the misunderstanding may be transformed into an opportunity that benefits each side without recourse to litigation. Moreover, one should be egoless in this situation. The wise always prefer peace to self-justification.

Trying to convince others with one's strength is foolish and destructive; such actions only provoke more difficulty. This is not the time to take risks. Any unnecessary aggression will only cause the conflict to deepen. One should seek the support of a just person in authority who will speak objectively and thus dissolve the difficulty.

LINE 1: *"Do not continue a small dispute. Things will eventually turn out right."*

The first line seeks to engage in conflict. However, since it is a yin line, it is too weak to hold its position and gets no results. One should now console oneself, avoiding dispute and possible litigation. Eventually, good fortune will result.

LINE 2: *"He recognizes that he cannot win the dispute and retreats. Thus, he creates no suffering for himself or his people."*

The second line represents a lesser leader. (The fifth line represents a great leader.) The second line fights for himself or his community; the fifth line fights for the entire nation. When one is involved in conflict with a person of superior strength or position, he should retreat. The second line is in dispute with the fifth. Since the fifth line is in a superior position, there is no way for the strong-willed second line to win; it has more than met its match in the fifth line. Thus, it is time for it to retreat in order to avoid a dispute with one of higher principles and purpose. By developing patience and tolerance, the dispute can be avoided.

LINE 3: *"One is satisfied with what one already has. Although there is some difficulty, things will turn out right in the end."*

The counsel of this line is to persevere with what is old instead of engaging in anything new and challenging. Be conservative. This line is between two yang lines, which is a place of difficulty, but there will eventually be good fortune if one is cautious. If one initiates new undertakings at this time in order to expand, trouble will arise.

LINE 4: *"It is not proper to take advantage of a high position to win a dispute. Discontinue the dispute. Peace brings good fortune."*

The fourth line is a yang line in a yin position. It wishes to use force to win its dispute with the weak first line. However, one should not insist on being victorious just because of one's righteousness or superiority. At this time, one should discontinue the dispute and try to make peace. The other party will therefore recognize the true righteousness of one's heart.   Good fortune results from exercising virtue instead of strength.

> **LINE 5:** *"It is appropriate to correct the dispute. Good fortune belongs to the one of true righteousness."*

This line is the principal leader of the hexagram.   One in this position should hold firmly to righteousness and extend it in all actions.   In this hexagram, the fifth line is the only one in an appropriate position to express righteousness.   With correct principles and judgment, one will be able to channel different energies in a positive direction and thus dissolve all disputes within oneself and among others.

> **LINE 6:** *"Receiving honors by winning disputes is certainly no great accomplishment.   Such superficial honors will surely be taken away, time after time."*

One may have a reputation for winning disputes. However, such a meaningless reputation will be challenged again and again.   Though the dispute may be won, there is no real glory in doing so and one will eventually lose one's peace of mind.

In ancient times, a leather belt was bestowed on a good warrior as an honor from the emperor.   But under these conditions,   even if a "leather belt" is bestowed, it will be snatched away many times.

In order to maintain the "best" reputation, one must continuously strive to win.   In this way, one's harmony and peace of mind are exchanged for brief moments of emotional gratification.   Is this a good use of one's strength?

SPECIFIC GUIDANCE

PERSONAL FORTUNE: There is some discomfort and worry.

MARRIAGE: The marriage will be an unhappy one with much quarrelling.   However, with a strong go-between, it might be settled.

HOUSING/FAMILY: A move is favorable because the house is not peaceful, and there are obstacles.

CHILDBIRTH: The baby will be a boy.

LOOKING FOR HELP: If the help is for other people, it can be achieved; however, if it is for yourself, it will not occur.

SOCIAL/GOVERNMENTAL POSITION: It cannot be achieved in a hurry.

TRADE/BUSINESS: Although it can initially be successful, later there will be problems.

SEARCHING FOR SOMEONE: You should not look for them; there will be a quarrel.

WAITING FOR SOMEONE: They will not come.

LOOKING FOR SOMETHING LOST: It can be found close to where you live.

HUNTING FOR THIEVES: They are hiding in the West. If someone wishes to tell you where they are, they can be caught.

LAWSUIT: The suit should not be started.

CLIMATE: There will be rain, but within three days, the weather will be fine again.

TRAVEL: Beware of quarreling with your traveling companions. Travel is not good.

DISEASE: Difficult to cure. There may be some pain in the heart, stomach or abdomen.

PERSONAL WISH: Difficult to achieve.

COMMENTARY
The Paradox of Truth

All opposites are united. A view that has integrated all opposites is balanced and can therefore help one reach the truth. Living with a balanced spirit allows one to avoid life's many diversions.

All polarities become the elements of life. This is illustrated by the paired feet and hands. Each becomes the other's source of support with every new step or movement. With the integration of polarities, one's life can regain its original balance.

One cannot expect beauty to last forever, goodness to remain constant, or the high to never fall. Every day is a "fair weather" day. Excitement occurs in every moment. The climax is built by low tones. Success is contained in every common minute.   The recognition of regularity, plainness, ordinariness and usualness is the fundamental element for achieving a balanced way.

By embracing integral oneness and dissolving discriminating opposites, one can keep his natural-born flexibility and thus live deeply within one's own spirit. This practice will allow one to transcend all worldly attachments and the unhealthy, contradictory, dualistic sphere of the human world.   Thus, one may achieve immortality.

Spiritual truth is sometimes paradoxical.   The following story is my own personal experience in the pursuit of enlightenment.   When I was young and engaged in the activities of youth, my father always reminded me of the importance of achieving enlightenment.   I told my father, "I am bright already.   What enlightenment should I look for?"

My father said, "The enlightenment you should have at first is to know that you are behind the darkness of your brightness."

I had not yet discovered that I was "behind the darkness of my brightness," as my father said.   I thought I was smart.   Taking pride in my smartness was probably my darkness.   I finally realized my own darkness and began working on it to discover real enlightenment.

After many years of cultivation, hard life and difficult times, I eventually felt very enlightened.   I went to my father and told him, "I don't need to look for the truth anymore.   All truth is here, now!   For people of starvation, the truth is to eat.   For people of over-consumption, to eat less is the truth.   For people of poverty, to be rich is the truth.   For people of illness, to be well is the truth.   For people of leisure, to work is the truth.   For people of constant work, to relax is the truth.   For people of a rigidly organized life, flexibility is the truth.   For people of sloppiness, to become well-disciplined is the truth.   For people of spiritual underdevelopment, to pursue enlightenment is the truth.   For people of deep spiritual development, helping to improve the confused world is the truth.

"The truth is always in the polar opposite.   We call Polaris the 'Northern' star, because we are south of it.   If we change our position, we see and name things differently.   This shows the relativity of yin and yang.   An achieved one can embody all truth with his single being. At the same time, all such truth is irrelevant to him."

My father said, "Tell me how can you embody all truth with your single being and, at the same time, make all such truth irrelevant?"

I pondered this question carefully and responded, "All such truth I mentioned is the use or function of the truth. It is not the body or the entity of truth. All uses of truth are specific expressions of it. Every moment and activity may be an expression of truth. Therefore, as the ancient achieved one said, 'One cannot depart from the truth for a single second.' All uses of truth are the truth. At the same time, since all uses of the truth are merely expressions of truth, they are irrelevant to the independence and wholeness of the body of truth."

"Can the use and body of truth be separated as different existing entities?" my father asked.

"No," I replied. "The use of truth and the body of truth cannot be separated. When one of them is perceived, the other also appears. When one of them is disregarded, the other also disappears."

"Well," my father said, "in this way, the existence of truth must have acknowledgment, otherwise it cannot be independent. Is this what you meant? Furthermore, is it not possible for truth to be disregarded or unnoticed, my beloved one?"

"No, sir. If it is the truth, it must always be independent, transcendental and absolute. Otherwise, how can it be truth?"

"My son, in your previous statement, you said that for people who are starving, the truth is to eat; for people of thirst, the truth is to drink and so forth. Now, may I ask you, if to eat and to drink are the truth, then are hunger and thirst the mother of truth? If hunger and thirst are the mother or substance of truth, they should be higher than truth itself. The substance of truth is immutable and unchangeable. What, then, is above your truth?"

After this illuminating discussion I continued to work on the amazing topic of truth. I was up and down with the truth. I was shaken by the pursuit of the truth. At the same time, I was also strongly enchanted by the enlightenment of truth. I was at work day and night with this puzzle. Finally, I developed two theories. First, that enlightenment is some place you can reach alone, without anyone's help. I called this the "theory of self-reaching." The second theory was this: You have been there, but you cannot share it with anyone or go there again, and only a like-minded person can understand what you say.   I called this the "theory of non-transmissibility of enlightenment."

I held to these two points to define the enlightenment of truth. As for myself, I thought that I was already at a certain level of enlightenment.   Before my next meeting with my father, however, I hoped to do some further preparation, just in case he gave me more trouble with the "truth."   Interestingly enough, the night before our meeting, I received an important dream.

In the dream, I was walking in a place where there were two cliffs with a deep ravine between them. I was on the higher side of the ravine.   On the other side, I could hear a woman of late middle age talking to a young man about her adoration of a religious "star" that had been shining for more than a thousand years.   She was saying that this star's life was the only living truth, and it would enlighten all followers with the truth.

Since I was on the other shore, I hurried to go over to her because I wished to correct the false belief she had.   I wanted to tell her that every person is the life of truth, and at the same time, no one is the truth itself.   Truth is not presentable by, or as, anybody or anything.   To do so would damage the truth.   Truth is Truth; it cannot change hands.

As I approached her, but before I could correct her, I noticed that on the same shore in another place a man was talking to some other people about the truth.   He felt that he had a better way of presenting it.   Again I thought I must go there quickly and stop him with my "theory of non-transmissibility," that the real truth cannot be passed.   When one wishes to describe truth, it is no longer the moment one experienced as the truth.   I went over to him to convey my thought: "If you hold this way of talking about the truth, the truth will no longer be the truth, but words."   However, when I was close enough to him, I discovered by the smell of his breath that he was drunk.   Immediately, I decided that what he had achieved must be alcohol truth.   Before I could begin my explanation he greeted me and invited me to his cellar to enjoy some good wine with him.   This friendly gesture made it awkward for me to immediately and straightforwardly pass my message to him.   I also began to feel some difficulty because he seemed beyond my help.   By this time, he was so busy with his wine that he had no time for anything else, and when he offered me the wine, I could not drink it since I discovered I had a toothache. At this time I also discovered my shoelace was loose and needed to be tied.

Suddenly I awoke and could not sleep anymore. I wondered what could be the meaning of this dream. It seemed to me that in spiritual achievement the problem is not enlightenment itself, but the "transmission" of enlightenment. The matters of enlightenment and darkness are on two different shores. It is easy for a person on the high side to descend to the low side, but it is very difficult to communicate with people on the low side. Also, on the low side of a steep ravine, the darkness influences people differently. This had just been illustrated in my dream.

I thought very carefully about which part of my dream was connected with the ultimate truth. The next morning, when I faced my father, he said in a clear voice, "When your shoelace is loose, tie it. When you have a toothache, keep away from drinking. In the freshness of the early morning, gather the chi. During the brightness of the day practice subtle virtue. In the darkness of midnight maintain enlightenment. People of deviation seem to have many chances to expound the truth, but truth never gives the Integral One a chance to express it."

7 　　
shih

military leadership

GUIDANCE: *"Military leadership. If an upright leader is selected, there will be no mistakes."*

In this hexagram, Earth is above Water. The five yin lines are united by one yang line. Although the yang line is in a yin position, it is still central and correct, thus it can assume the position of leadership.

The lower trigram represents a person or group charged with the responsibility of carrying out a great worldly mission. Water in the Earth expresses a boundless source of power that springs forth and flows over everything in its path. This image is very much like an army.

The inner hexagram of Thunder beneath the Earth depicts a potentially explosive situation, like a volcano. When thunder comes in the spring, it awakens all life with its power. With it also comes the rain that nurtures life. This potential power needs a wise and virtuous leader to control it.

Normally, the fifth line is the leader of a hexagram, but here it is too weak and therefore delegates its duties to its subordinate, the strong second line. It is imperative that the second line be responsible and capable of handling the challenges that come to it. If this position is given to an inferior leader, all will be endangered.

Fortunately, the leader in the second place is obedient and cooperative. Though some obstructions are encountered from the upper trigram, he responds capably to the situation and all people follow and support him. Thus, there is an opportunity for victory.

LINE 1: *"Strict discipline is needed from the beginning or there will be great misfortune."*

Since the first line is a yin line in a yang position, it is weak and creates problems. This line needs good discipline to strengthen itself in order for it to carry out orders from the second line. If one in this low position tries to evade its duty for selfish reasons, failure of the entire army will result.

LINE 2: *"Correctly balanced, one is assigned to be the general. The king empowers him. Good fortune. No problem."*

The second line is appointed and empowered by the king, the fifth line, to be the leader in this situation. The cooperation between them is expressed by the harmonious interaction of yin and yang. With such mutual trust and confidence, the second line carries out its assignment with ease.

LINE 3: *"The army will be defeated. Misfortune."*

The third line is a yin line in a yang position; it is the image of a defeated army carrying its dead and wounded. Although its intentions are good, its actions are weak.

Because of its inability to lead the group and its lack of strength in carrying out its intentions, there will be a great defeat.

LINE 4: *"The army retreats. No blame. Such actions do not contradict principles of good military strategy."*

The fourth line gives guidance on how to retreat. There is no blame because one's estimation of the enemy's position is correct. One should never feel humiliated by retreat. Only the stupid and headstrong continue in the face of unnecessary difficulty.

LINE 5: *"Like birds who have come to eat your seeds, the invaders are all over the field. This is the right time to resort to military action. No blame. However, if one who is young and inexperienced is sent to lead the army, defeat and loss of life will result. Possible misfortune."*

A good leader must know how to delegate responsibility. A good helper or general should be appointed and given complete authorization to carry out the mission. To give two generals equal power for the same assignment would create internal conflict and weaken one's strength. Internal conflict is often worse than external conflict because it can prevent the task from being fully accomplished. Thus, assignments should be clearly given, and the leader must carefully match the right person with the appropriate duty.

LINE 6: *"When the war is finished, there should be just rewards. The deserving should be given high positions in order to care for the nation. Those who are inferior should be rewarded with material goods but never trusted with high positions."*

Even though many people helped in accomplishing the mission, they may not be capable of effective administration in a high position. If so, negative forces would interfere with constructive plans for achieving peace.

Be mindful to give rewards that are appropriate to a person's merit.

SPECIFIC GUIDANCE

PERSONAL FORTUNE: This is a difficult time. Conflict may arise between husband and wife.

MARRIAGE: Although it can be successful for a while, afterward there will not be such good fortune.

HOUSING/FAMILY: If the family is large, many might become sick.

CHILDBIRTH: The delivery will not be very smooth. The baby will be a girl. If the fifth line is received, the mother will be in danger. If the top line is received, the baby will be in danger.

LOOKING FOR HELP: Even if you receive help, there is some doubt about motives.

SOCIAL/GOVERNMENTAL POSITION: If you have the help of powerful people, there will be good fortune.

TRADE/BUSINESS: It can be achieved and can be profitable.

SEARCHING FOR SOMEONE: There are obstacles to meeting them.

WAITING FOR SOMEONE: They will return.

LOOKING FOR SOMETHING LOST: It is difficult to find.

HUNTING FOR THIEVES: They can be caught.

LAWSUIT: The dispute can be cleared up by helpful people. All arguments and disputes should be avoided unless necessary.

CLIMATE: The weather will be fine.

TRAVEL: It is good to travel alone.

DISEASE: There may be complications that will be dangerous.

PERSONAL WISH: It can be achieved.

COMMENTARY
The Restoration of Normalcy

After ages of departing from the right way through insistently following its own will, mankind has lost its natural balance. Man's mind has become distorted and his very life untrue. Instead of having his energy centered and focused as it should be, it often floats upward and scatters, stimulating one or another of the sensory organs. This imbalance manifests as being self-centered, boastful, envious, jealous, quarrelsome, as gossiping, raving about the opposite sex, taking things too easily, assuming to be learned and having contempt for the stupid, finding fault with others, having an excess of desire and corrupting the morals of others or being overly ambitious.

The negativity of most people can be changed and refined through cultivation as self-awareness unfolds and self-completion evolves.   One should neither be inert nor frivolous, but should follow a normal balance.   To hold fast to the waves of your negative energy is dangerous. Return to the right way before you go out too far into the open sea.   Return to the shore of positivity and constructive creativity.   This safe shore is to be found in the transformation of your own energy elements and through spiritual evolution as taught in the Integral Way.   The Way teaches that physical and mental well-being are the foundation for high spiritual attainment.

8   比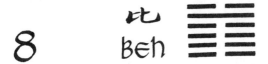
Beh

Fellowship

GUIDANCE: *"Fellowship.   Good fortune.   Be cautious, content and upright.   The undecided will join and follow.   The lofty will lose the opportunity and thus be isolated."*

In this hexagram, Water is above Earth.   All the yin lines are gathered by the unifying force of a leader, the yang line in the fifth position.   The unifying strength of the previous hexagram, Shih, depends on discipline.   In Beh, however, the position of leadership relies on prestige and kindness.

Water and Earth harmoniously support each other. Water flows freely throughout earth and, in the process, earth absorbs water.   Here, five yin lines assist the yang line, illustrating a situation in which the leader is at peace with his followers.   Thus, there is a spirit of fellowship among the followers as well as with the leader. The success of any endeavor depends on the strength and cooperation of the group. This is developed by maintaining a strong sense of receptivity and open-mindedness toward new members, new advisors and one another. Through harmony, peace and friendship, a goal that benefits the entire group can be attained.

LINE 1: *"Be as faithful as a full jug in making friends. Unexpected good fortune will come to you."*

The first line represents the early stages of fellowship; it is in a weak position. The fourth line can be a helpful friend to the first line, especially since it has the support of the fifth line. Thus, there will be good fortune.

LINE 2: *"Make friends out of innermost sincerity. Perseverance brings good fortune."*

Choose your friends by looking deeply within. It is not necessary to reach out socially or to let superficial or external motives influence your decision. By cultivating virtue and sincerity, good friends will naturally respond to you.

The second line is naturally harmonious with the fifth. It does not need to make a special effort to earn its friendship. Through self-cultivation it automatically attracts recognition from the wise one. One who is sincere and virtuous can be a true friend at any time and under any circumstances.

LINE 3: *"Fellowship with the wrong person."*

This line tries to respond to the top line, but it is a yin line in a yang position. This implies that one attempts to become friendly with an unvirtuous person.

LINE 4: *"Extend fellowship to good people. Perseverance brings good fortune."*

This yin line is in the right position and is close to the wise leader, thus it should completely support the fifth line without restraint. This is a golden opportunity to deal with human relationships. The wise friend and virtuous leader in the fifth position will appreciate your virtue and capability. This kind of cooperation will undoubtedly achieve greatness.

LINE 5: *"Glorious fellowship. The kind ruler leads the hunt, taking only the prey that runs in his direction. He does not go after those that run away."*

The image of a hunt is used to described the leadership qualities of this line. It was customary for a group of hunters to go into the woods and form a circle. While making a great noise, they would gradually close the circle and trap all the animals within. However, a virtuous leader in this position leaves an opening in the circle in order to give the prey a chance to escape. The leader expects his followers to be obedient and behave accordingly; those who hesitate or have doubts are free to leave. This is an attribute of a virtuous leader. He welcomes those who wish to help but holds nothing against those who choose to do otherwise.

LINE 6: *"No fellowship can be made. Misfortune."*

Isolation makes one useless. Without extending oneself to others, one can neither serve nor be served. Although isolation may be tolerable for a while, it eventually leads to danger.

SPECIFIC GUIDANCE

PERSONAL FORTUNE: Difficulty arises in the beginning, but afterwards there is good fortune. If you move quickly, things will be profitable. If you hesitate or procrastinate, trouble will arise and failure will result.

MARRIAGE: It can be successful.

HOUSING/FAMILY: The district and neighborhood are good, and there will be good fortune.

CHILDBIRTH: The delivery will be safe. If the baby is born in the spring, it will be a girl. If born in the autumn, it will be a boy. If the second and fourth lines change, the baby will be a girl.

LOOKING FOR HELP: It will be given to you.

SOCIAL/GOVERNMENTAL POSITION: The position is not a high one. To go forward at this time brings good fortune. Do not retreat.

TRADE/BUSINESS: A partnership will be profitable.

SEARCHING FOR SOMEONE: They are in a temple or with a woman.

WAITING FOR SOMEONE: They will leave a message.

LOOKING FOR SOMETHING LOST: Look in the Northeast. Though part of it can be found, part remains lost.

HUNTING FOR THIEVES: There are more than two thieves and they live in the East or the South. If you search immediately after the robbery, they can be caught.

LAWSUIT: You should make peace.

CLIMATE: Rain will soon change to fair weather or fair weather to rain.

TRAVEL: Travel brings good fortune if you do not go too far.

DISEASE: There is difficulty with heat in the chest and stomach. If it persists, it will be difficult to cure.

PERSONAL WISH: It will take a little time to achieve.

COMMENTARY
Natural Light in Relationships

The inner essence of the universe is benevolent.
People, within their true natures,
  functioning as a microcosm of the universe,
  are also benevolent and should, therefore,
  cherish humanity in their hearts.
Use tolerance and patience toward others.
Be loyal and forgiving, warm and sincere.
Extend your harmonious energy to others.
Do not complain,
  so as not to pass on your negativity.
Approach everyone with an open mind
  and without pushing yourself forward,
  but do not bare your heart
  when meeting for the first time.

Judge yourself well and others moderately.
Be forgiving, and forgive fully and frankly.
There is always a good reason
  to forget another's faults.
Remember, even the sages were not faultless.
Keep your tongue quiet
  so as not to provoke arguments.
Leave room for your own repentance
  and compensation
  in every affair.
Be flexible and yielding, and do not quarrel.
Bear an insult and keep your dignity.
To repress a moment of anger
  can save you much regret.
Strive to be selfless, not self-centered.
A self-centered person expects favors from others,
  while a selfless person gives to others
  and never asks anything in return.

Win people's hearts, and do not impose
  upon their wills.
With affinity, people will meet each other from
  a great distance.
Without affinity, even when face to face,
  they might never truly meet.
When people are of the same mind,
  their integrity will cut metal.
Do not have intimate dealings with unvirtuous people
  whose words mean little
  and whose actions are indecisive.
Do not nourish an unfaithful person.
If one associates with unvirtuous people,
  one will be negatively influenced by them.
Be fraternal and friendly to everyone,
  but keep your own balanced nature
  whole and untouched.
Do not speak of another's shortcomings at any time.
If you respect others,
  they will in turn respect you.
Be humble and willing to serve people
  whenever you can.
Thus is the nature and the absolute virtue
  of the universe.

9 小畜 shau chu

≡≡

small accumulation

GUIDANCE: *"Small accumulation. Proceed. This is like thick clouds that have gathered in the sky, but there is not yet any rain."*

In this hexagram, Wind is above Heaven. One yin line holds five yang lines together. The literal Chinese translation of Shau Chu means a small herd of cattle, a small gathering, or an accumulation.

The image of the wind blowing through the sky suggests clouds that are accumulating. Thus, this hexagram indicates a time to prepare for a large enterprise. This time is also beneficial for planning and exchanging ideas with others, removing psychological obstacles and smoothing any rough edges before initiating the work.

Because the fourth line is in the yin position next to the fifth line, which is the leader, its duties are those of an assistant or a minister. Since the yin line is the only one among all the yang lines, it represents a minister with a high level of responsibility. Thus, its energy is concentrated on a special assignment for the leader. Guiding a small group of people in this special work is appropriate for the fourth line, but being overly ambitious and usurping power will create problems.

This hexagram also implies that the demands of the time may be far greater than resources available; therefore, caution should be exercised. In its negative aspect this hexagram represents a wife who degrades her husband or a servant who tries to control his master. However, in a positive sense, small undertakings can be accomplished which can later lead to larger events.

LINE 1: *"Return to the original path. No blame."*

The first line cooperates with and responds to the fourth line. Furthermore, it acts correctly, carrying out its duties without going beyond its sphere of responsibility.

By tending to its own business, it avoids conflict and difficulty, and its position is a very comfortable one.

The literal translation of this line is: "Come back to
your own way. How can there be any problem in this?
Good fortune." Therefore, good fortune lies in keeping to
one's way. The yang line in the first position is not strong
enough to go beyond its capability. Since it is not strong
enough to act aggressively, there will be no problem. The
fourth line has power and is in the correct position. It
neither attacks nor harms the first line, so the whole situation is harmonious and there is no trouble.

LINE 2: *"Together, return to the original, right path.
Good fortune."*

The second line has the same energy and virtue as the
first. Since both are in low positions, they come together
and mutually adhere to the right path. They do not undertake anything too hastily or engage in reckless actions.

LINE 3: *"The wheel falls off the wagon. Husband and
wife quarrel."*

This line can represent a marriage or a vehicle. Both
are temporarily hindered in their progress as indicated by
the wheel falling off the wagon. This line illustrates the
importance of cooperation. Since the third line does not
accept control from the top line, and the fourth line does
not have enough energy to restrain the third line, confrontation and disharmony result and nothing at all is
accomplished.

LINE 4: *"Be confident. Wipe away the blood and
avoid the danger. No more trouble."*

Here, "blood" represents the worry and tensions which
arise when the small tries to restrain the powerful. Since
this responsibility rests on the shoulders of the fourth
line, anxiety arises. The real problem in this position,
however, is to avoid too much pressure and worry. If one
is sincere and scrutinizes everything, all will be well.

Though the fourth line is not innately strong, it does
have the necessary qualities of understanding and sincerity. Such qualities make it an excellent worker in this situation. Furthermore, it is supported by and in harmony
with the leader, the strong fifth line. Thus, by having a

moderate attitude and not being too aggressive, everyone will feel equally involved and strengthened. With cooperation, the task at hand will be greatly improved and danger will disappear.

LINE 5: *"Be faithful and cooperative with neighbors in order to successfully collect and distribute wealth."*

Because the fifth line has the same energy as the other four yang lines, it needs someone to gather the work and make connections. Thus, it relies on the fourth line to fulfill this responsibility. When the fourth line receives the fifth line's support, they can then share the profits. One cannot be rich alone.

LINE 6: *"The rain has come! One's kindness benefits all people. The woman's power becomes dominant like the full moon. Exercise self-restraint. If one wishes to do something independently, problems will arise."*

Rain depends on the accumulation of clouds. The accumulation has now been fully achieved, as represented by the yang energy coming to the top position. Thus, rain comes.

The upper trigram, Soen ☴ , also symbolizes an elderly woman. The image of a domineering wife expresses yin energy restraining yang. Although she may be correct in some things, the situation is still an uncomfortable one. The moon also represents the fullness of the yin energy. The negative atmosphere is still strongly influencing the situation, and this is not the time for creative yang energy to be active. Otherwise, impediments will be encountered.

SPECIFIC GUIDANCE

PERSONAL FORTUNE: Some people will create obstacles and cause trouble for you.

MARRIAGE: One may marry a divorced woman. If the question concerns a break-up, a reunion is possible after differences are settled.

HOUSING/FAMILY: Housing is spacious and it is good for two people to live together; however, living with young women is not good because there will be quarrels.

CHILDBIRTH: The baby will be a boy. If a divination is made in the autumn or winter, the baby will be a girl.

LOOKING FOR WORK: It can be achieved, but there will be quarrelling afterward. To rely on a woman will bring good fortune.

SOCIAL/GOVERNMENTAL POSITION: Achievement comes late, maybe in the 6th or 11th calendar month.

TRADE/BUSINESS: Difficult to achieve; much damage and loss.

SEARCHING FOR SOMEONE: They live outside the city in the valley or the wilderness.

WAITING FOR SOMEONE: They will not come.

LOOKING FOR SOMETHING LOST: Send a woman to look for it in the East.

HUNTING FOR THIEVES: They live in the Northeast and are difficult to find.

LAWSUIT: There may be danger and harm from a woman.

CLIMATE: It will rain. If there is wind, the weather will be fine.

TRAVEL: This is not a good time for travel.

DISEASE: Good fortune for a child. Danger for an adult.

PERSONAL WISH: Difficult to achieve in a short time.

COMMENTARY
Taming the Wild Horse Within Yourself

Bridle the mind, for it is like a wild horse. It needs to be tamed. First one has to know it is there, running on the plain. Then try to catch it, ride it, lead it by the reins and be watchful of its movements all the time. With firmness, gentleness and patience, the horse will be tamed and the master known.

One has to practice the healthy way daily and unconditionally. Without daily practice, the little progress one makes will wither away quickly. Be constantly aware of the movement of the mind. If it is negative, lazy or inconsiderate, subtly but firmly change the channel on the mind's screen to a positive and giving direction. At first it may seem unnatural not to follow the impulse of the mind, since one is used to following the self-willed mind without question. But being impulsive is not the same as being spontaneous. Spontaneity is a refined state of attunement with life in its united form.   Gradually, one's effort brings one to a higher state of energy.   One's mind becomes pure, little by little, and one's actions become spontaneously virtuous.

It will take many years to purify the mind.   Have courage and trust the positive nature of the universe and the positive nature of one's own being.   Practice daily; never skip a day.

10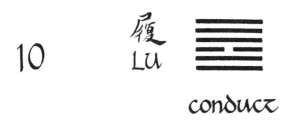

conduct

GUIDANCE: *"Conduct should follow the correct order so as not to cause trouble.   When treading on the tail of a tiger, avoid challenging its power.   Proceed with caution and awareness."*

This hexagram shows how a weak person conducts himself at the side of a strong one.   Chyan, Heaven ☰, is the moving power above Tui, Lake ☱, which is soft, gentle and still.   Since the powerful force of Chyan could easily overcome Tui, thoughtful conduct is necessary to maintain a harmonious relationship between them.

The third line is the only yin energy among five yang lines and is in a yang position.   Though the situation appears dangerous, the yin line remains safe, harmonizing the yang lines with her gentleness.   The *I Ching* describes this situation as "treading on the tail of a tiger."   By remaining true to one's nature, a weak person can achieve much more than he otherwise could.   When encountering the strong, one accomplishes much through humility, moderation and centeredness.   Meekness can harmonize great powers and thus avoid any confrontation and antagonism.

The first and second lines represent the way of naturalness, of simply being oneself, and they provide a good example of the fundamental guidance for conduct.   This is the way of Lao Tzu's teachings.   One needs no glamour, glory or high social position to add to one's natural well-being. When neither honor nor disgrace is imposed on a plain good life, one has good fortune.

LINE 1: *"Conduct yourself in accordance with your true, plain, natural being. No blame."*

The first line represents the inner-centeredness of one's natural being and simple way of living which results in forward movement in accordance with what is right and true. Since this line has no correspondence with the fourth yang line, it should be self-contained, independent, and only do what is within its means. Because the first line leads a plain, simple, normal life without seeking fame or fortune, it passes safely through the danger. By keeping to what one already has, happiness is attained.

LINE 2: *"Conduct yourself according to the simple path. Simplicity brings good fortune."*

The second line represents one who remains centered and undisturbed by external circumstances. Although he cannot respond to the fifth line, his conduct is correct. He is content living simply and alone, expecting neither a high position nor favors from above; thus, he is protected.

LINE 3: *"With poor vision and poor movement one treads on the tail of a tiger. Danger. The arrogant soldier offends the king by being too rigid."*

The third line presents the image of a one-eyed person or someone with partial vision. Because he cannot see the entire situation clearly, danger is present. A person is not capable of handling the situation with only one "eye." Being aggressive or ambitious at this time will cause danger. One is treading on the tail of a tiger and, if not careful, will be bitten.

LINE 4: *"With hesitation and prudence one approaches the tail of the tiger. Be careful of offensive, challenging behavior. Eventually, one is successful in accomplishing the task."*

Though the fourth line is in an incorrect position, it still has the power to complete its mission. By being very careful it can change danger to safety and misfortune to good fortune. Thus, one's intentions can be achieved.

LINE 5: *"Resolute conduct. It is difficult but proper."*

The fifth line is in the correct position and has the capacity for strong leadership. Through caution, good fortune can be achieved.

When the time comes to take action, one should be resolute but cautious. Although the problem is recognized, there is still some danger. Heed past mistakes and be receptive to new ways of accomplishing things. The whole meaning of life is continual self-cultivation, or the chance to positively reform oneself on a daily basis. Good fortune comes from the wisdom developed through understanding one's past.

LINE 6: *"Check the results of your conduct and make corrections. Great good fortune. You will celebrate your high achievement."*

The top line, being in a high position, can objectively review its actions. Though sophisticated, he remains on the right path and thereby achieves greatness and good fortune.

SPECIFIC GUIDANCE

FAMILY FORTUNE: Peaceful and prosperous.

MARRIAGE: Difficult to achieve.

HOUSING/FAMILY: The place is not a comfortable one.

CHILDBIRTH: The baby will be a girl. If born in autumn it will be a boy. If the baby is healthy, the mother will have some trouble.

SOCIAL/GOVERNMENTAL POSITION: It cannot be achieved.

TRADE/BUSINESS: Difficult to achieve.

SEARCHING FOR SOMEONE: They are difficult to find.

WAITING FOR SOMEONE: They will have a message for you.

LOOKING FOR SOMETHING LOST: It is difficult to find.

HUNTING FOR THIEVES: They are in the West and are easy to catch.

LAWSUIT: Good fortune.
CLIMATE: It will be fine.
TRAVEL: A long journey is better than a short journey.
DISEASE: Dangerous.
PERSONAL WISH: It can be achieved later.

COMMENTARY
The Natural Light in Everyday Life

If you are about to do something,
  consider its disadvantages first
  and see if you can do without it.
Use caution before taking action.
Restrain yourself from moving too fast
  and from dissipating your energy
  in too many directions.
Do not meddle in someone else's affairs;
  it will only complicate your life
  and bring confusion.
Preserve the serenity of your nature
  by observing the multiple activities of life
  and not participating.
As a spectator, you can see clearly
  that the participants are often lost in the maze.

Stay with the oneness of all things.
Do not talk more than is necessary.
Do not let your mind run from this subject to that.
Walk on the balanced path of Tao
  and you will be preserved.
Take moderation as your guide;
  even happiness should not be enjoyed to excess.
Cherish self-control
  and hold fast to the subtle law of nature.

Do not be a servant to material things.
Simplify your life by doing away with things,
  do not accumulate them.
Give away what you cherish most,
  and your desire for material things will diminish.

Be prepared for the future.
If you are prepared for difficulties,
  they become easy to overcome.

In taking action, be far thinking.
Consider the consequences at all levels.
If your motive is selfish or will harm others,
    restrain from taking action.
When you have attained your objective,
    use caution and do not overdo it.
Be heedful in the beginning to ensure a good ending.

Always try to help yourself
    before you ask help from others;
But never feel too proud
    to ask for assistance if you need it.

Keep your mind clear and you will be able
    to manage your affairs in good order.
A clear mind is an uncluttered mind;
    make it one-pointed and direct.

Manage public affairs with selfless judgment
    and fairness.
One must display honesty, generosity and earnestness.
Do not deceive people;
    the heart knows and cannot be deceived.

Be gentle in doing right; do not be violent.
Be sure that your conduct is in harmony
    with your understanding,
    even in small matters.

The essence of work is diligence.
 A successful life depends on
    doing the right thing at the right time
    and obeying the cosmic law.
Blessings come in many ways.
Do not look for happiness, and you will be content.

Continuously remove negativity within yourself.
One's good life is decided by one's virtue
    and a clean mind.
To endure difficulty, quit complaining.
To endure vexation and annoyance,
    avoid bitter comment.
If your mind is always occupied by distress,
    good fortune is sure to evade you.
When things get to their worst,
    they can only get better.

When something reaches its limit,
* it has to return to its opposite.*
This is the T'ai Chi of events.
Avoid involvement with people who are suspicious,
* easily pleased or angered.*
Listen only to proposals of a balanced view.
Walk away from idle talk.
Unite with people of outstanding character.
Collective purpose forms a fortress.
In uniting harmonized energies, we gather strength.

11

peace - harmony - good opportunity

GUIDANCE: *"Good opportunity.   In a time of prosperity*
something small is given and something large is returned.
Little effort brings a big reward.   Good fortune.   Proceed."

In this hexagram, Heaven is below Earth. The natural movement of light, Heavenly yang energy is ascending while that of heavy, Earthly yin energy is descending. As they meet and commune with one another, peace and harmony are achieved and great accomplishments are possible.

This hexagram is associated with February/March, the first month of Spring. The harmonizing natural energy of Heaven and Earth is the highest foundation for all living things and indicates a time when all things grow and prosper. One who follows this principle will be able to arrange his energy harmoniously, thus maintaining good mental and physical health and managing business and state affairs well.

The hexagram T'ai represents a time of peace, harmony and prosperity. The literal translation of the word T'ai means "best order" or "perfect condition." During such times the wise take the reins and correctly utilize the resources that benefit all. Achieving a peaceful, harmonious order is not easy, and maintaining such a situation is even more difficult. Thus, even in these times one must remain cautious and protect the peaceful fruit that has been harvested.

When the strong, positive energy of Heaven puts itself beneath the receptive, negative energy of Earth, a positive relationship and time of creativity are symbolized. Such an arrangement is especially indicative of a good relationship between a man and a woman. True love comes from a deep level of the mind; such harmony is not only the result of the present situation, but the resonance which the Chi of the two beings has developed beyond time and circumstances, probably throughout many lifetimes.

The affinity between people capable of selfless love originates from a remote spiritual background. Most people have experienced such a state at various moments in their life. Two essences that harmoniously merge are an expression of Tai. This perfect harmony of energy is also what causes one to be "in the right place at the right time," which is not just accidental, but the subtle attraction of individual energies responding to one another.

This is a time of renewed personal growth which brings success in self-cultivation. As positive energy becomes active, negative energy recedes. Physical, mental and spiritual energies are in balance and a perfect state of well-being results.

The *Tao Teh Ching* teaches us not to seek full expansion. An overly extended spring loses its resilience and cannot be renewed. In order to harmonize the forces of yin and yang, one should follow a moderate, balanced path and avoid all extremes. This teaching is the fundamental guidance of the *I Ching* as well as the *Tao Teh Ching*. This hexagram gives a clear image of that harmonious state and instructs one how to make that condition useful and enduring.

LINE 1: *"When pulling couch grass, many pieces are pulled up together because their roots are interconnected. Now is the time to undertake something. One finds correspondence from more than one person."*

Couch grass is a soft, slender grass with a sharp tip and edges, used to make huts in China. Its roots are interconnected, which signifies that a "good connection" will emerge to support one. This is the right time to proceed toward a goal.

LINE 2: *"Harmonizing all opposites with great courage is like crossing a river. Do not neglect the good elements that are distant. Egolessly refuse the influence of the bad elements that are close by. In this way, a balanced path can be maintained and great achievement can be accomplished."*

This line is in harmony with the fifth and is the central character in making peace. One should have the heart of Heavenly kindness with the great, encompassing capacity to include all differing energies. With this Heavenly-spirited purpose, and by firmly following the principle of balance, one can achieve the task of bringing harmony to all people.

LINE 3: *"No plateau is without a slope and no forward movement is without a turning back. One needs to maintain one's goal without being discouraged by difficulties. Have no worries and be faithful; thus enjoyment and blessings follow."*

The third line is between the ascending yang energy and the descending yin energy. It represents a position of transition. One must maintain control and be firm in approaching one's goal. Though this situation may appear beyond one's capabilities, with firmness good results can be achieved.

LINE 4: *"Cooperate with one's neighbors. With good intentions, share one's being with others."*

This yin line is in a yin position, therefore it finds response from the yang line in the first position. Relationships of this kind are good because they are based on sincerity. If money or power is used to attract followers, the bond will not last long, but here one's purpose is correct and honest, so there can be success.

The first line is connected with the other two yang lines; thus, there is a tendency to push forward. The fourth line normally corresponds to the first, but in its attempt to balance and harmonize the two groups of opposing energies, difficulties arise unless it can get the help of the third line. Harmony must begin with one's close neighbors so that a peaceful influence can develop.

LINE 5: *"One connects oneself with the lower. Great blessing."*

The high energy descends. The fifth and second lines unite, representing a leader who allies himself with people of lower rank. Such an action makes the nation strong and prosperous.

The good fortune of T'ai unites the achieved with the unachieved. Good fortune on a grand scale must not be enjoyed alone; it must be shared with everyone. The true meaning of T'ai is good fortune for everyone on all levels. Such a situation is beautiful, full of success and joy.

LINE 6: *"The protection is weakened. The defending wall of the city falls. There is not yet a need for the army; however, the people must stay alert in order to prevent trouble from happening."*

After good fortune comes misfortune. This line warns that one should now control and restrain oneself in order to maintain the situation and help minimize the inevitable decline. One must be careful at the peak of prosperity not to rejoice to the extent that one's duties and responsibilities are neglected. Otherwise, humiliation may result. Good times should always be valued and correctly used.

SPECIFIC GUIDANCE

PERSONAL FORTUNE: There is much worry connected with the gossip of women.

MARRIAGE: Although the marriage can occur, divorce will follow in the future.

HOUSING/FAMILY: The house is not a good one for a female.

CHILDBIRTH: The delivery will be safe, and the child will be a good son.

LOOKING FOR HELP: The help will be greater than one had expected.

SOCIAL/GOVERNMENTAL POSITION: One can obtain a promotion with the help of an influential person.

TRADE/BUSINESS: The buyer profits more than the seller.

SEARCHING FOR SOMEONE: There will be success if the fifth line is received.

WAITING FOR PEOPLE: They will not come.

LOOKING FOR SOMETHING LOST: It is not stolen and can be found nearby.

HUNTING FOR THIEVES: There are three or four persons hiding in the East near a body of water; they are difficult to catch.

LAWSUIT: Now is a good time to make peace. Profits are not gained by going to trial.

CLIMATE: There will be no rain.

TRAVEL: This is not a good time to travel alone.   One should travel with two companions.

DISEASE: It is dangerous if the condition has lasted a long time.

PERSONAL WISH: There will be no success if you hurry. It can be fulfilled in the long run.

COMMENTARY
The Natural Light in General Life

The five blessings of life are:
  health, longevity, virtuous behavior,
  prosperity and a natural death.
The five constant virtues are:
  propriety, benevolence, righteousness,
  wisdom and faith.
Those who live in accord with
  the universal subtle law are preserved.

Aim at human and spiritual nobility.
There is one word that we can use as a motto
  for our entire life: reciprocity.
What we do not want to be done to ourselves,
  we must not do to others.
The more we give to others,
  the more abundant our lives become.
In helping people and caring for life,
  our own lives will be very rewarding.

On entering a country, do not do what is forbidden;
  follow the customs.
On entering a house, respect the taste of the family;
  in this way there will be no improper behavior.
A wise man is free of perplexities,
  because he understands what is right and wrong.
A virtuous man is free of anxieties,
  because he tries his best in all undertakings
  and regards failure as a means
  to strengthen his character.
A man of courage is free from fear,
  because he strongly believes in his goals,
  regardless of the difficulties.

Do not desire to have things done quickly
  if they cannot be done thoroughly;
Success in work is founded on thoroughness.
Do not be greedy of small advantages,
  and great projects can be accomplished.
Be eager to inquire when in doubt;
  one who does not learn from others
  will remain ignorant.
The learned man may not be wise,
  and the wise man may not be learned.
Be aware of the difference between wisdom
  and learned knowledge.

True fulfillment in life is derived from hardship.
One can only appreciate the joy of fulfilled
  responsibility after shouldering the burden.
The best strategists are not impulsive;
  the best winners are not quarrelsome;
  the best rulers are not arrogant.
Things have their beginnings and their endings;
  events have their causes and their outcome.
To know which should be first
  and which should be last
  will bring one nearer to the truth of life.

Live with virtue and abide with the laws of nature.
Do not shallowly care for your own comfort
  and indulgences.
A man of leisure will never find success.
Be efficient in work and careful in speech.
Correct your faults and be humble.

Never tire of studying and practicing
  the right way of life.
If you do not practice and study,
  you will not grow to completeness.
Although the job is simple,
  one can never complete it without working.
Although the distance is short,
  one can never reach the goal without walking.
There is no definite route to success or failure,
  as they are very intricate;
The reason some succeed and others fail
  is that those who persist in a positive direction
  succeed, while those who do not will fail.

When Heaven is going to confer an important task
  on someone, first it makes his mind suffer
  and labors his body with heavy tasks.
It will present hardships,
  and defeat all his undertakings.
Through all these trials,
  it strengthens his mind and will
  so that he may overcome all difficulties.

If you want to enjoy a long and fulfilling life
  supported by the energy of Heaven,
  you should diligently cultivate virtuous action.
There is a right way and a wrong way to live.
The virtuous way may lead to disadvantage,
  but victory is assured.
The unvirtuous way may lead to prosperity,
  but failure is inevitable.
Take care to proceed on the right path.
If you stray, know that there is always a safe shore
  to which you can return.

If one's heart is wrongly pursuing evil,
  then even though it has not been accomplished,
  bad fortune will follow.
Consider the success and failure of others as your own;
  share in their fortune and misfortune.
Do not aggressively or unrighteously
  expose the faults of others,
  nor boast of your own excellence.
Do not hold a grudge toward anyone.
Live with humility.

12　否
pi

MISFORTUNE

GUIDANCE: *"Unfavorable situations. In times of adversity, evil ones are in positions of power. Good people cannot enjoy normal life. Much is given, little is received."*

In this hexagram, Heaven is above Earth. They appear to be in their proper order, but as expressions of natural energy, they are going in opposite directions. If the strong, heavenly yang energy could move downward toward Earth, and if the earthly yin energy could move upward toward Heaven, there would be harmony, as illustrated in the previous hexagram, Tai. However, here there is no intercourse or integration of these two energies. Heavenly yang energy ascends and moves further away from the earthly yin energy, which, in turn, descends and moves further away from Heaven. The distance between them increases, precluding their ever coming together.

Only when the great motherly energy of Earth and the great fatherly energy of Heaven come together can anything be created or accomplished. It is clear from an examination of both Pi and Tai that the arrangement of natural forces is very important in determining whether there will be union or separation of yin and yang.

Pi indicates adverse times or bad luck. During these times, a blockage is created and energy stagnates, thus this hexagram represents an unfortunate or desperate situation. However, in the natural energy cycle, good fortune is forthcoming after a time of misfortune. According to the top line: "When one is experiencing the bitterness of winter, the warmth of spring cannot be far off."

LINE 1: *"In times of adversity, evil beings congregate in large numbers. If one pulls a single blade of couch grass, one gets the entire bunch because the roots are* *all interconnected. This is a time to remain calm and upright."*

This first line is almost the same as the first line of the previous hexagram, T'ai. "When one pulls a blade of couch grass, the whole bunch comes with it." However, this is a yin line in a yang position, which resembles a person of inferior virtue. Furthermore, it has a strong connection with others of inferior virtue. Therefore, this line cautions that to undertake something at this time will result in a chain reaction of ominous events. One is not encouraged to go forward with an undertaking or relationship that one might wish to start.

LINE 2: *"In times of adversity, it is all right for ordinary people to be obedient. But one of self-cultivation should not compromise with the evil majority."*

The second line follows the leadership of the fifth line by offering to help. This line is tolerant and cooperative. Although a great person should keep to himself without becoming involved in the evil that surrounds him, tolerance toward his environment will help him endure. If he does get involved, his awareness will be distorted and his virtue will decline.

LINE 3: *"In times of adversity, one is humiliated by inferior influences. This is incorrect."*

The third line disgraces itself by trying to please those of evil inclination. As a consequence, it fails to maintain its virtue and takes their evil unto itself. Therefore, humiliation results. Though flattery can sometimes help one attain good position, this is not the way of a far-sighted individual.

LINE 4: *"In times of adversity, those who have faith in a virtuous deliverance will receive blessing."*

Everything is cyclical, and in every cycle there comes a point where things turn around. Great adversity was once overwhelming; however, it now starts to wane. Those who remain centered will go through bad times and eventually receive good fortune. The fourth line has departed from the darkness and is headed into the light. Now one must rebuild oneself calmly and firmly.

LINE 5: *"At the end of adversity, stay alert! A great one will plant his root deeply and firmly."*

The fifth line can stop the misfortune. A great one is always very cautious at the end of a crisis. If one is careless at the end, the crisis may be prolonged just as peace is about to be reached. Give constant attention to preserving the peace; then safety and the certainty of being prosperous again will be as sure as "the thick leaves that grow on a mulberry tree and the new shoots that sprout from the bamboo roots." Real safety comes from being prudent.

LINE 6:   *"After reaching its extreme, adversity is followed by felicity."*

It is a simple truth that when misfortune reaches an extreme, good fortune will certainly follow.

Master Lieh Tzu was poor and always seemed destitute. However, because he was a very wise man, his name became known to many. Word of his difficulty reached the Premier of the state who decided to help him unofficially by offering him a large gift of rice. When Lieh Tzu graciously but firmly refused this offer, his wife became very angry with him for being unrealistic and refusing the Premier's kindness. Lieh Tzu laughed, saying that neither she nor the Premier understood him. The Premier's gift was only in response to someone's good words about him. In this same way, the Premier could just as easily persecute him for a bad report which someone might give of him. The Premier's offering of the rice was not from his true understanding of Lieh Tzu. Therefore, the Master refused the rice.

In ancient times, if someone accepted another's support, it was the custom that the favor must be returned, even at the cost of one's life. If one were unwilling to die for such a person, then the favor should not be accepted. A righteous person would only give his life for a good cause. This is why Lieh Tzu refused help.

After some time, the country had a rebellion, and the Premier was killed along with all who had supported him. Lieh Tzu's foresight and wisdom were correct to put righteousness above the satisfaction of his family. One should be cautious in accepting help, even in trying circumstances. If one accepts the favors of others, they must be repaid.

But how does refusing corrupt gifts relate to this line? Misfortune is what builds a strong personality. Do not let material comforts and superficial glory destroy you. The virtuous strength of your personality should not be traded for such unworthy things. Misfortune has built all the great sages. It was through great difficulties that they were enlightened. Do not depend on good fortune. Depend on your own virtuous personality and normal life to make you the final winner. This is the key to reaching the Tao, the great path of life.

SPECIFIC GUIDANCE

PERSONAL FORTUNE: Presently it is not good, but later there will be good fortune. Be cautious and do not act recklessly.

MARRIAGE: It can be achieved, but there will be difficulty. It is suitable to marry late.

HOUSING/FAMILY: Nothing is ever smooth; trouble never seems to end. There also may be some disease or pain.

CHILDBIRTH: Not safe or peaceful. If it is the first birth, the baby will be a girl; if the second or third child, it will be a boy.

LOOKING FOR HELP: In the beginning, one has difficulty; afterward it is easy.

SOCIAL/GOVERNMENTAL POSITION: Not successful at this time.

TRADE/BUSINESS: It will be profitable for the buyer but not for the seller. It is good to wait before you sell.

SEARCHING FOR SOMEONE: Look in the Northwest to find them.

WAITING FOR SOMEONE: They will not come.

LOOKING FOR SOMETHING LOST: It can be found in the East or the South.

HUNTING FOR THIEVES: There are two who live in the woods, on the mountain or near the water in the east.

LAWSUIT: Not favorable; you may have wronged someone.

CLIMATE: It will be fine.

TRAVEL: If you hurry there will be some quarrel; if you wait, there there will be good fortune.

DISEASE: There is some dangerous problem around the heart, stomach or diaphragm.

PERSONAL WISH: Although there is difficulty in the beginning, afterwards there is success.

COMMENTARY
The Sacred Light of Natural Life

The universe never dies
  because it maintains its eternal constancy.
All creatures die
  because they allow their external environment
  to continually change their own natures
  and their virtues.
People are attracted by the outside world
  and do not feel content or sufficient
  within their own natures.
They follow what is attractive to them.
They always want to be something or someone else
  and, so doing, depart from their own good natures.
One dies every minute one departs
  from one's true nature.
Every minute is a new life to a true being.

As I awakened in Tao, I came to know:
  with Tao we receive life;
  Tao is the eternal way;
  Tao is the constancy of the universe;
  Tao is the origin of our vitality;
  Tao is the enduring spirit of life.

Moving about in the spiritual world,
  I abide with the eternal spirit.
I am content with my own nature.
The harmonized energy of the universe supports me
  and I live firmly with the eternal Tao.
I can alter confusion and dangerous situations
  by abiding in the true power of the
  subtle virtue of the universe.
I follow a regular, normal way of life,
  avoiding all extremes, excesses
  and extravagances.
I am plain, simple and true.

I never allow myself to daydream
   or wish to be a saint or other exalted being,
   only a being of wholeness.
I walk the Way,
   without concern for my future, past or present.
My emotions are softened, my desires few.
I keep my spirit untouched,
   my mind clear and detached,
   my body still and upright.
All my actions have a deep respect
   for the original stillness of the universe.
I use non-action or non-deviation
   as a gateway to true work.
Though peacefully engaged in life,
   I abide in the infinite simplicity of Tao.
This is the way to perpetual peace,
   true beauty, happiness and joy.
This is the secret of a natural life.

13 ZUNG REN

uniting with people

GUIDANCE: *"Proceed to unite with people.   Now is a suitable time to 'cross the great water' or undertake an adventure.   It is correct for people of self-awareness to pursue their goals."*

In this hexagram, Heaven is above Fire.   The energy of both Heaven and Fire ascends and spreads.   Fire, or sunshine, symbolizes illumination and strength.   Heaven, or the sky, symbolizes righteousness and openness.   Their natures are not something one can possess.   They exist for the benefit of all things.

All life needs sunlight.   Those who receive this light can attain health and strength.   The image of this hexagram indicates a fellowship or coming together in order to accomplish a common goal. The impartiality of sunlight is also emphasized.

In this hexagram, there are five yang lines with one yin line in the second position. Since this is the right position for the yin line, it becomes the receptive center of the lower trigram; thus, it responds to the fifth line, which represents the will of Heaven or a great leader. When the masculine and feminine characteristics of energy harmonize, everyone is united and the group gathers in order to achieve a common goal.

Hexagram #7, Shih (Military Leadership), is the opposite of this one. It has five yin lines and one yang line in the second position. The yang line in Shih represents a strong leader who helps bring the group together. There the weaker energy unites under the direction of the strong line in order to accomplish great things.

In Tung Ren, the gentle and harmonious energy of the weak line brings all the strong lines together. This line accomplishes its goal, not only because it is in the correct position, but also because it has the ability to see things in a larger perspective. Therefore, a person can gather the people in order to accomplish great tasks.

A further meaning of the hexagram can be seen as the harmony of people's minds. In public endeavors, most people generally cannot accomplish things single-handedly. A great task can be completed more easily and effectively when different energies combine to work as a group. Each position is essential for the completion of the entire task, and each person depends upon the others. Through unity, one accomplishes his goals or service to the world.

Because people no longer live alone in the mountains or wilderness, this hexagram is especially relevant to modern life. In spite of the fact that we all live together, most people are unable to cooperate with others or interact in a positive way. When people's egos obstruct their potential, their minds become rigid and narrow. Even when they have great abilities and intelligence, they are unlikely to achieve anything, as they do not know how to share their potential or participate with others.

If your pursuit is the accomplishment of a great collective goal, then what is most beneficial to the group is also most important to you. Likewise, whatever is important to you as leader is also important to the rest of the group. In this way, all obstacles can be overcome and all things accomplished.

LINE 1: *"Being united with people outside your door; no blame."*

A door is a place where people come and go. The first line represents someone standing at a door. Here one leaves the privacy of one's room, closes the door behind him and is seen by others. Hiding or staying behind a closed door implies no public spirit and no sharing. This line encourages you to leave your room, letting people get to know you and understand your public spirit and good intentions. Thus, there is no blame.

LINE 2: *"Being united only with members of one's clan. One cannot achieve a big goal."*

The second line implies that gatherings should not be limited to small groups, especially ones in which those within the group are already close to each other. If fellowship among people becomes a clique, humiliation will result.

The entire group needs the balanced energy of the second line to keep it together. Since the second line only responds to the fifth, there is a tendency towards an exclusive relationship. Such a situation cannot produce a good leader, a trustworthy helper or an effective organizer.

LINE 3: *"Being united with rebels who hide in a mountain wilderness. For three years, one dares not begin a big undertaking because he is already overly ambitious."*

The third line symbolizes an ambush. Its target is the top line situated on a high, open place. Since the third line is the upper line of the lower trigram and is also in an exposed position, its ambush cannot succeed. Therefore, it must wait three years before attempting anything.

The third line cannot be a great leader; it is a warrior who cannot accomplish anything that requires tolerance and an expansive view. It can only lead bandits. It lacks a sense of cooperation and is weak in public spirit. Its ambition to become a leader is greater than its sense of obligation to accomplish its work.

LINE 4: *"One attacks the strong city wall. If he becomes aware of his impropriety and corrects his actions, good fortune will result."*

Although both the fourth and the first lines are strong, the fourth is the superior. If it tries to subdue the first line, it meets with resistance, symbolized by attacking a city wall. However, when one understands that this action is wrong and immediately corrects it, there will be no bad fortune. Good fortune is the result of valuable introspection.

> **LINE 5:** *"A great meeting. In the beginning strong emotions are expressed. But, at last, obstacles are overcome. Laughter is expressed and all rejoice."*

There are two groups in conflict: the first and the fourth lines, and the third and the sixth. The hostility and confrontation is overcome by the power and virtue of the fifth line. In the beginning, there is resentment and anger, but through the cooperation of the second and fifth lines, all emotional obstacles are dissolved and great harmony is attained.

Leadership must be accompanied by a sense of cooperation and fellowship. The leader of this hexagram, the fifth line, attains cooperation from the virtuous second line.

In order to achieve any great goal, one must have the courage and strength to withstand all difficulties. There is no great goal that can be achieved without difficulty. Sometimes one feels that a goal is too difficult to accomplish, but true joy is experienced when one finally looks back and sees how beautiful and necessary the entire process was.

> **LINE 6:** *"To be united with people in a rural place. Neither trouble nor any big achievement can be expected."*

Here people are united for the purpose of achieving a far-reaching goal. Though this is correct behavior, it is less influential in uniting people than one might hope.

SPECIFIC GUIDANCE

PERSONAL FORTUNE: Your fortune increases by gathering help from friends.

MARRIAGE: The marriage will be accomplished. An older woman is not helpful to the husband.

HOUSING/FAMILY: Harmonious conditions.

CHILDBIRTH: Peaceful delivery. The child will be a noble son.

LOOKING FOR HELP: Asking two people for help will prove successful.

SOCIAL/GOVERNMENTAL POSITION: It will be accomplished. Two people will help you achieve success.

TRADE/BUSINESS: Successful.

SEARCHING FOR SOMEONE: They can be found.

LOOKING FOR SOMETHING LOST: It is in the Southwest. It was taken by some people and is hard to find.

HUNTING FOR THIEVES: They can be caught soon.

LAWSUIT: There are people who protect you. There will soon be harmony.

CLIMATE: First there is rain, then the weather is good. As the fifth line says: "In the beginning, there are tears, then comes joy."

TRAVEL: Good fortune.

DISEASE: Fever. The whole body is in pain. It is difficult to cure.

PERSONAL WISH: If your wish is upright, it will be accomplished late in life.

COMMENTARY

Create positive influences
  for the needs of our fellow people.
From this we must not walk away.
Have compassion for the inferior world.
Becoming one of the spiritual healing lights,
  you provide a model and spiritual influence
  for all spiritual beings.
The radiance of your smile, your speech,
  your conduct and your way of life
  weaves a cohesive and beneficial medicine
  for all sick minds and bodies.

Maintaining kindness, generosity and grace
  is the heritage of our heavenly kinship.
The virtue of heaven and earth
  gives birth to all things.

The nature of heaven and earth
  leads us to our heavenly home.
Through compassion we not only enjoy eternity,
  we unite with the positive energy of all life.

Worldly people desire life and fear death.
But, fear it or not, physical death is certain.
Immortality can only be achieved
  through many deaths.
As the impulsive mind dies,
  the shadow of life and death can be seen
  as the surface activity of non-conscious awareness,
  for nothing is ever really born or destroyed.
The luminosity of pure mind
  comes only with the death of desire.
As the mind dies, your spirit comes alive,
  realizing an unusual majestic light.

The sons and daughters of impurity
  count worldly enjoyment as blessings.
In doing so, they block the channels of super energy.
They cannot see death hiding
  in the pleasures they seek.
Though death many not be immediate,
  these pursuits sap their vital essences
  and carry the odors of a corpse.
Only the true sons and daughters of
  of heavenly, whole beings
  know the wonderful principle
  of receiving life through death.

14 大有 ta yuo

GREAT PROVIDER - GREAT HARVEST

GUIDANCE: *"Great provision. Great good fortune."*

In this hexagram, Fire is above Heaven. The order of
the sixty-four hexagrams, from Chyan to Wei Chi, is a
natural progression. But in Tung Ren, the preceding

hexagram, energy comes together to accomplish a great goal. In this hexagram the goal is accomplished, resulting in much productivity and a great harvest. For this reason, "Great Harvest" follows "Uniting with People."

Ta-Yuo has several meanings. First, it represents sunlight which provides for all life. On a human level, the one yin line in the important fifth position is like a radiant leader who unites all other forces. The fifth line is able to gather strength through cooperation and gentleness, which is the innate power of harmony, thus this hexagram is called "The Great Provider" and is symbolized by the sun. It is also called "The Great Harvest" because an auspicious time of great productivity is indicated.

The upper trigram, Li (or light), implies clarity and wisdom. This means that one is clear-minded. The three yang lines in the lower trigram represent healthy and creative energy. To have health, strength and clarity of mind indicate that one can be a leader of all people. However, since this is an abundant time, the *I Ching* cautions against over-extending oneself.

Fullness implies decline. The full moon will soon begin to wane. In order to maintain this positive condition, everyone within the group must cooperate. Even a single deviation from the spirit of cooperation will cause an immediate change in this success. If each person will carry out his duty mindfully, without creating obstacles for others, the situation can be safely maintained.

One who seeks high achievement or a position of great responsibility must have the same radiance as the sun. One who drowns himself in selfishness will never achieve greatness.

LINE 1: *"Because one is isolated, one has some minor difficulties but invites no real trouble from the outside world."*

The first line has no correspondence with the fourth. It can only correspond to the fifth line, which is too far away. Therefore, the first line is in an isolated position. There is no blame, however, because this is a natural situation. In this position, one should stay away from those things which may be damaging and especially do nothing to draw attention to oneself.

LINE 2: *"Proceed with a big carriage. No problem."*

The image of the second line is that of a large wagon carrying loyalty and devotion to the fifth line. It is large because it carries the first, third and fourth lines with it. Here, the energy is very strong and should be used most wisely. Be like a "great carriage" moving toward a noble destination.

LINE 3: *"An important public undertaking can be beneficial. A small personal matter should not be undertaken because it will cause trouble."*

The third line needs an unselfish and impartial public spirit. With these qualities, it will enjoy the great harvest. If one is selfish and desires personal profit, the result will not be as one wishes. This line is in the powerful and influential position of change from the lower trigram to the upper and should work unselfishly for the great harvest of the whole.

In *I Ching* numerology, odd numbers indicate something active and even numbers indicate something stationary. Thus, the third line indicates a time of transition. Gains will become losses and losses will become gains. In unstable circumstances one cannot think too much about personal gain or loss. Only with a great heart and mind can this situation be properly handled.

LINE 4: *"If one does not over-expand, there will be no problem."*

The fourth line indicates that one is nearing fullness, like a balloon that is ready to burst if any more air is blown into it. If one continues to "puff" oneself up, one inevitably invites trouble and danger. One should use one's energy to be peaceful and cooperate during these times.

LINE 5: *"Being receptive and sincere while maintaining power brings good fortune."*

This fifth line is a gentle line and is the energy that holds the five yang lines in this hexagram together. The true power of an able leader does not lie in being a hero, but rather in being able to organize people to do the right job for the betterment of the whole. He does not need to be superior in every detail.

LINE 6: *"Heavenly blessing. Good fortune. No problem."*

In most hexagrams the top line represents excessiveness and extremes, but here it is a wonderful line, representing high achievements. The top line is a great supporter of the fifth line, or leader. It teaches that it is not always necessary to put the person with the most wisdom in the position of leadership, nor should everyone strive to be a leader. One can achieve greatness in a supporting role such as a teacher, advisor or through practically assisting another.

The sixth line represents a wise person who seeks neither favor nor any special benefit from the world. Help and blessings from Heaven are naturally bestowed upon one who is like this line, humble and virtuous. This is the teaching of Lao Tzu as well as the *I Ching*.

SPECIFIC GUIDANCE

PERSONAL FORTUNE: Beautiful, blessed and healthy.

MARRIAGE: The marriage will be successful. The woman will be beautiful but short.

HOUSING/FAMILY: Good fortune results from sharing a dwelling.

CHILDBIRTH: The delivery may be unsafe. Be cautious of a miscarriage.

LOOKING FOR HELP: In the beginning people will doubt you, but eventually you can succeed.

SOCIAL/GOVERNMENTAL POSITION: With the help of an important person, the situation will be prosperous.

TRADE/BUSINESS: It can be successful, but be careful of losing money.

SEARCHING FOR SOMEONE: They can be found in the South or the East.

WAITING FOR SOMEONE: They will come.

LOOKING FOR SOMETHING LOST: It can be found.

HUNTING FOR THIEVES: They are difficult to apprehend.

LAWSUIT: The judgment will cause you some anxiety in the beginning, but eventually there will be good fortune.

CLIMATE: If the weather is rainy, sunshine will follow. If there is sunshine, then there will be rain.

TRAVEL: Do not leave immediately, wait for several days. Traveling West will be profitable.

DISEASE: Headache or eye trouble, difficult to cure.

PERSONAL WISH: Difficult to achieve. In regards to money or literature, there can be success.

COMMENTARY
Stay With the Fundamental After Achieving the Great

There is nothing more worthwhile in life than to follow Tao. Possessing wealth, fame, position, power, intelligence, wisdom, beauty, etc., does not really matter. The most magnificent of all things is Tao. Though Tao cannot be possessed, it can be embodied. As stated in Chapter 25 of the *Tao Teh Ching*:

"Humanity takes the example of Earth
*   to stabilize itself.*
Earth takes the example of Heaven
*   to rotate itself.*
Heaven takes the example of Tao
*   to purify itself.*
Tao takes the example of itself
*   to integrate and disintegrate*
*   all things and all lives."*

What do the luxuries of life, ornamental knowledge, psychological toys, social and religious vanities all mean to human life? Value your plain life. Do not do things that cause you to lose your original perfect balance. This is called "wu wei" (non-doing).

Although it does not matter if you do something, it does matter if you overdo it. This is called "wei wu wei" (do the non-doing). These are two important guidelines from the *Tao Teh Ching*.

Mind, desires, entrails and bones compose the main constitution of human life. Do not let the mind exhaust that which supports the body. If the mind is overused, the entrails become weakened. If one has too many desires, the bones become hardened and the marrow dried.

For people who lack spiritual integration, their lop-sided, dualistic-mindedness becomes an obstacle in achieving or maintaining the wholeness of mind and spirit. Thus, battles and wars never end, within and without. It is impossible to attain inner peace or outer harmony without the achievement of mental and spiritual self-integration. This is to say that whole-mindedness must be put above all the philosophical and religious conceptions that have been the source of strife among people and have led to mental and spiritual separation from the absolute truth.

15 chien

mode5ty · egolessness

GUIDANCE: *"Egolessness. The developed one reaches his goal. Benefit goes to the humble while failure awaits the arrogant."*

In nature, a mountain stands above the expanse of the Earth, but in this hexagram the mountain is below. Its high peak is humbled. In the human realm, this signifies someone who does not exaggerate his emotions or self-importance, but modestly maintains his equanimity. In addition to modesty Ch'ien can also be translated as egolessness, moderation or humility.

Here, the mountain willingly takes a position lower than the Earth, thus it is self-effacing. The *I Ching* guides us to follow this example in our daily lives. One should be moderate at all times and not over-extend oneself. Moderation and modesty are the means for being durable and ever-lasting. A person of self-cultivation does not flaunt his achievements or bemoan his difficulties. By cultivating the virtues of modesty and egolessness, one does not presume to be more special than others. The ego is overcome by practicing modesty in difficult circumstances.

The mountain symbolizes earnestness, honesty, receptiveness, modesty, and yielding without resort to force. The virtue of Ch'ien is most apparent when conditions are unfavorable. One must, at times, accept hardship and do things that are not in accordance with one's hopes or plans. When superficial pride dissolves, the real treasure of integrity can shine forth. By moderating ambition, one's virtue becomes brighter. When one's mind is humble one becomes more honest and natural, and this is sure to bring a positive response from the subtle realm.

The *Tao Teh Ching* teaches that the way of Heaven is to increase the insufficient and decrease that which is overextended. Thus, one of cultivation allows some latitude in his life in order to avoid extremes. In most situations, modesty is the most important virtue because it allows a person to recognize the shortcomings and inadequacies that are obstacles to growth. In the long run, overconfidence breeds failure.

In each line of the lower trigram, modesty gives rise to good fortune. Therefore, the upper trigram is benefited because modesty is used to harmonize people through cooperation and organization. In the same way, one can organize and improve oneself. Each line of Ch'ien illustrates how modesty and egolessness make one a victor.

The first line represents a realistic person. When in a low position, he is interested only in steady progress and does not seek hasty achievement. The second line is a gentle person who is honest and yielding. His virtue is recognized and his influence is far-reaching. The third line, the only yang line of the hexagram, is responsible for pulling together the energy of all the yin lines and he works hard without complaint. This line represents one who is modest and willing to accept assignments that are distasteful to others. Such a person eventually earns the cooperation of all. The fourth line is in a high position; because of his modesty, those above trust him, while those below are not jealous. Since he creates no obstacles, he is able to achieve great things. The fifth line is a gentle leader who does not take advantage of his powerful position. This line is yielding and benevolent and thus keeps order among his followers. The top line is self-disciplining. Here modesty also means not overextending oneself, but rather working on ways to better organize responsibilities. Even in military actions, he is able to recognize and overcome his shortcomings.

Ch'ien follows Ta-Yuo, the Great Provider. Therefore, one of great possession, whether it be wisdom, wealth, social position, or anything else that is abundant, must have modesty. Only with modesty can one apply wisdom or power in a beneficial and non-threatening way. For example, one with a strong voice who uses it to its fullest capacity is likely to disturb others.

Regularity and normalcy usually make things endure. However, most people prefer the excitement and intensity of things that are of a transitory nature. One of modesty understands that greatness is achieved by remaining low and humble. This is truly a wise way to live.

LINE 1: *"The egoless one who crosses the great water and engages in adventures obtains good fortune."*

One of self-cultivation seeks steady progress with determination and modesty. These attributes allow him to move from his lowly position and to make progress without being too hasty or aggressive.

LINE 2: *"Expressing oneself without ego. By keeping to this practice, one has good fortune."*

Discussions and disagreements are unavoidable. What is most important is how one expresses oneself in these situations. One of self-cultivation will be modest.

Remember not to overdo modesty. People who are too modest are usually just trying to manipulate others. Look closely to see whether you bring peace to others or create disturbance. Further, excessive modesty can be interpreted as weakness, which can create problems. That situation is illustrated by the top line.

LINE 3: *"Be egoless and take the hard jobs. Those who are dedicated succeed in life."*

The third line teaches one to selflessly accept unpleasant tasks and put forth his best effort. Such actions represent the divine way to deal with things and eventually lead to benefit and good fortune.

On the other hand, those who believe they are overworked lose this opportunity by withdrawing from the chance to learn more, practice more and develop further. They never stop to realize that the benefits of work far outweigh the difficulties. In the long run, one will solidify achievements and gather merit. Those with this virtue are the true pillars that support the whole structure.

LINE 4: *"If one remains selfless, there is nothing unbeneficial in this position."*

Although the fourth line is usually close to a position of authority, there is still someone in the fifth place who supervises him. The fourth line is only a secondary leader, but with modesty he gains support from those below him and the trust of those above him. There is nothing wrong or unfavorable for a person in the fourth position if he is modest.

LINE 5: *"Do not depend on personal wealth or strength. Instead, be a source of help in correcting disorders. Everything is beneficial."*

The fifth line is a weak line, but fortunately everyone in his community is virtuous and wise. This line is not special, but because of its modesty, people follow it. Thus it can overcome any problem that arises inside or outside of its territory. It obtains help to accomplish whatever it wishes to do. Opposition can be dissolved smoothly.

LINE 6: *"He uses modesty instead of aggression with outsiders to correct the confusion within his territory."*

The top line represents self-regulation within one's "territory." When dissatisfaction arises, one should overcome one's own shortcomings and not interact aggressively with the outside world. This is the true meaning of modesty. The top line is not in a central position, but it is in a good position for self-cultivation and self-discipline. Thus, one is strengthened through the virtue of modesty.

SPECIFIC GUIDANCE

PERSONAL FORTUNE: For a while things go smoothly, but gradually they become difficult.
MARRIAGE: It can be accomplished, but for the woman it may be a confused sexual relationship.

HOUSING/FAMILY: The house is close to a mountain, but it is not good for children.

CHILDBIRTH: The delivery will be safe.

LOOKING FOR HELP: In the beginning there is no success. If you ask again, you will succeed.

SOCIAL/GOVERNMENTAL POSITION: Difficult to achieve an important position. In the spirit of modesty, do not even speak about a high position.

TRADE/BUSINESS: Later, it will be profitable.

SEARCHING FOR SOMEONE: They will return by themselves.

WAITING FOR SOMEONE: They will come later or they will not come at all.

LOOKING FOR SOMETHING LOST: Look in the East or South, some place with bamboo, pliant bushes or trees.

HUNTING FOR THIEVES: They are nearby, in the Southeast, and can be caught.

LAWSUIT: Make peace; a lawsuit in this situation is not good. Righteousness is on your side.

CLIMATE: It will be rainy.

TRAVEL: There may be obstacles but no harm. If you are with a crowd there is good fortune.

DISEASE: Depression and congestion; difficult to cure.

PERSONAL WISH: You will obtain the help of others, but it will take a long time to achieve the objective.

COMMENTARY

The wise person avoids having interest
  in that which is extreme.
When he knows something,
  he knows that he knows it.
When he does not know something,
  he is also aware of that.
In this way he preserves true knowledge.
When he experiences trouble,
  he uses it to develop his wisdom.
He uses roundness in thinking,
  and squareness in conduct.
He does not murmur against Heaven
  or blame other people.
In knowing the first movement of things,
  he develops the brightness of his mind.

Cordial and gratified feelings
  are the assets of his life.
He is of a most natural and pleasing appearance,
  and his mind has a high degree of ease and peace.
He can be thus because
  he keeps his mind dispassionate
  and unaffected by the cares of the world.
If you have respect for the high spirits
  of the ancient sages
  and think of them as if
  they were in front of you,
They will then respond to you
  as friends and guides.
In this way, you can connect with
  the highest realm of the universe.

16   YU

COMFORT

GUIDANCE: *"A favorable time for expansion. Establish a new branch and set up a new state. Send out an army for protection."*

In this hexagram, Thunder is above the Earth. The first sound of thunder signifies the coming of Spring and is a time when all animals in hibernation become active again. This is a significant time when all things blossom from a period of inactivity into a time of liveliness and prosperity.

The Chinese name for this hexagram is "Yu." Its ancient meaning implies feeling relaxed, comfortable and without disturbance. Because of good preparation, this seems to be a time to enjoy life and have a good time. However, the *I Ching* cautions that a time of ease and smoothness is also a time to be careful of too much looseness, carelessness and overindulgence. Comfort often brings a sense of smugness which, in turn, can invite danger. However, the sound of thunder can awaken people before they become completely lost in their pleasures.

People who are wise find pleasure in virtuous ways. Good food and music become offerings to the Heavenly Realm, and joyful occasions are great times of unity and are good times to organize responsibilities, delegate duties and assign new tasks. If all energy was dissipated in movement and frivolity, there would be no preparation or defense against the time of decline that must inevitably follow.

The fourth line is not in a natural position of leadership. However, in this hexagram, it is in the position of strength and influence because it is the only yang line. Further, during times of order and peace the leader or fifth line can relinquish authority to the fourth line without major concerns. On the human level, this is a time to be careful and well-disciplined and not succumb to excessive indulgences.

LINE 1: *"One is greatly pleased with his achievements. Danger."*

The first line expresses self-complacency. One is endangered by such an attitude. This is a yin line in a yang position and is thereby weakened. But since it corresponds with the strong fourth line, its excessive self-assuredness can be curbed and disciplined by the fourth line's positive energy. The fourth line is the moving force of thunder, which restrains the sloppiness, self-indulgence and smugness of this line.

LINE 2: *"One is as solid as a rock and unshaken by the comforts of life. Good fortune."*

The second line represents one who remains aware while enjoying prosperous times. Appropriate to this position, it maintains a firm and disciplined attitude and never indulges in excessive merriment. The virtue of the second line is its ability to maintain self-control in all situations, whether joyous or sad. Following this example brings great good fortune.

LINE 3: *"Out of envy for the powerful, one resorts to flattery trying to please him. Such actions must be corrected without delay; otherwise, there will be remorse."*

The third line makes a constructive contribution to the fourth, but tries too hard to please. The third line should offer the fourth support, not flattery. This is a yin line in a yang position and thus signifies an improper attitude. However, in this situation, there is still a chance to correct oneself before it is too late.

LINE 4: *"Being a source of comfort and harmony, one attains greatness. Without suspicion, friends form a fellowship."*

The fourth line is the focal line of this hexagram and is in a position of harmony, organization and joyfulness. In ancient times, spiritual people wore their hair tightly bound on the top of their heads, held in place by a clasp. This line is like a clasp that holds people together. Through their support, one's goals and wishes can be easily realized.

LINE 5: *"One has an illness but does not die. Over-indulgence is like an incurable disease; however, with effort, clear-mindedness and self-respect, it can be overcome."*

The fifth line represents one who enjoys his comforts to such an extent that he forgets his responsibilities, loses himself and must then rely on the fourth line for protection. Such over-indulgence is like being sick. Lacking self-control, the fifth line becomes useless.

Here, the leader neglects his duty and relinquishes his power to his subordinate, the fourth line. He loses both himself and the importance of his position to these happy times. In such a situation, a leader must be especially alert. When the whole nation is celebrating, it is very vulnerable and must be protected.

LINE 6: *"Enjoyment based on self-delusion cannot last long. However, there is hope if one corrects oneself."*

The top line indicates that one's happiness is a result of self-delusion. If one changes and corrects oneself, trouble can be avoided.

SPECIFIC GUIDANCE

PERSONAL FORTUNE: Good fortune.

MARRIAGE: The woman's nature is damaging to the husband; she will need to be remarried.

HOUSING/FAMILY: The house will be badly damaged.

CHILDBIRTH: Unsafe. If the delivery is in the summer, the baby will be a boy.

LOOKING FOR HELP: It will come.

SOCIAL/GOVERNMENTAL POSITION: It can be achieved at a later time.

TRADE/BUSINESS: The price of merchandise will rise sharply and one will be able to make substantial profits.

WAITING FOR SOMEONE: After overcoming some obstacles, they will come.

LOOKING FOR SOMETHING LOST: It is difficult to recover.

HUNTING FOR THIEVES: The thief is a female who has escaped to the West. She cannot be caught quickly.

LAWSUIT: At first it is a big matter. Later it becomes small and in the end there is peace.

CLIMATE: It will be fine.

TRAVEL: Do not travel with a person who is weak.

DISEASE: Difficult to cure.

PERSONAL WISH: It is possible to fulfill.

COMMENTARY

In times of ease,
  one with a deep vision of life
  follows the way of immortality.
Love not the world of colored dust.
One hundred years pass in an instant.
In the time it takes to snap your fingers,
  we live and die.
Our temporary existence
  is as significant as a dew drop.
Yesterday a man rode his horse through the streets;
  today he lies sleeping in his coffin.
This is the glamour of life.

Like so many autumn leaves,
  all the stories of a man's life one day fall,
  and become a dream resting under the spring tree.

Start your cultivation early.
Learn to balance your life.
Make your mind and body firm.
This is important.

First weed your mental field,
  allowing not one particle of dust
  to remain in the lens of your mental eye.
When the mind is transparent and subtle,
  the soul becomes supreme.
Then you can use your power as you will.
But do not use it carelessly,
  it is not a plaything.
Accumulate too much wealth
  and it will prove not only burdensome,
  but disastrous.
Gain too high a position,
  and you will find it both dangerous and degrading
  to your true self.
Keep to the roots of your life;
  do not live unconsciously as in a vague dream.

The approach to true happiness
  should not be like a fire
  that dies as quickly as it flares up.
Truly happy people do not clutch at worldly things,
  but appreciate all that comes to them,
  living contentedly with their invisible,
  subtle and immortal natures.
Do not look for happiness
  in the excitement of the sensory world.
Rather, gain an understanding
  of the subtle laws of the universe,
  and it shall be yours.
True wisdom can save you.
Move rapidly to board the steady
  spiritual ship of safety.

17 隨 SUI ䷐

compLiance · foLLowinG

GUIDANCE: *"Compliance. Everything should go smoothly if one is faithful to one's highest principles."*

In this hexagram, Lake is above Thunder. The energy of the lake is gentle, while that of thunder is strong and active. The powerful force of thunder subordinates itself to the gentleness of the lake; therefore, positive things can be accomplished and good fortune will result.

One who is strong-willed usually does not like to obey or listen to those of lesser stature; thus, he is seldom able to accomplish anything that requires the cooperation of other people. However, if one is able to adapt to gentle people by virtue of self-discipline and an open mind, there will be great harmony and real achievement. Compliance is only possible when aggression, stubbornness and rigidity are put aside.

Compliance also means following one's highest principles. The manner in which one complies with his principles determines the kind of response one will evoke from the high spiritual realms. Like attracts like; following good principles and maintaining integrity will attract a beneficial response. Complying with negative forces will bring about disaster through the negativity that one attracts.

It is not difficult for the truthseeker to follow the good. The problem is knowing what is good. If an inexperienced person follows one who knows as little as he, the outcome can be disastrous. There are two extreme types of people in this regard: one readily gives consent to whatever other people think is right; the other stubbornly defends his opinions no matter what others think. Neither view is correct or balanced. What or whom one follows represents one's level of growth. This hexagram gives advice on how to choose and follow someone or something.

LINE 1: *"Going out the door and making friends with highly-achieved individuals without losing one's virtue brings success."*

The first line is the strong moving line of Thunder. It tells us that when the time is right, we should use our energy to change ourselves. Do not shut yourself in a room. Instead, go out and make friends with virtuous people; however, you should not unquestioningly accept the words of others. Instead, develop and broaden your views through your life experiences. This is a good time to reach out to others. When a new era or a revolution begins, one should depend on a group of strong people.

LINE 2: *"One who stays with what is small loses the opportunity to connect with what is great. In this case, you have a clear choice."*

The second line has a relationship with both the first and the fifth lines. The first line represents a close neighbor, while the fifth line represents a remote friend or relative. The second line should follow the fifth line, who is worthier than the first. If she takes the easy way out by simply following the first line, the opportunity to follow the great one will be missed, and she will lose her chance to be more useful. By being too greedy for small profits, we often lose the real chance to succeed in a great undertaking. This is the lesson of the second line.

LINE 3: *"Compliance with the great overcomes the attraction of the small. This choice brings positive results. One should be firm with one's decision."*

There are ways that lines can be integrated in a hexagram. One is the first line corresponding to the fourth; the second to the fifth; and the third to the sixth. In this relationship of 1 and 4, 2 and 5, and 3 and 6, each pair has both an odd yang number and an even yin number.

The other kind of integration is that of the first and second lines; the third and fourth; and the fifth and sixth. The number correspondence of 1 and 2, 3 and 4, and 5 and 6 can be integrated as harmonizing energy if the lines are in their correct natural order.

The third line in this hexagram has two choices for association; either the second or fourth line. But the second line cannot be a good leader for the third. Under these circumstances, it rightfully chooses the fourth yang line. It gives up the lesser second yin line in order to follow the greater fourth yang line.

The third line is a yin line in a yang position and tends to use craftiness or cleverness in its pursuits. When one makes a choice, one should not do so for self- ish reasons only. One who seeks only personal benefit from this situation may suffer. Good fortune can only re- sult when the action is not for personal, narrow-minded or selfish gain.

LINE 4: *"The follower attempts to surpass his leader. Even though this line may be correct, there will be trou- ble if it insists on its own way. Thus, it should remain in compliance with the leader. The clouds of suspicion will eventually disperse and brightness will reappear."*

The fourth line is a yang line in a yin position and is next to the strong leader, the fifth yang line. Although such a position enables him to dominate the lower tri- gram, he should not do so. If he does not use self-re- straint, the situation could become dangerous and the good order destroyed. If he recognizes and remains in this correct position, there will be no blame or trouble.

LINE 5: *"Being faithful to what is good brings good fortune."*

Both the top line, as an advisor, and the second line, as the leader of the lower trigram, offer faithfulness to the fifth line. The fifth line is a trustworthy leader and enjoys the loyalty of its followers.

LINE 6: *"The wise one is bound with an assignment at the holy mountain. He offers the highest compliance to the Heavenly will."*

A mountain symbolizes a high but inactive position, such as that of a special advisor. Some people are very valuable but may not be suited to being followers. The top line is a wise and virtuous person, but the leader in the fifth position does not insist that he be one of his fol- lowers. Instead, the leader "binds" the top line with re- spect and love and makes him a special helper. His spiri- tual assignment is to serve the leader and the world.

SPECIFIC GUIDANCE

PERSONAL FORTUNE: Very ordinary. One should temporarily keep still, at least until next year, which will be a good time for distant travel.

MARRIAGE: The marriage can succeed, especially if it is a strong man marrying a gentle woman.

HOUSING/FAMILY: Something strange will cause you shock.

CHILDBIRTH: The delivery will be safe, and the child will be a boy. If the fifth line is received, the mother will have some trouble.

LOOKING FOR HELP: It can be obtained.

SOCIAL/GOVERNMENTAL POSITION: Wait. This is not the right time.

TRADE/BUSINESS: Presently there is difficulty, but next spring will be more profitable.

SEARCHING FOR SOMEONE: They can be found.

WAITING FOR SOMEONE: They will come immediately.

LOOKING FOR SOMETHING LOST: It is not far away.

HUNTING FOR THIEVES: They are hiding in a field to the East, the wilderness or in a house close to water.

LAWSUIT: There will be a jail sentence.

CLIMATE: There will be heavy rains with thunder.

TRAVEL: Following others or going together is good. One should not travel alone at this time.

DISEASE: There are headaches and difficulty in eating and drinking. The problem is difficult to cure.

PERSONAL WISH: It can be accomplished.

COMMENTARY
The Triune of the Spiritual World

Follow what is indescribable. Ally with what is inexpressible. What is describable is only in the relative sphere of language. What is not expressible is the absolute truth as stated in Chapter 14 of the *Tao Teh Ching*:

"What you try to see,
  but evades your vision
  you say: Yi!
What you try to hear
  but evades your hearing
  you say: Shi!

What you try to touch
  but evades your hand
  you say: Hui!"

The invisible, the inaudible and the formless are expressed as a triune, but they form an undivided oneness. Because they are of the spiritual realm where intelligence fails to go, they evade all further inquiry. In spiritual terminology this is called "one chi transformed into three Pure Realms."

Yu Ching, or Immaculate Purity, is the name for the unnameable. This realm is for the original immortals such as Yuan Shih.

Shang Ching, or Unblemished Purity, is the name for the imageless. This realm is for the responsive supernatural beings such as Lin-Pau.

Tai Ching, or Great Purity, is the name for the formless. This realm is for the integral ones such as Lan-Chun.

These three Pure Realms maintain the universe totally and are interconnected and integrated in the Subtle Realm.

This Subtle Realm of the Triune is higher and more fundamental than the ordinary Spiritual Realm. It has been the testimony of all developed ones that the Triune is the foundation of the most Subtle Realm. To enter the High Realm is a great achievement.

The highest spiritual realm is the Great Pure One, the Tao, the Way and the Law. This is where all spiritual and immortal beings live. Tao is more subtle and original than the spiritual or godly realm. Here, there is no individuality, only various responses to different functions.

This is the secret of the great spiritual truth. A god can either be an ordinary human being or one who is highly developed. The latter is achieved and able to dwell in the Divine Immortal Realm. The former is an unsuccessful or degraded god who deviated from the Way and therefore dwells in the mortal realm. Surely, this is not the end for people who are unsuccessful in maintaining their spiritual integrity.

In our tradition, only the one who is able to break through the "three in one divided" (the invisible, the inaudible and the untouchable) can conjoin with the real, wonderful, spiritual world.

18 盅 KU

CORRECTING the CORRUPTION

GUIDANCE: *"Work against corruption. This is a beneficial time to engage in an adventurous task. Prepare carefully in advance and make a thorough inspection afterward."*

In this hexagram, Wind is below the Mountain. However, the gentle wind cannot penetrate the dense area at its base. A place that does not receive air becomes decayed and rotten, thus we have the image of corruption. Furthermore, the Chinese character for this hexagram represents a container in which worms thrive. Although the *I Ching*'s guidance enables one to recognize a particular situation, its main force lies in how to correct the situation, if necessary.

Here, corruption has already manifested and can no longer be ignored. At this time, a thorough examination of the situation before deciding on the appropriate way to take action is of utmost importance. The *I Ching* advises the use of extreme caution at the outset. If this advice is not followed, one may easily misjudge the situation and fall under the influence of corruption.

With a compromising attitude toward corruption, nothing is accomplished and one loses the opportunity to correct the problem. Correcting mistakes of the past is not an easy task, especially if one is in a position of responsibility and does not recognize the gravity of the situation. However, if one has sincere intentions and acts decisively, success will eventually come.

Patience, gentleness and tact are essential when correcting past mistakes, especially when loved ones are involved; otherwise disturbance and destruction will ensue. Since the present contains the positive as well as negative accumulations of the past, one must be very careful when correcting past errors not to destroy the positive aspects.

LINE 1: *"To correct the father's corruption, the son is called upon to help. No blame. Though there is some difficulty at first, good results will be brought forth eventually."*

The "father's corruption" represents the negative effects of past actions toward oneself or one's family. Correction must be handled with care, tolerance and gentleness. If force is used, there will only be resistance to change and nothing will be accomplished.

LINE 2: *"When correcting the mother's corruption, beware of being too rigid and stop before going too far."*

Whereas the "father's corruption" is social, the "mother's corruption" signifies a personal matter. Since emotions are involved, this problem must be handled with the utmost understanding and tact. Finding the correct balance in this situation is also necessary. If one's approach is too strong, hurt feelings will result. On the other hand, if one is not firm enough, the problem will not be corrected. Thus, one must proceed with great care.

LINE 3: *"Correcting the father's corruption with too much strength will result in some remorse; however, no big problem will arise."*

One's intentions and approach are appropriate; however, since too much strength is used, one meets resistance in correcting the social problem. If this yang line changes to a yin line, the result will be Meng ☶, Hexagram #4, or a situation which is not yet very civilized or well-developed. Misunderstandings and resistance from others may arise. One must be careful in one's approach because assertiveness will certainly hinder any progress that might be made.

LINE 4: *"Increasing the father's corruption. With an indecisive attitude, one cannot rectify the situation. Humiliation."*

One is not in an appropriate position to apply the correct energy and illuminate the corruption. Therefore, one's involvement will reinforce the problem and humiliation shall result.

LINE 5: *"Correcting the father's corruption, one enjoys high honors and continues the positive aspect of the father's creation."*

Correction is possible because of cooperation from the people, as represented by the strong second line. Correcting what is spoiled is not a negative undertaking. It can further and refresh the positive aspects of the past and stop the confusion of the present. Thus, the condition is corrected.

LINE 6: *"He does not wish to serve nobility, but withdraws in order to cultivate his own virtue."*

When there is corruption, correction will eventually follow. Has this not always been a fact repeated in history? Therefore, the wise ones give up foolish involvement in human affairs. Instead, they prefer a simple life of cultivation and self-improvement. If everyone would accept and follow this example, the world would naturally be corrected.

Developed people work on correcting themselves. This is the fundamental way to correct the corruption of humanity as a whole. If one changes one's own life, then there is hope for all life. A developed individual does not try to please the world with grandiose promises, nor does he try to entice those in positions of influence so that he might profit. By understanding his own goal and by working on himself, he corrects the corruption of humanity for all times.

SPECIFIC GUIDANCE

PERSONAL FORTUNE: There will be good fortune, but the old way needs to be changed and a new way embarked upon.

MARRIAGE: Not good. The couple may pass diseases to one another.

HOUSING/FAMILY: By taking care of family administration, one will be freed from temptation, damage or loss.

CHILDBIRTH: There is the possibility of an abnormal fetus. If the third line is received, there will be danger for both the new baby and the mother.

LOOKING FOR HELP: No success.

SOCIAL/GOVERNMENTAL POSITION: In the beginning there is no success; however, if a further attempt is made, there can be success.

TRADE/BUSINESS: The inventory will be damaged. Try to sell it fast.

SEARCHING FOR SOMEONE: Hurry. Use three people in your search.

WAITING FOR SOMEONE: They will come.

LOOKING FOR SOMETHING LOST: It can be found but is damaged.

HUNTING FOR THIEVES: They are in the Southeast and can be caught.

LAWSUIT: If you are dishonest, you may win; but in the end you will lose. The best way to settle the matter is without court action.

CLIMATE: There will be more rain and less clear weather. If the third line is received, the weather will be fine.

TRAVEL: Misfortune.

DISEASE: Although it is curable, be very careful. Someone has used a curse or black magic to make trouble.

PERSONAL WISH: Difficult to accomplish; do not indulge in the matter.

COMMENTARY
Divergence

The achieved spirit, unobstructed by worldly triviality, is easily misinterpreted as being passive, irresponsible, escapist, lazy, impractical or nonsensical. Such a negative misconception is prevalent among new students. For this reason, readers of Chuang Tzu mistakenly believe that they have learned everything from this great elucidator of Tao. However, the result of their studies indicate otherwise.

An ancient Chinese proverb says, "One assumes he has drawn a tiger, but the tiger turns out to be a dog." Finding such examples is not difficult; understanding the real spirit of an achieved one is not a simple task. The achieved spirit has no certain form. Thus, how can one hope to make it visible?

A few years ago, a party was given in order to introduce me to some people. I brought a rose with me from my garden for the hostess who was a regular patient of mine. She paid many compliments to this rose of Chinese golden redness. The guest speaker, who was introduced as an expert on oriental philosophy, then told the following story:

"Chuang Tzu, one of the great spiritually achieved ones, had a beautiful rose garden of great renown, and every year he would open the garden to the public. Many highly educated people would bring good wine to sip when they came to see the beautiful roses. Reports of this beautiful garden eventually attracted the curiosity of the Emperor, who owned the largest rose garden with the most lovely roses in the kingdom. In order to know whether the acclaimed beauty of Chuang Tzu's garden was true or just a rumor, the Emperor sent a notice to Chuang Tzu announcing when he would arrive to see the specially-cultivated roses. After receiving the king's notice, Chuang Tzu cleared the crowds, closed the garden, and prepared for the important visit.

"When the special day arrived, Chuang Tzu humbly greeted the Emperor at the gate. The Emperor was in high spirits, anticipating his promenade along the garden path. Everywhere, rose bushes filled the garden, but not one of them had even a single rose! The Emperor's consternation grew and grew until it reached a peak. Then suddenly, in the center of the garden, to the Emperor's great surprise, a single rose proudly and brilliantly blossomed. His Majesty's heart was immediately seized by an irresistible fascination with this rose. For a long, long time he stood there, lost in reverie. When his consciousness was restored, he declared this rose the true 'queen' of all roses.

"Dear friends," the speaker said seriously as he went on, "do you know why the Emperor made this rose the 'queen?' I will tell you. This was actually an ordinary rose, no more beautiful or extraordinary than any other, but before the Emperor's visit Chuang Tzu had cut and removed all the other roses from the garden, leaving only this one in an unexpected place. For that reason, the Emperor believed it to be a truly special rose."

When the speaker had finished his story, I was asked to comment. Having no other choice, I continued the story:

"Ladies and gentlemen, do you know what happened to the Emperor after seeing this wonderful rose? He missed the rose so terribly that he became seriously ill!

All his high ministers and generals knew the Emperor's illness was caused by his longing for this special rose, and in desperation, they hastily began to search for a rose of equal beauty. However, since it was wintertime, there were no roses for thousands of miles, and these were obstructed by snow and ice.

"Because their interest was first and foremost to restore the Emperor's health, they devised a special plan to bring, by way of fast horses, the best roses from the warm lands of the South. People living along this route thought there must be something very important happening on their southern border. No one realized that these fast horses were actually carrying just roses.

"The Emperor's health did not improve, however, and in order for him to rest peacefully, he needed to hold a rose in his hand at all times. But when he would awaken, he would discover the lovely rose scattered in petals and become even more ill!

"Since the trouble had developed from Chuang Tzu's rose, the helpless high ministers and generals finally decided to seek his help. Chuang Tzu was a 'clever' master, so he agreed to give his help. It took only a short time for him to take a beautiful rose to the royal court and let the old Emperor - who had not left his ivory sick bed since his illness began - hold it in his hands. No one and nothing had been able to help him feel better until finally he was able to hold one of Chuang Tzu's roses. Now, every time he awoke from his rest, he would see the beautiful rose in all its splendor, safely in his hands.

"The Emperor gradually recovered from his very unusual illness and could once again attend to the affairs of state. The people of the entire nation, after learning of his recovery, were thankful and very happy.

"Dear friends, are you interested in knowing the secret of the flower that Chuang Tzu took to the Emperor? Let me share it with you. It was an artificial rose, since there were no true roses in the kingdom.

"Confucius, who knew the story of the secret rose, once sighed and sincerely said, 'When worldly people are ill, artificial roses make them feel refreshed. However, it is not the artificial rose or artificial truth that deserves blame for lack of truthfulness. It is the intellectual mind which is attached to artificial, untruthful creation that makes people lose themselves!' Is this not true?"

19   Lin

Advancing

GUIDANCE: *"Advance. It is beneficial to go forward with a positive attitude, but be mindful of the cyclical nature of things."*

Yang energy moves forward and upward. In this hexagram, the two bottom yang lines, the growing force, are in the process of development. This expresses the natural tendency of yang energy. This is the primary energy of the universe and the great motivator of human behavior. It is very important to properly control and guide this yang energy in its early stages of growth. Otherwise, change will occur too quickly and difficulty will arise. Such is the warning of this hexagram.

Change is the reality of all phenomena, and all change comes about through the interaction and alternation of yin and yang. Each of the sixty-four hexagrams reflects a different stage of their interaction. The alternation of yin and yang can be most clearly seen in the twelve hexagrams which correspond to the twelve months of the year. Six of these hexagrams express the increase of yang energy, while the other six express its retreat. The first part of the cycle, in which the yang energy increases, is after the winter solstice:

Revival
(11th month)
Capricorn

Advancing
(12th month)
Aquarius

Harmony
(1st month)
Pisces

Strength
(2nd month)
Aries

Resolution
(3rd month)
Taurus

Complete Yang
(4th month)
Gemini

At this point, the second half of the cycle, in which yang energy decreases, begins after the summer solstice:

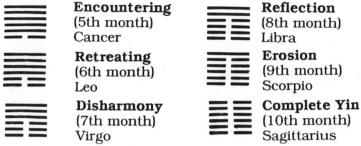

Encountering
(5th month)
Cancer

Reflection
(8th month)
Libra

Retreating
(6th month)
Leo

Erosion
(9th month)
Scorpio

Disharmony
(7th month)
Virgo

Complete Yin
(10th month)
Sagittarius

Though all things must change, we should never be discouraged. One must face whatever happens and learn not to push or interfere with the natural process of growth. If one handles oneself well in the early stages of growth, one's cycle will naturally be lengthened. Otherwise, things will happen too quickly and the cycle will diminish. Everyone should understand the guidance of this hexagram and take heed of both its encouragement and warning.

LINE 1: *"Advance impartially. One should start in this manner and continue in this direction. Good fortune."*

The first and the second lines, advancing yang energy, should practice broad-mindedness and impartiality toward all four yin lines without being attached to any of them. This will insure correct action.

LINE 2: *"Impartial advance without prejudice continues. Everything is profitable. Good fortune."*

This line is the closest to the four yin lines, which could create obstacles. If the yang energy becomes attached to any of the yin lines, progress will be stopped.

LINE 3: *"Easy advancement. If one abuses one's position, there will be trouble in the long run. If this tendency is corrected immediately, there will be no blame."*

When one's power is young and growing, there is a temptation to mistreat people by throwing one's weight around. There may also be a tendency to abuse one's health through indulgence. At this time, caution and restraint are needed if one wishes to continue advancing smoothly.

LINE 4: *"Correct advancement. No fault."*

The fourth line is harmonious and cooperates with the first line, which is appropriate. This makes a smooth advance possible for both.

LINE 5: *"Wise advancement. This is how the great should proceed. Good fortune."*

This is the best position for the first and second lines as they advance. This line has gained the wide acceptance of the people. It knows how to practice the principles of balance and harmony, and its moves are therefore suitable and beneficial.

LINE 6: *"Sincere advancing. Good fortune. No blame."*

When the advancing yang energy has reached the top line, it has accomplished its fullness in width and depth. Its maturity and mellowness are expressed by a kind heart. External growth matches internal growth. This line stresses cultivating inner growth, which should not be neglected by indulging in external activities. In this way, one advances toward good fortune.

SPECIFIC GUIDANCE

PERSONAL FORTUNE: Now is the best time.   The Chinese word "Lin" means occurring immediately.

MARRIAGE: It can be accomplished, but since the third line does a lot of talking there will be some quarreling.

HOUSING/FAMILY: Having a good house close to the water and living with someone is beneficial.

CHILDBIRTH: If the divination is made in spring or summer, it will be a girl; if in autumn or winter, it will be a boy. The delivery will be safe at either time.

LOOKING FOR HELP: It is difficult to achieve one's purposes.

SOCIAL/GOVERNMENTAL POSITION: Successful.

TRADE/BUSINESS: Profitable.

SEARCHING FOR SOMEONE: After a long time, you can meet them.

WAITING FOR SOMEONE: They will come very soon.

LOOKING FOR SOMETHING LOST: Hurry to look for it. If you wait too long, it will be difficult to find.

HUNTING FOR THIEVES: There are three or four people at the base of the Southeast mountain and they are difficult to catch.

LAWSUIT: If you sue someone, you will hurt yourself. If you remain peaceful, all will be benefited.

CLIMATE: It will rain for a long time without stopping.

TRAVEL: Good fortune for travel.

DISEASE: It is curable but very slowly.

PERSONAL WISH: It can be achieved.

COMMENTARY

To become one with Tao depends wholly on oneself.
To achieve the level of a shien, a heavenly being,
depends solely on your will.
It is possible.
True achievement is obtainable by all
when they stop clinging selfishly to their desires.
Detach yourself from the irrelevance
of worldly affairs.
Allow not one piece of dust to stain your true nature,
and it will clearly and freely shine through.
Then it will be impossible
for the world's evils and poisons
to present themselves to you;
evils that create untold difficulties and problems.
When action is the result of the desires of the mind,
you perpetuate the painful rounds
of life, death and rebirth.
You remain unconscious.
Avoid suffering the consequences of your actions
by ridding your mind of all desire
for or against anything.
If your desire to achieve is too strong,
you will disturb your true nature.
Instead of ascending to shiendom,
you will spiral downward into chaos,
your subtle nature no longer intact.
Even one impure motive will spawn
a disturbance in the mind,
causing you to lose the humility and
clarity established by Tao.

What you have already achieved,
  you can no longer enjoy.
Alas, your previous efforts shall all
  have been in vain.
Dissolve the poisons of greed and hatred,
  remove yourself from the passions of love,
  and they shall transform into sweet dew,
  cooling and purifying you.

20   觀   KUAN

CONTEMPLATION · POINT OF VIEW

GUIDANCE: *"Contemplation. After washing his hands and beginning the ceremony, with deep sincerity the officiant centers his mind. The hearts and minds of all the participants are attracted by his good example. Likewise, the way of the highly evolved inspires people to adore the divine order of the universe."*

In this hexagram, Wind is above Earth.   Just as a penetrating wind pervades everywhere, a good way of life and good teachings influence everyone they touch.

The two yang lines at the top of the hexagram represent models of virtue in times when negative forces are pushing forward.   The image of the hexagram suggests an altar or temple where an opportunity is provided to witness spiritual activity and to adore divine beings.   This is the reason a spiritual temple was traditionally called a Kuan.

The greater significance of Kuan, however, extends beyond the physical structure of a temple or shrine.   It represents a way of life that is cultivated and guided by constant self-contemplation.   Through such introspection, one remains unaffected by the pressures of worldly life and stays attuned to the deepest level of nature, which is the origin of the universal life force.   By following worldly changes, one becomes lost in the temptations of living superficially.   Therefore, Kuan is more than a temple.   It symbolizes a way of life: the practice of deep contemplation and the pathway to eternal unity. This kind of spiritual cultivation is necessary for one's complete growth.

One's mind reflects one's practices and vice-versa. Therefore, maintaining spiritual practice within one's "inner altar," or "kuan," nurtures one's divine nature in order to attain unity with all things.

This hexagram is also concerned with one's overall view of life, which may be determined by how broad and encompassing one's understanding is. Even if one has traveled in many countries and lived among many different people, one's view may still be very narrow.

The lines in this hexagram represent various levels of awareness. The first line represents a shallow vision and is called the "view of children." The second line represents the awareness one has from behind a door or screen, or from an inner room. One's view from such a place is not very expansive, nor does it allow a face-to-face encounter, thus it is called the "view of ancient, overly-protected ladies." The third line, the highest position in the lower trigram, has a clearer, more expansive view. The fourth line represents close contact and direct experience, thereby allowing a clear, objective point of view. The fifth line represents one of self-reflection. Being in an influential position, he is aware of his responsibility to set a good example for everyone. The sixth line represents reflection in one's spiritual life. With a sense of moral responsibility, one can only enjoy complete inner peace when the whole world is no longer in a state of confusion.

LINE 1: *"A child's vision. Though not a problem for the undeveloped, it can be disastrous for a developed individual."*

This line has the viewpoint of a child. There is no blame because one has not yet reached a level of sound judgment and developed vision. However, for an adult's vision to remain like a child's is shameful. Such a person will eventually be humiliated.

LINE 2: *"Vision from behind a screen, like a young girl who hides behind a screen and timidly peeps out. This does not deserve encouragement."*

One's vision is limited from a dark position, symbolized by a young girl who shyly peers out from behind a screen. For her, this is an expression of innocence; however, this is not generally a good way to observe things.

LINE 3: *"With the broad vision obtained by contemplating one's life, one can decide whether to go forward or to withdraw."*

Here the *I Ching* responds by throwing the question back. One is now in a position of change and indecisiveness. Going forward or retreating are both correct at specific times. One should now be observant and gather relevant knowledge from all sources in order to know which action is appropriate. Fortunately, this line has the clear vision and understanding that comes from contemplation. Since one wishes to remain disciplined, one does not imprudently push forward or allow oneself to become trapped by temptations or trouble.

When reflecting upon life, especially when one feels insufficient in some manner, remember that there is always someone in a worse position. However, when trying to cultivate virtue and maintain high standards, always look up to someone more developed. An ancient proverb states, "Look above for the standard of virtue; look below for the standard of life."

LINE 4: *"It furthers one to go forward to see the country and to be the honored guest of the king."*

This is an encouraging opportunity. Since one is now in a high position, one has the chance to observe all that is below. This is signified by "seeing the country as a guest of the royal court" or by seeing value and glory in one's surroundings.

One who is in a low position should look above for an example; one who is in a high position should not only look within, but should also survey his surroundings in order to better understand the situation. A good opportunity now appears for one's vision to expand through great experiences.

LINE 5: *"Reflecting on one's way of life, the great one knows how people are positively influenced."*

In this position, one's actions are being observed by all. Being in a position to influence others, one must be a model of righteousness and continually work on self-development.

LINE 6: *"With prudence, one contemplates one's life."*

In this position, one no longer has strong or direct influence over others. However, one can still offer a good spiritual example and should not discontinue constant self-cultivation. This line describes one of high virtue who follows the depths of Tao. The divine nature of the universe and universal love are what he adores. As a spiritual model, he serves others by quietly living according to the principle of Kuan, not by preaching eloquently.

SPECIFIC GUIDANCE

PERSONAL FORTUNE: Good fortune for one talented in art or literature. This is a profitable time to get out and make things happen; one should not stay at home.

MARRIAGE: Conflicts and opposition will arise.

HOUSING/FAMILY: If the house is located close to a shrine or temple, circumstances will be all right.

CHILDBIRTH: It will be safe. The first baby will be a girl; the second will be a boy.

LOOKING FOR HELP: One should rely on the help of a person in a high position or on an influential religious figure.

SOCIAL/GOVERNMENTAL POSITION: It can be achieved as you wish.

TRADE/BUSINESS: Successful.

SEARCHING FOR SOMEONE: One should look in the West.

WAITING FOR SOMEONE: They will not come.

LOOKING FOR SOMETHING LOST: One should look toward the Southwest.

HUNTING FOR THIEVES: They are hiding in a church. If one moves fast, they can be found.

LAWSUIT: One's actions are justified, and a peaceful settlement comes in the end.

CLIMATE: Although it will not rain, conditions are uncertain as to whether it will be cloudy or sunny.

TRAVEL: It is dangerous to travel alone; however, it is
   safe to travel to a remote place with companions.
DISEASE: It is difficult to cure.
PERSONAL WISH: There will be no achievement if you
   are in a hurry.

COMMENTARY

Tao is without color or form,
   yet from it emerges all wonders of the universe.
Subtly flows the Tao,
   deep within the fertile stillness,
   hushed within the profound quietude.
It is indeed the Great Reality.

Listen to the silence!

Religions, rich in color and form,
   are but creations of the mind of man.
Follow only mental creations
   and you will not even scratch the surface.

Watch the invisible!

Trace back to the root of your soul,
   found deep within your quiet reflections,
   and the ultimate truth unfolds itself naturally.

Feel what you cannot touch!

Self-cultivation will bring you safely
   from the shore of beingness
   to the vast ocean of non-beingness.
A system, the ferry boat,
   is discarded when the destination has been reached.
All man-made religions share the same ignorance;
   but through cultivating the root of life,
   one may achieve the great awareness.

Strive for it!

With the clarity of an illumined mind,
  penetrate the illusion of color and form.
Embrace the substance of Nature
  and merge with the Origin.
Obstacles will suddenly collapse,
  allowing your inner light to be seen and felt.
In this way, your spiritual flower will surely blossom,
  and you will bear the sweet fruit of immortality.
It is all within your reach,
  but first must come the cultivation,
  the practice, the self-discipline.
This is the true and traditional way
  of becoming one with the Tao.

Unstain and empty the mind;
  thus it will become the fine tool that will unite
  the scattered fragments of yourself into one whole,
  so that what is may become clear.
As the earth gives forth flowers and trees,
  all cultures, civilizations and religions
  are born of the mind.

Magical mind, even more magical when perfectly still!
As a clear and silent pond,
  so should be the mind.
Empty, relaxed, firm, undisturbed,
  thus, and only thus,
  able to know the Truth.
Draw your mind inward to your calm center,
  and all diverse and scattered thoughts will cease.

To follow the impulse of passion and desires
  is to stay trapped in bondage.
Only when you empty the mind
  can you verify and experience
  the wonders of the eternal realms.
But attach yourself, ever to this empty mind,
  and you remain yet outside the Tao.

Cling neither to emptiness nor to concepts;
  this is the proper way to mind your mind.
Guard and cleanse the gates of the six senses
  so that you will not be deceived by them.
The calculating mind cannot be trusted,
  because hidden in its roots
  are the distorted thoughts and feelings
  of pain, bitterness and sadness.

Boldly swing the sword of wisdom,
  and cut yourself free from the shell of illusion
  that binds and confines you.
Beware of being tricked by vanity.
Love, fame, profit and high position
  are the golden harvest moon
  bobbing on the surface of a lake.

Do not let the world disturb you.
Maintain unshakable quiescence
  and enjoy the exquisite peace.
In your experience of this aspect of true freedom,
  understand the real Void is not void at all!
Through unrelenting self-discipline,
  the hidden truths of the universe will unfold.

21   嗾 嗑   shih ho

Biting Through Hardship

GUIDANCE: *"Biting through difficulty brings success. It is necessary for one to cut through negative influences with decisiveness."*

In this hexagram, Fire is above Thunder.   The lines form the image of a mouth, which "bites through" difficulty.   The top and bottom yang lines are like the upper and lower lips.   The yang line within is what must be cut through and chewed.

The image of "biting through" represents the process of cutting away an evil force.   Thunder is the force of awakening; fire is the force of clarity and illumination.   With inner strength and light one can "bite through" the darkness.

The first and top lines receive the pressure and do the hard work.   The second, third, fourth and fifth lines do the punishing.   Although punishment is an external thing, it affects what is inside.   The inner lines represent the power that can overcome darkness.

Fire and Thunder present an opportunity for one in darkness to see himself clearly. Lightning is created by the interaction of these elements. It lights the way, allowing one to overcome ignorance and to move freely in the direction of righteousness.

This hexagram advises one to be decisive in overcoming the difficulty which lies before him. Since there is no suggestion of escape, avoidance, compromise or any other evasion, one must face one's destiny and determinedly "bite through" the darkness.

LINE 1: *"The toes disappear when the fetters are put upon the feet. No movement is possible."*

The first line represents the restrained, aggressive yang force of Thunder, the punishment and confinement, which may actually be of benefit. Aggressiveness and stubbornness toward oneself and one's environment must be restrained, as symbolized by the image of a common criminal with shackles on his feet. Such punishment and confinement is just and proper when negative tendencies arise. Good teachers and parents should know this in order to help the growth of their students or children. Discipline and punishment should be skillfully applied with decisiveness and directness. Why? Because too much shallow love spoils a child.

This line also applies to the limitations and obstructions of the environment, which can also serve as "fetters" toward progress.

LINE 2: *"He bites so deeply into the flesh that his nose disappears."*

This line represents the kind mother who, because of the deep love in her heart, needs decisiveness and correctness in punishing her children. To form good habits and a proper way of life, discipline and punishment should not be spared. If punishment is applied only lightly to the skin, it will have little effect as a restraining measure. It must be strong enough to be effective.

For this kind of effective punishment, the *I Ching* uses the image of biting into the skin so deeply that the nose disappears. Such a vivid illustration portrays a mother's love for her children as well as her understanding of the need for punishment as an educational measure.

The virtuous and kind often appear to be soft and weak; however, moral courage can transform gentleness into the highest form of power and decisiveness. Since the second line is a yin line in the correct position, it naturally does what is right. Therefore, there is no problem.

> **LINE 3**: *"One bites through preserved meat and encounters poison. There is a little trouble, but things will be all right."*

This weak line faces the darkness of the top line and symbolizes chewing meat which is no longer fresh, thus becoming poisoned. The individual in this situation is aware that the "meat" is not good but continues to eat it anyway.

This third line uses the "wrong" method to correct the stubborn evil at the top and therefore tastes the "poison." This means that one tries to give admonitions or criticism to someone whose darkness is already very deeply rooted. To continue this will only lead to trouble for everyone involved. Surely the wise would throw the "poison" away without hesitation!

> **LINE 4**: *"One bites on the bone with little meat and finds a metal arrow. Although this is certainly a difficult task, to face the challenge will bring good fortune."*

The fourth line represents a difficult task or time. This is like enjoying the meat that is next to the bone until one finally meets the hardness of the bone. In this situation, problems cannot be avoided and must be dealt with by "biting through." Such action is like "biting the bullet." Keep a positive attitude toward overcoming the difficulty. To continue "chewing" is the necessary process of breaking through.

"Hardness" is represented by a yang line in a yin position or a positive person in a negative environment. Thus, one must face the problem directly and thoroughly work through it. Overcoming the obstruction in this way will bring good fortune.

> **LINE 5**: *"Biting dry meat, one finds gold. When one deals with problems in a balanced way, there is no fault."*

One has unexpected good fortune. The hard, dried meat turns out to be a piece of gold, which means that one transforms difficulty into great fortune.

The fifth line is in a position of righteousness and its strength and power are applied in a balanced and just manner. The *I Ching* encourages one to confront the difficulty as required. It can be totally dissolved if the correct energy is applied without intimidation until victory is achieved.

LINE 6: *"The ears also have shackles on them. One no longer hears good advice."*

In this position, the shackles covering the ears are probably the result of one's own doing. One ignores the good advice available and rushes into trouble.

The following saying is appropriate to this situation: "You have ears but cannot hear; you have eyes but cannot see." One imprisons oneself by ignoring good advice and discipline. Stop this foolishness immediately while there is still a chance.

SPECIFIC GUIDANCE

PERSONAL FORTUNE: Good luck; your influence rises.

MARRIAGE: It can be achieved, but there will be many quarrels.

HOUSING/FAMILY: Danger. There is the possibility of fire.

CHILDBIRTH: If the baby is born in the autumn or winter, it will be a boy; if in the spring or summer, it will be a girl.

LOOKING FOR HELP: You need to ask two people. In the beginning, you are not successful, but finally you succeed.

SOCIAL/GOVERNMENTAL POSITION: It can be achieved, and the position will be a high one.

SEARCHING FOR SOMEONE: They can be found.

WAITING FOR SOMEONE: They will come.

LOOKING FOR SOMETHING LOST: It was stolen; you need two people to look for it in the Southeast.

HUNTING FOR THIEVES: You can catch them in the busy streets of the city.

LAWSUIT: It is justified.

CLIMATE: There will be thunder and rain.
TRAVEL: Good fortune.
DISEASE: Danger. There is a chance of high fever and
  even madness.
PERSONAL WISH: If you hurry, you can succeed. If you
  desire only profit, you will meet with calamity or disaster. The entire hexagram teaches using the brightness
  of the light and proceeding in a righteous manner.

COMMENTARY

When cultivating the Tao,
  rid yourself of illusion.
Cast off the limitations
  of the body and mind.
Do not get caught in conflicts
  between yourself and the world.
Only in this way,
  can whole and complete freedom be found.

Dissolve the difference
  between yourself and objects.
No longer be bothered by color or form.
Remove the dirty clothing
  of your pain and bitterness,
  and your true nature will instantly appear.

Though the Way is boundless,
  persistence will deliver you
  to the distant shore.
Continue on!
Do not stop before reaching your destination.
Succeed!
And experience the indescribable happiness of purity.

Work night and day in your efforts.
Courageously face all the tests and trials.
Here and now surpass all distinctions
  between yourself and Heaven.
Then, in one final step,
  you will be able to cross
  the bitter sea to the crystal shore.

Never, from beginning to end,
  lose sight of this goal.
When your cultivation is finally complete,
  full will be the merits and virtues.
Always remember,
    that in the nothingness of mind,
    the seed of a whole being can be found.

22   貢 BE

ADORNMENT · BEAUTIFICATION

GUIDANCE: *"Beautification. Proceeding with small matters
is profitable."*

In this hexagram, Fire is at the foot of the Mountain.
The mountain is an image of stillness. Flames contribute
to the beauty of this stillness in the vast wilderness. True
natural beauty is achieved through self-containment; there
is no superficial adornment in nature. Fire, set at the
foot of the mountain, gives warmth, grace and safety and
is a gesture of welcome and hospitality in ordinary life.

This hexagram is associated with art and civilization,
the process of the refinement of natural life. On a social
level, Fire gives light in order to conquer the darkness in
people in the same way that it illuminates the dark shadow of the mountain. Within an individual this light is
the power that can drive away inner darkness and guide
one safely through a dark environment.

One of self-discipline works on refining his character,
while a shallow person seeks external adornment in order
to express his value with such things as academic degrees, honors and other social decorations. Most people
know how to look better with superficial make-up, but few
know how to truly beautify themselves by polishing and
improving their personality and virtue. Those of self-cultivation combine outer grace with inner beauty. This is the
true beauty they reach for. Like all adornments, the benefits of this hexagram are limited to small matters.

LINE 1: *"Strengthening one's toes, one does not use a decorated carriage, but instead goes by foot."*

The toes are in the lowest position of the body and are a function of support. Here they symbolize the beginning of movement. People express their vanity with luxurious vehicles. By over-doing, the true function of their vehicles as an extension of their feet becomes obscure. People are often more willing to spend time in decorating their vehicles than in strengthening their feet by walking. And what have they gained? Even the most luxurious vehicle cannot replace a healthy pair of feet.

LINE 2: *"Beautifying his mustache, he is momentarily cheered up."*

"Manliness" is not expressed by a mustache. Instead, righteousness, broadmindedness, bravery, straightforwardness and other virtues are the natural attributes of manhood. Teenage boys often attempt to express manhood by growing a mustache, but in reality cultivating virtue is much more important than cultivating the symbols of manhood.

LINE 3: *"Continuously beautifying and refreshing oneself can bring good fortune unless one's virtue is covered by adornments."*

Civilization, education and religion can enhance a person, provided they are the results of a sincere search for personal growth. However, the beauty of what is real and natural should never be replaced by something merely decorative. Since this strong line is between two gentle lines, it is influenced positively by what is above and below.

LINE 4: *"With white hair and a white horse, he comes to court the lady. He is suspect in the beginning, but is accepted later."*

The color white expresses frankness. Although frankness and sincerity should be the highest values in life and in establishing relationships, most people evaluate others according to their appearances. Such sincerity is exemplified in the image of a white-haired man on an unadorned horse who approaches to court a young girl. At first the girl misjudges him, but his honesty and frankness convince her of his sincerity, and he is eventually accepted.

If one must be adorned with something, then let it be honesty and sincerity, for they alone will overcome all appearances.

> **LINE 5:** *"A small garden, a modest house on a hill and a simple gift taken to a wise one. These are the things on which a happy and lasting relationship are based."*

Be content with a simple garden and house. Comfort does not come from luxuries. The most valuable things in life are peace and safety. Indeed what they bring is true happiness!

> **LINE 6:** *"Decoration is not needed when one is plain and simple. Thus, there is no blame."*

Maintain simplicity. Why must we have titles or belong to special organizations? Decorations are not needed to prove that one person is better than another. Instead, one should be what one really is. Thus, one remains completely unaffected by the world and keeps the wholeness of one's being.

SPECIFIC GUIDANCE

PERSONAL FORTUNE: There will be some obstacles, and things will not go as desired. The correct thing to do is move away.

MARRIAGE: The beginning will be successful, but the marriage will finally end in divorce.

CHILDBIRTH: Not very peaceful.

LOOKING FOR WORK: Hurry up.

ELECTION: It will take a long time to accomplish.

TRADE/BUSINESS: Success.

SEARCHING FOR SOMEONE: You can meet them.

WAITING FOR SOMEONE: They will come.

LOOKING FOR SOMETHING LOST: It is close to the water and can be found.

HUNTING FOR THIEVES: They may be a family who lives in the Northeast. If the fourth line is the focus, they will be harder to catch. Otherwise, they can be caught.
LAWSUIT: In the beginning there is some happiness; but in the end, some worry. It is best to make peace.
CLIMATE: It will rain.
TRAVEL: Profitable.
DISEASE: Danger.
PERSONAL WISH: Difficulty.

COMMENTARY
The Light in Self-Cultivation

The goal of self-cultivation is to return to one's natural state of purity. Through cultivating the self, one can see one's true nature by the light of one's own unfolding intelligence. Turn inward and examine every part of yourself. Follow what is right, eliminate what is wrong. All things depend upon the harmony of one's will and the will of the subtle realm. Do the best you can, and leave the result to the subtle realm.

Maintain strict discipline under any circumstances. Relinquish worldly ambitions and abandon worldly cares. Do not live a shallow life. To be awakened to the path and still adhere to your old, inferior habits is disastrous.

Still the mind and its passionate nature. Learn to say "no" to friends and especially "no" to yourself. You will receive strength from conquering an overwhelming desire. It might seem easier to straighten the winding rivers and mountains than to alter the disposition of a rigid mind. Regulate your temper and cultivate your heart.

With undaunted determination, one can become a true immortal being if one has worked on his self-cultivation and transformed himself to a more subtle level of pure existence in body, mind and spirit. Human beings have the potential to evolve to this higher form of life.

23 剝 po
≣≣

erosion · decline

GUIDANCE: *"Erosion. Now is not a good time to go any-where."*

In this hexagram, the Mountain is above Earth. This image usually represents a stable condition, but here the yang energy is ascending and the yin is descending. This suggests that since the summit is without support, the base of the mountain is naturally eroding away. Where there is only one yang line above five yin lines, there can be no interaction; therefore, the result is one of separation or splitting apart.

This hexagram depicts the time of sunset. The following hexagram, Revival, is five yin lines above one yang line and represents sunrise or a time for renewal. Decline is associated with the months of October/November when yin energy has almost reached its fullest and Autumn makes the transition into Winter. Renewal is associated with the months of December/January when the yang energy first starts to assert itself again. It is well to remember that, in a situation of decline, the condition will always change to one of revitalization and renewed growth.

The five yin lines of this hexagram can be thought of as an evil or negative force, while the top yang line is the single force of virtue. Any situation that has one portion of virtue combined with five portions of evil is a dangerous one. Everyone must face the inevitability of decline at certain times in their lives - one cannot always expect to rise - but decline gives way to renewal, like a bare tree blossoming in the Spring. Po thus guides us to an understanding of the causes of decline and erosion and how to deal with them.

The single yang line cannot withstand the progressing negative force. In such an overwhelming situation, one should gather one's energy and not confront the evil directly. Storing energy in difficult times enables one to prepare for renewal.

Never compete with persons of inferior virtue, because doing so gives them the opportunity to undermine you. Also, when interacting with them, remain detached from personal credit or merit. There is no need to broadcast what you have done. By claiming credit, you only create enemies and eventually harm yourself.

During unfavorable times, one should remain especially grounded. Even when feeling fully supported by other people, one should not get caught up in a struggle with negative energy. Negative energy can be found not only in one's environment, but also in an emotional state or during a period of mental self-deception. One who lives a life that follows the fundamental integral path develops gentleness and self-containment. Thus, no negative force can destroy his balance and composure.

Problems arise when people do not see a situation clearly. In this case, struggle is useless and a waste of energy because all efforts are in vain. By being composed and attuned to the reality of the circumstance, it is possible to act in accordance with it. Not directly confronting evil in these circumstances does not mean admitting defeat but is simply the only strategy that will assure victory in the long run. Is this not the spiritual principle for handling all confrontation and strong negativity?

LINE 1: *"Erosion at the legs of the bed. Some danger."*

The first line suggests that the feet of the bed by which one is supported are beginning to be undermined. The image of a bed is used because it is during sleep that we are most vulnerable to negative influences. This line represents the beginning of danger and warns that one should be cautious of a shaky foundation in one's social, financial or general condition of life.

LINE 2: *"Erosion at the upper part of the bed's legs. Danger."*

Harm moves closer. When people are cruel, why stay close to them? Perhaps one is still "sleeping" or one's vision is covered by the clouds of selfish desire. By wishful thinking, the mind provides an opportunity for those of inferior virtue to come closer and closer.

LINE 3: *"He is the only good one during times of erosion."*

During times of erosion, the third line is not an un-
dermining influence like the others because it corresponds
to the top yang line. Among all five yin lines, only the
third can respond to the top and thus maintain normalcy.
A "pearl" is found among the "swine."

Though the yin lines wish to harm the top line, the
third line is able to stay removed from evil. Thus, his
light has not been extinguished by environmental influences like the others.

LINE 4: *"Erosion has developed close to the skin of
one who sleeps on the bed. Disaster is near."*

The erosive force has developed from the bottom three
yin lines until it now directly attacks the body. How can
danger be ignored?

LINE 5: *"A group of maids, like a school of fish, is
guided to the palace. There is no friction."*

Because the fifth line is closest to the yang energy, its
quality is changed. Even though there is only one yang
line, the entire situation can be harmonized by the broad-
mindedness of the fifth line. It is able to organize the
other four lines to serve the yang line and thus there is
no friction.

During times of moral corruption, normal human nature is usually severely eroded. The arrogance of modern
people who are aggressive and deny the divine order of a
harmonious universe is an example of this corruption.
Only the developed few of self-awareness, as represented
by the fifth line, follow the divine universal law during
times of corruption and recommend that others do the
same.

LINE 6: *"Only one fruit remains on the tree. If there
is one of great virtue in this position, he will acquire a
wagon by accepting support from others. An ordinary
person will lose his house by accepting the erosive
influence."*

The image of a tree is symbolized by all the lines of
this hexagram. Every fruit has fallen off the tree but one,
which represents one's last chance. If seeds are preserved
when crops are bad and famine is present, a chance for
survival still exists, but if people are self-indulgent and eat

the seeds of their revitalization, their way is damaged and the likelihood of survival greatly diminished. Many times people exhaust themselves by not knowing how to preserve the last of their energy for revival; thus, they lessen their chances for survival.

This is the time for one to fall in order to begin growing again, like the seeds of a fruit which have fallen to earth. One should not fear the fall but instead should have courage in order to gather energy for revival. Preserve the seeds and root of your life. This is the only way to change misfortune to good fortune. The danger that bothered you in the beginning is no longer a worry. This same principle applies to self-cultivation for longevity and and spiritual immortality.

SPECIFIC GUIDANCE

PERSONAL FORTUNE: Not very good. Your outlook may appear good but it is actually empty.

MARRIAGE: If you are female, the man will bring you harm. If you are a man, the woman will bring you harm.

HOUSING/FAMILY: If you are contemplating buying a house, you should instead find a simple, temporary dwelling like an apartment. Do not leave your own house at this time.

CHILDBIRTH: This may be the third delivery and may also be a premature birth. There will be shock at the delivery.

LOOKING FOR WORK: Big things cannot be achieved.

SOCIAL/GOVERNMENTAL POSITION: Although there is difficulty in the beginning, finally there is some achievement. The rewards do not last long.

TRADE/BUSINESS: If your capital is large and you can gather many goods, there will be some profit.

SEARCHING FOR SOMEONE: They are difficult to find.

WAITING FOR SOMEONE: They will come. This situation is like ripe fruit that is ready to fall from the tree.

LOOKING FOR SOMETHING LOST: There is not much chance of recovering it.

HUNTING FOR THIEVES: They are in the Southwest. If you wish to get things back, there is much difficulty.

LAWSUIT: In the beginning some money is lost, but finally peace will be made.

CLIMATE: If you expect the weather to be fine, it will rain. If you expect bad weather, it will be fine.

TRAVEL: It is only good to travel with a companion at this time; do not go alone.

DISEASE: Some implication of death.

PERSONAL WISH: If your wish is connected with money, then there may be some achievement although not complete. Others will continuously give you trouble, so be aware.

COMMENTARY

Do not mistake false illusions for reality.
Cast your light within
to look at your own reflection.
Worldly affairs are but empty dreams.
All the wealth in the world
is not worth any more
than one strand of your hair.

Where a being of wholeness comes from
can only be seen with a mind that is pure.
Rid yourself of all thoughts and mental activity,
and eye the origin of goodness.

Retreat, pull back, confine yourself,
keep still your mind,
and the outer world's temptations
will melt like ice.
Control each subtle square inch of your mind.
Eliminate mental confusions;
many there are.
Preferences and other worldly dyes
stain your body and mind.
Though it is difficult at first to discipline yourself,
good habits, once formed, come naturally.
You will be rewarded for your discipline,
truly and completely.
The happiness which will come to surround you
is unspeakable.

Once you no longer follow
    the moving stream of your consciousness,
    the rounds of life and death will be broken.
Take leave of false phenomena.
Surpass all form and you will discover
    that reality is the subtle nature
    that is everywhere, yet nowhere to be seen.
Follow reality like a road
    by cultivating your trueness.
Leave the limited concepts of form,
    and so progress toward the invisible,
    eternal infinitude.
The Sacred Method is simple;
    the seed needs only to be molded.

24   復 fu   ䷗

REVIVAL · RENEWAL

GUIDANCE: "Revival.   Proceed without harm and with friends.   The beginning of a new cycle comes on the seventh day.   One is benefited by going somewhere."

In this hexagram, Thunder is below Earth.   At this time, negative yin energy is beginning to decline and positive yang energy is returning.   Thunder grows and breaks through all obstacles; even Earth cannot stop its explosive nature.   This symbolizes revival and is a good time to gather supportive energy.

This hexagram is like the sun which moves across the sky from sunrise to sunset.   Each line represents both a different time of the day and a different day in the seven day cycle.   The first line is the seventh day.   When a new cycle begins, the second line becomes the first line of that cycle.   (See Figure 102.)

During the cycle of the seasons, many animals and insects hibernate in winter until the first clap of thunder awakens them in the spring.   Thus, they move from hibernation into a time of renewal.   The clap of "thunder beneath the earth" can also apply to the awakening of people who are in "hibernation" as a result of selfishness, narrow-mindedness and negativity in order for them to return to the positive sphere. If one's motivation is correct, righteousness becomes the supporting power that can help one overcome obstacles and thus return to the natural path of life.

The yang line is like a seed which has fallen to the ground. All revival needs a foundation from which to grow. The essence within the shape or shell of the seed is the real root or the "spirit" of life. Without spirit, there cannot be renewal, and without a peaceful environment, nothing can grow.

At this stage of renewal, yang energy as the main life force is weak. However this position does not hinder one's progress. Remember that, when negative yin energy, which is an obstacle for the life force, reaches its extreme, it creates an opportunity for positive yang energy to return. In the previous hexagram, "Erosion or Decline," the yin energy which was nearing completion was in control of the situation. In such a situation, one cannot stop the force of erosion; one must pull one's energy inward to prepare for the renewal that is to follow. But in this hexagram, negativity is giving way to light. This is the Heavenly Way. There has never been any evil force which has completely succeeded in eliminating the return of the light. This is called Tao or the subtle universal law.

LINE 1: *"Renewal. If one does not stray too far, return to the right path will be easy and without remorse. Good fortune. One should practice self-cultivation."*

When one has lost something, whether it be clarity of mind, money, opportunity or love, this line signifies the time is appropriate to let the period of loss or suffering end and return to normal.

LINE 2: *"Easy restoration. Good fortune."*

The second line is gentle and close to the first line, which becomes its model. When the second line sees that the first line returns, it follows. There is good fortune when one is inspired by the innocence or purity of others. To return to one's own true nature is the true revival.

LINE 3: *"Repeating mistakes, one is unable to maintain normalcy. Not good, but also no great problem."*

The third line is a yin line in a yang position; therefore, it is weak and vacillates. It wishes to improve but is too unstable to do so. Since the main direction of this hexagram is toward light and goodness, even though there is some momentary wavering, there is no great humiliation.

LINE 4: *"Independently, follow the right way."*

This is a beautiful line. It is among four other yin lines but is the only one that responds to the first line. All its comrades have strayed from the right path. However, it has the independence and sound judgment to follow the correct way and is uninfluenced by its peers.

LINE 5: *"Sincerely return to the right path. No remorse with self-reflection."*

The position of the fifth line is high and is also the center line of the top trigram. Although in a position of respect, it can still be humble. It has the capacity for reflection and can easily return to the correct path. Therefore, there is no difficulty. It earnestly admits its mistake and decides to return to the right path.

LINE 6: *"Fatally losing oneself, there is no return to the right path. One is dangerously heading toward disaster. If it is insisted that the army be used, it will be defeated, and it will take ten years to recover the losses."*

The positive influence is too far away from the sixth line, which is ignorant and stubborn. It continues to engage in harmful habits and follows the wrong path. There is no chance of its coming back, and it is lost. This calamity is self-created and will also invite response through natural calamity. If it has faith in violent conquest, it will surely destroy itself.

The top line is usually the position associated with extremes. However, if one can stop before reaching an extreme and be humble in seeking the right path without resorting to force, there will be good fortune. But the chances are that this line will do the opposite. It still insists on its way and relies on war rather than the practice of virtuous actions. Thus, it finally suffers a serious defeat like all tragic historical figures who resort to violence.

The attitude of the top line not only spells disaster for the individual, but for the whole world. The history of humanity is evidence of this truth and the need for renewal.

SPECIFIC GUIDANCE

PERSONAL FORTUNE: Good luck will come. It will be more profitable to await it quietly.

MARRIAGE: There can be success for a while, but eventually the marriage will split up.

HOUSING/FAMILY: If there is some disharmony within a family, the situation can be improved in the springtime.

CHILDBIRTH: The baby will be a boy. If the fourth line is emphasized, there will be danger for the mother.

LOOKING FOR WORK: You will be successful.

SOCIAL/GOVERNMENTAL POSITION: It is hard to achieve.

TRADE/BUSINESS: There is difficulty; there is conflict with another person.

SEARCHING FOR SOMEONE: You do not need an intermediary.

WAITING FOR SOMEONE: They will come.

LOOKING FOR SOMETHING LOST: It can be found in the East.

HUNTING FOR THIEVES: There is no definite place where they are hiding; thus, it is difficult to catch them.

LAWSUIT: You can be the winner.

CLIMATE: There will be sudden rains alternating with good weather.

TRAVEL: Go northward first, then to the Southwest.

DISEASE: Presently there is danger, but you will get well.

PERSONAL WISH: It can be achieved.

COMMENTARY
Self-Integration

Becoming spiritually integrated means giving up the false beliefs of a conceptual world and keeping one's own true nature deeply connected with the universe. The following guidelines will help you to self-revival:

1. Unify the mind and body so there is no separation.

2. Concentrate on inner vitality and on becoming pliant like a baby.

3. Purify the inner vision in order to reach immaculate accuracy.

4. Love all people and govern the country with serviceable virtue instead of resorting to the worldly approach of force.

5. Be receptive when the Heavenly door opens and closes. This brings forth the subtle changes that appear in the physical world.

6. Be crystal clear with an innocent mind.

7. Keep your mind and life unoccupied in order to live with the reality of each new moment.

25 元 妄
wu wan

innocence · unexpected happening

GUIDANCE: *"One meets the unexpected with innocence. It is good to proceed, and if one remains virtuous, it will be beneficial. Otherwise, it will be disastrous."*

In this hexagram, Heaven is above Thunder. Thunder is neither controllable nor predictable and can be either beneficial or destructive. Sometimes it brings needed rain, other times it brings lightning which can strike people or houses and create unexpected disaster.

Wu Wan deals with the occurrences in human life which are beyond one's control. Sometimes they are beneficial and sometimes not. This is why the ancients called this hexagram "unexpected happening" or "innocence."

Many good things come to pass because we organize and plan for them. Also, many good things come to pass when we are guileless and innocent of circumstances. However, there are other times when our innocence is a source of difficulty. Sometimes innocence is blind to the dangers that lie ahead.

There is at times a mystical power behind thunder. This truth can be verified when one has attained sufficient spiritual achievement. Generally, innocence is a great virtue, for it is close to nature, but one should understand that there are two kinds of innocence. One is the innocence of a child who knows nothing about time, society, positivity, negativity, etc., and lacks true knowledge. This is not the kind of innocence developed ones strive for. The innocence of the developed ones is the restored purity of the Integral Way after one has experience and knowledge of things. Though developed people have the capacity to do or to know negative things, they choose to remain innocent and to abstain from such things. This is the kind of innocence which is truly valuable. In order to overcome unhealthy desires, temptations and impulses, one must have knowledge of them. Thus, returning to natural innocence is the result of complete knowledge, cultivation and spiritual development and is quite different from youthful, naive or ignorant innocence.

The universe is very responsive to one's energy. This is the power behind the force of retribution. Therefore, one must always try to maintain virtue. Rewards and punishments, whether visible or invisible, are usually instigated by one's own thoughts and behavior. In other words, we are our own executioners. This subtle law is the invisible sovereign of all life and is not connected to any social code of morality.

Develop an awareness of the subtle universal law and follow the true knowledge. Cultivate virtue, for it is more powerful than any natural phenomenon and is the greatest insurance against natural calamities.

LINE 1: *"Guilelessness brings good fortune."*

With innocence and sincerity, one's intentions will be pure and one will be able to attain one's goal. The first line is a yang line. Since yang energy is the energy of movement, this line needs to go forward. When one moves with good intentions and sincerity, there will be no problems. This is the power of righteousness.

LINE 2: *"There can be no harvest where one has not been tilling and weeding. It is profitable to go ahead only if there is no scheming."*

One should be diligent in one's work, especially mindful of tilling and weeding, but not overly concerned with the harvest. By tending the fields, the crops will grow. This line shows the importance of remaining steadfast in one's work, rather than stopping to measure how much has been done. People frequently like to measure more than they like to work. Be where you are now.

LINE 3: *"Unexpected trouble. Someone keeps an ox in another's village and a traveler takes it away. It then becomes trouble for the villagers."*

This third line is a yin line in a yang position. The line to which it relates at the top is also in the wrong position; therefore, there is trouble. This is illustrated with an image of someone leaving an ox on your property and someone else taking it away. The first person returns looking for his ox and does not accept the explanation when told that you do not know where it is. This is called "undeserved misfortune."

A Chinese proverb says, "When you pass by a melon field, avoid trouble by not bending down to tie your shoe laces! When you pass by a plum tree, do not raise your hands to correct the position of your hat!" One should avoid unnecessary suspicion. In such situations, arguments are not very effective.

LINE 4: *"Having no guile incurs no fault."*

One is free from blame because one is virtuous and restrains impulsive movement. By keeping oneself upright, one can save much unnecessary trouble and be efficient in all aspects of life. A yang line finds itself in a yin position with two related strong lines in the first and the fifth positions respectively. In a situation like this, maintaining oneself in a simple way is appropriate.

LINE 5: *"Unexpected sickness. No medicine is needed. Happiness eventually comes."*

The literal Chinese translation of this line is, "The sickness is merely false and confusing symptoms." Because the fifth line is a healthy yang line and is in the right position, shadowy obstacles cannot really affect him. Also, some trouble happens to him, but it turns out to be a surprisingly good ending.

LINE 6: *"Be still. Any action results in disaster. No profit."*

One who is ignorant and ambitious will inevitably invite trouble. Because the top line is far from the center and there is no place to go, further movement will bring misfortune.

SPECIFIC GUIDANCE

PERSONAL FORTUNE: It appears good. Though you have a lot of money, you are sometimes sick because of difficulty with your spouse. A third person has trouble which involves you, and this troubles you.

MARRIAGE: It can be achieved and will be successful.

HOUSING/FAMILY: Prosperity; the family will grow.

CHILDBIRTH: The baby will be a boy. If it is a girl, the mother will have difficulty.

LOOKING FOR WORK: In spring and summer, it can be successful. In autumn and winter, it will not be successful. If you depend on a woman, there will be an obstacle.

SOCIAL/GOVERNMENTAL POSITION: If you depend on yourself, do not go any further. If you depend on outside help, it may be achieved.

TRADE/BUSINESS: It will be beneficial and profitable in the long run.

SEARCHING FOR SOMEONE: Do not look by yourself.

WAITING FOR SOMEONE: They will come.

LOOKING FOR SOMETHING LOST: It can be found, but do not ask for help from women.

HUNTING FOR THIEVES: They are hiding in a church in the Southwest and can be caught.

LAWSUIT: Keep peace.
CLIMATE: If the first line is emphasized, it will rain. If the second line is emphasized, it will be windy.
TRAVEL: Do not hesitate.
DISEASE: There seems to be danger in the beginning, but finally there is safety. As Heaven and Thunder indicate masculine energy. this condition will be more dangerous for women.
PERSONAL WISH: The time has not yet come; if you hurry, nothing can be achieved.

COMMENTARY
The Non-Glaring Light of True Wisdom

First know that without challenges,
*   one cannot become a sage.*
Without undaunted determination
*   to walk the right way,*
*   one cannot attain true wisdom.*
One should give up all kinds of strange paths
*   and return to the plain truth of nature.*

Flowery words are not to be trusted,
*   for the truth is simple and unadorned.*
Never tire of studying life.
Ceaselessly gather your chi
*   and keep it whole.*
Essence, chi and spirit
*   are the three jewels of life.*
When chi is high,
*   one can triumph over all negativity;*
When it is low,
*   one will be prey to it.*

Only with developed spiritual eyes
*   can one discern the marrow of wisdom*
*   in oneself and others.*
One must meditate and cultivate oneself for many years
*   before experiencing the high mysterious intelligence.*
Self-cultivation ennobles one's personality.
Keep your senses in perfect quietness.
Do not contend with anyone.

The struggle for supremacy
  destroys one's high spiritual quality.
When living with others, keep peace.
When living alone, beware of negative thoughts.
Never commit faults because you consider them small.

When nature sends calamities,
  it is still possible to escape;
When one creates the calamity oneself,
  one has to suffer the consequences.
Prevent disease by taking good care
  of yourself when healthy.
Do not treat anyone or anything with indifference.
Your behavior has serious consequences
  to your health, your family and your very life.
One who is noble in spirit,
  does not covet what others take pride in:
  their things, their occupations, or their interests.
If you see something you like,
  restrain the desire;
  follow what is in your own nature.

26 ta ch'u

GREAT AMASSMENT

GUIDANCE: *"Be firmly committed to your goal. This is not the time to keep to oneself but to engage in adventure."*

Great Amassment refers to the gathering of various forms of energy and the need to control it. The methods of control are symbolized by the domestication of animals, as depicted in lines four and five.

In Ta Ch'u, Heaven is below and the Mountain is above. The sign of Heaven expresses healthy, forward moving, active energy. The mountain remains still, holding together. Thus, the progressive yang energy of Heaven is restrained by the inactive yin energy of the Mountain.

This indicates a great accumulation of energy, like water that is dammed up.

From the Mountain, one can learn to remain calm and thus retain the strong, moving energy of Heaven. By following the example of the Mountain, one's virtue will increase daily and progress will be endless.

Amassing positive energy means gathering personal virtue, material support, information and knowledge. Knowledge of natural life is real knowledge and is full of beneficial power. However, this knowledge is not obtained from books. The ancient sages respected and learned from that which is living by being with nature. Their intuition was highly developed and they had an awareness of the principles of the natural subtle law. Guided in lives by their highly developed intuition, they naturally knew what would succeed or fail.

The principles of this hexagram can be applied practically by a leader or one who follows the integral way of living. A group is an accumulation of similar and dissimilar energies. In order to put these differing energies to positive use, the group must work collectively toward a common goal. If people do not cultivate and focus their energies while working together, their potential for achievement becomes scattered and their efforts useless. Such behavior is like electricity: if the wires are not connected to the generator, light is not produced. The same principle applies to water. If it is not properly controlled, it will either evaporate or flood its banks. One of the highest principles of natural law is to maintain balance. As stated in the *Tao Teh Ching*, "It is beneficial to reach for one thing at a time; it is confusing to grasp many things all at once."

This hexagram teaches how to amass positive energy and how to help people develop collectively in a positive direction. Its two yin lines function like a dam that contains water or a corral that confines cattle. Their main purpose is to accumulate energy and make it useful.

The sixth line is at the top of the Mountain. There, high energy has been accumulated; with such "strong capital," correct action can be taken to achieve the fullest prosperity. The fifth line is the central controller. The fourth line is the trustworthy helper who assists the fifth line in gathering the energy. The second line serves as an able helper who controls the lower part of the hexagram. It integrates the power of each position into the whole, like threads interwoven to make a fine piece of cloth or spokes that comprise a wheel.

In the ninth hexagram, one weak yin line holds to-gether five strong yang lines. Thus, there is a small amassment. But in this hexagram the centered, gentle energy of the fifth line, along with the cooperation of the fourth line, extends strong, positive control which leads to great amassment.

There are advantages in working collectively and short-comings in working individually. In relation to the whole, no one's energy should be wasted. Even an obnoxious, aggressive person can make a great general on a remote frontier border. A leader's responsibility is to unite the energies and make everyone useful. Since the leader is far from the people, able assistants and secondary leaders must be carefully chosen to assist in controlling the mas-ses. If such important elements are properly controlled, then all parts can be united.

LINE 1: *"There is difficulty if one goes forward; first be peaceful with oneself."*

The first line is restrained by the fourth. The upper trigram restrains the movement of the lower.

This is the time for self-cultivation. Do not waste en-ergy. You are like a young boy who has an abundance of energy but insufficient knowledge to utilize it constructive-ly. There is nothing beneficial in your actions at this ear-ly stage. Thus, you are most successful when you keep to yourself and do not press forward.

LINE 2: *"The wagon goes smoothly if proper balance is maintained."*

The second line corresponds to the fifth and is like a wild boar that is restrained by the leader in the fifth posi-tion. The second, as the strong axle, holds the wheel of a carriage. A carriage can make no progress if the control system is poor. One should now exercise self-restraint and be centered.

LINE 3: *"After training the horse well, you may cau-tiously pursue your goal."*

The aggressive third line at the top of the lower tri-gram is disciplined by the restraining force of the upper

trigram, Mountain.   Although this line is similar to the
first line, here the energy is stronger and the restraint is
greater.   Since this line represents the mind, it is like a
wild horse that must be tamed.   Only when it is under
control can it be useful.

First learn to harness the wild horse.   Later, when the
reins are properly controlled, one will be able to ride well.
Avoid rushing into activities; approach matters with caution and persevere.   Premature attempts at this time will
only cause trouble.

LINE 4:   *"Putting a headboard on young bulls bring
good results."*

The fourth line begins to restrain the lower, strong
yang lines as they try to advance.   The fourth line represents a board which is placed over the developing horns of
a young bull in order to guide its growth.   Without using
restraint, the bull's sharp horns will develop into dangerous weapons.   This line recommends that forms of discipline be practiced from the very beginning in order to encourage the growth of virtuous qualities.   Here, in its application to human relationships, the fourth line is a great
helper who assists the fifth line to establish constructive
leadership.

LINE 5:   *"The tusks of a castrated boar are tamed.
The herd is under control.   Good fortune."*

The fifth line also refers to restraint, especially to the
control of growing groups.   The literal Chinese version
says, "A gelded boar's tusks are good fortune."   This line
restrains the growth of evil by "gelding the boar."

In the human sphere, the fifth line represents an able
leader who knows how to correctly apply controls to himself and his work.   He knows how to "geld" disturbing energy from any source.

LINE 6: *"Attaining greatness; Heavenly blessing."*

Throughout each stage of this hexagram the yang energy has been gathered and stored.   This accumulated energy can now be put to good use and difficulties overcome.
True achievement and enlightenment are possible only
after the body, mind and spirit have been disciplined.   The
sixth line represents Heaven and is the highest phase of

energy transformation. By acting in accordance with the natural moral order, one will be able to achieve one's goal and thus experience success.

As a rule, when a hexagram is applied to the spiritual cultivation of an individual or group, the lower two lines represent physical energy, the middle two lines represent mental energy and the upper two lines represent spiritual energy. The lower two lines can also represent Earth, the middle two lines humanity and the upper two lines Heaven. It is valuable to use these principles in one's interpretation when it is the right occasion.

SPECIFIC GUIDANCE

PERSONAL FORTUNE: This is not a very good time. Following a period of two years (indicated by the fourth and fifth lines), good fortune and blessings will be attained. Your personal wish can be accomplished.

MARRIAGE: Although marriage can be successful in its early stages, it will eventually end in separation.

HOUSING/FAMILY: Live close to mountains or hills. Furthermore, there will be prosperity for your family.

CHILDBIRTH: Though the baby will be a boy, the delivery is dangerous.

LOOKING FOR WORK: Be patient; the job you want will come later.

SOCIAL/GOVERNMENTAL POSITION: You should wait until you are thirty to be of service to your country.

TRADE/BUSINESS: Prosperity and big profits will be earned in three months or three years.

SEARCHING FOR SOMEONE: They can be found unless the fourth line is emphasized.

WAITING FOR SOMEONE: They will not come.

LOOKING FOR SOMETHING LOST: The object is difficult to locate initially, but after a long period of time, it can be found in the Northeast and close to water or it may still be in your house.

HUNTING FOR THIEVES: They are in the Northeast and are people you know. If the fourth line is emphasized, they will be difficult to catch.

LAWSUIT: In the beginning, you feel confidence followed by a period of anxiety; finally there is peace.

CLIMATE: Due to a great accumulation of moisture, there will be rain for some time.
TRAVEL: A slow start brings good fortune.
DISEASE: There is difficulty in urination and elimination. The abdomen is distended. The problem is difficult to cure.
PERSONAL WISH: Be cautious. Haste makes waste.

COMMENTARY
Non-Possession

The body you are using does not belong to you.
It is the result of the interaction of the chi
  of light spirit and heavy physics.
One's spiritual nature is handed down
  from the divine Subtle Realm.
Why is it that we should lead our lives
  in selfish delusions?
In the midst of this material world,
  the deluded mind exhausts itself
  by endlessly chasing ups, downs
  gains and losses.
The moment the servant of death knocks at the door,
  it is too late to regret
  that one's life has been passed in vain.

In earlier days, we were enlightened
  by breaking through our illusions
  with the help of our masters.
Today we must strengthen our life source anew
  from the root.

We borrow this pure, clean, divine essence
  from Heaven.
It should be returned without contamination.
Do not stain it with dirt and filth
  or soil it with flaws and corruption.
It is an allowance from the divine Heaven
  and is handed to us for positive use.
Only fools try to possess it.

We come from nothingness and possess nothing.
Our only wish is to become eternally one
  with the harmonizing entirety.

Henceforth, we are awakened
  from the midst of our dream.
After awakening, there is nothing
  which can be recognized as the ego.
Deeply, from our hearts, we offer our lives
  in dedication to the reintegration
  of Heaven, Earth and Humankind -
  the spiritual integration of the universe.
Every worldly deed, whether for self or for others,
  is dedicated as an offering to the Subtle Origin.
We offer our worship as a direct response,
  with absolute sincerity to the Subtle Divine Realm.
All the shiens in Heaven are our witnesses.
Our resolution is as vast and deep
  as the mountains and oceans.
Thus, our hearts are rooted firmly.
We never evade our responsibility out of greed,
  because the net of Heavenly laws
  cannot be escaped.
We always maintain Heaven's ever-permeating,
  righteous chi.

27

pROVIDING NOURIShMENT

GUIDANCE: *"In nourishment, one should seek the right nutrition and not be tempted by what others enjoy."*

In this hexagram, Mountain is above and Thunder is below. The image is that of a mouth. The two yang lines, one at the top and one at the bottom, represent the upper and lower jaws. The yin lines within represent the cavity of the mouth and the teeth. Through the mouth, nourishment begins.

The Chinese word "I" means self-cultivation and nourishment that is obtained by living peacefully. "I" is both spiritual and material nutrition. The upper trigram represents the nourishment you give to others; the lower trigram represents the nourishment you provide for yourself. The upper trigram represents spiritual nourishment, the lower represents physical nourishment. The most beneficial nourishment is that which leads to a peaceful life by living simply.

To be peaceful is to be supportive of yourself and others. Physical nourishment is minor compared to spiritual nourishment, and people who spend their lives seeking nourishment for the mouth alone will never develop spiritually.

The lower trigram expresses selfish desires. Such desires are gratified through the mouth and only satisfy the lower sphere of life. The upper trigram wishes to nourish others through spiritual guidance and support. Just as wholesome food provides nourishment for the body, healthy communication is nourishment for the mind and spirit. The mouth is the opening where things both enter and leave the body, and it must be guarded well. Thus, one should use restraint in eating and care in speaking; be cautious of the inward and outward flow of energies. By cultivating this awareness, one's nutritional source will be pure and well-managed.

The image of an open mouth is symbolized by the four broken lines that form the shape of a mouth. The energy of the Mountain in the image of the upper jaw is still, while that of Thunder in the lower jaw is active. Expressions are formed at the corners of the mouth; thus, the shape of a smile or frown indicates a particular state of mind.

The image of Thunder indicates the speech of an authoritative or responsible person, a teacher, parent, elder or advisor. Though Thunder provides nourishment in a constructive way, the initial experience of it may appear destructive. But with Thunder comes rain, which fosters the growth of all vegetation. Likewise, the words and actions of a developed person also provide nourishment. Sometimes the "light-giver" is also the "thunder-giver." The shock of an achieved one's "thunder" can be the force which spurs one's development. A person of truth never relies on beautiful words. Only the truth endures; all else quickly fades.

Generally, people over-use their lower jaw through such activities as talking, kissing and eating. Highly developed people "use" their upper jaw for more spiritual communication and less physical communication; more breathing and less eating.

The entire hexagram is about nourishment. Nourishment is obtained from quietude, healthy food and inspiring speech. Providing nourishment to all people brings high spiritual achievement.

LINE 1: *"One gives away that which sustains one's good life by admiring what others enjoy."*

During ancient times, the tortoise (used as the image for this line), symbolized simplicity, inner quiet, wisdom and longevity. This particular kind of mountain tortoise needed only dew and air to sustain life. Here, the tortoise represents simplicity and peace, the highest nutrients for life. Be like a tortoise; maintain the modesty and ease that lead to a peaceful life.

Admiring and envying external things can cause you to lose the invaluable self-dignity which is the center of your well-being. Is it not better to lead a simple life and stay close to that which is natural rather than to be enslaved by vanity and luxury? Do not be buried in the treachery of your own impulses. By following the true rhythm of nature, your own nature is unified with the Great Oneness.

LINE 2: *"One neglects the constancy and stability which can benefit life and seeks nourishment from the wrong source. Misfortune."*

Since the second line has no support from the fifth line, it tries to obtain nourishment from the top line. When one separates oneself from the normal path and tries to attain things beyond one's natural capabilities, misfortune results. People frequently lose their real security in search of more security and thus exhaust their vitality. All people wish to be happy; only a few understand that real happiness cannot be obtained with the restlessness that is created by constant searching.

LINE 3: *"The wrong kind of nourishment. This kind of nourishment may look good for ten years, but in the end has no real benefit. Misfortune."*

The lower trigram, Thunder, indicates the lower jaw, the muscle activity affecting the lower part of the body and the physical impulses. This line is the boundary between those lines that seek external, material nourishment and those that are still and peaceful. It can create disorder for the upper trigram by being too active, too concerned with the lower part of the body. The more you eat, the less you can control yourself; finally your well-being will be destroyed. When speaking, choose your words well; when eating, select good food.

LINE 4: *"One desirous of good nutrition, like a hungry tiger, bears no blame for his good desires."*

The fourth line has the desires of a tiger. However, a tiger does not search for prey all day, but only attacks when it is truly hungry. In preparation for the attack, it lowers its front legs and head and makes an intimidating display before striking with its incomparable courage and power.

In contrast with other fierce animals, tigers do not kill more than they need to survive. Even as "king" among animals and having a healthy appetite, the tiger does not take advantage of all the nourishment provided by nature. Thus, it allows nourishment for others. Be like a tiger; do not abuse your powers. In action, a tiger is neither dependent on others nor impulsive. He chooses his nourishment and opportunities correctly. This is the virtue of the fourth line.

LINE 5: *"One relies on nutrition that has already been obtained; thus, one does not need to become more ambitious and aggressive."*

The fifth line is generally the ruler of a hexagram, but here the top line governs. The sixth line provides the nourishment and the fifth line manages the nourishment. It is important to cultivate oneself. Avoid distractions and improper nutrition. Exercise self-restraint, remain quiet and beware of danger.

Do not "cross the great water," as there is danger in taking risks at this time.

LINE 6: *"One becomes the source of nourishment. Though there may be some difficulties along the way, one can accomplish greatness by marching forward."*

The upper three lines indicate good fortune. The top line is the main line of the upper trigram, as well as the ruler of the entire hexagram. At this time, you should carefully observe all things and make wise selections; avoid the lower, blind impulses of desire. "Thunder" is not easily controlled. When using his mouth, the sage chooses only good food and righteous words. Thus, great fortune results and nourishment is provided for all.

SPECIFIC GUIDANCE

PERSONAL FORTUNE: One has plenty of money and property with the future possibility of obtaining fame. However, success will not be achieved with his or her spouse.

MARRIAGE: Marriage with the "mouth" implies fighting and arguing. This marriage will be a painful experience.

HOUSING/FAMILY: Housing should be near a mountain or hill, with a double front door. The foundation may be threatened by erosion and one should be watchful of fire.

CHILDBIRTH: The baby will be a boy. If the delivery is in the Summer or Autumn, the baby will be a girl. During delivery, the mother will become sick.

LOOKING FOR WORK: In the beginning there is difficulty; however, in the end there will be success.

SOCIAL/GOVERNMENTAL POSITION: Though there is no success now. After some time, good fortune will come.

TRADE/BUSINESS: Keep your old business. Investing in new ideas will not be profitable at this time.

SEARCHING FOR SOMEONE: It will be possible to meet soon.

WAITING FOR SOMEONE: They will not come.

LOOKING FOR SOMETHING LOST: Though the object is now mixed up with other things, it will later appear.

HUNTING FOR THIEVES: They are in the Northeast and can be caught.

LAWSUIT: While the issue is large in the beginning, it later diminishes. Do not rely on the help of others.

CLIMATE: It will be cloudy.

DISEASE: It is dangerous and one is unable to eat.   If the fourth line is emphasized, the disease will be difficult to cure.

COMMENTARY

Gently gather your energy,
  and quiet your wandering mind.
Carefully filter your desires
  to protect your vitality.
You will radiate with an auspicious light.
All of Heaven and its deities,
  all of Earth and its people,
  respect this kind of light.
The power you acquire and are able to use,
  is released by your tranquil mind.

Internal powers are far greater than external strength.
With calmness comes wisdom.
The clouds part, the moon becomes bright,
  and all directions shine with the light.
Surpass the sacred method with the sacred method,
  then no more method will there be.
You and the method become one.
The deepest, most wondrous silence
  comes by forgetting the active.
This is the level where you become the great king
  of the sacred method of liberation,
  at last able to enjoy its fruit.

True happiness can come only from
  rightful discipline and patience.
Use your courageous mental powers
  to withstand fear and anxiety.
The existence or non-existence of your physical body
  is not cause for worry.
True spirit has no worry or fear.
This is how to be a very developed being.

28 大過 ta kuo ䷛

GREAT EXCESS

GUIDANCE: *"Great excess. The main ridgepole is broken. Go ahead to help. It is preferable to proceed."*

In this hexagram Wind, or Wood, is below the Lake. The weak yin energy on the outside is trying to contain the strong yang energy within. Because the yin energy is not sufficient to control the yang, a great imbalance is created, which presents an image of imminent danger.

Such imbalance can be caused by great excessiveness and is called "Ta Kuo" in Chinese. "Ta" means "too big" or "too much"; "Kuo" means being "over." Ta Kuo results from being too strong or doing too much, in other words "excess." It is like a building with a large, heavy top and weak support, or a person with a great torso supported by thin legs. Because they are too weak to support such a heavy load, damage or danger is indicated. The original text of the *I Ching* uses the image of a beam or ridgepole sagging to its breaking point to represent this situation. Action must be taken to remedy the imbalance before destruction occurs.

When this hexagram is received in response to a question of timing or for some undertaking, it warns that the moment is one of conflict and confusion. In response to questions of health, it indicates that death may be imminent. In reference to a question about character or personality, it suggests that the individual is overly aggressive, egotistical, selfish, rigid or on the other hand, too passive, fearful or weak. Such a person can hardly be considered truly balanced. Nor will he ever be able to qualify as a leader or a valuable member of a group because his personality will prevent him from cooperating with others.

Inner and outer strength must be in balance. One needs a strong outer physical structure as well as firm inner principles to guide one's life. At the same time, however, the wise teachings of the *Tao Teh Ching* encourage softness, gentleness and receptivity. One whose demeanor is brusque or arrogant weaves a web of isolation for himself. Out of an inability to unite his merits with the merits of others, he eventually confines and frustrates himself. Likewise, one whose talents and intelligence are affected by passivity or fear will accomplish nothing. Excess of any kind makes greatness impossible to achieve.

This hexagram teaches the value of the central way. The central way is the way of doing things "just right," neither too little nor too much. Even things that are intrinsically positive can become counter-productive or damaging when done in excess. Neither must one interpret the central way as something done halfway as a compromise to quality. In either case, one misses the center, the "bulls-eye" of the target. The excessiveness symbolized here either misses the center or responds inappropriately to a situation. When one "misses the target," one creates difficulty for oneself.

The principle of centrality and appropriateness can be interpreted as harmony, balance, equilibrium, resonance, symmetry or spontaneous reaction in the correct manner to a situation. This is the way of the universe. The nature of the universe is also our nature and is the center of life for those who seek the truth. When one's behavior and emotions are correct and in harmony with circumstances, one's actions will hit the "bulls-eye."

LINE 1: *"It is like the soft white couch grass being suppressed beneath a weight. Because of its elasticity, it has no trouble taking difficulty and hardship."*

White couch grass was used in ancient times to make special seats for spiritual offerings. It symbolizes purity and sacredness. The first line shows the appropriate way to encounter strength by following the way of grass when the great winds blow. In laying low to the ground, the grass's softness and flexibility make it possible to endure the powerful wind.

This line is weak. Ahead of it are four strong lines. By not resisting their strength, it will remain safe. Remember that many strong trees are broken by fierce winds.

LINE 2: *"The withered weeping willow grows new branches. An old man marries a young girl. Everything is profitable."*

The second line is like an older man who marries a younger woman, represented by the first yin line. They still make a good team because the husband, as strong yang, works outside and needs a young wife as strong yin to work inside. For the strong to work without and the weak to work within is correct.

Right organization is expressed by the outer layer being tough and strong, characterized by mental strength and physical activity. The inner layer is soft and passive, characterized by emotions and the flow of subtle energies. For reasons of security and protection, those who work outside should be stronger than those who work inside. Yang means that which is visible and yin means that which is latent. The two become a team and now work with cooperation and harmony.

In developing character, one should have a gentle demeanor while firmly remaining true to inner principles. This is the meeting of good principles with the proper actions. The fulfillment of growth comes from one's faithfulness to subtle high guidance.

LINE 3: *"The ridgepole of the house is broken. Danger. Nothing can help it."*

This is the main line of the hexagram, which is the apogee of excess and the danger, perhaps even death. When excess of any process becomes visible, extinction cannot be far away. When a candle is burning out, the last few moments of light are the brightest.

The third line indicates one who isolates himself because he is too assertive and cannot cooperate with others. This is like a ridgepole sagging to the point of breaking.

LINE 4: *"This line is like the single purpose of a ridgepole; it supplies strength. There should be no other purpose. Good fortune."*

The strong is supported by the weak; the high is esteemed by the low. A friendly relationship exists when people of lower rank support their superiors. The strong fourth line is supported by the first line. This relationship serves as a solid base from which one can exercise strength. When used correctly, the strength of this line can benefit an entire community. However, if strength is abused or if one attempts to further express or display power, disaster will result. To moderately apply strength is the correct course in this position.

> **LINE 5:** *"The withered weeping willow is in bloom. An old woman marries a young man. Although they are neither blamed nor praised, the relationship does not last too long."*

The fifth line is like a warrior who marries an older woman, as represented by the top line. The strong warrior in the central position needs the gentle support of those below him in order to be balanced. However, he only gets this support by marrying an older woman of some influence. The result is far from perfect and just barely acceptable. Neither good nor bad.

The question is asked: "Since a strong fifth line is normally appropriate in this position, why does this particular yang line need support from a yin line?"

The answer is that a yang line in a yang position is generally in a correct position relative to the entire hexagram, but an excess of yang energy is present here. Thus, the excessiveness of this line needs yin energy to balance it. Unfortunately, the only yin energy available is the weak, old sixth line.

Another question one might ask is: "Why is the top line viewed as an old lady?" The top line is a yin line in a yin position which contains too much yin energy and can be regarded as a weak or old female. Thus, an overly strong man marries an overly weak or aged woman who cannot really support him. The overall situation is weakened by this imperfect match.

This line not only illustrates the effects of too much yang, but also the need to accurately match the energies in a situation in order for it to be correctly balanced.

> **LINE 6:** *"One's head disappears in crossing the water. Danger. There is no great blame for this."*

Now water covers the top of one's head; one is overwhelmed by the excess. At this point, what can the top line do? When danger has already been reached, the only thing one can do is not become too rigid or violent. Through calm and appropriate measures, one will be able to handle the dangerous situation.   Do not rely on strength or challenge the overwhelming situation with a daring attitude.   The problem can be diminished to practically nothing by responding calmly and gently. The following three principles are worth repeating:

1. Nothing should be done to excess.

2. All components of a situation must be well matched for there to be balance and harmony.

3. Flexibility, softness, calmness and patience provide hope in a dangerous situation.

In divination, this sign is an unfavorable one. But it does provide a great opportunity to understand the teachings of one of the wisest of all sages, Lao Tzu.

SPECIFIC GUIDANCE

PERSONAL FORTUNE: It will be poor, inharmonious and burdensome.

MARRIAGE: Not good.

HOUSING/FAMILY: The situation is suitable for living with others.

CHILDBIRTH: The baby will be a girl.

LOOKING FOR HELP: It can be found.

SOCIAL/GOVERNMENTAL POSITION: The position will not be good; forget it.

TRADE/BUSINESS: It is difficult to achieve.

SEARCHING FOR SOMEONE: They are difficult to find. If you receive a message, they can be found.

WAITING FOR SOMEONE: They will not come.

LOOKING FOR SOMETHING LOST: It has fallen into the water and is difficult to recover.

HUNTING FOR THIEVES: They are hiding in the West and can be caught.

LAWSUIT: There will be some problem or obstruction.

CLIMATE: It will be cloudy or rainy for a long time.

TRAVEL: A good time for travel.

DISEASE: It is serious but can be cured.

PERSONAL WISH: It is difficult to achieve.

COMMENTARY

It is not difficult to cultivate and understand reality.
The secret of achievement lies in
  the persistence of a pure mind.
Once you begin the sacred method,
  follow it only.
The constancy of your efforts
  will cause the wisdom of your soul to shine through.
Following different approaches
  disperses your energies,
  creates chaos and delays in your achievement.
Self-cultivation creates a firm, calm power.
Through it, your efforts and hopes
  to transcend the mediocre will be realized.
Stay with one method from beginning to end.
Avoid the temptation to change paths.
Honesty and sincerity are connected;
  each influences the other.
With them, all positive, subtle energy
  protects you.
Your subtle body has form,
  but is not limited to it.
True wisdom is quiet,
  independent and fragrant.
Persevere in connecting with the universal light.
Through it you will achieve
  the fullness and brightness
  within your own nature.
You yourself can experience and verify
  the greatness of eternal truth,
  and thereby voyage safely
  across the boundless spiritual ocean.
Know that your own intelligence can create blindness.
Be diligent in changing night into day.
It is easiest to progress with self-cultivation
  in a quiet, dark and separate room.
The grace from all the subtle worlds will come to you
  and make you the wise, firm seed
  of a heavenly whole being,
  a shien, a most beautifully developed one.

29 坎 K'an ䷜

the ABYSS

GUIDANCE: *"Confidence and mental stability are needed in times of difficulty. When the mind is no longer obstructed by external difficulties, the goal can be attained."*

This hexagram is formed by a doubling of the trigram K'an or Water. This is one of eight hexagrams where the basic trigrams are doubled, thus its image is reinforced. In this hexagram, each trigram consists of a yang line between two yin lines. The two yin lines form a ravine through which Water, represented by the central yang line, flows. Meeting with obstruction and entrapment are symbolized here.

The primary guidance of this hexagram uses the nature of Water as an example of appropriate conduct and self-development. The *Tao Teh Ching* also guides us to be like water:

> *Water always takes the lowest position.*
> *Obstacles do not hinder it.*
> *It accommodates whatever is in its path*
> *   and continues to flow forward.*
> *It never loses its direction.*
> *By remaining low it follows its true nature*
> *   and its fundamental direction is not*
> *   influenced by superficial obstructions.*
> *Water is always ocean-bound,*
> *   seeking to reunite with the whole.*
> *To follow the way of water*
> *   is to return to one's spiritual essence.*

Water never forms itself. In a square container, its shape is square; in a round container, its shape is round. Whether the container is made of crystal or of mud, the essence of water remains the same. Its surroundings do not influence or alter it. Likewise, a person who lives by his true nature is not affected by what others think of him. Since he does not become involved in disputes, his being remains unaffected.

The nature of Water is soft and yielding, yet it can wear away huge rocks. Lao Tzu used the following simple example to illustrate a profound principle: "To be soft is life; to be hard is death." This same principle is expressed in nature. The branches of a living tree are limber. If the branches are hard and dry, then the tree is dying or already dead. When one is young, one's bones are soft and pliant. As a person becomes older and approaches death, his bones become stiff and brittle. Likewise, to stiffen the mind with concepts and emotions also stiffens the spirit. By following the example of Water, one can learn the conduct that is appropriate to different circumstances.

This hexagram also signifies danger because the configuration of lines suggests a place like an abyss. One who adapts to danger and maintains inner integrity will not be hurt. One's true nature will not be affected even by great suffering, and one's spirit will remain unharmed. This is because the danger is external to one's spiritual essence. Yet, even in the absence of external difficulties, one's life can become an abyss by indulging in excessive emotions and cultivating narrow attitudes. With such behavior, one deviates from one's true nature. However, by remaining centered, one will be unaffected by difficulty. One can learn the order of the universe by observing its elements and movement. Following these principles can lead to an understanding of all situations in life and enable one to overcome all obstructions.

LINE 1: *"Facing doubled obstruction, one is entrapped. Misfortune."*

One enters a dangerous situation and is too weak to resist being trapped. This danger is caused by overestimating one's capabilities. Surely, this is not the correct way to deal with difficulty.

The first line is weak, yet in a position requiring strength. The first line normally corresponds with the fourth; however, in this situation the fourth line is also weak, so the first line does not have its support. From the onset, this line will experience difficulty.

LINE 2: *"Through calmness and clarity, one will gradually overcome difficulty."*

A yang line is trapped between two yin lines. This implies a dangerous situation from which one should seek a way out, though not too hastily. First, become centered so as not to be overcome by the situation. Then, by being practical and cautious, one can steadily work one's way out of trouble a step at a time. Strength in handling this difficulty lies in inner truth and knowledge.

LINE 3: *"Going further will cause danger and difficulties. Do not proceed."*

The third line is a yin line in a yang position. It is caught between two ravines and can go neither forward nor backward without falling into the abyss. Any movement at this time is dangerous. Over-estimation of one's ability to handle a difficult situation does not result in accomplishment. Therefore, one should not attack the danger directly.

LINE 4: *"Though small, a sincere offering will be blessed with peace and safety."*

The fourth yin line is in its appropriate position. If one's attitudes are sincere, like the sincerity expressed during ceremonies, then one may be freed from difficulty. In a meeting between the strong and the weak, faithfulness and truthfulness will help decrease any possible difficulty.

LINE 5: *"If water does not overflow, it reaches its own level; no fault."*

When one is neither proud nor complacent, one can reach full development without causing danger. One remains safe and without error. If in a good position, do not become overly ambitious. If emotions are strong, do not become too desirous. The emphasis here is on restraint.

LINE 6: *"Bound tightly and placed in thorns, one is never pardoned and thus not freed. Misfortune."*

The top line indicates that one's ignorance and stubbornness has caused danger. This danger or trouble is symbolized by an ancient form of punishment in which the criminal was bound with ropes and confined within a thicket of brambles. If the criminal was not pardoned within three years, he would not be pardoned at all. This symbolizes a weak person who enters a deep abyss as the consequence of not having enough self-restraint.

SPECIFIC GUIDANCE

PERSONAL FORTUNE: There will be a family separation. One will leave one's hometown or mother country.

MARRIAGE: It will be successful and may be between close friends.

HOUSING/FAMILY: Moving close to water and building a house there will bring success.

CHILDBIRTH: The baby will be a boy. There will be a shock after the delivery, but all will be safe.

LOOKING FOR WORK: It will be achieved later.

SOCIAL/GOVERNMENTAL POSITION: It will be difficult to achieve.

TRADE/BUSINESS: It is very profitable.

SEARCHING FOR SOMEONE: Look southward, near water.

WAITING FOR SOMEONE: People living far away will come; people living nearby will not come.

LOOKING FOR SOMETHING LOST: Quickly look near water. Delay will make it difficult to find.

HUNTING FOR THIEVES: They are hiding close to water, perhaps a mountain stream.

LAWSUIT: There is good fortune in seeking material benefits.

CLIMATE: There will be a long period of rain.

TRAVEL: It is dangerous. There may even be death.

DISEASE: The disease is hard to cure. There is danger.

PERSONAL WISH: There are some obstacles. If you pursue them in a hasty manner, there can be no success.

COMMENTARY
Water: The Example of Natural Virtue

The following are eight natural ways of virtue in which people of integral virtue can learn from Water:

1. Be content with a "low" position. Like Water, by remaining low, one may be safe and free from competition.[2]

2. Remain profound. A profound mind is as quiet as the deep ocean. Therefore, it is undisturbed by the waves on the surface.

3. Give generously. Water constantly gives without asking to be repaid.

4. Speak faithfully. The flow of Water always faithfully goes toward the sea.

5. Govern gently. Though Water moves with gentleness, it can overcome even the hardest obstacle under Heaven.

6. Work capably and adaptably. Water can fit what is square or what is round. It keeps its true nature in any containment or circumstance.

7. Take action opportunely. Water freezes in Winter and melts in Spring. Its inflexibility in the Winter is like death. Its softness in the Spring generates new life.

8. Never fight. Water does not fight for itself, thus it is beyond blame.

---

[2] This implies that humans like to be in "high" positions rather than "low" ones. This becomes a source of conflict for many. Those on a high tight rope always need to look for balance points. For the one who walks on the ground, a fully opened parasol or pole is a great nuisance.

30

離
LI

Radiance

GUIDANCE: *"Bright and progressive. Cultivating the heart will be prosperous. Good fortune."*

In the hexagram Li, both the upper and lower trigrams represent Fire and brightness, thereby reinforcing the meaning. Fire symbolizes beauty and illumination. It can also symbolize a mind that is too active, unstable, desirous and lost in search of external beauty.

Though Fire is beautiful, it is difficult to control. The mind is also like Fire and is difficult to control and keep still. Fire can manifest as desire and ambition which can easily burn a person if the Fire is not managed correctly.

Water is necessary to balance Fire. Without the interaction of Fire and Water, life would be impossible. Likewise, without the sun and moon to brighten the earth, cultivation could not exist.

In their natural aspect, Fire and Water represent opposing forces. At the same time, they are also cooperative forces that help accomplish each other. The yin-yang principle is demonstrated by these two forces.

The interaction of these two energies is very important to all life. In order to distinguish the light energy from the heavy, Heaven and Earth are used to represent yang and yin as the two great spheres of the universe. This energy division is represented in the diagram of the "Pre-Heaven" stage. (See Figure 105a.) However, after the development of Heaven and Earth, Fire and Water are the dominant expressions in the arrangement of the eight natural manifestations (Hou Tien Pa Kau), as shown in the diagram of the "Post-Heaven" stage on the next page. Having a good understanding of these two energies, Li (Fire) and Kan (Water), is very important.

Post-Heaven (Practical order)

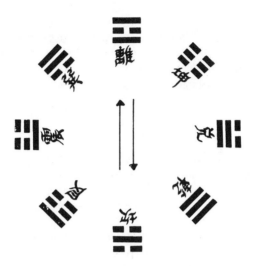

(Figure 113)

The composition of life is an interaction of Fire and Water, mind and body. These forces must not only be integrated and well managed in one's life, but also in one's body. The active mind is Fire; the body is Water. More specifically, Fire is emotions or desires and Water is the secretions. If these energies cannot be well-controlled, a person will not live peacefully. Yet, Fire and Water, when arranged and managed correctly, can interact harmoniously and thus benefit life.

In the hexagram K'an, Abyss ☵ , the formation of yang energy within yin energy is like water flowing in a ravine. In Li, yin energy within yang energy indicates that all the energy is radiating outward and that the center is empty, like Fire.

The original meaning of Li is "radiance in all directions," "beauty" or "illumination." In modern Chinese, it implies departure or "spreading." In ancient times, the character for Li represented the sun or source of light.

Furthermore, Li can mean "Fu Li": Fu, "clinging," and Li, "beautiful." The original Chinese character for beauty portrayed the eyes of a deer and represented the sun and the moon. Light from the sun and moon brightens the earth. Because of this light, we are able to enjoy beauty. But beauty must cling to something; it cannot exist independently of an object. A tree is beautiful because of its form, the shape and color of its leaves and its fruit and flowers.

On a practical level, this hexagram instructs humanity in the uses of brightness or mental illumination for the guidance of others. When one cultivates brightness, one's light will illuminate all directions. Those who receive this brightness will also reflect it. To perpetuate brightness is to radiate warmth in all of one's actions.

LINE 1: *"Prosperous beginning with some disorder. Be cautious. No blame."*

The nature of fire is movement. The first line is like someone who is about to begin a journey. Everything must be put in order before commencing. With proper preparation and a clear mind, reckless actions can be avoided.

This line is a strong line in the correct position and indicates movement with inner composure. It refers to early morning. This is the most important time of day. One should respect this sacred time and be peaceful in order not to violate the energy of the entire day.

LINE 2: *"Warm, beautiful yellow light; very good fortune!"*

The second line is a yin line in the right position. It is taken from the hexagram K'un, Earth. It is a beautiful line and expresses being centered and balanced, thus the second line is the most favorable one in this hexagram.

Youth is a time when one can mold one's emotional patterns. Such patterns are difficult to change later in life. A person should remember to continually refresh oneself by cherishing the spirit of the second line. It can give one renewed hope and the ability to break away from the past, which is merely a phenomenon of time and has no real substance.

The second line represents mid-morning, between the hours of nine and eleven a.m. This is the time when the sunshine is comfortably warm and not too strong. This line represents the golden time of youth, the decisive period which determines correct direction and development. This line also represents an emotionally balanced and harmonious life. Therefore, always keep the mind like the second line - young and hopeful.

LINE 3: *"The sun passes midday. Make good use of this time and be happy; otherwise, it will be too late to establish a good life. Possible misfortune."*

The sun has reached its highest point and begins to decline. One must now act in order to make the best use of the time. Do not waste this golden opportunity. To make a bad decision at this point could ruin the rest of one's life.

LINE 4: *"It comes suddenly, burns brightly and is quickly consumed."*

Expressing strength, like Fire, hastens death. One is doing things too hurriedly. This line represents midafternoon, between the hours of two and three p.m. The afternoon sun is descending, having passed its zenith. This line is like a meteorite or a shooting star; it moves with urgency, then suddenly burns up. Slow down!

LINE 5: *"He who feels truly sorry for being overly indulgent with luxuries will be able to regulate and correct his vanities. This is accomplished by feeling sympathy for those less fortunate. Good fortune."*

The Fire has reached its peak. One should be aware that the time of prosperity will soon be over, so moderation and self-discipline are most important. Good fortune comes only after much remorse and deep reflection.

This line represents late afternoon, between the hours of four and five p.m. There are only a few hours of light left. Everything is now at that level of maturity which is the best time of life. Value and use this light and the wisdom that has been acquired. Radiate and spread the light in order to help and influence others.

LINE 6: *"Now the king engages in conquering the rebels. He subdues the chief and punishes him. No blame."*

It is now sunset, the most beautiful time of day and the time for old age. This is the time to capture and overcome the main rebels and thus create a peaceful environment. "Rebels" can symbolize one's unreasonable desires, which disturb joy and harmony. Now is the time to handle confusion and temptation and to create balance.

SPECIFIC GUIDANCE

PERSONAL FORTUNE: Problems at the beginning improve with time; however, one has difficulty with one's spouse.

MARRIAGE: Having a beautiful marriage is not likely. Even future marriages will result in misfortune.

HOUSING/FAMILY: There is a chance of robbery or fire. Be careful.

CHILDBIRTH: Difficult, with possible miscarriage.

LOOKING FOR WORK: Obstacles make success difficult to achieve.

SOCIAL/GOVERNMENTAL POSITION: Advancement and success are possible.

TRADE/BUSINESS: Business will be profitable in the future.

SEARCHING FOR SOMEONE: They will not be found.

WAITING FOR SOMEONE: They will not come.

LOOKING FOR SOMETHING LOST: A woman may help find what is lost.

HUNTING FOR THIEVES: They have moved from North to South and can be caught with the help of others.

LAWSUIT: For the instigator, this sign is unfavorable and may be dangerous. However, the defendant has good fortune.

CLIMATE: It will be rainy or cloudy for many days.

TRAVEL: Travel to the north or west is not favorable.

DISEASE: Fever is indicated. It is curable for a man, but incurable for a woman.

PERSONAL WISH: One's wish is difficult to achieve.

COMMENTARY
Cultivating the Mind

The mind and the heart represent the Fire energy in our bodies. Only when they are harmonized with the body which represent the Water energy, can one achieve the correct goal of fundamental cultivation: good health.

Keep the mind clear,
it is more valuable than knowledge.
Inquire into the properties of things
and penetrate to their essence.

Do not be excessive in anything,
  not even in joy.
When joy is overabundant,
  it must turn to its opposite,
  and sorrow will overcome you.
When pleasure is carried through to its highest degree,
  it will bring about sadness.

Nourish the body with calmness.
Nourish the heart with giving to others.
The more you give to others,
  the more you will abound.

When righteousness lives in the eyes,
  they become bright.
If you keep negativity in your mind,
  calamities are sure to come.
If you keep your mind open and receptive,
  it can absorb knowledge very quickly.
The mind of a superior being
  is imbued with righteousness.
When the mind approaches true happiness,
  it becomes intelligent.
Keep the mind unoccupied, receptive and loose.
Do not hold on to anything good or bad.
Know that everything is in constant change.
Nothing is static.

Be thorough in your actions,
  but keep your mind empty.
Through creative non-action,
  one can extend the clarity of one's mind
  and the innocence of one's pristine spirit
  to embrace the eternal Tao.
When the mind betrays the pristine spirit,
  it becomes a monkey, jumping from here to there.
It becomes lewd, compromising and boasting.
Where is the beauty of your tranquil mind?
Cut deep into the core of your problems.
Cut out all falseness and conditioned ideas.
He who conquers his mind is really great.
Disarm it, conquer its willfulness.

Know that your mind is like spring water.
Its purity will emerge from the depths of your soul.
United with the spirit, it will express true beauty.

You will be earnest, contented,
  unconcerned with daily life, joyous.
You will be a useful vessel to assist others
  on the road of Tao.

We have to nourish the heart.
When we have little desire, the heart is content.

When we hold on to nothing,
  the heart becomes carefree.
Soon the heart is as a leaf
  trembling in an imperceptible breeze,
  as light as the dust on a butterfly's wings.

Closing the senses is perceiving life.
Perceiving no thing,
  be perceptive to the utmost depth.
Penetrate the impenetrable.
Perceive the imperceivable.
Such a small beginning
  to the wide, unlimited ascension.

31   咸   hsien

mutual attraction

GUIDANCE: "Mutual attraction brings about joyful love.
One will be profited by being upright and persistent. Marriage brings good fortune."

In this hexagram, Lake is above Mountain.   This
image represents the mutual attraction and interaction of
these two different kinds of natural energy.   The Mountain
is the youngest son of nature.   The Lake is the youngest
daughter.   Therefore, mutual attraction or love occurs
naturally.
  The Lake represents gentleness; its movement is descending.   Mountain represents strength and firmness; its

movement is ascending. These two different aspects of movement are in communion. While each retains its own natural characteristics, together they interact and harmonize. In human relationship, the Lake symbolizes a young girl and the Mountain symbolizes a young boy. They experience true love and share strong mutual attraction.

The ancient sages called this interaction "hsien" or "to touch the heart." A later Chinese word, "geng," is derived from "hsien" and can also be translated "to touch the heart." However, "geng" actually means to share a feeling of friendship or love - it is mutual appreciation and affection. At the highest level, "hsien," however, means universal love.

In this hexagram, the Mountain uses the moisture of the Lake and the Lake is contained by the Mountain. Through their interaction, everything is benefited. Likewise, marriage represents a relationship which fulfills reciprocal needs and brings about good fortune. A relationship which expresses a positive mutual attraction can also apply to family, friends, teacher and student, or business partnerships.

Hsien also indicates the mutual influence that exists between the strong and the gentle. In its highest meaning, Hsien is the mutual attraction between Heaven and Earth, the natural yang and yin energies. They attract each other, interact and bring about creative and productive results.

In true love, deep feelings are expressed without words, pressures, possessiveness or demands. The image of Hsien is that of the strong supporting the gentle from below. Such an interaction does not mean that one energy overpowers the other, rather that the relationship is one of interdependence. In a truly good relationship, the different qualities of each partner complement one another and combine to form a team.

One who expresses his strength aggressively rather than responsibly is feared. Such an aggressive approach can prevent or disrupt a good marriage. In such a case, the relationship becomes tyrannical instead of supportive.

The Mountain surrounds the Lake with empty space. When a person becomes empty, he is receptive to positive energy, love and other virtues. A selfish person, on the other hand, is filled only with himself, and this is the main source of difficulty between people. To be a good or able leader requires patience and the capacity to forgive. In a relationship, one should act appropriately at each level. If one's influence is too strong or is insufficient, the relationship will become imbalanced.

One must first attract people before trying to influence them. Being too strong may cause others to close their minds to one's influence. If a person does not want his real problem known, he will sometimes respond negatively to close friends, a spouse, a teacher or a healer. Therefore, one must develop discretion in order to know the appropriate level of intimacy in a relationship.

Opening one's heart and being influential requires virtue, which is the pure positive power of human nature. True virtue is true nature. Its purity and benefit are invariable and unalterable. A person of virtue cannot be influenced by flattery; he lives according to his genuine and sincere nature.

Here, different lines represent the toe, calf, thigh, hip, heart, neck and jaw to illustrate different levels of influence. In the *I Ching*, one of the natural energy correspondences between the lines is as follows: the first with the fourth; the second with the fifth; and the third with the sixth. However, the quality and degree of contact and influence the lines have on each other vary according to different circumstances.

All six lines have a common message. Good fortune will result from remaining centered, while restlessness and impulsiveness bring misfortune. It is important to respond to different situations appropriately, as illustrated by the other hexagrams; thus people will not waste themselves in an unnatural struggle as differing circumstances arise.

LINE 1: *"Attraction begins at the toes."*

The influence is in the toe, thus the attraction is shallow. Because this is only the beginning of mutual attraction, the position is not yet influential; however, it can be the start of a friendship. This is time to remain centered and not engage in premature action.

LINE 2: *"Attraction reaches the calf; disturbing. Now is the time to remain calm."*

The influence has now reached a higher level. This line is represented by the calf, which is associated with movement. However, one in this position feels uneasy and pushed. Remaining calm will bring good fortune. Seeking only to relate further on a physical level will destroy the prospect of a good relationship.

LINE 3: *"Attraction reaches the thigh. One who is too anxious and responds quickly meets trouble."*

The influence of the third line has reached a higher level and now touches the hip. In approaching someone by walking forward, one's toe moves first, followed by the calf and then the hip. The hip does not initiate movement. Therefore, one should only adjust to circumstances. Hastily pursuing one's desires will only cause humiliation. This line can indicate the sexual organs. In such a case it means the intimacy of a sexual response can be attained, but don't hurry.

LINE 4: *"Attraction reaches the heart. A correct response occurs and remorse disappears."*

The fourth line represents the heart and mind. The response has reached the heart; love and affection grow, but only when one's intentions are for a positive purpose will the response be a correct one. A relationship develops by allowing nature to take its course. Interfering with the natural process may hasten growth, but will destroy the fruit.

LINE 5: *"Attraction reaches the upper back. Neither response nor trouble."*

Here the attraction reaches the back of the neck. One cannot influence others at this time. However, there is no remorse. Touching the upper back is a light, friendly gesture with no expectation of anything in return. One wishes to move or influence others, but there is no response.

LINE 6: *"Attraction reaches the mouth. Conversation is brought about."*

The top line reaches the tongue and could result in flattery or pleasant talk. Maybe it also represents kissing.

SPECIFIC GUIDANCE

PERSONAL FORTUNE: Everything will be beautiful; however, one may lose oneself in love.
MARRIAGE: A beautiful marriage.
HOUSING/FAMILY: The family grows.
CHILDBIRTH: A boy will be born.
LOOKING FOR WORK: One will succeed later in life.
SOCIAL/GOVERNMENTAL POSITION: Successful.
TRADE/BUSINESS: The venture can be successful.
SEARCHING FOR SOMEONE: They cannot be found.
WAITING FOR SOMEONE: They are safely on the road.
LOOKING FOR SOMETHING LOST: It is close to water.
HUNTING FOR THIEVES: They are difficult to find.
LAWSUIT: Make peace; otherwise, a jail sentence is possible.
CLIMATE: It will be rainy.
TRAVEL: There will be some obstacle.
DISEASE: It is curable.
PERSONAL WISH: Your wish can be achieved.

COMMENTARY
Love

The mutual response of two young hearts presents the picture of love. This is illustrated by ☱ a young girl, and ☶ a young boy, and the mutual attraction shared between them.

When I was young, I focused more on my spiritual achievement than on experiences of love. After studying the important teachings of the three main cultural traditions - Taoism, Confucianism and Buddhism - I harmonized and expressed all three with the following words:

"Confucianism is my garment,
Buddhism is my cane and
Taoism is my sandal."

(For more information regarding this saying, refer to the commentary for Hexagram #45.) My young, proud mind seemed to be satisfied with this combination. However, one day I discovered that someone had added some new, handwritten words to each line of my writing on the wall of my study. These lines now said:

"Confucianism is my garment,
- *it is too short for you!*
Buddhism is my cane,
- *it is too weak to support you!*
and Taoism is my sandal
- *it has been worn out long ago!*"

My first response to this discovery was outrage.   I thought it must be my younger brother or elder sister making fun of me, but since it did not seem to be an ordinary joke, I immediately corrected my judgment. The person who wrote these lines had to have a vision higher than, or equal to, mine. I felt puzzled. Who could have done this?   Since the handwriting was not much better than mine, it could not be the work of a dignified adult. Also, this happened to be my personal study upstairs. I was the only one who used most of the upstairs rooms, except for the one used as the family shrine. After making many inquiries of my family, I discovered that some of my sister's girlfriends had visited us. One of them had been in our family shrine for a short while. She was the only daughter of one of my father's friends. She had to be the one who did this. She was famous for being the most beautiful girl in our town.   She was also well-educated and a lover of literature.

Though I had never paid attention to her before, I decided I must pay her a visit. I thought of the ancient one's saying: "Three people are walking together; one of them must have something I can learn." I dressed myself neatly and directly went to see her.

She received me in the small hall of their garden. After our greeting, I politely and straightforwardly requested an explanation of the addition I was certain she had made on my study wall. She flushed and suggested that if I would call on her for ten days she would then give me her explanation. I agreed to this as my respectful lesson. Thus, every afternoon I went to her house. We read some good, ancient poetry, played Chinese chess and did some gardening. Our friendship developed more with each day. When she tenderly touched the back of my hand, I felt that something had struck me, yet I liked it. Her eyes were the most beautiful poem I had ever read. The sweetness of her delicate smell intoxicated me. Her smile engulfed me.

Before very long, however, a difficulty surfaced in our budding romance. It appeared that she was especially attached to a novel entitled *The Red Chamber*. I could never agree with her belief that *The Red Chamber* held the truth of life and, likewise, she could never agree with my Kung Fu practice.

When we reached the end of our ten-day period together, I again requested her explanation of the lines she had written on my wall. She asked for my palm, upon which she wrote a Chinese character with her gentle, slim finger. The Chinese word struck me in the same way I was struck by her finger, moving lightly over my palm. It was the character for the word "love" or, more appropriately in this case, "affection."

Now I was even more bewildered than before. I could not refrain from asking her what connection could possibly exist between the love of which she spoke and her addition to my writing. At first she hesitated. Then finally, with apparent difficulty, she said, "You like to think very much of Confucianism, Buddhism and Taoism, but without the word 'love' nothing has any meaning in life. Have you ever thought of that?"

This was a real question for me. Since I had never experienced love, I had never truly pondered this question. I answered frankly, "I do not know yet. How do you know?"

"From *The Red Chamber*," she answered.

I frowned. I had read the book and did not like it. When I told her that, she responded, "What is wrong with a girl and a boy falling in love as described in that book?"

"I don't know. It seems like too much trouble to become involved in such complicated love," I replied.

"Well, it seems to me like Confucianism, Buddhism and Taoism give you even more trouble with all kinds of study and discipline," she argued.

"I haven't thought about that. However, you have given me your explanation. I shall now go home to discover, through my own cultivation, the true significance of that word."

Though it was time to say good-bye, her eyes kept staring into mine and I felt their warmth flow into my body. Gradually, her eyes became moistened, tears falling from them like a string of pearls. I did not know how to help her. After a long while with her handkerchief to her face, she said, "You are always contemptuous toward me and the other girls. You will not come to see me again."

"I don't know. I'll think about it," I replied.

"It will be too late to see me if you only think about it. I shall die only for love, like Blue Jade (the main female character in *The Red Chamber*). Can you understand?" she asked.

"I shall go home and study this book that you like so much."

She offered, "I would like for you to have my copy since it is the best version." She went into her inner room to get the copy of her "holy book" and gave it to me. I took the book and left.

Though we had several versions of *The Red Chamber* in our house, I had never been able to read through any one of them in its entirety. The main story described the life of Precious Jade, a young man of a noble and wealthy family. Although his youth was spent in an elegant garden with many beautiful girls as his companions, he fell in love only with Blue Jade. However, his family arranged for him to marry a girl for whom he had no love. Soon afterward, Blue Jade died from her disappointment in love. Precious Jade's family also suffered decline. Precious Jade himself discovered that his entire life was but an empty dream and thus decided to leave the dusty world to become a Buddhist monk.

Though this book was a good work of literature, the love it described was very narrow. I could not recognize any high truth with which the author could illuminate human life. However, since I wanted to be with my friend and because I still felt difficulty with the question of love, I turned to my mother for help.

My mother told me, "An ancient sage once said, 'Even a developed one feels trouble communicating with women and children.' Problems are created when people of different levels of development come together. Therefore, spiritual development sometimes makes it more difficult to be with ordinary people. If this shortcoming of a developed person is not moderated, it can bring extreme isolation to him. This would not be a very beneficial direction for anyone to go in, unless it is done so intentionally, with a positive purpose for some special cultivation.

"Love is a very important matter in life. Nobody can ignore it. In general, as you already know, love can be classified into two different categories: broad love and narrow love. Broad love is humanistic, and all the ancient sages were recognized for their broad love. Confucius (551-479 B.C.) and Mencius (372-298 B.C.) exalted humanistic love. Mo Tzu (501-416 B.C.) exalted universal love and made himself as a model to realize it. He led a life of absolute self-abnegation. He exerted himself to the fullest extent of his life by working for the peace of humanity. Lao Tzu valued natural impartial love as the highest level. Sakyamuni exalted compassion and equal love. In general, humanistic love is developed, peaceful, impersonal and dispassionate love. This is what human nature was born with and what human beings should continue to cultivate. Also, in general, narrow love can only be practiced between two people, like a boy and a girl, a man and a woman, a husband and wife, or among a group of people like a family, a circle of friends, a religious fellowship, a society, a nation or a race.

"The practice of narrow love is usually passionate. Passion is what makes love narrow. Passionate love can be a good experience during one's youth, but passion should be well-guided and controlled. Although the emotional experience of narrow love can be beautiful, it can also be harmful. Broad, humanistic or natural love, however, can be enjoyed throughout this life and all lives. Whether love is humanistic or passionate, it should always be guided by the principle of balance. If one loses his balance in the name of love, then that way of loving is unhealthy.

"All people are born with passion, yet different patterns of passion give people different temperaments. One's temperament is influenced by all the stages of one's pre-natal and postnatal life. Parents must take the great responsibility to smooth their own temperaments when raising children in their pre-natal and post-natal stages. An individual must also take responsibility to cultivate himself and regulate his own temperament when a certain level of growth is reached, or as the saying goes, 'An adult must take responsibility for his own ugly face.'

"Now we come to the matter of adjusting one's personal temperament. One's temperament is like one's dog: one needs to put a muzzle and leash on it when taking it in public. Surely achievement comes when one has cast off one's 'dog' nature which is molded by the environment.

"Passion is natural. It is something we are born with, but the way we express our passion is a matter of our environment. We develop that expression ourselves, thus it is controllable and reformable.

"Passion is like water. Water is always water, but in its different phases, the speed and shape of its flow vary greatly. It can be a swift current, a big flood or a torrent.

It can be slow moving, or stagnant and motionless. It can also be a rising or ebbing tide, overflowing or draining a stream, lake, ravine, river or ocean. When water meets heat, it becomes vapor; when it meets cold, it becomes ice. Dew, rain, hail, fog, frost, ice, snow and so forth, all come from water. The water always remains the same - it is the environment which causes its different characteristics. Passion is like that.

"Passion is only a part of the whole human mental being, however. There is still the higher sphere of the mind which needs to be cultivated and developed so that one can have good control over the passion of the lower sphere of the mind. A raft riding the torrents cannot carry many people. Danger may be lurking anywhere along the journey's path. Though one may enjoy the excitement of riding a raft in the torrents, this is not a normal, everyday practice. If one's passion is like a torrent, then one's life is like a raft. How dangerous that is! How long can the enjoyment of such excitement last? Is it worth exhausting one's life? This seems to be a poor model of normal, healthy passion.

"Love is a beautiful passion; however, when emotional force or possessiveness is attached to what one loves, the sublime state of pure love is degraded or damaged. Surely, a spiritually developed person can still feel personal love, but it is unattached and unoccupying love. This is the fine quality of true spiritual love. The nature of spiritual love is subtle. One can unceasingly appreciate beauty without creating the troubles which accompany its ownership. Therefore, a full life of appreciation can be lived without carrying the weight of worldly burdens.

"Out of one's humanistic love comes the courage to accept responsibility for the world. This is certainly not a rigid practice. Most ancient developed ones, if not living in the high mountains married to the beauty of nature, would travel around the world like a white cloud flying across the sky. Nothing could restrict them.

"The particular practice of love in our family is to reach the level of the very ancient developed ones. We follow the external patterns of secular life, but within this everyday life we fulfill the broadness of spirituality. In other words, we use the roughness of the world and the difficulties of practical life as the friction that creates our spiritual sparks. This is what people call enlightenment or inspiration. Though enlightenment and inspiration are only momentary experiences, they can mark where one has

reached.   Furthermore, the endurance of life, which is
built from the difficulties of worldly life, is our actual
realization of universal, impartial love.   The refinement of
one's passions and emotions becomes an important aspect
in this realization.

"Some people cannot see with their partial vision that
the truth is total.   They think there can be no existence of
individual happiness in the practice of humanistic love,
but the real truth is that individual happiness exists only
in the happiness of its completeness.   Can one have
happiness when the entire world suffers from a flood?
One can only fulfill one's own life through the harmonious
fulfillment of all lives.   That is why, in our family, we live
for ourselves as well as for the entire world, with a clear
spiritual direction."

Then my mother continued, "In the narrow sense of a
family, your father is our life-maker.   I am the homemaker and also a life-maker.   We are all makers of a
common life.   We fulfill our individual duty and also assist
the fulfillment of each other's duty.   I am eighteen years
younger than your father.   I respect and love him and he
has   much   tolerance   and   understanding   toward   me.
Actually, he treats the entire world this same way, but I
am the one who has the blessing to live with him.   Furthermore, your father is a man of spiritual development,
thus our love is mainly spiritual rather than physical.
Being spiritually linked is the source of our happiness.

"If love is true, the experience of love and deep joy
occur in the same moment.   It is not joyful to reminisce
about a particular moment of love in the past.   The enlightenment of love exists in each moment.   There is no
search that can find love, nor any occasion that can
create love.   You know love when your heart is open.   The
music is silent, but its harmony pervades your entire
being.   In that moment there is no separation.

"Love is the golden light of the sun rising within your
being.   It is the rose which has just opened its eyes.   It is
the freshness of dew or the caress of a wave on the
shore - all within you.

"But the dawn becomes noon and finally evening.   The
early morning dew evaporates.   The rose reaches its
fullness and its petals fall.   A wave reaches its crest and
returns to the sea.   Then, does love also die?   If the love
within us is living, does it also die when it reaches its
fullness?   Can one hold that certain moment of the sun's
first appearance on the horizon?   Can one make love

endure? At what point does the joy of love's presence become the need for its possession? When one fears it will go away or die is when the need for its possession arises. At this point love becomes contaminated with emotion and need, and its original harmony changes to dissonance. Love then reverts to the realm of duality, and the presence of Tao within our hearts is missed.

"Love can be fulfilled without becoming trapped in the web of emotional needs. We can learn from the virtue of a well which exists for all to take from. Its spring never runs dry. When our inner treasure is inexhaustible, we can provide limitless love and still remain independent and non-possessing.

"In our tradition, we can enjoy the sunrise within us every moment. Our love is as free as the blowing wind and as enduring as a flowing river. Since we continually renew ourselves, we do not fear losing love. Our cultivation becomes our lover, for our love is Tao. Thus, love never withers, for it is continually refreshed.

"When the time comes that you feel love for someone, be gentle. Love has a delicate nature. Never be rough with it or it will be completely destroyed. Always distinguish the difference between love and desire. Love gives pleasure; desire creates pressure. Desire, loneliness, tension and disappointment can all deteriorate the delicate nature of true love. To love is to be gentle. Tender love is truly beneficial in any circumstance. If love is not given gently, it becomes stormy. Stormy love, like stormy weather, can never last long. Generally this kind of love comes out of an imbalance in one's personality or from the pressures of an unhealthy environment.

"Young people may say tender love is weak love, but this is not true. Motherly love is tender love. An eagle soars in the sky and finds its prey among a group of small chickens searching for food in a meadow. It quickly dives to the ground, but before it can extend its sharp claws to capture its prey, the weak old mother hen has already spread her wings and gathered all her chicks under them. She puts herself, face to face, in confrontation with the aggressor. Love can give birth to courage and courage can subdue the strong. You have witnessed this great scene many times in our country life.

"I always tell your sisters that a woman should never become emotionally competitive with her man. A man does not like to have another 'manly' person in his private life. I also tell your sisters to be responsible in family life, but not bossy. A man may have enough bosses in his life outside the family. A woman must earn love and respect from a man by being feminine and by being faithful, not by fighting or competing.

"You feel troubled about correctly responding to the love that comes from this good girl. You can love her if it is your true response. This might be the first time you sail the oceans of love. However, there is nothing to be afraid of. When the current becomes rough, keep yourself centered as usual, and get complete control of your ship. As far as I can see, this girl is not a torrential type of girl. She is more like the beautiful flow of a brooklet; the poetic feeling of her presence can calmly be absorbed.

"However, do not develop your young spiritual love into sentimental love. The love of Precious Jade and Blue Jade is not a good example of pure love. It is not healthy to imitate it. Healthy love bears the fruit of deep rejoicing; nothing can alter it and nothing can be exchanged for it. The beauty of sentimental love can earn wide appreciation on a literary level. However, if it occurs in practical life, it must be the result of an emotional imbalance or feelings of insecurity. Above all, such imaginary love lasts for only a very short time. Her imitation of Blue Jade should not be encouraged by you through helping her all day to prepare a funeral for the fallen flower petals and then helping her bury them while singing the funeral hymn. I heard she has been doing this already for years. This is a silly matter, and it is ominous to accept the suggested destiny of Blue Jade in *The Red Chamber*.

"The challenge she makes on your young spiritual authority will surely benefit you. Remember, never be bothered about those who speak or write better than you. Always be mindful of achieving your own transpiercing vision of reality. She has not developed higher than you. Her motivation could be the need for your love. Now, restore your inner balance and give her an answer."

The same day, I wrote my answer to her and returned her copy of *The Red Chamber*. The following is what I wrote:

"Confucianism is my garment,
  - it is too short for me.
Buddhism is my cane,
  - it is too weak to support me.
Now I become a worshipper of *The Red Chamber*.

I am going to help Precious Jade secularize
   from his tedious life as a monk.
I am going to revive his Blue Jade
   with my immortal magic."

32   恒
        henG

constancy

GUIDANCE: *"Be constant; it is right.   Now is the time to be persevering and to undertake something."*

The upper trigram represents Thunder, a strong force. The lower trigram, Wind, is a gentle force.   Neither Thunder nor Wind has the attribute of constancy, so why is this hexagram called Constancy?   Wind and Thunder often occur together, but only at particular times and under certain conditions.   Neither Wind nor Thunder alone connotes constancy, but the laws and conditions under which they operate are constant and eternal.   If the universe were completely still without the generative energy of Thunder or the persistent action of Wind, there would be no life.   It is the movement of all the heavenly bodies and the incessant flow of energy that reflects the constancy of the universe.   On earth, it is the change of the seasons which expresses this constancy.

The energy cycles of all life are based upon an invariable Subtle Law.   All natural phenomena are in a continuous process of change, with constancy as the underlying principle.   On the human level, one's attitudes and disposition should be supported by the constancy of one's virtue.   Without a stable axis, neither nature nor civilized human life can endure.

This hexagram encourages one to be resolute and persevering.   These principles are especially applicable to married life, because married life needs constancy.   In terms of human relationships, the upper trigram represents an adult man, and the lower trigram represents an adult woman.   This hexagram is the inverse of the preceding one, Hsien, which involves courtship between a young boy and girl.   In the preceding hexagram, the boy is below the girl in order to gain her trust without intimidating her. However, Heng refers to the period after marriage, in which the man is above the woman, the order of the traditional family structure. In modern society, this pattern has changed since we no longer depend on physical strength for survival and a woman may represent the yang energy in a family.

The survival of any family, group or team requires perseverance. Relationships that have been organized as such cannot be secure without constancy. Without perseverance and constancy, members of the family, group or team will not be able to develop the tolerance and other virtues that are necessary for working together. After marriage, the roles of "breadwinner" and "homemaker" are defined and become the basis for team work. Thus, an individual's life patterns may change. Competing with another member or quarreling over changes creates disharmony. If the homemaker supports the breadwinner, a foundation of constancy can be established. In our culture, both man and woman may be breadwinner and homemaker at the same time to establish a prosperous family.

Persistence is the practical application of constancy. The lines indicate when persistence is appropriate and when one should desist and remain still.

LINE 1: *"Beginning things too quickly and precipitously is not a normal approach. No benefit; trouble results."*

The first line indicates the beginning stage. By persisting in matters not yet fully understood, troubles and obstacles are created. Hastily beginning projects for which one is not qualified will not be beneficial. At this time, one should not persist with one's opinion.

LINE 2: *"Be to the point. No remorse."*

Maintain the right position. Do not attempt either too much or too little, but instead strive for balance in all activities. In following the Path with sincerity and without deviation, there will be no regret.

LINE 3: *"One cannot maintain constancy. This can cause many problems. Continuing to be inconstant results in loss."*

When one does not persevere when it is necessary, there can be no virtue or constancy. Humiliation will result. The third line represents a person with emotional instability. Though he has deep understanding, he is not guided by correct principles. This description is based on the third line sitting between two improperly ordered lines, the second and the fourth, which makes him a "fence sitter." Therefore, he does not know when to go or stay, and he forfeits his true knowledge. He fears that those behind him cause troubles; however, his problems are created through his lack of dignity.

LINE 4: *"There is no prey in the field. One's constancy is wasted."*

You will not discover game while hunting in an empty field, regardless of how persistent you are. Do not waste your energy.

LINE 5: *"Persevering in being submissively virtuous is beneficial for followers, not for leaders."*

Being constant and submissive to one's leader or to a creative person in one's life is appropriate; however, the reverse is not correct behavior. A leader, a breadwinner, or the head of a family must have flexibility in order to deal with changing conditions. Life is less complex for one who stays at home and takes care of domestic matters or fulfills specific assignments.

The fifth line represents the benefit obtained by being settled and persevering. However, this benefit does not apply to the leader or breadwinner who must always examine the situation and make necessary adjustments. Peace and constancy should be kept within; responding to the situation with flexibility should be reflected outwardly.

In a hexagram where the number of yin and yang lines are equal, the fifth line can always tip the balance toward a favorable result. Thus, the fifth line has the responsibility of staying effectively organized.

LINE 6: *"Losing one's constancy, nothing can be achieved."*

The top line expresses extremes. Anything that is extreme cannot last long. This line is past the point of being constant and is like a government leader who has lost his power. The government eventually falls. After experiencing each stage of this hexagram, one becomes aware of the importance of being constant and can then apply constancy to what is correct.

SPECIFIC GUIDANCE

PERSONAL FORTUNE: There is some uneasiness. While friends and relatives may not be supportive, one's spouse is.

MARRIAGE: It will be successful. Good fortune.

HOUSING/FAMILY: Keeping the old building is more beneficial than building a new one.

CHILDBIRTH: The baby will be a boy. The mother will have difficulty during the delivery.

LOOKING FOR WORK: If one seeks an important job, one obtains a minor position. However, if one looks for a minor position, one receives an important one. Others may create obstacles, but they do not really stand in the way.

SOCIAL/GOVERNMENTAL POSITION: It will be quite successful.

TRADE/BUSINESS: Do not change locations. Stay at your current place.

SEARCHING FOR SOMEONE: One must hurry. Two people working together bring good fortune.

WAITING FOR SOMEONE: They will come.

LOOKING FOR SOMETHING LOST: The object is in the Southwest and will be difficult to find.

HUNTING FOR THIEVES: If they cannot be caught within three days, then it will take three years to know who the thieves are.

LAWSUIT: Though there may be some frightening experiences, there will be no real harm. In the Northwest, there may be someone who wishes to harm you.

CLIMATE: It will be fine.

TRAVEL: Arguments may arise. Check the route because there may be some hidden danger or thieves.

DISEASE: Restlessness.

PERSONAL WISH: It can be achieved with difficulty.

COMMENTARY

The natural principle expressed by one who is whole is the enduring spirit of life.

In the midst of all changes,
    remain undisturbed.
Whether the days are good or bad,
    whether dealing with virtuous or unvirtuous ones,
    do not leave the wholeness of your spirit.

What is the enduring spirit of life?
It is the same as the spirit of the universe,
    which is governed by constancy,
    regularity and spontaneity.
With its eternal virtuous nature,
    it nourishes and cares for all things.

Virtue is the inherent nature of life.
That which is inherent in the nature of life
    is inherent in your own nature.
In order to restore the enduring spirit,
    we have to practice its subtleties.
From nature,
    people are endowed with discernment.
They can actively change the rigidity of their mind,
    dissolving destructive tendencies
    and false images by means of
    practicing constant virtue.
Thus, they arrive at the delicateness
    of their spirit,
    which is creative, useful
    and beneficial to all.

33   遯 Tun

RETREAT

GUIDANCE: "Retreat. Small things will be profitable and correct."

In this hexagram, Heaven is above the Mountain. The positive yang energy is retreating, while the negative yin energy is advancing. The cyclic alternation of yin and yang is a natural process. For one of positive virtue, retreat at this time brings safety. Forward movement is untimely.

Regarding practical matters, this hexagram usually indicates a decrease in power, wealth and material possessions. While this situation may be difficult in the beginning, good fortune will follow eventually.

A person who is presently experiencing difficulty is not likely to resolve the matter immediately. However, if one truly understands the situation, there is protection in retreat. Being attached to position or profits will cause misfortune. This is a time to withdraw and move away from the danger. Doing so does not indicate weakness, nor is there blame for acting appropriately. A spiritually evolved person responds correctly to the situation and knows when to retreat.

The lines of this hexagram describe many different forms of retreat. For example, the first line is like an ostrich which hides its head while leaving its body exposed. The second line is flexible in tackling the difficulty. The third line withdraws its energy and is content with what it already has.   The fourth line seeks physical escape. The fifth line humbles itself in a position of leadership. The sixth line escapes by transcending the danger entirely.

The *I Ching* offers guidance according to the underlying principles of a situation. It is important to stress that an appropriate response does not follow a fixed, single source of action. A correct approach is one which properly corresponds to the universal natural law of changes. Thus, a period of increasingly erosive yin energy is not the right time for a righteous one to press forward. The time to undertake something is when yang energy is increasing.

Chyan, Heaven ☰ , usually represents strong, ascending energy, but here it means "to decisively rise up." Ken, or Mountain ☶, is usually associated with calmness and stability; however, here it means independence and detachment. The lines of the lower trigram do not feel happy with the good fortune of the top line because they are still attached to profit and success. The top line represents one of spiritual achievement who is free from worldly attachments. A person of self-development uses nature as his teacher. Thus, the highest wisdom is perceived as the simple, natural expression of the universe!

LINE 1: *"One must not wait until the last minute, the 'tail' of time. When the danger has already presented itself, it is too late to either diminish the danger or to escape. Going forward brings misfortune."*

Only by dealing with increasing danger at the earliest possible stage can trouble be averted. This line implies that the possibility of escaping the danger decreases as time passes. Here, danger is already present, and the problem cannot be avoided. Therefore, do not challenge the difficulty.

LINE 2: *"By being firm within, you can indirectly fight contention and entanglement."*

In this situation, one should be flexible, unassertive and not express sharpness. There is no way to escape difficulty; however, remaining outwardly soft yet inwardly firm, one will not be overcome by bad circumstances.

LINE 3: *"Stay away from evil forces. Going forward is dangerous at this time. However, turning back to private life to enjoy personal relationships brings good times."*

The line is in contact with the marching negative force. Emotional attachment to external fame and position will result in being hurt. Becoming involved in extensive public dealings at this time is unwise. There will be benefit in living within the limits of one's own privacy. Staying with your closest ties and showing no interest in public affairs is the way to evade the attention of those with evil intent.

LINE 4: *"Retreating in order to preserve one's purity is right for a developed being but is difficult for the undeveloped."*

What appears sweet is actually poisonous. While the attraction to the sweet is strong, retreating far away brings good fortune. The poisonous sweetness and strong temptation comes from the first line. However, a successful retreat is possible only for the developed being. His firm, virtuous character can help him to resist the temptation, while the undeveloped one cannot; he will be swallowed by the temptation.

LINE 5: *"Correct retreat. Good fortune."*

The purpose of this position is to provide safety and protection. In order to retain one's virtue, one must be inwardly firm but outwardly flexible. Here, retreat means keeping a low profile while being in a high position.

LINE 6: *"Comfortable escape. There is enough time and space in which to escape safely."*

This line represents one who is able to retreat with great freedom, thus he can be far from the danger. By acting appropriately, one can maintain distance from the difficulty and be at ease dealing with the situation. A developed being realizes that the highest level of retreat is self-cultivation. Spiritual achievement can enable one to transcend all turmoil. One who has achieved a high level of self-cultivation is above all worldly troubles and will live justly, righteously and harmoniously.

SPECIFIC GUIDANCE

PERSONAL FORTUNE: Great difficulties prevail.

MARRIAGE: The relationship cannot be successful and will bring misfortune.

HOUSING/FAMILY: There are problems with the doorway. It does not move in accordance with one's energy. Misfortune and disease will occur. One should move.

CHILDBIRTH: The delivery will be difficult.

LOOKING FOR WORK: There are good possibilities.

SOCIAL/GOVERNMENTAL POSITION: Though it is difficult to achieve, once achieved, it should be a very important position.

TRADE/BUSINESS: The time is not profitable.

SEARCHING FOR SOMEONE: They are difficult to find.

WAITING FOR SOMEONE: They will not come.

LOOKING FOR SOMETHING LOST: Finding the object will be difficult.

HUNTING FOR THIEVES: They are hiding far away in the mountains and to the Northeast.

LAWSUIT: It is justified.

CLIMATE: It will be rainy.

TRAVEL: Misfortune; there is trouble.
DISEASE: Emotional or imaginary illness; it is good to move to another house.
PERSONAL WISH: It will be difficult to achieve.

COMMENTARY

To achieve spiritual integrity in Tao,
  the emphasis belongs not on worldly affairs,
  but on keeping the mind still.
This you know.
As worldly interest lessens,
  spiritual interest increases.
As your mind becomes empty,
  the Tao fills your being.
With heart and mind pure,
  negativity and evil fail to lure.
Only by observing and correcting yourself
  can you eliminate the pain and torture
  you allow to occur.
Meaningless, deceptive,
  and vastly exaggerated
  are all worldly pleasure and pain:
  illusions we ourselves form.
What confusion and bewilderment they cause!
How they keep us from being free!
See through these obstacles
  and all hindrances in your path will disappear.
That these things are not a hindrance,
  enlightened people know.
Progress first by one step and then another:
  methodically, carefully,
  break through your confusion.

Silence is the ideal.
Merely talking about self-cultivation
  lacks any real benefit.
Allow Tao to penetrate
  and it will expand,
  filling your body and being.
Your way of life will be
  naturally smooth and straight.

Wholehearted you will be,
   with strong, protective power,
   forsaking the bitterness of life,
   content within yourself.
Because all lives are just like yours,
   all things are one body within you.
In this secret it is very clear,
   and with this comes the confirmation
   that you have the seed of a whole being.

34 大壯 ta chuang

GReat stRength

GUIDANCE: *"When great strength is correctly applied, it is a good thing."*

In this hexagram, Thunder is above Heaven. Both trigrams are images of strength. Ta Chuang is connected with the second month of the Chinese yearly energy cycle and corresponds to March/April of the Western calendar.

In contrast with the peaceful balance of yin and yang energy expressed in Tai ☷☰ , and Chi Chi ☵☲ , Ta Chuang expresses excessive strength. The image used in several lines of this hexagram is the goat, which symbolizes stubbornness and over-abundant strength. The gradual increase of yang energy in the Spring also indicates a preponderance of strength.

The force of the four yang lines easily overcomes the two weak yin lines. However, one with a gentle heart does not use strength to conquer. Though his force may be strong enough to dominate weak or inferior people, he still follows the principles of righteousness.

The use of force in a beneficial manner is the theme of Ta Chuang. Pressing forward aggressively creates problems, while allowing nature to take its course brings calmness. Hasty or impulsive movement can be damaging. We must remember to proceed slowly in times when we need to reform ourselves or influence others.

One who is too powerful or has a strong personality is not usually receptive to advice. Such a person generally prefers to go his own way and show off. Too much strength is like excess water flowing over a rim, but too much power usually creates opposition when it encounters a force with which it is incompatible. Such movement is also like an impetuous goat ramming its head against a fence.

When wishing to obtain additional information, one should be still and not exalt one's knowledge. Benefit is obtained through quiet humility. Power may also be acquired in this manner. Applying the principle of naturalness is more effective than forcing the situation.

Non-action is the term generally used to interpret the spiritual principle of naturalness. However, non-action does not mean that one does nothing, rather that one does not scatter one's energy. Allowing nature to take its course without interference is the real meaning of nonaction.

Energy should be gathered to the center so that one can become a positive transmitter or reservoir of energy and accomplish all things smoothly.

Each line guides us in the use of force. The first line represents energy that is gathered and cultivated. This accumulation can be used to observe and respond appropriately to the various situations that confront us. The second line recommends the use of self-restraint. In the third line, the choice is given between expressing virtue through non-action or ignorance through strenuous response. The fourth line indicates that this is the right time to apply strength. The fifth line represents a position of weakness and teaches how to deal with such situations. The top line advises using difficulty as a means of becoming strong.

LINE 1: *"Too much strength in the toes. The beginning stage makes moving ahead difficult. Such strength will surely lead to misfortune."*

In the initial stages of a situation or relationship, one should not invest all one's energy, power or money. Excessive interest shown in the beginning usually fades rather quickly.

Now is the time to observe and study circumstances and gather one's strength.

LINE 2: *"Caution in using strength brings good fortune."*

This line is strong but in a weak position; however, it has a good response from the fifth line. It is strong, yet it exhibits self-restraint. By not exerting its strength, it has good fortune.

> **LINE 3:** *"Those of self-development do not display their strength. Inferior people willingly show their strength and thus create a dangerous environment. Such a display of strength is like a goat attacking a fence. Because of its stubborn persistence, its horns become weakened."*

The third line is in a position to reflect upon the examples of the previous two lines. The first represents an ignorant person who does nothing to investigate the situation in the beginning. The second line represents a wise person who cultivates calmness before tackling the problem. Therefore, if the third line is virtuous, it will follow the example of the second line by keeping to the principle of calmness and strengthening itself. If it is ignorant and restless, it will follow the example of the first line and act without proper observation or planning. In such a case, it is like a goat that weakens its own horns. The third line is on the boundary between ignorance and wisdom. Thus, one has the choice of either acting like a goat or a wise human being.

> **LINE 4:** *"Continue marching in the right direction. All obstructions will disperse. Use strength correctly, in the proper place and at the right time."*

One should now gather and use all one's strength. This opportunity must be seized and not wasted. This yang line is the leader of the other three yang lines. It is the one which can remove the obstacles created by the two weak lines above. Toward this end, two guiding principles should be adopted. Independent actions should not be taken by any of the four strong lines, and there must be cooperation among them. The strength of great might must be an expression of righteousness, not aggression.

> **LINE 5:** *"One subdues oneself in order to end all confrontations. No remorse."*

One who is faced with a possible attack is advised not to fight. By avoiding force and using harmonious means to change the situation, one can be saved. Do not be discouraged, proud or discontent. The difficulty can be dissolved.

> **LINE 6:** *"The stubborn goat attacks the fence, but can neither achieve its goal nor retreat. No benefit. If one learns through one's difficulties, trouble will not last and there will be good fortune."*

The top line indicates that the goat has now learned its lesson. He can go no further; however, in the end he has good fortune because he has learned a valuable lesson. Through introspection and change, one's bad disposition or situation disappears and good fortune results. Self-developed people are educated and strengthened by obstacles and difficulties. One's development depends on breaking through these obstacles in order to benefit one's growth.

SPECIFIC GUIDANCE

PERSONAL FORTUNE: You will be prosperous.

MARRIAGE: Misfortune.

HOUSING/FAMILY: The foundation of the house is not good and may be dangerous.

CHILDBIRTH: The baby will be a boy. The mother will have difficulty because the yang energy is too strong.

LOOKING FOR WORK: There are difficulties at first. However, if the first or fifth line changes, ask for the job.

SOCIAL/GOVERNMENTAL POSITION: At the beginning, difficulty will be experienced. Later, the position becomes easier.

TRADE/BUSINESS: Success is difficult.

SEARCHING FOR SOMEONE: They can be found unless there is any special condition.

WAITING FOR SOMEONE: They will not return.

LOOKING FOR SOMETHING LOST: It is difficult to find.

THIEVES: Be careful. You may be robbed.

LAWSUIT: There will be something frightening.

CLIMATE: It will be rainy.

TRAVEL: Now is not a good time to travel.

DISEASE: The sickness is connected with the feet and is not dangerous.
PERSONAL WISH: It cannot be as you wish.

COMMENTARY
Premature Enlightenment

The following is an anecdote of an early spiritual experience I had before I obtained instruction on the true mind from my father. It helps illustrate the hexagram of "being overly strong."

In my home town there were several good libraries, as well as a number of good book stores. One day, having exhausted all the private libraries in our town, I ventured to the city in order to satiate my young desire for more knowledge, especially in matters of history and of spirit. It was a walk of fifteen li (approximately five miles) one way, so I carried my lunch with me in a package of lotus leaves.

Within this neighboring city, there was a Buddhist library in which I often found myself. It was set in a Buddhist temple and was especially nice and quiet for reading, except on days when there was a ceremony. During this period of my youth, I was a fervent reader of Buddhism and was permitted to read from any book on the tall, wooden bookshelves in this temple. Because my reading speed was fast, I needed only to stand in front of those tall book shelves to finish reading several books. To my annoyance, after a few days a monk began appearing who dusted the room in such a manner that I always had to move to make way for him. After this had occurred many times, I discovered that the monk was doing this intentionally. I finally said to him, "Please do not create dust while I am reading. It disturbs my eyes."

"Pardon me, but is it the 'dust' on the shelves which disturbs your eyes, or is it my work?" the monk queried.

This question made me aware of his implicit challenge, and I answered, "I came here to discover what the 'dust' is which covers the eyes of all good Chinese people and, to my surprise, I find one here who buries himself in dust as his profession."

The monk responded, "Well, well, I mistook a tiger for a dog. Come into my room. Let us share a cup of tea."

I accepted the invitation and went with him to his room. After putting the tea set on the table, he said, "If you answer this question correctly, I will serve you tea." I agreed, and he asked, "What is Buddha Dharma?"

"Have a cup of tea!" I replied. He poured the tea into my cup. I started to pick up the cup, ready to drink, when suddenly he seized my hand and said, "Wait a moment, you have not asked me yet."

"All right, what is Buddha Dharma?" I asked.

"Have a cup of tea, sir," was his reply.

We both laughed. After a sip of tea, he asked again, "What is the spectrum of achievement of Buddha?" I replied:

> *"Like wayfarer worn,*
> *up homeward hill paths,*
> *straining for scenes that*
> *anxious eyes may rest.*
> *Pavilion lone,*
> *its loved one gone.*
> *Vain kept the swallows their nest."*

Then it was my turn to ask him, and he said, "Here, within me, I leave no room for the old Buddha. Therefore, there is absolutely no Buddha shadow within me. What I have is my own spectrum of achievement, which may be worthy for entertaining my young guest. I make this offering; listen!"

He paused and then continued:

> *"Moon gleamed like frost.*
> *Breeze free like fluid,*
> *pure world without bound.*
> *Up crooked reaches fish leaped,*
> *on lotus leaves dew distilled,*
> *quietude without sound.*
> *Lo, a third time*
> *of time-telling drum in the late night.*
> *Loud dropped a leaf -*
> *broke me from dreams profound.*
> *Night stretched dim.*
> *The return missed,*
> *at dawn I paced the garden round."*

I could appreciate his answer and he also appreciated mine, thus through this meeting we became good friends.

At this time I was around seventeen. During that summer, I started to "preach" to my friends and, as my convictions were very strong, I felt there was no one more superior than I. I would use the corridor of our house at the side of the canal as the gathering place where people could enjoy the breeze while they listened to my talk. Usually when I spoke I would be giving my doctrine of self-authority to the neighborhood kids. This was what I usually said:

"Believe nobody. There is no God, there is no Buddha, there is no authority but yourself as the real authority of your life. In other words, I am the true God. I am the true Buddha. I am the true Way. I am the authority of my life. Therefore, there is no need to worship any sort of divinity. Do not go to the temple; do not go to the church; do not make pilgrimages to any place. Your holy land is within yourself. Most important, never recognize any authority. Deny all sages, and deny what our ancestors said. Your teacher, your parents, your grandparents and all other people are not the authorities of your life; it is no one but you."

I earned many new friends by using my young usurping "religious" ideas. Some families were troubled by my influence. My brother said I was mad. Some of the parents wished that my father would stop me. My father told them, "All great world teachings are premature or half-mature. False teachers find many followers; true teachers have few. False teachings make people strong and rigid; true teachings make people gentle and pliant. All teachings are for the purpose of growth. Should we obstruct the growth of our children?"

One day at noon, during our main meal, my mother sent my brother several times to get me. Instead of returning with him, I kept talking and talking, becoming wilder and wilder. When I finished, I walked into the dining room. To my amazement, there was no food on the table. I walked into the kitchen; there was no food there. I walked to the other part of the house; no one was around, except for my father. Being busy as usual with his patients, we had no chance to exchange any words. I went upstairs to my own room, since I wished to rest. My hunger, however, kept me restless and there was a constant noise in my belly. I rushed down to look again for my mother and the rest of the family. This time my father told me they were all out visiting friends and he was not sure when they would return. He said my mother had suggested it might be a good idea for me to fast for the rest of the day, so I returned to my room. From upstairs, I could look out to the front and see the canal, or from the back I could view the luxurious green fields reaching to the mountains. Here I could study, meditate, practice Kung Fu and do other spiritual activities. This was a great gift of my youth, where I could quietly lay the foundation for my future spiritual development without disturbance.

But this particular occasion was not easy for me. Because I held my doctrine, "Everybody is the authority of his own life," I thought surely my mother or sisters should not have to cook for me all the time. Furthermore, since I am the authority of my own life, why should I bother to eat? During the first part of this long summer afternoon, I was very determined to live by my convictions. Then as evening came, I noticed the setting sun was not as delightful as usual. The evening breeze which comes with the twilight of the stars was not as cool and pleasant as usual either. This night also seemed much longer than usual. However, being the authority of my own life, I thought I could at least make it useful for sleeping. Let me tell you, when your stomach feels full it is easy to sleep, but when your stomach is empty it is not so easy to reach calmness. Nevertheless, I went to sleep but suddenly awakened after midnight.

In the early hours of the morning, I began to examine my great spiritual system obtained from my own enlightenment. Reflecting on the condition of the empty stomach, the fresh brain, the music of the crickets and frogs below and the subtle light in the sky, it was easy for me to rediscover that no life could forget its physiological base and that no individual could claim authority over life. No food could starve a person. No air could suffocate a person. And on and on, until my self-authority became more and more thinly supported and, finally, I fell into a sound sleep.

When the morning sun awakened me with its golden smile, it was already thirty rules high (forty to fifty degrees). I washed myself and prepared for the great spiritual meeting in the corridor. At this meeting, my lecture changed.

"Ask no one to do for you. There is no God who does for us. Neither is there a Buddha who does for us. No one can play the self-authority. Every individual person must be self-responsible. We must deeply recognize the truth of self-authority; I must admit that. Worshipping, going to temple or making a pilgrimage goes against the truth of self-responsibility. The authority of life is truly self-responsibility. Deny the thought that there will be someone who can save us or who can do for use. If that were so, why would our ancestors need to leave their precious methods of self-cultivation for us? They just led us to what they had discovered. All sages and developed ones are self-responsible for their own development and extend their self-development to other people. Self-awareness is a deep sense of responsibility. If self-awareness causes you to become selfish or assuming, then your self-awareness is incomplete. Complete awareness makes you become fully aware of self-responsibility. Therefore, deny all wishful thinking, but be self-responsible."

At this time, I discovered my mother in the corridor. She smiled, awaiting the conclusion of my lecture. I finished, "Each life is self-responsible on all high levels, especially for individual spiritual development. We must continue self-improvement and pursue the ancient secret way of high achievement that has been left for us. Through self-cultivation, one can reach the true authority of the non-authority, the Tao. Otherwise, all speeches are just empty words. Therefore, my endeavors must be in this direction. It may be after years of cultivating that I can serve people who are self-responsible."

My mother then took me in to the dinner she had made and quietly watched me eat a hearty meal.

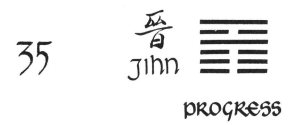

35 Jihn

PROGRESS

GUIDANCE: *"Go ahead to reach for prosperity, victory and honor."*

Fire is above Earth, thus presenting the image of the sun illuminating the earth. It is a time when all things flourish. A virtuous individual has an opportunity to return from darkness to light where his brightness, beauty and wisdom can be seen and appreciated by all. Through his own efforts, his virtue is brightened and his esteem recognized. Surely this is a prosperous time!

The judgment of Jihn is: "The powerful prince is honored with horses in large numbers. In a single day, he is granted an audience three times." This means one is glorified from the light-giving power above. A wise leader is one who is conscientious and in control.

Although the trigram Li, ☲ , appears in sixteen other hexagrams, only the Great Provider, ䷍ , and Progress, ䷢ , suggest that this is a time for self-developed virtuous people to manifest what they have cultivated. This is a time for action, a time for participating in activities of a high nature and for extending services outwardly.

The most important progress to be made is the development of virtue, which is achieved by continuous introspection, self-improvement and the gathering of energy. If one is impeded by external factors and cannot improve the situation, only the development of virtue promotes progress. As a result, everything changes.

The lowest trigram, K'un ☷ , is composed of all yin lines, making it hollow and receptive. Most of the Earth's energy comes from the sun, moon, other planets and stars. Because of its receptivity, Earth flourishes and teems with life. Be receptive like the Earth. Instead of pushing forward blindly and creating failures and tragedies, wait until there is an appropriate response from the outside. Progress is not achieved through impulsiveness. Without a clear mind, ambition is dangerous. However, progress can be made safely by responding to high spiritual influences.

There can only be prosperity when external circumstances harmonize with one's energy. If either the correct circumstance or the energy is absent, nothing can be attained. Misfortune results from trying to force the situation. Such forcefulness is like a ram butting its head against a wall in vain. When one maintains one's true nature, things happen naturally and progress is made.

Many people pursue careers and lifestyles that are contrary to their true nature. Although their ambitions may be fulfilled, they often harm themselves psychologically and spiritually.

Progress is an expression of energy movement. There is progress in regression and regression in progress, each contains the other. The most meaningful progress one can make is to become free from the physical laws of life. Such progress is only accomplished through self-achievement. When one serves one's spiritual essence, progress and regression are seen as the same phenomena!

During times of difficulty, one often experiences restriction or regression. However, an obstacle can be beneficial even though it halts one's movement, because it creates an opportunity to gather energy. Progress is made when difficulties are used positively. All achieved ones have had to break through difficulties.

> **LINE 1:** *"Move forward with strong intentions; however, maintain the right path. If the correct response cannot be made, there is still an opportunity for achievement. Do not be bothered if progress cannot be seen at the beginning."*

Progress at the beginning may not be acknowledged by others. However, real benefit comes from continuing in what is right. Even in an unfavorable position, one can remain flexible by holding to righteousness. The first line is a weak one in a strong position, indicating that progress is made by remaining still and allowing the energy to grow.

Sometimes progress achieved through strenuous efforts can be harmful. Let things happen naturally. Do not expect what is beyond your limitations. Though you cannot move forward at this time, you can maintain you true nature. No great progress can be expected now.

> **LINE 2:** *"Progress that meets with difficulty brings worry. Keep to the right path. By remaining upright, one will be blessed by the Divine Mother."*

The third line is an obstacle to the second. Though progress is made, it is done with caution and worry. When one remains calm and upright, good fortune comes. The second line receives help from the fifth line, although they do not directly correspond with one another. The upper trigram is sunshine; when it shines, the Earth is abundantly benefited. The positive influence of a female divinity or authority is symbolized by the yin line in the fifth place.

> **LINE 3:** *"All give their agreement; thus go ahead."*

This line represents another step forward. One's actions are correct. The lower trigram receives its essence from the Earth. Therefore, this connection is one of true obedience and harmony. The third line cooperates with the neighboring fourth. The third line receives the sunshine from above, which means that one is in the spotlight and success will surely come!

LINE 4: *"Being greedy with progress is dangerous. Surely, a big rat cannot hold a tiger's position."*

This yang line in the fourth position is surrounded by yin lines and cannot go anywhere safely. Its movements are like those of a rat - furtive, hesitant and cowardly as it tries to move out of its hole. At this time, nothing can be properly achieved. The right thing to do now is retreat.

LINE 5: *"In making progress, one should not worry about gain or loss. Go forward. A happy celebration awaits you."*

This is the principle line of the hexagram. By acting gently, there will be no problems. As the *Tao Teh Ching* teaches, accept favor and disfavor as the same.

LINE 6: *"If one persistently marches forward, one will encounter danger and confinement, like pushing oneself into the sharp tip of a horn. If one is disciplined and regulates one's actions, there will be good fortune. This is not the time to move ahead."*

Do not go further. Continuing in making progress becomes excessive. When expanding energy or progress reaches its fullest, it must contract, renew itself and start again. You cannot always continue to go forward. Doing so only makes the situation more and more confining.

SPECIFIC GUIDANCE

PERSONAL FORTUNE: Good fortune will come very soon.
MARRIAGE: It will be successful.
HOUSING/FAMILY: The front door of your house is not in the right position. Change it.

CHILDBIRTH: The baby will be a boy. Good fortune.
SOCIAL/GOVERNMENTAL POSITION: One must depend on friends. If the fourth line is received, no success.
TRADE/BUSINESS: Doing business with people from the Southeast is profitable.
SEARCHING FOR SOMEONE: Look in the mountains to the Southwest.
WAITING FOR SOMEONE: They will come.
LOOKING FOR SOMETHING LOST: The object is difficult to find but might be in the North.
HUNTING FOR THIEVES: Go to the Southeast. They may be found in a graveyard.
LAWSUIT: A long time is needed to resolve the situation.
CLIMATE: It will be fine unless the second line moves, in which case there will be rain.
TRAVEL: It is suitable for two people. The Southeast is a good place to go.
PERSONAL WISH: Your wish can be accomplished.

COMMENTARY
The Development of Life

Without proof of spiritual reality through direct contact with the existence of the vast spiritual realm, a true audience from high divine beings, and the experiencing of divine immortality before exuviating the fleshly life, one's striving toward spiritual development is only partially fulfilled.

The gift of expressible, sudden enlightenment does not bring about this fulfillment. Nor will intensive effort in the realm of personal growth techniques or religious practices necessarily lead one closer to the true immortal, divine world. You may, in fact, some day find that you have merely been enacting the ideas or principles of another rather than traveling the integral path to true fulfillment.

The blossoming mind will wither if it does not reunite with its true nature. You may feel that you have arrived at the root of universal life, but without the confirmation of the real experiences mentioned above, your spiritual development is similar to riding an elevator in a tall building. Though the elevator works, the doors open to nowhere.

True achievement comes from obtaining the true method. Practical spiritual cultivation, therefore, uses the expressible development that one has attained to serve the public and thereby integrate individual attainment as part of the whole. The main goal of methodical self-cultivation is the attainment of immortal life. Otherwise, what is the reason behind this madness to cultivate? Obviously, self-indulgence is a better way!

Do you believe there are immortals in the universe? By believing, how does one know that he is not being self-deceived? Surely, there must be a way. Yes, there are techniques that are taught in the natural spiritual tradition. One way is the Sacred Way of Summoning and Connecting with Divine Beings. This method of learning does not belong to the categories of hypnosis, witchcraft, modern parapsychology, psychic powers or religious theology. After learning this method and practicing the cultivation, a person can directly and truthfully connect with, and thus summon, pure spirits.

After sure-footed proof, one can know that the vast spiritual realm, in general, is divided into the categories of yin and yang. The yin category includes "general beings" of an ordinary life who may or may not have followed a particular religion. The yang category includes "true beings" of the universal eternal life who have attained total freedom and happiness. To receive such a universal citizenship, one must know all the methods of the tradition of the integral immortal beings. The traditional tuition is 1,000 ounces of pure gold. If you think that this price is too high, then the traditional measure of two hundred "catties" of pure gold will do. (One "catty" is about as heavy as an adult cat and is a traditional Chinese pound with 16 ounces.) But, the teaching can also be the reward to a virtuous individual.

Another method is the Secret Carriage to the Divine Realm. This cultivation is one of the highest spiritual secrets. Understanding this practice can enable one to enter the eternal divine realm, both before and after the exuviation of the fleshly body. This is death as it is known in the ordinary shadow world. After receiving and practicing this method, one establishes sure communication with the different levels of divine immortal and starry beings. Thus, one may become a member of the divine immortal world even during one's physical life. One who discovers and obtains this method shall be successfully saved from a "wasteful" life.

Having no subtle beings is not the world's problem; instead, the problem is too few people with accurately developed spiritual sensitivity. Having people who can know subtle things is not the world's problem; instead, the problem is having people who lack the knowledge that there are vast, different spiritual realms. Without the correct methods and practices, one is very likely to become lost in the profound spiritual world where only the chi of a person's cultivation is recognized. Nothing else should be valued, except the cultivation of chi. Different chi produces differences in people. The end that one will reach within their lifetime can be anticipated by the path one follows.

There are many valuable, secret methods of spiritual cultivation. All the effective methods have been introduced by Pao Po Tzu, (Master Kou Hong), an ancient developed one with a great heart, in a book entitled *The Pao Po Tzu*. Unfortunately, it has not yet been correctly translated into English. (The book was written during the Jing Dynasty, 265-419 A.D.) Pao Po Tzu's book contains a good introduction to over two thousand ancient, secret methods.

The truth of all sacred, secret methods of the spiritual tradition can be verified by one who correctly understands them. In order to arrive at a correct understanding, however, one must have the correct development to receive these special instructions. Not surprisingly, most of these instructions are strongly guarded and prohibited in order to prevent people from immaturely or prematurely practicing them. Unfortunately, as a result, the highest treasures of wisdom and technique are limited in their exposure to the world. Because ordinary opportunities to learn these methods do not exist, a long, long time is required to educate a good student toward true development and attainment. Only when a person is truly ready to receive the high spiritual methods will they be passed on. Only then will the student be benefited rather than endangered. This prohibition also extends to the master, who would otherwise suffer if instructions were given prematurely.

A safe and broad way to overcome the difficulty of learning these methods is available in my work entitled *The Heavenly Way*. This book contains three treatises. The first, "Straighten Your Way," was Pao Po Tzu's recommendation from his Master and the Masters before his Master. The second article is the traditional elucidation of Chapter 71 of the *Tao Teh Ching*. It says:

"To know what one knows
   is to be highly enlightened.
To not know what one should know is sick.
Only the one sick of suffering
   can be saved from the sickness.
The highly enlightened one is never sick;
   he is aware of sickness and, therefore, avoids it."

The third article, an exemplification from a deity with human experience, contains the invaluable essence of a safe practice. The standard and evaluation for what one must accomplish in preparation for becoming a virtuous person is accurately expressed in these three treatises. Actually, they serve as the Direct Way. And, at that, even one with the extraordinary luck of obtaining these methods, as revealed in the above treatises, still needs virtuous achievement as a foundation of personal energy.

36   明夷 MING YI

The TIME OF DARKNESS

GUIDANCE: *"At the time of darkening, one should correctly respond to one's difficulties."*

In the previous hexagram, the Sun was above the Earth, but in Ming Yi the Sun is below the Earth. This is a time when darkness rules the world. Applied to human circumstances, this is the time when one's light is obstructed and there is danger in one's development or life. The individual should protect his light by using his brightness, talents, capabilities, wisdom and intelligence to accommodate the darkness.

The image of this hexagram is that of light held below the Earth. If Fire is covered by Earth, it cannot illuminate. Without the presence of clarity and wisdom, one must dwell in darkness. However, even in times of darkness, light is forthcoming. Thus, one should not be sad, but instead should cultivate the spirit, maintain health and wait for good times to return.

Fire beneath the Earth also implies the energy of a volcano about to erupt, thus it may be a good time to go away.

The upper trigram is like a rigid, restricting mother who has a talented child. She is egotistical and threatened by the child's precociousness. Instead of ruining the harmony of the family, however, the child should hide his light and allow the mother to have her way.

The upper trigram can also represent an ignorant leader who has authority over a bright employee. In such a situation, the employee should protect his talents by keeping quiet. Any movement will only create additional pressures and difficulties.

During the Time of Darkness, one's shining wisdom may become a source of trouble. Most influential people who live in darkness are not able to recognize another's inner brightness. Out of ignorance and contentiousness, they often hurt or create problems for one who is wise.

The *I Ching* teaches that beauty can be the cause of troubles, but that troubles and difficulties can be an opportunity for growth and success. General education encourages people to flaunt their beauty and their talents or achievements. In doing so, the brightness of the mind is darkened.

Each line in this hexagram teaches that, in times of darkness, virtuous people are not accepted by society. At such times, wisdom and virtue should be concealed in plainness. The wise one uses this darkness as a protection so that others cannot see him.

LINE 1: *"On a journey, the wise one does not stay where people may create trouble for him. Even though there may be food or shelter ahead, he moves on."*

Those who are virtuous cannot avoid contact with society altogether, so they should be very selective in accepting favors. While some are acceptable, many others are not and can create problems and entanglements.

This yang line is in the correct position and corresponds to the fourth line. However, one should contemplate the entire situation instead of remaining in danger. Darkness will come very soon. But, as indicated by the first line, an opportunity still exists for one to escape. One who has foreknowledge of the approaching darkness should protect himself by departing early, otherwise one will be swallowed by it.

> **LINE 2:** *"As the result of darkness, one moves with difficulty, as if one's leg were hurt. However, a fast horse can carry one to safety while it is still twilight, before darkness completely surrounds one. Otherwise, time will run out."*

Now is the time to escape rather than staying to fight the darkness face to face. The second line is the center of the lower trigram, Light, and remains underground. However, the light is already being obscured by the obstacles above. Despite the danger, one must now use all the strength that remains to save the situation.

There are times when one should not succumb to darkness, but artfully and tactfully confront it, especially when dealing with one's own personal darkness. Usually, seeing the darkness in others is easier than recognizing and conquering it in ourselves. It is correct to use strength in overcoming inner darkness. No compromises should be made.

> **LINE 3:** *"The darkness can be overcome and its ring leader captured. Such a move should not be hasty, but instead should be an expression of righteousness."*

"Darkness" can also refer to the darkness within oneself. When one engages in an important task, one must first overcome one's inner darkness. Then one can be benefited by using the external darkness or difficulty as a tool for enlightenment.

The third line is a yang line in the correct position. It receives help from the second line and attacks the top line, which is the leader of darkness. Extreme care must be exercised when conquering darkness. Both the third and sixth lines are somewhat damaged by this situation.

Though there are times in which one may wish to avoid conflict, here it is not possible. Compromise cannot be made with evil. If the cause is righteous, one must not fear the consequence.

> **LINE 4:** *"At the entrance of darkness, one can preserve peace of mind only by departing at the right moment."*

The fourth line is the first line of the darkness. In such a situation, one can either go further into the depths of it or retreat, keeping himself upright and sustaining inner illumination. The lower trigram represents light, the upper trigram represents darkness. The fourth line is the boundary between them and can go in either direction. Since it corresponds to the first line and is only at the threshold of the darkness, it is still close enough to follow the light. Otherwise, it may succumb to hopeless darkness.

As stated in the original Chinese text, "Be out the door and gone." Since the darkness is still incomplete, one can effectively be guided by one's inner light.

LINE 5: *"In the middle of darkness, one can only adapt to the situation, but without giving up one's inner light."*

This line is the central line of the hexagram. Darkness is inescapable. During this time, it can be very damaging. Be very careful now not to lose your clarity. By keeping your inner light and adapting to the situation, the external darkness will be deprived of its influence under the law of cyclic movement.

NOTE: The principle of this line has been applied to various circumstances throughout history. One such instance is illustrated in the section following the Specific Guidance, and relates to this line in particular.

LINE 6: *"In the beginning, there is brightness. In the end, darkness swallows all things."*

This line symbolizes the time after sunset when darkness finally overcomes the light. However, there is still hope for this line. As Lao Tzu, says, "Big winds and storms cannot last forever." When there is darkness, light must soon return. Likewise, one's emotional storms and darkness will also pass.

SPECIFIC GUIDANCE

PERSONAL FORTUNE: You have complex problems. Maintain silence.

MARRIAGE: Though the marriage can endure, there are many arguments. This match is not a good one.

HOUSING/FAMILY: There is a bypass in front of the house which makes the energy confusing. The house is the cause of misfortune and the source of worry. If the parents live apart from the child, there will be less difficulty.

CHILDBIRTH: The baby will be a girl. The mother will shocked or frightened by something during the delivery.

LOOKING FOR WORK: There are obstacles.

SOCIAL/GOVERNMENTAL POSITION: A high position is not indicated here. If the position is indeed a high or important one or if the first line is received, there will be danger.

TRADE/BUSINESS: The time is not a profitable one.

WAITING FOR SOMEONE: They will not come.

LOOKING FOR SOMETHING LOST: The object will be hard to recover.

HUNTING FOR THIEVES: They are close by and it is possible to catch them soon.

LAWSUIT: A jail sentence is involved.

CLIMATE: It will be rainy.

TRAVEL: Do not make the trip. Misfortune.

DISEASE: It is dangerous.

PERSONAL WISH: It is difficult to achieve.

COMMENTARY
Fifth-Line Illustrations

The background of the fifth line of the 36th hexagram is a series of events which took place during the reign of the Emperor Jou (1154-1122 B.C.), the last emperor of the Shang Dynasty (1766 -1121 B.C.). It is also a story of how Korea began its history as a nation.

As a youth, Jou was receptive to the teachings of the wise counselors of his father's court. Eventually, he became overly confident of his own abilities and grew tired of the advice of his teachers and counselors. Thinking he was wise enough to rule alone and make his own decisions, he rejected the teachings of the virtuous way. The following is the legendary story of his excesses and corruption.

During one of the national festivals, Emperor Jou, along with the ministers of his court, went on a pilgrimage to the temple of a heavenly goddess. The statue of the goddess was so beautiful that the Emperor became entranced. He believed that, since he was Emperor, the goddess would come to him and be his woman. This blasphemous, licentious wish actually manifested in the form of a real woman, Tan Chi, who later became Emperor Jou's favorite. After taking Tan Chi into his confidence, he would not accept advice from anyone else. With this, the downfall and destruction of his empire began.

Separated from the correct path of life, Emperor Jou began to follow an extravagant lifestyle. Consideration for his country and everything else was lost in his constant desire to please his mistress. The demands placed on his people were extreme. Ponds were built in his court and filled with wine. His people were ordered to give him their best meat, which was hung on the trees of his garden for Tan Chi and her horde of attendants to enjoy. Beautiful girls were forced to pose nude as a human screen where he sat. He even built a great tower in hopes that the stars could be picked for her pleasure. He had his first wife put to death, and eventually his empire became corrupt because he was so cruel to the ministers who had faithfully served him and his father.

One day Tan Chi feigned illness. Although Emperor Jou ordered the doctors to help her, she did not respond to their treatment. Tan Chi told the Emperor that in order for her to become healthy again she must drink blood from the loyal heart of his key minister, who also happened to be his uncle. Not being able to refuse her, Emperor Jou ordered his loyal minister, Pi Kan, to allow his heart to be cut out as a demonstration of his allegiance to the Emperor. This order was given on an occasion when Pi Kan had advised the Emperor to desert Tan Chi and tend to affairs of state. Pi Kan faithfully accepted the Emperor's order, and Emperor Jou subsequently did the same thing to many other loyal ministers who advised him in a similar manner. The remaining wise ministers, whose lives had been spared, faced a serious moral dilemma. Being deceitful in order to please the Emperor was against their conscience and way of life. However, if they offered honest advice, they would surely be killed.

The old premier, Wen, after returning home from an assigned expedition, felt that his duty was to correctly advise the Emperor.   Wen informed him that he should not devote himself to Tan Chi, but instead should offer his devotion to his country.   Because of Wen's outstanding military achievements, the Emperor hesitated to kill him, and his life was temporarily spared.   When Tan Chi discovered what the Emperor had done, she devised a plan that would create doubt in Emperor Jou's mind about the loyalty of his premier. Her plan was to heat the inside of a hollow brass pillar and ask the premier to prove his loyalty by embracing it.   The Emperor declared that, if Wen were genuinely faithful, he would not die. The premier could not refuse the test.   However, just before dying, he cried out to the young emperor, "I will see that your kingdom is eliminated from the Earth! I choose this day for my death, while the Earth is still clean and not yet totally spoiled by you!"

Emperor Jou had another uncle, Chi Tzu, who was an *I Ching* practitioner.   He was inspired by this hexagram, and his experiences were later utilized by King Wen.   He realized that he could not overcome the power of darkness by revealing his light.   Therefore, he feigned madness by running around naked, dancing in the streets, gambling, losing money he did not own and selling himself to his creditors.   He became like a degraded slave and acted as though he enjoyed it.   In this way, he was able to stay alive.

When Tan Chi asked the Emperor if any of his loyal ministers were still alive, the Emperor replied that there were none except Chi Tzu, who was completely useless. After a time, however, Chi Tzu went to the region of Korea, where he was established as a feudal prince by the new dynasty.   Seeing the national flag of South Korea today, it is clear how much the *I Ching* influenced Chi Tzu and his descendants.

Emperor Jou's psychological problem was an obsession to prove his abilities by going beyond his father's influence.   However, he abused his power and became too strong.   His life was a great example of excess and imbalance, which manifested in an extremely negative manner.   He ultimately lost his empire and took his own life by burning himself to death.

The following is another story illustrating appropriate conduct during the time of darkness.

Originally, the *I Ching* was without words.   An author of some of the written text, King Wen, was a feudal prince during Emperor Jou's reign. The Emperor was intimidated by the reputed abilities of King Wen and was determined to find out if he truly had the power of foreknowledge. King Wen was then summoned and confined to the capital. As a secret test, Emperor Jou had the King's son killed and then served the boy's flesh in a soup. King Wen knew that to refuse the soup would prove he had foreknowledge of his son's death, so he drank it, passed the test to the Emperor's satisfaction and was released.

King Wen became the "seed of fire" for the upcoming revolution that would begin a new dynasty.

The following story is yet another illustration of dealing with the time of darkness. At the end of the Chou Dynasty (1122-256 B.C.), there lived a famous Master, "Son of the Spiritual Valley," who had two students. The elder student was very advanced in his studies, while the younger student, who was quite handsome, was rather negligent in his. The young student left his Master and traveled west to the State of Wei. There he became a general and married King Wei's daughter. The king placed the young man in charge of the entire army in order to attack the neighboring state of Chi.

Some time later, the King heard that the elder student was superior in wisdom and invited him to the court as an advisor. The wise Master, knowing that this situation would be dangerous, warned his elder student. However, the student thought, "I came to learn from you, Master, but now I have an opportunity to use what I have learned. Please allow me to take this honorable position." Although the Master advised his student that this was an inappropriate time for such an assignment, he realized that the student was intent on leaving. Before he departed, the Master said, "I have a secret letter for you. If you encounter extreme difficulty, open it and follow the directions inside. You will then be safe. But only in the most dangerous situation should the envelop be opened!"

The elder student then became King Wei's respected guest and was treated with much favor. It soon became apparent that he had more depth than the younger student, the King's son-in-law. The younger student, realizing how the king felt, knew that if something were not done soon, he would lose his position. Therefore, he told the king that the elder student's hometown was in the State of Chi and that he should not be told of the plan to attack it because he might be a spy. The king listened to this logic, agreed with the younger student, and put the elder student in prison in order to observe him. It was clear to the elder student how dangerous his situation had become and that his teacher's warnings were coming true. Remembering the letter given to him by his teacher, he quickly opened it.   On the page was written only one word, "Mad." He then knew that to survive, he must appear to be insane.

For a while the king's men observed the elder student intensely, but as his madness continued the king eventually lost interest. The young student, realizing that his purpose was accomplished, now felt safe.   However, because of the king's neglect in guarding the older student, he was able to escape. His foot had been cut off under King Wei's order, and he was filthy from having slept in the dirt.   Nevertheless, he was rescued and carried by wagon to Chi where he became a close advisor to their king.   He successfully protected that state and carried it to victory by his brilliant military strategy.   Unavoidably, the great commander of Wei was defeated, losing both his army and his life.   This student's name was Sun Tse, whose book on military strategy became one of the most influential works in history.

COMMENTARY

Cultivate the Tao as your own spiritual integrity,
*   and you need not worry about producing*
*   the proper fruit.*
Life is equal.
A sage has neither more nor less
*   than a mediocre man.*
No different are the rich and poor,
*   the noble and the common.*
Differently only in whether or not
*   there exists a will.*
If you can adhere to the sacred method,
*   cultivating yourself precisely,*
*   keeping clear as to your every motive and idea,*
*   then all good, positive qualities*
*   become firm and all traps can be avoided.*
You then become one with Tao,
*   unchanged even in death*
*   as you realize the eternal firmness of existence.*
This undecayed, everlasting spiritual body

is the highest true soul
which connects to the course of the universe.
Because the great harmony of non-action -
  different from no-action -
has such wondrous effects,
  the spiritual firmness of Tao is thus reached
  by the sincerity of daily life.
Impartiality is the key.
With it you remove all cause for worry
  over excessive conduct.
This is the correct and sacred way of a shien.
Cling to it firmly, strictly and finally.
The sprouting seed of a whole being
  makes steady growth.

37 chia jen

family

GUIDANCE: *"Family.   Profitable for a virtuous woman."*

In this hexagram, Fire is below and Wind is above. Fire generates warmth and light.   Wind is gentle and penetrating. These characteristics represent a family. Warmth binds a family together.   Without warmth, the essence of the family is lost and its energies become scattered.   On the other hand, excessive Fire creates intense friction, which brings conflict and discomfort to a family.

Because Fire is intensified by Wind, Water is necessary to balance it.   This harmonious cooperation of natural forces expresses the basic principle of the integration of opposites.   This principle also applies to the essential structure of human life.   Our two eyes, two hands and two legs express the cooperation of pairs, which is fundamental to the function of the whole.   The family may also be symbolic of the interaction of differing, conflicting natures.

The basic pattern of cooperation relies on the correct organization of diverse energies.   With this understanding, one should not feel troubled about the differences that exist within one's family.

The inner trigrams, Water and Fire, represent the integration of male and female energies, which is the foundation of a family. The way these energies interact determines the harmony of the entire family. Measures can be taken to balance a group in the same way that Water keeps the force of heat balanced. Discipline and mutual respect between a man and woman prevent arguments like a health regimen prevents disease.

Historically, the function of the family was to provide security and protection. However, the focus of modern life has shifted from a family-centered life to a socially-centered life. What was originally part of the family structure is now attempted individually within a larger collective context, which changes the real function of a family. As a consequence, the sense of unity within a family diminishes.

Modern education encourages individualistic tendencies, and these tendencies reshape the patterns of society. Emphasizing individualism or personal rights in a family or group unavoidably obstructs the integration of the whole. However, the physical and emotional needs of people are still the basis for marriage and family. Maintaining life by earning a living and continuing life by giving birth to the next generation fulfill the fundamental pattern of life. Therefore, the family is the first form of society.

Family life is seldom smooth, but its difficulties can provide real substance for refining one's nature. Using difficulty as an excuse for personal failure only obstructs self-development. When properly used, one's emotional difficulties become one's nutrition, one's fundamental education and the impetus for growth, although serious problems and extreme circumstances (as in the failure of a marriage) can damage one's health.

During times of difficulty one should independently strive to eliminate rather than emphasize confusion and negativity. Everyone has personal difficulties and is responsible for silently overcoming these troubles or miseries by oneself. Reinforcing negativity supports it, and eventually it is absorbed into one's nature.

Everything that happens has a positive reason, although it may seem disastrous at the time. By embracing a reflective attitude, one's mind can be cleansed of delusions and all negative influences, thus allowing the opportunity for spiritual growth.

LINE 1: *"Family life offers protection. Harmony and discipline among family members must be adhered to. Then there will be no reason for remorse."*

This strong line represents a necessary family principle that should be recognized by all family members in order to avoid possible scatteredness and difficulty. Such preventive measures become the guardian of the family. The significance of family life is the opportunity it affords to actually incorporate responsibility and security.

LINE 2: *"Without asserting herself, the female supplies food for the family. Correct actions bring good fortune."*

The second line represents the homemaker whose duty is to provide sustenance for the family. This line also represents the unity of the family, while the fifth line represents the image of father and husband.

When one is in such an important position as that of harmonizer of the energies of a family, the *I Ching* advises against using self-assertion. In this position, one is responsible for sustaining others through gentleness and submissiveness. Good fortune is the result.

LINE 3: *"Appropriate discipline should be used. The correct balance brings good results."*

The third line represents all the members of the family. Correct discipline, which is essential to good family life, should be applied to all members. Discipline should neither be too strict nor too lenient. If it is too easy or too harsh, it will bring humiliation.

LINE 4: *"Being dutiful enriches the family. Great good fortune."*

The fourth line represents a wise wife, who is a great assistant to the fifth line, her husband. She brings good fortune to the family by fulfilling her duty as helper.

LINE 5: *"The head of the family can enjoy his family life. Good fortune."*

The fifth line represents the husband, who has a harmonious relationship with the second line, his wife. The family flourishes under the loving guidance of his discipline. This beautiful picture shows that love and security bring true happiness.

LINE 6: *"Faithfulness brings order and union to a family. The fulfillment of duty brings good fortune."*

The sixth line expresses the achievement of family order, harmony and the strength of unity. With a sense of devotion to the whole, each member reflects upon his individual faults and corrects them. Thus, the family attains great fortune.

SPECIFIC GUIDANCE

PERSONAL FORTUNE: Now is the time for prosperity; however, if guided by negativity, you will be negatively influenced. Likewise, if guided by virtue, your virtue will increase. Therefore, be careful in your behavior. A man can profit with the help of his wife.

MARRIAGE: This is a good sign for marriage and match-making.

HOUSING/FAMILY: Make preparations in case of fire.

CHILDBIRTH: The child will be a boy. If the child is born in the Winter, it will be a girl. If the fifth line is received, difficulties will arise.

LOOKING FOR WORK: Now is not a fruitful time. Ultimately there can be success.

SOCIAL/GOVERNMENTAL POSITION: It will be difficult to achieve.

TRADE/BUSINESS: There can be success at this time.

SEARCHING FOR SOMEONE: As soon as they arrive, they depart. However, if the second or fifth lines are received, the people will not depart.

WAITING FOR SOMEONE: They will not come.

LOOKING FOR SOMETHING LOST: The object is in the South and difficult to find.

HUNTING FOR THIEVES: They are hiding in the North-west.

LAWSUIT: The trouble may have been caused by a woman, but there is no great harm.

CLIMATE: It will be rainy.

TRAVEL: Wait a while. Do not hurry.

DISEASE: It is difficult to cure.
PERSONAL WISH: It is achieved slowly.

COMMENTARY
The Virtue in Family Life

Female and male in harmony
* are the strong foundation of a happy marriage.*
When choosing a mate,
* outer beauty is not necessary,*
* but virtuous behavior is.*

If one's heart is good,
* noble children will be born.*
Hand down the right instructions to them
* and be strict, softened by gentleness.*
Do not possess your offspring,
* but guide them to form their character*
* so that they can stand alone*
* when their time comes.*
They will carry forth your virtuous behavior
* as their heritage,*
* and in turn will guide the next generation*
* on the right path.*
Be aware that your example
* carries through many generations to come.*
When instructing your children,
* example is better than precept.*
It is better to keep their life as simple as possible.
Even if you are prosperous,
* keep them always a little hungry and a little cold.*
It is a challenge in this affluent society
* to restrain oneself*
* and live as if there were no abundance.*
Spoiled children become weak adults.
Self-indulgence is the greatest misery of our times.

Limit your activities and those of your children.
Too many activities scatter their developing minds.
Make the home inviting
* with quiet activities and togetherness.*
Television is the biggest threat to a developing mind
* and brings disorder to the family.*
Cut your own desire,

and the desire of your children will lessen.
Teach them to be content with little.

Let them be aware of caring for others,
    as well as for themselves and the environment.
Your children, when very young,
    need to feel secure and loved.
Regularity and steadfastness on your part
    gives them security.
Strictness, softened by gentleness and forgiveness,
    makes them feel loved.
With these two virtues,
    the foundation for the harmonious development
    of their being is built.

Dare to stand back and watch
    their unfolding growth process,
    with reserve and respect for their own natures,
    interfering only at the right time.
Give them time and space to develop
    in accordance with their own divine plan.
In the early years it is easy to observe
    their divine natures,
    but soon the whole picture of their inheritance
    and self-created life patterns accumulated
    through many lifetimes will emerge.
We must stand by to exercise and encourage
    the positive side of their characters
    and encourage them to recognize and change
    their negative tendencies.

Use firmness and discipline,
    always softened by gentleness.
Form a T'ai Chi in everything you do.
Find the balance in interacting with your children.
Bring yin and yang into harmony in your own person.
To have a harmonious family,
    each member must be aware of his or her place.
If roles are reversed between male and female,
    disharmony is the inevitable result.
Great confusion starts in families
    when people use forceful means
    to insure their identities.
The evolution of the human race as a whole
    requires adjustment from both partners
    in a mature and gentle way.

Positively approached,
  we must grow in a flexible yin-yang relationship,
  giving both partners room for their personal growth,
  each fulfilling their role within their natures.

The wife's place is predominantly in the home,
  her nature being to shelter and nurture.
The husband's place is predominantly
  outside of the home,
  his nature being to provide and support.
The oldest child should teach the youngest;
  the youngest should follow the oldest.
In this way, harmony can be established.
Respect for the other person, young or old,
  should be the key word within
  and without your family.
Respect nurtures kindness.
With kindness you can win the hearts of the people.
Maintain economy without being stingy.
When you are careful and practical in monetary affairs,
  you have much to give away.
Never hoard money for selfish purposes.

In the family, cultivate the outer aspects of
  conscientiousness, respect and gentleness.
The practical aspects of the home are
  tolerance, flexibility and patience.
These virtues will make your home
  a shelter for all those who may enter.
People will move about contented with their own beings.
Natural affection will brighten their days.
Cultivate respect,
  follow the laws of nature,
  and abide in the principles of Tao.
Then your life will be useful, calm and fulfilling,
  and life's abundance will display itself within you.
When that happens, it will be found
  within the family,
  within your neighborhood,
  within your community,
  within the state,
  within the country,
  and ultimately within the whole world.
Such is the way.
Such is the law of subtle energy response.

38

暌
KWEI

opposition · disharmony

GUIDANCE: *Opposition. Only small things can be achieved.*

Fire is above Lake. The nature of Fire is to move upward, and the nature of Water is to move downward. When Fire and Water are in this relationship to one another, opposition or separation is expressed. On a human level, Fire, ☲ , represents the middle daughter and Lake, ☱ , represents the youngest daughter. Although they live together, they do not cooperate.

This hexagram indicates a time when people's minds are in opposition, thus difficulty prevails. At this time, one should not attempt to undertake or complete matters of importance. However, with sincere effort, the situation can be improved and, with cooperation, small achievements are possible.

Disharmony in the present situation stems from doubt and suspicion. Such growing suspicion may make others appear evil, dishonest or insincere. Only when disharmony is resolved will harmony and affection be restored.

With subtle changes, the entire situation can be transformed into a positive one. The second and fourth lines of this hexagram are yang lines in yin positions, and the third and fifth lines of the hexagram are yin lines in yang positions. This kind of unnatural arrangement represents an imbalance between the masculine and feminine principles. In this hexagram, the feminine energy is excessively aggressive. When a female uses a masculine approach, disharmony often results. In order for such a situation to improve, a woman should be softer and more placid.

In either a family or personal relationship, contention and confrontation may arise if a woman tries to change or lessen her femininity by taking on the attributes of a man. If a man and woman compete as individuals, they may eventually go their separate ways. Maintaining a relationship in which each partner has distinct interests, inclinations and goals is difficult. Common goals and interests, as well as complementary differences, present an opportunity for integration and harmony.

This hexagram also counsels us to avoid unnecessary confrontations and connections with people of inferior virtue. All the lines suggest self-discipline and cultivation as measures against impending difficulty. Now is the time to practice self-restraint by avoiding excessive behavior and exaggerated emotions. Thus, one will be secure in times of disharmony.

LINE 1: *"Since there is no communication, there is no opposition. Do not pursue a lost horse. It will return by itself. Meeting perverse, troublesome people causes no problem if the connection is only superficial."*

There is no communication between the first and fourth lines, which are both yang lines. Since there is neither contention nor closeness between them, there is no reason for remorse. When two strong forces meet, one should not attempt to impose one's will. Others will come and go of their own accord. Furthermore, one should be calm, simple and righteous in dealing with rough or negative people. Do not plant seeds of hatred.

LINE 2: *"Good communication can be achieved between a superior and a subordinate in reversed positions."*

This situation could be an awkward one. The fifth line should be a yang line but is yin, and the second line should be a yin line but is yang. However, through their cooperation, assistance and exchange of energies, they can be mutually benefited.

LINE 3: *"Action is curbed and movement is restrained when one confronts strength with strength. Adjusting to the situation brings a good ending."*

Difficulty is expressed by the third line, which is a yin line in a yang position. Here, the animal force, which is pulling the wagon, is restrained. Ongoing work suffers from frustration and difficulties. However, achieving harmony in the end is possible, as indicated by the correspondence between the third and top lines. Thus, one should reflect upon inner difficulty, rather than complain about outer circumstances. Through introspection and self-improvement, a person of inferior tendencies can improve himself as well as his environment.

LINE 4: *"Opposition is caused by isolation and separation. If one is sincere and has no bad intentions, harmony can be attained."*

Both the first and fourth lines are yang lines and show strong tendencies toward independence, thus they are isolated from each other. However, since both are frank and straight, if good communication can take place between them, understanding and cooperation can be brought about.

LINE 5: *"Opposition disappears. Close relationships are achieved among all people."*

The fifth line meets the second line with the virtue of harmony, like a gentle caress.

LINE 6: *"Isolation is caused by suspicion. Hostility is expressed toward those who come to make peace. Only when suspicion is dissolved is a good relationship possible."*

The top line expresses isolation. Although it meets the third line, it has no desire for closeness. Initially, one in this position treats all who approach with suspicion and resistance. However, after some time, he recognizes that the one who approaches is a friend. This situation is like an unexpected rainfall relieving hot, dry weather.

SPECIFIC GUIDANCE

PERSONAL FORTUNE: You must wait for success. This is not your day.

MARRIAGE: Marriage may result in argument. For a woman, remarriage may occur.

FAMILY/HOUSING: Disharmony exists between people of the same sex or between different families living together. The walls of the house will be broken. Now is the time to move.

CHILDBIRTH: The baby will be a boy. There will be difficulty in the delivery.

LOOKING FOR WORK: There are some obstacles.

SOCIAL/GOVERNMENTAL POSITION: It is difficult to achieve.

TRADE/BUSINESS: Do not hurry. Ultimately, there will be a large profit.

SEARCHING FOR SOMEONE: They are difficult to find.

WAITING FOR SOMEONE: They will not come.

LOOKING FOR SOMETHING LOST: Although you might try looking in the Northwest, the object will be difficult to find.

HUNTING FOR THIEVES: Wait, they will return. Do not hastily pursue them at this time.

LAWSUIT: Now is the time to make peace.

CLIMATE: It will be rainy.

TRAVEL: Now is a good time for travel.

DISEASE: The disease is severe and the cure will be slow.

PERSONAL WISH: Difficult to accomplish.

COMMENTARY

Ordinary worldly religions and teachings
  attract ordinary minds.
Their tenets, like haphazard vines,
  sprawl every which way.
Illusory and idealistic,
  they attempt to explain reality,
  but fall short,
  unable to penetrate
  their own spiritual blind spot.
They attract weak spirits
  who must cling to something
  stronger than themselves,
  who must encourage consoling illusions
  to cheat themselves.

Follow this crude way of trusting and believing,
  without self-development,
  and what you will experience is but a void.
After you experience the truth,
  you will know why shien cultivation

emphasizes self-realization and transformation.
Therein lies the answer
  to the puzzle of oral and written obstacles.

First, strengthen yourself,
  then you can influence your environment.
All parts of your body and spirit
  will become like hands and eyes.
Develop your mental ability
  until it is round,
  full and smooth as a pearl.
Then reap the reward.
Fearing danger no more,
  you will easily shake free of its bondage.
The subtle heavenly law
  will appear within you and through you
  because you have succeeded
  in the spirit of sharpness.
Truly, even while living in the world,
  you will come to surpass and transcend
  its mundane problems and difficulties.

Divine awareness always appears,
  helping you as you go,
  while leaving your spiritual ego
  in union with all beings.
Heaven, Earth and I are a union of one,
  for we are of the same origin.
Realize this
  and become the strong seed
  of a whole being.

39 JIEN

OBSTRUCTION

GUIDANCE: *"The good direction is where there is no abyss or high mountains, like the Southwest, but not the Northeast. One should go to the great leader who can work with people in breaking through obstructions."*

The purpose of the *I Ching* is to infuse the realm of human activity with the same clarity found in the principles of nature.   One can then apply these principles to personal life and make whatever corrections may be necessary.

This hexagram describes the time of obstruction.   In front is the ocean, which prevents forward movement. Behind is a high mountain, which prevents retreat.

In the post-Heavenly order of natural energy symbology, the Northeast is the Mountain, Ken ☶ , and the North is Water, K'an ☵ .   Respectively, they indicate difficulty and danger. However, in the South is Fire, Li ☲ and in the Southwest is Earth, K'un ☷. Together they represent a vast stretch of sunny region and an image of prosperity and promise.

During times of obstruction, one should be still and practice cultivation.   This opportunity should be used to gather energy, instead of complicating matters with impatience and struggle.   When one has a positive attitude, even the highest mountain seems lower and the deepest water more shallow.   Inner strength can make obstructions less imposing.   A self-developed person cultivates his virtue and is not defeated by obstruction.

If a person discovers a leak in his boat, the appropriate action should be to immediately plug the hole before bailing the water.   This principle also applies to relationships among family members, friends or lovers.   Reacting impulsively to obstruction or frustration is like reacting to the water instead of the leak.   Instead of being saved from loss, the difficulty is only exacerbated.

Emotional attitudes often prevent a person from advancing.   Lack of discipline, holding preferences, negative emotions and bad habits formed early in life are all obstructions to inner development.   Inflexibility often becomes the main obstruction to what is being sought. Such inflexibility is exemplified by the woman who yearns to meet a Prince Charming who will carry her away on a white horse.   Since no one meets her expectations and preconceived images, she fails to recognize her true "prince" when he appears riding a mule.

Attempting to fight an obstruction directly can often become an obstacle to breakthrough.   Instead of battling the difficulty head on, one can overcome the obstacle by simply letting go and ceasing to struggle.   Both benefit and growth can result from a so-called obstruction.

Obstructions are met daily when things do not go as planned. In the process of growth, obstructions are met thousands of times over and usually generate great despair. One who wishes to move forward, but is unable to do so because of restrictions, can respond by changing direction and taking another path, one that goes inward or upward. Sometimes what appears difficult is actually a protection or an opportunity for spiritual growth. All great achievements are obtained through the positive use of obstructions.

Some people, due to poverty, must work extremely hard just to get an education. However, the struggle for a better life often results in one's mind being stronger and less psychologically troubled than that of a person with no apparent difficulties. Both pain and suffering are necessary for growth and understanding. Sometimes, for a materially and emotionally spoiled person, the hardship of poverty can be a healthy psychological tonic. It is an opportunity to experience real life.

Listing all the things you consider obstructions and frustrations can be beneficial. These are actually the tools that Heaven has provided for your improvement, education and strengthening. No great person has ever grown without such "nutrition."

Many inventions are the result of breaking through a great obstruction. Without an obstacle there can be no breakthrough, whether in spiritual cultivation or on the mundane psychological level. Periods of smoothness naturally alternate with periods of disruption. Accidents usually occur when a circumstance does not require close attention, just as obstructions usually appear when one assumes that one's position is secure. Therefore, one who is cautious and careful will be safe.

Death seems to be the ultimate obstruction. It has been the impetus for the most highly developed to achieve great breakthroughs. They not only broke through this obstruction for themselves, but also for their fellow beings. This is how the sacred methods of cultivation were revealed. Unfortunately, they have been neglected by modern intellectual minds.

For every obstruction, there is a solution. Everything is created by the combination of yin and yang energy, which is a manifestation of natural law. Therefore, a person never has to be limited, either internally or externally, by nature. One who is attuned to the natural laws can prepare for any circumstance!

Physical life is very limiting and shallow. Not until the very last moments can one's true accomplishments be known. Temporary fame, wealth, glory and honor are not important. Knowing the real values of life enables one to gather essential, universal power.

When a person truly understands that the development of the universe and life are regulated by the same alternating yin and yang energy, he will no longer be limited by his own particular preferences. Day is followed by night. Progress is followed by standstill or regression. Sometimes life flows smoothly and other times we pass through periods of difficulty. All circumstances are relative, and life is a continuous cycle. By following the natural way of life, one will attract the supportive response of universal energy. Thus, frustrations over individual matters cannot arise.

LINE 1: *"If one moves forward, obstruction will be encountered. Honorable growth naturally comes to the one who keeps still."*

The Mountain cannot move to the Water; however, the Water can flow to the Mountain. There is obstruction for one who goes to the people. This is the right time to wait for the people to come of their own accord.

LINE 2: *"When one serves as a selfless minister to tackle all obstructions, one's strong sense of duty is correct. Any misunderstanding must finally disappear."*

This line represents someone who encounters an obstacle. One should courageously fulfill one's duty, without feeling too troubled by these misunderstandings and complaints.

LINE 3: *"Going, one meets with obstruction. Returning, one meets with a warm reception."*

In going forward to meet the top line, the third line encounters danger, the abyss. One should return and not advance at this time. If the third line returns, the first and second yin lines will welcome its help.

LINE 4: *"Going, one meets with obstruction. Remaining, one receives help and cooperation."*

This is the right time to receive help from others. If you allow things to come to you, instead of pursuing them, an obstruction can be dissolved or prevented. This image is indicated by the yin lines in the first and the fourth positions.

LINE 5: *"During the time of great obstruction, friends all come to help."*

In the midst of great obstruction, one must truly face the situation and work on it. Positive energy causes a beneficial response from like energy. The cooperation extends naturally to the second line and the others.

LINE 6: *"Going, one meets with obstruction. Returning, one joins the talents of others in assisting the great leader to break through obstructions."*

If one goes forward, there is obstruction; by keeping still, favorable change results. Obstruction cannot always remain obstruction.

The entire hexagram teaches that at the time of obstruction, inward enhancement is the main effort that helps to overcome the external difficulty.

SPECIFIC GUIDANCE

PERSONAL FORTUNE: Though this is a difficult time, success is possible.

MARRIAGE: There is no success. Even if the marriage endures, there will be quarreling.

HOUSING/FAMILY: There is danger from flooding mountain waters.

CHILDBIRTH: There is difficulty.

LOOKING FOR WORK: Success comes later.

SOCIAL/GOVERNMENTAL POSITION: There is difficulty at the beginning but success later.

TRADE/BUSINESS: There is an obstacle which prevents the transition from going through.

SEARCHING FOR SOMEONE: They are difficult to find.

WAITING FOR SOMEONE: They will not come.

LOOKING FOR SOMETHING LOST: It can be found in the Northeast near water.

HUNTING FOR THIEVES: They are in the Northeast, at the foot of a mountain. Look for them quickly.

LAWSUIT: The matter should be discontinued; otherwise it will be dangerous. Do not appear in court.

CLIMATE: It will be rainy.

TRAVEL: You will lose some money. A later date is more profitable for travel.

DISEASE: The problem is in the feet and can only be cured slowly.

PERSONAL WISH: There is difficulty in the beginning; however, after some time, there will be success.

COMMENTARY

To cultivate the Tao, spiritual integrity,
*   you must first exalt purity.*
Clean the mind of all stains.
Frequently review your judgments.
Hold firm to the pure motives
*   which inspired your cultivation.*
Bar the entrance of evil disturbances.
Do not allow the mind to change.
Even on the roughest roads,
*   keep it steadfast as it travels*
*   toward its destination.*
Let it not float, move or trap itself.

It is uncleanliness of body and mind
*   that causes the disorders of passion and virtue.*
Disorder makes peace impossible.
Evil powers are divisible by four:
*   external, internal,*
*   apparent and hidden.*
The most difficult are the hidden,
*   because your knowledge of their coming*
*   is prevented.*
You must recognize them
*   in their subtle beginnings.*
*   Work to refine your precious wisdom,*
*   and you will not need to retreat*
*   from the world to avoid its temptations.*

Your all-important balance
  is damaged by too much inharmonious
  mental activity.
If mental disorder arises,
  you are the evil powers' slave.
Of the few principles in cultivating Tao,
  the key one is keeping your real mind pure,
  undivided, unscattered.

Self-discipline alone
  will correctly develop your divine nature.
The subtle body,
  which will manifest itself,
  is the basis of your immortality.
It is possible to become a thief
  of your own balance.
Have caution on the road you travel
  to become a whole being.

40   hsieh

dissolution of the problem

GUIDANCE: "The friendly direction is the Southwest, from whence comes the strength of dissolution. If one wishes to go forward in the new correct way, early movement brings good fortune."

In this hexagram, Thunder is above Water. Although Water in the form of ice is the obstacle, Thunder has the strength to break through it. The first sound of Thunder in Spring proclaims the time of melting ice. Thus, a promising time is beginning, like a breeze coming from the warm Southwest.

After obstruction comes resolution. The guidance of the previous hexagram, Obstruction, is to keep still and gather energy, but Hsieh indicates that the obstructive force has started to diminish and a new cycle is beginning. This is the right time to positively dissolve all problems.

The following illustration from Chuang Tzu can be used to exemplify Hsieh. There was once a butcher who always used the same knife. Although he used this knife for many years, it remained without a nick and never became dull. Summoned by the king and asked how he was able to keep the knife freshly sharpened after so many years, the butcher replied, "In my eyes the cow is already separated, bone by bone, muscle by muscle, and tendon by tendon. When I use my knife, I do not cut with brutal force. In my vision, the cow - being already separated with empty space between its bones, joints and tendons - allows my knife to pass smoothly through these empty spaces without resistance."

Most people's minds and hearts have many nicks from continuously trying to "cut through" life, but by following the example of the butcher, one would not need to use brutal emotional force to overcome difficulties. Problems could be resolved naturally.

Hsieh also means to "untie," which implies untangling the psychological knots in one's life. The *I Ching* teaches that entanglements within can be dissolved through forgiveness. A person who can forgive others can have peace of mind. Certain actions may seem unforgivable; however, hostility, pride, jealousy or other emotional attachments are like thick clouds that gather and obstruct the clear sky. When one has a forgiving attitude, an offending action is forgotten and one is no longer influenced by negativity. Thus, one becomes independent and one's balance is no longer threatened by those who trouble him. Instead of being at the mercy of external reality, one creates his own reality by forgiving others.

With Thunder comes rain, thus the difficulty has ended and the drought is relieved. This is the image of dissolving worries, tensions and hostilities. The lines of this hexagram represent the gradual stages of dissolution.

LINE 1: *"Keep to what is right and in accordance with the time and circumstance. No blame."*

The beginning of Spring, when the ice starts to melt, is a time of regeneration. Likewise, as a problem begins to dissolve, one should use the time to prepare for recovery. In this early stage, one is advised to keep still because the energy is not yet ready for use. Any action would be premature.

LINE 2: *"Three foxes are captured with one arrow. Good fortune is brought about by correct action."*

If one remains inactive at this stage, one's opportunity will be lost. This is the time to advance toward one's goal.

The second line represents a strong righteous individual who supports the entire situation. Though the three yin lines above it are an obstacle in its path, it overcomes all obstructions by being like an arrow - direct and unhesitating.

LINE 3: *"A greedy undertaking brings humiliation."*

This yin line in a yang position represents an incompetent person who takes a high position. Being weak or unqualified is not a disgraceful matter as long as one does not attempt to take a position beyond one's capabilities. This line is like a newcomer who invites humiliation through arrogance.

LINE 4: *"When truly helpful strength is attracted, the obstruction can be dissolved."*

The fourth line can dissolve the obstruction of the problem and make progress if his strength is not pulled away by the third line, his closely related neighbor whose focus and purpose are on excessive self-protection with only self-interest. Thus, when he disentangles himself from the influence of the third line, he will be able to gather the understanding and cooperation of the second and sixth lines to solve the problem. Wrong cooperation brings no positive result. Faithfulness to one's correct direction will attract truly helpful friends.

LINE 5: *"Dissolution is brought about by the virtuous one. His faithfulness makes the negative forces recede."*

The fifth line unites with the second line in order to resolve the great problem of removing negativity. Only by being faithful to each other can a cooperative solution to the problem be discovered. The disappearance of negativity is proof of success for the virtuous.

LINE 6: *"Standing on a high wall, the prince shoots the eagle. No remorse. Disorder and confusion dissolve."*

The peak of energy has been reached and is now past. In this position, one can be of benefit by turning back to help others. Only through cooperation and friendly communication can the problem be resolved.

SPECIFIC GUIDANCE

PERSONAL FORTUNE: This is the time for you to cheer up, take action and get out of difficulty.

MARRIAGE: There is no success, not even in the future.

HOUSING/FAMILY: The situation is neither beneficial nor auspicious. Stop communicating with neighbors or with one who continues to come to you.

CHILDBIRTH: The baby will be a boy.

LOOKING FOR WORK: Because there are obstacles, there will be no success.

SOCIAL/GOVERNMENTAL POSITION: If the third or fifth line is received, there will be success.

TRADE/BUSINESS: The undertaking can now be accomplished.

SEARCHING FOR SOMEONE: They are difficult to find.

WAITING FOR SOMEONE: They will not come.

LOOKING FOR SOMETHING LOST: It is difficult to find.

HUNTING FOR THIEVES: They are difficult to locate.

LAWSUIT: A long time is involved. If the third or fifth line is received, trouble will arise.

CLIMATE: It will be rainy for a long time with possible wind. Lightning may be dangerous at this time.

TRAVEL: The journey will be beautiful. Good fortune.

DISEASE: There is danger.

PERSONAL WISH: This is a profitable time. However, if you wait too long, success will not be possible.

COMMENTARY

To become one with Tao,
    or to become a shien, an immortal being,
    newly achieved and born in heaven,
    there is one, only one requirement:
    keep a consistently calm mind.
Keep it peaceful, transparent and
    still as the water of a clear, quiet lake,
    and you will enjoy the subtlety of great bliss.
When dealing with
    minor problems or major disasters,
    stay calm and still as a holy mountain.
When dealing with the pleasurable,
    maintain strict discipline.
In this way,
    when the unpleasant presents itself,
    your mind will not be disturbed.

Those who would embellish rites and rituals,
    succeed only in trying to impress others.
There is no power to be gained.
Nor is self-cultivation a tool
    for exacting respect from your community.
It must show its effectiveness
    on all occasions,
    especially in times of great difficulty.
Every day, in each ordinary situation,
    you can realize the benefit of self-cultivation.
No special time is reserved for this.
The calm power derived from your daily practice
    can transform what seems to be a disaster
    into a blessing.
Quietude can change misfortune into good fortune.
Understand the elusive quality of your body and mind.
It is easy to keep the mind calm and the emotions
    peaceful in ordinary situations,
    but how difficult it is when problems come!
Learn this and you will be qualified
    to sit in the seat of the Lotus,
    to look deep within yourself.

Be as a person of iron -
    your mind firm, unshakable -
    and you will become the favorite child
    of the family of whole beings.

41 損 suen ䷨

SACRIFICE · DECREASE

GUIDANCE: *"Reduce that which is excessive. Great good fortune without doubt. Go ahead with the great task. If one is sincere, one's simple offering will be blessed by the Divine Realm."*

The literal translation of Suen is to "decrease" or "reduce." The Lake is at the foot of the Mountain. The Lake erodes the Mountain, hence the image of the Mountain above the Lake can be viewed as being unfavorable or even damaging. The height of the Mountain is in great contrast to the depths of the Lake.

On a deeper level, Suen is expressed by the interacting energies of the mountain and the lake. The energy of the Lake, ☱, is more active than that of the Mountain, ☶. Thus, strong, active energy seeks balance and decreases in order to strengthen weaker, passive energy. This process is of benefit to both the Mountain and the Lake. As a form of energy cultivation, Suen demonstrates how balance can be achieved by decreasing emotional and mental contaminations or burdens.

Water from the Lake decreases through evaporation. It then returns in the form of rain, nourishes the Mountain and finally replenishes itself. Thus, decrease is a very important and necessary process for the completion of this cycle. Furthermore, as Decrease evolves into T'ai, Peace/Prosperity, ䷊ , the perfect union of yin and yang is achieved. T'ai becomes the accomplishment of Decrease.

A very important principle of the *Tao Teh Ching* is represented in this hexagram: "The way of man is taking from those who lack and giving to those who abound. The way of Heaven is taking from those who abound and giving to those who lack." One must look inwardly to determine what should be given away or made as an offering.

In Suen, an offering is represented by the inner trigram, Thunder, which signifies a bowl. This image symbolizes the ancient Chinese practice of making offerings to one's ancestors and to Heaven and Earth in gratitude for an abundant harvest.

One who truly understands the principles of increase and decrease can avoid difficulties in life and relationships. People seek what they think is beneficial and try to avoid or get rid of what they consider unfavorable. This is a daily enterprise. But do we truly understand what is beneficial and what is not? Frequently, what initially appears helpful actually ends up bringing misfortune. Conversely, what originally seems to be disadvantageous later becomes a great blessing. Both increase and decrease are part of the same cycle and occur at their appropriate times. Thus, in maintaining balance, the essential adjustments to be made are in one's attitudes and actions. Desire, anger, arrogance and anxiety are obstacles for a peaceful mind and can directly affect one's health. Applying the principle of decrease to the emotions can help restore harmony.

Mathematics views the principles of increase and decrease as mutually exclusive. However, according to the principles of the *I Ching*, when something is decreasing, it is also increasing, and vice versa. The interaction of these two phenomena occurs simultaneously. Therefore, in the "mathematics" of the *I Ching*, less is sometimes more, and more is sometimes less.

LINE 1: *"Give friendly help. Correctly sacrifice yourself in order to benefit others and there will be no problem."*

This strong yang line aids the weak yin line in the fourth place. In this position, put aside self-concern and offer help in accordance with the situation.

LINE 2: *"Stay with what is right. Movement should not be attempted at this time."*

This is the time to maintain one's energy. Staying where one is without attempting to increase or decrease is beneficial.

LINE 3: *"When three people walk together, their group is reduced by one. A person traveling alone acquires a* *friend. Likewise, a single purpose will attract friendly help. Too many directions will lose help."*

Harmony is best maintained between two people. A person who is alone finds a companion, but adding a third person brings mistrust and upsets the balance of energy. If one's scope, purpose and goal are broad enough, the involvement of many people can be helpful. Even so, the main focus of energy must remain between two people in order to maintain and support the integrity of the plan.

LINE 4: *"One decreases the seriousness of his disease with a friend's help. Rapid recovery brings happiness."*

One becomes conscious of the problem and works to solve it. Such progress brings joy. Since the first and fourth lines correspond to one another and are in their correct places, healing becomes possible.

LINE 5: *"Be receptive to all benefits that come to you. This is certainly good fortune blessed by Heaven."*

This line is yin in a yang position, which represents a leader who is not very strong. Nevertheless, it has support from the Heavenly Realm, as indicated by the sixth line, which serves to protect this hexagram. Thus, one is blessed and has good fortune. This blessing is the result of the union of the Heavenly realm and the human realm, which can be symbolized by a big turtle.

LINE 6: *"With sufficient strength, no increase is needed. Maintaining a righteous balance brings good fortune. This is the right time to do something that will help people and to accept an assistant who is without a family."*

If one is increased without depriving or taking advantage of others, there is no blame. The energy offered by the lower trigram strengthens the upper trigram. Since the top line is now sufficient, it offers its strength to serve others. Thus, success is achieved.

SPECIFIC GUIDANCE

PERSONAL FORTUNE: At this time, one's fortune is very unstable.

MARRIAGE: There is success. The Mountain symbolizes a young man and the Lake symbolizes a young girl.

HOUSING/FAMILY: Pay particular attention to safety needs. There is difficulty in family relationships.

CHILDBIRTH: There is difficulty.

LOOKING FOR WORK: You will get the job, but money will be lost in the process.

SOCIAL/GOVERNMENTAL POSITION: Although there is difficulty in the beginning, the position can later be achieved.

TRADE/BUSINESS: After several attempts, success.

SEARCHING FOR SOMEONE: They can be found.

WAITING FOR SOMEONE: They will not come.

LOOKING FOR SOMETHING LOST: It is difficult to recover.

HUNTING FOR THIEVES: They are difficult to apprehend. Look in the Northeast.

LAWSUIT: There is possible benefit for you, but misfortune for others.

CLIMATE: It will be rainy.

TRAVEL: This time is not good for travel. Someone may trick you.

DISEASE: It is curable.

PERSONAL WISH: Nothing can be accomplished in a hurry.

COMMENTARY
Absolute Freedom

Living in the world, we are sometimes benefited through increase. At other times, we are benefitted by decrease. As Chapter 48 of the *Tao Teh Ching* says:

*"In learning, the increase of knowledge
and skill should be seen daily.
In cultivation, the decrease of coarseness
in character and impurity in mind
should also be seen daily
in order to reach the true essence."*

Spiritual truth is derived from the unfolding of a natural mind. Such an experience can be described as the complete "opening" of the mind, like a fully-blossoming flower - totally liberating the mind, untying the entanglements of the mind, unveiling the truth or revelation of the ultimate truth. All of these terms carry the same connotation but differ vastly with personal experience. Such practices and pursuits of spiritual achievement are high above common religious worship.

Among all the great books ever written about the nature of truth, Chuang Tzu's is the highest. His teachings, however, are difficult to translate. Unfortunately, there was no correct translation available to English speaking people before. This fact is not due to English Sinologists being unskilled, but it is like using an oil painting technique to copy a Chinese brush-painted masterpiece. The work of art can be well-copied and may look the same; however, to the eye which has seen the original, a distinction can be made between its authenticity and the copied work. A translation cannot convey the original meaning of the natural unobstructed spirit. Also, the original book itself is easily misunderstood. Thus, not only could one incorrectly interpret its effect, but one's thinking might be contorted as well.

Among the hundreds of thousands of readers of that great book, perhaps only one will be able to restore his original nature. Why? Because merely reading a book and getting a vague impression of its meaning without the direct training and guidance of a truly achieved one is not enough. It is difficult to reach the level of an achieved master. Furthermore, it is not a matter of understanding, but a way of living. One can follow nothing until one has experienced the real model. People in their general lives and religious practices have specific ways of expressing what they do, such as a cook, a carpenter, a farmer, a teacher or a minister. However, an achieved master has no trace of anything discernible. From him you see nothing.

Has anyone ever seen a real dragon? A real dragon does not show itself. How can people with undeveloped eyes see the really achieved one? They only see his human shape. Seeing him is less interesting than seeing an attractive movie star! Moreover, there is no benefit from just seeing a really achieved one. Spiritual benefit is not based on one's understanding - it is based on direct reunion with the subtle truth. A person who says he knows that someone is an achieved master does not know the

master at all. This person covers himself with shallowness. This is like the many attempts to make "Chuang
Tzu" a subject to be studied. Learning Tao is not like
studying someone. Tao is not to be understood. Tao is
just what is.

Once I wrote some Chinese calligraphy in strong, black
ink on a piece of paper and put it on the wall of my
study. It read:

> *"I sit with vulgar people.*
> *I stand with vulgar people.*
> *But where I live*
> *   is not where vulgar people can reach!"*

I truly believed that I had achieved this. My elder sister happened to see the writing, and on one occasion, she
and my younger brother found an opportunity to quiz me
about it during dinner one summer evening. (We were all
teenagers at this time.) Hoping to shake me from my diamond throne of spiritual achievement, she began this way:

"You use big characters to tell the world that you sit
with vulgar people and that you stand with vulgar people,
but is it not we who sit and stand with you? Since the
writing refers to 'us' as vulgar people, then what are you?"

My younger brother continued, "Where you live is not
where vulgar people can reach! But to us, living under
the same roof means that you are the same as us!"

This was one of the "wars" in which I was under attack because of my own foolish "achievement." Thus I
had invited this invasion.

Our eldest sister never failed to act as an arbitrator,
as she did on this occasion. She said, "Be quiet. He
means that his spirit no longer follows this same vulgar
track."

"We doubt that he is achieved in such a way that dis-
tinguishes him from us!" my second sister and young
brother sang in unison.

"You only reveal your own vulgarity by insisting on interfering with his personal spiritual endeavor!" my eldest
sister said.

Although my eldest sister thankfully saved me from
embarrassment, I still did not fully realize my mistake.
When the defeated "knight" retreated to the kitchen, my
mother was already washing the dishes. As she worked,
she repeatedly murmured, "Everything is Tao. Everything
is not Tao." I thought she might be trying to teach me to

recognize that kitchen work is also the performance of Tao, as she often did.   However, in front of my mother, I acted like a little child again.   I started to touch everything in our old-fashioned Chinese kitchen.   Every time I touched something I would say, "This is Tao, that is Tao," and continued to do so until there was nothing more that I could put my finger on.   After I stopped my frivolous actions, my mother said, "What you can touch is the Tao with form.   Show me the unformed Tao."

For a moment I was dumfounded.   Then, pointing at the empty space I said, "This is Tao, that is Tao."

My mother simply said, "No, this is East and that is South."

Then I moved my finger in all different directions and said, "This is Tao.   That is Tao."   But everywhere I pointed, my mother proclaimed the direction and the space, such as left and right, front and rear, upper and lower, and so forth.   There was no place my finger pointed without direction or name.   I hastily pointed at myself and then at her.   I continued to be given a name, a form, a describable being or a definable meaning.   Finally, I gave up.   There was no hope of expressing the unformed Tao. She gave me time to collect myself, but by now, I had tried everything in vain.

Then my mother said with a very slow and clear voice, "Since your 'Tao' is with form, you bind yourself with your own vulgar triviality.   How can you enjoy the absolute freedom of being with Tao?   Tao is neither with form, nor is it formless.   This is why I repeated to you, 'Everything is Tao, everything is not Tao."

At that moment I received a new light which pierced the darkness of my self imposed cocoon.   My mother led me to discover the imperfection of spiritual achievement.

During the following months I completely reworked myself without mercy.   During that Winter, around the time of the Chinese New Year, it began to snow.   We stopped most outdoor activities and gathered in the kitchen, my mother's "empire."

My mother asked me to express my yearly achievement by writing a poem with snow as the topic.   This is what I wrote:

> *There is no trace of snow when it is fine.*
> *There is no trace of being fine when it snows.*
> *Before the birth of Heaven and Earth,*
> *   neither trace could be found.*

I read the poem to my mother. She then asked me to present it to my father. My father read it with a smile. After I repeatedly insisted on having his comment, he finally said, "I am happy to see that you can connect all changing events to the unchangeable, true nature of the universe, but your poem lacks the vividness of life. Such beliefs could lead to the narrow practice of a religion. Tao is life. If Tao is what you choose, then come back to the real life!"

In this very moment, and with the help of my father's seldom-used mystical sword, the thick layer of my mental obstruction was peeled away. Thus, I immediately received true freedom from spiritual bondage.

In later years, due to the drastic changes in the world I was in another place, far away from our old home. Undaunted, I shouldered the responsibility of passing the truth as a healing, awakening means for individuals to cultivate an integral life. In this endeavor I met tremendous difficulties from all directions, but with the innermost light of my true nature, I overcame all obstacles (which actually stirred my growth). On one occasion, I had a chance to write to my elderly father to assure him that in all aspects of life, I was all right. I wrote him in the wintertime, after the snow had fallen in the high mountains. I missed my family very much and was especially worried about my parents who, at that time, were living under tremendous pressures. Finally I got an answer from my father. In his letter he wrote:

> *"When it is fine, I am trouble-free.*
> *When it is snowing, I am also trouble-free.*
> *No matter how the world changes,*
> * I always remain trouble-free."*

He expressed his unobstructed spirit in this poem during a time of the adversity of the Chinese nation.

Generally, when people have a comfortable life, their natures are buried under material enjoyment. When they live under adversity, their natures are bent and damaged. Those of real achievement can not only enjoy comforts, but can also withstand adversity. Clouds do not really hinder the sky, and neither does the sky hinder the clouds. The real usefulness of spiritual achievement is similar to drinking water - only the one who drinks shall know the true flavor.

42

益
YI

BENEFIT · INCREASE

GUIDANCE: *"Benefit. This is the right time to go ahead, to engage in an adventurous task."*

In this hexagram, Wind is above Thunder. When these natural energies meet, they strengthen one another. Thus, an increase in power results. While the character Yi means "to benefit" or "increase," it also signifies an empty bowl ready to be filled. The lower trigram, Thunder, represents the bowl, and the upper trigram, Wind, represents emptiness. Just as the bowl's usefulness lies in its emptiness, a person must also become empty in order to receive benefit.

The phrase "to cross the great water" is often used in the *I Ching* to indicate the time to begin a new venture. In ancient times, when travelers or hunters would reach a great body of water, the question would arise as to whether to cross the water or turn back. This hexagram suggests that we courageously go ahead.

The hexagram Benefit, as well as that of #41, Decrease ☷☳ , is better understood when one understands the relationship between yin and yang. All things can be expressed in terms of yin and yang. Yang energy generally moves upward and forward, yin moves downward and backward, and neither can exist without the other. Every form of existence is a relative complement to another existence, as symbolized by the T'ai Chi diagram ☯ . Thus, yin and yang contain each other and encompass both the visible and invisible realms, the manifest and unmanifest planes of the entire universe.

Whenever one aspect of this inseparable pair is singled out, its opposite is automatically formulated. For example, the existence of beauty suggests ugliness, good suggests bad, difficulty suggests ease, long suggests short, high suggests low, loud suggests soft, before suggests after, etc. Each derives its meaning from its opposite. On the dualistic plane, this principle applies to all things.

The hexagrams for Increase and Decrease can be understood when T'ai ☰, Peace, is used as the reference for balance and harmony. In the energy formation of Tai, the heavy, feminine energy of Earth is above the light, masculine energy of Heaven. Since earthly energy descends and heavenly energy ascends, the two energies peacefully interact and prosper. This interaction represents the ideal integration of yin and yang. The situation of Peace serves as the standard from which Increase and Decrease obtain their positive meanings.

Yi, ☰☰ , Benefit/Increase, comes from Pi, ☰☰ , Misfortune/Disharmony, or Uncooperativeness. The bottom line of the upper trigram, Heaven, sacrifices itself and moves down in order to help the bottom line of the lower trigram, Earth. The upper trigram then changes to Wind and the lower trigram changes to Thunder. Thus the situation changes from misfortune to Increase, and the hexagram Yi results.

There are many aspects of Increase which are not beneficial and many aspects of Decrease that are beneficial. When one maintains a broad perspective, one can be receptive to all changes. Often one suffers from that which is thought to be not beneficial or unprofitable, yet what appears not to be beneficial can sometimes be of great benefit. Being mindful of this can provide healthy protection.

LINE 1: *"Undertaking a great task is suitable at this time. Great good fortune."*

This yang line is in the correct place. Generally, the first line is too weak to take major action, but in this hexagram the first line receives help from the fourth line. Therefore, the yang energy of the first line is balanced and strengthened by the harmonizing and cooperating energy of the fourth line. Obstacles are thus overcome and supreme good fortune results.

LINE 2: *"Accept the great benefit. Good fortune results in keeping to that which is correct. One offers one's virtue to the Divine One and constantly receives good fortune. Benefits also come from without but are not the result of one's actions."*

This yin line is in the correct position and receives support from the fifth line, Heaven, the one who is above or the one who may be a leader. This line expresses the receptiveness of the lower trigram. Its benefit is the greatest of all the lines in this hexagram. The blessing of this line is equal to the fifth line of Decrease. It is the result of the union of the Heavenly Realm and human realm, which is symbolized in the Chinese version by turtles. If one can maintain a spirit of openness and cooperation, good fortune will surely come.

LINE 3:   *"One is benefited by hardship. When one keeps to the right path, there is no blame. At this time, public trust needs to be earned and established."*

Taking the unfavored position sometimes becomes the means of obtaining positive results. What is unfavorable often evokes the opposite response. Good fortune is frequently hidden within misfortune. This means for a person to take care of the difficulty, but not take credit if there is any benefit. One would even win the friendship and appreciation of others by so doing. One should now discover and put into use these benefits of difficulty. This is similar to drinking bitter herbal medicinal tea, which tastes bad but brings good results to improving one's healthy life. It is often going through hard experience that helps one achieve higher.

LINE 4:   *"By keeping to the right path, one receives consent and obedience from the public; thus, one leads all people toward the right place."*

As the Wind stirs, it becomes beneficial. Likewise, the downward movement of the fourth line aids the first line in carrying out its duty. Great good fortune and prosperity result. If movement is made now to benefit others, there will also be benefit for oneself.

LINE 5:   *"If one has a heart that seeks to benefit others, there will be good fortune. One's virtue will be expressed and benefited. This benefit is the result of one's own accomplishments."*

Now is a peaceful and prosperous time. The harmonious fifth line, with its wonderfully kind heart, gives support and benefit to the second line. Thus, their relationship is correct and great good fortune is achieved.

LINE 6: *"Remain firm in your decision to benefit others. Trouble is created when one stops giving and begins taking."*

The strength of this line is excessive, thus over-ambition is represented. Normally, the sixth and the third lines correspond with each other, but here both lines are in incorrect positions and their correspondence with each other is not beneficial. With the support and good will of the neighboring fifth line, this situation can be redeemed from one of complete misfortune.

SPECIFIC GUIDANCE

PERSONAL FORTUNE: It is good.

MARRIAGE: It will be a good marriage.

HOUSING/FAMILY: Repair is necessary. Beware of fire.

CHILDBIRTH: It will be a peaceful delivery.

LOOKING FOR WORK: The job you seek does not exist.

SOCIAL/GOVERNMENTAL POSITION: A high position is not in accordance with the time.

TRADE/BUSINESS: Successful.

SEARCHING FOR SOMEONE: They are difficult to meet.

WAITING FOR SOMEONE: They will come late.

LOOKING FOR SOMETHING LOST: The object can be found.

HUNTING FOR THIEVES: They are difficult to locate.

LAWSUIT: Think about the case. Do not proceed.

TRAVEL: If you hurry, there will be trouble. Now is not a good time to travel alone.

DISEASE: There is danger.

PERSONAL WISH: It is difficult to accomplish.

COMMENTARY
Attaining a Practical Mind

Everyone looks for benefits and favors for one's life, but does one really know what is beneficial and favorable? The true essence of life is chi. It is chi that builds life.

One who would truly develop the vision to know this truth, should be willing to engage in the cultivation of chi.

What is chi? Chi is the mother of all things and all beings. It is the subtle essence of the universe. This statement could never satisfy an ordinary intellectual mind, but the use of the mind represents only one way in which chi moves. Recognition of the deep truth depends on long years of self-reflection and cultivation. Through actual cultivation, one is able to discover the subtle existence of chi.

In order to seriously begin the cultivation of chi, a peaceful mind is necessary. This should be practiced not with a passive purpose, but with a positive and creative purpose. In human life, a peaceful mind can nurture personal vitality. Here is where all personal enterprises of spiritual and worldly achievement start.

Sometimes knowing how much progress one is making is not easy, but the following discussion should help you obtain your preliminary goal.

Conceptual recognition of the contradictory nature of worldly things comes from mental objectivity, but this does not help eliminate the conflicts that are experienced in real life. Thus, conceptual development may only be helpful as a first step. The way taught by the ancient developed ones for attaining a peaceful, undisturbed and unattached mind is the withdrawal of one's mental being from the outer layer of worldly tensions to the unified core of universal life.

A peaceful, undisturbed and unexcitable mind can be achieved by nurturing chi. A dialogue between Mencius and one of his students explains this important practice. (Mencius, a popular teacher in China, who lived from 372 B.C. to 289 B.C., was a later-generation student of Confucius' teachings.)

"Master, if you were put in the position of the premier of the State of Chi so that you could fulfill all good principles as you had always wished, you would be the equal of a king dealing with major affairs of state. Would this opportunity excite you?" inquired the student.

"No," said Mencius. "When I was forty, I had already achieved an undisturbed mind."

"Then," said the student, "you must have surpassed even the ancient brave man, Men Pei, who did not fear anything on land or in water. Richness, nobility or even fear for his own life did not disturb his unexcitable mind."

Mencius replied, "It should not be so difficult. Koa Tzu, your fellow student, achieved a passionless, undisturbed mind even earlier than I."

"Master, is there any sure way of reaching a passive, undisturbed mind?" queried the student.

Mencius said, "There are several ways. Pei Kung Yu's method was to control the skin and not react to heat, cold or pain. His eyelids did not blink with any agitation, and he did not turn his face or close his eyes to anything fearful. But if one single hair on his body was damaged by anyone, he would become as insulted as if he were publicly beaten. It did not matter whether that person was in ordinary clothes or a king of ten thousand chariots, his revenge was taken in defensive action. If bad words were spoken to him, then the same would be returned by him. This was his way of keeping the vigor of his mind.

"The method of Men Shih Shr was to face defeat as one would face victory. He estimated the enemy before marching and measured the chance of triumph before engaging in war. He said, 'I do not let my mind think I am the winner, but neither do I let fear disturb me.'

"These are but two ways among many to achieve an undisturbed mind. The first way, that of Pei Kung Yu, suggests facing bad situations fearlessly. In other words, exerting the vigor of the mind instead of depressing it. The second way, that of Men Shih Shr, stresses the centering of one's mind before putting it to good use. I cannot say which is the stronger way, although I do think that Men Shih Shr's way may be more practical.

"I remember Tsen Tzu taught one of his students the following, 'You wish to be powerful? I heard my master, Confucius, say that, when the most powerful one inquires into a matter with his mind and finds out what is not right, even if he faces a simple, ordinary person, he still feels fear. If he inquires into a matter with his mind and finds out what is right, even if there are thousands and thousands of people who say it is wrong, he still faces it.'"

Mencius continued, "From viewing this, I think Tsen Tzu's way is the most important."

The student asked, "Master, may I venture to ask your way of cultivation and how it differs from Kuo Tzu's way? You mentioned that he achieved his undisturbed mind earlier than you, but he has followed you for some time."

Mencius responded, "Kuo Tzu's principle for reaching an unperturbed mind is this: 'Do not think about the unjust words people speak to you and do not resort to emotions when people disagree with you.' The main guidance of his way is 'do not.' But from my understanding, the rational mind is the center. The emotional force is connected to the whole body. When the rational mind reacts to a situation, the emotional force follows. Therefore, keep the rational mind peaceful and do not violently stir passion."

"Master, you have pointed out that when the rational mind reacts to a situation, emotional force follows. It seems that the whole matter is the mind. But you also say to keep the rational mind in peace and to not violently stir the passion," said the student.

Mencius replied, "When the mind is in control, it 'moves' the emotions, but when the emotions are in control, they 'move' the mind. For instance, when one who has been walking falls down and becomes angry, it is emotion that moves the mind."

"Master, may I venture to ask the advantage of your way?" queried the student.

Mencius responded, "I think, first of all, that I understand people's words and the meaning behind all that is said. I especially cultivate the boundless inner power of personality in order to maintain the unperturbed mind."

"Master, may I venture to ask, what is the meaning of the boundless inner power of personality?" asked the student.

"This is difficult to express; however, this power is the greatest and the mightiest. It can only be successfully nurtured in a peaceful and harmless mind by using righteousness and by following the Way. Thus, it can extend to any sphere of the universe. Otherwise, it evaporates. Why? Because the power is obtained by accumulating righteousness and the correct way of life. It cannot be obtained by occasional righteousness. When one's behavior does not agree with one's mind, then this power becomes deflated.

"Therefore, I think Kao Tzu has not known that the power is within us. Cultivating this power must be done with gentle care. There is no room for negligence, nor is there anything extra that can be done in order to help it grow.

"Do not do as the person who lived in the State of Sung. He thought his young crops did not grow fast enough, so he went to the fields to pull them up a bit higher. Quickly finishing his work, he returned to his family. He told them, 'I am so tired now. I helped all the crops grow today.' His father went to the fields to see them, but they had all wilted."

From this dialogue we can understand that Mencius' undisturbed mind is not a negative practice but a power that is nurtured within. This boundless power can be cultivated by a pacified mind. Mencius was benefited by his own cultivation and he lived to an old age, smoothly, wisely, healthily and successfully.

From Mencius one can have a complete understanding of cultivating Tao. One does not need to do anything extra, but one should keep away from all negative things.

43   KUI

RESOLUTION

GUIDANCE: *"Resolution dissolves evil forces. One should obtain the cooperation of all righteous forces. Isolated and hasty actions are inappropriate. The advancement of cooperative, virtuous energy is wise."*

Traditionally, the character 夬, Kui, meant change, or more specifically, revolution. Gir, the 49th hexagram which has become known as Revolution, actually means "reformation." However, Kui more clearly depicts a "revolution" than does Gir.

In this hexagram, Lake or rain is above Heaven. The image is that of high clouds gathering in the sky. Rather than emphasizing the individual trigrams, the hexagram as a whole (five yang lines below one yin line) will be considered.

When yang energy is allowed to grow to completion, fulfillment and true achievement result. However, the yin line at the top of this hexagram becomes an obstacle to the generating power below. Thus, the five positive energies must break through the negative energy above. After a firm decision is made to break through this negative energy, complete yang energy can be attained.

The yang energy can undoubtedly remove the evil force at the top, but the hexagram suggests the need for caution each step of the way.   People cannot withdraw from every evil that is encountered.   If they were continually overcome by problems and inconveniences without ever reforming them, the destructive force would eventually take charge.

Whether the circumstance involves overcoming an obstacle in one's environment, an internal deficiency or a bad habit, caution should be exercised.   Dealing with negativity is similar to tending a flower garden.   If weeds are brusquely removed, the flowers may also be injured. Likewise, one should be careful not to harm the energy one is trying to nurture.   Instead of directly attacking the problem, one should try to balance the whole situation. Only when one's strength is organized can the obstruction be faced and the resolution be achieved.

Another important aspect of this hexagram is how to deal with sickness.   A minor ailment which is not quickly and effectively dealt with can become the root of a more serious problem.   Thus, one should draw from one's reservoir of energy in order to deal with the problem while it is still localized.

At times, a person overreacts by focusing on the problem instead of seeing the situation as a whole.   Throwing away an entire piece of fine cloth instead of simply cleaning the soiled spot seems absurd, yet there are many similar ways in which one loses clarity by acting impulsively.

The most effective principle to use in dealing with a situation like a revolution is to decrease and fundamentally correct any bad habits or shortcomings.   People often resort to artificial solutions such as alcohol or drugs to relieve tension or to help them get to sleep, but this is like asking a thief to catch a thief.   By not depending on outside crutches, one's true energy can become stronger and more effective.

Regardless of the difficulty the top line manifests, understanding its strong and influential nature is very important.   This yin line appears amiable, but is actually quite vicious and devious.   Thus, one's resolution must not be too reckless or forceful.   One who does not understand evil is vulnerable to its influence.   Having a firm resolve, supported by virtue, clarity and strength, is important at this time.

The dynamics of this hexagram can be further understood from its position in the natural cycle of energy rotation. It is associated with the third month of the Chinese calendar. This is the transition from Spring to Summer, when the yang energy increases and yin energy declines. The peak of Summer, when yang grows to completion, is full of sunshine, and the entire earth abounds with life. Thus, the pressures of life can be eliminated as the yang energy continues to advance during the time of resolution or revolution.

LINE 1: *"Strength is expressed by the toes. Even pushing ahead cannot solve the difficulty. Premature resolution brings humiliation."*

This line represents the toes. The shortcoming or obstacle is still far away. In the beginning stage, one should not attempt to tackle the difficulty directly, because he is still weak. Without support and coopera- tion, success is impossible. Furthermore, premature action yields an incorrect result. One's strength is inade- quate at this time to deal directly with the problem.

LINE 2: *"Strength is expressed by shouting. It is necessary to keep guard, even in the deep night, in order to protect oneself from a surprise attack."*

The energy has now grown. Darkness is above. This line represents a mouth and only allows a cry of alarm. One should be careful and not react in a shallow and impulsive manner. In these first and second stages, only observation is appropriate, not direct action. The dark- ness cannot be removed by a premature, radical or emotional response. Keep to what is right.

LINE 3: *"Hostility is expressed by the cheeks. One excites his enemies. Danger. Like a defiant child going out into the rain, one is sure to get wet. However, one's righteousness can be proven with fortitude."*

The strain of breaking through the negative force in the top position manifests in the expressions of the face. It is not wise to confront the problem alone. If one does engage in the task by oneself, difficulties may be encoun- tered and one may even fail to attain one's righteous goal. At this time, avoid expressing any antagonism in order to achieve your purpose.

LINE 4: *"One is restless and hesitant. One does not listen to trustworthy words, but remains indecisive, intending to avoid the danger, but lacking the necessary courage to eliminate the evil."*

The literal translation of this text is: "There is no skin on his buttocks." Without skin, how can one sit calmly? This indicates restlessness and impulsiveness. The fourth line represents a person who ignores advice and attempts to circumvent the problem. However, since one is not in a position of leadership, one should accept and follow the orders of the leader, the fifth line.

NOTE: Compare this line to the third line of Kou, Hexagram forty-four.

LINE 5: *"Keep to the right path when walking among weeds. Firmness keeps one from corruption."*

This line is in the position of the leader. This is the time to make responsible decisions.

LINE 6: *"Helplessness. Danger is present."*

The top line represents the force of evil. The literal meaning of the Chinese term for "evil" generally refers to destructive or negative energy which obstructs forward movement.

Everyone knows the story of the boy who cried wolf. At the crucial moment, his lack of credibility allowed negative energy to triumph. Beware of a sweet face that conceals a dark heart. To be able to recognize evil is an important form of true knowledge. Sometimes it is difficult to recognize that which works against one's development.

In a situation of danger, the *Tao Teh Ching* advises non-action. If one focuses by cultivating the right energy, there is no room for the negativity to grow. If one does not clash directly with an obstacle, it is as if there were no obstacle.

The *Tao Teh Ching* does not advise starting revolutions. Instead, it emphasizes the great benefit that results from cultivating normal growth. If a person displays aggression toward evil, he is actually practicing evil. Most heroic stories depict "evil" as something that must always be overcome. Such actions make the world an arena for strife. Evil is usually just the aggressive growth of a tendency that was once normal. Instead of competing with negativity, or fighting evil with evil, one should concentrate on one's own normal growth.

SPECIFIC GUIDANCE

PERSONAL FORTUNE: This is a very strong and vigorous time. It is the right time to spend some money, but not to accumulate things for oneself.

MARRIAGE: The marriage will not be a good one.

HOUSING/FAMILY: This is not a good place to live. There will be a flood which creates unrest.

CHILDBIRTH: The baby will be a boy.

LOOKING FOR WORK: Difficulty in the beginning. Success will come after some time.

SOCIAL/GOVERNMENTAL POSITION: No success.

TRADE/BUSINESS: Not successful.

SEARCHING FOR SOMEONE: Not much chance in finding them.

WAITING FOR SOMEONE: They do not come.

LOOKING FOR SOMETHING LOST: It can be found in the West.

HUNTING FOR THIEVES: They have already gone to the West and will be difficult to locate.

CLIMATE: It will be cloudy.

TRAVEL: One will become lost.

DISEASE: Danger.

PERSONAL WISH: An obstacle makes one's wish difficult to achieve.

COMMENTARY
The True Mind

The main guidance for becoming an integral being is: "If even one small portion of yin energy (the dualistic function of the mind) remains, then one will not become a shien. If even one small portion of yang energy (the integralness of life) is not complete, one will not become a shien."

In the science of self-cultivation, chi belongs to the yang category and mind belongs to the yin category. All thoughts are a digression from one's essence, and essence is what enables one to maintain wholeness.

In the hexagram Kui, ▰ , Resolute Change, the yang energy can be completed only when the remaining yin line on the top is eliminated. In self-cultivation, only when the untruthful mind is regulated can the wholeness of spiritual life be attained. Let the following discussion probe our minds.

To wonder if there is a God or no God is a typical question of the dualistic mind which can only respond with "yes" or "no." If you look deeply enough, you will find that the true nature of the mind is not dualistic, nor is the true nature of the universe. The self-nature of the universe can be called God.

Look at the mind. It is hardly substantial. It reveals itself only through its function and work. The insubstantial is called the true mind. Grasping this, one is able to enter the formless realm of the life of the universe which never ceases. With it, the universe operates in an organic way and is identified as subtle law.

If the true mind is the only thing recognized, then what is matter? Mind and matter permeate each other and interact well. Looking from the unmanifest truth to manifested matter, one will see things having forms which are limited in truth and short of time. To look from the unmanifest to the manifest sphere, one will not be bewildered by the diversity of forms which derive their essence from the oneness of the subtle origin. The only way to remain integral is to maintain a balance between the unmanifest and manifest spheres of the universe. Who can really deny the oneness of the integral universe?

The following illustrations may be useful in attempting to explore the true mind.

In China there was a famous master who led a group of his students on a hike in the mountains in the early spring. Eventually they came to an unusual place where, to their surprise, they discovered a beautiful peach tree in blossom. Everybody was enchanted by its brilliant rich pinkness and remained silent as they enjoyed its extraordinary beauty. For some time they were unable to take their eyes away from it.

After a long while, the master posed several questions. First he asked, "Is the universe with or without a mind? If it is without a mind, who brings about the beauty?

Must not there be a universal mind behind the ordinariness to present such beauty?

"Secondly, if the universe has a mind, should not this tree blossom in the city so that more people could experience its exquisite creation?

"Thirdly, without you and I to experience this tree, does its beauty still have meaning?"

When I was a young man, I formulated answers to these questions as follows: "The self-nature of the universe gives birth to the peach tree and to all beauty. It is the self-nature of the peach tree to produce flowers, as it is the self-nature of people to respond to the beauty of its flowers." Was I correct?

Once, during a time of confusion, a rebellious army came to attack a region of China. Understandably, the people of this region began to flee. Among those refugees was a group of young scholars who passed by a plum garden. The fruit on the trees was red and fully ripened, the branches drooping heavily under their weight. Eagerly, everyone began picking and eating the fruit. Among this group of students, however, was one young man who did not eat the fruit. His companions were surprised and asked him why he did not pick any plums. This garden now, during the time of confusion, belonged to no lord. The young scholar answered, "Truly, the trees and the whole garden belong to no master now, but within each of us there is a master, whether there is one outside of me or not. No irresponsible behavior should be done by a person of responsibility."

The next story is about a young man who fell in love with his cousin. The cousin refused to marry him because of their close blood relationship. Although it was acceptable in ancient China for a cousin on the mother's side to be married to a cousin on the father's side, the young girl still refused the young man's love, and he became greatly saddened. After some time, the young man became rich. In his innermost heart, however, he felt empty and began to desert his current wife and three children. He drank, took drugs and kept a mistress who looked like his cousin. He spent a great deal of money on this girl because of her resemblance to the cousin he had truly loved.

The young man knew that he was squandering his life and money and believed it was solely because of his disappointment in love. Do you believe his reason was real? Then why, when the opportunity to marry his cousin later occurred, did he feel his love no longer existed? Which was real to him, his mind or his love? If his mind was the true reality, it could not be altered. If the love had been reality, why was it alterable? Can true love be changed by the passage of time? Is there ever "true love" between girls and boys? Must true love be expressed by possession? Why does the difficulty of obtaining things always make them more desirable, and why are the most common goods the most valuable in terms of human survival?

The fourth story takes place in a temple. An old master once declared, "The true mind is not a formed mind. The mind that is formed is just a response to circumstance, thus it is not the unformed, true mind. When sailing on the ocean, one is not aware of smooth water, but when the water becomes rough one quickly notices it. Which part is the true ocean? Which is not?

"The 'false' mind is the conceptual mind that has taken form by reacting to specific situations. What is formed is no longer the 'substance' of the mind - once expressed, it becomes matter. True mind has no shape, no form, no direction and no preference. Ordinary people pay attention only to the reactions and formulations of the conceptual mind and neglect the quietly existing true mind, but one who practices the Integral Way values the original, unformalized mind more than its reactions to specific events. Similarly, people of vulgar religions worship expressed spiritual events while those who practice the Integral Way worship the unexpressed subtleness of integrity."

In the neighborhood of this temple, there happened to be a fox's nest. Foxes are smart animals and they like to imitate humans. One moonlit night the local foxes had a spiritual meeting like that of their neighbors. The old leader of the foxes, who was sitting in front of the group, began his lecture with "The true mind is not conceptual. The conceptual mind is not the true mind..." and so on, until a dog appeared. At this time, all the foxes rushed away. It is easy to talk like a master, but it is hard to cultivate and maintain an undisturbed, true mind.

The old master had something more to say, "The wooden fox has a true mind." Do you believe this? If you do, are you an idiot? If you do not, are you a fool? Tell me, what is the truth behind this?

At the age of six, I used to play in the carpentry workshop of a neighbor. He specialized in making round shaped wooden vessels, hence his tools were somewhat different from those of a regular carpenter. One day, I wished to make something of my own and played carelessly with some newly sharpened chisels. Being unskilled at using the tools, I inevitably chiseled my left index finger instead of the wood. It was a deep cut and the finger was almost gone. It bled profusely and was very painful. With my mother watching nervously and my brother and sister surrounding me, I cried bitterly as my father put medicine on the finger and confidently mended it.

My father quietly asked me, "Why do you cry so nervously?"

"It hurts!" I yelped.

"How do you know you are in pain?" he asked.

"I feel it! My mind feels it."

"Then it is pain and not your mind," my father calmly corrected me.

At that time I did not understand what my father said. I was too busy with the pain to ask further questions. Years later my father took my hand, looked at the scar on my left index finger and asked, "Do you feel pain now?"

"Of course not," I replied.

He continued, "Didn't I tell you that it was pain and not the mind? Pain will pass, but not the mind. Ordinary people complain with their mind. An achieved one dissolves the real trouble."

Dear friend, can you give equal attention to the troubled mind and the true mind? Which serves you more? Have you ever known the existence of the true mind as being the quiet, faithful servant of your life being? Yet is it not always neglected by you? You may complain with your mind and exaggerate your troubles, but is it your mind which creates stories to separate you from the truth, or something else which does all of this? Is it the unformed true mind or the false mind which lacks simplicity and clarity that causes you unnecessary confusion? Who should be charged with the responsibility? Can you accurately use your mind? Or does your mind command you? Can you separate the rough waters of the ocean from the peaceful waters, or should one separate the roughness from the peacefulness? In other words, should we create separation between troubles and the mind in spiritual practice? What is the real value of this? Please ask yourself.

44　姤　KOU ☰☴

εncountεr · mεεting togεthεr

GUIDANCE: *"Encounter. It is like an overly strong woman who has difficulty in being a good wife. Do not marry such a woman."*

Heaven is above the Wind. The blowing Wind touches everything in its course, thus there is encounter. The situation appears to be smooth. The image suggests that everything will go as one wishes. However, hidden danger approaches in the form of the forward yin line below. Negative force has begun to grow again as yang energy has reached its fullest strength. One should be careful of this situation and heed the warning of this hexagram.

The image here is that of five men competing for one woman. The situation is one of potential contention and struggle. This single element of feminine energy can spoil the union of five men. The woman cannot marry all five; peaceful order depends on her ability to respond correctly to each of them. She must maintain composure and conduct herself well; otherwise she becomes a source of trouble.

The yin line here represents any negativity, darkness, shortcoming or bad habit. The entire hexagram suggests that this negative energy will eventually overcome the positive, for the yang is structured in such a way that it submits to the power of yin and thus becomes susceptible to the dark influence. This process, a cyclical movement of natural energy, represents gradually coming under the control of some inner negativity, bad habit or physical illness. The developing yin energy exerts more and more influence as it aggressively advances toward the five yang lines. In the human sphere, changes can be made to alter the situation. Therefore, one should now be cautious and maintain his position, otherwise the situation will deteriorate.

This hexagram may also apply to a great task in which a person of inferior virtue becomes involved. Since the five yang lines do not cooperate and hold to correct principles, a way is provided for the erosive power of an evil force to grow. Although such a situation is not a favorable one, it is a natural phase of the cyclic energy rotation.

This hexagram is associated with the fifth month (June/ July), just after the apex of Summer, when yang energy is at its highest. At this point, yang begins its decline and yin energy increases as Winter approaches. The situation symbolized by this energy formation actually serves as a warning. In life, a person is usually overcome by a problem through negligence. As the *Tao Teh Ching* advises: "Handle difficulties when they are still small."

On the whole, this hexagram employs the image of a man in the fourth position wishing to meet the woman in the first position, but he is unable to do so. He has four competitors and she is ambitious in her desire to conquer. Moreover, her contact with some of the other lines precludes any involvement she might have with the fourth line. There is no chance for a correct response between them, because each is in the wrong position. The first line should be yang, and the fourth line should be yin. Although the literal Chinese translation for this hexagram means "to come together"' it is impossible to do so.

On the positive side, this hexagram describes the energy involved in spreading culture's nurturing influence. Such efforts touch everyone and help to develop an entire society. Yin and yang continuously interact in every aspect of life; thus, this principle can be applied to all experiences.

Great things may sometimes be attained when we are aware of our limitations and shortcomings. Such an awareness allows us to work at preventing these limitations from overtaking us. By beginning with something small, something great may be accomplished in the end.

LINE 1: *"The restless sow is firmly restrained. The rolling wagon is safely stopped. Good fortune. However, if one goes ahead, there is trouble."*

For one of youth and inexperience (represented by the first yin line) self-restraint will prevent danger. The opportunity of the present circumstance appears to be propitious. However, in reality it will not foster positive growth.

If one in this position acts aggressively and radically, like a young girl who tries to make contact with all the men she meets, danger and misfortune will surely result. This yin line, like a hungry sow, is restless and causes disturbance.

If this line changes to yang, everything will turn out well. Then this hexagram evolves into Chyan, the Creative or Heaven. There could be nothing more beautiful than pure yang energy!

LINE 2:   *"There is a fish in the kitchen.   It is not for outsiders."*

Here there are five men and one woman. Competition exists here because the second line is centered and in a naturally responsive position to the first. The first line is the fish which belongs to the second line. If the second line takes charge of the situation while matters are still controllable and before things become "messy," order will be maintained.

If the second line can exert its yang energy in the beginning to put the "fish" safely under its control, there will be no overall problem.

LINE 3:   *"The skin of the buttocks is hurt.   One is restless and hesitant.   Neither good fortune nor a big problem exists because there is still no real connection."*

Restlessness makes one uncertain in movement. However, no great loss has yet occurred. The position of this line is similar to the fourth line of Hexagram #43, Resolution. Line three, confronted with danger, would like to move forward but is unable to do so. Line four in #43, although faced with difficulties, continues to push forward. Such movement, however, only creates further problems. If it would relax and not be persistent, its problems would subside; however, it pursues its own impulses and creates more obstacles.

The lower trigram of #44, ☰, is the direct opposite of the upper trigram of #43, ☱ . The second line of #43 and the fifth line of #44 both have direct contact with and respond to the yin line in each hexagram. Both the third line of #44 and the fourth line of #43 wish to be in direct contact with the yin line, but are unable to do so.

Seeing things clearly at this point can prevent further problems.

Energy correspondence occurs in two ways. Relationships are formed between the first and the fourth, the second and the fifth, and the third and the sixth lines. The first and second, third and fourth, and fifth and sixth lines also form a unit and correspond. In hexagrams #43 and #44, the second principle applies. The first and second lines in #44, and the fifth and sixth lines in #43, form a harmonious bond which excludes the third line of #44 and the fourth line of #43.

LINE 4: *"There is no fish in the kitchen. Movement brings danger. One is separated from reality. This is like a government that is separated from the people."*

Both the first and fourth lines are in the wrong positions for a correct response. Furthermore, there is rivalry and competition among the yang lines for the yin energy below. The fourth line has traveled far in order to court the first line, but she is no longer available.

LINE 5: *"The big tree overshadows. It provides a supportive framework and protects the gourds. The gourds will ripen and fall naturally. The vines will also wither, but the tree remains stout, upright and unshaken by matters which occur naturally."*

The other four yang lines represent the image of ripe gourds or melons hanging precariously from a weak vine represented by the first line. They can fall at any time. However, if the fifth line can stay firm and stout in order to unite the other four yang lines, it will be able to determine the outcome of the situation. With the cooperation of the second line which is in the front line of combat, the approaching difficulty can be faced. The fifth line should do its best without becoming discouraged by knowledge of the inevitable consequences of the growing negative force. This will be its only good opportunity.

LINE 6: *"Meeting at the tip of a horn. Nothing can be achieved, though there is no grave danger."*

This line describes one who is proud and isolates himself from his leader and the rest of the group. He is narrow-minded, uncooperative and goes his own way. There is no blame for this, because he stays far away. He has lost his ability to cooperate with others and has backed into the tip of a horn, hoping for the feeling of limited security. His self-interest makes life even more narrow and confining. Eventually he has no courage to resist the evil and cannot maintain himself. He thus loses the opportunity to return to the normal, broader scope of life.

SPECIFIC GUIDANCE

PERSONAL FORTUNE: Small matters bring good fortune. Large undertakings are not profitable, especially for men.

MARRIAGE: Possible success for a time, but no harmony in the end.

HOUSING/FAMILY: The place is not auspicious.

CHILDBIRTH: Easy. The ripe watermelon on the weak vine falls simply and naturally.

LOOKING FOR WORK: Rely on a woman to help you.

SOCIAL/GOVERNMENTAL POSITION: Successful, but not profitable.

SEARCHING FOR SOMEONE: They may be in the South, with a relative's family.

LOOKING FOR SOMETHING LOST: Difficult to find, but if you rely on a woman, it can be found.

HUNTING FOR THIEVES: They are in the Southwest and can be caught.

LAWSUIT: A long time is needed.

CLIMATE: It will be cloudy and windy.

TRAVEL: Travel to the North will be auspicious. Do not be kept by a woman, this is not good fortune.

DISEASE: Some danger.

PERSONAL WISH: If the wish is too big, disaster.

COMMENTARY
The Untrue Mind

Just as in the hexagram Kou, ☰, where the aggressive yin energy cannot harmonize with the higher yang energy, at a deep level the mind cannot harmonize with nature and thus the untrue mind is formed. The following story is one of my early experiences in dealing with this problem.

It seems impossible to know the true mind unless you first learn to recognize the untrue mind. Once I asked my father about this. He said that he could help me study the fundamental principles of Chinese medicine, but that the high practice of the traditional healing art could not be put into words. It is a matter of skill achieved through development. In the same manner, the question of true mind is a matter of real achievement and practice, it is not a matter of discussion or information gathering. My father wished for me to discover the answer myself and thus be truly benefited by that which I had accomplished.

Because of the frustration of wanting to understand all spiritual truth in one second, I put myself through years of active inquiry, study and experience and so began my spiritual journey. One of those experiences is related in the commentary entitled "Premature Enlightenment." The following experience occurred before my premature enlightenment and was several years before I had received the truth. This story is but one episode in the long process of my spiritual cultivation.

Some years after my initial exploration of the nature of true mind, I remarked to my father, "I have discovered that the true mind is not the colorful construction of all religions. Nor is it the atmosphere created by the many different churches and temples. Neither is it the different doctrines and rituals practiced in various ceremonies and celebrations. These practices are just various expressions of human custom and are not the ultimate, immutable truth. None of them has any solution to the question of life and death; they are merely useless decorations for the plain process of human life and death. Not one of them is the result of the discovery of truth. They serve only as psychological coverings or artistic beautification to human disappointment and despair. Beneath all these different forms of entertainment, these ornamental measures, lies utter impoverishment and helplessness. Such religious practices go against the true mind. To follow a religion is to proceed in the opposite direction of the true mind."

I paused here for approval from my father. He responded, "What you say is not the practice of the true mind. The practice of the true mind is not the practice of criticism. In all the examples you mentioned, there is the opportunity for the important practice of non-bewilderment within any confused situation. In other words, the practice of the true mind as an accurate response on these occasions is the fundamental practice of clarity. The true mind is responsive, but it does not lose its clarity because of its own responsiveness."

At that particular moment I felt I had received the key and I expressed my gladness and good understanding. I said, 'Truly, truly, though the criticism was perceived through my achieved clarity, I separate my mind from the clarity when I criticize. Knowledge is something that has already been established, while clarity is the unformed, true mind. It can be compared with the relationship of the sky and clouds, knowledge being the clouds which hinder the clarity of the sky. From now on, I shall keep myself to the fundamental virtue of mind-clarity without deviation or separation by established knowledge or emotion."

My father responded, "Be careful, son. Clarity is only one virtue of the true mind. There are still equally important practices of the true mind, such as the practice of sincerity, the practice of freedom from temptation, the practice of the Mind of Non-Evasion In Any Moment, the practice of the Mind of Composure and Peace, the practice of the Mind of Non-Dissipation, the practice of Dispassion, the practice of the Unattached Mind, the practice of the Impartial Mind and the practice of the Mind of Harmony, among many other virtues. These are all important in attaining clarity of the mind.

"Among all virtues of the mind, only clarity and sincerity are basic powers of the true mind. Neither can be separated from the other. To have sincerity without clarity is foolish. To have clarity without sincerity is to be a disinterested bystander of worldly people and matters. Any single virtuous practice is a rigid or dogmatic practice. Obviously this is not the way to reach Tao.

"Also, be sure that a specific virtue is not neglected when facing a specific circumstance, otherwise you will lose the correct response of the true mind. Tao is the totality. Tao cannot be put into partial practice. The practice of a single virtue has helped some people earn fame as a so-called saint, but in reality this is using the entire being to fulfill what is a partial expression of life. This is why ordinary religious people are in danger of losing the view of the wholeness of life. This is one extreme. On the opposite side, ordinary non-religious people use their entire being to fulfill a single desire or emotional attachment. This is another extreme. Thus, cultivating the

wholeness of life is the complete development of an individual human being. If one has reached an understanding
of the wholeness of life, one can see that many past religious leaders and saints died before they had developed
themselves completely. In other words, they died for the
sake of only one part of their integral being. As heavenly
models, this was misleading and actually a serious matter
of personal underdevelopment. They set incomplete
examples which have misled those who followed. The
highest examples of complete virtue are not even recognized by most people since the leader with complete,
absolute virtue works quietly and subtly. When he has
accomplished his task and completed his duty, people say:
'It is we ourselves who have made it so.' Leaders who
have plain good virtue attract followers who like to be with
them and who respect and honor them. The forceful
leader creates a strong emotional response among people.
Among these virtuous beings, only the one of complete virtue
is the one we follow with complete willingness!"

At this moment, my previous enlightenment was
revealed in all its shallowness. I struggled with my young
pride and said, "Now I understand that the true mind is
the balanced mind. The true mind is the integral mind.
The true mind is the crystal clear mind. The true mind is
the transcendental mind, and the true mind is the
natural, unspoiled mind. It contains all positive virtues.
The fragmentary insistence on one or a few chosen virtues
is dangerous. Now I truly understand what the ancestors
said: 'Rigid practice is the thief and robber of the way of
the true mind."

May father said: "Well, even I can agree that now you
have something. The mind is part of our entire being.
The mind is the latecomer of our life being. In our life,
there are some things which are more fundamental. The
work you did with your mind was to remove the poisons
of the vulgar mind. There are not many more secrets of
the mind. The secret of life is chi, which precedes all
human life and continues to exist after the human flesh-
life has transformed. After studying the game of the
mystery of the mind comes the more important cultivation
of chi. One who only learns the mind may speak better,
but achieving real spiritual growth is another matter.
Herein lies the importance of cultivating chi."

45　　苹
　　　TSUI

CONGREGATION · GATHERING the essence

GUIDANCE: *"Congregating goes well. The great leader harmonizes the people of his nation with the temple of their common ancestor, Heaven. All people have the opportunity to be close to the leader during this time. A great sacrifice should be made as an offering. This is the right time to move forward and be creative."*

In this hexagram, Lake is above Earth. Lake represents joyfulness, and Earth represents obedience. Wherever there is water, there is life, and vegetation thrives. Animals also congregate where vegetation and water abound. Thus, this hexagram represents a peaceful and happy gathering of life.

The literal translation of T'sui means "to gather the essence," to gather those of harmonious spirit in order to unite their minds for a virtuous purpose. The gathering of diverse energies to accomplish a common goal is like gathering one's energy within. If the leader has a joyful spirit and the followers are obedient, their coming together becomes a beautiful gathering of good will. This kind of gathering promotes health and growth. However, one should still weed out harmful elements and maintain good order to enable one to be more productive.

A gathering of good, positive energy is an opportunity to renew oneself. After gathering one's essence or positive energy, one should then extend a loving universal nature to others. When something or someone seeks our help or advice, we should respond with our best energy. This is called uniting all virtues with one's universal love. Actually, this opportunity exists at every moment. No time is better than the present.

A more profound example of "gathering" occurs when one cultivates and gathers subtle energy. The gathering of spiritual energy is even more important than the gathering of food, because food supports only physical life.

A Divine Immortal is someone who has assembled the most highly refined energy. This is achieved by gathering essential energy every moment. It is through this continual practice of energy refinement that one can achieve the "crystal," "diamond" or "subtle" body. Though the physical body must disintegrate, the subtle body continues to live in the immortal realms. In the Integral Way, this is the highest meaning of gathering or assemblage in one's personal cultivation.

> **LINE 1:** *"Even if one has unquestionable sincerity, the correct purpose of the gathering may not be clearly understood. Confusion may still arise. Clarity and order are brought about by patience, firmness and the demonstrated sincerity of the group. Then the gathering becomes a happy one. There is nothing wrong. Proceed."*

In any gathering, order must be established in the beginning. The first line is a yin in a yang position which indicates scattered energy in the early stages. However, with help from the fourth line, the confusion can return to order.

> **LINE 2:** *"Recommendations bring good opportunities. There will be no trouble if one's sincerity has not altered. One need not worry that one's offering is insufficient."*

The second line, being at the center of the lower trigram, gathers all three yin lines together as a bridge to the fifth line. This gathering is for a spiritual purpose. In ancient times, such a gathering was signified by the ringing of a bell or gong. The fifth line, or leader, is able to gather others through the strength of his virtue and spiritual practice. Since the second line corresponds to the fifth, it brings everyone together in dedication to him.

> **LINE 3:** *"Aggressive tactics to join create difficulty. Although this appears unprofitable and small problems may arise, cautiously moving ahead is correct."*

This line is in an inappropriate position and thus suffers some frustration. It represents one who is overly eager to reach the top and, as a result, invites misunderstanding and creates an uncomfortable response. One who receives this line should try to avoid arrogance and doing things single-handedly. To do so will only result in isolation.

LINE 4: *"Great good fortune comes with brave conduct."*

Both the first and fourth lines are in incorrect positions. Correction of the situation comes from an interchange and integration of their energies which produces a positive influence.

This situation represents a virtuous person who is in an incorrect position. However, he does the right thing at the right time by selflessly supporting the weak beneath him and by being a good advisor to the leader in the fifth position.

LINE 5: *"One cannot depend on one's power and position to gather obedience. One must have great purpose, firmness and correctness. Only then is one safe from error."*

This virtuous leader guides people with his good spirit and is able to bring them together. He is benevolent and considerate to all the lines beneath him. He takes care of them and gives them protection. The lower trigram is also good-willed and reflects this goodness to the upper trigram. Thus, their interaction creates a harmonious union.

LINE 6: *"Sighs and tears. No blame."*

A real spiritual gathering must be a selfless matter for all concerned. The leader must know how to reflect good will and must be the catalyst for the integration of that good will. However, this line expresses a circumstance in which one is removed from others through pride and feels remorse for not having participated.

SPECIFIC GUIDANCE

PERSONAL FORTUNE: Although you will be safe, you should still be careful. Even during the most peaceful of times one should not neglect potential danger.

MARRIAGE: Can be achieved.

HOUSING/FAMILY: Be careful about floods.

CHILDBIRTH: A baby girl. Good fortune.

LOOKING FOR WORK: It is good to cooperate or unite with military people.

SOCIAL/GOVERNMENTAL POSITIONS: Success later.

TRADE/BUSINESS: Success.

SEARCHING FOR SOMEONE: Look in the Southwest and you can meet them.

WAITING FOR SOMEONE: They will come.

LOOKING FOR SOMETHING LOST: Look in the Southwest. However, it is difficult to find.

HUNTING FOR THIEVES: They (three people) are in the East and can be caught.

LAWSUIT: Good fortune.

CLIMATE: There will be drought for a long time.

TRAVEL: It will be dangerous. There will be quarreling.

DISEASE: Difficult to cure.

PERSONAL WISH: Can be accomplished.

COMMENTARY
No Idolization

Among the undeveloped, "idolization" is often used to assemble people. However, in cultivating spiritual growth, "idolization" can be an obstacle if it is incorrectly applied. The following gives instruction and guidance as to its influence in spiritual matters.

> *"Confucianism is my garment,*
> *Buddhism is my cane, and*
> *Taoism is my sandal."*

This "three-in-one" spiritual movement was the actual response of a vast number of Chinese people in the Tang Dynasty (618-906 A.D.) to the rise of Buddhism, which prospered because of the support of the royal court and thus became the third most important element in Chinese cultural life. Most Chinese scholars accepted this new cultural condition by considering Confucianism, Taoism and Buddhism as the three legs of a cauldron. In ancient Chinese symbology, the Caldron represents unification, thus Confucianism, Taoism and Buddhism became the harmonizing forces in the lives of Chinese people.

My family's work of cultural integration involved only the awakening of the Chinese people. Our real cultural foundation was the *Book of Changes* which expresses the principles of balance, symmetry, evenness, equality and harmony. Sometimes this book is considered mystical because its principles are expressed with signs instead of words. Many scholars have been perplexed by the signs of this book's ancient metaphors and concise language. The key to the *Book of Changes* is to maintain balance in all situations involving change. With such eminent guidance for life and culture, it is not unusual that Chinese scholars would adopt an attitude of harmonization amid the cultural conflicts of their time.

Under the high principles of the *I Ching*, these three schools functioned mainly as different educational sources for the majority of Chinese people. Though each appeared to be independent of the other, each actually absorbed the other in the course of time. In our present generation, a careful scholar would have no difficulty discovering that present-day Confucianism absorbed Taoism. Taoism also absorbed Confucianism. Buddhism also combined with religious Taoism.

Hermetic Taoism unavoidably responded to the new situation by adopting a principle of "balanced cultivation," which meant keeping conceptual training on a level with spiritual training. After the Tang Dynasty, some ancient leaders from the Taoist tradition actually became the practical leaders of this new spiritual integration, with achievements that have been recorded throughout history.

My father was in his late years when I was born; thus, when I was in my teens and began to know and understand things, my father had already achieved spiritual maturity and could enjoy his high achievement. I greatly benefited by the broad background he provided me.

The three lines which begin this chapter were an inspiration to me. I wrote them on a piece of paper and put them on the wall of my study. The words happened to be heard by one of my father's serious friends who was most appreciative of them. This man shared the words with all his friends because they actually expressed the harmonizing attitude of Chinese people: they adopted Confucianism as their social and family mode; they adopted Buddhism as their emotional support; and they practiced Taoism in their practical life.

On one occasion I met my father's highly developed friend and he remarked: "I heard that you wrote: 'Confucianism is my garment, Buddhism is my cane, and Taoism is my sandal.' At your age, how much can you know about Confucianism, Buddhism and Taoism? Now, you must tell me. If your answer does not meet with my satisfaction, I will not let you go home. I shall keep you here in my study to finish reading my long years' collection of good books."

My answer was: "You asked about my garment; please ask the tailor. You asked about my cane; please ask the cane-maker. And you asked about my sandal; please ask the shoe-maker."

He seemed surprised and pleased. After a moment he exclaimed: "Your answer is unbelievable! If it were from the mouth of an aged master, it would be very meaningful, but it came from a young boy like you. However hard it is to believe, I am convinced. A father tiger never gives birth to a dog son."

He then asked his family to come into the living room to meet me. Now I could leave with a light heart. However, this matter was not yet over. He later repeated our dialogue to his good friends. With bewilderment and skepticism, this group of friends met to discuss the matter and, wishing to discover the truth about me, invited me to their meeting. I sat quietly among all these elders of my father's spiritual kingdom.

While everybody was leisurely sipping their tea, the chair elder said to me: "We heard of Mr. Lin's profound experience with you. He told us about your conversation and gave you a high evaluation for spiritual achievement. We have hoped for someone in the younger generation to be able to do something for the world, but this is not something that can be expected of a particular person without the real approval of the Divine Realm. Spirituality has its own unmistaken standard of what is true and what is not true. Now we would like to see for ourselves how you present the tradition in front of us, since you say: 'Confucianism is your garment, Buddhism is your cane, and Taoism is your sandal.'

"We are not concerned with how much you have read about Confucianism or Buddhism, or even how much you know about Taoism. What we would like to know is that if Confucianism is the garment, Buddhism is the cane, and Taoism is the sandal, then who is the user? Now tell us, who is the true one who dresses himself in the garment, holds the cane, and wears the sandal? This is all we need to know. It is a rule that you not hesitate in answering the question."

"The awakened Chinese people," was my answer.

Everybody seemed quite satisfied, but the examination continued. "What do you mean by the awakened Chinese people?"

"Six thousand years ago there were no teachings of Confucianism, Buddhism and probably none of Taoism either. Furthermore, those people did not consider themselves as "Chinese" people who were different from other people. People such as they are the ones who truly use and enjoy all of these teachings. Clothing should be made to fit the people; people should not be made to fit the clothing."

Their level of interest seemed to be increasing, thus the questioning continued.

"Why do you specify the 'awakened' Chinese people and not all the people of China and the rest of the world?"

"This is the level the 'awakened' Chinese people have reached. When all the people of the world reach this same level, freedom from religious and philosophical conflicts can be realized and the harmonization of the human spirit can be reached."

"You said that six thousand years ago, there were no teachings of Confucianism, Buddhism, nor were there written words of Taoism, and that the people of China did not know they were "Chinese." And that people such as those are the ones who truly use and enjoy all of these teachings. And furthermore that clothing should be made to fit the people; people should not be made to fit the clothing.' Exactly how much of this is your own contribution?"

"I do not claim original credit for this point of view. Rebellious people also use these words, but what they say has no true spiritual value. My spiritual value was obtained from serious cultivation, thus I do not speak out of rebellious ignorance. From spiritual achievement I am able to reach the truth. I value the healthy spiritual education that the past human race developed. I deny anything which can be an obstruction in reaching the truth."

"Wait a moment," one of them exclaimed, "this is the point we really need to know. Now, what is the truth you have reached, and by what books were you inspired? Quickly, tell us!"

In this room was a table on which were many different important books and translations of world religions. At this moment I was inspired and stacked all the books into one pile as a stool and sat on them. Someone then passed me one copy of Lao Tzu and one copy of Chuang

Tzu, and said: "Take these also, to make you sit higher."
When I refused, he demanded the reason.

I answered: "I know what is beneath me, and what is
not beneath me."

"That is an evasive answer. What is your real
answer?" he demanded.

"In response to your demand, I can see you are
worried that I idolize these books as my innermost
precious spiritual treasure. I would ask that you recognize that I have not idolized anything. I earnestly give
recognition to Lao Tzu, the source of my spiritual nursing,
and to Chuang Tzu, who postulated that even the intimate
truth - Tao, the great true Oneness - cannot be idolized.
Thus, allow me not to be an ungrateful student and
friend."

One of the elders then slowly explained the following
to me: "This point is the most important heritage of our
spiritual family. Though it is already clear to you, it is
absolutely necessary that it be made explicit. It must
never become confused or mixed up. The spiritual
practice of some traditions of the world is to deny the
idolization of anything. But as a consequence, one consciously or unconsciously begins to idolize oneself instead.
This is a practice of shallowness and rigidity and is a
spiritual dead end. Some spiritual traditions deny all
nameable things, yet affirm 'oneself' or the 'self,' thus they
have reached nowhere. The one who follows the true path
knows that everything in the universe is already oneself.
There is nothing that can be denied without 'self,' nor is
there anything that can be affirmed as 'self.' If everything
is denied, then the 'self' is affirmed. If the 'self' is denied,
then who is the one making the denial? None of them
has reached the breakthrough of the two-sided spiritual
practice of yin and yang. In other words, they have not
reached spiritual unity.

"In our spiritual family ('family' meaning the followers
of the true path), when we deny the idolization of
anything, our purpose is not to affirm 'self' but to present
the wholeness of Tao, which is already an integration of
everything, including the 'self.' This is the reason Tao is
indefinable. Total harmony and spiritual unity can be
achieved when idolization of all things is removed. This is
not accomplished with a negative spirit, as in other traditions, but it is achieved by following a balanced and
harmonized path which leads to Tao. Tao is the integrity,
the wholeness, of the origin. Thus we do not accept any

name for the unspoiled naturalness of the great reality of the oneness. As you know, this is how your father guided all of us."

Finally, they seemed to have reached an understanding that they need not trouble me with further questions. Spiritually I had almost reached their level. Then, the atmosphere of the meeting changed again. Another elder asked: "We feel satisfied with the growth of your positive spirit. On a practical level, it can be interpreted as: no life should be sacrificed, nor wars fought for religious reasons or conceptual conflicts. To illustrate, the common people of China eat swine; however, the Chinese Islams do not. There were two villages in the western region of China. One village raised and ate swine, while the Islamic village did not. This incident was enough to cause a great battle between the two villages. This is a simple example of exaggerating a 'principle' and then using it as justification for conflict.

"Another example of this principle from history was the Crusades. What did people who participated in those persecutions accomplish except exaltation of religious prejudice?"

Another elder then said: "The real problem is not the pervasion of religious prejudice, it is the darkness of people's minds. Thus, they find excuses to fight over religious teachings. There is no way to correct this except by the spiritual development of the entire world. Achieved people know the 'true mind' and do not fall prey to idolization of religious leaders or doctrines.

"When one holds tightly to a concept, clarity is lost. If clarity is lost, the situation can never be rightfully handled. Having a 'leader' is no longer a good concept because emotions have now become the 'ruler.' Even if a good idea is presented, by idolizing it - putting it into a rigid mold - its connection with the original truthfulness is lost and much harm can undoubtedly be caused.

"For example, in one of our big cities, there was a young girl who wanted to marry a boy with a completely different culture and religion than hers. Her parents were opposed on the principle that marriage alone would be difficult for two young people, but to bridge two entirely different worlds of cultural and religious upbringing would be an impossible task. They considered this relationship to be an especially bad match because of their strong attachment to their own religion and they feared that such a marriage could dilute the religious beliefs of the next generation.

"The boy and girl were idealistically in love and believed they could transcend their cultural differences and find a common ground. The influence of the discouraging parents on both sides, however, strongly affected the couple and eventually the young lovers killed themselves.

"Another example is one's love for nation. Such a situation is similar to one's idealistic love for a child, in that emotions dominate; thus, one's ability to be clear and right-minded is lost. The issue of politics is similar to the issue of emotions in that both are the real reasons behind the actions which affect most people."

After further discussion, the eldest member made his stately conclusion and directed it towards me: "It will not be very far in the future when darkness will over-power this part of the world. You are the one who will be able to provide the light. If our material possessions and anything else can be preserved, and if you need them, they will all be at your command. We also realize this could be our wishful thinking; however, this is the way for us to express our concern and support in awakening the entire world toward spiritual maturity without creating conflicts by idolizing spiritual images or human authorities. When people are not truly spiritually developed, power can make them mad. Power can be useful in helping to accomplish great virtuous merits when entrusted to the hands of virtuous world leaders."

When he finished his talk, he asked me to read the following chapter of Lao Tzu, and said, "After reading this, you may go."

This is what I read:

"When people of the world live in accordance
with the way of universal harmonization,
horses are used for agricultural purposes.

"When people of the world do not live in accordance
with the way of universal harmonization,
then horses and even pregnant mares
are driven to the battlefield and bred there.

"There is no greater calamity for a nation,
as well as for an individual,
than not to find one's own sufficiency
through peaceful measures.

"There is no greater mistake for a nation,
as well as for an individual,
than to be covetous of more and more
goods of another,
and thus become involved in contention."
(Chapter 46 of the Tao Teh Ching)

46   sheng   卅

RISING

GUIDANCE: *"This is a great opportunity to go forward to*
meet a great person.   No worry.   A southward expedition
brings good fortune."

In this hexagram, Earth is above Wind or Wood.   Like
a new sprout, Wood energy moves through the earth as it
grows upward.   This is the natural way of development.   It
is a gentle energy, abundant with life.   Earth symbolizes
obedience and Wind symbolizes gentle penetration.   When
they come together, great prosperity and high achievement
are the outcome of their natural interaction.

Steady growth is based on the accumulation of many
small progressions.   Power or wealth must come in small
increments to be well-utilized.   If they are obtained too
suddenly, one might go mad.   It is important that one is
not given more than he can handle at any one time.
Sometimes people are too anxious to progress, and their
ambition creates problems.   They forget that they are born
with the perfection of nature and that life itself is a slow
continuous process.

In youth, one always thinks of the future; in old age
one only remembers.   When the mind lingers only in the
past or future, growth is no longer possible.   This hexagram counsels one to emulate a young sprout by maintaining calmness and balance and allowing growth to evolve
naturally.

LINE 1: *"Rising is approved by everyone. Great good fortune."*

The first yin line is in a low position, like a tree which has its roots deeply planted in the earth. The second and third lines are like the trunk of a tree which extends from the earth. The roots beneath the earth consume water; the body of the tree absorbs sunlight. A prosperous life is expressed by this image of growth.

The first, second and third lines are cooperative, and together they promote mutual growth. This rising is agreed upon by everyone.

LINE 2: *"With sincerity and piety, as in making an offering to Heaven, one obtains happiness."*

During youthful development, one's offering is usually small, yet the intent is sincere. Here, the second line is moving toward the fifth position, from an inferior position to a superior one. It is the strength of this sincere spirit which enables it to rise. The upper trigram is weak and without the support of a strong leader. Thus, the second line can rise to the fifth position and assume leadership.

LINE 3: *"Rising to enter an unobstructed area. Have no doubts."*

This yang line is in the correct position and easily moves upward. Before it lies an empty, unobstructed territory. Movement proceeds without trouble or doubt.

LINE 4: *"The prince makes a great offering at the Western Mountain. Good fortune is naturally brought forth."*

This lines indicates promotion to a high position like that of an important minister. Because of his gentleness, this minister has been assigned by the King to perform the great offering to Heaven on the high mountain of Chi. This is clearly a good and enjoyable situation.

LINE 5: *"Correctness brings good fortune. Rising, one nobly achieves his goal."*

Greatness is obtained by the accumulation of small achievements. This line represents one who has risen from a low position to a high and is now the central line of this hexagram.

In meditation, images and signs sometimes appear. As a basic principle, regardless of whether these images are high beings or evil demons, one should remain calm. Most images are the result of being too ambitious, which causes the mind's clarity to be lost. When one is emotionally affected, one's spiritual energy is also influenced and, as a result, cannot grow well. Promotion, progress, and achievement which do not come at the right time cannot be considered fortunate. By accumulating small virtues one becomes great. This is the secret to the achievement of greatness.

> **LINE 6:** *"Continued rising brings self-impoverishment. One enters the realm of delusion."*

This is no longer the time for growth but for service. One who continues to rise will only reach darkness. This is an important time to move downward to support inferiors in the third position.

Do not fossilize your mind with fragmented intellectual knowledge. Open your mind to the subtle truth of the universe. Otherwise, you will become stagnant.

SPECIFIC GUIDANCE

PERSONAL FORTUNE: Things get progressively better and better.

MARRIAGE: It can be achieved.

HOUSING/FAMILY: A small household in the beginning grows larger.

CHILDBIRTH: The baby will be a girl.

LOOKING FOR HELP: Success will come later.

SOCIAL/GOVERNMENTAL POSITION: It can be achieved.

TRADE/BUSINESS: Profitable.

SEARCHING FOR SOMEONE: Look in the Northwest.

WAITING FOR SOMEONE: They will come.

LOOKING FOR SOMETHING LOST: It is in the Southwest, but is difficult to find.

HUNTING FOR THIEVES: If you hurry, they can be caught in the Southwest.

LAWSUIT: Good fortune.

CLIMATE: Although the weather will be rainy, soon after it will be fine again.

TRAVEL: This is the right time to go North if you are in the South. Going forward brings good fortune, hesitation brings misfortune.

DISEASE: Dangerous.

PERSONAL WISH: There is success, but nothing is accomplished in a hurry.

COMMENTARY

The timeless body of a superman was originally ours to have, but we destroyed ourselves with uncontrolled passions and lust. In our desire for wealth, fame and sensual love, we drowned.

Though we live a hundred years, time will pass quickly - empty pursuits will see to that. If our lives are conducted like a sloppily-run business, we will end our years with nothing.

Thus, always keep your mind empty, like the great space of the universe. Do not obstruct the smooth course of the waters and clouds. Flowing smooth and free, so should the mind be kept clear of sticky impediments.

Keep the same innocence inside as out. This is the way to wholeness. It is within you, the immortal, spiritual, subtle body. Do not mistakenly go begging and searching outside for it.

The road to becoming a Shien is clearly marked. It is your impatience and desires that blind your spiritual eyes. If you remove all covers and obstacles right here and now, you will know the origin of your life. A long pilgrimage is not necessary to find your source. If you get sidetracked on an evil path, try though you may to achieve self-cultivation, you will be moving against the Tao. Stay whole, stay clean, stay firm - and in one moment you can experience everything of Tao and become an adored child of Heaven.

47　囲 KUN ䷮

BesieGeᎠ · enᏒᏒΑpped · exhΑusᏒeᎠ

GUIDANCE: *"Entrapment. This is a time to keep to one-self. A great person nourishes his personality to alter his future. No blame, though now his words are not trusted."*

In this hexagram the Lake is above Water. The character K'un is formed by the image of a tree, 木 , surrounded by a very tight and confining environment, 囗 , resulting in, 困 , which is unable to grow freely and fully.

There are several other interpretations. For example, one is completely surrounded by water and can go nowhere. This situation is like being exiled on an island. Another is that of a lifeless, dry lake which has been drained by the larger body of water below and which represents exhaustion. The inner trigrams, Wood above Fire, symbolize a tree on fire or a situation of being "beseiged by enemies."

Each of the six lines represents a different stage of "entrapment" as applied to spiritual, mental and physical life. People are trapped by emotions, desires, fears, attachments and other "enemies" which the mind creates. These mental traps are usually just shadows of one's impulsiveness. However, when the mind becomes strong and balanced all so-called "enemies" disappear, both internally and externally. On the spiritual level, there are no real confinements other than those which we create.

The hexagram K'un indicates that this is an unfavorable time for development, especially for those who do not know how to use a situation for spiritual growth. Rather than lament over one's troubles, one should accept circumstances, gather and store energy for positive efforts, and wait for better times. No situation can last forever.

The *I Ching* offers helpful principles based on the laws of nature. If a person is self-developed, entrapment does not lead to despair but is a time to practice that which has been cultivated. Knowing the limitations of a circumstance can enable one to create the best possible opportunities from it and thus enjoy the fruits of any time or situation.

One's achievement is not really hindered by danger or difficulty. For a wise person, adversity and frustration actually become fertile soil for spiritual growth. When things run too smoothly, or if one becomes too accustomed to comfort and ease, there will not be enough strength or tolerance for overcoming an obstacle. There- fore, do not think of difficulty as something undesirable. The greater the difficulty, the greater the opportunity for growth.

Everyone has experienced confinement, restriction or bondage. Shallow people become depressed and forfeit self-responsibility, but those who practice self-cultivation make use of these occasions to learn. One has the choice of making the situation either positive or negative. Even in adverse times, the true nature of happiness can be maintained.

The normal tendency of people is to avoid difficulty. However, in times of being entrapped, the *I Ching* teaches stillness and quietude. During such times the mind is usually unbalanced, actions are not centered, and words are not believed. It is crucial to calm oneself, to gather and center one's energy, and to face, accept and exper- ience the difficulty. After one's eyes adjust to the dark- ness they will be able to see again. Likewise, after one adjusts to a new situation there may be an opportunity for reform, or a new solution to the problem may be found.

At this time nothing can be accomplished by emotional outbursts or through struggle. Facing difficulty is a test of one's personality. One cannot hope to develop integral- ly without encountering any trials or difficulties. In an artificially protected environment, growth is stunted. One who understands the principle of self-development and spiritual cultivation can reap true benefit even during times of entrapment.

Most people make sharp distinctions between what they believe to be good or bad fortune. However, if one knows how to cultivate oneself, any situation can be beneficial and productive. In good situations one can extend his kindness and talents selflessly to others. In confinement, one can cultivate oneself. As the ancients have said: "In times of adversity, cultivate yourself. In times of prosperity, help the world."

LINE 1: *"Entering a dark valley, one is trapped by bushes. For three years he cannot see the light."*

Desire is like a dark valley which does not allow things to be clearly distinguished. One is trapped in the bushes, unable to find a way out. This difficult situation takes a long time to dissolve. To struggle in such entrapment proves futile. Only by becoming calm and slowing the mind down can the situation possibly decrease or disappear.

When one is inwardly balanced and not dependent on external forces such as reputation, beauty, property or position, one is able to make adversity a spiritual pilgrimage. One who is impressed with wealth, position and fame becomes easily trapped by desire.

There is a story about a person who was confined to a dark cell for three years. During his confinement he developed the ability to see in the dark. With this special ability he later discovered many hidden treasures. Do not despair if you find yourself in darkness. Instead, profit from it!

LINE 2: *"Entrapped by feasting and honor. It is wise to keep to one's spiritual practices. To undertake a major expedition is dangerous. With self-awareness and patience, there is no great difficulty."*

The second line is trapped by favor. Favor which damages one's character is not truly favorable. When favor is bestowed, it is often in exchange for something, and the price one pays may be too high. Some people in high positions compromise their principles for favor. This line warns that accepting such favor may result in misfortune. Declining what is believed to be "favor" is often difficult; however, with reflection, one can learn to recognize misrepresentation and thus avoid the trap.

LINE 3: *"Entrapped by rocks and thorns and nowhere to go. One cannot meet one's close companion or wife. Danger."*

One is trapped by ignorance or egotism which causes isolation. Though there is correspondence with the top line, two strong lines are barriers to the connection.

LINE 4:   *"Trapped in a golden wagon, one moves slowly. This is a pity, but things turn out well in the end."*

The wagon represents an opportunity which comes late and slows progress. For a while there is humiliation. Although this line is weak, if it practices patience there is hope.

LINE 5:   *"One is in great distress and trapped by a difficult mission. Success comes only through slow and gradual progress. Spiritual practice should be maintained in order to strengthen oneself inwardly and to prepare oneself to accept the Heavenly blessing when it comes."*

This line represents one who is trapped by his kindness and gentleness. One is in a high position due to his virtue. Some people take advantage of such kindness. However, it is inappropriate for a virtuous leader to respond to evil with evil. One in a high position cannot counter-attack inferior people who try to blaspheme or disgrace him with their ignorance, aggression, or shallowness. The obstacles here are not one's own shortcomings, but rather the darkness of others. One can only allow the reality of one's own correctness and virtue to prove itself. In this way, one regains the faith of the people and one's virtue will be blessed by the Heavenly Realm.

LINE 6:   *"Entrapped by wild vines. One's arrogance causes discomfort. Thus he must be humble and gather himself in order to break out of bondage. Good fortune."*

Here one is trapped by self-aggrandizement or pride. This is a volatile situation; however, if one is remorseful and takes corrective actions there can be a change, a new start which will bring good fortune.

SPECIFIC GUIDANCE

PERSONAL FORTUNE: This time is not good. Remain calm and wait for better times.

MARRIAGE: The husband will die young.

HOUSING/FAMILY: The wife has some difficulty or sickness. Also, there may be a problem with the plumbing or water supply.

CHILDBIRTH: If there are no unusual circumstances, the delivery will be safe. If the fourth line is received, the baby will be a girl.

LOOKING FOR WORK: Difficulty at the beginning, but afterwards success is possible.

SOCIAL/GOVERNMENTAL POSITION: Difficult to achieve. If you succeed, your life is in danger.

TRADE/BUSINESS: Not successful.

SEARCHING FOR SOMEONE: They can be found.

LOOKING FOR SOMETHING LOST: Difficult to find.

HUNTING FOR THIEVES: They are hiding in the Southeast and can be caught.

LAWSUIT: Dangerous.

CLIMATE: It will be stormy with lots of rain.

TRAVEL: Good and profitable if the direction is in the Northwest.

BORROWING MONEY: No success.

DISEASE: Dangerous.

PERSONAL WISH: Difficult to achieve.

COMMENTARY
The Mystical Change of the Person
Who Succeeds in Connecting his Energy
with the Subtle, Divine Energy of the Universe

One is no longer tempted by former bad habits, nor does one chase after worldly pleasures. Old physical maladies gradually and completely disappear. The mind is right, and the body reflects one's righteousness.

One stands firmly on one's own two feet. Deep calm pervades one's internal and external atmosphere. One finds one has both the time and the energy to accomplish any task. One purifies oneself and is at peace with one's environment. One never becomes violent and has untiring patience with one's fellow beings. One is worry-free and always has a joyful heart. One is never jealous of another's prominence nor greedy for the possessions prized by others. One has no ambition to live a vain or luxurious life.

Because one eats simply, one maintains serenity. One keeps one's physical desire subdued and one's virtue high. One develops true and deep knowledge, dissolves all obstacles, and extends oneself to meet the straight and eternal Way. Thus, one experiences uncritically that concepts of life and death are merely the ebb and flow of the eternal breath of Tao.

One dissolves one's ego and with it all internal and external conflicts. One does not seek one's own longevity or personal happiness, nor does one struggle to hold onto material things. One does not use the speakable as truth to suppress those who are silent. One has no desire to go beyond one's means or ability. In one's pure mind, one holds no illusions or strange thinking.

One nurtures a firm character through selfless giving and self-oblivion. One never emphasizes that which one does as right, nor does one claim credit for one's undertakings. One knows things thoroughly from beginning to end. Virtuously, one knows there are certain things one will never do.

One avoids involvement in contests for worldly profit or glory. One is amiable and useful. One embodies harmonious equilibrium and creative appropriateness. One enjoys ease, both internally and externally. One strives only to surpass one's own virtue. One obeys the universal Spirit in order to evolve higher. Before touching the formed, one rests in the unformed. One enlightens oneself and never tires of awakening the world.

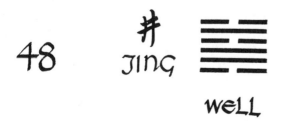

48   **JING**

WELL

GUIDANCE: *"A village can be changed and the people can move away, but a well cannot be changed or moved, it remains the same. When water is drawn from a well, the bucket or jar must be raised from the bottom in such a way that it does not hit against the sides of the well. Otherwise, the bucket or jar may be broken and the goal remain unachieved."*

In this hexagram Water is above, Wind or Wood is below. The lower trigram, ☴, when interpreted as Wind, is like air-pressure forcing underground water to surface. As it surfaces it becomes a fountain for all to enjoy. This kind of water is fresh and flowing in contrast to the water in a pond which is still and stagnant.

When the lower trigram is interpreted as Wood, it becomes the bucket that draws water from the ground. Thus, the image of a well is formed. This interpretation can also represent a tree that brings underground water up into the branches and the tips of the leaves.

In ancient China, a small community was comprised of eight families who often shared a central plot of land which contained a well for everyone's use. Thus, the character for a well is 井 . As the surrounding community changes, the well remains constant and stable. The well is not concerned with gain or loss. Its function is to provide sustenance for all.

An important aspect of this hexagram is the quality of the container and the method in which one draws water from the well. Likewise, a student or spiritual follower who uses the correct approach with his teacher obtains spiritual growth and also leaves the way open for other students to follow. One who abuses the well, or teacher, hinders that which can serve everyone.

The mind can be compared to a well. Its ideal state is one of clarity and quietude amidst the activities of daily life. Though the environment and those who come to the well change, the well remains true to itself. The message of this hexagram is to follow the example of the well by being peaceful and resourceful.

The image of the well can also be used to represent the different levels of our being. The water at the very bottom of the well is muddy, like the mind that is stirred by passion and desire. The rest of the water in the well can be compared to potential mental clarity. At this level, the particles that cloud the water have settled. Likewise, the particles of one's mind can also settle, allowing the mind to become stabilized and clean, thus returning to its original state. The top part of the well, from the water to the rim, symbolizes one's spirit.

The railing which surrounds a well is like the discipline which is needed to guide the mind. The well's

openness, usefulness and resourcefulness are characteristic of an unspoiled mind, and these attributes are the
source of public virtue and unselfishness. One's self-
development becomes like a well when one offers one's
service to others. On the highest level, individuality is
replaced with public service. However, just as there are
people who resourcefully draw from the well, there are
also those who dirty the water. Thus, one must take care
to keep the well and the mind in good shape and beware
of those who abuse or soil it.

Some people dig only three to five feet for water, and
upon striking rock, dig another hole and then another.
Because of their shallow effort, water is never reached.
An ancient proverb says that it is better to dig one well
deep enough to reach water than to dig nine shallow wells
which provide nothing. This principle applies to all life
endeavors. One must willing to work through the "rocks"
and difficulties in order to reach water. Of course,
knowing whether there is water or not is important. If
indeed there is, then one's hard work is rewarded by clear,
flowing water.

On another level, beyond the issues of commitment
and perseverance, this hexagram deals with the integral
development and spiritual achievement of an individual.
Knowing where to dig requires a deeper knowledge. Those
who rush about making many attempts at digging never
allow themselves enough time to "sense" where the water
is. Such intuitive ability is the result of one's self-
cultivation and development. Thus, one who is developed
depends upon his intuitive and spiritual achievement to
lead him to "water," instead of wasting a lot of energy
searching in many different directions.

In studying the individual lines of this hexagram, each
level of one's being can be analyzed through the metaphor
of the well. As the lines move from the bottom to the top,
the water becomes increasingly clear and more useful.

LINE 1: *"There is only dirt in the bottom of the well.
Nobody comes to drink from it; even birds avoid it. It
seems forsaken."*

The first line, being in the lowest position, is the base
of the well. The muddiness of the water at this level
renders it undrinkable. This image implies an unsettled
mind which is clouded by desires and attachments. One

whose mind is soiled is generally useless and avoided by others.

However, this situation can be used as an inducement for self-improvement. Although the lotus originates from mud, its beauty is not in the least bit soiled. Similarly, all achieved beings have worked through all kind of struggles and trials in order to transcend the turbulence of their minds.

LINE 2: *"The fountain of the well is weak. Only frogs can prosper there. One's bucket is leaking; no water can be drawn."*

Sometimes, one may hope to obtain information or help from someone who is not in position to offer it. The quality of one's readiness, preparation, or ability to draw sustenance from the well is indicated here. Such a quality is like the rope which holds the jug. It must be long enough to reach deeply into the well in order to draw the water. The fact that the well is too deep may not be the problem. It is possible that the rope is too short.

This line also represents the relationship between the well and the one who draws the water, or the relationship between a teacher and a student. One who cannot reach the depth of the water may not be ready for, or making full use of his teacher. What matters most is the degree of one's willingness and receptivity to learn.

LINE 3: *"The well is clean. It would be a pity not to drink from it. Likewise, a great leader's clear-mindedness is a source of blessing to all, for he is the only one who knows how to put the right person in the right job."*

Now the well is clean. The remaining dirt in the water settles to the bottom so that the water can be drunk. Unfortunately, such a valuable process is ignored. Why? Is it the destiny of the well, or because of poor insight on the part of the people?

LINE 4: *"Rails are placed around the well for protection. Correct."*

A well, or any source of continually flowing water, requires maintenance and care. Though one has much to offer, one still needs self-discipline and firm principles in order to make oneself most effective.

LINE 5: *"Pure, clean water is available to all."*

This line represents a well of cool, sweet water which is ready for consumption. One's helpful and useful personality is available as an example to all.

LINE 6: *"Do not cover the well. It should be constant in providing sustenance. Great good fortune and high achievement."*

The water in the well continuously replenishes itself. It sustains all, without favor or condition. One who emulates the virtue of the top line has the spirit of open-mindedness and universal love and benefits all who come to drink.

> *It is sad to see.*
> *The well is deep.*
> *The water is shallow.*
> *The rope is short.*
> *The bucket is broken.*
> *If one cannot reach the depth of the well,*
> > *perhaps one's shallowness*
> > *keeps him from tasting the sweet waters;*
> > *perhaps the water in the well is too shallow.*
>
> *One who is limited is unable to know*
> > *the limitations of the well.*
> *Both situations can be seen,*
> > *but they cannot be solved by inflexibility.*
> *They can only be remedied by further development.*
>
> *May the water from the Heavenly fountain*
> > *cleanse our being.*
> *May the water from the Heavenly fountain*
> > *quench our spiritual thirst.*
> *May the water from the Heavenly fountain*
> > *cure our wounds.*
> *May the water from the Heavenly fountain*
> > *bless us all.*

SPECIFIC GUIDANCE

PERSONAL FORTUNE: Keep to yourself, otherwise there will be more damage and less profit.

MARRIAGE: Half good, half bad.

HOUSING/FAMILY: If the house is too close to water, it will not be peaceful.

CHILDBIRTH: Neither safe nor easy.

LOOKING FOR WORK: Some time is needed, but there is success.

SOCIAL/GOVERNMENTAL POSITION: Not successful.

TRADE/BUSINESS: Difficult to succeed. If the business is successful, it will also be very profitable.

SEARCHING FOR SOMEONE: Difficult to find them.

LOOKING FOR SOMETHING LOST: It can be recovered.

HUNTING FOR THIEVES: Difficult to catch them.

LAWSUIT: A very long time is needed. The dispute is over land.

CLIMATE: There will be rain for an extended period of time.

DISEASE: An acute illness with a slow cure.

PERSONAL WISH: Difficult to achieve.

COMMENTARY
Purity of Mind

When the full moon arrives in the heights of the sky,
a breeze blows over the water.
I believe there are not many
who know the taste of purity.

-a poem by a nature poet of the Chin Dynasty (265-419 A.D.)

A pond of half an acre
is like a mirror reflecting the sky.
From high in the sky often comes
the shadow of flying clouds,
making their visit then quickly passing.
How can I attain such purity?
Because within me there is a living fountain.

-a poem by a philosopher of the Sung Dynasty (960-1279 A.D.)

These are two poems my father brushed in red ink on Chinese bamboo paper. When I was five, he made me copy his written characters in black ink, as my initiation into ancient Chinese cultural life. In my time, pre-school education was given to children by their parents. I was not special. However, the material my father adopted was different from what other families used, and it was this which was engraved upon my innocent heart.

It is the true knowledge of all developed people that no life can be free from troubles, but the mind can be trouble-free after spiritual achievement. The unaffected mind is often illustrated by analogy with the sky and clouds. The passions or emotions with which people react to troubles are like the clouds, or the "substance" of the mind. The true mind, which can take the troubles and reactions and yet remain unchanging, is like the sky.

Various reactions to the occurrence of "clouds" covering the "sky" - i.e., the passions, emotions, or pain which overcome the mind - developed into different attitudes or modes or responses toward the problem. An intellectual would conclude that since it is the "clouds" that cause the trouble, it is the "clouds" that should be dispersed. In the view of some Buddhist teachings, it is the "sky" which should be destroyed since it is the canvas on which trouble can occur. Most other religions invite thieves to catch thieves. They chase thieves away, but invite new ones to come. This is simply substituting an artificial faith or a strong image to support the falseness of the reacting mind.

In contrast, developed ones apply the principle of naturalness, leaving the "sky" as the "sky" and distinguishing it from the "clouds" which come and go and which can therefore never really affect the vastness and profundity of the "sky," that is to say, the true mind.

Intellectualizing or analyzing the clouds, or "tearing down the sky" (denouncing the mind completely as the way of solving all problems at once), or using thieves to govern thieves, are all ways of responding to the same phenomena. However, in spiritual understanding, the "clouds" enable the beauty of the sky to be appreciated, and the beauty of the "sky" is what gives significance to the "clouds."

On a conscious level, it is easy to see the association of "clouds" and "sky" with pain and with the mind which experiences pain. When one appears to exist, the other is also present. Balance should always exist as the normal relationship between the mind and its feelings. The elementary practice of the true, unaffected mind can help one reach the true path. For a balanced mind there is nothing to talk about; for an excited mind, there is always much to discuss. To maintain quiet-mindedness is an achievement, though it is not a rigid demand in spiritual cultivation. Nothing can be rigidly practiced in the Integral Way, because it is not a dogmatic religion.

Once a man whose life had been full of misery came to seek guidance from my father. In order to retreat from his previous worldly life, he had gone to live in a temple in the mountains. Usually, a visitor who had traveled a long way would stay with us for several days. My father received this guest in our garden. As a pupil and attendant of my father, I could see from our guest's eyes, eyebrows, and overall face that although he had retreated from the troubled world, his mind had not completely retreated from his past troubles. During this meeting my father offered him no guidance; instead, my father was more involved in watching a young cat chase a butterfly and its shadow around a flower bush. The butterfly flew here and there, lower and higher, nimble and elusively, while the young cat anxiously tried to catch it. My father's involvement with this scene naturally directed our attention to the cat. The butterfly now flew away, but just as the cat began to relax, it flew back again. This repeated challenge and provocation made the cat even more intent in its desire to catch the butterfly. "To catch it" became the sole necessity of the cat, because it seemed the cat would not admit failure, as I could understand through my own excited blood flow.

Presently, my father had to leave to take care of a patient, and the guest and I were alone in the garden. Without moving our eyes away from the scene of the cat and the butterfly, he asked me, "What does your father teach you now?"

"He asks me to recite the ancient medical books."

"Medicine has no Tao," he commented, and continued, "Start early. Do not be too late to learn the Tao, as I was. My life was full of events. Now my mind is full of misery. My life was eroded by all those unworthy experiences. What you cultivate in one day now may take me long years to achieve."

"But my father once told me, 'The ancient medicine is Tao in a narrow way of practice. Tao is medicine in the broad way of practice. Other than the healing effects of

Tao as medicine, our tradition has little to offer the ordinary world."'

The man was astonished to hear my answer. Just then, the cat suddenly jumped to catch the butterfly, which barely escaped.

After we both recovered from the tension created by watching the great chase, he retorted: "If the Tao is medicine, there should be no incurable disease. If this is so, then why has all my family died? As you can see, many people have died from disease."

His retort made me impatient. I was busy taking sides in the great chase - sometimes I took the side of the cat, and other times, the side of the butterfly. I always silently "hurried" the one who moved more slowly. At the same time, I was anxious about the "real catch."

Then I exclaimed, "My father said that there is no incurable disease. There are only incurable people."

"Ah!" was his only utterance. I was not sure if his "ah" was aimed at me, at the danger of the butterfly, or at the pathetic expression of the cat's failure. I decided his "ah" was for me, not fully understanding what he meant.

I continued: "Healers are for general diseases, but a person must take responsibility himself for the important matters in his life. He is the one who must live the life he has molded. If he plays the destroyer of his life and then asks others to play the rescuer, can anything be achieved?"

"Ah! Ah!" was the sound he made, but his bodily posture sank. I continued, "Spiritual cultivation, as I know it, is to be self-healing or self-regulating at the fundamental level. Self-development and self-achievement are at an advanced level. However, each step must be taken with good spirit and accomplished by oneself. Only when the dough is ready should the yeast be applied. Otherwise, it is a waste to make a long journey with any great master."

This time he made no response at all. Instead, he slowly stood up and picked up his bag, moved his eyes from the still active cat and turned his face. He began with a sigh, then slowly and with integrity said: "I have received medicine from your venerable family. I did not waste my trip. After some years, I shall return to express my gratitude if I have proved I am worthy." Then he bowed and left.

Years later, during the great invasion and bombing, people who lived in the cities or important towns left because of "the tension of the times," as the Chinese people called it. I was sent to a temple in the mountains. I was greeted there by the keeper, with whom I felt some familiarity and was asked to take a seat in the main hall. He then sublimely saluted me in a very traditional way, took from his big sleeve a piece of rice paper that was folded into a square, and handed it to me. I opened the paper which contained a neatly written poem:

> *"Worldly life is but a cat*
> > *endlessly chasing the shadow of a butterfly.*
> *Nothing is real.*
> *Long ago I stopped playing the cat's game.*
> *The long ignorant one finally becomes a spiritual tiger*
> > *in the secluded mountain."*

Suddenly, I recalled who he was and we had a good laugh. I enjoyed the several weeks of my stay there. Besides having the good energy of the mountain, I also had the company of a spiritually developed one.

Not long ago, one of my American students asked the meaning of the "Heavenly Gate" referred to in Chapter 10 of the *Tao Teh Ching*. At the same time, someone else asked the meaning of "destiny." I immediately recalled this story and gave my answer for the meaning of the "Heavenly Gate" as follows:

When the Subtle Gate opens, one receives life; when it closes, one's life is transformed. The Subtle Gate is continually opening and closing; therefore, one's destiny is continually changing.

The opportunity arises for one to receive life when the Subtle Gate opens widely. When one's star looks dark, one may believe that the Subtle Gate leaves only a "narrow pass" for him, but how many "narrow passes" or critical moments occur in one's life? Are such moments also met by others? Actually, because of one's own tension and restlessness, one nervously and mistakenly pulls the invisible string to hasten the closing and opening of the "Subtle Gate," thus disregarding the natural rhythm of life.

The Subtle Door is a door of no door, a gate of no gate. It is the constantly changing level of the mind which separates the reality of the continuous transformability of our destiny from the unsentimental cycle of life. The feelable destiny and other emotions and passions are all misbeliefs from our life. The tensions of the mind breed such misbeliefs. Misconceptions or incorrect feelings build a self-deceptive psychological life.

49

革

GIR

REVOLUTION · REFORMATION

GUIDANCE: *"A successful revolution is a matter of proper timing and correct implementation. Only when the goal is just and carefully approved, can a righteous and beneficial revolution be achieved."*

In this hexagram, Lake is above Fire. These two natural forces have opposing natures and must carefully interact, because an excess of one can conquer the other. Separately, each represents a different stage of growth and energy. Together, they express disharmony.

Gir means "the hide of a cow" and symbolizes the virtue of tenacity, endurance, strength and protection. Such virtues are essential for change. In family relationships, the upper trigram represents a young girl and the lower trigram represents a woman. When disharmony and contradiction exist, then improvement or reform becomes necessary.

Fire also indicates Summer, and Lake indicates Autumn. During the transition from Summer to Autumn, the cycle of yang energy is gradually replaced by yin energy. In the five elemental energy phases, Lake belongs to the phase of Metal. When these energies interact, the heat from the Fire causes the Metal to be reformed. Furthermore, Fire signifies sunshine and Lake indicates westwardness, which implies the rotation of the earth and the alternation of day and night. The ancients understood this energy arrangement as revolution, reformation, change, or the reshaping of things.

Revolution can also be an expression of replacement or transformation. The process of revolution can be one of continuous renewal and refreshing change. However, in worldly life revolution often manifests as rebellion. On a deeper level, revolution refers to development or evolution towards maturity. Such a process is like stripes gradually emerging on a tiger as he grows. This kind of change occurs as a natural result of growth and is a process which starts subtly and goes on to be clearly expressed in its influence. Whether revolution occurs individually or within a society, its positive effect depends on the correct goal and appropriate timing.

This hexagram encourages one to let go of the old in order to proceed with what is new and right. When dealing with revolution, an individual should adjust to external conditions and avoid either a premature or delayed response. If this process is not carried out in an appropriate manner and at an appropriate time, the attempt to improve or reform the situation, or oneself, will certainly become destructive. Thus revolution must be in accordance with inner and outer reality.

Movement is a natural and necessary occurrence. There is nothing that is always still. That which is kept from movement and change becomes stagnant and decayed, like water in a swamp. In our bodies, cells are dying and new ones are being generated every moment. Our energy changes daily, but our minds tend to resist change. Many habits and patterns of thinking are established in a search for security. Many people deplete their life energy by seeking security in relationships, careers, possessions, etc. while completely disregarding the constancy that exists in change. Change is the true security of the natural law that underlies the order of the universe. All things in nature and the entire universe follow their own natural revolution. The essential nature of a human being is no different from that of the universe. Every moment of life is a time for self-renewal and continued self-evolution.

These principles can be applied to one's own darkness and inadequacies. Recognizing and understanding this darkness is difficult. One's dark areas cannot be pointed out by others. One must independently determine what is undesirable in one's life and then decide if one is willing to change. If not, the difficulty may become an obstacle that can affect one's future and perhaps destroy happiness and good fortune.

Many people spend a lot of time and energy trying to help others before putting their own lives in order. Likewise, some nations are aggressive and meddlesome in the affairs of other countries, but are unable to hold their own country together due to internal conflict. Thus, the following principle applies equally to a nation or an individual:

"In order to serve outwardly, people or nations must first reform themselves inwardly."

In recent history the word "revolution" is almost synonymous with "rebellion," which is characterized by conspiracies, killings and wars. This hexagram does not emphasize that kind of revolution.

How should a peaceful revolution be accomplished? Basing their thought on the philosophy of naturalism, the ancient composers of the *I Ching* noted that there was tension between the two trigrams, Lake and Fire. The upper trigram was designated as the government and the lower trigram as the people or the revolutionaries. Gir gives guidance as to how the lower trigram can most effectively accomplish a peaceful revolution.

The fourth line is the minister, or premier, who is the one responsible for the ineffective administration and who becomes the object of the revolution. Although the entire society is involved, a revolution always needs the power of a single individual to start it and to successfully carry it to completion.

The fifth line symbolizes the authority of a society. In a democracy, this line represents the president or congress. In a constitutional monarchy, it is the king or queen. Most important, the fifth line implies that revolution can clearly bring about a change for the better. Revolution was very much approved by the ancient sages as a legitimate method of bringing about change.

The top line represents the outcome of the revolution. Here, only the positive results are described. There is no mention of the struggle for power or the confusion and disorder that usually result.

There is no suggestion of war in these lines. A peaceful revolution can not only save many lives, but can sometimes avoid the destruction of an entire nation.

LINE 1: *"Keep still. Be firm like cowhide. Do not move recklessly."*

Since the first line has no response from the fourth, it cannot presently do anything other than gather energy. Reformation or revolution must take place at the right time; otherwise, one's actions will be premature.

The first line indicates that the time is too early to initiate outer reform. However, this is the right time to begin reforming one's bad habits and mistakes before they become firmly rooted and uncontrollable.

LINE 2: *"This is the right time to go ahead. No fault."*

The second line responds to the righteous principle of the revolution. This line has the cooperation of the fifth line, thus reformation can proceed and will surely succeed.

LINE 3: *"In a revolution, being too aggressive is as bad as being too conservative. Adhere to advice and make necessary corrections. Thus, one gains the faith of the people."*

There is difficulty in keeping still as well as in taking action. One must first look for understanding and support from others. Thus, the third line seeks advice from the corresponding sixth line in order to diminish all obstacles and resistance.

LINE 4: *"Remorse disappears. Be faithful in reformation. Good fortune comes with change."*

The fourth line represents a person who is in a position of public service and cannot respond to the demands of the people, indicated by the first line. Thus a source of contention arises. Because both the first and the fourth lines are yang lines, there is no correspondence between them. The fourth line is the one in an inappropriate position and should be the one to change or reform. Thus, revolution is brought forth.

Only by reforming itself will the fourth line be able to rightfully serve the people beneath, represented by the first line. Its function as minister or general of this hexagram is fulfilled. After the change, harmony is possible.

LINE 5: *"This is a great change that can be seen by all. Even before making a divination this change can be trusted. It is as clear and obvious as the stripes on a tiger."*

This line represents a great revolutionary matter. Its purpose is just and clear. With this support, a successful revolution can be accomplished. Because its goal is correct, the achievements of reformation are like the stripes on a young tiger which have fully developed.

On a personal level, the fifth line represents the mind and heart which guide the correct reformation that comes from within and without.

LINE 6: *"People of self-cultivation change themselves from the inside, like the growing spots on a panther. Ordinary people change themselves superficially through their obedience to external pressures. In both ways reformation is accomplished. Now is the right time to keep peace and good order. To further the revolution is destructive."*

The top line can represent a deep or superficial change. Thus it expresses the outcome of reformation on different personal and social levels. People of development reform themselves deeply and thoroughly. Shallow and narrow people only change themselves superficially. The face indicates that the change can be seen.

SPECIFIC GUIDANCE

PERSONAL FORTUNE: Something unusual will happen which will show the inadequacy of your material forces - possibly money or material goods.

MARRIAGE: The marriage can be accomplished, but the husband will be controlled by his wife. She will eventually ask for a divorce.

HOUSING/FAMILY: Be careful about fire.

CHILDBIRTH: Safe.

LOOKING FOR WORK: It can be found.

SOCIAL/GOVERNMENTAL POSITION: Difficult to achieve.

TRADE/BUSINESS: Successful.

SEARCHING FOR SOMEONE: They can be found.

WAITING FOR SOMEONE: They will not come.

LOOKING FOR SOMETHING LOST: It is difficult to recover.

HUNTING FOR THIEVES: They are hiding in the Northwest and can be caught.

LAWSUIT: Something arises for no reason. The problem starts from the outside. If you change your presentation, the suit can be won.

CLIMATE: If it is raining, conditions will improve; if the
weather is fine, there will be rain. These are changing
times.

TRAVEL: Two people traveling together is good.

DISEASE: Difficulty.

PERSONAL WISH: Difficulty in the beginning, but the
wish will later be fulfilled.

COMMENTARY
The Work of Awakening

Language awakens the minds of people, chi awakens
the chi of people. The world needs both a truly awakening language and a truly awakening energy.

There is nothing more significant than for one to keep
awake.   There is also nothing more meaningful than to
awaken others.   The awakened one maintains wholeness
and constant balance.   He does not participate in mob
movement, nor does he give up the world. He lives among
worldly people without being discouraged by their ignorance, stubbornness and aggression.   He maintains his
awakened nature.

By what method did he achieve himself? By what method
will he help others? What is the reality of awakening in the
natural and supernatural spiritual tradition?

Some of the more secret methods of spiritual achievement
are only allowed to be passed on to three human beings every
seven hundred years. Some others are only allowed to be
passed on to one human being every thousand years.
These methods support a person's high achievement. To
limit the spreading of such secret methods, there are different Heavenly prohibitions accompanying different levels
of achievement. When I look at the misguided direction of
the general human culture, I wish Old Heaven would allow
us to remove all these prohibitions. If the truth of life
and of universal formation were totally revealed to all,
would this not end all arguments and wars among people,
and would this not be a beautiful thing?

I have often asked myself: Should I risk breaking the
Heavenly prohibitions in revealing the general sacred
truths for the purpose of correcting the improper educational guidance in schools and society? Should I tell people that the first important objective in their education is

to recognize their own true nature? Can I tell people that they have a divine nature, or should I just tell them that human nature is already semi-godly with the potential of restoring its "other-half" - its divine nature?   Can I show the truth, through self-cultivation, of how a human being can give birth to a spirit which can further one's visible life?   Can I show the truth that, through cultivation, one human life can give birth to numerous spiritual beings? Can I reveal the truth that through correct cultivation, the essence of each organ in the human body can transform into a "womb" for a spiritual baby, which can later become independent in the universe with complete senses and capabilities?   Can I tell people that their own spiritual development directly determines the quality, capability, virtue and destination of the spirit which could be born from them?

Have I enabled people to see the value of the balanced way: that neither the narrow practice of religion nor the self-indulgence of the secular way is correctly centered? Can people, through my work, understand that the paths of idealism and materialism are both one-sided and miss the mark?   Can I tell the world's people the truth of life so that they may re-evaluate and readjust all the school books which have already gone astray by their partial vision from the truth of life and of the universe?

Why must spiritual truth be limited to certain individuals? Why cannot spiritual truth become public education?   Why does spiritual achievement become a domain which only a few specially developed people can share and enjoy?

I often ask myself such questions. In order to soothe my burning compassion for my fellow people of the world, I remind myself of the following.

In my own experience, if the secret gate were suddenly opened to an ordinary man or woman, this person would surely become mad.   One's mental capacity is not prepared for this spiritual achievement. Thus, the Heavenly prohibition should be regarded with the clear understanding that it is actually Heaven's protection. This protection is not only for an individual who is interested in learning, but is also a protection for others who might immaturely practice what they have learned.

The incorrect knowledge system of the ordinary world is part of the process for human growth. Children ask for cookies and toys, not truth. In the same manner, intellectual knowledge systems of human life are the toys which general people play with in their life. The truth of life is simple and clear. If people wake up, they can see it.

There are three main obstacles which serve as poisons and thus prohibit people from seeing the truth: ignorance, stubbornness and aggressiveness. How can an achieved one help? If the achieved one is passive towards these people, then he will give up the world to live in seclusion. If he is active and responds to the world's people, his warmth gathers their ignorance, stubbornness and aggressiveness to himself. Hundreds of times, he may tell himself to leave, but where can he go? Where are there people of no darkness, no obstinacy and no aggression? Should he retreat to become a hermit, as did the ancient ones who traversed the Silent Way? The demands of their generation were much different from this one. If he should want to stop after giving a class, a talk, or writing a book, there always comes the same response from the Old Master:

> *Do it without anticipation.*
> *Do it without assertiveness.*
> *Do it without self.*

A hundred times he may answer the Old Master, "It is no fun!" But he may always answer himself, "Is there anything more fun than awakening people? One must keep oneself wholly and constantly awakening!"

Language awakens the minds of people. Chi awakens the chi of people. The world needs more than just awakening energy and awakening language.

50   ZING

cauldron · harmonization & stability

GUIDANCE: *"The cauldron is stable and well-balanced. Good fortune. Everything goes smoothly."*

In this hexagram, Fire is above Wind or Wood. After revolution comes reconstruction, reorganization, and the re-establishment of peace and order, thus the cauldron represents stability.

The image of the cauldron has several meanings. In ancient times it was used for cooking royal feasts in which offerings were made to Heaven and one's ancestors. Exemplifying the universal spirit of humanity, these offerings expressed ancient people's harmonious relationship with the spiritual realm and their deep gratitude for the good life they enjoyed together. After the offering, the food was then portioned to the older people, people of wisdom and people of merit as a token of respect from the emperors.

In addition to cooperation, unity, harmony, security and stability, the cauldron also symbolizes the newly-established order which follows reformation. The cauldron also indicates a big family.

In spiritual development, Ting symbolizes internal cultivation via external "burning." Each of the sixty-four hexagrams applies to personal cultivation; however, Ting especially applies to the entire process of internal "cooking" or self-cultivation. It teaches how one can mature to ripeness and mellowness.

When Fire is over Wood, the process of cooking is represented. In China, a great leader was compared to a good cook. Energy naturally transforms from Wood to Fire and cultivates that which serves as a life support, such as properly prepared "food" or wisdom.

In the Integral Way, the entire universe is thought of as a cauldron. Life on earth is the product of the interaction and integration of Water and Fire. It depends on the warmth and light of the sun, which represents Fire in nature and the heart in the human body. Life also depends on the moon, which represents Water in nature and the various emotions in a person. Life is based on the harmonious intercourse of this Fire and Water externally, and that of the heart and the mind internally.

In self-cultivation, one's body can be likened to a cauldron which blends the diverse energies. Therefore, people must develop their awareness of the art of "cooking": blending the natural, internally and externally, to reach the real, wholesome being.

The *I Ching* teaches us to extend the principle of the cauldron by serving others. A wise leader gathers the materials (fire, water, food, etc.), then prepares and offers them to all beings of the human and spiritual realm. As a symbol of a balanced life, Ting expresses the unity which extends from one's inner self to one's immediate family, to all of mankind, and to the entire universe. Since order is essential to unity, a leader must care for the young and encourage all people to follow the guidance of the principle of balance.

The cauldron transforms that which is raw and hard into something ripe and soft. This process implies that the young and unripe will become the useful essence of the nation. Thus, Ting encourages the wise one to understand his duty and his responsibilities and to stabilize his efforts in order to help and guide the well-being of all people. Following the progression symbolized by the levels of the cauldron can help one fulfill one's duty in life and develop accordingly. Thus, the first three Sagacious Emperors of ancient China valued the cauldron as the symbol of a well-ordered society.

Each of the six lines of this hexagram represents a different section of the cauldron. The first line represents the foot of the cauldron; the second, third and fourth lines represent the body; the fifth line represents the side handles, and the top line represents the lid.

LINE 1: *"One leg of the three-legged cauldron is not well set and the cauldron inclines to one side. However, one may use this occasion to clean the inside. In a family relationship this situation is like a second woman who, though not formally married, gives birth to a son and thereby contributes to her importance in the family."*

When a cauldron is titling to one side, it can be easily cleaned and purified. Although such a situation appears unfavorable, it can be of some positive use. In order for it to become a positive situation, a third partner or an assistant is needed to effect the balance of a family or social circumstance. Eventually, the importance of such a contribution will be recognized.

The hexagram as a whole means that if balance cannot be maintained by two, a third element of support should be made use of. The image of a cauldron symbolizes such a situation, its three legs maintaining balance.

In the situation in question, a third party may be needed, like a second woman who comes into a family when the primary wife cannot, by giving birth, continue the lineage or provide for the elders in the family.

LINE 2: *"The cauldron is filled. One is self-contained and does not let a companion who becomes unbalanced upset him. Thus, there is no blame."*

This line should naturally correspond with the fifth line, but the neighboring first line disturbs it. If the second line firmly resists this temptation and unites with the fifth line, it will have good fortune. This line shows the cauldron full of ingredients which need to be safely contained while the cooking process takes place.

Cleaning the cauldron is part of the preparation; however, cooking is the real work. Do not let the importance of this time be upset by the enticement of the first line.

LINE 3: *"The ears (handles) of the cauldron do not work. Though the good food is ready, it cannot be served. One feels regret at not enjoying the food before the rain comes."*

Although this is a yang line in a yang position, Wood and Fire are unfortunately in excess. The cooking is accelerated until the contents of the cauldron are boiling. This implies that one's talents and measures are too strong. Instead of using the cauldron properly, one spoils the food by poor handling.

LINE 4: *"The leg of the cauldron is broken. Food falls out of the cauldron and is spoiled. The great minister fails to fulfill his duty and is privately punished. He receives no faith from the public."*

This line symbolizes the good order of a nation, family or any relationship that has failed. It is like the over-abundance of food in a cauldron; it cannot be cooked very well. Likewise, a person who is too proud, too full of false information or tries to learn too much at once prohibits the proper balance for a correct result. In cooking, one must be cautious not to over or under cook the food. In such a situation, proper management as well as the art of "cooking" are of utmost importance. This same principle also applies to embarking on an education, running a business or governing a nation.

LINE 5: *"Strong golden handles of the cauldron with yellow ears, firm union and upright management bring good fortune."*

"Yellow," being the middle color in the spectrum, expresses being well-balanced and centered. The fifth line is the lid and "ears" of the cauldron which, when adjusted, allow the heat and steam to work within and prepare the food. This line implies the need for proper control in cooking.

> **LINE 6:** *"The strong jade handle on top of the lid does not become overheated. Great good fortune. Everything is in its right order and correctly prepared. The food nourishes the wise and virtuous. The country is well-governed by the top minister."*

The lid should be opened and the food served. Thus, the top line represents the handle of the lid, the able minister whose proper conduct leads to the good fortune of a nation. Although this is a strong line, good management was provided which enabled the right nourishment to be served to all. Thus, the virtue of the cauldron is complete.

SPECIFIC GUIDANCE

PERSONAL FORTUNE: Very prosperous.
MARRIAGE: It can be achieved; however, there will be some quarrels.
HOUSING/FAMILY: Be careful about fire.
CHILDBIRTH: Unsafe.
SOCIAL/GOVERNMENTAL POSITION: Obstacles in the beginning. Later, success.
TRADE/BUSINESS: The business will succeed and you can easily make a fortune.
SEARCHING FOR SOMEONE: They are in the North and are difficult to find.
WAITING FOR SOMEONE: They will come.
LOOKING FOR SOMETHING LOST: It is in the Northeast and difficult to find.
HUNTING FOR THIEVES: They are in the Northeast and difficult to catch.
LAWSUIT: If the suit continues, it will be difficult to stop. Make peace now.
CLIMATE: Following rain, the weather will be windy.

TRAVEL: Okay for three people traveling together. If only two go, then money will be lost.

DISEASE: Dangerous.

PERSONAL WISH: Difficult for the time being.

COMMENTARY
No Separation

The spiritual application of the hexagram Ting, Harmonization/Balance, is illustrated by the following story.

As a young boy, I esteemed enlightenment above all else. I knew there were many things of high spiritual value to be learned in my tradition, but I nonetheless thought of enlightenment as the "express train" which could take me directly to the subtle origin of all lives, as well as to the six breakthroughs, the milestones of self-development, which would mark my high spiritual capability and free me from further dependency on other spiritual beings.

Until I was in my late forties, the attainment of such enlightenment and breakthroughs were my highest achievements. Naturally, these achievements made my life and work more effective, whether in healing or teaching, but I realized there was more to learn.

For an enlightened one, the world is the altar on which he offers his cultivation. One who is enlightened is no longer spiritually connected to people on a common, undeveloped level. An enlightened one, returning to the people of the world, is like a well-disciplined child going outside to play in the "mud." Regardless of how clean he was before going outside, he will get at least somewhat dirty, yet return to the world he must. As a gift to humanity and as the virtuous realization of his own being, an enlightened one must fulfill his natural and supernatural responsibilities. (Just as the sun, moon and stars in the vast sky are the sources of illumination for an entirely dark world, how could people live in darkness without the light of a developed one?)

Even though the enlightened one has reached the level of spiritual achievement, the fact remains that the world is not naturally morally-ordered. Therefore, an achieved one must continue to safeguard his offering from the harm of evil when extending his being to the world. It must be remembered that what one has, after achieving enlightenment and the six breakthroughs, is the purified, responsive yang energy of a human being. Thus, such a one needs even more spiritual protection from the shadow realm of evil spirits and evil people. Even with pure yang energy, without further development through the real divine method, without learning how to protect oneself from being used as a tool of evil ghosts, one is still vulnerable, or sometimes even more vulnerable, to spiritual attack from the inferior world. People who suddenly become possessed have been attacked because they relinquished their self-control and rational behavior. Even though such evil is the product of undevelopment, it may still cause much harm. The offensive evil cannot be punished, and the traditional, righteous spiritual power cannot be extended over the evil ones. Though enlightenment has been achieved, spiritual dominance is still foreign.

I realized that, although I had experienced many high spiritual peaks, my cultivation was still incomplete. When enlightenment carried me from darkness to the light and from wrong to right, its function was accomplished. However, lightness and rightness are still within the relative realm. Thus, enlightenment is really just the beginning of developing oneself beyond the level of duality. Though the function of enlightenment is to improve one's consciousness and fundamental concepts, it still does not reach the reality of the real spiritual beings.

You might well ask: what is a real spirit, and what is the real immortal realm? What is the connection of one's spiritual being with the immortal realm? Such questions had been at the center of my ancestors' spiritual endeavors, and now they were mine. I realized that up to this point, I had been unrealistic, achieving myself mostly through idealistic efforts. As I now discovered in my cultivation, I was only partially developed, with what is expressible only on a human level.

In order to fill the gap that existed between the spiritual realm and a human being with a flesh body, I decided to once again become a beginner and to learn the real divine practices of my tradition and become thoroughly trained in the details of the ancient methods outlined by Pao Pu Tzu.

At first, my efforts were concentrated on making contact with a particular Heavenly being. Then I developed my connection to the divine ones with special spiritual functions. Finally, I worked on the total, unifying spiritualization of my own being.

The main harvest of my advanced spiritual cultivation, which began in my late forties, was to end the separation between universal beings, my spiritual being, and my human being. This reunion can also be expressed as a metaphor: "The body is an empire, while the universe is a body."

Now, anywhere I go and every place I stay, I meet spiritual beings of good will, joyful communication and great harmony. What a truly supernatural privilege to enjoy the reality of no separation.

51 震 chen

The Arousing · Force of Thunder

GUIDANCE: *"Terrifying Thunder keeps people alert, but this is all right. There is an undisturbed joyful meeting among those who follow the correct way of conduct. Although a loud thunderclap brings shock, the ceremony is still kept in good order."*

The image of Thunder, in which yang energy is beneath inactive yin energy, expresses a force which has been obstructed but which suddenly bursts forth in an explosion. In this hexagram both trigrams represent Thunder. When an image is doubled, as it is here, the impact of the natural force is twice as great.

Although the generation of all life is dependent on the harmonious integration of elements within the natural world, shock is sometimes necessary to disrupt complacency and inertia. The purpose of Thunder in our lives is to arouse and awaken us. As a symbol of awakening, Thunder can be manifested by one's teacher, parents, a natural phenomenon, or one's own inner being. In all stages of development, people need the force of Thunder.

An old Chinese proverb says: "When a good horse sees the shadow of the whip, it begins running at full speed." Alertness is what makes a good horse. Lazy horses, even with coaxing or a thrashing, are still inert. Often too, one acts like a rebellious child trying to violate teachings and disciplines one knows to be true. During such times, Thunder helps to rouse one from foolishness or complacency.

A developed being or true spiritual teacher who practices the virtues of Thunder in his teachings does not flatter people in order to gain power over them, but rather seeks to awaken them. Undoubtedly, one experiences difficulties in being with such a teacher. To consider such shocks as punishment is to devalue the awakening that one's teacher is offering. However, the use of shock for growth and development must be very precise in its timing and purpose.

Chen represents the time of Spring when all life is renewed. This is a time of joy and hope for those who have a sense of awe and reverence within. The time is favorable for self-cultivation and helping others, thus good fortune results. The power of awe can stimulate one to set one's own life in order, as well as the lives of others. Such a person can be entrusted with matters, whether large or small.

Calmness is always necessary in fulfilling great responsibility. It is especially important in dealing with shock and confusion. In this hexagram, the *I Ching* encourages a person to exercise responsibility with the same calmness, steadiness, intensity and reverence that he would use if performing a sacred rite. If one's energy is scattered or disordered, one will be easily jolted by every shock that comes along, but one who is centered will act appropriately, regardless of what confronts him.

Shock and confusion are not always caused by a destructive act. Sometimes they are the result of too much of a good thing. The following story illustrates how even happiness may cause shock.

Many years ago in Hong Kong there was a coolie who, hoping to become rich at horse races, invested in a ticket. He put the ticket stub in a bamboo pole which served as his tool for making a living and in which he carried all his possessions. By and by, he discovered that he was the winner of the grand prize. So extreme was his excitement over his fortune finally changing, he took his bamboo pole, the symbol of his poverty and toil, and threw it into the sea.   Later when he went to collect his winnings he realized his ticket was still inside his life-long friend.

As the story illustrates, the hexagram emphasizes the importance of maintaining a clear, calm mind at all times.

Is there any real retributive force?   The notion that lightning will strike the evil-doer has been a common belief for ages.   Though modern thinking has changed, the reality of retribution, in all its various forms, is still just as exact as it always has been.   True retribution, however, is much more subtle and profound than lightning striking someone directly.   Though the evil doer may not literally be struck, he will surely suffer retribution in some form or another.   According to the universal law of natural energy response as taught by Lao Tzu, violent action invites an unnatural death.   Thus, retribution is inescapable.   Good will attract good friends and a good life; negativity will attract enemies and danger.   This is a basic principle of life.   Unfortunately, religious theories are often too subjective to accurately explain this simple truth.

The development of ancient tribes began with the awakening force of Thunder.   Thunder would come without warning, and what lightning chose to strike was just as unpredictable.   It was the awe and fear of these two powerful forces which made people begin to reflect. Without a deep understanding of the truth behind these mysteries of nature, inaccurate interpretations arose. Those who feared Thunder saw in it a wrathful and vengeful God who dominated and subjugated them.   Conversely, those who were stimulated and awakened by thunder channeled its power to aid in their inner quest for truth. Thus, the response to Thunder led to superstition on the one hand and a deep understanding of its significance on the other.   To the achieved, Thunder was a responsive, benevolent and life-giving force.   The result of this realization was religious advancement without and spiritual development within.

One who receives this hexagram should reflect upon his chosen path, stage of spiritual growth, and the spiritual patterns which he accepts.   Such patterns determine who one really is.

LINE 1: *"A warning comes like Thunder. Joy comes when one corrects his behavior and puts his life in order. One is benefited by fear."*

One can change a fearful circumstance into something positive through correct conduct. This line is in the right position, and this is the time for growth and achievement. Though apprehension may arise in achieving one's goal, rightful actions and a sense of awe can lead to success.

LINE 2: *"Fear-evoking Thunder comes. One loses one's fortune by hurrying to safety. Do not bother searching for fortune right away. It can be regained in seven days."*

Shock comes. One leaves one's treasures behind and goes to a high place to escape danger. There is no need for one to pursue possessions at this time for they can be restored. When the natural event is over, one regains his senses. It will be a time for renewal and the overcoming of difficulty. The threat of survival makes one stronger. This time should be used for retreat and introspection. In the end, nothing is lost and there will be good fortune.

LINE 3: *"Terrified by Thunder, one cannot conduct oneself calmly. Be cautious and correct one's conduct. There is no real trouble."*

In most hexagrams, the first and second lines represent the Earth, the third and fourth lines represent Man, and the fifth and sixth lines represent Heaven. This line shows a person who is beginning to gain awareness of the laws of nature. One now has an opportunity to apply one's limited understanding and to make slight progress without any serious mistakes. The third line should be yang, but instead it is yin. If one tries to change, there is no difficulty, because in the attempt, one may become self-correcting. One should be cautious in this position but not lose the spontaneity which is needed to act correctly.

LINE 4: *"Lightning hits the mud. It gives no power and no light."*

This line is not in its correct position. It is between two yin lines and is the center of the upper nuclear or inner trigram, Water, and the top line of the lower nuclear or inner trigram, Mountain. Thus, the image of lightning hitting mud is formed. Energy is being wasted.

If a person allows himself to be influenced by desires instead of good judgement, or if he allows his mind to become so stagnant that he cannot see clearly, then what can be done to help him?

This entire hexagram shows various levels or situations in which one experiences shock. This line has the ability to improve itself and can be the source of thunder. In other words, the shock can come from within or without.

> **LINE 5:** *"Thunder shocks repeatedly. Difficult communication. One must be careful and put everything in order. There will be no damage if one makes no mistakes."*

Though this line is the leader, it finds no response from the second line and is too inexperienced to be in such a shaky situation. A person in a high position, yet insecure about his ability to do the job well, must be cautious. The *I Ching* often encourages boldness, but not in this situation. Sometimes one needs to respond with a little fear which, if applied constructively, can be very useful in life. Furthermore, any aspect of one's being that can be used in a positive direction should not be rejected. If one keeps the right position, even in a difficult situation, then nothing is lost in the end. However, if one is warned of the difficulty and still does not know how to prepare for the shock by setting everything in order, the situation will turn out negatively. Having a firm goal and doing the best with what one has is of utmost importance.

> **LINE 6:** *"Being extremely shocked causes one to behave rashly. No further movement should be made. Shock hits a neighbor but does not affect oneself. There is some misunderstanding over one's marriage agreement. This indicates that one's mind is not peaceful. Though there is a threat, there is no real problem. However, it makes one cautious with one's neighbor."*

In spite of all the turmoil, this line is in a good position to observe all things thoroughly. If one does not attempt movement and simply utilizes this position, all goes well. However, one who tries to imitate greatness without the necessary inner development is an impostor. One cannot attain greatness by imitation and will only become the source of gossip among neighbors. One must also be careful that friends do not become enemies. True cultivation enables one to attain what is real, regardless of whether the results are recognized by the neighbors.

SPECIFIC GUIDANCE

PERSONAL FORTUNE: This is a time of good luck. Cheer up and face the difficulty; after a while you can have a good time.

MARRIAGE: If the bride or groom comes from the Northwest, the marriage will be good and successful. If either one comes from the Northeast, it will not succeed.

HOUSING/FAMILY: There is shock associated with the house and one should move.

CHILDBIRTH: A boy will be born, but there will be some shock during the delivery.

LOOKING FOR WORK: Difficulty.

TRADE/BUSINESS: Good fortune will result.

SEARCHING FOR SOMEONE: Meet with them half way.

WAITING FOR SOMEONE: A message is coming.

LOOKING FOR SOMETHING LOST: It can be found in the East and West.

HUNTING FOR THIEVES: They are in the Southwest and can be caught.

LAWSUIT: Make peace or there will be great harm.

CLIMATE: It will be stormy with thunder.

TRAVEL: Travel to the South is good, travel to the East is bad.

DISEASE: Danger in the beginning; later, good fortune.

PERSONAL WISH: There are obstacles and difficulties.

COMMENTARY
Stay with the Unshaken Fundamental Path of Tao

According to the generally accepted philosophical view, the law of cause and effect is supreme. Nothing is excluded from it. All things are the product of a cause or an effect. However, Tao, the path of all, takes another view, for to what cause does the origin of Tao belong since it originates itself? Therefore, Tao is above the law of cause and effect.

One way to put it is that Tao itself is the law - it is self-natured. Tao is the first nature of the universe, of divinity, of matter and of humankind. While other things have a second or even a third nature, Tao has only one absolute nature. Tao is all nature. It is the first principle which is completely beyond reasoning. Therefore, to look for Tao by using reason or thought is like climbing a tree in search of fish eggs.

In Tao, all causes and all effects merge into oneness. There is no confrontation between what causes the shock and what receives the shock.

52   Ken

Keeping still · impediment

GUIDANCE: *"Impeded by the back, one cannot see the front. Walking in the empty court, one cannot see the man."*

Here, the double Mountain represents an insurmountable blockage which necessitates stillness. In the previous hexagram, Thunder, the yang lines are kept from rising because of the two yin lines. In this hexagram, the yang energy reaches the top of the mountain and its activity is impeded. The stage of yang energy development represented here is young and shallow. When yang energy is not yet mature and not deeply rooted, it is appropriate to keep still.

The virtue of Mountain is its stillness. Growth is generated and maintained without strain. Unlike a Mountain, human life is not permanently established unless people know the virtue of stillness. Since they do not know when to stop unnecessary activity, they continue to follow overly active desires and thus their organs and senses eventually become exhausted.

The backbone indicates stillness and peacefulness and is unenslaved by desire. Thus it is associated with the stillness of a Mountain. The vertebrae of the spine can be compared to the ridges along a Mountain peak, the correct position of each vertebrae along the spinal ridge being essential to the serenity of the whole.

With calm and inward focus, one can clear the mind of selfish thoughts and desires and maintain the tranquility of a Mountain. Keeping still, however, does not mean being inactive, but rather that one acts correctly and without strain in any situation that presents itself.

The inner trigram, K'an $\equiv\equiv$, is in a central position in this hexagram. Stillness of the mind brings about clarity and brightness. When one's mind is disturbed, inner energy is unsettled and peace is difficult to achieve. An unaffected mind is the mark of true achievement. A person of self-cultivation knows how to remain centered. His attention is not easily "robbed" by external circumstance or desire.

Two adjacent Mountains represent a huge impediment. Such a situation is not easily overcome. Realizing the nature of the problem, one becomes still, gathers energy and remains uninvolved with this circumstance. To continue to attack the problem is a waste of energy and serves only to create distress.

The balancing force of activity is stillness. Stillness and activity complement and lend significance to each other. Since humankind is prone to activity, the correct application of stillness can make these activities more effective and meaningful.

LINE 1: *"One's toe is impeded. Nothing furthers. There is no problem in keeping still and being firm in these circumstances."*

The first line corresponds to the toes where movement begins. In order to walk, one must first move the toes to take a step. If one knows where to step, there will be no trouble; but if one does not know when to stop, peace and satisfaction are never obtained. This weak line must keep still and remain firm; thus, there will be no difficulty.

LINE 2: *"The calf is impeded. One cannot help his companion. This results in regret."*

This line corresponds to the calves. It is wise enough to remain where it should be. The third line, however, is stubborn and does not listen when advised to keep still. The second line is saddened because he cannot help; thus, he can only mind his own business in this situation.

LINE 3: *"One's sides, or waist, are impeded. The rib cage expands. One's heart burns with restlessness. Being held in bondage by too much ambition is endangering."*

In a time of stillness, one's mind burns with the restless desire to move forward. One cannot move physically, but tries to race ahead mentally. It is correct at such times to allow things to develop naturally without using force. There is no reason to expand oneself. Using the mind to interfere with the body will only create tensions in life.

LINE 4: *"The trunk of the body is held still. No blame. One should now stop all activities."*

By keeping the trunk and body still in this situation, the mind is calm and the heart at peace. One is wise enough to fulfill one's duty. Thus, impulsiveness and restlessness are controlled and one brings no trouble on oneself.

LINE 5: *"One's cheeks are kept still. Words must be put in good order. No blame."*

One should only speak when one has something worthwhile to say. One should listen well and put ideas in order to help insure correct movements. Then one's words become effective and useful.

LINE 6: *"Profound stillness and honesty, like the top of a mountain, brings good fortune."*

This line represents the honest spirits at the top of the head. Here stability and peace of mind are expressed as the highest conditions of all.

SPECIFIC GUIDANCE

PERSONAL FORTUNE: This is the time to retreat and keep still.

MARRIAGE: A successful marriage can be achieved.

HOUSING/FAMILY: In this house, both the man and the woman have something to worry about.   This is not an auspicious sign.

CHILDBIRTH: It will be a boy.

LOOKING FOR WORK: Success.

SOCIAL/GOVERNMENTAL POSITION: Achievement later in life.

TRADE/BUSINESS: It can be successful, but do not be greedy for something extra.

SEARCHING FOR SOMEONE: They are in the Northwest.

WAITING FOR SOMEONE: They do not come.

LOOKING FOR SOMETHING LOST: It is still in the original place and can be found.

HUNTING FOR THIEVES: They are in the Northwest and not far away.

LAWSUIT: Must be righteous and squarely handled.

CLIMATE: It will be rainy.   However, if there is already wind, the weather will be good.

TRAVEL: Some doubt makes one feel uneasy.   If one pushes on in the journey, one will meet with danger.

DISEASE: Difficult to cure.

PERSONAL WISH: Cannot be achieved.

COMMENTARY

Build a house of Tao on a foundation of virtue.
With virtue there is union.
Subtle power comes not just from within ourselves,
*   but from Heaven, Earth and all living things*
*   working positively through us.*
The mind embraces all positive virtues.
Without being separate, you contribute to all things,
*   creating a solid immortality with the whole universe.*
Strengthen your virtues and become
*   forever, naturally firm, beyond decay.*

Obediently follow the great Tao with a single mind
*   and all anxieties will fall away.*

The inferior mind is the origin
 of all trouble and sickness.
To treat your illness, first treat your mind.
As the impure mind becomes active,
 all manner of negative obstacles arise.
As the mind calms, shadows and hardships disappear.
A harmonious mind breeds no disease.
Pride and self-neglect both breed imbalance.
To know the cause is to know the cure.

Do not think of Tao as a theoretical arrangement.
The improvement of your life
 depends on honest self-cultivation.
Cultivate the awareness that obstacles are impurities.
Melt through your mental formations
 to the eternal reality.
Unite with the final truth.
Treat your mind and body with your mind and body.
Trace differences back to their origin.
Through the truest cultivation,
 discipline, proof and gain,
 become the son or daughter
 of the highest heavenly family.

53　　　漸
　　　　JEN

GRADUALNESS

GUIDANCE: *"Be gradual like a woman planning to marry. Good fortune comes by firmly keeping to the right way."*

In this hexagram, Wind or Wood is above Mountain. Mountain suggests quiet, while Wind represents gentle movement. Together they suggest gradualness. The upper trigram, Wood, is like a tree slowly growing on a mountain. The inner trigrams of Water and Fire enable Wood and Mountain to interact harmoniously. The inner trigrams also suggest the union of male and female energies, or of any positive relationship. This type of internal harmony encourages the gradual development of a good relationship.

The Mountain suggests a young man, and Wind suggests a woman. As they gradually come closer together, their relationship culminates in marriage. If they follow the natural order of development, success is assured. However, if they rush unto the relationship, it probably will not endure. The relationship will benefit both sides if they remain detached in the beginning, observe circumstances and slowly reach a point of mutual friendship before becoming more closely involved. Thus, there will be no remorse.

Obviously, this principle is not limited only to marriage. Marriage is simply a metaphor for the gradual development of any relationship or situation.

The meaning of this hexagram is further illustrated by the gradual step-by-step process of geese migrating to distant lands. Each line of the hexagram represents a different resting place in their long journey. In cold weather they fly southward; in Summer they go northward. Geese symbolize stability as they unerringly follow the rhythm of the seasons. They also display order in the formations in which they fly and faithfulness in their mating habits. When one dies, the other never chooses another mate.

Wild geese are water birds and gather on river banks. From there, they travel over the plains to the highlands. Thus, they symbolize the wind gently blowing over the mountains.

Gradual progress leads one to higher levels. The Mountain, when it refers to a young man, means inexperience. He suffers emotional difficulties because he still knows little about handling problems. At an early stage, it is sometimes beneficial to follow a leader in order to gain an opportunity for development. By slowly showing one's talents and earning the trust of superiors, a relationship can mature. Therefore, one has an opportunity to be useful in any situation and to share life meaningfully with others. Conversely, if one engages in work for a superior person but perceives it as an obligation rather than a privilege, one's efforts will not be positive, nor will they be received with appreciation. The energy offered to one's spouse is received in the same manner.

LINE 1: *"The wild goose comes to rest on the shore. A young man feels insulted and is the object of gossip.*

There is no problem because he follows the natural order."

This line is like a budding young man whose conduct and movements are still inexperienced and immature. The first and fourth lines usually correspond harmoniously. However, in this situation, the fourth line cannot respond because both are yin lines. Therefore, the first line remains isolated. This is a time for patience. To seek promotion at this time would only evoke criticism.

When a goose flies toward the shore, it chooses landmarks to help keep it from getting lost. If one keeps one's goal in mind and avoids hasty action, one will be ready when opportunities arise.

LINE 2: *"The wild geese gather to rest on a rock, happily enjoying the communion and feast. It is a joyous occasion."*

This yin line is in its correct place and therefore attracts a response from the fifth line. The literal translation of the Chinese text is: "When you find food and supplies, they are not only for you." This line represents one who has plenty. Like a wild goose who shares its good fortune, a person is also benefited by sharing.

LINE 3: *"The wild geese gather and stay in the lowlands. A man will leave and not return. A woman will be pregnant but not give birth. One should now defend oneself."*

This yang line is in a yang position, but is in conflict with the sixth line which is also yang, thus it must be very careful. Since the third line is the top of the lower trigram, it is usually in a difficult and dangerous position by being excessive. Such a position is like a wild goose who flies too high and becomes lost or a pregnant woman who cannot give birth safely.

Socially, it is inappropriate to be too aggressive. However, if others are aggressive or hostile, then it is correct to defend oneself. That is why the last line can also be interpreted: "It is advantageous to resist robbers." In this position, strength is appropriate because one must defend one's position or one's people.

LINE 4: *"The wild geese come to rest on a branch. There is no problem because the rest is temporary."*

The fourth line represents a resting place which is not very comfortable. The upper trigram symbolizes a tree. The goose flies to the branch but cannot linger because its feet are flat, and it cannot easily perch there. Therefore, one does not feel comfortable remaining long.

LINE 5: *"The wild geese come to stay at the summit. Though a woman fails to conceive in three years, this is an extraordinarily good and strong marriage."*

The second and fifth lines are both in their right positions. This represents a good marriage with strong love. He is strong, she is submissive, which makes the marriage bond firm. As a result, there is great security and happiness.

Having a child is symbolic of love. The union of the second and fifth lines is hindered by the two lines between them. Since the summit of love has been reached, there is unavoidable envy and opposition from without. This is why "pregnancy" or "fruit" cannot soon be born. Although there are difficult times, finally all troubles are overcome and a strong union is attained.

LINE 6: *"A single wild goose flies too high. This is not appropriate for it. When it rejoins its group, their flying formation is a beautifully ordered parade."*

One who is too idealistic or who keeps himself in an inappropriate position cannot be of practical value. In this case, his development lies beyond the material plane.

When geese fly, they sometimes form a single line. At other times they fly in V-formation. To the ancient Chinese, such patterns were once source of inspiration in the formulation of Chinese characters. For example, ➖ means "one" and the character for "man" is 人. This expresses the value of traveling in groups.

SPECIFIC GUIDANCE

PERSONAL FORTUNE: One's fortune is like a tree on a high mountain when springtime comes. In the Spring it prospers, in Winter it is less prosperous.

MARRIAGE: Successful.

HOUSING/FAMILY: The house will be peaceful and safe.

CHILDBIRTH: If the baby is born in Autumn, it will be a boy; if born in the Spring or Summer, it will be a girl.

LOOKING FOR WORK: It can be achieved later.

SOCIAL/GOVERNMENTAL POSITION: It can be achieved.

TRADE/BUSINESS: It will gradually become profitable.

WAITING FOR SOMEONE: They will come.

LOOKING FOR SOMETHING LOST: Difficult to locate.

HUNTING FOR THIEVES: They have not gone far and, if pursued, can be caught.

CLIMATE: It will be rainy.

TRAVEL: For good fortune, go to the East. Traveling to the North is not good at this time.

DISEASE: It will become dangerous, stronger and more severe.

PERSONAL WISH: There are obstacles, especially with money.

COMMENTARY

The key to Tao cultivation lies in the eyes.
The eyes gather color and form which,
*   when too active, hinder cultivation*
*   and drain energy.*

Hold all six gates serene and pure.
Remove all distraction from the ears and eyes
*   to keep your energy full and your spirit whole.*
Keep the mind from wandering.
The subtle body is like nature and Heaven.
It receives all and holds nothing.

The origin of suffering lies in the body of flesh.
Make it the altar of self-cultivation.
Trickery and deceit do not benefit the body.
What may seem good for your body
*   may damage your mind,*
*   and a damaged mind holds no home for the soul.*

Adding a title to your name,
*   or a decoration to your personality,*
*   is not the way of a whole being.*

True benefit is found in the efforts
of your own deep soul.
Real benefit is not found in social reputation.
True gain is measured deep within yourself.
For the Sacred Method to be real
and practical in the realm of life,
to be a Heavenly whole being, a Shien,
one must have deep spiritual roots.

Choosing an heir to the Sacred Way
must be done with care.
This is not the same as doing favors
for the whole world.
Love and value the Sacred Method.
Do not carelessly throw it away.
Observe those with true spiritual affinity
for the way of eternity
and those without.
The Grand Masters of the Sacred Method
bid us again and again
to fully protect this treasure
in a cautious way.

54 歸妹
KUEI MEI

MARRIAGE

GUIDANCE: *"An improper match makes a regrettable marriage. No benefit."*

In this hexagram, Thunder is above the Lake. The energy of Thunder is moving, forceful and masculine like the eldest son. The energy of the Lake is gentle, joyous and feminine like a young woman. This interaction is like a man influencing a young woman. Kuei Mei represents a deep relationship such as marriage or an important partnership. Normally, marriage is a happy circumstance, but here there is a hint of unpleasantness.

Since the literal Chinese translation of Kuei Mei is, "a woman returns to where she belongs," there is a suggestion that something is out of place. Not one line in the hexagram is in a proper position of correspondence, most being yang lines in yin positions, and vice-versa. Even the first and last lines, although they are in the correct positions, do not harmonize with their corresponding lines because they are of the same energy. The yang first line cannot harmonize with the yang fourth line, nor can the yin sixth line correspond with the yin third line. Furthermore, as the third, fifth and sixth lines are all yin lines, yin energy is above the yang. This is like a woman who lords over her man in marriage. Therefore, the guidance here is a warning.

The preceding hexagram (Jen) also discusses energy in terms of marriage, but there marriage is successfully achieved in gradual stages. This is the only way that a normal, healthy and happy marriage can be attained. However, in Kuei Mei, a "bossy" girl marries a strong man and friction results.

This hexagram also gives advice on how to maintain a good marital relationship. Lake, which is a manifestation of yin energy, is naturally receptive to the action of Thunder, whose energy is yang. Unfortunately, Lake also represents the mouth and tongue, which indicates that quarreling and fighting are inevitable.

Harmony is the real essence of marriage. Here one can clearly understand how important the receptive feminine virtue is in maintaining a harmonious relationship.

Most *I Ching* scholars have emphasized the impropriety of a female aggressively courting a male in an attempt to establish a marriage. They have also stressed that it is not right for a woman to marry only to acquire a good name and social position. What is truly important is that the female maintains her dignity as well as the feminine virtues that distinguish her from a man. This is the primary guidance of this hexagram.

LINE 1: *"It is not a very good match. One leg is shorter than the other and one sees with only one eye. A good relationship can still exist, however, if one is willing to be submissive and helpful to one's partner."*

The first line is a yang line in the right position, but it cannot find an appropriate match among the strong yang lines in the second and fourth positions. This is like someone who is lame or blind in one eye - although in-convenienced, he is still able to function somewhat normally.   If there is sincerity and perseverance, things will work out satisfactorily.

LINE 2:   *"It is still not an ideal match, but one can have a solid, peaceful relationship in ordinary circumstances."*

In an ideal marriage, a good initial match is of primary importance. A good match resembles well-paired eyes and limbs; their interdependence brings about completion and fulfillment. This line is similar to the first line in that nothing great can be achieved. Although this, too, is not a well-matched relationship, it is not quite as limited as the situation described in the first line.

LINE 3:   *"A reluctant match. The marriage will become disharmonious."*

The third line is a weak line in a strong position and has no response from the sixth line. Therefore, she must wait for a better opportunity. If she does not wait and decides to rush into marriage anyway, she will suffer.

LINE 4:   *"A late marriage. One must wait."*

This is a yang line in a yin position which means that the marriage will not occur as soon as this line wishes it to.   Since this person is virtuous, has firm goals to achieve, and engages in continuous self-improvement, he will eventually find a good marriage partner. If the right opportunity arises, it should be accepted unless there are delays. If so, one should be patient and maintain an appropriate style of life until the time is right.

LINE 5:   *"A harmonious marriage. Modesty and virtue result in a good relationship."*

The relationship between the second and fifth lines implies an alliance between the noble and the plain. Their energy correspondence is symbolized by the relationship between a young noblewoman of high development and a common, less developed man. Originally, the marriage between a princess and an ordinary man was the image used to described this situation. Because of their differences, she should be humble and subordinate herself to the man she married. Only in this way can there be a harmonious interaction of energy between them.

To maintain a good marriage, the female must sometimes have more tolerance and a better temperament than the man. Generally, masculine energy is more inclined to impatience. If a woman does not understand a man's shortcomings and tries to compete with him, the marriage will be ruined. Even if she is a wise and capable person, she must also have humility and patience and occasionally be able to subdue her pride if she expects the marriage to last.

Here, the emperor allows his young sister or daughter to marry a commoner in order to ally royalty with the common people. This also implies that in some circumstances, the wife develops to a higher level than her husband. In either case, the woman must be extremely tolerant in order to enable the relationship to work. By showing respect for her husband, and creatively working to harmonize the family, the relationship can be a positive one.

An honorable, happy marriage cannot be chosen or bought, but can only be earned. Virtue is the foundation for such a marriage. When one understands the reality of a situation, one should respond to it objectively, rather than reacting emotionally. Surely the ideal way to develop a beautiful relationship is gradually, but if one is involved in the special circumstances expressed by this hexagram, tolerance becomes a tool for the wise.

LINE 6: *"A mismatch. An empty basket is brought by the girl. The man performs a bloodless sacrifice. No benefit to the relationship."*

Although this yin line is in its correct place, it has no correspondence with the third line, which is also yin. Since the positions are not right for marriage, there is friction. Nothing good results from this match because of insincerity. The ceremony is only superficial, like a basket without fruit. Only if there is a change in character can there be any hope.

SPECIFIC GUIDANCE

PERSONAL FORTUNE: For a while something good seems to be happening; however, this situation eventually disappears.

MARRIAGE: Can be achieved, but hard to prolong.

HOUSING/FAMILY: It cannot last long.

CHILDBIRTH: Normally the child will be a girl. If it is a boy, both the mother and son will be endangered.

LOOKING FOR WORK: If you depend on a woman, it is easy to accomplish.

SOCIAL/GOVERNMENTAL POSITION: Although you look for something small, you attain a high position.

TRADE/BUSINESS: Not successful.

SEARCHING FOR SOMEONE: They are difficult to find if they are women.

WAITING FOR SOMEONE: They will come.

LOOKING FOR SOMETHING LOST: It can be found.

HUNTING FOR THIEVES: They are in the Southeast and are hard to catch.

LAWSUIT: Suitable to make peace.

CLIMATE: It will be rainy with thunder.

TRAVEL: Not good to travel with a female.

DISEASE: Dangerous.

PERSONAL WISH: Some obstacles.

COMMENTARY
No Bondage

After the good conditions of life are met - health, finances, security, a solid relationship, a good living environment, etc. - and one decides to raise children, one should have a clear understanding of this commitment. If one becomes a mother or a father and lives in a normal society with a normal pattern of life, then twenty-five years of self-sacrifice should be anticipated.

The traditional purpose and benefit of marriage is to raise children. In order to provide psychological security and healthy growth for the young, a binding marriage is very practical. Aside from this particular purpose, a binding marriage is harmful, especially for natural spiritual cultivation. If the marriage is not a case of feeding each other the three poisons (ignorance, stubbornness, and aggressiveness), each person will still someday inevitably suffer the hidden erosion that comes about as the result of sharing the same bed or the same room.

Human beings are changeable animals. Of two people who are married in their early twenties, each may grow at a different rate, thus their personal development does not occur at the same pace. A match that was good ten or fifteen years earlier can seldom maintain this mutual pace and direction of development, and the distance between even a well-matched young couple widens. The harm of social, religious, or familial binding affects each person of the couple and, in particular, influences their moral responsibility to remain independent persons.

Love can be expressed in marriage, but it cannot be expressed in bondage. When one feels the bondage or obligation of a relationship, true love quickly dies.

All lovers dedicate themselves to each other with great respect and appreciate the love they receive. However, when they marry, their love often becomes an obligation and they come to take what love there was for granted. Thus, true love ceases to exist. If there is no true love, then how can such a relationship be called a marriage? It is a marriage with no "soul," a sad result of social custom and environmental conditioning.

A marital law which protects only one of the spouses is unjust. Marriage should be decided by the two people who love each other, and they should make the decision jointly. Divorce should be decided in the same manner. A good marriage cannot be established if one person does not love the other. Similarly, if the husband or wife no longer feels love, a divorce is in order. Any prohibition of divorce is inhuman, and anything inhuman is immoral. Alas, many immoral ways are inhumanities whose persecuting force has continued from the old, faded, insensitive customs of society or religion.

The improvement of married life can often be accomplished by taking a marriage "vacation." When a couple experiences difficulty, they should take a vacation from each other for a while instead of deciding to divorce as quickly as they married. If both parties recognize that the difficulty stems from emotional friction, then the true problem is not one of love, and adjustments can be made accordingly. Thus, the marriage "vacation" offers a positive function. If divorce is the only answer, then a marriage vacation can also help each side see more clearly. No church, court of law, any other authority or outsider can determine the existence of a marriage between two people who are involved in love and life together. Other people should merely be witnesses to the decision.

If a divorce ensues, a husband should not take material profits from his wife. Likewise, the wife should not ask for money from her husband. But, if they so desire, they can offer each other a gift. As to distributing the wealth, if each party is working, then it should belong to the individual who created it. If only the husband has worked and is well off, and the wife has kept the home and is without a skill, the husband should make arrangements to adequately provide for her well-being. If there is equity in their life together, then the wealth should be equally divided. The children should belong to either one side or the other. A determination should be made as to who is more practically able to care for them.

A couple who has reached middle or old age after having been together for many years must maintain virtue in divorcing. The situation may be one in which the children are independent and the wife has no means or skill with which to support herself. Many women in this situation fear divorce, but the man should practice the virtue of a faithful old friend by offering to provide total or partial financial support for his wife for the rest of her life. The wife should practice her virtue of tolerance by not trying to deprive her husband of his natural rights. The fruits of their life should be shared equitably without creating deep worries for either side regarding old age.

In ancient Chinese society, marriage was not bondage. Marriages were based on organizing life to fulfill the practical responsibilities of maintaining their life, and rearing the next generation. The relationship between husband and wife did not emphasize emotional love. Their individual roles were based on mutual energy performance. While the wife devoted herself to the responsibilities of a household, the husband could pursue all kinds of development and was not strictly bound by the narrow sense of marriage. The woman found happiness and enjoyed respect as the one who nurtured her children, while the husband extended himself outwardly. Being a wife made her head of the household, and her position was not altered by any newly-created relationship. If a new woman or several other women were enjoyed by her husband, she welcomed them as sisters. In ancient marriages, there were no emotional expectations. The wife could enjoy her life and status without interfering with, or playing against, the life of her husband. The center of her life was her children and home. However, I do not think this kind of peace between husband and wife will ever return. A painless marriage must be organized differently today. Otherwise, the unhealthy environment of modern life, or the fear of being married, becomes a problem which causes men and women to lose the root of life and home.

The problem is not one of marriage or of staying together or of making friends. In totality, the problem is one of finding the right partner. Even so, the right partner is always in a process of change.

A good marriage is a balance of love, respect and tolerance. A less than good marriage can sometimes last because of emotional dependency, loneliness, insecurity, or social expectation. If marriage is motivated by the pressures of loneliness, the communication within that marriage will never be complete. This type of marriage is made out of emotional imbalance, and the chance for divorce is already there, but hidden.

Marriage is too high a price to pay in order to drive away loneliness. There are alternatives. Engaging in art or participating in spiritual community activities are two positive methods to drive away loneliness and retain emotional balance.

Loneliness can cause people to become imbalanced; it cannot be neglected. All too often loneliness is the source of many bad habits, many bad marriages, many bad occupations and many criminal actions. For a spiritually developed person, loneliness, or being alone, is a good time for self-cultivation or work. So whether one is alone, in a marriage, or within a group, life must continue to be viewed as a process of cultivation.

During the time the *I Ching* was written, at least 3,000 years ago, highly developed spiritual men and women came together on high energy days to harmonize their energies. Following the old traditional methods conducted by the elders, they practiced the subtle harmonization of yin and yang. In the villages of those ancient times, boys and girls lived separately. The girls usually lived with their families and the boys usually lived in groups. Sexual activity occurred only when a certain age and level of physical maturity had been reached.

For a mind longing for sexual satisfaction, subtle energy integration and cultivation is the best solution. It is the best cure for sexual craving which ordinary playboy style sex will never achieve. The latter brings about venereal disease, monetary and energy expense, and the loss of one's true personality. Unfortunately, the subtle method is only available those who are spiritually developed.

On several occasions and places in this sacred book, I have revealed that the Integral Way is not the rigid practice of religion which insists upon celibacy. Nor is it the secular way which promotes sexual indulgence. In the Integral Way, one can perform the energy harmonization that remedies the imbalance of natural physical desires without resorting to masturbation or going to any special place. Furthermore, energy harmonization can occur respectfully with, or sometimes without, the knowledge or agreement of a partner. When one is harmonized within, he or she is ready to be re-charged with the different kind of sexual energy the universe provides.

If mental love exists between two people, and if they are virgins and are correctly guided, they can directly become subtly integrated and rank as angels. If they are not virgins, then the couple has more work to do in the subtle integration. If they use their relationship for ordinary sexual intercourse rather than for conceiving a child, it becomes the downfall of their spiritual cultivation.

To suppress love in one's mind or regard the opposite sex or sexual activity as sinful is the narrow practice of religion and is both inhuman and immoral. From this perspective, I appreciate the great value of the different levels of yin and yang harmonization in the Integral Way. The correct practice in this aspect can be learned from my work. One can refer to *Eight Thousand Years of Wisdom,* the book about natural harmony and my other books for guidelines for correct sexual practice.

It is not that marriage is bad; rather, it is people who create the problems. They cannot control themselves and harmonize their personal, individual energy.

In the small community of a family, and between husband and wife, brothers and sisters, or parents and children, if one does not maintain a consistent level of one's personality, then the hurt which results is unavoidable. One does not need to study people around the world to see that they poison each other. One merely needs to experience life with those under the same roof to discover that the poison there is stronger than in other places. Total spiritual development in a family is important in order to avoid such poison, but if just one member of the family or group does not develop himself, then his or her behavior becomes a source of unhappiness for the entire family. However, spiritual development cannot be demanded of anyone.

The best way of living is to live independently and to enjoy a life with no disturbances, especially for one who aspires spiritually. To know one's own range of health or how far one should keep oneself from people depends upon one's personal development and needs.

For a spiritually developed person, the Old Master has set this example: "Keep a healthy distance away from people and live with a sufficient amount of private space, even within a family. Yet work selflessly among them."

Note: Spiritually-aware people may think the way of subtle intercourse is the same as tantra, but this is not so. Tantric sex requires penetration or a "plug-in." Subtle Intercourse does not require a "plug-in;" it is a communication somewhat like a wireless telephone. It can be practiced anywhere, even with great distances between the two partners, and is far more effective than tantra.

There are three levels of techniques available to our modern times for yin/yang harmonization:

1) For fun. There is no need for this tradition to be taught here since several books on sexual techniques have been translated and are available in book stores.

2) To maintain energy and rejuvenation. At this level, one can not only enjoy sexual activity, but can at the same time pacify the restless mind and enjoy high achievement, rejuvenation and longevity.

3) To approach immortality. This level is the highest means of cultivation.

For more information on this, see *Harmony, the Art of Life*.

One way which served as the most secret and most effective method of rejuvenation and longevity was through dual cultivation which was only practiced in ancient China. This method no longer exists in our drastically changed world.

Among all the available practices for maintaining and improving health and preparing for visible and invisible sexual cultivation, one should be trained in two typical methods that can be practiced before and after sexual cultivation.

1) The Natural Way of Vitalization through Breathing Methods: a unique method to strengthen personal vitality and improve one's physical power and sexual endurance.

2) The Natural Way of Life Endurance through Energy Guidance: a special way to work on the glands and the internal flow of energy. It is applied by a series of quiet sitting movements which enforce one's vitality to slow down the aging process and prevent weakness.

For more information, see *Attune Your Body with Dao-In* and both volumes of *The Life and Teaching of Two Immortals*.

55   fonG

OVER - CAPACITY

GUIDANCE: *"At the time of over-abundance, the king en-joys full growth and has no worry, but he should remain properly motivated for expansion and correctly direct his strength.   Thus, the great attainment of fullness can be maintained and enjoyed."*

In this hexagram, Thunder is above Fire. When these energies interact, over-abundance is expressed. The lower trigram, Li ☲ , is an expression of clarity and illumina-tion. The upper trigram, Chen ☳ , is an expression of movement and shock. Light illuminates, while the power of Thunder awakens. A person with power and light can guide others on the right way.

One's attitude should be like the sun at high noon: bright, sustaining, and enlightening. This hexagram il-lustrates the benefits that come from nature's fullness. A developed being uses such fullness to serve everyone.

According to the natural law of balance, when some-thing reaches its point of fullness, decline must follow. Everything in the universe follows this cycle. If one has more than enough, he should not hold onto everything for himself. If one is given something, he should not be given more than he can hold comfortably. Over-abundance is like light which has become too strong: vegetation dries up, the land becomes parched, and nothing can flourish. For humans, this light becomes blinding and prevents them from seeing clearly. Fong teaches the practice of control in a situation of abundance.

The guidance of the Chinese text indicates that a truly selfless leader who is experiencing a time of abundance is not discouraged by the knowledge of inevitable decline. He simply continues to radiate warmth and clarity to all, just like the midday sun.

During times of abundance, however, most people become apprehensive about losing their wealth and cannot really enjoy it. They become excited and over-indulge, eventually hurting themselves. Controlling oneself at a time like this is crucial. If a person maintains virtue and centeredness, disaster will not follow easily.

Although it is a natural law that fullness is followed by decline, through self-cultivation one can maintain fullness or lessen the severity of the decline by transmuting and refining desires into essential energy or wisdom. With wisdom comes appropriateness and virtue.

Appropriateness is maintaining a delicate balance between over and under-reaction. It is like shooting at a target. If one aims too high or is too weak, he fails to hit the target, but when one hits the bullseye, one is in resonance with one's virtue.

What is fullness? What is excessive for one person may not be for another. The minds of different people have different capacities and capabilities. The degree of capacity and capability will be decreased if one tries to hold too much at one time. However, when a person cultivates virtue, his physical and psychological capacities are not limited, they are strengthened.

Thus, one's capacity becomes infinite. The single force that can overpower any spiritual limitation is one's natural virtue. When one follows natural virtue, one's true chi becomes wisdom and one's actions and reactions become spontaneous and appropriate. Eventually one's virtue will blossom fully and freely. A wise person can illuminate the space of his own steps, while a highly virtuous person can light up the space of history's steps.

LINE 1: *"The rich guest gets along well with his rich host. Fullness brings creation without excess."*

The first line goes to meet the host, the fourth line. Though both lines are yang, they work well together, because this hexagram combines clarity with action. As long as this line does not overdo anything or act too aggressively, good progress can be made.

> **LINE 2:** *"The decorative covering of the house is excessive. One does not have much light. Darkness brings narrowness and suspicion. With plain honesty, one can again restore one's clarity."*

The literal translation of this line is: "The pole star cannot be seen in the sunlight." One's visibility can be hindered by being in an overly strong light. This is to say, one's strong ambition can negatively affect the brightness of one's mind.

This line implies that one who seeks external prosperity rather than striving firmly for internal clarity will meet the obstruction of darkness. With honest reflection, one can regain the light by removing the decorative coverings such as false knowledge or superficiality. Although the second line attempts to give good advice or tries to help the fifth line, he elicits suspicion. Thus, he turns back to cultivate himself. This line suggests that every person should develop his own truth and clarity and not reach out with blind ambition. For people who are in a superior position, let those who are wise discover your true value and capability by themselves.

> **LINE 3:** *"A broken arm impedes usefulness, but no blame. Too many banners flying in the air to protect people from the strong light blocks the light."*

When the light is extremely bright, it is blinding and one's vision is obscured, like not being able to see after staring at the sun. Here, the sun has already passed its zenith and is declining. The banners (the top line) now become an obstruction. The literal Chinese words are: "One breaks his right arm but there is no problem." This means that the top line hopes to become an able helper, but instead he becomes an obstacle covering the light with his inappropriate behavior. Although a broken arm cannot cause much trouble, one is unable to achieve anything of significance because of it.

> **LINE 4:** *"The decorative curtains of a house are so thick that one lives in partial darkness; however, his association with a good ally brings positive results."*

The fourth line, a yang line in a yin position, is hindered by its improper position. Thus, there is darkness. But by having proper correspondence with the first line, the misfortune can possibly be turned into good fortune. Even when one is in a bad position and time, an opportunity may still exist to achieve safety or bring forth good fortune through correct associations.

LINE 5: *"Celebration and good reputation will be brought forth. Good fortune."*

Help comes from without, from the second line. The fifth line, being a weak leader, should extend his receptivity and openness in order to receive the support of able helpers from the fourth and second positions, as well as from the entire lower trigram. Though one is weak, one can achieve success with assistance.

LINE 6: *"A big house has all the luxuries, but look in the house - there is no one inside. For three years no one can be seen there."*

The top line has already passed fullness and is now in a period of decline. The value of abundance is in decline and resembles one who hides and does not put himself to good use. This is like keeping a mansion for only one person to live in. Arrogance brings isolation. One should stay within the light and be useful rather than occupied only with self-serving interests.

SPECIFIC GUIDANCE

PERSONAL FORTUNE: This time is the height of your fortune. Be careful.

MARRIAGE: Not successful.

HOUSING/FAMILY: Live beside or on a mountain. Good fortune.

CHILDBIRTH: Misfortune.

LOOKING FOR WORK: Though there is difficulty in the beginning, it can be achieved later.

SOCIAL/GOVERNMENTAL POSITION: A situation is developing.

TRADE/BUSINESS: It can be achieved.

SEARCHING FOR SOMEONE: They cannot easily be found.

LOOKING FOR SOMETHING LOST: It is in the East and can be found.

HUNTING FOR THIEVES: They can be caught.

LAWSUIT: Although things look good in the beginning, there may be problems later.

CLIMATE: It will be rainy, with floods.

TRAVEL: Go slowly.

DISEASE: Very severe.

PERSONAL WISH: It can be achieved slowly.

COMMENTARY

Be gentle in doing right.
Do not be violent.
Be diligent in all undertakings, even in small matters.
The essence of work is diligence.
A successful life depends on doing the right thing
*   at the right time and obeying the cosmic law.*
Blessings come in many ways.
Do not look for happiness
*   and contentment will come naturally.*

Continuously remove the negativity within yourself.
One's good life is decided by one's virtue
*   and clean mind.*
To endure difficulty, avoid complaining.
To endure vexation and annoyance,
*   avoid bitter comments.*
If your mind is always occupied by distress,
*   good fortune is sure to evade you.*
When things reach their worst,
*   they can only get better.*
When something reaches its limit,
*   it turns into its opposite.*
This is the T'ai Chi of events.

Avoid involvement with people who are suspicious,
*   easily pleased or angered.*
Listen only to viewpoints that are balanced.
Walk away from idle talk.
Unite with people of outstanding character.
Collective purposes form fortresses.
In uniting harmonized energies, we gather strength.

56　旅　LU ䷷

CRAVELING

GUIDANCE:　*"Traveling. On a journey, only minor under-takings go well."*

In this hexagram, Fire is above Mountain. The image is a vivid one. Fire is "traveling" or spreading across a Mountain, sustained by trees and driven by the wind. Wood or Wind is implied by the inner trigram, Sun ☴. Sometimes the burning is so rapid that in a matter of hours the Fire may travel a hundred miles without being contained.

Only small matters should be undertaken at this time. Like a "rolling stone which gathers no moss," the fast movement of the Fire does not allow the accumulation of anything big. At this time there is good fortune in achieving small things.

Traveling includes several factors: the traveler, the road, the destination, the lodging and the service. Those can also symbolize elements of one's internal process. The "lodging" represents one's center, which is reached through stillness and calmness. The "journey" represents the movement of one's energy and the process of refining it. The patterns of yin and yang are expressed in life through the interaction of stillness and activity. The way one manifests and expresses his energy in relation to the world determines the quality of his "service." Each moment in one's life is part of a journey. This hexagram provides an opportunity for one to reflect upon the destination of his journey. If one's destination is exclusively extroverted, he will become fixed in his outwardness or never finish doing the work of accomplishing himself. If one's destination is exclusively introverted, he will never be able to manifest it. The *I Ching* teaches the balanced way of being neither overly extroverted nor overly introverted.

A balanced personality can be attained by integrating one's spiritual purposes with a practical life style. Only by achievement at both levels can an individual and all of humanity progress.

Since life is energy in movement, the destiny of travel cannot be avoided. For the many disturbances encountered along the way, the image of a Mountain inside and Fire outside expresses a good principle by which to live: keep still within and active without. One cannot avoid life by hiding in the mountains, because life exists there as well. But one can avoid the disturbance of the external world by remaining centered and calm like a mountain. The I Ching teaches one to make good use of the contradictory quality of life by uniting opposites in a harmonious balance.

Life is movement, and movement cannot be stopped. One should neither fear to move nor lose the stillness within. Life is the projection of one's energy, like an arrow aimed at a target. It is possible to hit the "bulls eye" and accomplish the purpose of life, but unfortunately most people miss the target by shooting their "arrows" aimlessly. Life's travels must include a destination in order to judge whether the methods that have been set are beneficial and worthy. If one's goals are in harmony with the universe, then the right internal energy will manifest at the appropriate time.

Do you know the destination of life's journey? Is it internal or external? Look inside to discover the correct meaning of your journey. You have already shot the arrow. Where is it going?

LINE 1: *"Traveling. Do not argue over small expenses or trouble will arise."*

The first line is a yin line in a yang position and applies to the lodgings and the traveler. If the hotel is unreasonable in its charges or services, or the guest is too miserly or demanding, conflict is bound to arise. In such a situation, unpleasantness is created for both sides. Getting involved in such trivial matters is an unnecessary waste of time and energy. When traveling, one should be tolerant of the different customs of the host.

LINE 2: *"Staying in the right place, one protects one's proper ties and finds a good helper."*

This line is in its correct position. The traveler is safe and has everything he needs. The second line represents a traveler who is self-disciplined, modest and reserved. In traveling, three things are important in determining whether one's travels will be pleasant or not: a good place to stay, adequate resources and helpful people.

LINE 3: *"The lodgings catch fire and one loses his helper. Stubbornness causes the trouble."*

The "lodge burning down" suggests a traveller with a quick temper and reckless in his actions. This line also describes someone who is stubborn, opinionated and unwilling to adapt to the circumstances of his travels. Such arrogance can only cause trouble. Arrogance can destroy one's attainments and achievements in all circumstances, particularly while on a journey.

LINE 4: *"Traveling to a shelter. One meets with gain but must constantly keep alert. Such temporary lodging makes one feel uneasy."*

Although the traveler has shelter, his life has not adjusted to the new environment and he feels restless and out of place. He needs to protect himself, which makes him feel unsettled.

LINE 5: *"Shooting a pheasant. Though the arrow is lost, fame is earned."*

The fifth line is the center of clarity in the upper trigram. In ancient times, statesmen introduced themselves by offering a pheasant. If the statesman shot the pheasant himself and used only one arrow in the process, he was commended. Such a person is represented by the fifth line.

In this position, one's task is completed and all difficulties are removed. One is accepted by society and receives honor. The price has been paid and one now receives the reward. Although hardships have been suffered along the way, one's destination has finally been reached.

LINE 6: *"The bird's nest is burned. The cattle are lost. The reckless traveler laughs in the beginning but cries in the end. Misfortune."*

The top line represents a traveler who, through un-reasonableness and lack of consideration, has no place to stay. In addition, he has lost his belongings.

This line describes a person who is extreme and has no consideration for others. He does not understand the Chinese proverb: "To give convenience to others is to earn convenience for oneself."

SPECIFIC GUIDANCE

PERSONAL FORTUNE: This is not your best time. There may be some trouble.

MARRIAGE: This is not a suitable partner nor a good marriage.

HOUSING/FAMILY: Buy a small house. Be careful of fire.

CHILDBIRTH: The baby will be a girl.

LOOKING FOR WORK: Do not go through an agency. Apply directly. Make your own recommendations.

SOCIAL/GOVERNMENTAL POSITION: Difficult to achieve.

TRADE/BUSINESS: It can be successful.

WAITING FOR SOMEONE: They will come.

LOOKING FOR SOMETHING LOST: Look in a far place. It can be found.

HUNTING FOR THIEVES: Difficult to catch them.

LAWSUIT: It will be rainy.

TRAVEL: This is not a good time for traveling.

DISEASE: Danger.

PERSONAL WISH: Small things can be accomplished; big things cannot.

COMMENTARY

Life is a journey.
What is your destination?
Which path will you follow?

The Natural Integral Way differs
  from all ordinary religions and teachings.
We think all people are born
  with the same basic qualities:
  organic, rational and divine in nature.
Right cultivation nourishes these qualities
  enabling fulfillment and union with true life.
Instead of dividing ourselves many times,
  we must nurse the powerful chi.
Books alone will not uncover it.

At birth a person is full,
  then one chi is transformed from the three purities.
To achieve the three purities
  means the fulfillment of the three natures of life.
To develop and fulfill your organic nature
  is to extend to the Realm of Great Purity.
To develop and fulfill your rational nature
  is to extend to the realm of Crystal Purity.
To develop and fulfill your spiritual nature
  is to extend to the Realm of Utmost Purity.
Thus, the realms of life extend to the realms of purity.

The fulfillment of this energy
  is the way of Heaven and Earth.
It has no beginning or end.
It is unchanged and never exhausted.
If not distorted or disturbed,
  it brings proof of immortality.

Because of your place in life,
  there is need for discipline and cultivation.
But this need not be done in the mountains
  as a hermit.
Work with all the changes and patterns
  that life presents you.
Utilize the sacred methods
  to attract the help you need.
Practice it constantly to practice it correctly.

Talk brings no real benefit.
Do not swim in theory, going round and round.
To deepen in reality, cultivate the Tao.

57 soen ䷸

gentle wind · submissiveness

GUIDANCE: *"Submissiveness can further one in achieving minor things. It is good to assist a powerful leader with a great goal."*

In ancient times, before societies were created, people followed the example of nature with unspoiled minds. From Wind or air, they learned obedience and submissiveness. All things depend on Wind for survival. From the gentleness of Wind, one can learn how to give and take. From the force of the Wind one can learn how to balance and control oneself. Wind is an energy which acts by invisible ways, yet achieves visible results. One cannot see the Wind except by its effect on something. It exists as an interaction of subtle energy, yet expresses itself substantially.

In this hexagram, Wind symbolizes the subtle, influential energy of spirit. It also represents the eldest daughter and the attributes of gentleness, softness, femininity and obedience, which are characteristics of a woman who has reached the mellowness of maturity.

In both trigrams, there are two forceful yang lines above one gentle yin line. Each yin line expresses the true nature of Wind, which is gentleness. One who seeks guidance from this hexagram is counseled to wait for the right time in his growth to pursue what he wishes to achieve. Great achievements cannot be expected in the beginning.

For a correct understanding of the hexagram as a whole, one must consider the inner trigrams: Fire is above and Lake is below, which indicates that one has a good heart. When a person instructs with a righteous heart, others will naturally follow. When the Wind blows, the grass bends. This is a good sign, especially for teachers and advisors.

Here one is wise but weak and must therefore seek outside support. There are two strong leaders in the second and fifth lines. By following and assisting strong leaders, one can achieve a righteous goal, but if one is alone, not much can be achieved. Likewise, on an inner level, even with little physical strength, the power of the mind can bring success. As subtle energy accumulates, what one develops and reinforces within will become manifest in the processes of thinking and doing. Since the nature of one's thoughts determines what will occur, it is important to maintain firm-mindedness and high virtue.

Those who are weak need the help of someone of strength and virtue to make their purposes concrete. Otherwise, even righteous purpose and wisdom are not sufficient. In Chinese history, there are many wise men who assisted strong leaders as advisors in order to achieve great purposes.

We can emulate the virtue of Wind and thereby benefit all life by radiating a good influence. This is the highest natural effect of positive self-development.

LINE 1: *"Hesitation. It is correct for a soldier to resolve indecisiveness."*

This is a gentle, weak line in a strong position. Its tendency is to hesitate and be indecisive. At this time, one needs the spirit of a soldier and should go forward decisively and with perseverance. Firm intention will eliminate doubt.

LINE 2: *"Enlightened instruction should be given to eliminate foolishness and confusion."*

Soen also represents Wood. The second line is the symbol for a wooden frame, like a low table, altar or bed. The first yin line represents the feet which support the frame. In ancient times, exorcists would search beneath the bed for negative spirits and evil influences and drive them away. It was also a practice to use a table as an altar, a tool for guidance and civilization.

This symbol can be interpreted in two ways: it encourages us to seek out negative influences, and it is also a vehicle for understanding and enlightenment.

This line counsels one to accept service and assistance and to accumulate this information in order to make a sound decision. In this way, negative influences can be eliminated. Being receptive to all sources of help enables one to accumulate the information and energy necessary to make proper judgments and take correct action.

The second line advises one to follow the principle of gentleness. By using virtue and wisdom to guide people, rather than using strength to conquer and subdue them, one wins their obedience and cooperation.

LINE 3:   *"Being overly submissive, one loses one's confidence."*

The gentleness of the third line is excessive and dependent. It cannot make a firm decision and stick to it, nor does it carry out its responsibilities.

One in this position does not have faith in himself or in others and, as a result of hesitation and inertia, lacks a creative spirit. Thus, he loses his opportunity and suffers humiliation.

LINE 4:   *"Remorse disappears. One obtains three kinds of game in the hunt and earns merit."*

The fourth line is close to the leader and offers cooperation and assistance. The literal translation of this line is: "One may have an abundant harvest and catch plenty of game in the hunt." In ancient times, game was caught for three purposes: as a spiritual offering, for feeding guests, and for one's own household. This line is an example of acting appropriately to fulfill all three needs.

LINE 5:   *"With gentleness, be firm in your principles. Remorse disappears and all things are benefited. With good preparation, the reform has begun. With careful inspection throughout, it is successfully completed. Good fortune."*

Change must be made gradually and with deliberation. When one wishes to begin something, it should be started gently. If one wishes others to follow a command, it should be made with gentleness. It is also important to give notice before implementing a new plan. Enough time should be allowed for adjustments in order for the new transition to be gradual and smooth. When reform is undertaken, be like grass in the Wind, willing to bend but not break.

LINE 6: *"Being too subservient, one loses property and protection."*

If, as in the third line, one is too polite, gentle or hesitant in expressing expectations, one will surely lose this good opportunity. In this important position at the top, one cannot afford to be weak. Such weakness will result in the loss of what has already been accomplished. Although one should normally be yielding, like the Wind, there is no more room in which to yield. On this level, continuing to yield only invites danger. One must be firm in principle and express one's desires and goals. Any weakness or gentleness displayed at this time will only cause more trouble.

SPECIFIC GUIDANCE

PERSONAL FORTUNE: Smooth and peaceful.
MARRIAGE: Difficulty at the beginning. Later, it will be easy.
HOUSING/FAMILY: It is suitable to live close to a temple. Two people should live together.
CHILDBIRTH: If you make a divination in Summer or Autumn, the baby will be a boy. If the fifth line is received, it will be a difficult delivery.
LOOKING FOR WORK: Look quickly.
SOCIAL/GOVERNMENTAL POSITION: Although there is some difficulty in the beginning, success will eventually come.
TRADE/BUSINESS: It can be successful.
SEARCHING FOR SOMEONE: They can be found.
WAITING FOR SOMEONE: They will not come.
LOOKING FOR SOMETHING LOST: Hard to find.
HUNTING FOR THIEVES: They are hiding in a church in the Northwest and can be caught.
LAWSUIT: Make peace.
CLIMATE: It will be windy.
TRAVEL: Suitable for two people traveling together, but not suitable to go to the Northwest.
DISEASE: Danger.
PERSONAL WISH: Partially realized.

COMMENTARY
Spiritual Renaissance

Soen means to follow. What do we follow? On what occasion should we be obedient? Let us ponder this spiritual matter.

As a child, I often had the opportunity to see folk people walk barefoot over burning coals at religious festivals. Several times I even saw people with bare feet climb high ladders made of sharp knives. When I was older, I saw someone put a wide knife blade to his chest with his left hand and, with his right hand, use a rolling pin to hit it completely into his chest. Throughout this amazing feat, the performer continually summoned spirits. When the knife was removed, not only was there no bloodshed, there was not even a scratch.

Over the years, I experienced many such extraordinary religious and magical powers. Sometimes I enjoyed them and felt quite amused, but since these feats of magic were not my real interest, I never thought to learn or practice them. Most were without true spiritual development and simply demonstrated "brutal" human faith. Faith that is not guided by reason is brutal; it is a remnant of primitive, undeveloped human tribalism.

Once a divine being said to me, "Humankind's growth is slow. It seems that it has not evolved beyond the 'brutal' stage. For example, modern religions still follow the track of earlier, undeveloped human tribes. They continue to exalt a forceful image of past religious leaders to lord it over present-day people who lack true spiritual knowledge. A certain over-used book is infused into the minds of ordinary people; its far-fetched interpretations are produced to fit all situations, while the 'living book' of individual self-cultivation for personal growth is suppressed.

"History is a good book; it demonstrates that old tracks of a failing vehicle should not be followed. When a book containing experiences of brutal struggles of the past is used as the model for present and coming generations, is it not intended to use mixed-up religious emotions to lock people into the same tragic patterns as past generations?

"Hundreds of different interpretations have been given for this book, but they merely compete for authority on something which fundamentally is not a matter of truth or untruth, but rather one of faith. When faith, which is an emotional force itself, is used to guide all other emotional forces, the result is disaster. The stronger an emotional force, the further it is from the truth.

"Surely, throughout the history of humankind we have witnessed many misunderstandings and failures due to the lack of spiritual development. They are so obvious that it is not necessary to be spiritually advanced in order to recognize them. Even the initial leaders of Communism knew them well and they utilized these old techniques to push their "new" religion onto people. The form was altered, but the same darkness was imparted. Of course, one would not wish for the world to remain constantly unchanged, but one can wish the quality of human existence to continue to improve. Until the darkness of the human world is totally dispersed by humankind itself, people will never be able to see the light.

"The first Renaissance brought about a change in forms. Let us hope that a new Renaissance will bring about a change in the 'brutal force' which is cultivated by modern civilization.

"Modern people take a meticulous approach to studying the material sphere, but they are lax in studying the reality of the spiritual realm. If the same vigor that is applied toward studying the material sphere could be applied toward studying spiritual reality, dominating, undeveloped religions would cease to control those who are spiritually undeveloped. Most human disputes, based as they are in ignorance and misdirected energy, could then be stopped."

The new Renaissance of humankind is not impossible, but, as most of you know, the strength of the collective good-will of humankind has been misguided and misused. If each of us were to correct this in ourselves, who would say that a new Renaissance of balanced human nature and the above conversation were merely the illusion of a man of cultivation?

58 兑 ZUI

JOYOUSNESS

GUIDANCE: *"One can enjoy what one is doing and still be firm with one's principles."*

In this hexagram, the trigram Lake is doubled. The inner trigrams represent sunshine and Wind. This is the image of a beautiful place which can only evoke joyousness. In both trigrams, the yin line above the two yang lines represents one who acts with receptivity and gentleness but who holds to firm principles within. When one achieves such inner and outer harmony, life is naturally joyous.

True happiness and joy are the results of virtue and constancy, not of emotionalism. The *I Ching*'s guidance in this respect is very clear: sentiments and emotions should be governed by the principles of balance and appropriateness. However, one should not try to suppress emotions, because emotional rigidity is just as unhealthy as emotional indulgence. Most people think that life without so-called "joy" and "pleasure" is boring and worthless, but pleasure is actually as elusive as a shadow. If one tries to catch it, it no longer exists, and when it reaches its peak it becomes its opposite - sorrow. Pleasure is only momentary. It cannot last. Thus, learning what comprises true joy and happiness is real spiritual evolution.

Tui guides us to develop an inner, constant peace of mind that is not upset by external circumstances. People who seek happiness from others, or who seek only to please others, will never discover their fountain of joy within.

When one only perceives things emotionally, reality changes according to mood, but when one's energy is centered, one is not affected by external circumstances and is thus closer to knowing the true virtue of joy. In handling joy, as well as other emotions, one should follow the example of the ocean. Its surface is rough and excited, but its depths are very still.

The promise of constant, subtle joy may encourage one to attend to internal growth and to look deeply within to see what obstructs joy. The achieved mind is like an endlessly clear sky. No cloud can block the brightness of this innate purity and joy.

LINE 1: *"The joy of harmony and independence. Good fortune."*

The first line is a yang line which has no response from either the fourth or second line. It is unattached and independent. This joy comes from inner harmony and is like the pure, spontaneous joy that one feels when experiencing a pleasure for the first time.

LINE 2: *"The joy of faithful friendships. Remorse disappears."*

Sincerity and faithfulness cause others to trust you. Pleasing others in order to achieve yourself is not necessary. This line makes friends through sincerity. In remaining unaffected by closer, inferior acquaintances like the third line, it wins the true friendship of the upright.

LINE 3: *"One tries to please superiors with flattery. Misfortune."*

This yin line is in a yang position. It has a weak personality with strong ambitions and is attracted to worldly people and pleasures. It seeks wealth and power by making itself known to others. Its joys are temporary and superficial; therefore, humiliation and misfortune result.

LINE 4: *"One hesitates to curb the lower passions, but when this is accomplished there is much joy and celebration."*

This is a strong line in a weak position, thus it is restless and hesitant. Because it is between the weak third and the strong fifth line, it has strong desires, yet is also aware of higher joys. In such a position, one must choose which way of happiness to strive for. Of course, the easiest way is to stay with worldly pleasures. However, this line has the ability and strength to rise above them. When one makes the decision to firmly follow one's virtue, pure joy and bountiful blessings will indeed come.

LINE 5: *"Be alert in order to avoid exploitation."*

This line represents a strong leader in the correct position. However, if he places his trust in the wrong person, disaster will surely result. The sixth line represents an unvirtuous person who attempts to influence others through flattery and exploitation. The fourth line represents an able helper who does not seek favor, but wishes to provide the leader with correct advice. A clear head is needed in this situation.

LINE 6: *"Evil temptation."*

This yin line is above two yang lines.   It is very scheming and negative and only wishes to please others. In the end, it pleases no one. Like attracts like. Inferior people will be attracted to evil and become trapped; however, the virtuous will attract good friends and benefit greatly.

SPECIFIC GUIDANCE

PERSONAL FORTUNE: It is stable, but be careful about illness.

MARRIAGE: There will be some quarrels.

CHILDBIRTH: Peaceful and safe.

LOOKING FOR WORK: It can be found.

SOCIAL/GOVERNMENTAL POSITION: It can be achieved. Rely on the support and strength of friends.

TRADE/BUSINESS: In order for it to be profitable, you need to depend on people's help and assistance.

SEARCHING FOR SOMEONE: They can be found.

LOOKING FOR SOMETHING LOST: Difficult to find.

HUNTING FOR THIEVES: Difficult to catch. They are hiding in the Northeast.

LAWSUIT: Make peace.

CLIMATE: It will be rainy.

TRAVEL: In the beginning there is some loss, but afterwards there is happiness.

DISEASE: Severe and dangerous.

PERSONAL WISH: Difficult to achieve.

COMMENTARY

One can be amused by beautiful words.
One also tries to frequently please others
  by what he says.
Are we aware of what we say?
Much speech is not good.
Less speech is favorable.
Speechlessness is best.

Unite your energy to the mystery of the universe,
   and in the quiet depth within yourself
   you will meet the totality of universal truth.

Keep the three mystics (mouth, mind and will)
   firmly united in one.
Roaming, thinking and myth-creating are wasteful.
Hold fast to the true origin of life.
This is of real value to cultivation.
To follow many religious teachings is confusing.
To follow their essence is useful.
To follow some plain truth of nature is best.
Too many methods bewilder.
Use only one path to the most subtle realms.

The deepest mysteries are found
   without any teachings.
Only by being of the highest spirit
   can you be among the Shiens, the whole beings.

59   huan

dispersion

GUIDANCE: "Success.   The great leader distributes his love impartially to all people. He builds temples in order to regain the spiritual focus which people have lost due to their scattered minds.   He needs great courage, like that which is needed to cross the great water. There is help in the upright and the firm."

In this hexagram, Wind is above Water.   How does their interaction indicate dispersion? In the yearly energy cycle, Water belongs to Winter and Wind belongs to Spring.   When Spring winds blow over winter ice, the ice begins to melt and disperse.   Also, Wind blowing over the surface of Water causes it to spread in all directions.

Huan also suggests entrapment. The lower trigram, K'an or Water, usually represents an abyss, danger or entrapment. Through the virtue of the Wind, however, that which was dammed up and stagnant is now free to move again.

The upper trigram, Sun, is Wood. Wood over Water symbolizes a boat which, with the help of Wind, can pass over difficult waters. Thus, now is a suitable time to go far away or communicate with people who are at a distance.

If one is guided by clarity and calm, one can successfully avert or correct problems and handle the aftermath of dispersion. There may be some worry over losses, so one should be careful. Although this hexagram does not express absolute good fortune, it is for the most part very positive.

There are many examples of how dispersion is used as an aid in breaking up congestion. For example, when ominous clouds gather and create stormy conditions, the Wind comes and blows them away. When one catches a cold, because the ventilation between the inside and outside skin has become congested, a warm bath which causes sweating will break up the congestion and health will be restored.

Dispersion is especially valuable in self-cultivation. When strongly influenced by desire, ambition or misunderstanding, one must remove the obstruction or there can be no real progress. Once the "frozen ice" is dissolved, joy can be restored.

Sometimes people remain unforgiving or hold a grudge. Such a condition is more unhealthy for the grudge bearer than for its object. Knowing that dispersion starts from within, then through forgiveness balance can be restored. To forgive is to disperse the blockage and dissolve the tension.

LINE 1: *"Dispersion begins. Rescue comes like a strong, fast horse with the cooperation of friends."*

The first line is weak, but in this position should be strong. Since it has no correspondence with the fourth line, it seeks support from the strong second line.

Although the danger is not yet serious, one must act quickly or it will be too late. Fortunately, its neighbor is a yang line which carries the weak first line to safety.

LINE 2: *"He quickly goes to the rescue. Remorse disappears."*

The second line is also in an incorrect position. Furthermore, its moving yang energy is hindered by the surrounding yin lines, like a wild horse trapped within a ravine. It does not receive help from the fifth line, which is also a yang line.

However, the second line is the beginning of the inner trigram Chen, which represents Thunder or the feet and connotes movement. Although it is unable to help itself, it gathers its energy and helps the first line, which is in even greater trouble. Even though one has much strength, it will go to waste if not used to benefit others.

LINE 3: *"Dispersing one's strength for the salvation of the world. There is no remorse in this."*

The third line is a yin line in a yang position. Along with the fourth line, it is an assistant to the leader, the fifth line. The third line renounces itself in order to help others. First one must rid oneself of everything which serves as a barrier to the understanding of others. Although nothing can be accomplished for oneself in this position, one can be of great benefit to others.

LINE 4: *"Leaving one's small group, people surprisingly come to support you. Great good fortune."*

The fourth line is in its correct position, but has no correspondence with the first line. He becomes independent and gains high recognition as a loyal minister to the king. He dissolves established bonds in order to completely and selflessly dedicate himself to serving others. In return, he is greatly benefited.

LINE 5: *"Dispersing one's treasures to help the world. There is no fault in this."*

This line is a strong, wise and able leader. The wild horse in the second position is too strong and ambitious to correspond with it. However, the ruler is able to tame him.

Since the fifth line is the strong center of the trigram Wind, he exemplifies the power of gentle persuasion and so gives of himself to one and all. The fifth line has accumulated much wealth and strength and is therefore in a position to help many people. He gives away his accumulations, his strength and his "sweat." Just as sweating can help break through a physical crisis, giving of oneself can help break through a social crisis.

> **LINE 6:** *"Dispersing a crisis that could lead to bloodshed. One must keep far from this danger."*

The top line is trying to disperse trouble by avoiding it. One should prepare another place far away in order to avoid the present danger.

SPECIFIC GUIDANCE

PERSONAL FORTUNE: Things are running smoothly now, but be careful of a change in your attitude.

MARRIAGE: Separation.

HOUSING/FAMILY: If there is a lake in front of the house, the owner will not feel at peace.

CHILDBIRTH: If born in Spring or Summer, it will be a boy. If born in Autumn or Winter, it will be a girl.

LOOKING FOR WORK: You get it, but afterwards you lose it.

SOCIAL/GOVERNMENTAL POSITION: Though there is difficulty in the beginning, afterwards it can be achieved.

TRADE/BUSINESS: Difficult to achieve.

SEARCHING FOR SOMEONE: They are in the South and can be found.

WAITING FOR SOMEONE: They will not come.

LOOKING FOR SOMETHING LOST: Difficult to locate.

HUNTING FOR THIEVES: Difficulty.

LAWSUIT: Take action slowly. Do not hurry.

CLIMATE: It will be rainy.

TRAVEL: Not good for a long trip.

DISEASE: Danger.

PERSONAL WISH: It can be achieved.

COMMENTARY
From Three to Five

Dispersion occurs when human intelligence grows above spiritual capability, when one or a society is unable to be held as one piece. Intellectual divergence arises from the different capabilities that people have for understanding and knowing things. Arguments and wars breed in the warm bed of divergence.

Real peace cannot be achieved until the entire knowing capability is achieved by both the individual and the total human race. Tolerance must be worked at when dealing with such differences. The real strength for such tolerance is only obtained through a higher vision.

Many years ago, a new group of religious leaders from a large city wished to begin a united religious movement. They sought my father's support and expressed their broad-minded views to him in this way:

"All religions are the same. Some people call the universal divinity God, others call it Allah, Brahman, Tao or some other name. The lotus flower sits above its root and its stem and is known by different names in different places, but the lotus sits at the top and is actually the essence of them all. Therefore, God, Allah, Brahman, Tao and the various other names really mean the top, the essence. Religious conflict is totally unnecessary. Religious teachings should serve people, not cause them to fight over their religious differences.

"A new universal religion with an equal view and no prejudice is needed now to break through the religious obstacles which have continually hindered a close and peaceful relationship among people throughout the world."

My father greeted them warmly and, during the abundant meal he shared with them, he spoke of his personal efforts in this direction. "I lost my father between the late Spring and early Summer when I was eight years old. At that time, our village and ten neighboring villages were suffering severely from an epidemic of smallpox. It happened that my father was the only doctor people would trust with their young ones' lives, so for three to four months he refused no house call when there was a child with a high fever. Without concern for his own health, without proper rest or food, he fought this vicious, life-taking disease with a firm will day and night and succeeded. Not a single life was lost. Finally, when the difficult period had been overcome, he returned home one evening from a house call. The starlit sky was hushed in silence as he approached the stone bridge crossing the canal. He lifted his over-worked legs, step by weary step, until he finally reached the bridge. In the dark of midnight, the arched bridge of slippery green stones made it difficult for him to cross the canal. The silence surrounded him and everything was peaceful, except for the one thunderous splash from the water. His neatly-cut slim silhouette disappeared from the top of the bridge. At that moment, ten villages and our neighborhood lost a good doctor and I lost my father and teacher of Tao.

"When I was fourteen, I became an apprentice to a tailor who specialized in making religious robes and clothing for priests and monks and nuns of different orders. During this time I had the opportunity to live in one temple after another working for a master of some religion or another. When I was nineteen, I took all my earnings plus my family savings of several hundred pieces of silver and became a military officer. I inherited my rank from one of my ancestors who had served in the army of the Ching Dynasty (1644-1911 A.D.)

"My unit was stationed on a beautiful mountain with several famous temples and many hermits who cultivated themselves in the stone caves. The army was sent there because of outlaws who often made this sacred place their den. To pass the time, the soldiers would shoot at monkeys, but since it was such a task to operate the old-fashioned rifles, the monkeys usually disappeared before the soldier could fire a shot. Nevertheless, a rifle in hand always suggested authority, and in my innocent youth I vaguely sought to have some feeling of authority over life and death.

"As I patrolled the different places of the mountain, I became familiar with almost every spiritual person living there. One day, at a place called the Temple of the Benevolent One, I met a traveler. He was a beautiful old man with a lovely moustache and beard and a strong aura around his peaceful being. After a normal greeting I immediately recognized him as a highly achieved one, and a special friendship was formed. Feeling at ease, I asked him about Tao. His straightforward answer surprised me: 'To be an authority of life is to learn the Tao.'

"I laughed and said, 'I am already an authority of life. If I wish, I can kill almost anything on this mountain.'

"'Perhaps you can,' he replied, 'but, it seems to me that killing is not the authority of life. When the chi of death extends itself to someone's hand to execute its work, one becomes the slave of death. An authority of life is the opposite: one who can control his own life can bring life to all others.'

"I paused momentarily to reflect on the wise words this old man had spoken and then continued. 'As a matter of fact, my father was a doctor. He brought life to many families, but lost his own. Thus, a family of long lineage in Tao has been interrupted by his death, and now I have no way to continue his work or career.'

"'See, you are not an authority of life. A person who is an authority of life can determine and achieve what he is going to be. No matter how difficult, all obstacles on his path can be overcome if he applies his utmost sincerity. Tell me if I am not right.'

"After a long, inspiring conversation, I knew I wanted to become his pupil and to follow him wherever he might go, but when I expressed my desire to become his follower he refused, saying, 'I am like an unanchored boat. I am not suitable to have a pupil. But I will make you this promise, every few years I will come to see you.'

"'How will you know where I am?'

"'Do not worry, I shall meet you anywhere, just as I have picked you from among the many soldiers here.'

"I parted from him reluctantly, and since I had also finished my three hundred days of killing authority, I was free to embark on my re-awakened spiritual journey.

"With my skill in making clothes, I visited many spiritual people living in temples, and even some hermits. I stayed here and there for different periods of time in order to learn herbology, acupuncture and the Integral Way from the many spiritual teachers I encountered along the way. Whenever I heard of anyone who had made some special achievement in his cultivation, I would go there and insist on becoming his pupil. During this time I also finished reading all the books my father had left.

"Ten years passed, and all my teachers thought I was fully skilled and completely knowledgeable in handling all diseases and spiritual problems. With my old, worn robe, oil-paper umbrella, and three pieces of silver, I went to a town to begin my work. This was thirty-five years ago when I was in my thirties. Every day I treated patients, and every festival day I taught people. Soon I found it necessary to develop centers and temples for my teachings, as many people came to accept and practice them. At the opening of one new center I gave the following talk:

"'Give up the prejudices of different religions and utilize the essence of them all. Recognize the different functions of all teachings. What one can do, another cannot. What Confucius offers is on the level of the general relationship of family and society. What Sakyamuni offers is the consolation of psychological emptiness and the end of death. What Lao Tzu offers is the value of remaining pure and unattached. We need them all. There is no reason for an ardent follower of one religion to be the cruel enemy of another.

"'We are not poor cooks, however, who merely throw a variety of foods together in one dish. We have the highest example from the I Ching: the principle of balance. A normal mind is a balanced mind. We should not allow prejudice or the extreme nature of some religions to obstruct our minds and cause difficulty in the practical sphere of life or in the harmonious relationship of mankind. With this principle, I shall call our path the Path of Three-in-One. But it is not limited to three-in-one. The teachings of all great world religions can be melted into one great pot to nourish us. However, I shall still call our group Observers of the Path of Three-in-One. Heaven is one, Earth is one and all religions which are a human development, are one. In a fundamental sense, the body, mind and spirit are reintegrated. Not only do we harmonize with all beings and all world religions, we also unite with all Heavens and Earths in the entire universe.'

"While I was joyfully expressing this new spiritual direction for humanity, I was surprised to see my old friend, the achieved one, among the listeners. He was carrying the same big bamboo hat on his back and was smiling calmly as he sat on one of the seats and quietly listened to my talk. As I went over to greet him, ready to invite him to our home, I was surprised to notice that he appeared exactly as he had the day I last saw him many years ago. When I reached him, he said he wished to see me in the garden to have a word with me.

"After accompanying me to the garden he said: 'What you say is on the conceptual level. The mind is describable; the spirit is not. Tao, as a path, began before recorded history. Thus, there are some things which cannot be described or written about in books. You say that you have gotten the essence of spiritual learning, but according to all truly achieved sages what can be spoken is actually the dregs and is not the essence. You can feed an ordinary horse with general fodder, but you cannot feed a dragon with the

food of ordinary people. If this is what you have fed yourself, how do you expect to continue the work of the dragons,
your achieved forefathers? Have you really learned spiritual
truth? Work on this. I will see you in the future.'

"I knew I could not keep him for more instruction. I
stood there motionlessly in the garden as he left, while the
large crowd somewhere in the distance was enjoying what
I had just fed them.

"Beginning at that moment I rearranged my schedule.
Almost every afternoon I went to a particular mountain
and stayed in seclusion. I meditated on top of a large
stone which had a legendary connection with an ancient
achieved one. I knew that in order to learn the high truth
of life, no ordinary teacher or book could help me. My
teacher had to be the old man, my old friend. I thought
of him day and night when my mind was clear, and especially when I meditated in seclusion. By doing nothing for
several years in my meditation except to think of the old
man, I discovered that my mental capability had improved
considerably. One afternoon, during the good weather of
autumn, as I was recovering from deep meditation, I discovered an erect, unusual human form in front of me. It
was no one else but my old friend!

"He smiled and asked, 'Why do you invite me here?'

"I knew this was the opportunity I had obtained
through the practice of utmost sincerity over these long
years. I corrected my posture and knelt in front of him.
'Other than to learn Tao from you, I have nothing to beg,'
was my prompt reply.

"He laughed and said: 'Tao is too big to put into
words. One can only learn a way to reach Tao.'

"'That is what I meant.'

"'From very ancient times there have been many
methods which were left to be passed on. Some of those
methods are used to affect people's vision, such as making
oneself disappear, making the sun or moon move eastward, cutting the rainbow in half, spilling beans and
transforming them into an army, moving a mountain from
one place to another, emptying water from the ocean and
so forth. Some ways can cause the full response of nature, such as summoning the wind and rain or thunder to
subdue an evil demon or summoning an army of spiritual
beings in an important event, or causing flesh to grow
again on a skeleton. Some are personal, practical achievements such as traveling to the sun, the moon, and all
other stars; making oneself invisible, standing in the sun

without casting a shadow; taking a single step and yet traveling thousands of miles; enjoying whatever one wishes that is unobtainable by ordinary people; entering the smallest space, and so forth. Now, what do you wish to learn with such sublimeness?'

"'I wish I could meet my father.' I could not help but ignore all those other interesting methods and directly state what was deepest in my heart. To be with my father again was the only serious wish in my life, although I was soon to discover it would take a long period of cultivation in order to be fulfilled.

"He laughed again. 'You are wishing to make this proof your achievement. But, as you told me, you lost your father when you were a small child.'

"'As I learned, there are five ways of exuviation for one who has achieved himself spiritually. He could have passed through any one of the five ways to dissolve his physical body: spontaneous dissolution (instant departure from any position one chooses and at any time), water dissolution (to be drowned in water), fire dissolution (to be burned in fire), weapon dissolution (to let another person use a weapon on him), and earth dissolution (to make the earth split, bury oneself, and then close it again without a trace). I am certain my father did not die an ordinary death. He must have passed through water dissolution.'

"'How did you know all this? How could you know it was water dissolution?'

"'I read one of my father's secret books and also recall his special virtuous practice. He had clearly made his preparation to enter the Divine Immortal Realm.'

"'In what way would you like to meet your father? As he was in the ordinary world, so that you might see him honorably revered as a human noble? Or would you like to see him as a real divine being?'

"'I would like to see him as a real divine one.'

"'Do you know there are only two important sentences which can describe a divine being? The biggest has no exterior. The smallest has no interior. A divine being is a being who can have the greatest size, or any size or form he chooses for his transformation. Just as a human stretches and bends his body, a divine being stretches, becoming larger than the universe, and bends, becoming smaller than a grain of sand.'

"'I would like to see him as the largest body,' I replied.

"'If he appears as the largest body, you will never recognize him. For example, once when you were on this mountain you felt lost, until suddenly you came to this particular place. Everything was so attractive and precious to you, so beautiful and wonderful. Do you recall how you felt when everything was bathed in abundant sunshine? You were totally enveloped by the charm of this natural environment. Were you not puzzled that you did not know where you were or know how to find this place again afterward? But you did experience it, and you could remember everything in detail, right? Actually, that was your father's divine being; you came into his being. You were active in his being, but you never recognized your father. This is why the divine being can be defined as 'the biggest has no exterior.'

"'Yes, it has always puzzled me. Thank you for breaking the riddle. It is no wonder that there are many legends about people going to places as enchanted as a fairyland, yet not being able to find it again. Now I understand this experience of entering a divine being. It is like a rose placed in a room with its fragrance pervading the entire room. One enters into the being of the rose when one sits in the room, enveloped by its fragrance. Now, please, I would like to see my father in the smallest size.'

"'You could not see him that way either. For example, when you see things, he can be riding on your eyebrow; when you hear things, he can be sitting in your ear. He can be with you any time and any place he wishes, but you cannot see him. It is not his fault that you cannot see him; rather, it is your fault that you have not yet achieved yourself. Your father has been with you many times. There are also hundreds and thousands of divine beings who have visited you, but you have never been able to see them.'

"'Is there a way in which I can meet my father as I see you, the way I talk to you and touch you, as a solid fact which my unevolved human mental pattern can recognized?'

"'You can have the ability from the ancient divine methods to be whatever you wish, as well as to be the size you wish. Your method will be ready for you in your inner room. When you are achieved, I shall bring you to meet your father. Goodbye until next time.'

"He disappeared in the blink of an eye. I hurried home to my inner room. The divine book was on the desk. From that moment on, I gave up conceptual activity and completely engaged myself in real, useful cultivation.

"Another fourteen years passed as I diligently cultivated myself. One late summer afternoon, I was at one of
our connected temples, resting by the side of a pond. I
was surrounded by weeping willow trees with their long,
pliant branches dancing gracefully in the gentle breeze. I
watched the lotus flowers in full bloom. In this great
tranquility, I saw a familiar figure appear on the surface of
the lucid water. Immediately, I turned and stood up to
greet my old friend.

"He said, 'I have made an arrangement with your
father. He wishes to meet you. We think you are ready!

"'When? And where?' I asked excitedly.

"'Right now. And here. Make arrangements to have
no disturbances for seven days.'

"I followed his instructions and made the arrangements. Under his further instructions we meditated there
at the side of the pond. The tall cupola of one lotus was
the destination we were to reach and enter.

"After I entered the cupola it was no longer a cupola,
but a complete universe. I walked with my old friend and
occasionally we talked cheerfully. It took us three days to
reach the center where, on the central mountain, a figure
was sitting gracefully and comfortably. I hastened my
steps until I reached where he sat. With every part of my
being, I recognized him. He looked the same as he had
when I was eight years old, when he had patted my head
and then left to make his last house visit. I almost burst
into tears with great rapture on finding my father. Finally, after all my valuable toils, I met him.

"My father took my hand and said, 'Let us travel together to see the world. I arrived not long ago.'

"It seemed that all the things I wanted to say to him
became like ice exposed to sunshine; they all suddenly
disappeared and the three of us happily traveled the interesting world of the cupola.

"Almost seven days had passed when my father said,
'Your body is still important. You have seen me as you
wished, and we have had a wonderful time together. This
is not a departure, but a new communication to start
hereafter. The secret of life and the secret of the universe
are very ordinary to us, but these secrets are beyond the
general human mind. No disturbance should be given to
ordinary people or to yourself by telling of your experience. This is a traditional prohibition.'

"I bowed to my father, as a human father, who accepted my great human tradition salutation. Then my old

friend and I flew back to the shore. After this experience, I revised my view of life and of the world."

Being a student and pupil of my father, I was captivated by this wondrous story as it was being told. I was a bit amazed and uncertain, however, when a small distinct voice arose and said, "Oh, oh, your father made a mistake; he used the food worthy of a dragon to nourish the common people!"

The voice said this with such loud laughter that my ear itched. I could see my father must have received this message at the same moment, for he concluded his story like this:

"From that time on, I corrected my teachings from the Path of the Three-in-One to the Path of the Five-in-One. Dear friends, the Path of the Five-in-One means that the five elementary forces of nature within oneself need to be harmonized. It also means that the five great harmonious relationships and duties on the human level should be fulfilled, especially the five blessings of Hsin (the divine immortal tradition started before written history): longevity, wealth, health and peace, constant observance of virtue, and natural life. This was the real religion of unspoiled minds, but how can unspoiled minds have such great demands? They did not obtain these five blessings in the relative sphere. They obtained them by birth and by living correctly every moment in life. If we could restore the unspoiled happy mind, what then would we have to unite?"

60   chieh

SELF-RESTRAINT

GUIDANCE: *"Self-restraint helps one to progress. Anything overdone cannot last long."*

In this hexagram, Water is above Lake. If there is too much Water in a Lake, it will overflow and cause damage to the surrounding area. If the water level is too low, life will be undernourished.   Likewise, one's energy must be balanced for life to flourish.

A person's energy can be managed in much the same way that Water is regulated by a dam.   If the energy becomes too full, the dam will break; if the energy is depleted, there will not be enough in reserve for times of need.   This is a time of self-control, self-discipline and self-restraint.

This hexagram also gives guidance on how to correctly govern people with wise laws, reasonable controls and moderate restraints.   Restraint that is rigid or harsh cannot be adhered to, will reap negative results and thus will not endure.

Most people impose limitations on themselves by holding a narrow point of view or unreasonable fear.   Both are obstacles that hinder necessary breakthroughs.   Fear, emotional need, desire, pain and guilt can all distort clear vision.   Unfortunately, most people never get beyond such self-imposed barriers.

Limitation is a necessary aspect of life and can provide a positive impetus for proper growth because of the opportunities it presents for breakthrough.   A great tree was once a seed which had to push its way out of a shell and then out of the earth.   Some limitations serve as a natural guard against premature action.   A child crawls before it walks.   How else could it develop enough strength in its legs to support its body?   A tree will not bear fruit until its branches are able to support it.

As people grow up in competitive societies, they become engrossed in worldly life, seek all kinds of extravagances and thus lose their natural self-restraint.   They seek external power and wealth without developing the inner strength necessary to allow a proper balance.   Through over-indulgence they ruin their health by living unnaturally.   For example, when one eats too much, one's internal organs are harmed.   When one speaks too much, one's lungs and mind become weakened.   On the other hand, extreme self-denial is also harmful and can provoke rebellion.   One who does not sleep properly or engages in rigid limitation also suffers harmful consequences.

Sometimes people try to impose rigid self-restraints as compensation for excesses, like a bandit who in his later years practices religious austerities.   Some people try to compensate for excess by making unrealistic promises and commitments to others.   But one who truly knows himself is aware of all his limitations and neither over-extends himself nor makes promises that cannot be kept. When one knows one's real capacity, commitments and goals can be set that are realistic and beneficial. If one becomes exhausted or quits halfway, nothing will be accomplished.

In natural spiritual education, self-restraint is symbolized by bamboo which is hollow within and has a joint at regular intervals. The joints make the bamboo stronger and more flexible. If the bamboo did not grow joints sectionally, but grew in one unsegmented piece, it would never be able to support itself.

The appropriate and positive use of natural limitations and healthy temperance in all aspects of life is the primary guidance of this hexagram. Restraint allows one to know one's limits. By recognizing them, one can be free within them and thus conduct oneself properly in any situation. By not expecting more from a circumstance than is possible, and by not striving for impossible goals, one will be able to conserve one's energy for other needs. Each line of this hexagram offers guidance for different stages of restraint.

LINE 1: *"Definite self-restraint. One stays within one's house. No blame."*

Maintain restraint, otherwise trouble arises. The first line represents Water at the bottom of the Lake and indicates that the Water is well contained without any danger of flooding. One should stay calm and not try to exceed one's limitations. Such self-restraint is beneficial, because one is acting appropriately. At this time do not be active. Keep yourself safe.

LINE 2: *"Self-restraint with flexibility, versatility and movement. To stay behind one's door is dangerous."*

This line is the opposite of the first one. Here, trouble is caused by the Water not going "out." The level of Water in the Lake has reached its point of safety. In order to avoid danger, it should continue to flow outward normally. A sudden, strong flow would be disastrous to the surrounding area.

LINE 3: *"Lack of self-restraint brings trouble. This condition could cause one to sigh over his state of helplessness."*

The third line is at the top of the trigram Lake. Thus, there is an abundance of water and much strength is needed to maintain a normal flow so that flooding will not cause trouble and waste. The third line is a weak one in a strong position; if it is not aware of the problem in advance, it will be too late to control it later on.

LINE   4:   *"Comfortable self-restraint.   One feels confident by following a step-by-step plan."*

"Self-restraint" can mean doing things rhythmically and systematically. Moreover, the practice of self-restraint can bring about positive results in maintaining a good creative relationship. The fourth line is a yin line in the correct position, which means that one is loyal to the leader in the fifth position. The fourth line works well with self-discipline. He uses his position correctly to support and cooperate with the leader, and he carries out all his duties efficiently and successfully.

LINE   5:   *"Enjoyable, sweet self-restraint.   Good fortune. Everything furthers."*

This line represents a strong leader in the right position. Such a person controls and regulates his life by imposing restraints in a natural way. By regulating himself appropriately, there is benefit. As master of his own life, he gains the love and respect of others. Thus, he enjoys the benefit of his habitual self-restraint.

LINE   6:   *"Bitter self-restraint. The level and standards of self-restraint are too high.   Although no serious remorse will be created, extremes in practice will eventually not be able to last long because they are an abnormal approach."*

This position indicates too much control, unreasonable discipline and abnormal self-restraint. Thus, difficulty or trouble arises.

The example of a ruler and his people is a good analogy for the higher and lower aspects of one's being. The top position, the ruler, has better vision than most of the people; however, ordinary people reject discipline because they do not understand its benefit. The reason for their rejection is that their perception is limited by short-sightedness. On the other hand, if the discipline is too harsh and idealistic, it is not practical and becomes devoid of meaning.

This line applies to a virtuous individual who has set his standards too high, thus his discipline becomes embittered. Here the *I Ching* suggests that one should not be too severe and should moderate one's idealistic expectations to more normal, practical standards.

Anyone in a high position should avoid being stubborn and inflexible and should not seek to accomplish things that are beyond his ability. Overly severe discipline brings no real benefit in the long run.

SPECIFIC GUIDANCE

PERSONAL FORTUNE: This is not the right time for great prosperity, you need to wait.

MARRIAGE: Successful.

HOUSING/FAMILY: Good fortune, but be careful about thieves.

CHILDBIRTH: Peaceful. The baby will be a girl.

LOOKING FOR WORK: You need to ask again and again before finding work.

SOCIAL/GOVERNMENTAL POSITION: Not successful.

TRADE/BUSINESS: Difficult to achieve.

SEARCHING FOR SOMEONE: Hurry, and perhaps you can find them.

WAITING FOR SOMEONE: They will not come.

LOOKING FOR SOMETHING LOST: Difficult to find.

HUNTING FOR THIEVES: They are in the Northwest.

LAWSUIT: You should make peace.

CLIMATE: It will be rainy.

DISEASE: Danger.

PERSONAL WISH: Difficult to fulfill.

COMMENTARY

"To Do is to Be" and "To Know is To Do"

Discipline and self-restraint are the means of reaching achievement. In fact, they are "achievement" in themselves. In order to avoid an unnatural and immoral result of discipline and self-restraint, the relationship between the discipline and the disciplined must be clearly understood.

Any given action is a reaction to previous behavior, and all behavior and actions are part of all other actions, thus their interaction composes all of life's activities. When we are hungry, we eat. In this case hunger is the cause and eating the effect. We eat in order to satisfy our hunger.   Then, when we eat in order to satisfy our hunger, eating becomes the cause and the satisfaction or extinction of hunger becomes the effect.   The matter of eating and the satisfaction of hunger are actually of one origin and not two as it may appear.

The one origin is the life force.   The entire universe is but a life force called primal energy or universal Nature. Every phenomenon, including non-existence, is a diversified expression of this universal life force or Nature which is self-regulated toward all events in life, big or small.

In the *I Ching* or *The Book of Changes*, this life force of the universe is called Chyan ☰ .   The expression of the sixty-four hexagrams make this universal self-regulation traceable.

On a human level, the only constant factor on which we can rely throughout all generations is the virtue of universal cyclic change.   Among all changes and variations, the basic pattern of change has been found in the interaction of yin and yang from which the oneness of primal energy can be recognized.

The relative nature of human cognition is surpassed by spiritual power.   An absolute being is one who has extended his knowing and being beyond the relative spheres of general conceptual life.   Such spirit of absoluteness is obtained through the experience of the relative patterns of the function of the mind and finally goes beyond such a relative mind to reach the unity.

According to this vision, the highest power in the responsive universe is the power of virtue.   The power of virtue maintains the constancy of the universe.   Without this constancy, the universe would be in a state of chaos. All of our activities, good or bad, follow a specific, corresponding pattern or channel of energy.   Regardless of circumstances, we should keep our virtue constant. Whether we are rich or poor, noble or common, whether we are having a good day or a bad day, we must always have the same good virtue towards ourselves and others. We should follow the example of Nature, whose constant virtue enables all beings to have the potential of enjoying their life within their own period of time and development.

As human beings, we are all born with the potential to develop our understanding and our ability to know that the constant virtue of the universe exists behind the chanegable, superficial phenomena. Our confidence in Nature first grew from the constant virtue of the universe. All of the world's cultures, religions and sages spoke to their different communities and times in an attempt to describe the truth of life, but their colorful descriptions were variable and never sufficient. Behind all changing phenomena is the hidden, enduring virtue of the universe which, as the universal cycles evolve, remains eternally positive, creative, constructive, productive and affirmative. Because the universe maintains its constant virtue, it never dies. Creatures die because they allow their external environment to continually change their nature and virtue. People are tempted by the outside world and do not feel content and sufficient within their own being. Thus, when they see this, they want to be like this. When they see that, they want to be like that. They forsake their own good nature in the pursuit of something or someone else. They die, not from the moment they physically cease to breathe, but rather in each moment that they lose their constant virtue.

Then what is Tao? Tao is but the eternal Way. Tao is the constancy of the universe itself. It is our original, divine, vital energy. With it, we receive life. Without it, we cease to live. Maintaining the enduring spirit of life is the first principle of the Integral Way. As we remain undisturbed by the changeable face of life, our happiness will never cease and our positive energy will never die but will exist firmly with the eternal Tao.

In ordinary daily life, our primary endeavor is to keep our enduring, positive attributes, whether we are having a good or a bad day. We accept any external change as it is. Relatively speaking, if we keep our virtue, we can enjoy our good days more fully and we can soften and mitigate the discomfort of our bad days. Through virtuous behavior we can even alter possible dangerous situations because of the trustful, stable, true power of constant virtue.

To be virtuous means that we follow the constant Middle Way, not allowing ourselves to run into extremity, violence or radical attitudes. One does not wish to become a Buddha or an angel or any other exalted being. Neither does one want to become evil under any circumstances. We would rather keep our original virtue. We keep our spirit pure and untouched, our mind clear and detached, and especially avoid emotional demands such as emotional prayer and love. We keep our body still and upright (but keeping still does not mean sitting in a corner or lying in the fetal position).

All action must hold a deep respect for the original, productive quietness, the creative nothingness, the most integral, active non-action. Through integral active non-action we can extend the clarity of the mind and innocence of the pristine spirit to embrace the eternal Tao. We spontaneously maintain all our simple, daily activities within the energy track of our life and follow the universal principle of normalcy. This is the way of perpetual peace, beauty, true enjoyment, happiness and spiritual joyousness. This is the secret of a natural, spiritually based life.

In Tao, to know is to do and to do is to be. If our knowledge or our spirituality and morality cannot be manifested in our daily lives through our thoughts, attitudes and behavior, it means that we do not truly know them. To know means to have mentally and spiritually attained and experienced it. For example, the true knowledge of benevolence is at the same time the manifestation of benevolence in our nature. To know benevolence is to be benevolent.

For instance, a baby may crawl into a busy street because of the negligence of its young mother, and a passerby may reach out to save the baby from danger. To know is to do. This natural logic expresses the truth that there is no separation between the knower and that which is known or between the doer and that which is done. This truth disproves the erroneous idea that there is separation and duality between what one is and what one thinks, knows, does or experiences on any level. Through such incomplete understanding, mankind dogmatically created such concepts as karma, retribution and the law of cause and effect.

In order to correct the old misinterpretation of natural truth, and to reveal the unchangeable fact that we are what we do and think, this ancient book of the unspoiled mind (the *I Ching*) is presented as an expression of the spiritual truth of behavior. It is, at the same time, a manifestation of the truly wise and virtuous energy of the ancient sages. When a fragrant flower emits its beautiful scent, this is an act complete in itself. The conduct of the follower manifests the nature of a fragrant flower. It does what it is. Otherwise, it would be impossible to recognize it as a fragrant flower. In the absolute realm of spiritual truth, to do is to be. To know is to do. In reality, this is absolute truth.

The act of knowing is the activity of mental energy which forms itself into a specific pattern. The principle "to know is to do" means that the mind extends itself in the projection of mental energy, creating patterns and images which are spontaneously reflected or mirrored back to the mind. In the relative realm, the form or patterns the mind holds may be classified as "good" or "bad." The principle "to know is to do" is different in the relative realm, as one may know something and not necessarily do or be that which one knows.

Comparatively speaking, to truly know something is different from being aware of it. In the realm of mankind, one may discern something as good and thus do good, and one may discern something as bad, but not necessarily do it. This is the basis upon which mankind's codes of ethics and reflections on morality were built. The spiritual, absolute realm transcends duality. In this realm, the mind plays a passive rather than active role - its function is that of a highly sensitive transmitter and receiver which spontaneously knows things without the necessity of previous experience and without having to discriminate between being or doing good or bad.

61 chung fu 中孚

faithfulness

GUIDANCE: *"Faithfulness can make even dolphins and swine trust you. It encourages one to engage in a great adventure, such as crossing a great body of water."*

In this hexagram, Wind is over Lake. This image is as natural and regular as the changing of seasons, the waxing and waning of the moon, and the changing of the tide. All of these cycles are expressions of faithfulness.

Here, two yin lines are surrounded by four yang lines, which represent an open heart and a clear mind. These qualities are at the root of faithfulness. Although our original, unspoiled minds have become distorted, our faithfulness can be restored through the practice of virtue.

In addition to the hexagram's central yin energy, each trigram has a yang line in its center, which expresses inner strength and truthfulness. Because of the position of these yang lines, the image of faithfulness is greatly strengthened.

The inner trigrams, Mountain ☶ and Thunder ☳, also contribute to this hexagram's internal harmony. Mountain and Thunder represent rest and movement respectively. An appropriate balance of the firm and yielding, stillness and action, allows one's faithfulness to influence others.

Wind and Lake also represent obedience and joy. In human relationships, they represent an older woman exerting a positive influence over a younger one. By integrating these good qualities, one can achieve what one undertakes.

The upper trigram, Wind, can also symbolize Wood, and the central openness of the yin lines suggests a boat on a lake. The lower trigram, Lake, symbolizes Metal. The interaction of these trigrams suggests a metal tool that is used to chisel out wood in order to make a boat.

This hexagram also symbolizes a bird's egg. The first and top lines represent the shell of the egg; the second and fifth lines, the white part; and the third and fourth lines, the yoke. Through the faithful nature of the bird, an egg is hatched and a new life brought forth. If the mother bird were irresponsible or careless in brooding her eggs, then what would be the outcome?

The image of a bird's egg can be applied to each line of the hexagram. The first line is like the mother brooding over her eggs. The second line shows life slowly taking form, like the embryo developing within the egg. The third line represents the stage where the baby birds may or may not hatch, the outcome depending on the mother bird's responsiveness. The fourth line indicates that the birds will hatch very soon; and the fifth line, that the eggs have already hatched. The top line is like a little bird learning to fly. In the beginning there is exhilaration and expectancy, but then it flies too high and there is sadness.

Regarding directions and seasons, Wind is associated with the Southeast and with Spring.   Lake is associated with the West and with Autumn.   In the five elemental phases of energy, Wind belongs to Wood and Lake to Metal.   It is between Spring and Autumn that growth and development are completed.   However, in the interaction of these same energies at their elemental level, Metal destroys Wood.   Therefore, the shell of the egg must break in order for the bird to hatch; the wood must be cut in order to make a boat.

These examples show how the interaction of these energies has both creative and destructive properties. Both are necessary in the process of development as we reconnect ourselves with the truth.

LINE 1:   *"Faith or single-mindedness brings peace and good fortune. Diverse intentions bring disharmony."*

From a broad point of view, this line is fortunate because of its position and correspondence with the fourth line.   The fourth line represents one who is single-minded and self-reliant.   However, if he loses his focus of purpose and correct position,   he will also sacrifice peacefulness. It is a blessing to maintain faithfulness steadfastly; otherwise, one is like a woman who is the mistress of two men. Only confusion can result.

LINE 2:   *"The crane calls out from the thicket, and the young respond to her call. This is like saying, 'I have something good to enjoy. Let us share it together."*

This line is the center of the lower trigram.   Though it is a yang line in a yin position, it is in a position of leadership.   It is firm and faithful to its principles, thus it is beneficial to the entire community.   Good communication with everyone brings great happiness.   In the literal Chinese translation, this mood is symbolized by the sharing of a goblet of wine.

The image of a crane is used because it is a lake bird and its call can be heard in the autumn, the season which corresponds with the Lake.   The image of Lake is also associated with an open mouth.   Furthermore, this line is at the beginning of the inner trigram, Thunder, which indicates movement.

The activity of the open mouth is like a crane calling out.   Her young can hear and recognize her call from a great distance, even when she is hidden. This means that one's influence and service to others are not limited by space. It also implies that there is a response to one's heartfelt wish.

LINE 3: *"One meets one's opponent. There could be either a battle or a celebration and could lead to singing or weeping."*

The third line is too weak for its position and corresponds to the top line which is too strong for its position. Therefore, even though there is correspondence, it is inappropriate. They relate to one another in a confusing manner, lacking high principles.

The third line relies on the top as its source of strength, since it has lost its own center and is not independent. Because others are not present to render aid, it is indecisive and vacillates greatly.

The third line is at the base of the inner trigram, Mountain, which connotes stillness. It is also at the top of the lower trigram, Lake, which represents excessiveness. This is a difficult situation and guidance is needed, but neither the top line nor the weak neighboring lines can be counted on. The *I Ching* advises one in this position to gather his energy to his center and to cultivate sincerity. Although this is a difficult time, it is good for growth.

LINE 4: *"The moon is almost full. The mare runs away from her mate, but offers her loyalty to the leader. No blame."*

The fourth line corresponds to either the neighboring fifth line or to the first line. In ancient times, a pair of horses was used to draw a chariot. The fourth line is like the mare; her mate could be the yang line in either the first or the fifth position. If she chooses the fifth line, she is benefited. If she disregards the fifth line in favor of the first, there will be misfortune. Fortunately, the relationship of the fourth line to the fifth has almost fully ripened, like the moon approaching fullness. The pending full moon suggests that the opportunity is an important one.

The fourth line should advance towards the fifth selflessly rather than manifest the selfishness attendant upon attachment to the first line. She should sacrifice personal affection in order to serve the fifth line for a purpose which is more important than her own needs.   Through such action, one in this position can create good fortune. When in conflict over the issue of faithfulness, one should choose the righteous way and sacrifice selfish personal views.

LINE 5: *"Faithfulness gathers good people. No remorse."*

The fifth line is the virtuous leader of this hexagram. The influence of its deep sincerity and high principles, in addition to its ability to communicate, is the central force which unites all.   One who has the sincerity of this line will be successful in whatever is undertaken.

LINE 6:   *"The rooster flies too high.   Pomposity brings danger.   Correct this."*

The sixth line is like a rooster that wishes to fly to Heaven.   This describes an inferior person who is attempting to reach too high a position.

A rooster who flies from one high tree to another only invites misfortune, but one who stays on the ground can easily find worms.   A person who thinks that flying is better than staying low, even though that is his position, creates difficulty.

The *I Ching* teaches balance, especially on the spiritual path.   One who believes that he must ascend to some artificial,   religious heaven is no different from the rooster that tries to fly too high.   One must be honest, not deluded.   If one cultivates virtue and health, builds a strong life foundation and establishes relationships that are harmonious, spiritual attainment will be the natural result. One whose faith is misplaced only creates trouble and confusion for himself and the rest of the world.

SPECIFIC GUIDANCE

PERSONAL FORTUNE: Be careful, initial prosperity will decline.

MARRIAGE: Although it can succeed, there will be some difficulty and misfortune in the future which will involve lawsuits.

HOUSING/FAMILY: It will last a long time, although there may be some difficulties.

SOCIAL/GOVERNMENTAL POSITION: It can be achieved.

TRADE/BUSINESS: Difficulty.

SEARCHING FOR SOMEONE: They are hard to find.

WAITING FOR SOMEONE: They will come.

LOOKING FOR SOMETHING LOST: It is hard to find.

HUNTING FOR THIEVES: They are in the East and can be caught.

LAWSUIT: If you hurry there will be profits. If you wait, there will be trouble.

CLIMATE: It will be windy.

TRAVEL: Good fortune.

DISEASE: Dangerous.

PERSONAL WISH: Can be achieved.

COMMENTARY
Reality

Looking carefully into the truth of spirituality from its origin, one finds that it can only be expressed by the sign ☰☷ . In this hexagram, two broken lines are between four solid lines, which represents a pure, open and empty mind. In the last five thousand years of cultural development, numerous beliefs, customs and doctrines have been created and established that have either promoted or deterred the spiritual growth of mankind. The fact that differences exist should not be the "problem" that it often is in today's society. Instead, humanity should develop the understanding that these differences are only varying recognitions and expressions of different levels of spiritual achievement.

Spiritually developed people are greatly amused and entertained by these colorful differences. They can enjoy the variation without becoming attached or confused. Being on the level of high truth, they do not need to accept or reject anything that was created by people of different times and geographical backgrounds, but such confusion has been the cause of many wars and conflict among undeveloped people.

Collecting the truth of religious reality, as it pertains to the evolution of the rational mind, is very valuable. In this way, spiritual confusion can be eliminated and the true spiritual essence can be reached. Let us follow the inquisitive mind of an excellent businessman and learn from his experiences in the search for truth.

In a large Chinese city lived a successful business-man. When he was in his teens, he was a Confucian scholar, as were most young men of general education. He came from a very poor family, and when his parents died he was forced to give up his studies and become part of the business world. Through hard work and fortunate circumstances he made a substantial fortune by the time he reached his forties. In his personal life, he enjoyed nice houses, beautiful gardens and the comforts of a family. He satisfied himself and his family with the best foods, even delicacies he had never dreamed of in his childhood.

His beloved parents remained deep in his memory, however, and it troubled him that they could not share and enjoy his prosperity. One of his old friends suggested to him a conventional solution.

"It is an easy matter and will only cost you the equiva-lent of 'one hair from nine cattle' to send your parents to Heaven. Why don't you invite all the different religious groups to perform their rituals to guarantee your parents' ascension to Heaven? This is the way to fulfill your filial duty to your deceased parents."

"But which way works?" the rich man asked.

"Who knows? This is our conventional way. You can see for yourself that this is the custom of all Chinese people when their parents die. They send for Taoist priests, Buddhist monks and nuns, and others to perform different rituals that will allow the dead to ascend to Heaven. One of these methods will probably work, but who knows which, since each one claims to be "the way."

The rich man decided to follow his friend's advice. With some help, he was able to choose the best groups for this special occasion and great rituals were performed for forty-nine days. As people flocked to see them, his feelings changed from sadness to pride. Although he experienced and observed many rituals and ceremonies concerning death, after the busy days had ended he again expressed concern to his friend by asking, "Did any method work?"

"This is the conventional way, as I previously told you. No one seriously questions it. People pay for these rituals in order to feel that they have helped their deceased ones. This is the only answer I know."

The businessman said, "Surely, you and I are successful businessmen. In the business world we have learned
to be realistic. I do not mind the money being spent, but
I do wonder which way works. I would like to do more for
my parents."

"This is not like buying goods for such a good price
that you should buy more!" said his friend.

Reluctantly, the rich businessman gave up the idea of
doing more, but year after year the many religious
questions about death grew deeper in his mind. As he
began approaching fifty, some of his old friends passed
away, and he noticed that his body was not as strong as
before, so he began contemplating things he had never
before taken seriously.

He had many experiences that had helped him solve
many problems and difficulties in both his business and
daily life, but now he needed a new idea. If money could
send people to Heaven, he would surely have no problem,
but going to Heaven only occurs after death and no one
could prove that it really happens. Taking it for granted
was certainly a great risk! He did not mind spending
money on rituals if they were effective, but if they were
not, then his good soul could be ruined. This might be a
serious mistake, especially since his wealth would not be
well used. He also thought that if money could buy
permission to enter Heaven, all the evil people who had
grand rituals performed or who made donations to temples
would also go to Heaven. How could such a place as
"Heaven" be so undiscriminating?

After careful thought, he reached the logical conclusion that money could offer no assurance of going to
Heaven. Finally, there came the light from his good
business mind that although money could not buy
Heaven, it could buy the truth of "reality." Thus, he
decided to interview different knowledgeable religious
people, and other experienced ones, in order to obtain this
"truth" from their learning and experience. He would pay
them, of course, as in any other business transaction.

As a good businessman, the adventurousness of this
enterprise appealed to him. Though he did not mind
paying the price, the goods must be real and worthwhile.
If he could gather the correct information to prepare
himself for going to a different world, then the money
would surely be well spent. At least he would be the only
one to blame, regardless of the result.

His idea was not difficult to carry out; only special arrangements needed to be made. A list of good teachers who could present their traditions and practices was prepared. Through the help of experienced friends, the businessman wished to filter out similar theories and practices of the different religions in order to extract the essential truth of each. He was so anxious to know the reality of all these different teachings that he was willing to pay a great sum, with "essence" being his only demand. Since he did not have much time for a great deal of theory, and in order to avoid complication, only the most important teachings were given. His good mind, which had been used so well in the business world, was now being applied as a meticulous buyer in the religious market.

Years passed and he became very knowledgeable about all the great religions, including their histories, doctrines and rituals. He remained self-motivated by his untiring inquisitiveness. During the process of learning, he sometimes became subject to the prejudices, confusion and contradictions of particular religions until he was able to attain some degree of enlightenment. Due to this benefit, he could deeply reflect and clearly understand that all dogmatic religious subjectivity, confusion and contradiction are merely conceptual. In other words, they are merely many different creations of the mind.

Surely, this was not what he had originally hoped for. He wished to achieve something deeper and broader than just the general understanding of religions. He now knew that general teachers could not meet his needs. They could only teach him some small things, most of which were theological exaggerations designed to accommodate psychological weaknesses. The structures of those religions did not go beyond the emotional or conceptual level, thus they amounted to no more than toys, tranquilizers, substitutes, compensation and escape. Surely, this shallowness was far from spiritual reality, so he decided to find a teacher who was really achieved, one of the ultimate truth, to be his model.

Finding such a teacher was very difficult. Only after searching for many years and using many sources was one of true achievement finally found who would accept the businessman as his student. Before this teacher arrived, the rich man received guidance from his advisor on how to greet a truly achieved master. In the teacher's presence he should only present a request or a question and avoid initiating conversation or asking personal questions such as the teacher's age. These questions would find no answers. The rich businessman learned this etiquette and promised to follow it carefully. When the meeting occurred, he welcomed his teacher very respectfully, but forgot how to conduct the conversation without asking his teacher's age. The teacher smiled and after a long pause, said:

"The ageless past is my yesterday. The endless future is my tomorrow. From this immeasurable present, at the point of this instant, you and I are meeting. The Realm of Timelessness is where I live, where neither time nor age are measured. Using no measurement, we can accept people as they really are."

The businessman suddenly recalled the warning he had received from his advisor. He immediately begged forgiveness and straightforwardly presented his wish to learn Tao.

The teacher demanded twelve fish of pure gold, each weighing one catty (16 Chinese ounces of gold) to be placed in a boat along with other offerings. The boat would set sail and be secluded from the worldly life of people. Only deaf sailors and servants would be allowed to help in the boat.

After everything was prepared, and on a very auspicious day, the teacher and pupil sailed out to sea accompanied by a few sailors and servants. The servants helped prepare the offerings in the manner of traditional ritual and then retreated behind their partition at the rear of the cabin. Only the teacher and the pupil were left together. They ceremoniously made offerings to the Heavenly Realm. Then, to the amazement of the rich businessman, the teacher took the gold fish and threw them one by one into the ocean. The pupil's first instinct was to stop him, but he dared not since the fish no longer belonged to him.

Finally, he gathered his courage and asked the master, "May I venture to ask the meaning of this?"

The teacher's answer was simple: "I just wanted to see the fish swim again."

"I am afraid that probably cannot happen."

"Why not?"

"Lifeless gold cannot be made into living fish."

"Is it that your gold is not good enough?"

"All gold is lifeless, venerable sir."

The teacher then smiled and gently said to his pupil, "I am glad you also know that."

At first the rich pupil was stricken, realizing what an expensive lesson he had just been taught, but he immediately said to his teacher, 'Thank you sir. Hereafter, your pupil will not value all those lifeless things. I will maintain single-mindedness in order to learn Tao from you."

"Being a truthful one, what do you already know about the achievement of Tao?"

"I know thus far in order to learn Tao, self-cultivation is more valued than common worship. The purpose of self-cultivation is to achieve natural self-mastery, self-discipline, self-dependence, self-continence, self-improvement, self-restraint, self-communion, self-command, self-possession, self-realization, self-sufficiency, self-contentment, self-effacement, self-renunciation and self-surrender. However, among all of these words, none can be considered an exact meaning for spiritual self-cultivation; they are only a measure."

"What makes self-cultivation different from other paths?"

"In all popular religions, authority exists outside of, not within, one's life. Therefore, worship is considered to be the most important practice of all general religions. In spiritual learning, however, one begins with a foundation of sincere practice and the recognition that the authority of life is within one's own being. One thus achieves the realization of true inner authority. Therefore, the process of self-cultivation is the main feature of spiritual learning.

"I do not mean that because spiritual learning stresses self-cultivation, one should turn away from the Divine Realm. I mean that only through one's own self-cultivation can one attain spiritual growth. Through this process of growth, one can connect deeply with the Divine Realm.

"In the real practice of deep spirituality, one realizes the divinity within oneself; there is no real separation between the universal nature and one's own divine nature. In the practice of popular religion, a divine authority is established outside of one's own being. As the followers of these religions miss the spiritual truth of oneness and become dualistic, the Divine Realm becomes even further removed from their lives. In practicing self-cultivation, however, one should not put too much emphasis on one's personal, individual divinity in order not to lose connection with the total divinity.

"There is nothing wrong with the level you have reached," continued the teacher, "what else do you wish to learn?"

"Not the conceptual level, but how to truly achieve Tao," the man answered.

"In order to achieve Tao and become divine within and without, one has to complete one's virtue. Only by realizing and cultivating one's virtue can the secret of achieving Tao be passed on to a person," the teacher replied.

"Your pupil will do whatever you suggest," said the businessman.

"Did you ever lose your virtue as you made those lifeless fish?"

The businessman collected his thoughts and prudently made the following statement, "No sir. I assume you are asking if I lost my virtue in my financial enterprises. I have truly known that I dare not sever my root of life from its heavenly source, and have made a continuous effort to keep myself on the right path. Within this busily changing world, I am a man of diligence, sincerity, honesty, earnestness, duty, prudence, carefulness, fortitude, bravery, temperance, order, decency, courage and cleanliness. Among my friends and acquaintances I have earned a reputation as a man of righteousness, faithfulness, loyalty, trustworthiness, justice, helpfulness, kindness, gentleness, harmony, cooperation, courtesy, politeness, consideration, understanding, forgiveness and charity. In my own work of business management, I am a man of fidelity, propriety, correctness, exactness, precision and efficiency. I am also scrupulous in making money and frugal in spending it. For this, my family has occasionally complained. However, I believe I am frugal, not miserly. Every evening before going to bed, I write in my diary as a means of introspection. I have practiced this for many years. While this is my realization of self-virtue in everyday life, I truly know this is not something I did for others. I did it for myself, and it is nothing to be proud of. I have not accumulated any merit for the world. I have been self-centered with my love, and my purpose in life has been to obtain worldly strength. I was a man of the world, yet I recognize that divinity and Heaven are manifested by their boundless, virtuous love; that spirits can be made to respond to sincerity; and that the nature of the universe is the fundamental reality of the universe. The virtue of nature is to be truthful. Virtue is long-enduring; any other kind of power or force is short-lived. Virtue is gentle and subtle; power or force is strong and conspicuous. I am vaguely aware that through self-cultivation one can restore the virtue of one's nature regardless of birth, education or social background, but I made virtue the decoration of my life, the hallmark of being well-bred, an exhibition of my high social standing. I was wrong. Since I became interested in Tao, I now know that virtue exists in the honest, plain nature of a human being and can be expressed in various ways. Plain nature is invariable at any given time.

"My virtue was fragmented. I did not have integrity. Although my enlightenment is late, I now know that all virtue can be summarized into one word: goodness. Goodness is the first nature of all beings. When goodness is used to describe the first nature, it is the nature of truth, beauty, sacredness, perfection, completeness and greatness. In reality, the first nature cannot be specified by any particular virtue. Thus, it is truly integrally virtuous.

"Evil and sin caused by experiences within the social environment are distortions of the original, true nature. Self-contamination and bad habits are actually our second or false nature. Usually, someone who remains trapped in this way of living is referred to as one who has lost his original nature. Understanding this, I know that our original nature is invariable nature itself. It is the path, the Way. Consequently, following the path is truly self-realization and self-accomplishment.

"The first nature of human beings is the very nature of Heaven and Earth and, by extension, the nature of the entire universe. All correct spiritual education is aimed at the restoration of this original nature. This restoration does not require one to 'work' on anything. As I was told, the purest guidance of 'non-doing,' 'non-making' or 'non-deviating' is the only proper method. In order to recover our lost nature and reintegrate the many deviations from this nature, one has to eliminate contaminations from one's practical daily life. Such contamination is sometimes called using 'expedient measures' and, in certain situations, may be the most appropriate or the only way to react.

"But persisting in 'expedient measures' can become a means for corrupting one's nature. For example, in ancient Chinese society, bodily touch or extreme closeness between sisters and brothers, fathers and daughters, mothers and sons, brothers-in-law and sisters-in-law was strictly forbidden in order to avoid antagonisms or the possibility of interbreeding. Once the ancient sage, Mencius, was challenged with a question: 'If a sister-in-law fell into a well, should a brother-in-law reach his hand in to save her?" Mencius responded that he should, for this was an example of an expedient condition, not a normal one.

"However, if expedient behavior becomes habit-forming, such as helping one's sister-in-law in everyday situations, then many troubles may arise. In this same manner, soldiers carry out many evil orders during war; however, such expedient actions should not become habitual in one's daily life after times of war.

"Evil and sin can be defined as actions and behavior which occur at improper times and places. They are not absolute. Evil people and real sinners are those who become attached to expedient behavior once they discover this is an easy way of solving problems or accomplishing their purpose. Therefore, these expedient measures become habits, routines, and eventually a way of life. People who cultivate themselves do not need to work in order to reclaim their original nature; instead they need to constantly cleanse and purify the dirt that they touch. One must be careful not to let habits become the master of one's life.

"In cultivating the Integral Way, one cultivates the virtue of self-integration. In meditating on the Integral Way, one awakens the virtue of one's original nature. Awakening and enlightenment are not a form of spiritual loftiness, but come from a thorough realization of virtue.

"Cultivating Tao restores the integrity of the innate, universal, natural being. Cultivation restores purity to mental and physical contamination. Cultivation reintegrates the fragments of worldly distractions and de-unifying experiences. To be integral is to be one with the true, deep nature of the universe.

"Because the nature of human beings is the nature of the universe, the authority of life is internal. The authority of judgment is also internal and parallels the growth of human self-awareness. Punishment and guilt, misery and suffering are the results of deviating from one's original nature. Reward, contentment and true happiness all come from the constancy of embracing one's original nature. The highest morality is not linked to the demands of society, but comes from total inner harmony and balance. Thus, high morality is not a result of preaching; it is a result of self-recognition.

"The Integral Way is indescribable because it is total integration, but among all individually expressed virtues, truthfulness and sincerity are pivotal. With sincerity, one can realize one's true integral being. Virtue is like a beautiful flower, with one's integral nature as the root. The realization of virtue does not come from working fragmentedly on the surface of one's personality. Virtue must be whole, not partial. This is called 'Integral Being.'

"People all know that being virtuous is a valuable thing, but only a few know that being virtuous can be used as a 'secret measure' or 'weapon' for a nation, a family or a person to improve inner and outer being. Virtue should be practiced in a secret way as a silent path. Otherwise, one might turn virtue into something superficial and thus not be benefited by one's practices. By taking credit for virtuous actions, the mind is easily disturbed and sometimes even destroyed. Examples of this behavior are apparent in situations of worldly conflict. Therefore, the subtle, secret virtue is highest.

"What I have sincerely done through all the many years of preparation is just for this moment, in order for me to be worthy to receive the treasures of Tao. I present this to you for your inspection, sir."

The master responded, "The virtue I inquire about is much more fundamental than you might think. It is basic to all human life and does not involve philosophical understanding. Please, tell me: Do you eat well? Do you sleep well? Do you eliminate well? Do you do well with women? Do you walk well? These are some of the virtues of a normal, healthy life. If one has trouble with any of these, one may wonder what were the true reasons their life was ruined. I hope you have not neglected these."

"In all honesty, venerable teacher, with regard to these very personal things my life is thus: after years of beneficial and unbeneficial pursuits I have a stomach ulcer, so I cannot eat well. In terms of sleep, I have frequent insomnia, so I cannot sleep well. In terms of elimination, I have habitual constipation, so I cannot have good bowel movements. In terms of urination, I have kidney stones, so I cannot eliminate well. In terms of sex, I cannot have an erection, so I feel impotent. In terms of walking long distances, I have gout in both knees, so I cannot walk far. In terms of ..."

The teacher stopped him. "That is enough to tell me that you have lost the virtue of a basic life. What kind of spirituality do you expect to learn from me?"

"To integrally achieve in Tao," was the determined response.

"First," instructed the teacher, "restore all the virtues of a basic life. I do not need to question you further in order to find out whether you are worthy. Only when you restore these basic virtues shall the secret of Tao be passed on to you."

The rich businessman followed the special instructions and method his teacher passed on to him and restored all the "virtues" he had lost. In his later years he enjoyed the health of a total being. On various occasions, many of his old friends would visit him and ask how to cultivate Tao. He always laughed and gave an answer like this:

"As I was taught, the spiritual realm is not very different from doing business in the ordinary world. One needs to be practical about one's personal cultivation. One must first fulfill all aspects of life in order to live a life of completeness. This does not involve enormous material possessions, rather, a life of completeness is in itself the very essence of life. It cannot be achieved without being practical or down to earth.

"I have come to understand that spiritual achievement is purely personal. One's practice must be subtle and secret. In other words, be a god in the Subtle Realm and not a force in the human realm. This is spiritual virtue. One should be a spiritual model for people, while being careful not to present a dominant spiritual image, since this only creates conflict. If one loses spiritual virtue, one's teachings may sound beautiful, but they have no real spiritual value. Do not be confused by the great world religions. Do not mistake scarecrows for real beings. Do not choose a religion which will make you narrow and prejudiced. Always respect real spiritual education which can help you grow. Total human spiritual growth can only be realized through individual spiritual growth. By practicing true piety, which is not misguided toward a narrowly defined, limited spiritual image, one can find a connection with the totality of universal life. By achieving clarity, one can transcend shallow cultural and religious conflict. This clarity also allows one to be indifferent to the troublesome, vulgar world of ignorance, obstinacy and aggression.

"I have learned to cherish the truth in life. I believe the truth within me to be the same truth of other lives. It is not the truth which causes troubles; it is the inflexibility of many different interpretations which causes the major problems in the ordinary human world.

"The main thing I have gained from my search and the self-cultivation which I now enjoy and can share with others is this: depart from the wasteful past. Refine and enhance the essence of your being in order to live a universal life of endless bounty."

The businessman enjoyed great personal benefits as a result of learning Tao and his spiritual growth was much advanced. One day, to his surprise, he was paid a visit by Master True Gold. On this precious occasion, he sought further instruction. After this visit from his teacher, the man further taught his friends. "After learning Tao, we are proud of our good health. Having good health is nice, but it is not the total meaning of achieving Tao. If so, lions and tigers and other wild animals that have good health would be achieved in Tao. We also enjoy the high view that we have cultivated. But are you aware that you are taking advantage of that which is low to build that which is high? Surely, there should be no pride in this achievement either. Moreover, you inflexibly apply the principle of balance to all situations, which tells me you do not truly understand what balance is.

"Contrary to popular misconception, balance is not something that is half of this and half of that, though it can be equivalent and symmetrical. The correct application of balance is not a "middle" or "halfway," nor an attitude of compromise.

"In ☰☰ and ☰☰ different cycles which are beginning should be handled accordingly.

"In ☰☰ and ☰☰ different centers of strength are formed; one is broad-purposed and the other is narrow-purposed.

"In ☰☰ and ☰☰ responsibility is given; one undertaken with humility, the other with caution.

"In ☰☰ and ☰☰ duties are assigned to assistants. Privileges also shift to them. One accepts some with confidence and others with fear.

"In ☰☰ and ☰☰ correct centers are recognized; one supportive of kindness and the other of egoless power.

"In ☰☰ and ☰☰ competition is expressed; one with aggressive dominance, the other with virtuous resolution.

"In ䷿ and ䷿ the energy is different, but in the same formation.   Here, the balancing center is the fifth line.   When the center lines are all strong, ䷿ , the second line expresses safety, but in ䷿ the top line sacrifices itself for the rest.   In ䷿ , not only does the vitality of the masculine energy return, but also that of the feminine in ䷿ ; and, as the vitality of the masculine energy leaves, so does the feminine.

"In all sixty-four hexagrams there must be a balancing line.   The application of this principle is unlimited.   For example: the proportion of ocean water to earth surface is 70/30.   In this case, it is the necessary and appropriate balance.   Similarly, the hemispheres of the earth, like the hemispheres of the brain, are not a 50/50 division.   Their true equivalence or balance comes instead from the way in which they interact.

This same general principle applies to everything.   In diet and nutrition, for instance, the correct balance is not 50% yang-natured food to 50% yin-natured food, rather it is four portions of yang-natured food to one portion of yin-natured food.   (Note: this can be interpreted as a balanced proportion between alkaline and acid foods.)

Also consider the "lopsided" but nonetheless healthy balance within the human body, such as the vast number of red blood cells (i.e., the yung, or nutritive blood) working harmoniously with the small band of white blood cells (the wei, or protective blood).   By virtue of their respective functions, it would create havoc if they were equal in number.

"Extending outward into the social sphere, we can observe many instances in which the idea of a 50/50 balance should not and will not work.   It would only be a source of misery.   For example, when a country attempts to spend half or more of its budget on national defense, resulting in the necessary neglect of all other positive and beneficial causes, such as education, transportation, technological development and social welfare.   In this case, true "balance" would be achieved at a level closer to 70/30, with the military being apportioned the lesser share.

"Analogously, ever reflective of Nature, the sixty-four hexagrams express a different pattern of energy formation. In each hexagram, one appropriate point must be found. Only when that point is discovered and realized can balance, harmony and good cooperation exist.

"In every situation, there is an area or zone in which a harmonious balance of yin-yang is maintained. If the boundary for this zone is overstepped, one will meet destruction, and the particular transgression will naturally meet its appropriate retribution. Regarding individual life, the trouble will affect the person, his family, and all that he is associated with. On a larger scale, the effect is naturally much bigger. There have been many people in history who have tried to cross the harmonizing boundary line of yin-yang, even to the limitation of extremes at both ends, and have thus met destruction as a result of their personal ambition. In all matters and relationships, this inviolable line of harmony can never be ignored.

"Those of development should learn how to muffle their voices and not only understand the importance of realizing their virtuous being, but also keep it unknown to others. Never be proud of building something outwardly, but at all times, embody the unborn, imperishable and Immortal One."

小過
62 shiao kuo

minor excess

GUIDANCE: *"Minor excesses cause trouble. It is not safe for the bird to fly high; it should stay low. One should not attempt large undertakings at this time."*

In this hexagram, Thunder is above Mountain. When there is a storm above a Mountain, it is better to keep low. If a bird soars too high, it becomes caught in the storm. When personal weakness predominates over inner strength, one should not go beyond one's capabilities or position. However, such times of weakness are not necessarily dangerous if one acts in accordance with the natural principles that govern the situation. Thus, this is a time to be humble and not to undertake important matters.

In this hexagram, two yang lines are within and two yin lines are on each side. In quantity, yin energy exceeds yang, yet in strength, yang energy exceeds yin. The two central yang lines are not in a good position for leadership and are unable to control the situation. Leadership requires strong energy. The yin line in the center of each trigram is in a position of leadership, but it does not have the strength necessary to control the circumstances either. For this reason, much of the yin energy is unrestrained.

The symbol represented is that of a bird flying into a storm. The central yang lines represent the bird's body and the surrounding yin lines are its wings, hence the image of a bird flying proudly into a storm with wings outstretched. Imagine its fate!

The yin lines are also birds who fly too high, spreading their wings too wide and thus being unable to control themselves. The higher they fly, the more they are endangered; their pleas for help cannot be heard at such a distance. However, in a lower place they can gather together. Thus, this hexagram suggests remaining low and still. One who is too ambitious or too proud places himself in a difficult situation. One who is humble receives help.

The image of a flying bird also represents something that is unattainable. It can be seen flying and heard singing, but it cannot be touched. This implies a time when one is unable to accomplish anything of great significance. When there is a tendency toward excess, one should not become involved in things of great importance.

Examples of minor excesses are miserliness, gluttony, displays of grief or pain, and impositions on others. When one goes beyond the point of appropriateness, trouble results.

LINE 1: *"The bird tries to fly. Danger. Be humble."*

The first line is a yin line in a yang position which, in this case, means that one should be more prepared than one is. This line has a tendency to move forward without looking, to act before correctly understanding the situation, and to talk when it should be listening. One in this position is like a bird which attempts to fly before it is ready. Lacking the strength demanded by the situation, it meets danger that cannot be averted.

LINE 2: *"One should stay at one's level. Do not attempt to reach what is too high."*

This is a yin line in a position of leadership. It is weak, but it is in its right position. Although one cannot achieve anything of great importance, there is no problem if one keeps to what one can do and does not go beyond one's position.

This can be explained another way. Because the fifth line is also yin, there is no support from it. Thus, the second line goes to the fourth for help. The literal Chinese translation is, "One can only attain the standard of being a grandmother instead of a grandfather. One can only attain the standard of being a minister instead of a leader." This means that, due to one's limitations, one can only give help and support to others without attaining great achievements oneself.

LINE 3: *"Being overly-confident, one neglects proper protection and invites trouble."*

This line is at the top of the Mountain and is exposed to the Thunder above. Therefore, one must be careful even in a small matters. Furthermore, this is a yang line in a yang position, but in this situation its strength and pride, which are due to egotism, are exaggerated since both leaders in upper and lower trigrams are weak. The third line invites trouble by showing off. He feels too confident and expresses himself without regard for his leader, the second line. Also, he has not protected himself well and is thus susceptible to flattery and compliments from those of inferior virtue.

LINE 4: *"Resistance will result from any forceful action due to haste. In correcting restlessness there will be no fault."*

Although the fourth line is strong, it is limited by its weak position. If it can humble itself before the leader in the fifth position, there will be no problem. Now is an especially important time to be flexible. One should not try to exceed one's position but should modestly remain where one is. This line is a warning.

LINE 5: *"The clouds are thick, but it does not rain. One shoots birds in the nest."*

This line is in the position of leadership, but it is weak. Instead of being a leader, it is more like a young prince whose talents and abilities are not yet fully developed and whose style of leadership is not as strong as it should be. It is possible for this line to enjoy something which has already been done. However, this is not the correct position to start any new plans or to engage in major undertakings.

LINE 6: *"The bird flies too high. Danger."*

The top line exceeds its situation instead of just meeting it. One should establish limits that can be respected and achieved. Excessiveness and an attempt to maintain a high or lofty position will only invite danger.

The principle of keeping low is clearly exemplified in this hexagram as well as the previous one. The natural spiritual philosophy of being low can be understood by contemplating these two hexagrams. They are specific examples of learning from the virtue of nature.

SPECIFIC GUIDANCE

PERSONAL FORTUNE: Disease is difficult to prevent.

MARRIAGE: Success is difficult to achieve.

HOUSING/FAMILY: If there are two masters of the house, there will be no benefit.

CHILDBIRTH: Difficult.

LOOKING FOR WORK: Although it can be achieved, it will not be a high position.

SOCIAL/GOVERNMENTAL POSITION: Difficult to achieve.

TRADE/BUSINESS: There will be difficulties.

SEARCHING FOR SOMEONE: If you go searching with someone else, they can be found.

WAITING FOR SOMEONE: They will be late.

LOOKING FOR SOMETHING LOST: Hard to recover.

HUNTING FOR THIEVES: They are difficult to catch.

LAWSUIT: Make peace.

CLIMATE: It will be rainy.

TRAVEL: It is best to stay home.

DISEASE: If it is not serious, it can be cured by keeping still.

PERSONAL WISH: Hard to achieve.

COMMENTARY

Avoiding Excess in Everyday Life

When practicing self-cultivation,
  be truthful.
Continually assess your achievement.
With the Sacred Method of Harmony,
  dissolve the concept of self.
Prove that beingness and emptiness are connected
  and mutually transforming.

Life and death are superficial phenomena.
The way of life and death is one, not two.
Control the energy,
  and true living continues endlessly.

Because your energy is not yet refined,
  you become disturbed
  during the early stages of cultivation.
Eventually, the essence
  of the abdominal center appears,
  changing to sweet and fragrant chi.
Breaking through the three main points of the spine,
  these energy transformations
  can have the following benefit.
Rising up from the kidneys,
  the energy penetrates directly into the brain,
  becoming spiritual light,
  the energy of life and regeneration.

To achieve and constantly maintain the three spheres,
  agile vitality, calm mind and high pure spirit,
  proves that you are already a shien
  living in this world.
Govern your body with your spirit
  in order to progress to a higher level of life.
You are asked not only to inwardly cultivate
  your spiritual essence,
  but also to live harmoniously in the world.
To live in the world,
  we must complete the three natures of life
  (the divine, the human, and the transcendent)
  and become integrated with
  the virtue of mellowness.

To measure the success of self-cultivation,
do not use the conceptual gauges of
failure, success, sharpness or dullness.
Look only for the purity that comes from
sublimating confused discrepancies.
This comes from uniting with Tao.

A broken ship cannot journey long on the ocean.
In parting from the Truth to cling to false worship,
deception and exaggeration bring only emptiness.
From an impure, dirt-filled world you can grow
to become a tall, pure lotus.
Forsake all wasteful wandering,
all nonsensical talk and theories.
Nourish yourself with the true chi of original oneness.

63   chi chi 既濟

AFTER CROSSING THE WATER

GUIDANCE: *"The 'Water' has been crossed. This is the time after completion. Things go well. Small achievements can be attained, and accomplishments should be protected. Otherwise, the good fortune in the beginning becomes confusion in the end."*

In this hexagram, Water is above Fire, and all lines are in their correct positions. Although Water has no substantial form, it does have great inner strength, characterized by the upper trigram where the yang energy is within and the yin energy is without. Fire, on the other hand, is strong without but hollow within. This is expressed by the lower trigram where yin energy is within and yang without. The combination of inner emptiness in the lower trigram and outer strength in the upper trigram represent a harmonious and balanced situation.

Water and Fire represent two opposing natural elements. When they are in good order and harmonized their energy is creative, but when their relationship is

unharmonious their energy becomes destructive.   Therefore, true harmony is not simply a matter of opposites
confronting one another, but rather of how they interact.
When the elements of any situation are balanced, they
respond like two partners assisting one another toward a
mutual purpose.   If neither is excessive, everything is all
right.   For example, putting Water above Fire in cooking is
the correct relationship.   However, even in this situation,
if the Fire is too strong, the Water evaporates and
disappears.   Likewise, Water in excess can extinguish Fire.
Thus, the balance and management of energy is extremely
important.

The tendency of Water is to descend, and the tendency
of Fire is to ascend.   Therefore, when Water is above Fire,
their relationship is one of integration.   It is this integration which brings forth all life.   Furthermore, since every
line in this hexagram is in its correct position, things are
now in proper balance.   Nothing more needs to be done,
because completion has been reached.

Since the natural movement of universal energy is
cyclical, the state of completion is just one phase of an
entire cycle.   In natural energy movement, a period of fullness is always followed by a period of decline.   The I
Ching teaches the natural truth that when something has
been accomplished, or when a life circumstance reaches
its peak, one should be aware of the cycle of decline
which will inevitably follow.   People generally focus on a
particular goal or plan without paying attention to what is
to follow.   Even when they get off to a good start in a
relationship, a job or any undertaking, few are able to
remain persevering throughout.   One who is consistently
mindful will never fall, but if one's achievement or accomplishment makes him proud or overly confident, his
balance will soon be lost.   This is how people often bring
about disorder after success.

The I Ching teaches one to give equal consideration to
all phases of any development because each phase is just
as important as the next.   Each stage is reality at that
particular time and must be dealt with accordingly.   Every
situation or circumstance in life is an opportunity to learn
how to maintain balance and appropriateness.   Though
disorder approaches after completion, one can adjust to
the reality of any new situation by following the guidance
of the I Ching.

When matters have been brought to completion, it is
time to attend to small details and tie up loose ends.

This is not the time to engage in new undertakings. Thus, the natural cycle of decline can be avoided. Even when aware of this pattern, one must still refresh oneself, continue one's progress, and not let past achievements hinder future prosperity.

> **LINE 1:** *"The wheels are controlled. Beware of getting wet at the onset of crossing the Water. Caution can save one from fault."*

One should be prudent and cautious when undertaking a great task. This is illustrated by a young fox attempting to cross the Water. By not rushing, it is able to prevent its tail from getting wet. Thus, there is safety in undertaking the crossing. One should restrict impulsive activities and reflect on what is about to take place before rushing into something.

> **LINE 2:** *"The curtain of a lady's carriage has fallen somewhere and causes delay. There is no need to search, for it will be found in seven days."*

Although the undertaking has already started, a minor problem causes a delay. There is no need to worry, because in seven days one can start again.

In ancient times, when a lady rode in a carriage, there was usually a curtain over the window to protect her from being seen. If the curtain was missing, she was not to travel at that time.

The second line is the leader of the lower trigram and is at the heart of the Fire. Though this line is in its correct position, the lower trigram is confronting the upper trigram, Water, which indicates trouble. However, after seven days, the second and fifth lines will meet because the cycle of all six lines will be complete. Thus, one should keep things in proper order so that one can proceed when the time is right.

> **LINE 3:** *"It takes three years to achieve victory, which is accomplished through the careful selection of qualified people. However, one feels exhausted when victory is finally reached."*

The third line is at the top of the trigram Fire and is also the strong center in the inner trigram, Water. This implies strength and clarity in times of danger. A highly qualified person is required to accomplish a difficult task which takes three years. When the task has been completed and success is achieved, one must be very careful not to employ or trust someone of inferior virtue. Otherwise, the fruits of the difficult labor will be snatched away.

> **LINE 4:** *"One needs to be prepared for a leak in the boat at all times by keeping materials at hand to plug the hole. This causes one to remain tense."*

The fourth line warns: One must check for leaks before sailing in heavy waters.

The fourth position is the second line of the inner trigram, Fire, and the first line of the upper trigram, Water. This causes a situation of contention in which appropriate action must be taken. The fourth line is also like a noble person who benefits others by being considerate.

> **LINE 5:** *"The eastern neighbor kills a cow in making an offering. This is no more meaningful than a sincere, modest offering that is given from the heart.'*

In ancient times, after matters were completed, offerings of gratitude were made to Heaven in the form of sacrifices. This line shows the effect of two different types of offerings: the grand display of a slaughtered ox, and a simple but sincere offering from the heart. Actions done with sincerity are always more valuable than those done for show.

It further indicates that during the time after completion, one must not be wasteful.

> **LINE 6:** *"One finally gets his head wet. Danger."*

People are usually careful in the beginning and careless at the end, but one should be careful during all phases of a venture. If one is as careful at the end as the beginning, the task can be completed and the effects will be positive. If in "crossing the water" one is careless at the end and becomes excited, he may fall in and get his head wet.

Do not cause yourself to fall into the Water by being overly confident or excited about your near success. If so, your happiness may turn into disaster.

SPECIFIC GUIDANCE

PERSONAL FORTUNE: This is the height of your prosperity. You must be careful about inevitable decline, however, or something bad might happen.

MARRIAGE: Haste brings danger; slow movement brings good fortune.

HOUSING/FAMILY: Peaceful.

CHILDBIRTH: If the baby is born in the Spring or Summer, it will be a girl. In Autumn or Winter, it will be a boy. There will be no obstacle.

LOOKING FOR WORK: It takes three attempts to find the right position.

SOCIAL/GOVERNMENTAL POSITION: In the beginning there is much hard work, but finally there can be promotion to a high and important position.

TRADE/BUSINESS: It depends on some important person's strength to be successful.

SEARCHING FOR SOMEONE: They can be found.

WAITING FOR SOMEONE: They will come.

LOOKING FOR SOMETHING LOST: Difficult to find.

HUNTING FOR THIEVES: They are in the neighborhood and can be caught.

LAWSUIT: Afterwards, peace can be made.

CLIMATE: It will rain.

TRAVEL: It is good for people traveling together to go to the Northeast. One should not travel alone.

DISEASE: Dangerous.

PERSONAL WISH: Difficulty and obstacles.

COMMENTARY
The Integral Life

No one can neglect the importance of the material sphere in maintaining life. This is an obvious fact which people may tend to over value by taking the view that one's physical life is the entirety of one's true being. The spiritually developed individual knows that the limitation of a lifetime is a limitation of view, and that it falls short of the total reality of life.

In human life, each individual has a subtle essence which can be treated as the core of one's being. This subtle essence is formed prior to the physical form and returns to the subtle sphere after the physical form ceases to exist. This subtle, spiritual essence can be weakened and scattered, or strengthened through personal life experience.

Most people have not discovered this truth of life, thus they make a cheap trade by mis-using the eternal subtle essence to serve the needs of their material life. On the other hand, it is also an error for people of spiritual quality to focus solely on the subtle and neglect the material. They do not fulfill the balanced path of life and thus lose the opportunity of wholistic development in life. Worst of all, many people become lost in the confusion of the multiple misconceptions of cultural religious viewpoints which are limited by the background of time and affected with only short term goals.

The following story presents the reflection of a universal mind to another open mind of a high human being.

Several million years ago, astral beings lived on energy islands in space. Some of these islands were close to our solar system, and over a long period of time these beings witnessed the small planet earth becoming a balanced field of different energies that radiated from far and near-by stars and planets.

After some time, this balanced planet became a place on which a new specimen of life could thrive and propagate. The appearance of this new specimen, which was highly intelligent and which had a perfectly shaped physical body, gave all the astral beings such great joy that they came to earth to play with and teach these human beings.

To their astonishment, the astral beings recognized that this new species grew so intelligent that the original balance and well-being of individuals could no longer be maintained. Extreme tendencies became more and more prevalent. As human beings became increasingly superficial, they eventually lost the spiritual essence of their life. This improper development caused the astral friends great concern, and most of them stopped visiting the earth as often as they used to.

One astral family, however, could not bear to see the darkening of the human race. In order to help mankind rediscover its original balance, integrity and clarity, this family decided to take upon itself the task of enlightening their spiritual human friends. Thus it was that some six thousand years ago those very kind astral beings came to this world and took human form in order to help humanity overcome its difficulties. They knew that taking human form could hinder their own spiritual clarity, but an effort had to be made.

They decided that the two hundredth cycle of the yellowish planet, Saturn, as it orbits the Sun, would be the time for them to meet again, (One orbit of Saturn around the sun takes approximately 30 years) and that their meeting place could be the top of Kun Lun mountain, the designated station point for space traveling. They also decided that after their meeting they would restore themselves to divine immortality and play no more reincarnating games in the human realm.

For six thousand years, these astral beings had many human lives. They were good swimmers in the stream of life. Just as a swimmer holds his breath and submerges his head into the water, then lifts his head up into the fresh air, the astral beings would complete each life cycle, occasionally leaving the water to take a rest and sit on the shore. With such attained freedom, one does not become attached to either the joy of swimming or the leisure of sitting on the shore. Whatever is done is done with the highest freedom.

Time came for the meeting. Although all the astral beings lived in different places, had different kinds of lives and different appearances, a strong summons was simultaneously felt in each of their hearts. One by one, they all came to Kun Lun mountain in the Western region of China where gatherings of immortal astral beings often take place.

They all arrived on time and quietly refreshed themselves. Although they recalled who they had been and the work they had performed on earth, they had completely awakened from their experiences of human life. Their total integrity was restored.

Before returning to the Divine Immortal Realm, however, each of them offered some insight on what they had witnessed in the human realm. What follows are their conversations, as reflected in the mind of one of their human friends. We should regard it as advice the immortals have offered to us.

Chia, from the East of Kun Lun said: "I have witnessed both the growth and decline of our human friends. They have become trapped by their own creations: social systems, religions and other such weapons. Their common problem is the lack of spiritual clarity. Although they can intelligently handle small matters, they are unable to perceive the whole. They enthusiastically pursue external or material expansion which results only in upsetting their naturally well-balanced lives. Greed leads them away from their innermost spiritual source. Unlike the ancient, integrally developed human beings, modern intellectuals can see very tiny things in hidden places, but due to the lack of inner awareness, they are unable to see the vast spiritual truth, even if it was a cart of firewood right in front of their eyes! Being able to see a detail in the material sphere can be useful, but insisting that what one sees is the total truth is a serious mistake that can create unnecessary conflict and disharmony among human societies."

Yi, from the Southeast of Kun Lun, said: "I am concerned that our human friends have misguided their emotions in the direction of darkness. It is not religious emotion or pure piety that creates problems, but war-like religious structures with dominant doctrines, aggressive temperaments, and racially ignorant prejudice that eventually lead all followers into an abyss.

"Piety, like any other human emotion, can have a positive effect if it is well-balanced and correctly guided. If not, it can negatively influence both an individual and the entire human race.

"With their spiritual focus misguided and misused, our human friends have lost their natural direction and seek the temporary relief that some religions offer. They cannot see that the most important element of a religion should not be fear of some god who is a source of power or force. The positive basis of all true religion is sincerity, not fear. Whatever form sincerity or piety takes is strictly superficial. A religion is only the framework or house for one's piety. Once this is understood, then one can also understand that piety within and between all people is the same; the only difference is in its various expressions and interpretations. Without sincerity, all religious worship, sacrifice, offerings, and rituals become meaningless. Thus, competition or contention among religions is fundamentally groundless."

Bing, from the South of Kun Lun, said: "If our human friends knew that piety is their own internal, boundless treasure, and if their piety were correctly guided and conducted, then they would discover the universal truth of all life.

"No one should be forced to only one way of interpreting the truth. It is more appropriate to show people true sincerity. A sincere person is a developed one; discrimination cannot affect one of pure piety and sincerity. Although stories can describe piety, they are only stories. Religious conflicts exist because people insist that their interpretation is the only conceivable one. Although ordinary religion serves as a means of interpretation, the higher truth is indescribable personal sincerity.

"People and societies that are oppressed tend to respond to religions with rigidly narrow social views. Also, without a negative environment, people might not engage in individual spiritual growth. However, they should not settle for the kind of worship where only a single element of piety is expressed, but should inwardly recognize their divine nature.

"External religions worship the shell of spiritual custom such as what God looks like, what kind of robe God wears, what kind of crown is on God's head, what God holds in his hand, etc. But the True Path values reaching the purity that is beyond desscription or interpretation and achieveing subtle integration with the high spiritual reality of the universal nature. Awe is merely a preliminary passion or an emotion to support religion as the establishment of an external image of authority. True piety and a pure mind, however, enable one to remain inwardly centered and to achieve the highest spiritual level: a serene mind and the stability of pure spiritual energy.

"Divine beings respond differently in different situations. They respond in ways that communicate certain messages, or in ways that are only understandable to a particular person. The appearance of a divine being is a message or a communication in itself. However, a defined form or single interpretation cannot be ascribed to a divine being. In most situations, if a person is developed enough, he will be the only person who receives and understands the message. To become dogmatic is thus harmful.

"The highest Divine Realm, as achieved by the most ancient developed people, is correctly expressed as the 'Three Purities:' The Form of the Formless, The Image of the Imageless, The Shape of the Shapeless. This means that the divine form is not limited, the divine image is not a single image, and the divine shape is not one definite shape. The Divine Realm reflects an image that does not have to wear white, purple, or any other specific color or garment. Nothing can be defined in the real Divine Realm. Thus, the true highest Divine Realm, the true origin, is the mother of all images, all forms and all shapes.

"Recent converts, or people who are born into a particular religion, are usually not objective about their religion. They are touched by stories which only temporarily correspond in some manner to their emotions and life experiences. As strong sympathizers and firm believers, they reinforce the same patterns of emotion and follow the same pattern of destiny as the religion they follow. This is not a natural, healthy attitude derived from spiritual growth and deep individual awareness.

"The general purpose of established religion is to teach people to worship a single spiritual image for the purpose of authority and power rather than to guide them to achieve true spiritual growth. Individual development is curbed by dogma, which causes people to eventually stray from a liberal-minded, meditative and reflective spiritual path.

"Unfortunately, piety is often only accepted when it is practiced according to a particular, established way. However, this kind of practice becomes the source of religious confusion and conflict in the world. Thus, a complete spiritual education must have two elements which are of equal value for individual development: the practice of pure piety guided by personally developed awareness, and self-cultivation for harmonized development."

Ding, from the Southwest of Kun Lun, said: "The spiritual confusion of the human world is indeed expressed in its religions. Religions have misused the emotion of sincerity or piety; thus, followers never have the opportunity to correctly reach the exquisite reality of spiritual truth. When one's sincerity is aimed at a target such as God or salvation one must be developed enough to know whether that direction is the correct way. Although most religions use the emotion of sincerity, it is usually misguided. Even with piety, one needs the right direction. However, one does not need to travel far. One's own true essence is the gateway to the high spiritual realm. A pure human mind is like a mirror, and describable images are its reflections. What one projects into the mirror is the image it will reflect.

"Many people have misused the good name of religious faith as a tool for expressing their mischievous qualities and narrow-mindedness. Making a public declaration and spectacle of one's own piety does not necessarily indicate real spiritual growth. Such people have been known to criticize, attack and burn those of different beliefs in order to demonstrate the strength of their piety, but in reality they are totally lost.

"Piety must be rightfully expressed. With true, pure piety, a person will never be wild. With pure piety, one will always be gentle. With true piety, one will never do evil. With pure piety, one will always cherish and maintain purity and clarity."

Geng, from the West of Kun Lun, said: "The false beliefs of our human friends have definitely led them in the wrong direction. The Divine Realm exists above the human realm, but the dominance of a narrowly-defined spiritual realm of strong emotional force is not a true expression of the Divine Realm.

"The Divine Origin, which is expressed as the Subtle Realm, is indescribable, but a society or individual should always be open to various religious interpretations. All interpretations stray from the indefinable Subtle Truth, but such differences can offer further growth, even though they represent only a certain level of mental development. A natural, truthful and sincere mind is above all interpretations and is the totality of spiritual truth.

"A social design, which was given the term 'religion' by earlier leaders, cannot be good for all times and all people. Any religious or political system which imposes rigid patterns on a society must inevitably lead to suffering, pressure and tension. Any benefit, including military 'strength,' is ultimately nullified by the resulting deadlock of inflexible conditions. Compare this to a society that is naturally free and has less armed strength; the people stay open-minded, free, natural and harmonious.

"Those who extend their minds directly to the reality of the spiritual realm and who are not perplexed by the outer forms of religion, should be respected. They can live within a rigid worldly structure without losing their clarity of mind. Even while amassing material wealth they can value the spiritual truth without becoming lost.

"Most religions do not intend to guide people in the direction of total spiritual growth. They practice religious enslavement instead of true awakening or enlightenment. Only a developed person can embrace the universe.

"When one embraces the universe, all divine beings are harmonized and connected with him.   One does not need to pray in order to obtain their response.   It all depends upon whether one uses one's mind broadly or narrowly.   Spiritual connectedness is just a measure of what one can achieve.

"The integral path can open the eyes of its followers to see the true purpose of spiritual development.   It can also pass on to them methods for their spiritual self-cultivation which will allow them to reach true spiritual reality.   Engaging in such practices is indeed personal and real, and is the way to reach the true Divine Origin."

Hsin, from the Northwest of Kun Lun, said: "There is some dispute among modern minds as to how the world began.   Those who hold the view of idealism believe the world started as the creation of God.   Those who hold the view of materialism believe the world is based on matter. However, long ago some ancient achieved human beings reached the level of discovery that the origin or potency of the universe is chi.   The first stage of pure existence is neither mind nor matter, but chi.   Mind and matter are merely different expressions of this primal chi.   Existence is not a matter of different 'origins,' but of development. Thus, existence can be developed as mind and matter.

"Mental energy is a more highly developed stage of chi derived from grosser, material energy.   It is the essence of the external material shell.   However, essence cannot be without its gross base.

"The origin of energy has no form.   It is pure chi, which is the original form of everything.   Thus, the origin of the universe cannot be defined as being either material or mental, it is simply chi.   Disputes between materialists and idealists, therefore, have no basis, but are merely the expressions of a limited point of view.   Insistence on such partial views becomes the source of disintegration for human society.

"Standards for evaluating success and achievement in the world today may stress material progress, but if material progress goes against human nature, then imbalance occurs and a crisis will develop.   In any age, the principle of balance should be the highest guideline.   It should also be applied to general religious practices.   Religious life has many different levels: social, personal, emotional and spiritual. Fundamentally, if one is to avoid the downfall of human nature, one must become aware enough to rise above all established doctrines which damage the original naturalness and oneness of human nature. Only the unspoiled, natural followers of the ancient integral path can maintain the direct embodiment and fulfillment of truth in their lives.

"If one seeks individual realization of everlasting spiritual life, the methods still exist. The path of total integration is not only valuable for spiritual, mental and physical health and development, but it can also prepare one for high achievement. Actualization of such achievement has been proven by our ancient human friends who achieved themselves through these truthful methods."

Ren, from the North of Kun Lun, said: "In very ancient times, divine immortals could communicate with the unspoiled minds of their human friends. All beings, including humans, are born of Heaven. No group of people is especially favored by God, nor are there individuals who are God-forsaken. Heaven favors those who are virtuous, regardless of their tribe or religion.

"Through virtue and spiritual development, spiritual ascension can be attained. However, it can never be achieved by emotionally worshipping and begging God to do what one wants because one is unable to accomplish it for oneself. Unfortunately, due to the present confusion of people, they cannot follow the education that their immortal friends gave them.

"In ancient times, the divine immortals taught their human friends that universal harmony is the basic virtue of life. Obedience and harmony were originally expressed toward the wholeness called Heaven. This faith was handed down before recorded history, and it recognized two very important elements: the omnipresence of the subtle heavenly law (Tien Li), and the unimpeded individual conscience, which is able to know the existence of the heavenly law without searching for it. These were the sole moral strengths of the ancient developed ones before the invention of religion. To unspoiled people, heavenly law is the mind, and the mind is the heavenly law that true knowledge is born within.

"Artificial religions, on the other hand, make people behave decently out of fear of being punished by Heaven. This fear is widely preached by all religious leaders and is the degradation of human spiritual dignity. Thus, people are losing the true knowledge of their deep inner root of universal life.   Fortunately, the healthy ancient faith has been preserved in three different sources: Lao Tzu, Confucius and Mo Tzu.   Lao Tzu interpreted the faith of Heaven as keeping to the original nature.   Confucius' philosophy of humanism was based on the fact that heavenly law is not beyond human nature.   And Mo Tzu put it into the solemn practice of universal love.

"Ancient developed people recognized Heaven as their subtle supporter.   Interpretations of Heaven as a dominion that is different from what the ancients knew came from later religions.   Heaven (Tien) is the universal subtle law residing above all ruling forces.   Mo Tzu elucidated it thus: 'Heaven desires righteousness and detests unrighteousness.   If I lead people under Heaven to live a life of righteousness, I do as Heaven desires; then Heaven will respond to me with what I desire.   What I desire are blessings and benefit.   What I detest are calamities and harm.   If I lead the people under Heaven to live a life of troublemaking and evil doings, then I do not as Heaven desires, but as Heaven detests.   How do I know what Heaven desires and detests?   By the fact that under Heaven the one who is righteous lives a natural life, and the one who is unrighteous usually dies unnaturally.   One who is righteous enjoys life, one who is unrighteous suffers.   One who is righteous receives peace, and one who is unrighteous suffers being disordered.   Heaven desires that people live happily and not die unnaturally.   Heaven desires people to be self-sufficient and joyful and not suffer from self-created poverty and difficulties.   Heaven desires that people live peacefully and not struggle in disorder and confusion.   This is how I know that Heaven desires what is righteous and detests what is unrighteous.'

"This was the invisible law engraved in the minds of these developed people.   Can one separate heavenly nature from human nature? The social code of ancient developed people depended upon self-recognized natural moral law and, as a result, there was mutual understanding and consideration among all people.   Even though there were leaders in an ancient system of government, the society was naturally ordered without being specifically organized. Modern people may think the old natural societies were backward, yet they were more normal in a healthier, human way.   Modern people may think they were random and unorganized, yet they were natural and organic. Modern people may think they were inefficient, yet they

were relaxed.   Modern people may think they were un-
systematized, yet they were flexible.

"The ancient faith of humanism did not function as a
regimented system of law or religion which rigidly forced
its demands on people.   The foundation of ancient society
did not depend on emperors or officials for the establishment of order; it depended on an invisible moral force in
every individual which was further established within the
family.   Family discipline was the real foundation of social
discipline.   Parents took responsibility for the behavior of
their children, and the elders took responsibility for the
young.

"For almost 5,000 years moral law was the foundation
of that society.   Until the present time, though the
dynasties have changed, the social code did not.   The faith
in the Subtle Law of Heaven and humanism was the real
ruling power of the unspoiled mind.   The ancient
emperors were not the real rulers; on the contrary, they
were the ones who enjoyed the good nature of their
people.   The real leader on the spiritual throne of China
was universal humanism.   The society developed naturally,
stage by stage.

"However, the seeds of confusion in thinking sprouted
like weeds, and the Old Sage, Lao Tzu, saw correctly that
the decline of human nature would be inevitable.   He
beckoned people to return to their original nature, for
when one returns to the true mind of simplicity, there is
neither confusion nor contention.

"Surely, human life is now much more highly developed than animal life, so why don't humans have
peace?   Although wild animals are not more highly evolved
than humans, they have no organized wars.   Competition
and war have made all divine beings sad to see the backward direction of human nature.   If the human race continues to follow the darkness of its impulsive blindness, it
may lead itself to the point of self-elimination.

"The natural faith of humanism, or universal love, is
the mellow fruit of and for all people.   The ancient developed people directly recognized and applied the principle
that heavenly law is the human mind, and the human
mind is heavenly law.   They maintain naturalness without
deviation from the truth.   A developed person should keep
to the balanced, broad perspective without becoming reli-
giously dogmatic.   Humanism, or universal love, should be
one's contribution to total human life.   This is the essence

of the individual in human society and it should be the
goal of the entire human race."

Gwei, from the Northeast of Kun Lun, said: "The important achievement of the ancient developed people is
their holistic comprehension of the universe. This wholeness is the basic expression of the primal chi as numerous small T'ai Chi's with indistinguishable qualities,
whether mind or matter. The symbol of T'ai chi is ☯ .
Chi is the foremost foundation of the universe before it
develops into the distinguishable sphere. T'ai chi is many;
T'ai chi is one. It can be the smallest and the subtlest
entity of the universe before any shape is formed. In totality, T'ai Chi is the boundlessness of the universe.
        "Through manifestation comes the dimension of mind
and matter. Even in the ultimate development of both,
whether ideological or materialistic, both are still
completely within the scope of T'ai Chi. In its pure,
original state, mind cannot be separated from matter, nor
can matter be separated from mind. Nonetheless, an
artificial, intellectual separation was made. It was a
dichotomy with no basis, the result of a partial vision of
the manifested level. On the subtlest level, chi, or first
stage of pure, original existence, cannot be called mind or
matter. However, it can develop as matter or as mind. It
is not different to begin with; it is only perceived as being
different.
        "Indeed, the growth of the universe is like the growth
of all human life. In its early stages, there was the indistinguishable oneness, akin to babyhood, when neither the
mind nor the body considered themselves separate or different from each other.
        "In the second stage, spirits became active on the
gross material level. Spirits were no more than the subtle
essence of the gross, bulky material base.
        "In the third stage, different levels of spirits formalized
themselves with harmonious energy to become life. To
take the form of life is to follow the cycles of life and
death. To remain a spiritual being is to keep enforcing
one's true essence and thereby to surpass the cycles of
life and death.
        "In the fourth stage, the appearance of human life was
the perfect projection and formation of high spiritual
beings.
        "In the fifth stage, the partial development of hu-
manity's awareness brought about the divergence of mind

and body. The result of this dualistic vision was confusion and conflict.

"In the sixth stage, the original human nature was lost by confused creations and social competition. The downfall of humankind portends dangers which are beyond humanity's own capabilities to handle and control.

"In the seventh stage, in which vast destruction is approaching, self-awareness finally grows individually within people and on a cooperative basis. The value of human preservation becomes recognized, and human beings will again appreciate the truth of immortality.

"This is where the further development of human life after 'death' (the death caused by pursuit of worldly pleasures) is revealed. Possibilities exist in one's lifetimes to cultivate, develop and direct the subtle essence in order to enjoy everlasting spiritual freedom."

Mu, from the Upper Region of the Central Land, close to Kun Lun, said: "In order to give real hope to our human friends, it is necessary for them to focus on cultivating the essential quality of their intrinsic nature. All human external characteristics - what school a person graduated from, what position he holds in society, how much money the person has made or plans to make - is not our concern. There is only one true concern: the quality of a person. It is the quality of a person, the way one cultivates, develops and achieves oneself, that is the true measure of nobility. This is the only way to be ranked among the Divine Immortals.

"Needless to say, if one seeks spiritual maturity, there is nothing above the direct spiritual disciplines of the Integral Path. If one seeks continual life without influencing or accepting the interruption from the transformation of lives, the highest secret of the Integral Path is what one should acquire. This is all the truth we can reveal.

"Many animals have the peculiar habit of taking the indirect route home. They prefer the winding path. However, there is no such detour for a human being to take before reaching his or her own 'home.' Studying all the religions in the world may be fine if a person does not become entrapped by them. However, it is mostly a waste in terms of the spiritual maturation necessary to arrive 'home.' One who leads a life of self-cultivation will have the opportunity for full, spiritual growth; one who dogmatically follows a religion will not.

"One who wishes to restore his divine nature through self-cultivation must first recognize that his nature is the universal divine nature. He must then realize the universal divine nature in his life by extending universal love with the principle of balance. Since his life-being is also a life-being of the universal divine nature, he must give his love equally. Therefore, through realization of universal divine nature through one's self-cultivation, human and divine nature are reunited as one. Thus, any achieved one recognizes himself as being the same as God.

"A child's heart enjoys all kinds of different things. It is never bothered by conceptual differences. People, whether young or old, should meet each other with the heart of a child. This is the most important element of the human spirit and the best interpretation of humanism. The spiritual goal of a human being should be the restoration of a child's heart and a fully and healthily developed mind with high intuition and insight."

Syh, from the Lower Region of Central Land, close to Kun Lun, said: "Nature causes death to purify all lives. People accelerate this 'purification' with misdeeds directed towards themselves and others. The content of their lives is that of following the demands of their blind impulses without experiencing true inner growth. Eventually, they will be weeded out by wars of competition, unnatural accidents and disease, and will endlessly repeat such cycles.

"People of self-awareness, however, continually purify themselves instead of relying on the cycles of nature to do it for them. They cultivate inner spiritual wisdom which becomes the true growth necessary to awaken them from blind worldly impulses.

"By responding to force with force, the human race has inevitably led itself deeper and deeper into new problems and difficulties. Can our human friends return to their original nature? The entire society cannot return to a rustic, natural life, but individual human friends can maintain their good human nature.

"As Lao Tzu says, 'Reaching the Truth calls not for complicating our minds, but rather for returning to simplicity and enjoying peace.'"

64 WEI CHI 未濟

BEFORE CROSSING THE WATER

GUIDANCE: *"Before crossing the Water, things go well. It is like a young fox which cannot keep its tail above the Water in order to keep it dry; thus it must wait to cross during the season when the stream bed is dry. If the young fox rushes ahead and is unable to keep its tail dry, there will be trouble."*

This hexagram is the opposite of the preceding one, "After Completion," in which Water energy descends and Fire energy ascends, creating harmony. But in this hexagram, the opposites do not integrate. Fire is above, Water is below, and every line is in an incorrect position. Since Fire flames upward and Water flows downward, the two energies have no interaction and move away from one another. Chi Chi (Hexagram 63) deals with the time following completion, while Wei Chi offers guidance for the time just before.

Everything appears hopeless. However, if within this unpromising situation one applies one's strength toward improving circumstances and achieving one's goal, an opportunity for accomplishment will be provided.

At this time matters should be handled carefully and prudently. Although the overall feeling is one of disintegration, each individual line is still able to integrate with its corresponding line. Thus, the potential for harmony and success still exist. As stated in the *Tao Teh Ching*: "Misfortune is the root of good fortune. Good fortune also can be the root of misfortune."

The image of this hexagram is that of a young fox crossing a frozen stream. Because of his inexperience, he is not as cautious as he should be and gets his tail wet before completing the crossing. "Getting wet" means running into trouble. The lower trigram (Water) indicates danger because of inexperience, while the upper trigram (Fire) expresses clarity and strength. Together they indicate the completion of a task. The opportunity is there.

Looking back on the course of history, after social order has been established, disorder inevitably follows. A new order is then created, only to be followed by another time of disorder. This cycle goes on forever.

What is good fortune? What is bad fortune? Both are necessary within the natural journey of life and they exist in order to make one understand things differently. The *I Ching* does not value any particular social or environmental change over any other. Instead, it emphasizes valuing and adapting one's innermost light to all phases of the cycle. One should neither worry nor be overly attached to any situation, regardless of what it is. A bad time is the seed of a good time; this is the eternal way of nature. When one identifies with external changes, one is always lost in troubles. Is it not better to adjust one's inner virtue in order to cope with the outside? In this way one will outlive all troubles. By maintaining a calm mind, one will be able to experience the spectrum of events without being affected by them.

Nothing can avoid or escape the cyclic law which the *I Ching* reflects. Everything is continually changing. Within change, however, there remains an unchanging, insubstantial "substance." By identifying with the invariable essence of universal nature, one will constantly be in contact with this subtle source of life. With such harmony, how can superficial changes, alterations and variations be so deeply troubling?

Not to aggressively correct the attitudes of others is the most important thing in life. To correct oneself and have constancy towards one's true being is essential. Other things and people are not your worry. By following this principle, the changing attitudes of those who are close will not affect your emotional balance. People can be weakened by too much love; on the other hand, the hardships that one experiences can be strengthening. Through them one may learn from the environment and derive positive benefit. The strong are those who have been exposed to the harshness of nature; those who have been overly protected become weak.

In human relationships, one should never try to make emotional pets out of one's partner or children, otherwise one spoils them. All people need independent growth.

If the energy of the people is too aggressive, the world will be in turmoil. If their energy is too weak, there will be no progress. When either extreme manifests, doubts and jealousies, strengths and weaknesses always come into play. When yin energy is expressed negatively, it becomes jealous and suspicious. When yang energy is expressed negatively, it becomes aggressive and rigid. However, by removing negative elements, good energy will naturally produce a sense of well-being in one's life. In this way, a happy and harmonious relationship can be achieved whether it involves a couple, family, society, nation or the entire world. If humanity can properly adjust to the interplay of yin and yang, harmony will naturally be restored.

This hexagram completes the cycle of the sixty-four hexagrams. The *I Ching* always gives transcendental truths. One of them is that an end is really just a beginning. In the natural cycle of energy, a new beginning resides in that which has just been accomplished.

LINE 1: *"The young fox gets its tail wet crossing the Water. No good fortune."*

The first line is like a person who is weak and inexperienced, lacking in wisdom and a proper sense of timing. He is like a young fox who, planning to cross the Water without accurately gauging the distance or his capabilities, gets his tail wet.

LINE 2: *"To stop the vehicle from moving ahead is correct. Good fortune."*

The second line, a yang line trapped between two yin lines, signifies that this is not a good time for action. One should apply the brakes, maintain oneself correctly, and not become restless.

LINE 3: *"It is not time for a crossing. Going further brings danger. One should make preparations for crossing the great Water later."*

This line is at the top of the lower trigram, K'an. There appears to be a correspondence with the sixth line, which would suggest that it is heading out of danger into clarity and safety and that the goal can be achieved. But since the third line is also the base of the inner trigram, Water, it is incapable of handling the situation. Although the goal cannot be accomplished singlehandedly, it can be accomplished with outside help.

LINE 4: *"The proper person is sent to conquer. The victory is achieved in three years and great rewards are received. By being upright, one will overcome difficulties."*

The fourth line is a yang line in a yin position, hence there is some limitation. All one's strength is necessary in order to meet the challenge and hardship included in achieving the goal. If strength can be gathered, one may move forward and remorse will disappear. Before taking action, however, what was previously done must be corrected. Such action requires courage, impartiality and perseverance. Although results will not show immediately, the goal can be achieved by overcoming difficulties.

LINE 5: *"To be upright is to have good fortune. No regret. The inner light of a righteous person overcomes all obstacles."*

Although the fifth line, which is in the position of leadership, is a yin line in a yang position, it is supported and helped by the strong second line. The fifth line represents a humble, civilized, faithful and enlightened person. One should depend on his wisdom to accomplish the mission.

LINE 6: *"One falls into the Water and gets his head wet by becoming overexcited after successfully crossing the Water. He loses self-control in his rapture. How can he keep his success long?"*

Since this line is at the top of the hexagram, he is about to accomplish something great. He is so excited by his achievement that he sacrifices self-discipline and creates trouble for himself. As a yang line in a yin position, he is over confident and will surely be humiliated by losing the trust of his supporters. A Chinese proverb regarding excessive drinking says: "When happiness is enjoyed to its extreme, sadness results." Prudence at the beginning of a matter and care in the completion of one's work is always required in daily life.

SPECIFIC GUIDANCE

PERSONAL FORTUNE: Now is a time of turmoil, and therefore a time to be careful.

MARRIAGE: Although there is difficulty in the beginning, it can be achieved later.

HOUSING/FAMILY: Not harmonious and peaceful.

CHILDBIRTH: Peaceful.   If the lower line is received, the baby will be a boy.   If any of the lines of the upper trigram are received, it will be a girl.

LOOKING FOR WORK: It can be found.

SOCIAL/GOVERNMENTAL POSITION: It comes later, which is fortunate.

TRADE/BUSINESS: Difficulty in the beginning;   later success.

SEARCHING FOR SOMEONE: They will return of their own accord.

WAITING FOR SOMEONE: They will not come.

LOOKING FOR SOMETHING LOST: It can be found.

HUNTING FOR THIEVES: He is right in front of you and can be caught.

LAWSUIT: It is good to make peace in this instance.

CLIMATE: Rain.   After the weather clears, there will be a drought.

TRAVEL: Suitable for short distances only.

DISEASE: Danger.

PERSONAL WISH: It can be achieved.

COMMENTARY
The Unspoiled Natural Religion

Long, long ago I was in a vast land.   The people of this land knew of nothing other than their honest life. They lived by earnest means.   They all shared the same understanding: if one does not like what a person does to them, then one does not do that to another.

In this community no generation had ever started a war or made war any part of their livelihood.   Their language was very simple: all words were one syllable, the most common being "Oh" and "Ah."   The former was a peaceful greeting for all occasions and the latter was the first sound in everybody's name.   All of the people in this community maintained the same unorganized faith which had not been designed by anyone but had evolved naturally.

This was long ago, when people enjoyed a good, natural life. Many years later, suddenly confronted with outside worldly contention, this simple community struggled to maintain its own natural way. However, as new leaders adopted new philosophies and new ways, the people became lost. It seemed as though there was no one left who could recognize the original faith.

I was taught the original faith by my dear Father, Mother, and ageless Master. It had been handed down by the unspoiled ancient mind to provide help for those who needed it. Today, an unspoiled mind no longer exists because of the confusion brought about by human cultures and religions. My experience is no exception, but my faith, which was derived from unspoiled Nature, keeps my mind whole and in good use.

I make the following simple notes in order to retain the original guidance from the natural Divine Realm in my memory and as a means by which people can dissolve all later human prejudices.

The Natural State of Heaven is Impersonal

The original, unspoiled human mind understood that Heaven is impersonal. However, as it became tainted and confused, so did its view of Heaven, which became personal and anthropomorphic. A pure human mind is an extension of Heaven. All distorted images of Heaven stem from later mental development that was narrative in nature and that does not reflect the natural source of human life.

The value of faith in an impersonal Heaven lies in its not being named or insisted upon by the human mind. No one can justify a conceptual position by claiming divine right or authority. In contrast, ordinary religions, however, are created out of human concepts and explanations, thus providing opportunities for people to take sides, and engage in all kinds of savageries to defend or spread such doctrines. Any religion that deviates from the impersonal purity of divinity eventually becomes a source of conceptual confusion that will spread contention.

One who cherishes faith in an impersonal Heaven lives a life of unselfish achievement. He does not gather people in his name or teach them to worship him or try to dominate them in any other way. Just as the heavenly bodies offer their light without asking for anything in return, his devotion and work are offered without expectation of personal recognition or reward. Because he truly knows that Heaven or God has no name but can be referred to by all names, he achieves the "Being of Heaven," the non-partial "Being of Wholeness."

Heaven Has No Name

If we use human conceptions to describe Heaven, surely we limit it and make it partial. One's expression of Heaven is limited by one's knowledge and vocabulary, thus confusion and conflict are often created. The ancient, natural faith in Heaven is impersonal and has no particular name. So it is with all Gods; they cannot be defined by conceptual attempts.

The original human beings also had no name. All natural life is without a name. Why then must God have a name? As soon as God is defined, he ceases to be universal and is no longer the truth. God represents all beings and things of the universe and should have no particular name. To create a name for God is to separate him from his oneness.

Heaven is Limitless

The natural faith of the unspoiled ancient mind recognized that God has no particular shape or form, but the spoiled human mind has since dressed God in distinctive robes. In order to dress God, there must be a suitable tailor and the best cloth. How ridiculous! Giving height, weight, or other personal attributes to God is ludicrous and untrue.

Human mental development has become one-sided and tainted with conceptions. People no longer respond to the bare truth without an explanation or mental interpretation. In ancient times, people did not need mental interpretations because they had direct correspondence with Divine Beings. There were no conceptions which separated real beings from perceived ones.

Modern people have a chronic need to use their minds to interpret the facts of their life experience. Their lives depend on their minds' interpretive systems to explain the meaning of everything, even their feelings. Truly, they do not live a real life; they live by thinking. Thus, they have destroyed their real nature. Their minds have become very complicated and they live in a distorted, conceptual world instead of the real one. Even the simple fact of love or making love is, throughout its duration, continuously defined and described to the mind. All these words and concepts appear in the mind to separate experience from reality. In the same way, modern artificial faith has lost all sight, through its various interpretations, of the natural truth which the ancient developed ones once recognized and followed. Thus, we must recover the real nature as the ancient developed ones.

Heavenly Love is Impartial

The ancient, unspoiled faith believed that God is impartial love. God does not only love people because they are yellow, as yellow as gold, or because they are white, as white as jade. God loves gold, jade, and all colors, and no color. God is impersonal love. The love of men is partial and limited; the love of God is not. God never limits love to one culture or gives partial love to another. Partial love is created through one's own partial reflection. However, such a reflection also gives one much responsibility: it is to repay Heaven in gratitude for this love, and not to become prejudiced. The secret of inviting God's love is to be natural and virtuous. God loves the natural and virtuous.

God Has No Myth

The existence of Heaven is natural. It did not originate in the narrative mind of later human beings. Mythology is the primitive attempt to explain the phenomena of nature. Surprisingly, the ancient faith in Heaven has no mythology. From ancient writings engraved on the bones of oxen, we know certain rituals and the specific purposes and times that offerings were made, but there was no particular myth that was the authorized story of God and Heaven.

There were, however, many myths that mankind devised for himself. One of these was a myth about the first man, who was called Pan Gu or "Disc Head." According to the myth, the sky and earth were originally like a great egg. Pan Gu worked on this lump of energy with his ax to form the sky, the earth, and so forth, thus becoming the first man and ruler of the universe. This is not a myth about Heaven, but the origin of human beings. It originated much later than the longer period of untraceable, ancient times.

There were no myths until the development of the *I Ching* system which used "lines" to tell how the universe began, how it is now, and what it will be like in the future. But the *I Ching* is not a myth; it is an expression of the direct spiritual experience of the natural growth and development of Nature and mankind. It is a wordless interpretation, and was thus the first direct way of expressing the truth.

Human Nature is Heavenly Nature

Another trait of the ancient natural faith is belief in the oneness of Heavenly nature and human nature. True human nature is Heavenly nature; there is no distinction or separation between them. The concept of Heaven and man as two separate entities developed in later times. The idea of God as divine and man as vulgar is a divergence from the truth. The duality, separation and multiplicity of later generations formed our human nature in a complicated mold, but originally it was the same as Heavenly nature.

One is Many/Many are One

Another essential aspect of natural faith in a universal divinity is that, "One is many, and many are one." Religious conflicts over the question of many gods or one God, polytheism or monotheism, came about in later generations along with philosophical conflicts about monism or pluralism. But the ancient unspoiled mind was not confused. It knew clearly that the Subtle Origin is one and that its manifestations, duplications and multiplications are many. Therefore, one is many and, at the same time, many are one.

When the Divine Realm responds to different people at different times for different purposes, it is multiple. In its unmanifest state, it is one. Therefore, in the unspoiled ancient mind, there was never confusion about one God or many gods as there is today in modern religions. One God is many gods; many gods are one God. If we talk about many gods, we are referring to the different responses of the Subtle Realm to a particular group of people at a particular time. The divine nature of the universe is one, but its responsive function is multiple. To insist on one God, or on many gods, is to take a partial, limited view of the Divine Nature or Oneness.

God is the Model of Virtue

Another aspect of the natural faith in Heaven was the recognition of God as the model of virtue. In later times, God became recognized as a model for domination. The ancient faith was practiced by Fu-Shi who interpreted the natural truth with the line system, by Shen-Nung, the developer of agriculture, and by other ancient sages who all served mankind. The troubles of the world became their troubles, yet they did not hesitate to resign when their work was done, for they were not attached to their positions. They never thought in terms of capitalizing on their influence by becoming powerful leaders. The term "Ti" was used as a title for God and the human virtuous leaders. Ti has been incorrectly translated in English as "emperor." In Chinese, however, the character for Ti is the image of the stem from which the fruit or flower is sustained. Thus it is the emperor (Ti) who serves the people (the fruit or flowers). In broader terms, God is the stem from which all human beings obtain the sustenance of life. This was the ancient simple faith.

God Provides His Model in the Human World

The ancient developed people were pure people. Those who served the public were capable and virtuous. They received no salary for accepting this responsibility; they freely offered their talents and capabilities to society. Therefore, people trusted their leaders as the elder sons of Heaven, though everybody was considered to be a son or daughter of Heaven.

In later times, usurpers in Chinese history stole the name "Son of Heaven" and used it to rule people. Therefore, no single person, group, or class should be entrusted with the same responsibility as the ancient leaders. No one can believe that modern dictators are the elder sons of Heaven.

For spiritual reasons, one must be personally responsible for oneself. People can no longer naively have faith in their leaders. Generally, if a good leader is chosen, there is safety; if not, then people find themselves in difficulty. Therefore, we must restore the authority of virtue in our own being and become harmonious with other people.

Natural Faith has No Particular Rituals

Another quality of the ancient natural faith is freedom of worship. Confucius gathered and organized all the ancient forms of worship and presented them as the only correct form of worship. Although his purpose was to exemplify the ancient way, it unfortunately limited human piety to formal ritual and thus harmed the naturalness and originality of the ancient unspoiled faith.

During ancient times no one forced people to follow an organized form of worship. Their worship was free. The diversity of their worship grew out of natural differences of expression, however, they were all linked and unified by the same belief in Heaven. There were no problems or conflicts over differences, because a real faith and connection with Heaven existed.

Everything Under Heaven is Equal

Another trait of the ancient unspoiled faith of Heaven was the absence of distinctive social classes. Some societies of later generations have had a strong faith in Heaven, however, they have also created strong class distinctions among people. Class distinction is not the ultimate truth. God loves everybody. There are no special classes worthy of special favors.

God does favor the virtuous, however. The practice of virtue does not belong to any class. Certainly there are natural distinctions among people. Some are wise and some are less developed, and some have great potential while others will never attain greatness even if the opportunity is offered, but these are merely differences, not classes. Such differences are natural. They represent the essence a person develops throughout one or many lifetimes. Surely, there is a difference between a phoenix and a crow, but differences are not the basis on which we can establish respect or disrespect, preference or dislike. In the natural unspoiled faith, no such distinction exists. Social classes are an artificial human establishment and thus a violation of nature. They go against the Heavenly Way.

A Correct Way of Life is the Natural Religion

In the ancient natural faith, religion was nothing other than the correct way of life. There was no need to establish anything else, for the correct way of life was good faith. In later times, people established a religion apart from their lives because the correct way of life had been lost.

When there is a common respect for life, everybody can reach an agreement, but when religions are established on the basis of differences, conflicts arise. Such religion is untruthful because it is unnatural.

Natural Life is the Blessing of Heaven

The ancients recognized that worldly blessings are the rewards of Heaven. To be healthy, to eat and sleep well, to have a balanced mind and live naturally is to be blessed by Heaven. To receive life is the blessing of Heaven. To live peacefully is a blessing in itself. Whatever happens in a normal life is already a blessing. One does not need to look elsewhere for happiness. This only leads to imaginary happiness.

Natural Religion did not Start with the Preaching of a Particular Book

There was no book from which to preach the ancient unspoiled faith of Heaven. This faith was practiced by seeking divine guidance through a responsive system of change. Important events were engraved on ox bones which have continuously been discovered in underground excavations.

The Book of History was compiled by Confucius from ancient documents which described communities, wars, significant worship of Heaven, ceremonies, celebrations, and more. They also revealed the ancients' simple faith in Heaven. We know that the virtuous leaders of ancient society were recognized as the eldest sons of Heaven. Public decisions, however, were not made by these leaders, but were left to errorless, divine guidance.

During those times there were no distinctions. People knew that the source of all life was nature. Out of respect, they called this nature Heaven or "Ti" (God). To distinguish where they lived, they called it Earth. Earth was the small Heaven; the entire universe was the big Heaven.

This was the only faith for 5,000 years of written history, until recently when new standards were established. These new standards have brought much confusion.

A Natural Religion Seeks Only Divine Guidance

The natural unspoiled religion always sought Divine guidance through divination. Many ancient tribes throughout the world used some system of divination to help them make decisions in life. This system of inquiry expresses high wisdom since it can encompass all knowledge. Its method is as systematic as scientific and as logical as exact mathematics. It is a highly dialectic philosophical system.

What is the benefit of such a system, however? Though we are modern educated people, we are impulsive most of the time, and this leads us into difficulty. Indeed, all wars are the result of impulsiveness. As we reflect on our actions, in the hope of curtailing our impulsiveness, perhaps it seems unreasonable to exalt an ancient system above modern high technology. One important advantage of divination, however, if that the activity of divination has a calming effect which to some extent tames the impulsiveness in itself. This is how ancient people subdued and educated themselves.

In contemplating the actions of human beings, it is not a question of who is better and who is worse. Rather, it is a matter of who is more reasonable and who is more impulsive; this is what makes the difference. The marvelous aspect of ancient societies was that opinions and decisions affecting the public were not determined by individuals or leaders alone, but by the subtle guidance received through divination.

With this understanding, the differences between natural faith and social religious doctrines can more clearly be seen. It is a question of faith in the natural Subtle Law or in human dogma and doctrines. The ancient faith was not dogmatic. On the contrary, it was founded on the principles of appropriateness and balance in response to change. This is the most essential point in the ancient faith in "always seeking correctness."

The ancient developed people, with their natural unspoiled faith, truly understood and believed that the universe became manifest and was arranged through Subtle Law, which is highest above everything. Behind all human activity is Subtle Law. It is the ultimate law of the universe and of human life. Divination makes an aspect of the Subtle Law apparent and provides guidance in understanding and making a decision about a particular event.

On the basis of these principles, one can decide one's behavior and actions with or without divination. Ancient people had a strong faith in the Subtle Law and followed it exactly. They did not go beyond their own "lines" of duty. This faith was neither blind nor impulsive. On the contrary, it was built by experiment and experience. It was only through experience that the correct interpretations and illustrations of the Subtle Law could be found. We need to rebuild our own faith so that we too can live harmoniously and in accordance with the Subtle Law.

Certainly there can be no harm in following the examples of our ancient ancestors. Without a true and natural faith, modern people have become lost. When the ancient ones received guidance from the Divine Realm, they had no fear. They had no consideration of personal benefit or even of life or death. They integrated their lives with the Subtle Realm and received the instruction of the Subtle Law through either divination or their own discoveries of invaluable principles. Thus they lived a wholehearted life rather than a fragmented one. Since they had a closer connection with nature, they enjoyed many things. Their minds were not like modern minds which are trapped in thinking. Modern people's way of living is not real living. It is only formalized thoughts, imagination, and interpretations of their own system, which is not a true system.

When you consider the wholeness and simplicity of natural religion, you can see that it is modern people who have become superstitious through the fragmentation of a magnitude of dogma in their minds.

Three Elucidations of the Natural Religion

Before any book was written or any religion was developed, a natural faith existed and was practiced. Later, religion developed and was influenced by specific social backgrounds and problems. Religion was the response to a particular human situation; it does not represent a true faith. This is why we value the unspoiled natural religion.

The unspoiled religion has no particular book. Actually, all of human history is a book of testing the faith of religions, no matter whether they have succeeded or failed.

Generally speaking, we value every life experience that is connected with the internal and external development and evolution of human life. Whatever is true and natural is where God resides. There is no need to doubt this.

Any particular book, no matter how profound, represents only one interpretation of the Heavenly Realm. An accurate account of history can be a religious book if it records all actions, great deeds as well as great mistakes and transgressions. By reflecting on such events, human beings can better understand their troubles, how they spoil themselves, how they destroy themselves, and how they deviate from their true nature. All good books illustrate the natural, Heavenly Way and thus serve in the discovery and rediscovery of the natural, correct way of life.

In China, three correct elucidations of the natural truth were presented, each somewhat differently, by Lao Tzu, Confucius and Mo Tzu. Lao Tzu served to guide people back to their natural root. During his time there was already much divergence and deviation. He taught people to restore themselves through nature, because only nature can provide the correct direction of life. Anything interpreted by the later spoiled mind is misleading.

Confucius valued humanistic love, or "ren." Within the pit of the apricot, peach or plum is "ren," the essence of life. This means that all life is life-centered. Therefore, in order to realize personal life and to enjoy co-existence one must realize humanistic love.

Mo Tzu expressed two main elements with his teaching: following the Heavenly will, universal love, and non-aggression.

In terms of the ancient tradition, all three serve equally as primary illustrators of God and Heaven. There is also value in the good interpretations of other religions. However, it is necessary to make some adjustments in order to avoid racial and all other artificial prejudices.

By seeking the oneness of spiritual truth, together we assist the transformation of human society and help establish total progress for the entire human race.

Part Four:
Five Examples of
Ancient I Ching Practitioners

夫易廣矣，以言乎遠則不禦，以言乎邇則靜而正，以言乎天地之間則備矣。夫乾，其靜也專，其動也直，是以大生焉。夫坤，其靜也翕，其動也闢，是以廣生焉。廣大配天地，變通配四時，陰陽之義配日月，易簡之善配至德。

FIVE EXAMPLES
OF ANCIENT I CHING PRACTITIONERS

I
The Virtuous Leader, Wen Wong
The Widely Accepted King Wen

I would like to introduce an ancient sage whose immense virtue not only helped lay the foundation for the Chou Dynasty (1122-249 B.C.), but who also provided a virtuous influence for all of Chinese culture. He is commonly known as Wen Wong.

The *I Ching*, as we know it today with the complete system of sixty-four hexagrams, was the work of Wen Wong. He recompiled earlier versions of the text and reorganized the ancient knowledge, making excellent improvements. Having devoted an entire lifetime to the daily practice of the *I Ching*, he was highly qualified to do this. Thus I have chosen him as the first example of a great *I Ching* practitioner in the early part of human history.

Following this introduction are two articles adapted from Maoshing and Daoshing's lectures on February 13, 1983, during the Chinese New Year's celebration at the Shrine of the Eternal Breath of Tao in Malibu, California. Both of these will give you a good picture of the life of the virtuous King Wen.

Our family's ancestors were descendants of the Yellow Emperor. Now, this branch was the original supporters of Wen Wong who later were entitled as feudal lords on the land of Ni. Hereafter, naturally we adopted Ni as our family name to differentiate ourselves from other branches of the Yellow Emperor's descendants. Wen Wong was a descendant of one of the original experts in agriculture, Shen Nung, whose influence in agriculture greatly helped to build the foundation of Chinese society. King Wen's grandfather was a farmer named Gu Gung who was elected as leader of his community. Under his leadership and expertise in farming there were abundant harvests year after year. People were well fed and had a surplus. A nearby tribe, however, was jealous of Gu Gung's success and sought his land and people. When the people heard of their neighbors' ambitions, they became very angry and planned to defend themselves, even if it meant going to war, but Gu Gung said, "Since ancient times people have chosen their leaders because of their ability to benefit everyone by their leadership. Now another tribe wants my people and land. Neither the people nor the land belong to me or to those planning to invade. How can I be the cause of a war and in turn harm the people who elected me?" So Gu Gung gathered a few of his helping hands and, along with his family, left the land. Many more people followed him to the new settlement and an even larger community was formed. This was the beginning of the State of Chou, which was formed naturally, like many other original communities all over China. Although these natural communities eventually elected kings and dukes, and the emperor was elected by the leaders of these smaller communities, it is not really accurate to refer to it as a feudal system, although that term is the closest modern equivalent we have for such a system.

After Wen Wong took his position, the community became even more successful than during his ancestors' time and the "state" became even more renowned and respected than before. During this time, the empire of the Shang Dynasty (1766-1121 B.C.), the central power of the country, was fast declining. The last emperor of this dynasty had forsaken spiritual guidance and the laws of Nature. He was cruel, lustful, and so corrupted that he had the pool in his garden filled with wine, and the trees in his courtyard draped with meat. He taxed people heavily, tortured the innocent, and was despised by those he governed. Wen Wong, on the other hand, shared work with the farmers, even though he was recognized as a feudal lord. He taxed the people justly, and even had ample provisions to feed hungry travelers. He was respectful of the old and friendly to the young. No one in the state ever locked their doors at night because no crime existed! Because of his virtuous leadership, many wise men came forward to support him.

Once, two nearby states had a dispute over their boundary and they came to Wen Wong for advice. When they arrived in the State of Chou, they were surprised to see how tolerant his farmers were over the boundaries between their fields. Nobody needed to be aggressive. They also saw how considerate the young people were to the elders. The heads of the two states were embarrassed by their petty quarrelsome dispute and realized their immaturity. By following the good examples set by the State of Chou, they were able to establish a peaceful and mutually respectful atmosphere between their two states when they arrived home.

In today's modern society our advanced technology allows us to have almost anything we want materially, from computers to high speed jets, laser beams and nuclear weapons than can destroy us many times over. It seems we have almost everything, yet we lack one very important thing: virtuous leadership. The world can be built with computers, high speed jets and nuclear fusion, but without virtuous leaders it can easily be destroyed. Virtuous leadership is essential to the prosperity and longevity of a country. When a leader is virtuous and follows the harmonious order of nature, people will become peaceful; thus the whole world will be in harmony.

But how does one become virtuous and achieve this? It all starts within oneself. A person must first love himself, then he will love others. When a person considers his own life and death as precious, then he will consider the well-being of others as equally precious. To be virtuous means to follow one's own true nature and to serve others the way one serves oneself. This is my goal; I hope it is yours as well.

(from Maoshing's lecture)
I have been taught that to use virtue in leading or guiding people is the most beneficial way to organize a society and manage a country. In Chinese history we find a good example of leadership in Wen Wong who used his virtue to guide and serve his people. The foundation of his education was his sincere lifetime study of the *I Ching*. Before him, there were already two versions of *I Ching*: *Lien San*, developed by Sheng Nung, and *Gai Tsen*, developed by Shang Tung. After studying these works for many years, Wen Wong decided to further organize the *I Ching* based on the new social development of his time. His insightful reorganization was called *Chou I* and has become the *I Ching* as we know it today. Through his diligent work with the *I Ching*, his wisdom and virtuous personality were developed. By observing natural phenomena around him, he discovered the guidelines which would help people follow the most natural course of spiritual life. He was then able to teach others how to use the *I Ching* and thereby rise above difficult situations by avoiding things which might go against the harmonious order of universal nature.

Under his leadership, when a person committed a crime, that is, when he violated the natural harmony, Wen Wong drew a circle at the location of the crime and made the person stay inside the circle and reflect upon the matter until he could see his mistake and was willing to repent. With this form of corrective punishment there was hardly any crime in his land. People were able to sleep without closing or locking their doors.

Wen Wong also restricted the production of alcoholic beverages, because he saw how the Shang Dynasty had been weakened through the misuse of alcohol. At that time, group hunting had become the favorite and luxurious sport of the kings and lords. They would invite hundreds of people to their hunting parties and in the course of their sporting games would wreak havoc on the farmlands. Wen Wong disliked this kind of negligent indulgence and banned it entirely.

Because of his virtuous reputation, Wen Wong attracted many virtuous people to come to his land and humbly welcomed all of those who chose to follow him. Sometimes he would not even have time to enjoy his meal because he would be so engrossed in listening to the virtuous advice of these people. Eventually his reputation spread throughout the entire region of ancient China. More and more people began moving to his land, and his influence became widely accepted.

Wen Wong loved the natural life. That is the reason he valued the lives of all his people. His own life was simple and virtuous, and the people's lives were peaceful and satisfying. Today, after thirty-one hundred years, even though his physical life is over, his virtuous model is everlasting. In this modern world people tend to emphasize only the physical aspects of life. With all our modern technology, people are still only looking for sensory pleasure. Where does this lead? To unsatisfying and depressing lives! To have true fulfillment in our lives we must learn to be virtuous. We must live a life without stress, a peaceful, spiritual life. When we cultivate virtue, we then appreciate the existence of life itself and truly enjoy the happy lives we received from the Great Nature. This should be our goal, and Wen Wong the example in our hearts and our work. I hope that you can all benefit from the good example he was given to us.

(from Daoshing's lecture)

Although we are not the kings of countries, we are kings in our own lives. In the Taoist tradition, we do not aspire to be rulers, nor do we place high value on being a ruler, but we really do care to know about respected and virtuous leaders.

There is a famous classic novel called *Fung Sheng Dang* which tells the story of two groups: one group under the leadership of the tyrant Jou Wong, the other under the leadership of Wen Wong. *Fung Sheng Dang* shows us, in a metaphorical way, how to rule our own lives. Which part of your mind do you use to rule your life? Your emotions, your lower desires, or your wisdom? Sometimes you hear a small voice from your heart. Be careful! What is the source of this voice? Is it from the villainous King Jou or the virtuous King Wen? If it is the virtuous King Wen Wong's advice, then you are in harmony with universal order. If you follow the small voice from the tyrant King Jou, however, you will be guided to abuse and emaciate yourself. Everyone has two sides, two rulers in his mind and heart: one good, one bad. Here we emphasize the good side, that of Wen Wong.

Everyone is here on the planet Earth with one purpose: survival. Different people use different ways to ensure their survival. Many people do not firmly adhere to the strength of virtue. From the truth of history you can see that even though Jou Wong was physically stronger and had an entire empire, he was the one who was defeated. Wen Wong was a small leader of a small community. How can the leader of a small community finally win the heart of a whole nation? The evil king really overthrew himself, by abusing himself and his power. As spiritual people, we worship power: not the power of evil, but the power of virtue.

People ask how we can reach a peaceful world order. We begin by reaching a peaceful order within ourselves; this we can do, this is under our own rulership. First begin by asking yourself, "Do I rule myself well?" People always talk about survival, but do they talk about how to survive? There are two ways, means, attitudes, or modes of earning a living. One is to use our own energy to make an honest living; that is, to produce what can support our life. The other way is to hunt; that is, to conquer by force or depend on luck. The way of the hunter is the lazy way: only when he is hungry does he hunt.

The first way of survival is by working, as in farming or industry. Step by step, one depends on one's continued work until results come. These people live by honest work.

As to the second way, many people are still hunting! They do not like to sit at regular work. They are only looking for opportunities to come into power. When we look at the world leaders of today, how many of them are honest workers? Certainly there are some earnest workers among them, but mainly they are hunters.

Physical power is easy to recognize, but spiritual or virtuous power is difficult to recognize. You may recognize a person's strength and not be able to compete with it, but just as your teeth are much stronger than your tongue, which one remains through old age? Therefore, we must never rely on our strengths to win, but on our patience and tolerance. Virtue is much more enduring than that which can be attained by strength. This is what we can learn from King Wen.

There are many kinds of religion, but since most simply prepare you to die, they are not very useful unless you are already worn out. I recommend the principle passed down from Wen Wong which does not teach you to go but to stay and live, to embrace life, to revere the heavens and to exalt the virtuous nature of mankind.

(Master Ni resumes)

Developed ones worship the initial spirit. Initial means new; everything is new. I will illustrate initial spirit two ways.

One day, over ten years ago, I went to a lake called Jen Ching Lake in Asia and took a walk along its shore. Along the way there were beautiful summer houses and, as it was raining, I decided to step inside so I would not get wet. Inside I discovered one group of young people, and another group of people of all ages. The young people were enjoying themselves despite the heavy rain and were not dismayed or frustrated. At the same time I could hear the other group loudly complaining, "Bah, why did we choose today to come here?" Can you tell which group maintained their initial spirit and which was worn out by life and had lost theirs? If we have our initial spirit, how can we complain? Every day we are born anew, and anything can happen. If we have our initial spirit, then we can enjoy everything, and experience the joy of life.

At times all of us have some trouble or complaint. This is okay as long as we do not let the matter hang heavy over our heads. We should not let ourselves become dominated by feelings of disappointment, dismay or frustration and make these our daily manner of life. It really is not necessary if we can maintain our initial spirit.

As I mentioned there are two kinds of religion. One tells you to go to a better place. The other says, "We have just started. We want to keep things going! We like it...we love it...this is life!" So what do we have to complain about? There is nothing to complain about! We are brand new to life! You may say there is a lot of difficulty in your life. But when you are new to life, you have the courage to meet that difficulty. What is the truth of your complaint? Of what value is your frustration or dismay or defeat? None! Unless you sell yourself cheaply. When you are new, nothing can trouble you.

This initial spirit is what we value, not the worn out religions that represent a spirit that is worn out from constant persecution - or from constantly persecuting other people. If you lose your initial spirit, you feel pain. Of what value is your pain? If it has any value, it is to remind you to remain true to your initial spirit.

With initial spirit, one thing we must not neglect is completion. When you are young and impatient it is easy to jump from one thing to another, haphazardly digging here and there, scattering your good energy. The virtue of initial spirit may be there, but the virtue of completion is not. Through cultivation you will come to realize that without the virtue of completion, the initial spirit of our true nature cannot manifest its goodness in the world.

So, my dear friends, this is what King Wen had to offer: initial spirit and a sense of completion. He also valued the strength of virtue. These qualities, which Wen Wong had, I too have engraved in my bones, and I wish for you also to have. This is why I recommend Wen Wong as our first example of a responsible life.

II

Chang Tzu Ya, The Hermit Fisherman

This is the story of another great man who lived early in Chinese history, around 1154 B.C., when the power of the Shang Dynasty prevailed. Emperor Jou, its last emperor, had once been a man of strength and bravery, but in his later years he became corrupted by lascivious pleasures. He filled his ponds not with water, but wine, and dallied away his days with women. He was famous for having women pose as swaying trees, full of flowers, while he luxuriated among them. The faithful and trusted ministers left by his father tried to advise him to stop his excessive enjoyments, but their only reward for their truthfulness and straightforwardness was to be executed one by one. Can you see how this man of excess gradually eroded his support, thus causing the "ridgepole" of his government to sag dangerously to the breaking point, as illustrated in Hexagram 28 of the *I Ching*, "Great Excess?"

One of the ministers of the royal court was a talented achieved one named Chang Tzu Ya (1154-1115 B.C.). He recognized that Emperor Jou had reduced his court to a pack of fawning sycophants who appeased him in order to benefit from his weakness. (How common this is in the courts of all dictators!) Seeing how hopeless the situation was, Chang Tzu Ya fled the court to become a hermit fisherman on the River Wei. People of truth rarely abandon themselves to mundane authority.

Chang Tzu Ya became known as the man who could fish with a straight hook. This was a metaphor for his honest attitude toward life; opportunities came to him like schools of fish, but only those fish willing to bite the "straight hook" would be taken. Refusing to use any crookedness, he at first suffered from poverty and hunger. However, after many years of "straight fishing" he caught the big fish, King Wen, the revolutionary leader whose son had allied with all the other leaders to overthrow the corrupt Emperor Jou.

King Wen, who was being held prisoner by the tyrannical Emperor Jou, was finally released. Soon after, he was awakened by a startling dream in which a terrifying bear with wings jumped on him. The next morning he asked his close ministers what this powerful dream meant, and they told him it was an image of a strong personality whom he would be able to trust as general to fight against his enemy, Emperor Jou. King Wen immediately embarked on a hunting trip and eventually arrived at River Wei where he encountered an old fisherman. After exchanging a few words with the hermit, King Wen knew at once that this was the man who had appeared in his dream! King Wen promptly requested Chang Tzu Ya to return with him to his court where he appointed him as his highest advisor. Later, King Wen's son, Wu, with the aid of Chang Tzu Ya succeeded in revolting against the unrighteous Emperor Jou.

Two principles can be learned from this story. First, before one's real talent has been fully discovered, one should keep it to oneself while continuing to refine one's virtue and knowledge. Second, the talent should be put to use only for a good purpose and without thought of self-aggrandizement.

Part of the treasures of the spiritual tradition are stories of people like Chang Tzu Ya and Chu Ku Liang. Both had sympathy for people and helped remove their misery. They also exemplify true leadership as described in the *Tao Teh Ching*, although Chang Tzu Ya lived about 700 years before the *Tao Teh Ching* was written and Chu Ku Liang's life was much later. However, as achieved masters, both had a special spiritual trait in common: detachment from the fruits of their labor. After helping with an important mission, they did not accept any of the glory. Such detachment, so rarely seen today, truly emanates from the Heavenly Realm. There is so much to learn from these men. Without calling attention to themselves, they quietly accepted the proper moment to serve. Shunning excess, they accomplished great things; thus they were able to hit the target dead center.

All eminent military advisers were produced from the spiritual tradition. They offered their wisdom and talent only whenever the big society found itself in trouble. With deep training and being well versed in the *I Ching*, he could even use it without any form of divination. In this manner, he brought the success of an epoch of peaceful times which lasted 800 years.

III
Fang Li, The King's Advisor

I would like to introduce Fang Li, another great and wise man who lived during a time when many small countries were warring. The country called Yu (which, incidentally, is my home province) had been conquered by its neighbor Wu, which is now the area called Shanghai. The king of Yu, having been captured and enslaved by his conqueror, was searching for a means of revenge in order to restore his kingdom. However, since he was slave in the enemy's household, his chances for success were slim.

Fortunately, two of his talented ministers were still faithful to him: Fang Li, a spiritually developed one, and Wen Chung. These astute advisors suggested a plan to Yu. First, he must convince the King of Wu that he had abandoned all hope of restoring his kingship and appear willing to continue as a slave. Then, should the right opportunity arise, he must serve the king in a way that would gain his gratitude and favor. Such an opportunity would soon appear.

King Wu had become gravely ill, and his doctors could not diagnose the problem without an accurate analysis of his stool. Unfortunately, such an analysis included its being tasted directly, but even the king's wives and trusted ministers refused the job. At this time, Yu was serving as keeper of the king's horses. Soon, a message came, and Yu was asked if we would perform this task. Seeing this opportunity as part of his greater plan, Yu agreed to help. Appreciating Yu's help and aware of his humility in bowing to such disgrace, King Wu trusted him and decided to grant him his freedom. He further agreed not to challenge Yu's kingdom as long as Yu would render all extra crops to him. The motive behind this demand was that Yu and his people would never be able to gather sufficient strength to fight if there was no storage in the barns. One of King Wu's insightful ministers warned him that by letting the "tiger" return to the mountain, the seeds of his destruction would surely be planted, but King Wu persisted nevertheless.

When the King of Yu returned to his land, he followed the advice of Fang Li and Wen Chung. He first combed the entire country for dozens of beautiful, well-trained girls to send to King Wu. Although the King of Wu suspected that they were spies, he could not resist their beauty. The most famous spy among them went to Wu and said, "Great King, you conquered our whole country, why do you fear a weak woman like me?" So King Wu let himself enjoy the lovely women and drink the delectable wines they offered. Every day his weakness increased as he passed his hours in sensuality and sleep.

Meanwhile, back in his own country, King Yu deprived himself of all personal pleasures and slept on top of firewood and grass. From the top beam of his house, he hung the bitter gall bladder of a bear to remind himself of the bitterness of his ordeal. After ten years of rigorously training an army and civilians alike, King Yu conquered his neighboring rival. His power had become indomitable. He had avoided all excess and gone straight for the target.

After completing the successful mission, the time came for rewarding the two helpful spiritually developed ones. Fang Li was a truly achieved man who knew that during times of difficulty, people come together to accomplish a goal, but during times of ease they separate to compete for benefits. He also knew that once a task is completed, it is time to leave. Thus, Master Fang Li changed his name and became a businessman. Three times he made a great fortune and three times he gave it all to the poor. Because he was an achieved man, he knew the real meaning of money; to him, a worldly life was just a game. He had entered the world with clean hands and he wanted to leave the same way.

Wen Chung, however, could not be persuaded by Fang Li to do the same. He prepared to stay and bask in the glory of success. Wen Chung argued, "Slowly, through many years, we have finally accomplished something. Let me stay with my king to enjoy the benefits and glory." Shortly thereafter, Wen Chung was thought to be a threat to the king's power and was slain.

If one wishes to become developed spiritually, one must learn to take gains lightly. One's duty should be done without concern for personal gain. After the play-game is over, one should go to another plateau and remain unattached to the rewards. The worldly mode should only be used to support the true work of spiritual achievement.

When practicing the principle of non-excessiveness, one should always remember and follow the examples of Masters such as Chang Tzu Ya, Fang Li and Chu Ku Liang. When the world was in danger, they came to help. When their service was finished, they simply washed their hands and left. Their actions exemplify great spirit, a quality which is often lacking in today's world but which is greatly needed.

Fang Li was the student of Chi Zang or Wen Tzu, the number one student of Lao Tzu. He could understand a situation as clearly as putting something in his palm. He organized the principles of the *I Ching* so concisely that Chu Ku Liang could write them on a feather-made fan.

IV
Chang Liang, The Liberator

During the Chou Dynasty (1766-1121 B.C.), the country now called China was a nation unified culturally, socially and politically. During this time, there were many small country-states, each with its own king. Heading all these states was a central figure, the Emperor. This arrangement was very similar to the political structure of the United States today. Near the end of the Chou Dynasty, the power of the central government became weak, and individual states began fighting in order to gain control over each other and the central government. But in the year 248 B.C., after a long period of confusion, the State of Chin finally succeeded in reuniting the country.

When Chin was a small, rustic western state, its region was more suitable for raising cattle than promoting agriculture. Thus, aggressive and forceful qualities developed among its people and produced good generals, warriors and fighters. Eventually, Chin succeeded in conquering all surrounding countries. Present day China was named after Chin by those outside of China, though people living in China called their nation "the Middle Land."

The First Emperor of Chin was a cruel conqueror. He was the first to ascend the throne through the strength and vigor of his personality instead of being appointed or recognized by a previous emperor or king. Indeed, in the virtuous culture of ancient China, there were none like the first Emperor of Chin.

The power of the unified nation was soon enhanced and expanded. After achieving his goal, the Emperor eventually began contemplating his life and death. Being an ambitious man, he sought only physical immortality, which is a shallow, incomplete understanding of immortality. Being a man of power, he was able to locate a spiritual book which contained the secret of everlasting life. Unfortunately, the book was written in ancient mystical words and he was only able to understand one sentence: "The one who shall come to destroy Chin is Fu." He interpreted the word "Fu" to mean a tribe from the northern part of China, and wishing to have perpetual protection for his empire, he mobilized the whole country to build a great wall which would stretch for more than 2300 kilometers and thereby thwart any possibility of attack. Ironically, it was not the northern tribe of Fu which destroyed him, but Fu his second son. He never realized that the enemy was right in his house!

In the northern part of China, in a small country called Han, there lived a young man named Chang Liang who decided to take revenge on the first Emperor of Chin. Since there was no way to organize an army to remove the Emperor by force, Chang Liang sought an assassin for his secret plan. He was eventually led to a man named Chuan Chu, who had a reputation for bravery. Chang Liang discovered that Chuan Chu's mother was very weak and suffered greatly, so he decided to help make her life comfortable, and thus treated her like his own mother.

One day Chuan Chu said to Chang Liang, "You are so kind to me. I could not find a better friend in the world. Please, if you have any request, just ask. I would do anything you wish. I would go into water or fire for you."

Chang Liang, "I know of your fame as a brave man, and I admire your courage. I have a secret plan to assassinate the brutal killer, Emperor Chin."

The brave young man, after making his sincere offer and hearing the details of the plan, agreed to do it. His only request was that someone take care of his mother, which Chang Liang promised to do. Chuan Chu then prepared his weapon, a spearhead which could be hidden near his breast, and left to carry out his vow.

Some time later, Chuan Chu heard that the Emperor of Chin was traveling from the West to Tai San, a sacred mountain in the East, looking for secret spiritual books to make himself immortal. Since the Emperor's caravan was very long, Chuan Chu decided to use the time while the caravan was passing to fulfill his duty. Hiding until the Emperor's chariot was within reach, Chuan Chu threw the first spearhead with all his strength at the target. The Emperor's first minister fell dead. The Emperor immediately ordered the whole country to look for the one responsible for this attack.

Chang Liang, who was full of vengeance and convinced that it was necessary to use teeth to repay teeth and blood to repay blood, was easily discovered as being the instigator of this assassination attempt. All his strength and energy had been spent on this misadventure and now there were public rewards being offered everywhere for his capture or knowledge of his whereabouts. Wishing only to maintain his life and save himself from arrest, he escaped to a rural place called Shah-Pi where he hid, feeling hopeless and confused.

One day while taking a walk he came to a bridge which crossed a dry stream bed. There he discovered an old man who called out to him as he approached, "Hey fellow, go to the stream and fetch my shoes!" At first, Chang Liang was appalled by the insolence of the old man and decided to continue on his way. But he reconsidered his position and thought, "I am no longer an heir or a noble of the royal court, I am now a refugee. Maybe I should help this old man by doing him this service."

So Chang Liang went down to the dry stream, picked up the shoes and brought them to the old man. The old man said, "Put them on my feet." Such a gesture was very humiliating for Chang Liang. However, he smiled, swallowed his pride and anger and submitted to serving the old man.

The old man then said, "Seven days from now, very early in the morning, be prompt and come to this spot. I shall reward you with something you may need for your future career." Then he quickly left.

Since going into hiding, Chang Liang had continuously tried to devise a way to save himself and overthrow the Emperor, but as he was having no results, he thought, "What can I lose by meeting the old man?" So he went to the designated spot at the appointed hour. When he arrived, the old man was already there and said, "How can a young person like you be so negligent as to break a promise to be prompt? As you can see, I was here long before you. Now I suggest that after another seven days we try again. At that time, if you do not miss me by being late, you will find something that may interest you."

Chang Liang had no expectation that the old man could really offer him anything of value. However, he felt that to decline such a strong request from an old man of dignity was ignoble, so once again he went to the arranged spot. This time, he arrived much earlier than the appointed hour, but was surprised to find the old man already there. "You are tardy again," the old man said. "Try again to meet me here after seven days."

Chang Liang could feel the strength of the old man's words piercing his heart with their simplicity. After the victory of overcoming his own pride and self-importance, he decided to make whatever efforts were necessary to comply with the old man's request, even if they were greater than anything he had ever done before. He knew that it was not the old man who was making him so determined, but something deep within himself that had to be reformed and that would prepare him for a new phase of life.

The next time, instead of arriving earlier, he decided to wait at the spot the entire night. When the old man found him, he handed him a package and said, "If you wish to triumph over the strong, evil one, there is a chance. By studying the book contained in this package you shall become the teacher of kings and emperors in all future times."

Chang Liang politely asked, "May I know your name, sir?" The old man replied, "When you succeed in overcoming the tyrant, you may meet me at the foot of Mount Ku Chen in the North of Chi."

From that day on, Chang Liang intently studied the book. These are the great truths he discovered and applied to his life:

"The universal moral order cannot be violated.
Although strong and ambitious people
attempt to compete
*   with the silent sovereignty of Tao,*
*   no one has yet succeeded.*
Nor will there be anyone in the future
*   who will succeed."*

"It is foolish to fight strength with strength
*   or attempt to replace evil with evil.*
Are the teeth not stronger than the lips?
But which last longer?"

"To be headstrong is to be the disciple of Death.
To be gentle is to be the pupil of Life."

"The biggest enemy of human life
*   does not exist outside oneself.*
No, the biggest enemy of human life
*   exists within oneself."*

"He who wishes to conquer the world is ignorant
*   and does not know himself well.*
To compete with the ignorant is ignorant.
To teach the ignorant requires a kind hand
*   and enduring strength.*
The stubborn and the ignorant will bury themselves
*   in the ashes of their ambition*
*   if they do not develop receptivity."*

"A truly great conqueror learns
*   from the non-competitive Tao,*
*   which cares for all*
*   with uniform gentleness and immutable silence."*

These treasures helped Chang Liang unlock his puzzled mind and once again left him with the great task of overthrowing the cruel and ruthless Emperor of Chin. He was able to bring about this feat and thereby established the new Han Dynasty (206-219 A.D.).

Chang Liang was grateful to his teacher who had changed his life from one of definite failure to one of great success. At times, he went to the foot of Mount Ku Chen in the North of Chi in search of his teacher, but as the highest teacher is not identifiable, he could only discover a huge piece of yellow stone which resembled the old man of natural dignity and nobility. In his honor, Chang Liang entitled the book he had received, *The Book of Old Man Yellow Stone*. Practically, it is the introduction of special use of the I Ching.

V
Chu Ku Liang, The Mountain Hermit

In Chinese history there was a period known as the time of the Three Kingdoms (200-264 A.D.). Like today, this was an era of turbulence and confusion. During that time there was a wise hermit named Chu Ku Liang who lived on a mountain ridge called Wu Lu Kang, which means "mountain ridge of the resting Dragon." As you may know, a dragon signifies good energy or high talent.

Chu Ku Liang had been trained as a military strategist because of his keen awareness and intelligence; however, he chose to spend his life on the mountain as a farmer in pursuit of a simple, natural life. In those days, a good commander and strategist had to thoroughly understand the cosmological aspects of nature in order to properly plan maneuvers, whereas today, most generals are head-strong and fight blindly without taking universal subtle law, historical evaluation and astrological influences into consideration. With high moral achievement, talent, knowledge and wisdom, Chu Ku Liang chose to stay in his mountain hermitage where he cultivated and relished a life of repose.

"The Song of the Great Hermit Lien Fu' was a favorite poem that Chu Ku Liang had written and like to sing. It went like this:

"Who was the first to awaken
from the big dream of life?
I can only be aware of my own awakening.
As I finish my sleep in the warm spring morning,
   from that humble hut the beautiful red sun,
   the light of my life,
   slowly rising, enlightens me."

One morning a group of ardent young soldiers, who had undertaken the task of liberating the country from its constant turmoil, arrived outside Chu Ku Liang's hut. They had great courage and, having amassed a large army, they had already fought successfully in several areas. Lacking a brilliant strategist, they sought Chu Ku Liang and were told where he might be found; but it was not Chu Ku Liang's wish to meet with them.

The leader of the group, Lu Bei, was an insightful man who recognized the hermit's worth. He persisted in trying to influence Chu Ku Liang, despite the other men's perception of Chu Ku Liang as a mere civilian with a small frame and slender body, too weak to even bind a chicken. Nevertheless, Lu Bei returned three times to Chu Ku Liang's hut to show the hermit his sincere intentions. Standing outside in the snow, he repeatedly read from the engraved words on the door:

> *"I am indifferent to worldly gain,*
> *so I keep to my simple life.*
> *I keep calm, so I reach far spiritually."*

Finally, Chu Ku Liang agreed to help these men, and together they successfully occupied the rich lands of Szechuan, a very important base for resistance against the evil forces. The growing army consisted mainly of villagers and local farmers, but with the support, planning and teaching of Chu Ku Liang, they accomplished great things.

This story demonstrates two principles. First, one should not be self-assertive when trying to accomplish large goals. Lu Bei, a man of responsibility and power, was wise enough to humbly seek assistance from a man of superior talent and intelligence. Second, once a goal has been deemed virtuous and worthy, one should willingly offer once's service. Chu Ku Liang was a developed one; he preferred to embrace a quiet rural life and renounce wealth and power. But a man of talent must be prepared to utilize his talent if the goal is just. In order for Chu Ku Liang to judge whether the time was right, the people honorable, and the purpose correct, he had to listen carefully to the promptings of his deep insight before serving Lu Bei's army. The approaches and attitudes on both his part and Lu Bei's were just and correct. Therefore, their combined forces were able to cooperate and accomplish great things.

Years later, Chu Ku Liang had the supreme chance to enjoy respect and fortune. In 221 A.D., Lu Bei was still on the throne after having ruled the country since the initial victory effected by Chu Ku Liang's strategical genius years before. But now Lu Bei was dying. His son was still too young to assume the position of Emperor. Lu Bei asked that Chu Ku Liang visit him before he died. During their conversation he told Chu Ku Liang, "You are an intelligent man. My kingdom was built with your help. But now I am going away, and my son will be an orphan. If you would like to help him, then do so. If you would like to have the kingdom, it is yours, for this is also a fair request." These were the last words Emperor Lu Bei spoke to Chu Ku Liang.

Throughout his entire life Chu Ku Liang never sought to alter his role as an assistant. Even after he became old and weak, he still guided the army on six expeditions to protect the kingdom. Now he decided to remain and help the empire by establishing the ten year old boy on the throne. Twice he wrote letters to the boy-king stating that he was only a farmer from the mountains but would offer his help. "Your father," he wrote, "appreciated me and invited me to help. I humbly offered my knowledge and life. Now that your father is gone and you are on the throne, I continue to offer my faithfulness to you. I am old, and the external world seems to have become strong. All I can do is offer my best. I will diligently work without retaining even one ounce of my vitality. I will continue to fight for you until the end of my days."

Chu Ku Liang knew that fame was not important. If he had wished to become a king, he would have been a king, but his joy was self-cultivation and the realization of virtue. Because he led a simple and detached natural life, his spirit still lives transcendentally. Few people in human history can equal the spiritual merit that Chu Ku Liang achieved. Chu Ku Liang touched my young soul. He set a good example for me, as well as for others. I respect the virtue of his accomplishment-without-attachment. Our task today is no different than Chu Ku Liang's as we shoulder the responsibility for spiritual integration. Remember, his wisdom and virtue was derived from the lifetime study of the *I Ching*.

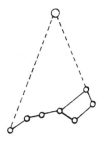

Part Five:
Epilogue

易无思也，无为也，寂然不
动，感而遂通天下之故，非
天下之至神其孰能与于此。
夫易，聖人所以極深而研幾也。
惟深也故能通天下之務，惟神
也故不疾而速，不行而至。

Epilogue

In this age of deviation from our original nature, distortion and confusion have become more and more prevalent with each passing year. Theological, conceptual, and physical conflicts have become more pronounced among humankind. At this time a call is being sent forth from an Ancient One; he beckons, "Come back, come back to your true nature. Stop fighting with one another. Return to the oneness of the unnameable universal origin." Some hear his call and live quietly, happily and peacefully. But those who cannot hear go further into divergence and deviation. They choose conflict rather than peace.

I have heard many times, "To be or not to be, that is the question." In the Integral Way this question is not meaningful. The real dilemma is how to be. Indeed, this is the real question, and a solution can be found. If you do not agree that how to be is the real problem, then simply reflect on the state of the world at the present time.

Although there have been all kinds of system and constitutions to regulate how to be, have any of these methods actually found the true way of harmony? On the contrary, confusion among people today is greater because of the proliferation of systems. However, the Integral Way, through the experiences of different times and different places, has put all its attention on how to be in accordance with one's true nature and has thus discovered that the truth of life is to live virtuously, harmoniously, simply and naturally. This is the plain way to a happy life and is the essence of a natural spiritual life.

In the Integral Way, there are three basic principles of life which serve as a foundation for individual and collective health in this overly-sophisticated world. They are: freedom from ignorance, freedom from tension, and freedom from pressure. Because we all need to fulfill the basic demands in our lives, evading the tensions and pressures of our unnaturally institutionalized world is difficult. These tensions and pressures have already reached a level where they are damaging to the health of the human organism. Even a spiritually developed person who lives in the modern world and works to be free from ignorance must continually work on eliminating tensions and pressures.

The deviation of humankind from its true nature began with the development and divergence of different religious traditions. Some people are evil because their religion is evil; some people are aggressive because their religion is aggressive. Such religions are misinterpretations of the natural truth; their descriptions of the spiritual world and understanding of human problems are incomplete and incorrect. Therefore, the priority of today's cultural and religious leaders should be to develop self-awareness, to be courageous enough to start anew and not to be confused by what has preciously been taught.

If conventional and inaccurate views continue to obscure people's true spiritual vision, they will certainly never be able to see the Truth or teach it to others.

Obviously, contemporary human beings have highly developed intellects, but they are frequently blind to the natural spiritual truth. As a consequence of this combination of highly-developed intellect and underdeveloped spiritual knowledge, people cannot control their minds when a conflict arises between thought and faith. The primary reason that atheistic communist regimes have arisen in the world is because modern people are disappointed in their conventional beliefs.

Look at the two opposing world views. One believes in a dominant god, the other in an atheistic, totalitarian political system. The former is childish; the latter is ignorant. One is born of a limited view of the universe; the other is the result of human arrogance and an incomplete know- ledge of modern science. One is a misunderstanding of the real, spiritual world and is attached to a primitive dualistic view of God; the other is the madness of material attachment.

Both viewpoints have led the majority of human beings into a world of immorality and deviation. Each calls the other an enslaving system. But I do not know any system that is not enslaving to some degree. If there has to be a system, let it be natural and original. If people are not willing to return to their original simplicity, there will be far more enslavement to come.

To deeply inquire into the modern problem, we must ask who is truly responsible. As modern human beings, can we excuse ourselves from responsibility for society on all levels? Spiritual truth can be learned from verifiable methods which ancient achieved ones developed through many generations. I am willing to challenge the modern myth of materialism with methods passed down from my forefathers, but the problem is not materialism alone. I am willing to work with a group of advanced scientists to conduct thorough research into the truth of human life, and to offer the methods of the ancient sages which are the key to unlocking the knowledge of those elements which really and ultimately constitute life. My goal is to not leave the world in the darkness of rigid monotheism of ignorant atheism.

The fundamental error on the popular level comes from dualistic religion. This, being the root of human difficulty, is what makes finding the solution so difficult. People are still following incorrect conventional beliefs and childish convictions inherited from their ancestors, themselves only partially developed. With such an incomplete and inaccurate view of the spiritual realm and of human life, these inadequate traditions have been misguiding people for generations. If we continue to follow their example, the world will surely remain in darkness.

People hold rigidly to the names, concepts and "isms" they have created. Their world is limited by all kinds of unnatural thoughts and inharmonious principles. Although they may think they are becoming more spiritualized and civilized, such things only serve to develop them in what is actually a negative direction. Only when people sift through all the confusion handed down by their ancestors and reassess the limitations of modern knowledge will they truly have a chance to find the Omni-Present Truth through spiritual techniques. The discovery of these traditional spiritual treasures will guide people to the rediscovery of their natural true being.

One may think that the Integral Way is just another name. There is nothing wrong with names if they reflect reality; however, they frequently do not. The term "Tao" is different. It is used to indicate something unnameable, indescribable and indefinable. Everything has its own way; yet all ways follow only one way which exists for all times. Thus it is called "Tao" or "The Way." It is undiscriminating and indistinguishable.

Natural spiritual teaching represents the self-awareness of human nature and the spirit of universal integration. Today, however, conceptual conflicts and confusions among human beings are unprecedentedly violent.

The following parable from the ancient Master Lei Tzu illustrates the spirit of my work. There are two big mountains, Tai-Shing and Hwan-Hou, which encompass seven hundred square miles and reach to a height of fifteen thousand feet. They lie south of the state of Chi and north of the place called Ho-Yang. There, facing the two mountains lived an old man, later known as the "Foolish Grandpa of the North Mountain." At that time he was close to his ninetieth year. After many years of detouring around these two opposing mountains he finally decided he had had enough inconvenience. He summoned his family and told them, "Let us use all our strength to level these two mountains. Then we will be able to reach the southern part of the state of Yu and the shore of River Han directly. Do you agree?"

Everyone agreed with the old man except his wife, who objected, "With your strength you cannot even move a small hill! How do you expect to do anything about the mountains of Tai-Shing and Hwan-Hou? And also, what will you do with all the stones and dirt you remove?"

"Throw them far away into the Ocean of Bo," was the unanimous reply. Then the grandpa started toward the mountains with his son and grandson. They carried tools to break stones and dig dirt and used simple bamboo containers to carry them far away to the Ocean of Bo. A neighbor's child of seven or eight also hurried to help them and returned home only once a year as the seasons change from summer to winter.

A clever old man who lived close to the river laughed at them and tried to stop them, saying, "The mountains are so extensive and you are so unwise. With such limited life and strength, you will not even be able to move a big tree on the mountain, let alone all the dirt and those enormous rocks!"

The Foolish Grandpa of North Mountain answered with a long sigh, "Your mind is narrow and stubborn; you clearly cannot see through the matter. Though I will cease my work someday, my son and grandsons will still be here to carry on. My son will beget children too. This will continue, generation after generation, ceaselessly. The mountains will not grow larger, so there is no reason they cannot be leveled." The clever old man could not say anything more.

A deity overheard this conversation, and fearing that the old man would not stop his work, went to tell the Supreme Divine One about it. The Supreme Divine One, however, felt moved by the sincerity of the Foolish Grandpa and ordered the two sons of the giant Kua-O to carry both mountains away. One was to be carried east of the Northland and the other to the south of the state of Yung. Thereafter there were no more obstructive highlands or big rocks between the south of the State of Chi and the south shore of the Han River.

In this spirit, and out of the same "foolishness" as the Grandpa of the North Mountain, I welcome others who are as "foolish," naive and as innocent as I, in the hope that they might continue the work of worldly spiritual integration.

In the Integral Way, we value purity and naivete. More importantly, to become positively sophisticated without losing the naivete and innocence of one's original being is the highest spiritual virtue. It will not do to merely withdraw from possible temptations. Think of the white lotus flower which derives its beauty from the sedimentary mud without becoming muddy. Its meaning can be implemented in modern life: to live in a glamorous modern city without losing one's innermost serenity; to give understanding to modern material research without giving up the vision of the whole and its subtle essence; and to live with the enormous pressure created by human ignorance without being emotionally squeezed. It is essential to be fully equipped with modern material knowledge and means without damaging the recognition of the spiritual integrity of human life and the universal nature.

Each individual who is on the Path, seeking the natural Truth, should continue his forefathers' work for his own sake and for the people of the world. All people should methodically cultivate themselves and evolve to the validity of natural truth. To be a developed person is not to assume world leadership under the guise of religion, or to start any new "isms." Instead, it selflessly serves those people who truly wish to become spiritually mature. Where and how a spiritual person starts to work is where and how the entire human race needs to work in order to liberate itself from the darkness of blind impulses, ignorance, stubbornness and aggression.

If human life has not turned away from its natural course, then why does one spiritual individual need to call out and ask people to return to nature? If human society has not lost real, natural, normal qualities, then why does a spiritual person need to ask one to reconsider the value of the ordinary in human life?

However, never feel discouraged. People can only work out solutions to their natural needs when they realize that the central work of human life is liberation from ignorance and darkness. When this goal is achieved, a beautiful and peaceful life without tension and pressure can be achieved.

The following is the "formula" which can serve to dissolve the conflicts and confusion of the human world.

LIST OF FIGURES

About Master Ni

The author, Master Ni, says he is lucky; everywhere he goes, he gives lectures without speaking very good English and yet people listen and understand. Perhaps 10% of the communication is by understanding his words; the rest is his personal sincerity and energy. However, he feels that it is his responsibility to ensure that people receive his message clearly and correctly, thus, he puts the lectures and classes in book form.

It is his great happiness to see the genuine progress of all people, all societies and nations as one big harmonized worldly community. This is the goal that makes him stand up to talk and write as one way of fulfilling his personal duty.

What he offers people comes from his own growth and attainment. He began his personal spiritual pursuit when he was ten years old. Although his spiritual nature is innate, expressing it suitably and usefully requires world experience and learning.

When he is asked to give personal information, he says that there is personally nothing useful or worthy of mention. He feels that, as an individual, he is just one of all people living on the same plane of life and therefore he is not special. A hard life and hard work has made him deeper and stronger, or perhaps wiser. This is the case with all people who do not yield to the negative influences of life and the world.

He likes to be considered a friend rather than be formally titled because he enjoys the natural spiritual response between himself and others who come together to extend the ageless natural spiritual truth to all.

He has been a great traveller. He has been in many places, and he never tires of going to new places. His books have been printed in different languages as a side offering to his professional work as a natural healer - a fully trained Traditional Chinese Medical doctor. He understands that his world mission is to awaken many people, and his friends and helpers conjointly fulfill the world spiritual mission of this time.

This list is according to date of publication, and offers a way to study Master Ni's work in order of his spiritual revelation.

1979:   *The Complete Works of Lao Tzu*
        The Taoist Inner View of the Universe
        Tao, the Subtle Universal Law
1983:   *The Book of Changes and the Unchanging Truth*
        8,000 Years of Wisdom, I
        8,000 Years of Wisdom, II
1984:   *Workbook for Spiritual Development*
1985:   *The Uncharted Voyage Toward the Subtle Light* (reprinted as
                Awaken to the Great Path and
                Ascend the Spiritual Mountain)
1986:   *Footsteps of the Mystical Child*
1987:   *The Gentle Path of Spiritual Progress*
        Spiritual Messages from a Buffalo Rider (originally
                part of *Gentle Path of Spiritual Progress*)
1989:   *The Way of Integral Life*
        Enlightenment: Mother of Spiritual Independence
        Attaining Unlimited Life
        The Story of Two Kingdoms
1990:   *Stepping Stones for Spiritual Success*
        Guide to Inner Light
        Essence of Universal Spirituality
1991:   *Internal Growth through Tao*
        Nurture Your Spirits
        Quest of Soul
        Power of Natural Healing
        Eternal Light
        The Key to Good Fortune: Refining Your Spirit
1992:   *Attune Your Body with Dao-In*
        Harmony: The Art of Life
        Moonlight in the Dark Night
        Life and Teachings of Two Immortals, Volume I: Kou Hong
        The Mystical Universal Mother
        Ageless Counsel for Modern Times
        Mysticism: Empowering the Spirit Within
        The Time is Now for a Better Life and Better World
1993:   *Internal Alchemy: The Natural Way to Immortality*
        Golden Message (by Daoshing and Maoshing Ni, based on
                the works of Master Ni, Hua-Ching)
        Esoteric Tao Teh Ching
        The Way, the Truth and the Light
        From Diversity to Unity: Spiritual Integration of the World
        Life and Teachings of Two Immortals, Volume II: Chen Tuan

In addition, the forthcoming books will be compiled from his lecturing and teaching service:

Gentle Path Tˈai Chi Ch'uan
Sky Journey Tˈai Chi Ch'uan
Infinite Expansion Tˈai Chi Ch'uan
Cosmic Tour Ba Gua Zahn
Immortal Wisdom
By the Light of the North Star: Cultivating Your Spiritual Life
Seeing the Unseen: The Reality of Universal Spiritual Beings

BOOKS IN ENGLISH BY MASTER NI

The Time is Now for a Better Life and a Better World - *New Publication*
What is the purpose of achievement? Is it just self-preservation or is it to exercise whatever you have attained from your spiritual cultivation to serve the public by improving the life of the majority of people? Master Ni offers his profound vision of our modern day spiritual dilemma to help us awaken to combine our personal necessity with the better survival of universal society. 136 pages, Softcover, Stock No. BTIME, $10.95

The Way, the Truth and the Light - *New Publication!*
Of all teachings by famous worldly sages, the teaching of this highly exalted sage in this book expresses the Way closest to that of Lao Tzu. The genuine life of this young sage links the spiritual achievement of east and west which highlights the subtle truth. 232 pages, Softcover, Stock No. BLIGH, $14.95

Life and Teaching of Two Immortals, Volume 2: Chen Tuan - *New Publication!*
The second emperor of the Sung Dynasty entitled Master Chen Tuan "Master of Subtle Reality." Master Ni describes his life and cultivation and gives in-depth commentaries which provide teaching and insight into the achievement of this highly respected Master. 192 pages, Softcover, Stock No. BLIF2, $12.95

Esoteric Tao Teh Ching - *New Publication!*
Tao Teh Ching has great profundity in philosophy and spiritual meaning, and can be understood in many ways and on many levels. In this new previously unreleased edition, Master Ni gives instruction for spiritual practices, which includes in-depth information and important techniques for spiritual benefit. 192 pages, Softcover, Stock No. BESOT, $12.95

Golden Message - A Guide to Spiritual Life with Self-Study Program for Learning the Integral Way - *New Publication!*
This volume begins with a traditional treatise by Master Ni's sons about the general nature of spiritual learning and its application for human life and behavior. It is followed by a message from Master Ni and an outline of the Spiritual Self-Study Program and Correspondence Course of the College of Tao. 160 pages, Softcover, Stock No. BGOLD, $11.95

Internal Alchemy: The Natural Way to Immortality - *New Publication!*
Ancient spiritually achieved ones used alchemical terminology metaphorically for human internal energy transformation. Internal alchemy intends for an individual to transform one's emotion and lower energy to be higher energy and to find the unity of life in order to reach the divine immortality. 288 pages, Softcover, Stock No. BALCH, $15.95

Mysticism: Empowering the Spirit Within - *New Publication!*
For more than 8,000 years, mystical knowledge has been passed down by sages. Master Ni introduces spiritual knowledge of the developed ones which does not use the senses or machines like scientific knowledge, yet can know both the entirety of the universe and the spirits. 200 pages, Softcover, Stock No. BMYST2, $13.95

Life and Teaching of Two Immortals, Volume 1: Kou Hong - *New Publication!*
Master Kou Hong was an achieved Master, a healer in Traditional Chinese Medicine and a specialist in the art of refining medicines who was born in 363 A.D. He laid the foundation of later cultural development in China. 176 pages, Softcover, Stock No. BLIF1, $12.95.

Ageless Counsel for Modern Life - *New Publication!*
These sixty-four writings, originally illustrative commentaries on the *I Ching*, are meaningful and useful spiritual guidance on various topics to enrich your life. Master Ni's delightful poetry and some teachings of esoteric Taoism can be found here as well. 256 pages, Softcover, Stock No. BAGEL, $15.95.

The Mystical Universal Mother
An understanding of both masculine and feminine energies are crucial to understanding oneself, in particular for people moving to higher spiritual evolution. Master Ni focuses upon the feminine through the examples of some ancient and modern women. 240 pages, Softcover, Stock No. BMYST, $14.95

Moonlight in the Dark Night
To attain inner clarity and freedom of the soul, you have to control your emotions. This book contains wisdom on balancing the emotions, including balancing love relationships, so that spiritual achievement becomes possible. 168 pages, Softcover, Stock No. BMOON, $12.95

Harmony - The Art of Life
Harmony occurs when two different things find the point at which they can link together. Master Ni shares valuable spiritual understanding and insight about the ability to bring harmony within one's own self, one's relationships and the world. 208 pages, Softcover, Stock No. BHARM, $14.95

Attune Your Body with Dao-In
The ancients discovered that Dao-In exercises solved problems of stagnant energy, increased their health and lengthened their years. The exercises are also used as practical support for cultivation and higher achievements of spiritual immortality. 144 pages, Softcover with photographs, Stock No. BDAOI, $14.95 Also on VHS, Stock No. VDAOI, $39.95

The Key to Good Fortune: Refining Your Spirit
Straighten Your Way *(Tai Shan Kan Yin Pien)* and The Silent Way of Blessing *(Yin Chia Wen)* are the main guidance for a mature, healthy life. Spiritual improvement can be an integral part of realizing a Heavenly life on earth. 144 pages, Softcover, Stock No. BKEYT, $12.95

Eternal Light
Master Ni presents the life and teachings of his father, Grandmaster Ni, Yo San, who was a spiritually achieved person, healer and teacher, and a source of inspiration to Master Ni. Some deeper teachings and understandings on living a spiritual life and higher achievement are given. 208 pages, Softcover, Stock No. BETER, $14.95

Quest of Soul
Master Ni addresses many concepts about the soul such as saving the soul, improving the soul's quality, the free soul, what happens at death and the universal soul. He guides and

inspires the reader into deeper self-knowledge and to move forward to increase personal happiness and spiritual depth. 152 pages, Softcover, Stock No. BQUES, $11.95

Nurture Your Spirits
Master Ni breaks some spiritual prohibitions and presents the spiritual truth he has studied and proven. This truth may help you develop and nurture your own spirits which are the truthful internal foundation of your life being. 176 pages, Softcover, Stock No. BNURT, $12.95

Internal Growth through Tao
Master Ni teaches the more subtle, much deeper sphere of the reality of life that is above the shallow sphere of external achievement. He also clears the confusion caused by some spiritual teachings and guides you in the direction of developing spiritually by growing internally. 208 pages, Softcover, Stock No. BINTE, $13.95

Power of Natural Healing
Master Ni discusses the natural capability of self-healing, information and practices which can assist any treatment method and presents methods of cultivation which promote a healthy life, longevity and spiritual achievement. 230 pages, Softcover, Stock No. BHEAL, $14.95

Essence of Universal Spirituality
In this volume, as an open-minded learner and achieved teacher of universal spirituality, Master Ni examines and discusses all levels and topics of religious and spiritual teaching to help you understand the ultimate truth and enjoy the achievement of all religions without becoming confused by them. 304 pages, Softcover, Stock No. BESSE, $19.95

Guide to Inner Light
Drawing inspiration from the experience of the ancient achieved ones, modern people looking for the true source and meaning of life can find great teachings to direct and benefit them. The invaluable ancient development can teach us to reach the attainable spiritual truth and point the way to the Inner Light. 192 pages, Softcover, Stock No. BGUID, $12.95

Stepping Stones for Spiritual Success
In this volume, Master Ni has taken the best of the traditional teachings and put them into contemporary language to make them more relevant to our time, culture and lives. 160 pages, Softcover, Stock No. BSTEP, $12.95.

The Complete Works of Lao Tzu
The *Tao Teh Ching* is one of the most widely translated and cherished works of literature. Its timeless wisdom provides a bridge to the subtle spiritual truth and aids harmonious and peaceful living. Also included is the *Hua Hu Ching*, a later work of Lao Tzu which was lost to the general public for a thousand years. 212 pages, Softcover, Stock No. BCOMP, $12.95

The Book of Changes and the Unchanging Truth
The legendary classic *I Ching* is recognized as the first written book of wisdom. Leaders and sages throughout history have consulted it as a trusted advisor which reveals the appropriate action in any circumstance. Includes over 200 pages of background material on natural energy cycles, instruction and commentaries. 669 pages, Stock No. BBOOK, Hardcover, $35.00

The Story of Two Kingdoms

This volume is the metaphoric tale of the conflict between the Kingdoms of Light and Darkness. Through this unique story, Master Ni transmits esoteric teachings of Taoism which have been carefully guarded secrets for over 5,000 years. This book is for those who are serious in achieving high spiritual goals. 122 pages, Stock No. BSTOR, Hardcover, $14.50

The Way of Integral Life

This book includes practical and applicable suggestions for daily life, philosophical thought, esoteric insight and guidelines for those aspiring to serve the world. The ancient sages' achievement can assist the growth of your own wisdom and balanced, reasonable life. 320 pages, Softcover, Stock No. BWAYS, $14.00. Hardcover, Stock No. BWAYH, $20.00.

Enlightenment: Mother of Spiritual Independence

The inspiring story and teachings of Master Hui Neng, the father of Zen Buddhism and Sixth Patriarch of the Buddhist tradition, highlight this volume. Hui Neng was a person of ordinary birth, intellectually unsophisticated, who achieved himself to become a spiritual leader. 264 pages, Softcover, Stock No. BENLS, $12.50   Hardcover, Stock No. BENLH, $22.00.

Attaining Unlimited Life

Chuang Tzu was perhaps the greatest philosopher and master of Tao. He touches the organic nature of human life more deeply and directly than do other great teachers. This volume also includes questions by students and answers by Master Ni.   467 pages, Softcover, Stock No. BATTS $18.00; Hardcover, Stock No. BATTH, $25.00.

The Gentle Path of Spiritual Progress

This book offers a glimpse into the dialogues between a Master and his students. In a relaxed, open manner, Master Ni, Hua-Ching explains to his students the fundamental practices that are the keys to experiencing enlightenment in everyday life. 290 pages, Softcover, Stock No. BGENT, $12.95.

Spiritual Messages from a Buffalo Rider, A Man of Tao

Our buffalo nature rides on us, whereas an achieved person rides the buffalo. Master Ni gives much helpful knowledge to those who are interested in improving their lives and deepening their cultivation so they too can develop beyond their mundane beings. 242 pages, Softcover, Stock No. BSPIR, $12.95.

8,000 Years of Wisdom, Volume I and II

This two-volume set contains a wealth of practical, down-to-earth advice given by Master Ni over a five-year period. Drawing on his training in Traditional Chinese Medicine, Herbology and Acupuncture, Master Ni gives candid answers to questions on many topics. Volume I includes dietary guidance; 236 pages; Stock No. BWIS1 Volume II includes sex and pregnancy guidance; 241 pages; Stock No. BWIS2. Softcover, each volume $12.50

Awaken to the Great Path

Originally the first half of the *Uncharted Voyage Toward the Subtle Light*, this volume offers a clear and direct vision of the spiritual truth of life. It explains many of the subtle truths which are obvious to some but unapparent to others. The Great Path is not the unique teaching, but it can show the way to the integral spiritual truth in every useful level of life. 248 pages, Softcover, Stock No. BAWAK, $14.95

Ascend the Spiritual Mountain
Originally the second half of the *Uncharted Voyage Toward the Subtle Light*, this book offers further spiritual understanding with many invaluable practices which may help you integrate your spiritual self with your daily life. In deep truth, at different times and places, people still have only one teacher: the universal spiritual self itself. 216 pages, Softcover, Stock No. BASCE, $14.95

Footsteps of the Mystical Child
This book poses and answers such questions as: What is a soul? What is wisdom? What is spiritual evolution? to enable readers to open themselves to new realms of understanding and personal growth. Includes true examples about people's internal and external struggles on the path of self-development and spiritual evolution. 166 pages, Softcover, Stock No. BFOOT, $9.50

The Heavenly Way
A translation of the classic Tai Shan Kan Yin Pien (Straighten Your Way) and Yin Chia Wen (The Silent Way of Blessing). The treatises in this booklet are the main guidance for a mature and healthy life. This truth can teach the perpetual Heavenly Way by which one reconnects oneself with the divine nature. 41 pages, Softcover, Stock No. BHEAV, $2.50

Workbook for Spiritual Development
This material summarizes thousands of years of traditional teachings and little-known practices for spiritual development. There are sections on ancient invocations, natural celibacy and postures for energy channeling. Master Ni explains basic attitudes and knowledge that supports spiritual practice. 240 pages, Softcover, Stock No. BWORK, $14.95

Poster of Master Lu
Color poster of Master Lu, Tung Ping (shown on cover of workbook), for use with the workbook or in one's shrine. 16" x 22"; Stock No. PMLTP. $10.95

The Taoist Inner View of the Universe
Master Ni has given all the opportunity to know the vast achievement of the ancient unspoiled mind and its transpiercing vision. This book offers a glimpse of the inner world and immortal realm known to achieved ones and makes it understandable for students aspiring to a more complete life. 218 pages, Softcover, Stock No. BTAOI, $14.95

Tao, the Subtle Universal Law
Most people are unaware that their thoughts and behavior evoke responses from the invisible net of universal energy. To lead a good stable life is to be aware of the universal subtle law in every moment of our lives. This book presents practical methods that have been successfully used for centuries to accomplish this. 165 pages, Softcover, Stock No. TAOS, $7.50

MATERIALS ON NATURAL HEALTH, ARTS AND SCIENCES

BOOKS

101 Vegetarian Delights - *New Publication!* by Lily Chuang and Cathy McNease
A vegetarian diet is a gentle way of life with both physical and spiritual benefits. The Oriental tradition provides helpful methods to assure that a vegetarian diet is well-balanced and nourishing. This book provides a variety of clear and precise recipes ranging from everyday nutrition to exotic and delicious feasts. 176 pages, Softcover, Stock No. B101V, $12.95

The Tao of Nutrition by Maoshing Ni, Ph.D., with Cathy McNease, B.S., M.H. - This book offers both a healing and a disease prevention system through eating habits. This volume contains 3 major sections: theories of Chinese nutrition and philosophy; descriptions of 100 common foods with energetic properties and therapeutic actions; and nutritional remedies for common ailments. 214 pages, Softcover, Stock No. BNUTR, $14.50

Chinese Vegetarian Delights by Lily Chuang
An extraordinary collection of recipes based on principles of traditional Chinese nutrition. For those who require restricted diets or who choose an optimal diet, this cookbook is a rare treasure. Meat, sugar, diary products and fried foods are excluded. 104 pages, Softcover, Stock No. BCHIV, $7.50

Chinese Herbology Made Easy - by Maoshing Ni, Ph.D.
This text provides an overview of Oriental medical theory, in-depth descriptions of each herb category, over 300 black and white photographs, extensive tables of individual herbs for easy reference and an index of pharmaceutical and Pin-Yin names. This book gives a clear, efficient focus to Chinese herbology. 202 pages, Softcover, Stock No. BCHIH, 14.50

Crane Style Chi Gong Book - By Daoshing Ni, Ph.D.
Chi Gong is a set of meditative exercises developed thousands of years ago in China and now practiced for healing purposes. It combines breathing techniques, body movements and mental imagery to guide the smooth flow of energy throughout the body. It may be used with or without the videotape. 55 pages. Stock No. BCRAN. Spiral-bound, $10.95

VIDEO TAPES

Attune Your Body with Dao-In (VHS) - by Master Ni. Dao-In is a series of movements traditionally used for conducting physical energy. The ancients discovered that Dao-In exercise solves problems of stagnant energy, increases health and lengthens one's years, providing support for cultivation and higher achievements of spiritual immortality. Stock No. VDAOI, VHS $39.95

T'ai Chi Ch'uan: An Appreciation (VHS) - by Master Ni.
Master Ni, Hua-Ching presents three styles of T'ai Chi handed down to him through generations of highly developed masters. "Gentle Path," "Sky Journey" and "Infinite Expansion" are presented uninterrupted in this unique videotape, set to music for observation and appreciation. Stock No. VAPPR. VHS 30 minutes $24.95

Crane Style Chi Gong (VHS) - by Dr. Daoshing Ni, Ph.D.
Chi Gong is a set of meditative exercises practiced for healing chronic diseases, strengthening the body and spiritual enlightenment. Correct and persistent practice will increase one's energy, relieve tension, improve concentration, release emotional stress and restore general well-being. 2 hours, Stock No. VCRAN. $39.95

Eight Treasures (VHS) - By Maoshing Ni, Ph.D.
These exercises help open blocks in your energy flow and strengthen your vitality. It is a complete exercise combining physical stretching, toning and energy-conducting movements coordinated with breathing. Patterned from nature, its 32 movements are an excellent foundation for T'ai Chi Ch'uan or martial arts. 1 hour, 45 minutes. Stock No. VEIGH. $39.95

T'ai Chi Ch'uan I & II (VHS) - By Maoshing Ni, Ph.D.
This exercise integrates the flow of physical movement with that of internal energy in the Taoist style of "Harmony," similar to the long form of Yang-style T'ai Chi Ch'uan. Tai Chi has been practiced for thousands of years to help both physical longevity and spiritual cultivation. 1 hour each. Each video tape $39.95. Order both for $69.95. Stock Nos: Part I, VTAI1; Part II, VTAI2; Set of two, VTAI3.

AUDIO CASSETTES

Invocations for Health, Longevity and Healing a Broken Heart - By Maoshing Ni, Ph.D.
This audio cassette guides the listener through a series of ancient invocations to channel and conduct one's own healing energy and vital force. "Thinking is louder than thunder. The mystical power which creates all miracles is your sincere practice of this principle." 30 minutes, Stock No. AINVO, $9.95

Stress Release with Chi Gong - By Maoshing Ni, Ph.D.
This audio cassette guides you through simple, ancient breathing exercises that enable you to release day-to-day stress and tension that are such a common cause of illness today. 30 minutes. Stock No. ACHIS. $9.95

Pain Management with Chi Gong - By Maoshing Ni, Ph.D.
Using easy visualization and deep-breathing techniques developed over thousands of years, this audio cassette offers methods for overcoming pain by invigorating your energy flow and unblocking obstructions that cause pain. 30 minutes, Stock No. ACHIP. $9.95

***Tao Teh Ching* Cassette Tapes**
This classic work of Lao Tzu has been recorded in this two-cassette set that is a companion to the book translated by Master Ni. Professionally recorded and read by Robert Rudelson. 120 minutes. Stock No. ATAOT. $12.95

Order Master Ni's book, *The Complete Works of Lao Tzu,* and *Tao Teh Ching* Cassette Tapes for only $23.00. Stock No. ABTAO.

How To Order

Name:

Address:

City: State: Zip:

Phone - Daytime: Evening:

(We may telephone you if we have questions about your order.)

Qty.	Stock No.	Title/Description	Price Each	Total Price

Total amount for items ordered_____

Sales tax (CA residents only, 8-1/4%)_____

Shipping Charge (see below)_____

Total Amount Enclosed_____

Visa _____ Mastercard _____ Expiration Date _____

Card number:_____

Signature:_____

Shipping: Please give full street address or nearest crossroads. If shipping to more than one address, use separate shipping charges. Please allow 2 - 4 weeks for US delivery and 6 - 10 weeks for foreign surface mail.

By Mail: Complete this form with payment (US funds only, No Foreign Postal Money Orders, please) and mail to: Union of Tao and Man, 1314 Second St. #208, Santa Monica, CA 90401

Phone Orders: You may leave credit card orders anytime on our answering machine. Please speak clearly and remember to leave your full name and daytime phone number. Call (800) 578-9526 to order or (310) 576-1901 for information..

Shipping Charges:

> *Domestic Surface: First item $3.25, each additional, add $.50.*
> *Canada Surface: First item $3.25, each additional, add $1.00.*
> *Canada Air: First item $4.00, each additional, add $2.00*
> *Foreign Surface: First Item $3.50, each additional, add $2.00.*
> *Foreign Air: First item $12.00, each additional, add $7.00.*

All foreign orders: Add 5% of your book total to shipping charges to cover insurance.

_____ Please send me your complete catalog.

Thank you for your order

Spiritual Study through the College of Tao

The College of Tao and the Union of Tao and Man were established formally in California in the 1970's. This tradition is a very old spiritual culture of mankind, holding long experience of human spiritual growth. Its central goal is to offer healthy spiritual education to all people of our society. This time-tested tradition values the spiritual development of each individual self and passes down its guidance and experience.

Master Ni carries his tradition from its country of origin to the west. He chooses to avoid making the mistake of old-style religions that have rigid establishments which resulted in fossilizing the delicacy of spiritual reality. He prefers to guide the teachings of his tradition as a school of no boundary rather than a religion with rigidity. Thus, the branches or centers of this Taoist school offer different programs of similar purpose. Each center extends its independent service, but all are unified in adopting Master Ni's work as the foundation of teaching to fulfill the mission of providing spiritual education to all people.

The centers offer their classes, teaching, guidance and practices on building the groundwork for cultivating a spiritually centered and well-balanced life. As a person obtains the correct knowledge with which to properly guide himself or herself, he or she can then become more skillful in handling the experiences of daily life. The assimilation of good guidance in one's practical life brings about different stages of spiritual development.

Any interested individual is welcome to join and learn to grow for yourself. Or you just might like to take a few classes in which you are interested. You might like to visit the center or take classes near where you live, or you may be interested in organizing a center or study group based on the model of existing centers. In that way, we all work together for the spiritual benefit of all people. We do not require any religious type of commitment.

The College of Tao also offers a Self-Study program based on Master Ni's books and videotapes. The course outline and details of how to participate are given in his book, *The Golden Message*. The Self-Study program gives people an opportunity to study the learning of Tao at their own speed, as a correspondence course, or for those who wish to study on their own or are too far from a center.

The learning is life. The development is yours. The connection of study may be helpful, useful and serviceable, directly to you.

- -

Mail to: Union of Tao and Man, 1314 Second Street #208, Santa Monica, CA 90401

_____ I wish to be put on the mailing list of the Union of Tao and Man to be notified of classes, educational activities and new publications.

Name:_____

Address:_____

City:_____State:_____Zip:_____

Herbs Used by Ancient Taoist Masters

The pursuit of everlasting youth or immortality throughout human history is an innate human desire. Long ago, Chinese esoteric Taoists went to the high mountains to contemplate nature, strengthen their bodies, empower their minds and develop their spirit. From their studies and cultivation, they gave China alchemy and chemistry, herbology and acupuncture, the I Ching, astrology, martial arts and T'ai Chi Ch'uan, Chi Gong and many other useful kinds of knowledge.

Most important, they handed down in secrecy methods for attaining longevity and spiritual immortality. There were different levels of approach; one was to use a collection of food herb formulas that were only available to highly achieved Taoist masters. They used these food herbs to increase energy and heighten vitality. This treasured collection of herbal formulas remained within the Ni family for centuries.

Now, through Traditions of Tao, the Ni family makes these foods available for you to use to assist the foundation of your own positive development. It is only with a strong foundation that expected results are produced from diligent cultivation.

As a further benefit, in concert with the Taoist principle of self-sufficiency, Traditions of Tao offers the food herbs along with the Union of Tao and Man's publications in a distribution opportunity for anyone serious about financial independence.

Send to: Traditions of Tao
           1314 Second Street #208
           Santa Monica, CA 90401

Please send me a Traditions of Tao brochure.

Name _____

Address_____

City_____State_____Zip_____

Phone (day)_____(night)_____

Yo San University of Traditional Chinese Medicine

"Not just a medical career, but a life-time commitment to raising one's spiritual standard."

Thank you for your support and interest in our publications and services. It is by your patronage that we continue to offer you the practical knowledge and wisdom from this venerable Taoist tradition.

Because of your sustained interest in Taoism, in January 1989 we formed Yo San University of Traditional Chinese Medicine, a non-profit educational institution under the direction of founder Master Ni, Hua-Ching. Yo San University is the continuation of 38 generations of Ni family practitioners who handed down knowledge and wisdom from father to son. Its purpose is to train and graduate practitioners of the highest caliber in Traditional Chinese Medicine, which includes acupuncture, herbology and spiritual development.

We view Traditional Chinese Medicine as the application of spiritual development. Its foundation is the spiritual capability to know life, to diagnose a person's problem and how to cure it. We teach students how to care for themselves and other, emphasizing the integration of traditional knowledge and modern science. Yo San University offers a complete Master's degree program approved by the California State Department of Education that provides an excellent education in Traditional Chinese Medicine and meets all requirements for state licensure.

We invite you to inquire into our university for a creative and rewarding career as a holistic physician. Classes are also open to persons interested only in self-enrichment. For more information, please fill out the form below and send it to:

Yo San University
of Traditional Chinese Medicine
1314 Second Street
Santa Monica, CA 90401

☐ Please send me information on the Masters degree program in Traditional Chinese Medicine.

☐ Please send me information on health workshops and seminars.

☐ Please send me information on continuing education for acupuncturists and health professionals.

Name _____

Address_____

City_____State_____Zip_____

Phone(day)_____(evening)_____